THE ANNALS
OF
AMERICA

"Armistice Night" by George Luks

"Armistice Night" by George Luks

THE ANNALS OF AMERICA

Volume 14

1916 - 1928

World War and Prosperity

William Benton, *Publisher*

ENCYCLOPÆDIA BRITANNICA, INC.

Chicago London Toronto Geneva Sydney Tokyo Manila

The editors wish to express their gratitude for permission to reprint
material from the following sources:

Appleton-Century-Crofts for Selection 1, from *The Century Magazine*, Vol. XCIII, 1917, Copyright 1917 by The Century Company.

J. J. Augustine, Inc. for Selection 17, from *Race and Democratic Society*, by Franz Boas.

Brandt & Brandt for Selection 122, from *John Brown's Body*, by Stephen Vincent Benét, New York: Holt, Rinehart and Winston, Inc., Copyright 1927, 1928 by Stephen Vincent Benét, Copyright renewed 1955, 1956 by Rosemary Carr Benét.

Columbia University Press for Selection 10, from *Our Chief Magistrate and His Powers,* by William Howard Taft, New York: Columbia University Press.

Ernst, Cane, Berner & Gitlin for Selection 78, from *The Nation*, Copyright 1923 by Nation, Inc., Copyright 1951 by Sinclair Lewis.

Harry Emerson Fosdick for Selection 63, from *The Christian Work*, June 10, 1922.

Harcourt, Brace & World, Inc. for Selections 65, 66, 67 from *Civilization in the United States,* ed. by Harold F. Stearns. Also for Selection 74, from his volume *Poems 1923-1954*, Copyright 1923, 1951 by E. E. Cummings. Also for Selection 97, from *Poems 1923-1954*, by E. E. Cummings, Copyright 1926 by Horace Liveright, Copyright 1954 by E. E. Cummings.

Harper & Row Publishers, for Selection 54, abridged from *Hail Columbia!* by W. L. George, Copyright 1921 by Harper & Brothers, renewed 1949 by Coutts & Co.

Harvard University Press for Selections 84, 115, from *This Was America*, ed. by Oscar Handlin, Cambridge, Mass.: Harvard University Press, Copyright 1949 by the President and Fellows of Harvard College.

Holt, Rinehart and Winston, Inc. for Selection 9, from *Chicago Poems*, by Carl Sandburg, Copyright 1916 by Holt, Rinehart and Winston, Inc., Copyright 1944 by Carl Sandburg. Also for Selection 36, from *Cornhuskers* by Carl Sandburg, Copyright 1918 by Holt, Rinehart and Winston, Inc., Copyright 1946 by Carl Sandburg. Also for Selection 79, from *Complete Poems of Robert Frost*, Copyright 1923 by Holt, Rinehart and Winston, Inc., Copyright 1936, 1942, 1951 by Robert Frost, Copyright © 1964 by Lesley Frost Ballantine. Also for Selection 110, from *Ballads and Poems*, by Stephen Vincent Benét, Copyright 1931 by Stephen Vincent Benét, Copyright © 1959 by Rosemary Carr Benét.

Houghton Mifflin Company for Selections 89, 109, from *The Autobiography of Will Rogers*, Copyright 1932 by Curtis Publishing Company, Copyright 1949 by Rogers Company.

The Jewish Publication Society of American and American Jewish Committee for Selection 81, from *Louis Marshall, Champion of Liberty: Selected Papers and Addresses*, ed. by Charles Reznikoff, Vol. I.

Grace Nail Johnson for Selection 121, Copyright © 1928 by Harper's Magazine, Inc. Reprinted from the November 1928 issue of *Harper's Magazine.*

Alfred A. Knopf, Inc. for Selection 23, abridged from *A Book of Prefaces*, Fifth Ed., by H. L. Mencken,

CODED SOURCES IN THIS VOLUME

PRFA   [United States Department of State] *Papers Relating to Foreign Affairs.* Compiled annually since 1861 except for 1869 with supplements issued periodically. Title changed to *Papers Relating to Foreign Relations of the United States* in 1870 and to *Foreign Relations of the United States* in 1947. Washington, 1862 *et seq.*

Record   *Congressional Record.* A record of the proceedings of Congress from March 3, 1873, to date, arranged by number of Congress and by session. Washington, 1874 *et seq.*

TWA   *This Was America.* Edited by Oscar Handlin. Cambridge, 1949.

United States Reports [Supreme Court].

250 U.S. 616	Vol. 250, pp. 616ff.;
251 U.S. 417	Vol. 251, pp. 417ff.;
261 U.S. 525	Vol. 261, pp. 525ff.;
268 U.S. 652	Vol. 268, pp. 652ff.;
273 U.S. 536	Vol. 273, pp. 536ff.

Contents

WORLD WAR
AND
PROSPERITY
In Pictures

The Great War 83-100

The coming of war in 1914 was the first of a series of shattering
events that ended America's isolation. Wilson's first futile response
was a neutrality consistent with his moralistic view of foreign
affairs; when American participation in the war could no longer
be avoided, the war itself was raised to the level of a crusade.

Postwar Reaction 219-234

The Versailles Treaty crushed the idealism of Wilson's crusade;
it also sowed the seeds of the next war. Disillusionment and
retreat were the national mood, and the return to comfortable
Republicanism seemed the natural path. The leftover enthusiasm
of war, together with a fervent desire not to be further disturbed,
led the country into the first of its Red Scares.

Though Progressivism was dead, two reforms that had
been long fought for were adopted in the postwar period.
Women's suffrage and Prohibition were both achieved by
Constitutional amendment. The former had none but salutary
effects and persisted; the latter was an altogether unpleasant
experiment and was soon abandoned.

The call for a return to "normalcy" was heeded almost
universally. The daily life that had been really only marginally
affected by war quickly resumed its course, and the nation
moved into the prosperity of the 1920s, disturbed only by the
economic distress of the farmers.

There was an apparent national determination to forget both war
and disillusionment in what seems in retrospect to have been an
orgy of adulation. This was the Roaring Twenties, and while it is
this aspect of the decade that is best remembered, most of the
noise was in fact produced by a relatively small group of people.

Introduction

By 1914 Europe had spent fifty years making itself inflammable; when the match was finally applied it was no time at all before the entire continent was ablaze. Before it was put out, the fire engulfed almost the whole civilized world.

The "match" was the murder of Austrian Archduke Francis Ferdinand at Sarajevo, June 28, 1914. Exactly one month later Austria-Hungary declared war against Serbia, which appealed to its ally and protector, Russia. On July 29 an Imperial Council at Potsdam decided on war against Russia, which had already begun to mobilize, and also against France. By noon on August 1 a state of war existed between Germany and Russia, and the next day Germany invaded France, formally declaring war on August 3. The next day German troops crossed the Belgian frontier, which England had said it would guarantee; at midnight England declared war on the Kaiser.

The month of August, one of the most frantic and terrible in the history of mankind, saw a million men die on the Western and Eastern fronts and also saw the battlelines drawn — in northeastern France — for a war that would eventually endure longer than anyone had imagined possible, and that would kill a hundred million human beings and destroy much of the wealth amassed in a century of peace.

There was a great debate, and much soul-searching among high and low, about the question of America's participation in a war that it seemed possible, at least at first, to confine to Europe. Secretary of State William Jennings Bryan, true to his Populist background, did not want war, nor, for various reasons, did a lot of others, including the President himself. One good reason was that the country was totally unprepared for such a war — a far cry, as the more astute observers recognized, from the Cuban adventure of fifteen years before. The out-and-out pacifists were opposed to any war, and the many first and second generation Germans were opposed to a war against Germany. And then there were those — and they were not a few — who were unsure of which side we should go in on, if we went in at all. (For American views of the war in Europe in 1914, 1915, and 1916, see Volume 13, Selections 97-98 and 112-118, and in this volume, Selections 3-4 and 11-14.)

But things happened thick and fast. The pressures built up. And thousands of men were dying in Europe every week. It could not go on, people said, it had to stop; and if we had to join in the fighting to stop it, and thereby kill more men, we would even do that. In the end it was above all the Germans themselves, with their unrestricted submarine warfare from February 1917 on, who made the choice inevitable. (The Germans knew that the policy was a gamble, but they were willing to take the risk. And there were evidently some German officers and statesmen who believed Germany could win even with America in the war.)

There is not space here to tell the story of the events leading up to the war, and of the war itself. But a few of the famous phrases that marked the period may jog our memories. (It was probably the first war in history that was fought as much with slogans as with guns.) "Our whole duty, for the present, at any rate," said Woodrow Wilson in April 1915, "is summed up in the motto, 'America first.'" A month later, he was saying that "there is such a thing as a man being too proud to fight." "Out of the Trenches and Back to Their Homes by Christmas" was the slogan of Henry Ford's peace delegation, sent to Europe to stop the war in December of that year. This venture of course was a farcical failure. In January 1916 Wilson had changed his tune. "There may at any moment come a time when I cannot preserve both the honor and the peace of the United States," he told a largely German audience in Milwaukee. "Do not exact of me an impossible and contradictory thing." He put it a little more strongly a week later, in Des Moines, when he declared that "America cannot be an ostrich with its head in the sand." And on March 3 he referred to a group of eleven Senators who by filibustering tactics had prevented passage of a bill to arm American merchantmen as "a little group of willful men." Nevertheless, he ran and won in the fall elections on the slogan "He Kept Us Out of War." Later, he said that this had not meant he would *continue* to keep us out — but there were those who felt he had betrayed a sacred trust.

In January 1917 Wilson was calling for "peace without victory." His government was indeed making efforts to end the war short of a surrender on the part of anybody, but the combatants would not go along. The Germans thought they could win, and the Allies thought that if they refused to take half a loaf, America would be forced into the conflict and they could then have all. It was the Allies who were right. Publication of the Zimmerman Telegram, revealing attempts of the German Foreign Office to arrange for a Mexican-Japanese attack on the U.S. West Coast, forced Wilson's hand. On April 2 he asked Congress for a declaration of war, saying that "the world must be made safe for democracy," and Congress complied five days later. On July 4, 1917, as the first contingents of U.S. troops were trickling across the Atlantic, Charles E. Stanton, chief disbursing officer of the American Expeditionary Force in France, made a speech in Picpus Cemetery, Paris, at the grave of Lafayette. He was moved by his consciousness of an old debt that was now about to be repaid, and he summed up his feelings in four very famous words. "Lafayette," he said, "we are here."

There were other slogans. "Bonds or Bondage," said the posters during the first Liberty Bond drive, in 1917. "Food Will Win the War" said other posters in the summers of 1917 and 1918. "Force, force to the utmost!" cried Wilson in an address in April 1918, and before the fall offensive of that year General Pershing is supposed to have proclaimed: "Hell, Heaven, or Hoboken by Christmas!" And the soldiers sang "Over There," and "K-K-K-Katy," and "Hinky Dinky Parlay-Voo." Fifty thousand Americans were killed, and about a quarter of a million were wounded. This was bad, but not as bad as the influenza epidemic of the winter of 1918-1919 that killed 500,000 American men, women, and children. Everybody agreed that it was a part of the cost of the war. (For various views of American participation in the war, see Selections 15-22, 25, 27-30, and 32-33.)

Wilson announced his Fourteen Points as the basis of a final peace in January 1918, and stuck to them until the war ended on November 11 of that year, and throughout the Peace Conference that opened in Paris on January 18, 1919. The first Point was the most important: "open covenants, openly arrived at." But the wily Allied negotiators — Lloyd George of Britain, Clemenceau of France, Orlando of Italy — were not going to accept it because a Presbyterian minister in the guise of the President of the United States told them to. They spent the spring secretly dividing up the world among them, and in the end produced the Versailles Treaty, presented to the Germans for their signature on May 7, which settled almost nothing and was, William Allen White said, "the peace that passeth understanding."

Wilson thought he had won the Fourteenth Point but finally lost it. It called for the formation of "a general association of nations" that came into being — but that the United States did not join. Wilson knew there was opposition, although the polls showed that the majority of Americans were in favor of U.S. participation in the League of Nations, and he set out on a speaking tour on September 3, 1919, to put the case for the future, as he saw it, to the people. "I can predict with absolute certainty," he said, "that within another generation there will be another world war [if America does not join the League]. . . . What the Germans used [in this war] were toys as compared with what would be used in the next war." But he suffered a collapse on September 25 — he was only 63, but he had been worn out by his terrible efforts of the past year and a half — and for the rest of his term was a sick, indeed a dying man. Perhaps if he had remained healthy he could have won over the recalcitrant Senate to his view, but at any rate he did not. And if America had joined the League, World War II might have come all the same. (For the Fourteen Points, see Selection 31; and for discussions of the Versailles Treaty, and of America's participation in the League of Nations, see Selections 34 and 38-41.)

The war and the peace that followed it were not all that happened in the eventful years covered by this volume. The first nationwide highway building program since the 1830s was inaugurated in 1916; the cause, of course, was the automobile, then as now a social force of immense power (see Volume 13, Selection 25). The next year witnessed the Russian revolution; the Czar abdicated on March 15, 1917, and the Bolsheviks took over in October. (See Selection 33.) There was a "red scare" after the war (see Selections 36, 47-48, 56, and 90-91) that in many respects was a preview of things to come a generation later during the McCarthy period of the 1950s, and that in a few respects was even more violent partly because it did not last so long. Probably the most memorable occurrence was the conviction of Sacco and Vanzetti in 1921 (see Selections 103-104). And the end of a great era of American history came in 1921, when quotas for immigrants were passed by a Congress that for the first time institutionalized the perennial fear of "degeneration" of the country's blood (see Selections 50, 81, 89, 99, 109, and 122).

The 1920s saw the culmination of two century-old reform movements, the one for prohibition, the other for woman suffrage. Prohibition, called by Herbert Hoover "a great social and economic experiment, noble in motive, far-reaching in purpose," lasted only until 1933. Despite the nobility of the motive, the experiment did not work, as Ring Lardner pointed out in some of the most trenchant prose written during the decade. Prohibition went into effect in January 1920; "the night before," said Lardner in 1925, "everybody had a big party on acct. of it being the last chance to get boiled. As these wds. is written the party is just beginning to get good." (See Selections 87-88, 102, and 115, and in Volume 15, Selection 25.)

The party was not really so good for everybody. A lot of people, especially young people, drank more liquor than they ever had before; but liquor being illegal, it had to be supplied by men who were outside the law. Racketeers took over the business, in which they — or their descendants — still have an influence, and since vast sums of money were involved, the outlaws gained great power quickly. And they were ruthless to each other. A report written in the 1930s told how one "mob" kidnapped a member of a rival gang: "What they did to him was a warning to others. They took him into a dive and beat him so badly as to cripple him. They strung him up by the thumbs for that portion of the lesson. Then they placed a strip of gauze that had been smeared with some infectious matter over his eyes, and taped it securely. When they finally tossed him out into the street . . . he was on his way to blindness. . . . He quit the business." (See Volume 15, Selection 26.)

Woman suffrage was another matter. It went into effect in the summer of 1920, but many women were apparently dazed by their newfound freedom, with the result that the proportion of eligible voters actually voting in the national election of that year was the lowest in our history. But women soon learned to use the franchise, which they did with good effect in the years that followed, until by the 1940s they were constituting more than half the voters in national elections. (See Selection 25 for some earlier problems of suffragettes.)

Two new Presidents occupied the White House during the 1920s: Warren Gamaliel Harding, who set the tone of the decade with his call for a return to "normalcy" (grammarians never forgave him this coinage) but had troubles with his friends and followers (see Selections 58 and 82-83); and Calvin Coolidge, who took over after Harding's death on August 2, 1923, and won reelection in 1924. His slogan was "Keep Cool with Coolidge," and perhaps the best known thing about him was his taciturnity — he once remarked: "If you don't say anything, you won't be called upon to repeat it" (see Selections 77, 101, and 111). A third President, Herbert Hoover, was elected in the fall of 1928, as the volume draws to a close; but his story belongs in the next volume (however, see Selection 118 herein).

Political events were hardly what concerned people the most. It was an era, as Westbrook Pegler later said, of "Wonderful Nonsense," and the doings of flappers in short skirts who danced the Charleston to the new jazz beat caught the public imagination more than the antics of elderly men in Washington. It was also a period — if we allow it to extend back to 1914 or 1915 — in which a number of America's now classic authors published either their first works or notable new ones. Edgar Lee Masters' *Spoon River Anthology* came out in 1915 (see Volume 13, Selection 119). The Provincetown Playhouse was also founded in 1915, and soon was presenting new plays by its extraordinary young "find," Eugene O'Neill (see Selection 65). The same year saw the publication of Carl Sandburg's *Chicago Poems* (see Volume 13, Selection 99, and in this volume, Selections 9 and 36), and people were reading and beginning to talk about Robert Frost's first two books, published a year or so before (see Volume 13, Selection 92, and in this volume, Selection 79).

People were also reading Ezra Pound, who had already published half a dozen books (see Selection 24); one of his best readers was the young T. S. Eliot, whose *Prufrock and Other Observations* was published in 1917 and whose *Wasteland* appeared in 1922. F. Scott Fitzgerald's *This Side of Paradise* came out in 1920 and was a portent of the future, not only in society but also in literature — *The Great Gatsby* saw the light in 1925, and other important books by Fitzgerald in the following decade (see Volume 15, Selection 25). Sinclair Lewis' *Main Street* was another portent; it was one of many books by authors who were not enchanted by the gilt and glitter of what R. L. Duffus called "the age of play" (see Selection 78 and 88, and in Volume 15, Selection 14).

John Dos Passos helped to inaugurate the war weariness and disillusionment that marked the period of *entre deux guerres*, and the generation that was called "lost" by Gertrude Stein, with his *Three Soldiers* (1921). It was a theme that was taken up and perhaps improved upon by Ernest Hemingway in a volume of stories, *In Our Time* (1924), and in a novel, *The Sun Also Rises* (1926). Their disillusion, if not, strictly speaking, their war weariness, was shared by Lardner, whose *How to Write Short Stories* (a collection thereof) also appeared in 1924 (see Selection 100) — a year that was notable, as well, for the first performance of George Gershwin's *Rhapsody in Blue* (see Selection 66). Other writers who were being talked about were Vachel Lindsay (see Volume 13, Selection 90, and in this volume, Selection 46), E. E. Cummings (see Selections 74 and 97), and Lewis Mumford (see Selection 85); not only being talked about but doing much of the talking was H. L. Mencken (see Selections 23, 68, and 100).

In addition, two magazines that were a far cry from any and all of these emerged during these years. They were the *Reader's Digest,* which began publication in 1922, and *Time,* the first issue of which came out in 1923. Both would have a great effect on the minds of Americans in the ensuing decades.

The above may give the impression that everyone was reading. Of course it isn't so; they were making money (see Selections 37, 44, 53, 59, 62, 64, 71, 86, and 108), and trying to ensure a lasting peace and to prepare for the next war (see Selections 93 and 119) — and going to the movies! The new art (or industry — moviemakers still seem to have trouble deciding which) was very new then; the first Hollywood feature film was made in 1913 (it was called *The Squaw Man* and starred Dustin Farnum), and the first talking picture did not come out until 1929. Some great films were made nonetheless, among them D. W. Griffith's *Birth of a Nation* and Charlie Chaplin's *The Tramp* (both in 1915), and people discussed the movies and worried about their "influence" even when they weren't going to see them. (See Volume 13, Selections 24, 47, 64, 85, and 107; and see, in Volume 15, Selection 3.)

In short, the period covered by this fourteenth volume of *The Annals of America* — it is the first time we can honestly say it — was in some respects very much like our own.

Chronology:1916 - 1928

1916

Feb. 10. Germany declares that all armed merchant ships of the Allies will be sunk without warning after March 1. **Feb. 17.** Fearful that the U.S. will be drawn into the war, Representative Jeff McLemore proposes resolution aimed at official limitation of travel by U.S. citizens on Allied ships. **Feb. 24.** President Wilson tells Senate committee that he refuses to approve "abridgment of the rights of American citizens." **Feb. 25.** Senator Thomas P. Gore introduces even stronger antitravel resolution in the Senate. **March 3 and 7.** At White House insistence, resolutions are tabled in both Senate and House.

Feb. 18. U.S. Senate ratifies Bryan-Chamorro Treaty between the U.S. and Nicaragua after delay of 18 months caused by efforts to insert Platt Amendment of 1901; Treaty grants the U.S. sole rights to canal route, as well as 99-year lease of two islands and the Gulf of Fonseca as naval bases. The U.S. and Nicaragua both ignore Central American Court of Justice decision against the Treaty.

Feb. 22. In House-Grey memorandum, the U.S. and Great Britain agree on peace negotiations and U.S. participation in war; Colonel Edward House, President Wilson's personal adviser and emissary, has agreed with British Foreign Secretary Sir Edward Grey that on indications from France and Great Britain, the U.S. will call for negotiated peace. In case of refusal by Germany, memorandum states that the U.S. might well enter war against Germany.

March 7. Newton D. Baker is appointed secretary of war after forced resignation of Lindley M. Garrison in previous month. Garrison has resigned after President Wilson refused to accept his plan to transform state guard units into a continental army, because Wilson fears loss of congressional backing.

March 24. Following secret orders to sink any ship in the English Channel, German submarine torpedoes the unarmed French ship *Sussex,* injuring American passengers. **April 18.** President Wilson, resisting demands for a break with Germany, sends strong note stating that unless Germany discontinues such methods of warfare, the U.S. will break off relations. **May 4.** Germany agrees to ultimatum.

April 29. Socialist Labor Party meets and nominates Arthur E. Reimer of Massachusetts for President. **June 7.** Republican Party at Chicago meets and nominates Supreme Court Justice Charles Evans Hughes of New York for President and Charles W. Fairbanks of Indiana for Vice-President. On the same day, Progressive Party nominates Theodore Roosevelt for President, but Roosevelt refuses nomination and supports Hughes; this move eventually breaks up

Progressive Party, and its national committee supports Hughes, while a later conference at Indianapolis refuses to. **June 14.** Democrats meet at St. Louis and renominate President Wilson, with Vice-President Thomas R. Marshall as his running mate. **July 19.** Prohibition Party meets and nominates J. Frank Hanly of Indiana for President. Socialists hold no convention, but Allan L. Benson of New York is nominated for President in mail vote. Democrats campaign for Wilson with slogan "He Kept Us Out of War," which gains him many votes in states that have given women the suffrage. Hughes loses votes by failing to disclaim support of German-American and Irish-American groups that criticize President Wilson's foreign policy.

June. National Defense Act authorizes five-year expansion of Regular Army to about 220,000 men and establishes National Guard of more than 450,000 men and Officers Training Corps in colleges, as well as making some steps toward industrial mobilization. **Aug. 29.** Council of National Defense is established; six Cabinet members and expert civilian staff are to survey industrial, technical, social, and economic preparedness for possible war. Congress also passes "Big Navy" Act, largest naval appropriation up to this time, authorizing a construction program intended to make the U.S. fleet equal to any two others.

July 11. With automobile and truck production almost double that of the year before and 3,500,000 vehicles on the roads, President Wilson signs the Shackleford Good Roads Bill, which provides for $5 million in federal funds to be given to states that will supply equal amounts for road-building programs.

July 17. In Rural Credits Act, farmers and farmers' cooperatives are enabled to participate through Farm Loan Banks in financial reserve and credit facilities like those provided for banking and industry by Federal Reserve Act of 1913.

July 18. Britain denies commercial privileges to American companies and individuals whom it accuses of trading with the Central Powers. **Sept. 6 and 7.** President Wilson signs retaliatory Revenue Act and Shipping Board Act, both of which seek to control discrimination against blacklisted companies by foreign ships in U.S. ports. Acts are not put into effect, since Britain relaxes restrictions on listed companies.

Aug. 4. Denmark and the U.S. sign treaty providing for U.S. purchase of the Virgin Islands (Danish West Indies) for $25 million; the U.S. has feared that Germany wants the islands for a naval base. A governor is to be appointed by the President, and islanders are to have local home rule. U.S. citizenship is granted in 1927.

Aug. 11. Warehouse Act passed by Congress; law authorizes crop-financing loans to farmers, based on storage of certain major crops in authorized places, and begins a series of federal farm assistance programs that continues to the present day.

Aug. 29. Congress passes the Jones Act (Organic Act of the Philippine Islands), which restates the intention of the U.S. to establish Philippine independence when a stable government is formed and sets up machinery for self-government.

Sept. 2. Germany, after military successes, but fearing that the U.S. will enter the war, asks whether the U.S. will mediate. President Wilson declines to take any steps until after the fall elections. **Nov.** Wilson drafts peace mediation plan calling for a conference of nations involved, but the Allies will not consider any proposal.

Sept. 20. National Research Council is established to coordinate and stimulate wartime scientific developments; Council is continued after war.

Nov. 7-9. For three days presidential election is in doubt until final California count shows the state to have gone Democratic by fewer than 4,000 votes. Final popular vote is Wilson, 9,130,000; Hughes, 8,538,000. Electoral vote is Wilson, 277; Hughes, 254. Democrats keep control of both House and Senate.

Nov. 29. U.S. establishes military government in the Dominican Republic to guarantee financial stability; U.S. forces and administrators have been in the Dominican Republic for a decade, but renewed disorders in public life and increase in the public debt through failure to collect revenues lead to full U.S. occupation, which is continued until 1924.

Dec. 12. Germany states to all neutrals that the Central Powers are willing to negotiate a peace. Dec. 18. President Wilson abandons his November plan and merely asks the Allies and the Central Powers to state their war aims. Germany makes no statement. Dec. 30. The Allies decline to consider Germany's December 12 offer.

Dec. 29. Congress passes Stock-Raising Homestead Act, which doubles maximum homestead allowance to 640 acres of grazing land; act excludes mineral and coal-mine land.

Michigan, Montana, Nebraska, South Dakota, and Utah establish state Prohibition. By this date, through political maneuvering and the influence of the clergy, the Anti-Saloon League has been largely responsible for dry laws in 24 states, with a combined population of about 32,500,000 people.

By this year U.S. commerce with the Al-

lies is almost four times that of 1914, increased from about $800 million to about $3 billion; in the same period, trade with Germany and Austria-Hungary has dropped by about 70 percent.

John Dewey publishes *Democracy and Education*, in which he outlines ideas of late "progressive education" movement.

In this year there are 254,000 miles of railroads, more than at any time in U.S. history; since this peak, mileage has steadily declined to the present day.

1916 - 1917

March 15, 1916. General John J. Pershing begins pursuit of Francisco ("Pancho") Villa into Mexico. Villa's forces have shot 16 American engineers invited by President Carranza's government to run idle mines and have several times conducted raids into New Mexico and Texas, one of which has resulted in the death of 17 Americans. Nov. 24. Joint U.S.-Mexican commission signs agreement to withdraw U.S. troops from Mexico and set up U.S.-Mexican border guard system, but Carranza refuses to accept agreement. Jan. 28, 1917. Faced with prospect of war with Germany, President Wilson finally orders General Pershing to discontinue vain search for Villa and his guerrillas; search has resulted in frequent protests from Carranza government, although originally it had approved the move. Pershing withdraws on Febrary 5. After Carranza is reelected and new constitution adopted, the U.S. recognizes new Mexican government.

July 30, 1916. German saboteurs blow up munitions dump on Black Tom Island, New Jersey, causing $22 million damage. Jan. 11, 1917. Large foundry in New Jersey is blown up. Both acts of sabotage are later found by a claims commission to be the work of Germany, and the U.S. is awarded $55 million damages in 1939, but Germany never pays.

1916 - 1927

Atomic research progresses during this period as the concentric-shell theory of atomic structure is developed by Gilbert N. Lewis and Irving Langmuir; William D. Harkins predicts that atomic nuclei contain neutrons, although they are not actually discovered until 1932; Arthur H. Compton demonstrates the corpuscular structure of radiation; and Clinton J. Davisson with Lester H. Germer discovers that electrons have wave characteristics similar to those of light.

1916 - 1928

Carl Sandburg publishes his *Chicago Poems* in 1916; collection is praised and criticized widely. In *Cornhuskers* (1918), *Smoke and Steel* (1920), and *Slabs of the Sunburnt West* (1922), Sandburg covers a wide range of subject matter. Edwin Arlington Robinson gains an immediate reputation when he publishes *The Man Against the Sky* in 1916. His Arthurian legend cycle, *Merlin* (1917), *Lancelot* (1920), and *Tristram* (1927), gains him further attention; between 1921 and 1928 he is awarded the Pulitzer Prize three times.

1916 - 1929

U.S. painters, influenced by French artists, such as Marcel Duchamp, who have moved to the U.S. at the beginning of World War I, experiment with Cubism and abstraction, although some change to a purist style. The work of many painters of the period, however, is an objective record of the local scene: examples are Eugene Speicher's portraits and Edward Hopper's and Reginald Marsh's city paintings. Most

prominent painter of the period is John Marin, whose paintings — largely watercolor seascapes and landscapes — show influence of Expressionism, as well as Oriental style.

1917

Jan. 16. German Foreign Secretary Zimmermann sends coded note to German minister in Mexico instructing him to try to make an alliance between Germany and Mexico if the U.S. should enter the war in Europe. Mexico, supported by Germany, is to retake former Mexican areas of Arizona, Texas, and New Mexico; it is also to try to persuade Japan to transfer its allegiance to the Central Powers. **Feb. 24.** The British Navy, having intercepted and decoded Zimmermann's message, gives it to the U.S. ambassador to Great Britain, who sends it to the State Department. **March 1.** State Department authorizes newspaper publication.

Jan. 29. President Wilson vetoes literacy test for immigrants, stating that literacy is not a criterion of fitness to become a citizen. Act is passed over the veto; it requires all immigrants older than 16 to be able to read between 30 and 80 ordinary words in English or some other language.

Jan. 31. Germany informs the U.S. that unrestricted submarine warfare will be resumed on the following day; submarines will attack all Allied and neutral ships except for one U.S. ship per week that will be allowed to go to and from England under specific conditions.

January. The Allies send outline of peace demands to the U.S.; plan includes not only payment of indemnities and evacuation of occupied territories but also requires the reorganization of all Europe after the expulsion of the Ottoman Empire. **Jan. 22.** President Wilson, after receiving Allied terms, speaks to the Senate, outlining his own program and emphasizing the necessity of an international organization to establish and maintain lasting peace; he also stresses that peace achieved now cannot endure unless it is a "peace without victory."

Feb. 3. The U.S.S. *Housatonic* is sunk after warning by a German submarine. On the same day, President Wilson announces to Congress that the U.S. has broken off diplomatic relations with Germany. **Feb. 7.** The Senate approves Wilson's decision.

Feb. 23. Smith-Hughes Act provides federal funds for states to aid state vocational education programs; states are to match amounts contributed by the federal government.

March 1. House of Representatives, spurred by news of Germany's Mexican note, passes Armed Ship Bill at request of President Wilson, who feels that arming U.S. merchant ships will cut down submarine attacks and thus avert war; but a handful of senators, led by Robert M. La Follette, filibuster until close of Senate session, and Senate is unable to vote on bill. **March 8.** Secretary of State Robert Lansing advises Wilson that he can legally arm ships without approval of Congress. **March 12 and 13.** State Department announces that ships in war zones will be armed, and the Navy instructs armed ships to fire on submarines. By March 21, four more U.S. merchant ships have been sunk in European waters.

March 2. Organic Act for Puerto Rico makes Puerto Rico a U.S. territory and its inhabitants U.S. citizens and sets up a U.S.-style government with a governor appointed by the President.

March 15. Czar Nicholas II of Russia is forced to abdicate in revolution; temporary moderate government is formed. Errors of

incompetent supreme command under Kerensky who becomes minister of war in May and prime minister in July result in continuing defeats of Russian Army by Germans, and by end of summer, Russians are crushed. **Nov. 6-7.** Lenin leads October (November, new-style date) Revolution, overthrowing Kerensky and setting up Communist organization. **Dec.** Russia signs armistice agreement with Germany and in March 1918 signs separate peace, the Treaty of Brest-Litovsk. Russia's withdrawal from the war frees great numbers of German troops for service on the Western Front.

March 21. Urged to declare war on Germany by all members of his Cabinet on the previous day, President Wilson calls for a special session of Congress. **April 2.** Wilson asks Congress for a declaration of war against Germany, saying that the war is for world peace, and that "the world must be made safe for democracy." **April 4.** War resolution passes the Senate. **April 6.** The House passes the resolution, and President Wilson signs it. (War against Austria-Hungary is not declared until December 7.)

March 31. General Munitions Board is established to coordinate war industry, but lack of organization and weak enforcement powers make it relatively ineffectual.

April 16. Congress charters Emergency Fleet Corporation, capitalized at $50 million, to purchase, lease, and build merchant vessels.

April. By this time, U.S. private loans to the Allies have reached more than $2 billion since first permitted by the U.S. government in September 1915. Most of these sums are spent in the U.S. for food and munitions, helping stimulate war prosperity boom.

April-December. The U.S. mobilizes for

war. **April 14.** Committee on Public Information is established; it is the most vigorous and comprehensive propaganda agency of the U.S. government up to this time. **April 24.** Liberty Loan Act is passed; sale of bonds to the public provides financing for U.S. war effort and war supplies for the Allies. Five loan drives from June 1917 to April 1919 raise more than $20 billion. **May 18.** Congress passes Selective Service Act; under this and later supplementary acts, 24,200,000 men aged 18 to 45 register, and almost 3 million are drafted; more than 2 million men serve overseas. Many individuals serve in Allied units, especially before U.S. war declaration. **June 15.** Espionage Act is passed; it provides severe penalties for activity that hinders the war effort or aids the enemy, and includes post-office censorship measures to control circulation of seditious publications. **July 28.** General Munitions Board is replaced by War Industries Board; under financier Bernard Baruch after March 4, 1918, the Board has effective power in economic aspects of war, aids technological step-up, rationing, standardization of industry, and purchasing. **Aug. 10.** In Lever Food and Fuel Control Act, Congress authorizes price-fixing and other measures to control domestic industry and domestic consumption; Act prohibits use of grains and sugars for the manufacture of liquor. Administrator Herbert Hoover, in charge of food, achieves self-control by consumers and much extra effort in war production. **Oct. 3.** Congress passes War Revenue Act, providing for increased corporation and personal income taxes, excess profits taxes, and luxury taxes. Act makes these taxes the major source of federal revenue during the war. **Oct. 6.** Trading with the Enemy Act is passed; the government is given control over all foreign trade, the power to censor foreign mail, and the right to seize and dispose of U.S. property of enemy citizens. **Dec. 26.** U.S. Railroad Administration is established; government takes over control of most available track

on behalf of the war effort and, later, waterways and express systems. Control continues until March 1, 1920.

May 4. U.S. Navy begins convoy duty in the North Atlantic for troop transports and merchant ships; later the Navy pursues submarines and joins the British Navy in attempt to keep the German fleet out of the North Sea.

June 14. General Pershing arrives in Paris to direct U.S. overseas army. **June 26.** First U.S. troops reach France at Saint-Nazaire. **July 4.** Colonel Charles E. Stanton, for General Pershing, says, "Lafayette, we are here," at the tomb of the French general.

August. Two-way communication by radio telephone from an airplane to the ground is made. In same month two airborne planes communicate with each other over Langley Field, Virginia.

Nov. 2. U.S. and Japan sign Lansing-Ishii Agreement. Japan, having joined the Allies in 1914, has tried to increase her powers in China over protest of the U.S., which seeks to maintain its Open Door Policy. Japan has signed secret agreements that confirm its aims in China with many of the Allies and tries also to persuade the U.S. to agree. The resulting Lansing-Ishii Agreement grants Japan "special interests" in China owing to contiguity; Japan interprets this as meaning it has political rights despite its avowal to respect the Open Door Policy and territorial integrity of China.

In *Wilson* v. *New*, the U.S. Supreme Court upholds the Adamson Act, which sets eight-hour day for railroad workers in interstate commerce. Act has been passed hastily in 1916 to avoid national railroad strike. Court holds that although Act fixes wages, Congress has the power to set standards in emergencies.

Three experimental plants in Texas produce first helium in quantity; but production is not fast enough to be useful for military balloons in France, and most helium produced has not been shipped from the U.S. at end of the war.

First Pulitzer Prizes for biography and history are awarded; fund has been set up by bequest from publisher Joseph Pulitzer of *St. Louis Post-Dispatch* and *New York World.*

Hamlin Garland publishes *A Son of the Middle Border,* stimulating Middle Western regional literature; it is the first of 15 semihistorical works. Garland wins the Pulitzer Prize for biography in 1922 for *A Daughter of the Middle Border.*

Expatriate American poet T. S. Eliot publishes in England his first book of poems, *Prufrock and Other Observations,* which, with his *The Waste Land,* published in 1922, sets an entirely new style of poetry. During this same period, Eliot gains a firm reputation as a critic.

Julius Rosenwald Fund is chartered to serve "the well-being of mankind"; its funds ($30 million in 1929) aid Southern rural education, race relations, and the health and education of Negroes; it is dissolved in 1948.

1917 - 1918

Oct. 16, 1917. Four women who have been arrested for picketing for women's suffrage before the White House are given six-month prison sentences. Others are arrested in the following month. Jan. 10, 1918. House of Representatives adopts (Susan B. Anthony) resolution to submit a women's suffrage amendment to the states for ratification. Sept. 30. President Wilson, citing the increase of 1 million in women workers since 1915, urges women's suffrage on the Senate as a "necessary war measure"; proposal is not carried, although New York State has passed a suffrage amendment in the previous year, and there are strong movements in other states.

1917 - 1920

Dec. 18. Eighteenth Amendment to the Constitution is adopted by Congress and sent to the states for ratification; by this time 29 states have enacted Prohibition laws of one kind or another. The Amendment is ratified by January 29, 1919, and goes into effect on January 29, 1920.

1918

Jan. 8. In speech to Congress, President Wilson outlines the Fourteen Points, which he feels must be basis of peace. Feb. 11. Wilson supplements the Fourteen Points by the "Four Principles." "Five Particulars" for peace with Austria-Hungary are announced on September 27.

March 21. Weakened by British naval blockade and deterioration of its submarine campaign, Germany tries to defeat the Allies on the Western Front before large numbers of troops can arrive from the U.S. April 5. By this date, Germany has split the British and French armies by penetrating British 5th Army lines and has reached within 10 miles of British war supply dump at Amiens. Only 2,200 U.S. troops have taken part in the action. April 9. As Amiens drive is slowed, Germans launch attack to the north near Armentières and achieve a significant advance but cannot take advantage of gap in British lines.

March. Daylight saving time goes into effect.

April 14. With President Wilson's consent, General Ferdinand Foch of France is made supreme commander of the Allied armies. General Pershing puts U.S. troops at Foch's disposal, although he is determined to keep U.S. Army a separate unit.

April-June. The U.S. enacts further war mobilization measures. **April 5.** War Finance Corporation is formed to support war industries through loans and bond sales; authorized financing is set at $3,500,000,000. **April 8.** National War Labor Board is created to mediate labor disputes. **May 16.** Sedition Act is passed; aimed at Socialists and pacifists, Act broadens Espionage Act of 1917. It provides severe penalties for any verbal or other form of criticism of virtually any phase of the war effort. Under Sedition Act, Representative Victor L. Berger, Socialist elected in 1910, is indicted for pacifist activities and is refused seat in the House when elected again this year, and Socialist labor leader Eugene V. Debs is sentenced to 10 years in prison. **June 8.** War Labor Policies Board is formed; function is to prevent interference with the war effort by equalizing labor conditions.

May 28. American troops, in first U.S. offensive, capture Cantigny.

May 30. Having beaten back the Allies from Reims to Noyon and having taken Soissons, the Germans reach the Marne River on a 40-mile front, about 50 miles from Paris. **June 3-4.** A full division of U.S. troops with parts of other divisions, added to the Allied forces at Château-Thierry, help French stop the German drive at that point.

June 3. In *Hammer v. Dagenhart*, Supreme Court finds federal law that forbids interstate shipping of products made by child labor unconstitutional, holding that law violates rights of the states; Justice Holmes dissents, asserting that Congress may control interstate commerce in any way. Similar decision in 1922 finds 1919 Child Labor Act invalid.

June 6. In first large-scale participation of American troops, about 27,500 infantry and marines attack German lines and recapture Vaux, Bouresches, and Belleau Wood by July 1.

June 9. Germans, having advanced far enough to threaten Paris, launch a great attack along a front between Noyon and Montdidier. French troops and 27,000 Americans, briefly forced back for about six miles, by June 15 are able to hold the Germans at that point.

July 15. Germans attack from both east and west of Reims, making almost no progress to the east but crossing the Marne River on the west. Once across the river, however, they are held by Allied troops, including 85,000 Americans. By this month, more than 1 million U.S. troops have arrived in France, and Marshal Foch is able to take the offensive for the first time. **July 18.** French units with 270,000 U.S. troops attack eastward between the Aisne and Marne rivers to eliminate the German pocket that threatens Paris. **Aug. 6.** By this date the pocket has been crushed, and the Allies have swung northeastward to a line between Soissons and Reims.

Aug. 8. British troops, supported by about 54,000 Americans, strike eastward along the Somme River. Offensive in this area continues for three months.

Aug. 10. General Pershing, who, since first put in command of U.S. forces, has insisted on a separate U.S. Army, organizes the 1st U.S. Army under his own command, although he remains commander of the American Expeditionary Force. Marshal Foch, convinced of the competence of American troops, agrees.

Aug. 17. French troops, accompanied by about 85,000 Americans, attack northward along Soissons-Reims line toward the Belgian border, which they near by November 11. U.S. troops, however, have been withdrawn by mid-September to take part in planned Meuse-Argonne offensive to the east.

Aug. 21. British, aided by 108,000 American troops, attack in Belgium from Ypres; battle continues until the Armistice.

Sept. 12. In preparation for future attack on German supply lines (Meuse-Argonne offensive), more than a half million American troops, aided by some Allied air units, all under General Pershing, attack bulge in German lines at Saint-Mihiel; within a day, the bulge has been cut off. At the cost of 7,000 U.S. casualties, 16,000 German prisoners and more than 400 pieces of artillery are taken.

Sept. 26. Huge pincer offensive, planned as a joint effort by Marshal Foch with Allied leaders, begins with U.S. troops concentrated between the Meuse River and the Argonne Forest. U.S. objective is main supply railroad and iron mines being used by Germans. Germans are gradually worn down until end of October, when they suddenly give ground and retreat eastward and northward until November 11, when the Armistice is declared. Prolonged battle costs about 120,000 American casualties.

Sept. 29. General Erich von Ludendorff, aware that the German Army is near collapse and alarmed by the surrender of Bulgaria, urges the German government to request an armistice. **Oct. 3.** Prince Maximilian of Baden becomes chancellor of Germany and immediately sends peace note to President Wilson, saying that Germany will accept Wilson's Fourteen Points as a basis for peace. **Oct. 30.** Austria also requests an armistice.

Oct. 16. Congress passes wartime measure that prohibits entry into the country of aliens who advocate overthrowing the government by force. In 1920 an additional act is passed that allows deportation of alien anarchists and enemies of the U.S.

Oct. 24-Nov. 4. Italians, with a small contingent of U.S. troops, achieve final defeat of the Austrian Army in a ten-day offensive at Vittorio Veneto.

Oct. 25. President Wilson appeals to the people to retain a Democratic Congress as a demonstration of confidence in his policies. Appeal is widely disapproved, since Wilson had declared a moratorium on politics during the war; 26 Democratic seats are lost in the House and 6 in the Senate, resulting in Republican majorities in House and Senate.

Nov. 5. President Wilson, having spent almost a month in armistice negotiations, finally transmits Allied peace terms to Germany. Delay has been caused by refusal of the Allies to accept Wilson's Fourteen Points and by Wilson's reluctance to deal with the German government, which he feels does not represent the German people. Suggestion that the U.S. will negotiate separately with Germany finally has persuaded the Allies to accept the Fourteen Points but with some reservations.

Nov. 6. German representatives start for France to negotiate an armistice. Three days earlier, revolution has broken out and is sweeping the country. The German fleet has mutinied when ordered on a hopeless mission against the British Navy. Turkey and Austria have surrendered. The Allied offensive continues on all fronts. **Nov. 9.** Kaiser William abdicates, and Prince Maximilian resigns in favor of Socialist Friedrich Ebert; Germany becomes a republic.

Nov. 11. With home and military situations as they are, Germany has no choice but to accept drastic terms of Armistice, which is signed at 5 A.M. in Marshal Foch's railroad car in the Forest of Compiègne. Hostilities cease at 11 A.M. In the U.S., where the news is received at 3 A.M. New York time, the wildest demonstrations in U.S. history take place.

Nov. 18. President Wilson announces that he will attend the peace conference, incurring wide criticism in the U.S., where he is called "egotistic." Republican criticism is strongest when it is announced that Wilson's peace commission lacks a member of the Senate and contains only one Republican.

Estimated casualties of World War I: Total Allies: of 42,189,000 who have served, 5,152,000 dead, 12,831,000 wounded, 4,121,000 prisoners or missing. Central Powers: of 65,039,000 who have served, 8,538,000 dead, 21,219,000 wounded, 7,751,000 prisoners or missing. U.S.: of 4,355,000 who have served, 126,000 dead (about 50,000 in battle and the rest of disease, especially influenza, which has devastated U.S. military camps), 234,000 wounded, 4,500 prisoners or missing.

The Education of Henry Adams, first published privately in 1907, is published after the author's death and becomes a best seller. Booth Tarkington publishes his study of three generations, *The Magnificent Ambersons*. Both receive the Pulitzer Prize in the following year. Willa Cather publishes her novel of prairie life, *My Antonia*. First installments of *Ulysses*, by James Joyce, appear in the *Little Review* and are burned by the U.S. Post Office Department as obscene. Book is banned from the U.S. until 1933.

The United Lutheran Church in America is formed from 45 divided synods when members reach an agreement on a common doctrine.

1918 - 1919

In several cases the Supreme Court upholds war power of the U.S. government. In *Arver* v. *U.S.*, the Court finds that conscription is authorized by the Constitution in Article I ("to declare war . . . to raise and support armies"); a temporary Prohibition measure, passed to conserve grain and sugar, is called a valid exercise of government wartime powers; and in *Northern Pacific Railway* v. *North Dakota*, the Court finds that the seizure and operation of railroads comes within granted war powers.

September. Influenza epidemic, traveling westward from Europe, begins in eastern U.S. and spreads to 46 states. Before it subsides in 1919, it kills about 500,000 people, disrupts services, shuts down war plants, suspends the draft in some places, and causes panic throughout the U.S. Throughout the world at least 20,000,000 people die, and one billion are sick.

1918 - 1927

May 15, 1918. New York City to Washington, D.C., flight is beginning of first scheduled airmail service in the U.S. Stamps cost 24 cents (reduced to 6 cents by November). **Sept. 10.** In first one-day Chicago to New York City airmail flight, overall time for delivery of mail is less than 13 hours. Daily service is begun in following year. **July-Aug. 1920.** First airmail flight between New York City and San Francisco. Air transport grows rapidly as private bidders are given airmail contracts. Regular night flights begin in 1924. Aerial navigation is aided by installation of radio beacons in 1925, and Air Commerce Act is passed in 1926; Act provides for government backing of civil airlines and building of airports. **Sept. 1, 1927.** Airlines and American Railway Express Agency cooperate to establish air express.

1919

Jan. 18. Paris peace conference opens without Germany or its associates. All major matters are discussed privately by President Wilson of the U.S., Prime Minister David Lloyd George of Great Britain, Premier Georges Clemenceau of France, and Premier Vittorio Orlando of Italy.

Jan. 25. Peace conference agrees, after urging by President Wilson, that a League of Nations must be an integral part of the peace treaty. **Feb. 3.** Commission, headed by Wilson, starts writing draft of League of Nations Covenant. **Feb. 14.** Draft is submitted to conference, and on the following day, Wilson leaves for the U.S.

Feb. 26. Opposition to the League already having grown in the U.S., President Wilson finds that Senate and House committees on foreign relations and many senators are unwilling to consider peace treaty that contains Covenant. They insist on first considering treaty alone. Wilson resists this proposal.

March 14. President Wilson arrives in Paris for negotiations on peace treaty. Although the Allies generally have agreed to Wilson's Fourteen Points, every Ally has an exception to propose in its own favor. Wilson's peace of conciliation becomes impossible in view of concessions he must make to every nation's territorial and economic demands. In addition to compromises on the peace treaty, Wilson, on the advice of senators in favor of the League, proposes amendments to the League Covenant that specifically exempt the U.S. from some of its measures; pro-League senators hope that these amendments will gain support of anti-League forces.

March 15-17. American Legion is formed in Paris when delegates from 1,000 units of the American Expeditionary Force meet.

April 19. Theater Guild, New York City, opens first play of many successes; Guild has been organized to improve and encourage American drama.

May 7. The completed peace treaty with League Covenant attached is submitted to Germany. **June 28.** Germany signs treaty. **July 10.** President Wilson presents treaty to the Senate for ratification. Senate opinion is divided three ways: Democrats for immediate ratification; moderates who want the U.S. to join the League of Nations with reservations to protect U.S. interests; and anti-League senators who refuse to accept the Covenant under any circumstances; 6 of the latter are on the 17-man Senate Foreign Relations Committee. Senate hearings and vigorous public debate continue until September 10, when Senate Committee submits 49 changes.

August. Communist Labor Party of America (present-day American Communist Party) is formed in Chicago after split from Socialist Party; Communists adopt platform and symbol of the Third International.

Sept. 3. President Wilson starts tour of country, convinced that if he takes his case for the League and the treaty to the people, popular pressure will force its ratification. He is opposed by a large national propaganda campaign and by two senators who make their own tour at the same time. Wilson makes about 37 speeches, traveling to 29 Middle Western and Western cities by September 25. **Oct. 2.** Having become ill in Colorado and returning to Washington, Wilson has a stroke, which eliminates him from treaty discussions.

Sept. 9. About three-quarters of 1,500-man Boston police force goes on strike.

Widespread looting occurs. Governor Calvin Coolidge calls out entire State Guard and breaks strike, saying that no one has a right to strike against the public safety.

Sept. 22. U.S. Steel Corporation workers strike when management refuses to discuss issues, mainly union status questions. Strike lasts for almost four months. Steel and coal industry unions have not been so successful as others in membership gains and in dealing with employers since the war.

Oct. 28. Volstead Act is passed over President Wilson's veto; Act provides enforcement power for Prohibition amendment. Almost immediately, after distillers and liquor distributors go out of business, criminal elements (bootleggers) take over, their operations growing steadily through the 1920s.

Nov. 6. Senator Lodge presents a resolution of ratification of the peace treaty after the 49 changes of the anti-League senators have been defeated; resolution contains only 14 reservations. **Nov. 18.** President Wilson, unwilling to make even this more moderate compromise, writes to pro-League Democrats, urging them to vote down the new resolution, since it provides "for the nullification of the treaty."

Nov. 19. Wilson supporters accede to his request and, with anti-League Republicans, block ratification, since their votes make a two-thirds majority impossible. Although a compromise is worked out in the following weeks, the final ratifying resolution still contains reservations that Wilson will not accept, and he again asks his followers to vote against it. The final vote once more fails of a two-thirds majority, and the U.S. never joins the League of Nations.

Financial cost of World War I to the U.S., including loans to the Allies, is about $41,500,000,000, more than half of which has been raised by borrowing; 1917 public debt of $1,300,000,000 has risen to $26 billion by 1919, a per capita debt of $246.

In *Schenck* v. *United States*, the Supreme Court unanimously upholds the Espionage Act, finding that free speech does not include the right to encourage resistance to conscription and that it must always be under control, especially in wartime.

Sherwood Anderson publishes *Winesburg, Ohio*, short stories of "average" people. James Branch Cabell publishes his version of the Faust story, *Jurgen: a Comedy of Justice*. Henry L. Mencken publishes the first edition of *The American Language*, which appears in various editions and with various supplements until 1948.

1919 - 1920

Dec. 22, 1919. About 250 alien "anarchists," Communists, and labor agitators are deported and sail for Russia. Fear generated by wartime hysteria and by Russian agitation against Western nations and in behalf of the Bolshevik Revolution in Russia leads to "Red scare." **Jan. 2, 1920.** Federal agents in nationwide raids arrest 2,700 persons; mass arrests, police espionage, and raids continue into May.

1920

Feb. 13. Secretary of State Robert Lansing leaves office; President Wilson has accused him of conducting unauthorized Cabinet meetings during Wilson's incapacity and has requested his resignation.

Feb. 28. Congress passes Esch-Cummins (Transportation) Act, which releases the railroads from government wartime control on March 1, greatly extends the powers of the Interstate Commerce Commission as concerns the railroads, and establishes a Railroad Labor Board to handle labor disputes.

March 19. Although Versailles Treaty ratification and Covenant of the League of Nations are finally defeated by the Senate for second time on this date, the U.S. takes part in work of many League technical commissions until the League is terminated in 1946 in favor of the United Nations.

May 5. Socialist Labor Party meets and nominates W. W. Cox of Missouri for President. **May 8.** Socialist Party meets and nominates Eugene V. Debs of Indiana for President, although he is serving a 10-year sentence for sedition. **June 8.** Republicans meet at Chicago and nominate Warren G. Harding of Ohio for President; nomination is engineered by party bosses, who are unable to engineer vice-presidential nomination; this goes on first ballot to Calvin Coolidge, governor of Massachusetts. **June 28.** Democrats meet at San Francisco and nominate Governor James M. Cox of Ohio for President on the forty-fourth ballot; Assistant Secretary of the Navy Franklin D. Roosevelt of New York is named Cox's running mate. **July 11.** Farmer-Labor Party (formed on June 12) meets and nominates Parley P. Christensen of Utah for President. **July 12.** Single Tax Party meets and nominates Robert C. Macauley of Pennsylvania. **July 21.** Prohibition Party meets and nominates Aaron S. Watkins. Republican platform vaguely advocates an "agreement among nations" to preserve peace but is against the Covenant of the League of Nations; Harding campaigns from his home, stressing a "return to normalcy." Democratic platform is in favor of the Covenant, as well as the Versailles Treaty, but leaves the door open for reservations to the Covenant to protect U.S. interests.

May 20. In a joint resolution, Congress declares war with Germany and Austria-Hungary ended, but President Wilson vetoes the resolution.

June 5. Congress passes Jones (Merchant Marine) Act, which, in addition to repealing measures passed during the war to regulate shipping, seeks to build up the U.S. Merchant Marine by various procedures.

June 10. Congress passes Water Power Act, which sets up the Federal Power Commission to regulate generation of electric power from navigable streams and waters of public lands and transportation on these waters.

Aug. 26. Women finally get the vote when the Nineteenth Amendment to the Constitution is declared ratified. By this time, 15 states have passed women's suffrage laws.

Nov. 2. In election, Harding wins decisively with a popular vote of 16,152,000 to Cox's 9,147,000; Debs polls almost 1 million votes in spite of being a federal prisoner. Electoral vote is Harding, 404; Cox, 127. Harding's victory dashes President Wilson's hope that the election will result in a national referendum in favor of the Versailles Treaty and the League Covenant.

Dec. 10. President Wilson's disappointment over his failure to get popular backing for the League of Nations is partially softened when he is awarded the 1919 Nobel Peace Prize.

U.S. census of this year shows a population of 105,711,000, almost a 15 percent increase over 1910; this includes 5,736,000 immigrants, fewer than in previous decade; to the present day, immigration has never again been so large. Movement of population shows 4,189,000 more people moving westward than eastward and 430,000 more moving northward than southward. For first time, rural population is smaller than urban. Only 6 percent of the population is illiterate, almost 2 percent less than in 1910. Bureau of Public Health finds average life expectancy at birth is 54.1 years.

In *Missouri* v. *Holland,* the Supreme Court finds that Congress may gain from treaties powers that it is not given in the U.S. Constitution; acts of Congress are controlled by the restrictions of the 10th Amendment, but treaties are not; therefore, powers not enumerated in the Constitution may be assumed by means of treaty.

1920 - 1922

Aug. 20, 1920. First regular licensed radio broadcasting is started by Station WWJ in Detroit. **Nov. 2.** First national service begins when Station KDKA in East Pittsburgh broadcasts Harding-Cox election returns; KDKA has been operated experimentally by Westinghouse Electric and Manufacturing Company. **1922.** WEAF, New York, broadcasts first-known commercially sponsored program.

Eugene O'Neill's first full-length play, *Beyond the Horizon,* opens, and in the same year, *The Emperor Jones;* in 1921 *Anna Christie* is produced, and in 1922, *The Hairy Ape.*

1920 - 1925

Sinclair Lewis' novel *Main Street,* a satire of small-town life, receives national attention in 1920; he continues the theme with *Babbitt* in 1922. F. Scott Fitzgerald publishes his enormously successful novel *This Side of Paradise,* as well as a volume of short stories, *Flappers and Philosophers,* in 1920; *The Beautiful and the Damned* (1922) and *Tales of the Jazz Age* (1922) are followed by his major work, *The Great Gatsby,* in 1925.

Edith Wharton publishes her novel of 1870 New York society, *The Age of Innocence,* Pulitzer Prize novel of 1921. John Dos Passos publishes *Three Soldiers,* novel reflecting postwar disillusionment, in 1921; *Manhattan Transfer,* dealing with city life, is published in 1925.

1920 - 1927

April 15, 1920. Paymaster and guard for Massachusetts shoe factory are killed during payroll robbery. Three weeks later, Nicola Sacco and Bartolomeo Vanzetti, Brockton, Massachusetts, workmen, are arrested and charged with the murder. **July 14, 1921.** Nicola Sacco and Bartolomeo Vanzetti are convicted of murder. Worldwide protest results, since many people believe the immigrant laborers have been convicted for their anarchist beliefs rather than for murder. Many attempts are made for retrial on ground of false identification, but all fail, even when, in 1925, a convict confesses that he and others were responsible. **April 9, 1927.** The men are sentenced to die, the Massachusetts Supreme Court having refused to reverse the decision. Bowing to protest throughout the world, Massachusetts governor appoints investigating committee, which later advises him not to exercise clemency. **Aug. 23.** Sacco and Vanzetti, still protesting innocence, are executed.

1921

March 4. President Harding, referring to the League of Nations in his inaugural address, says, "We seek no part in directing the destinies of the world."

May 19. Congress passes law to limit immigration; called the Quota Act, it allows only 3 percent of 1910 immigration from any country in one year and puts an overall limit of 357,000 on annual immigration.

June 10. Congress passes Budget and Accounting Act in effort to reform U.S. budget practices. Act creates Bureau of Budget and provides for annual submission to Congress of a budget for the coming year, accounting of the past year's expenses, and recommendations on financial measures. **June 21.** Charles G. Dawes is appointed director of the budget.

July 2. Congress, in joint resolution, declares World War I ended. **August.** Separate treaties with Germany, Austria, and Hungary are signed and ratified shortly thereafter.

July 21. General William ("Billy") Mitchell, assistant chief of the air service, demonstrates the superiority of aircraft over ships and the military value of concentrated bombing when massed planes sink a former German battleship in test off Virginia coast. Mitchell, outstanding U.S. air combat commander of World War I, is a strong advocate of a separate air force.

Aug. 9. Veterans Bureau is established; directly under the President, the Bureau is to coordinate all veterans' welfare action.

Aug. 15. Congress passes Packers and Stockyards Act to eliminate manipulation of prices and monopolies in meat-packing industries; regulations are to be enforced by the Department of Agriculture. **Aug. 24.** Similar legislation, the Future Trading Act, is designed to control speculation in grain; Act is voided by the Supreme Court in 1922 and another passed, to be enforced under the interstate commerce power.

Aug. 16. Department of Labor estimates that unemployment throughout the country has risen to more than 5 million. End of wartime boom has brought business depression. Many industries have announced drastic wage cuts, in some cases up to 22 percent. **Sept. 30.** National conference on unemployment proposes a program to provide jobs and advises manufacturers and retailers to reduce prices. Agricultural depression is most severe and long lasting, with forced sales of farms, foreclosures, and bankruptcies increasing steadily into the middle Thirties.

Nov. 2. National Birth Control League and Voluntary Parenthood League are combined to form American Birth Control League in New York City; League is headed by Mrs. Margaret Sanger. In the same year a New York physician is convicted of disseminating birth control information for selling *Married Love* by Marie C. Stopes.

Nov. 5. President Harding proclaims November 11, Armistice Day, a national holiday. **Nov. 11.** First burial ceremony is held at the Tomb of the Unknown Soldier (present-day Tomb of the Unknowns) at Arlington (Virginia) National Cemetery.

Nov. 23. Congress passes the Sheppard-Towner Act, which provides funds to states for maternal and infant welfare. Act is widely criticized as interference with states' rights.

Clayton Antitrust Act of 1914 is considerably weakened as to labor union protection when the Supreme Court finds in *Duplex Printing Press Company* v. *Deering* that anti-injunction clauses of the act do not apply to secondary boycotts by labor unions.

1921 - 1922

May 27, 1921. Congress passes Emergency Tariff Act, which raises tariffs on most agricultural products, a reversal of the reductions achieved by the Wilson administration. **Sept. 21, 1922.** Protective Fordney-McCumber Tariff Act is passed; it raises duties on manufactured goods and, in an attempt to protect farmers, places even higher tariffs on farm products than those of the previous year.

Nov. 12, 1921. Washington (D.C.) Conference convenes, with all major powers represented except Russia, which has not been invited. Seven treaties are made among Great Britain, France, Japan, Italy, the U.S., and four other nations, involving limitation of warships, restrictions on use of submarines, outlawing of poison gas, rights to Pacific island territories, joint consultation in case of aggression in the Pacific, guarantee of the Open Door Policy in China, and various other Pacific area questions. Conference adjourns in February 1922.

1921 - 1924

1921. The South is swept by whippings, tarrings, brandings, and destruction of property of Negroes and white sympathizers; most activity involves the Ku Klux Klan, and many incidents seem to be unmotivated. 1922. Klan activity has become so violent in the Middle West that Oklahoma is placed under martial law to control terrorists. 1923. *Baltimore Sun* and *New York World* expose activities of the Ku Klux Klan in the South, North, and Middle West. Louisiana refuses to indict offenders, even though evidence of torture and murder is given, but Indiana Grand Dragon is convicted of second degree murder. 1924. Klan has an estimated 4 million members, but by 1930 the number has decreased to about 30,000.

1922

Feb. 18. Congress passes Capper-Volstead Act, which encourages consumer and producer cooperatives and exempts various agricultural associations from the antitrust laws.

April 15. Senator John B. Kendrick of Wyoming calls upon Secretary of the Interior Albert B. Fall to explain information received from Wyoming that the Teapot Dome oil fields are in fact leased to Harry F. Sinclair's Mammoth Oil Company when the Senate has set them aside for the U.S. Navy.

May 23. Anne Nichols' play *Abie's Irish Rose*, whose underlying theme is religious prejudice, opens in New York City and runs for more than five years, the longest run of any U.S. play to this date.

May 30. Lincoln Memorial is dedicated in Washington, D.C. It has been designed by Henry Bacon in Greco-Roman style, with 36 columns to represent the states of the Union at the time of Abraham Lincoln's death, and contains a colossal seated statue of Lincoln by Daniel Chester French.

June 22. Bitter antiemployer feeling in railroad and coal strikes culminates in murder of strikebreakers by union miners in Herrin, Illinois. Labor union membership declines by almost one-third in this decade because of 1921-1922 depression, federal court attacks, and employer opposition.

Nov. 7. In fall elections Republicans lose 76 House seats and 8 Senate seats but retain majorities in both houses of Congress.

Explorer and film maker Robert J. Flaherty opens his pioneer film *Nanook of the North*, made during a 16-month stay with the Eskimos; later termed "documentary," the film sets a standard for such works.

Winner of international competition for an architectural design for the Chicago Tribune Tower is a Gothic-style building, but the massed modern tower of Finnish second prize winner Eliel Saarinen has far greater influence on future building design. Saarinen moves to the U.S. in the following year.

1922 - 1925

Feb. 9, 1922. Congress authorizes World

War Foreign Debt Commission to renegotiate international war debts — postwar relief loans as well as war loans — which amount to more than $10 billion. Britain and France, especially, with debts to the U.S. totaling about $7,682,000,000, have argued for cancellation of debts by all countries, but President Wilson has been adamant. When arguments are advanced in 1922 for reduction of the debts, President Harding also refuses, as President Coolidge does later. **Nov. 14, 1925.** Because of severe financial depression in Europe, the U.S. finally agrees on drastic reduction of debts, as well as of interest rate, but still insists on partial payment. This stand creates anti-U.S. sentiment in Europe, which in turn results in isolationist feeling in the U.S.

The *Reader's Digest*, publishing condensations of material from other publications, is founded by De Witt Wallace in 1922 in New York. In 1923 Henry R. Luce and Briton Hadden found *Time*, a weekly news magazine. H. L. Mencken and George Jean Nathan begin publishing the *American Mercury*, containing literary and critical pieces, in 1924. Henry Siedel Canby begins publishing the *Saturday Review of Literature* in the same year. Harold W. Ross founds sophisticated weekly magazine, *The New Yorker*, in 1925; James Thurber becomes editor for a short time in 1927.

1922. Albert H. Taylor and Leo C. Young demonstrate results of research into radio detection, the forerunner of radar. **1925.** Pulse-ranging radar similar to present-day technique is first used for investigation of the ionosphere by Gregory Breit and Merle A. Tuve.

1922-1927

1922. Technicolor process for moving pictures makes commercial debut, but it is not used widely until about 20 years later. **1923.** Lee De Forest demonstrates sound on movie film; the first full-length movie using sound (*The Jazz Singer*, starring Al Jolson) is shown in 1927.

1923

March 4. Congress passes Intermediate Credits Act, which expands and strengthens agricultural credit system and encourages farm cooperatives in an effort to counter agricultural depression.

March. Emphatic protest by Indians results in defeat of Bursum Bill, which would have transferred Pueblo lands to white settlers without compensation. In the following year, Pueblo Land Board is established to set amount of compensation, which is not paid until 1933.

May 4. In spite of President Harding's warning that federal authorities will have to take over Prohibition enforcement, Governor Alfred E. Smith of New York signs legislation repealing New York's Prohibition enforcement act.

July 28. President Harding becomes ill suddenly on return trip from Alaska and is rushed to San Francisco, where he dies on August 2. **Aug. 3.** Calvin Coolidge is sworn in as President by his father in Vermont at 2:30 A.M., when the news reaches him.

Dec. 6. In President Coolidge's first annual message to Congress, he supports a World Court, enforcement of Prohibition, lower taxes, and government economy. This is the first time an official presidential message has been broadcast.

In *Adkins* v. *Children's Hospital*, the Supreme Court calls unconstitutional a 1918 District of Columbia act that seeks to set minimum wages for women.

In *Wolff Packing Company* v. *Court of Industrial Relations*, Supreme Court finds that a state legislature cannot control an industry on the ground that it is involved in the public interest merely by stating that it is in this category. In a later similar decision, Justice Holmes dissents, holding that states have the right to enact any legislation not specifically prohibited by the federal Constitution. By 1934 Court has come to agree with Holmes's opinion that any industry may be in the public interest and thus liable to state control.

By this year, about 13,300,000 automobiles are registered in the U.S., slightly less than triple the number in 1917; this number is two million less than the number of telephones being used in the same year.

Du Pont Company acquires rights to manufacture cellophane from a French company; first U.S.-made cellophane is produced in Buffalo in 1924. It has been produced in Switzerland since 1912.

The Covered Wagon, voted one of 10 best movies of the year by *Film Daily,* sets the style for Western spectacles and is the beginning of popularity of Westerns which continues to the present day; production costs have been $350,000, and it nets $1,500,000 on the road.

E. E. Cummings publishes his first book of poems, *Tulips and Chimneys,* written in original poetic and typographic style; this is followed by *XLI Poems* in 1925 and *& and is 5* in 1926.

1924

Feb. 8. Commonwealth Land Party (Single Tax Party of 1920) meets and nominates W. J. Wallace of New Jersey for President. **May 11.** Socialist Labor Party meets and nominates Frank T. Johns of Oregon. **June 3.** American Party meets and nominates Judge Gilbert O. Nations of Washington, D.C. **June 5.** Prohibition Par-

ty meets and nominates Herman P. Faris for President and Marie C. Brehm for Vice-President. **June 10.** Republicans meet at Cleveland and nominate President Calvin Coolidge for reelection and General Charles G. Dawes of Illinois for Vice-President. **June 24.** Democrats meet at New York and nominate John W. Davis of West Virginia for President and Governor Charles W. Bryan of Nebraska for Vice-President; nomination of Davis follows 16-day battle between supporters of Alfred E. Smith and William G. McAdoo; and Davis is not nominated until the 103rd ballot. **July 4.** Progressive Party is formed in Cleveland by Conference for Progressive Political Action, representing farmers and workers; new party is backed by the American Federation of Labor, Farmer Labor Party, and Socialist Party. Convention nominates Senator Robert M. La Follette of Wisconsin for President and Senator Burton K. Wheeler of Montana for Vice-President. **July 11.** Workers' (Communist) Party meets and nominates William Z. Foster for President. Republican platform supports lower taxes, higher tariffs, economy, arms limitation, and international cooperation to keep peace. Democratic platform advocates competitive tariff, disarmament, and the League of Nations, and strikes at Harding administration graft. Progressives favor freedom of labor union action, government ownership of water resources and railroads, and child labor limitation, and denounce corruption, monopolies, and administration finance program.

Feb. 12. George Gershwin's *Rhapsody in Blue,* a new kind of symphonic jazz, is performed for the first time, with Gershwin as piano soloist accompanied by Paul Whiteman's orchestra. In the following year, Gershwin produces a sequel, *Concerto in F,* commissioned by Walter Damrosch, and in 1928, his symphonic poem, *An American in Paris,* which includes French taxi horns among its instruments.

Feb. 27. A treaty is signed with the Dominican Republic that supersedes that of 1907; an election is held, and in July, when a president is inaugurated, U.S. Marines are withdrawn.

April 9. Dawes Plan on German reparations is reported. Reparations due from Germany have been fixed at 132 billion gold marks in 1921, a figure that has been accepted by Germany after an Allied threat to occupy the Ruhr, with its great coal and iron industries; but the mark has collapsed, becoming worthless by 1923, and Germany has defaulted on payments; France and Belgium, angry at Germany's failure, have occupied Ruhr. A committee, headed by Charles G. Dawes, has been appointed to investigate German finances. Dawes Plan calls for Allied supervision of the Reichsbank; total reparations are left undetermined, with a graduated plan of payment and a loan to Germany of 800 million gold marks. Total reparations are finally set by Young Plan, which becomes effective in 1930.

May 19. Soldiers Bonus Bill is passed over President Coolidge's veto. President Harding has vetoed a similar bill in 1922, but veterans' organizations persistently have put pressure on Congress. All veterans under the rank of major are given 20-year annuities, based on $1.25 per day for overseas service and $1 per day for service in the U.S., on which they may borrow from the government.

May 26. Congress passes second quota law, which cuts immigration to half of 1921 quota; new annual quota is based on 2 percent of nationals from each country present in U.S. in 1890; change of date from 1910 to 1890 is made to reduce number of immigrants from southern and eastern Europe, about 70 percent of 1910 entries. Act is to control immigration until 1927, at which time a survey of national origins will be the basis for an immigration limit of 150,000. Strongly opposed, second quota law is not put into effect until 1929. Neither 1921 nor 1924 quota law applies to citizens of countries in the Americas and Canada.

June 2. Congress submits proposed constitutional Child Labor Amendment to the states for ratification, but opinion that the issue is a matter for state legislation is so strong that only 26 of the necessary 36 states have ratified it 26 years later.

June 15. Congress passes act making all native-born Indians full U.S. citizens.

July 1. "Hate America" meetings are held in Tokyo on this date, officially called "Humiliation Day," because of U.S. Immigration Act of 1924 that prohibits all immigration of Japanese persons, who are considered "ineligible to citizenship." Act follows earlier California and other state laws that restrict ownership and right to rent agricultural land.

Aug. 24. Congress passes Agricultural Credits Act in effort to forestall bankruptcies and dumping of surplus farm goods by dealers; dealers and cooperatives are granted loans to allow them to hold goods.

Nov. 4. President Coolidge is elected by popular vote of 15,718,000 to Davis' 8,385,000. Electoral vote is Coolidge, 382; Davis, 136. La Follette receives almost 5 million votes but carries only Wisconsin, with 13 electoral votes.

Nov. 30. Radio Corporation of America demonstrates wireless telegraph transmission of photographs from New York to London; process takes about 25 minutes per photograph.

J. Edgar Hoover is appointed head of Bureau of Investigation (established in 1908 and renamed Federal Bureau of Investigation in 1935), and Bureau is immediately reorganized to eliminate political considerations.

Lewis Mumford publishes his social history of architecture, *Sticks and Stones*. In Paris newspaper reporter Ernest Hemingway publishes *In Our Time*, a collection of short stories that sets a new terse style in prose. Columnist Ring (Ringgold Wilmer) Lardner publishes his collection *How To Write Short Stories*, which, with earlier stories, revives an American tradition of vernacular satire; *The Love Nest* and *Round Up* are published in 1926 and 1929, respectively.

By this year, there are 2,500,000 radios in the U.S., as opposed to 5,000 sets in 1920, used mostly by professionals.

Name of Trinity College in Durham, North Carolina, is changed by the trustees to Duke University to comply with conditions of multimillion-dollar trust fund established by tobacco millionaire James B. Duke.

1924-1927

Congressional committees investigating rumors that have started in 1922 find that graft and corruption have been rife during the Harding administration. Officials appointed innocently by Harding have used their offices for personal gain; departments involved are Interior, Navy, Justice, the Veterans Bureau, and the Office of the Alien Property Custodian. Secretary of the Interior Albert B. Fall is found to have accepted a bribe and leased naval oil reserves at Teapot Dome, Wyoming, and in California to a private oil company; eventually, he is sent to prison, and Secretary of the Navy Edwin N. Denby, who has been innocently involved, is forced to resign. Attorney General Harry M. Daugherty, in conjunction with members of the "Ohio Gang," a

group of grasping politicians, is found to have accepted bribes from Prohibition law violators, as well as failing to act on graft he knew existed in the Veterans Bureau; Daugherty, although not convicted, is forced to resign by President Coolidge. Colonel Charles R. Forbes, head of the Veterans Bureau until his resignation in 1923, is convicted of fraud, bribery, and conspiracy. Colonel Thomas W. Miller, Alien Property Custodian, is convicted when it is found that he has been taking part in wholesale looting of alien properties. Harry F. Sinclair and Edward L. Doheny, to whom the Wyoming and California oil fields have been leased, are acquitted of bribery and conspiracy, although more than $300,000 has passed between them and Secretary Fall. President Harding's sudden illness is thought to be the result of receiving a long coded message from Washington during the congressional investigations.

1925

Jan. 5. Mrs. Nellie Tayloe Ross takes office as governor of Wyoming; she is the first woman governor in the U.S.

May 5. Tennessee schoolteacher John T. Scopes is arrested for teaching the theory of evolution, forbidden by state law. **July 10-21.** In "monkey trial," which attracts enormous public attention, Scopes is defended by Clarence Darrow and Dudley Field Malone; William Jennings Bryan is one of the prosecuting attorneys. Scopes is convicted and fined $100 (later reversed on a technicality by the Tennessee Supreme Court). **July 26.** Bryan dies, supposedly as a result of the strain of the fundamentalist versus modernist trial, in which he has been subjected to a withering examination by Darrow of the fundamentalist literal interpretation of the Bible.

September. Colonel William ("Billy") Mitchell, outspoken advocate of a strong, independent air force, who has proved in 1921 that capital ships can be sunk by airplanes, accuses the War and Navy departments of "incompetency, criminal negligence, and almost treasonable administration of the National Defense." **Dec. 17.** Court-martial finds Mitchell guilty of insubordination, suspending him from the service for five years. Mitchell resigns as of February 1926. During World War II, he is posthumously restored to the rank of major general, and in 1946 Congress has a special medal struck in his honor.

October. Florida land boom reaches peak just before its collapse; period of speculation in Florida real estate is said to be greatest business stampede in U.S. history.

By this year, personal and corporate income and estate and gift taxes make up almost half of U.S. government revenue; customs duties have dropped to 14.4 percent of revenue, as opposed to about 57 percent in 1890.

Simon Guggenheim and his wife establish the John Simon Guggenheim Memorial Foundation in memory of their son; function is to "further the development of scholars and artists by assisting them to engage in research . . . under the freest possible conditions."

Theodore Dreiser publishes his novel *An American Tragedy,* based on the Grace Brown murder case; it brings him greater acclaim as a novelist than he has yet known.

1925 - 1927

C. Francis Jenkins demonstrates television; his work has been based on that of European scientists. First actual transmission of television signals occurs when the president of American Telephone and Telegraph Company in New York sees and speaks to Secretary of Commerce Herbert Hoover in Washington, D.C.

1926

Jan. 27. U.S. Senate approves American participation in Permanent Court of International Justice at The Hague, with certain reservations to protect U.S. interests; when one reservation proves to be unacceptable to the Court, the U.S. does not actually join. The U.S. has urged establishment of the Court in 1899 and 1907 at two Hague conferences, and Court has been formed by the League of Nations in 1920. Continuing efforts are made by Presidents Coolidge, Hoover, and Franklin Roosevelt to enroll the U.S. in the Court, but, largely because of the isolationist propaganda of the Hearst newspapers and "Radio Priest" Father Charles E. Coughlin, all efforts finally fail in 1935.

Feb. 26. Congress passes Revenue Act, which reduces income and inheritance taxes and removes many excise and nuisance taxes.

March 7. Radio Corporation of America, American Telephone and Telegraph Company, and British General Post Office hold first successful transatlantic radiotelephone conversation between New York and London.

April. Book-of-the-Month-Club begins enrolling members, acquiring 40,000 in the first year; new form of book distribution revolutionizes book publishing.

May 5. Sinclair Lewis rejects the Pulitzer Prize for his novel *Arrowsmith,* saying that such prizes make writers, "safe, polite, obedient, and sterile."

July 2. Congress establishes the Army Air Corps, in the same year that Colonel "Billy" Mitchell, who has advocated a separate air force, resigns from the Army after being court-martialed.

Oct. 25. The Supreme Court holds that the President has power to remove executive officers, thus voiding the Tenure of Office Act of 1867 requiring the consent of the Senate. The Act had been passed to tie President Johnson's hands, and his defiance of it was the cause of his near impeachment.

Nov. 2. In fall elections, Republicans lose seats in both Senate and House, and Progressives gain.

Congress passes Air Commerce Act, which,. through Bureau of Air Commerce, provides for federal aid to development of the aviation industry, establishment of navigation guides and airports, and licensing of pilots and aircraft.

Drs. George R. Minot and William P. Murphy discover first successful treatment of formerly fatal pernicious anemia when they use liver diet; in 1934 they share the Nobel Prize for Medicine with George Hoyt Whipple for their work.

1926-1927

Historian, poet, folklorist Carl Sandburg publishes the first two volumes of his biography of Abraham Lincoln, *The Prairie Years* (the four-volume *The War Years* is published in 1939); in the following year he publishes his collection of folksongs, *The American Songbag.*

National Broadcasting Company is organized as first nationwide radio broadcasting network in 1926; Columbia Broadcasting System is organized in 1927.

1926-1929

May 9, 1926. Richard E. Byrd, with

Floyd Bennett, makes first flight over the North Pole and is awarded the Congressional Medal of Honor. In 1927 he and three others fly from New York to France with first official mail service, and in 1929, on his first expedition to the Antarctic, he flies over the South Pole.

1927

Jan. 27. U.S. Senate unanimously resolves that Mexican-U.S. conflicts be settled by negotiation or arbitration. Formerly permanent oil land concessions of U.S. oil companies have been limited to 50 years by the Mexican government, and a law has been passed limiting the amount of land that can be owned by aliens. **Sept.** President Coolidge appoints Dwight W. Morrow ambassador to Mexico. **Nov. 17.** Morrow's efforts are so successful that the Mexican Supreme Court voids limitation clauses in oil land law, and in the next month Mexican Congress grants unlimited concessions on lands used before 1917.

Feb. 10. President Coolidge calls for naval-limitation conference of five major powers at Geneva, but France and Italy do not attend. **June 20-Aug. 4.** Conference, attended by Britain, Japan, and the U.S., accomplishes nothing, since Britain and the U.S. are unable to come to terms on restriction of cruisers. Eighteen months later the U.S. starts building fifteen 10,000-ton cruisers.

April 17. To an open letter of inquiry about his affiliation with the Roman Catholic Church, Governor Alfred E. Smith of New York, who is being considered as a Democratic presidential nominee, answers, "I recognize no power in the institution of my Church to interfere with the operations of the Constitution of the United States."

May 21. Charles A. Lindbergh is greeted by 100,000 anxiously waiting people in Paris when he arrives in his monoplane, the

Spirit of St. Louis, after a 3,600-mile, 33½-hour solo flight from New York. Lindbergh, 25 years old, has been competing for a $25,000 prize offered for the first nonstop flight from New York to Paris.

July 29. Bellevue Hospital in New York City installs first electric respirator (later called iron lung), originally designed for use in almost any kind of respiratory failure.

Nov. 13. Holland Tunnel, first underwater tunnel for vehicles built under Hudson River, opens; running from New York City to Jersey City, it is a double tunnel with two lanes in each direction.

Dec. 27. *Show Boat,* a new kind of musical comedy, opens in New York City; by Oscar Hammerstein II and Jerome Kern, it is adapted from Edna Ferber's novel.

Vernon L. Parrington publishes first two volumes of his *Main Currents in American Thought;* third volume is issued in 1930. Charles and Mary Beard publish first two volumes of their history *The Rise of American Civilization;* third volume, *America in Midpassage,* is published in 1939.

Ole Edvart Rölvaag publishes his finest novel, *Giants in the Earth,* which, like others, deals with immigrant pioneers.

1927 - 1928

April 6, 1927. French Foreign Minister Aristide Briand unofficially proposes an agreement between the U.S. and France to outlaw war. **June 11.** Secretary of State Frank B. Kellogg formally acknowledges the proposal, and Briand submits a draft about a week later. **Dec. 28.** Kellogg, having consulted the Senate Foreign Relations Committee, changes the draft to include all nations. Pact outlaws war as an instrument of national policy but does not reject defensive war. No sanctions are provided except force of world opinion. **April 13, 1928.** Draft of the Kellogg-Briand Pact is sent to other nations; eventually 63 countries sign it.

Aug. 2, 1927. It has been assumed that President Coolidge will run for office again, but he announces from South Dakota, "I do not choose to run for President in 1928." Near the end of his term, in December 1928, although he has encouraged financial speculation and ignored economic problems, Coolidge tells Congress, "The country can . . . anticipate the future with optimism."

1927 - 1933

April 1927. President Coolidge sends Henry L. Stimson, preceded by U.S. Marines, to Nicaragua to settle differences between President Adolfo Díaz, U.S.-supported Conservative, and revolutionist General César Sandino, one of several who support Juan Sacasa over Díaz. Withdrawal of Marines in 1925 has led to renewal of civil war. In spite of U.S. supervision of elections, internal warfare continues until 1933.

1928

Jan. 16. Pan-American conference at Havana is opened by President Coolidge. Latin-American nations attack U.S. claim to the right of intervention in internal affairs of Western Hemisphere nations under 1904 Roosevelt Corollary to the Monroe Doctrine. The U.S. gradually modifies the Corollary; in a series of hemispheric conferences, the Monroe Doctrine is transformed into one of hemispheric solidarity and mutual responsibility.

April 13. Socialist Party convention meets and nominates Norman Thomas of New York for President. **May 12.** Socialist

Labor Party meets and nominates Frank T. Johns, who is later killed and replaced by Verne L. Reynolds. **May 25.** Workers' Party meets and nominates William Z. Foster. **June 12.** Republicans meet at Kansas City and nominate Secretary of Commerce Herbert C. Hoover of California for President and Senator Charles Curtis of Kansas as his running mate. **June 26.** Democrats meet at Houston and nominate Governor Alfred E. Smith of New York for President and Senator Joseph T. Robinson of Arkansas for Vice-President. **July 12.** Prohibition Party meets and nominates William F. Varney of New York. Republican platform supports a federal farm board to stabilize agriculture, a protective tariff, and current foreign policy. Democrats also favor a farm board, promise enforcement of Prohibition (although Smith calls for repeal of the Eighteenth Amendment), call for more freedom for labor in disputes, and demand changes in foreign policy.

May 3. For the second time, Congress passes the McNary-Haugen Bill for relief of farmers who are still caught in an agricultural depression. Bill has come up four other times since 1924. President Coolidge vetoes bill for the second time on the grounds that it would tend to fix prices and encourage overproduction.

May 15. Congress appropriates $325 million for Mississippi Valley flood control over a 10-year period.

May 22. Congress passes Merchant Marine (Jones-White) Act, providing federal aid to U.S. private shipping by subsidized mail contracts, and doubling sums available — up to $250 million — for loans for new ship construction. Act also allows sale of U.S.-owned ships to private companies at low prices.

July 30. George Eastman at Rochester, New York, shows a group of viewers the first color motion pictures ever exhibited; original films show colorful subjects, from flowers, goldfish, peacocks, and butterflies to pretty girls.

Nov. 6. Herbert Hoover wins election by a landslide, with 21,392,000 votes to Smith's 15,016,000. Electoral vote is Hoover, 444; Smith, 87. Hoover takes 40 of the 48 states, including 5 states of the Solid South; against Smith are his unpolished background and his Roman Catholic religion.

Vesto M. Slipher, after observations of 43 spiral nebulae, demonstrates at Lowell Observatory, Arizona, that the nebulae are steadily moving away from the earth at increasing speeds.

Franz Boas, professor of anthropology at Columbia University, publishes his attack on the master race theory, *Anthropology and Modern Life*.

Stephen Vincent Benét publishes his epic poem of the Civil War, *John Brown's Body*. Edna St. Vincent Millay publishes famous sonnets in the volume *The Buck in the Snow and Other Poems*.

Italian conductor Arturo Toscanini becomes conductor of the New York Philharmonic-Symphony Orchestra; he has formerly conducted the orchestra of the Metropolitan Opera. Continuing with the Philharmonic until 1936, he then joins the NBC Symphony, remaining for 17 years.

Walt Disney released first Mickey Mouse cartoon, *Plane Crazy;* in the same year he produces *Steamboat Willie*, the first animated cartoon to use sound.

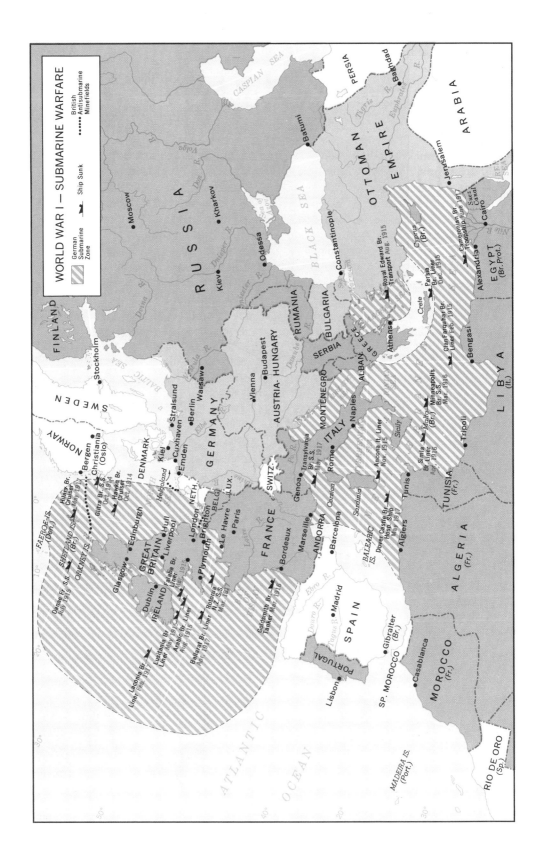

WORLD WAR I — SUBMARINE WARFARE

German
Submarine
Zone

British
Antisubmarine
Minefields

Ship Sunk

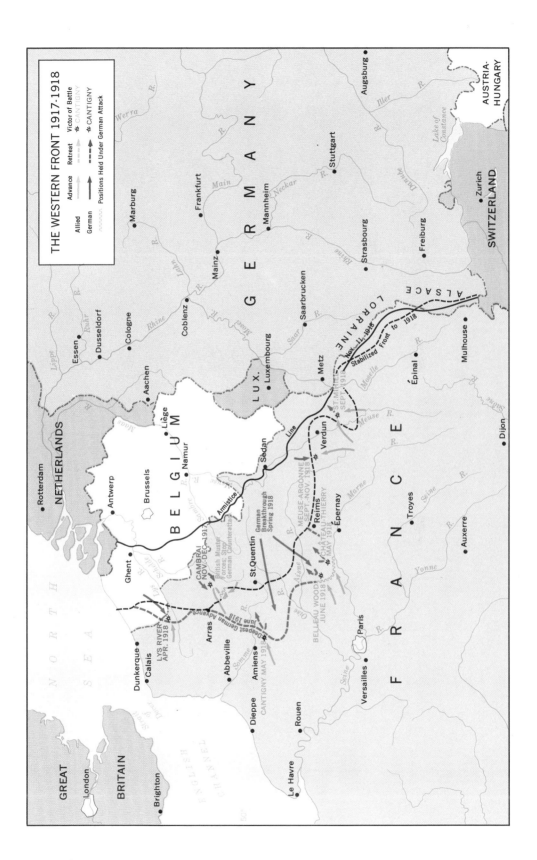

THE WESTERN FRONT 1917-1918

Allied   German

Advance

Retreat

Victor of Battle
✳ CANTIGNY
✳ CANTIGNY

Positions Held Under German Attack

GREAT
BRITAIN

London

Brighton

NORTH
SEA

NETHERLANDS

Rotterdam

Antwerp

Brussels

BELGIUM

Ghent

Liège

Namur

Dunkerque

Calais

Dieppe

Le Havre

Rouen

Abbeville

Arras

Amiens

CANTIGNY MAY 1918

LYS RIVER
APR. 1918

Deepest German Advance
June 1918

St.Quentin

CAMBRAI
NOV.-DEC. 1917

British Muster
Forces; Stop
German Counterattack

Armistice

German
Breakthrough
Spring 1918

Sedan

Line

Verdun

ST.-MIHIEL
SEPT. 1918

MEUSE-ARGONNE
SEPT.-NOV. 1918

Reims

Épernay

CHÂTEAU-THIERRY
MAY 1918

BELLEAU WOOD
JUNE 1918

Paris

Versailles

Troyes

Auxerre

Dijon

NETHERLANDS

Essen

Dusseldorf

Cologne

Coblenz

Aachen

Marburg

Frankfurt

Mainz

Saarbrucken

LUX.

Luxembourg

Metz

Épinal

Mulhouse

Zurich

SWITZERLAND

AUSTRIA-
HUNGARY

Augsburg

Stuttgart

Mannheim

Strasbourg

Freiburg

Lake of
Constance

GERMANY

LORRAINE

ALSACE

Stabilized Front to 1918

Nov. 11, 1918

FRANCE

Werra R.

Main

Neckar R.

Rhine R.

Lahn R.

Moselle R.

Saar

Meuse R.

Marne

Aisne R.

Oise R.

Somme R.

Seine R.

Yonne R.

Saône R.

Iller

Danube

Rhine R.

Lippe R.

Ruhr R.

Maas R.

Schelde R.

Lys R.

Sambre R.

ENGLISH CHANNEL

Strait of Dover

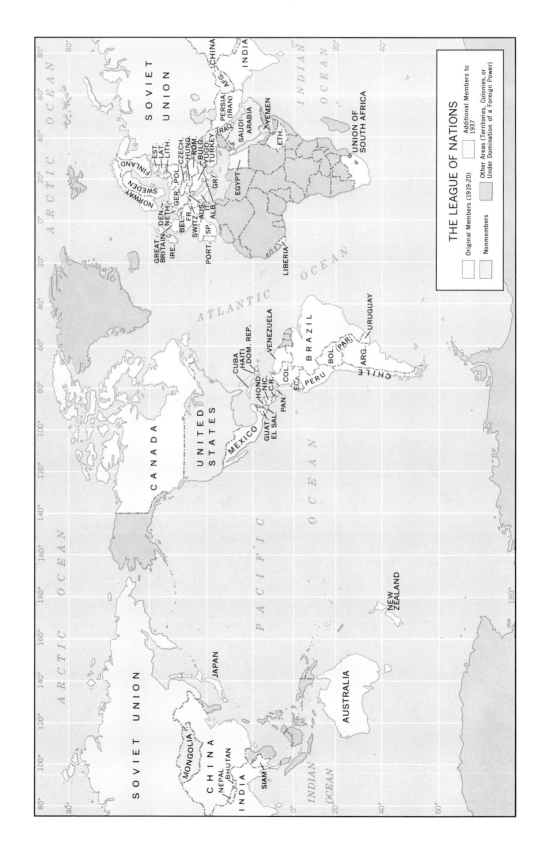

THE LEAGUE OF NATIONS

Original Members (1919-20)

Additional Members to 1937

Nonmembers

Other Areas (Territories, Colonies, or Under Domination of a Foreign Power)

ARCTIC OCEAN

SOVIET UNION

CHINA

INDIA

INDIAN OCEAN

PERSIA (IRAN)

AFG.

IRAQ

SAUDI ARABIA

YEMEN

ETH.

UNION OF SOUTH AFRICA

EST.

LAT.

LITH.

POL.

CZECH.

HUNG.

ROM.

BULG.

YUG.

TURKEY

GR.

FINLAND

SWEDEN

NORWAY

DEN.

NETH.

GER.

BEL.

FR.

SWITZ.

AUS.

ALB.

GREAT BRITAIN

IRE.

PORT.

SP.

EGYPT

LIBERIA

ARCTIC OCEAN

ATLANTIC OCEAN

CANADA

UNITED STATES

MEXICO

CUBA

HAITI

DOM. REP.

VENEZUELA

GUAT.

EL SAL.

HOND.

NIC.

C.R.

PAN.

COL.

EC.

BRAZIL

PERU

BOL.

PAR.

ARG.

URUGUAY

CHILE

PACIFIC OCEAN

SOVIET UNION

MONGOLIA

CHINA

NEPAL

BHUTAN

INDIA

SIAM

JAPAN

NEW ZEALAND

AUSTRALIA

INDIAN OCEAN

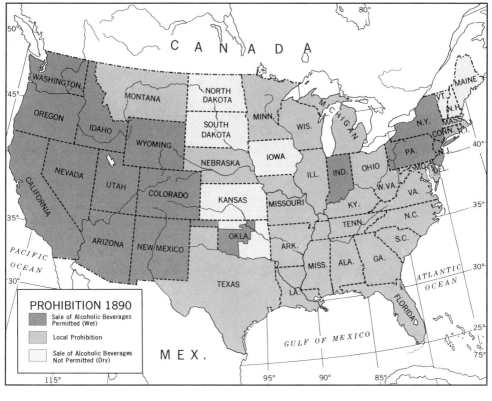

PROHIBITION 1890

Sale of Alcoholic Beverages Permitted (Wet)

Local Prohibition

Sale of Alcoholic Beverages Not Permitted (Dry)

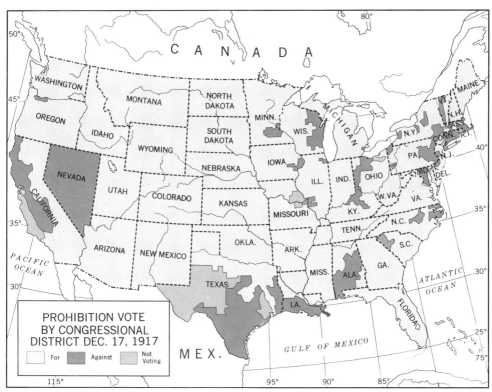

PROHIBITION VOTE BY CONGRESSIONAL DISTRICT DEC. 17, 1917

For   Against   Not Voting

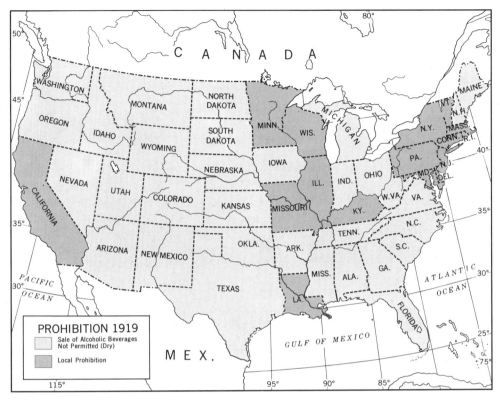

PROHIBITION 1919

Sale of Alcoholic Beverages
Not Permitted (Dry)

Local Prohibition

PROHIBITION TODAY

Sale of Alcoholic Beverages
Permitted (Wet)

Local Prohibition

Sale of Alcoholic Beverages
Not Permitted (Dry)

1916

1.

CARL VROOMAN: The Revolution in Agriculture

By 1916 scientific methods had been applied to agriculture on a large scale, but though the Department of Agriculture, in conjunction with land-grant colleges and state experimental stations, had directed valuable agricultural research, most of the results of these efforts had not yet reached the small farmer. Many individual farmers with modest holdings were suspicious of scientific discoveries and preferred their traditional methods. Carl Vrooman, assistant secretary of agriculture under President Wilson, addressed himself to the problem in an article published November 1916, a portion of which is reprinted here.

Source: *Century Illustrated Monthly Magazine,* November 1916.

AGRICULTURE, though one of the oldest of the arts, is the youngest of the sciences. Less than two years ago, for the first time, the American Academy for the Advancement of Science admitted agriculture into the family circle by giving it a place on its program and in its organization. Thus agriculture has become a sort of modern Cinderella. For thousands of years the servant and drudge of civilization, at last she has found the magic slipper and is making her debut as a veritable and acknowledged princess, a royal dispenser of bounty and happiness.

As a result of recent scientific and economic developments along agricultural lines, we are today in the midst of an agricultural revolution that seems destined to be as significant and as far-reaching in its effects upon civilization as was the Industrial Rev-

olution of the 18th and 19th centuries. In the light of these developments, agriculture appears, not only as the youngest of the sciences but also as the most important.

What this new science will do for the world ultimately, it would be inexpedient to attempt to prophesy. Therefore I shall endeavor to confine myself to a discussion of what the new agriculture may confidently be expected to do for this country in the near future; that is, when our farmers in general have learned to make a profitable application of the principles of scientific agriculture that already have stood the test of experience.

From data as unquestionable as the multiplication table, we may affirm that the new agriculture will accomplish certain definite results:

First, it will show the farmer how to increase his yields of standard crops anywhere from 25 to 100 percent, and, what is almost equally important, the percentage of such possible increase as will yield him a maximum profit.

Second, it will show the farmer how to market his produce to better advantage while at the same time reducing the relative cost of farm produce to the consumer.

Third, it will show the farmer how to make his purchases more advantageously.

Fourth, upon a solid foundation of increased yields, increased profits upon what he has to sell, and lower costs for what he has to buy, it will enable the farmer to build a splendid superstructure of more intelligent, more enjoyable, and more purposeful living. . . .

In the last half century, the Department of Agriculture has spent some $250 million, largely in research and experiment, to the end that American agriculture might be put on a high plane of efficiency. The results of this research and experiment have been agronomy and animal industry — a vast, but largely undigested and uncoordinated, mass of information about how to grow crops and "critters." During this entire period, the department has been accumulating and hoarding a vast store of facts about how to increase production.

Thus, during the first fifty years of its existence, the department was chiefly a bureau of scientific research that gave the farmer, from time to time, an assortment of miscellaneous scientific information that he might or might not be able to utilize to his financial advantage. Unfortunately, a world of practical problems that destroy the farmer's peace of mind and involve the success or failure of his business — namely, his business and economic problems — were virtually ignored. In other words, for the first fifty years of its life the department hopped along on one leg, the scientific leg. Happily, during the last three years, a miraculous thing has happened: the department has

grown another leg, the leg of business and economic efficiency. Now it begins to walk, and we confidently expect in the near future to see it going forward with giant strides.

During the last three years, for the first time in its history, the Department of Agriculture has had at its head an economist. Under the direction of Secretary Houston it has achieved a new point of view and a new conception of its mission. For half a century the department has used its utmost endeavors to show the farmer how to fight the chinch bug and the armyworm, the cattle tick, and the Hessian fly, and other insect pests, but had not even so much as attempted to show him how to protect himself from the yearly toll levied upon the fruits of his toil by such human pests as the usurer, commercial pirates posing as legitimate middlemen, and the other business parasites of the agricultural world.

The farmer who makes two blades of grass grow where only one grew before may be a good agronomist, but if he cannot sell his second blades at a profit, he is a poor farmer. In other words, farming is primarily a business. Very few practical farmers till the soil to demonstrate principles of agronomy. They produce crops to live rather than live to produce crops. Even more than large production they want *profitable* production. Upon the realization of this fundamental fact is founded the agricultural renaissance which recently has been begun.

It seems strange that a fact as simple as this should have been overlooked for many years. Every farmer, at one time or another, has been brought face to face with the paradox of big crops and small returns. He has often been forced to the conclusion that the larger crops you raise the less money you make. And statistics all too frequently have backed up this conclusion. In 1912, for example, the country produced 677,758,000 more bushels of corn than in 1913, and yet the farmers received $171,638,000 less. In 1906 a wheat crop 101,174,000 bushels larger than that of 1907 brought $64,104,000 less. In 1906 the corn crop, too, was unusually large — more than 150 million bushels larger than in 1909 — and it brought the farmers $500 million less. . . .

The capital that the average farmer has invested in this country now pays him a return, in addition to the mere wages he gets for his labor, of anywhere from nothing to 5 percent per annum. If the apostles of the new agriculture could not promise the farmers any larger returns than that on the additional capital they are advising him to invest, it is hardly probable that their new gospel would strike any responsive chord in the farmer's heart. However, it has been demonstrated repeatedly that for the additional capital which the farmer is advised to put into lime, phosphate, or potassium, into better seed, purebred bulls and boars, into siloes, tile, and hog-tight fence, he can realize not only the 5 or 6 percent that farmers ordinarily hope to get on their money, but the 10 or 15 percent that businessmen usually expect on their investments, or even considerably more. . . .

The profits of the farmer can also be increased by various other legitimate devices for increasing the efficiency of his marketing methods. For example, in the past a large proportion of the poultry of this country was shipped to market alive. The result was a heavy transportation charge, heavy shrinkage en route, and other attendant evils, such as deterioration in the quality of the poultry. The Department of Agriculture worked out an entirely new system, in accordance with which the poultry is killed and chilled before shipping. The new method improves the quality of the product for the consumer, prevents any loss of weight in transit, and cuts down the cost of transportation. Thus the farmer is enabled to get a larger price for his product, the consumer is required to pay no more than before for the same quality of poultry, and the middleman who per-

forms a useful social function is allowed to receive his legitimate profit as before. No one is injured, and everyone connected with this industry is benefited. . . .

If the new science of agriculture and the movement toward scientific business efficiency can be developed in the light of this truth, capital and labor will become so much more productive than ever before that there will be plenty and to spare for everyone who is willing to perform a real economic service to society for a legitimate remuneration. It is high time for both farmers and businessmen to learn that it is more profitable to work together for their common interests than to squabble with one another over conflicting interests, real or imaginary. This means cooperation.

The true spirit of cooperation is the most vital need of the day in the agricultural world, and indeed in the world at large. Without that spirit no considerable advance along the lines of the new agriculture is possible. Here and there a person will be able to apply some of its teachings on his own hook, but nobody can carry into effect all or even a majority of those teachings unless he is able to work together with his neighbors in some of the many possible varieties of cooperative community effort. The cooperative spirit is as necessary to the realization of the possibilities of the new agriculture as is cement or mortar to the erection of a gigantic edifice of brick or stone. I believe that this spirit will prevail, that even now it is prevailing, and that we are on the threshold of a new and more splendid epoch. . . .

While detailed figures are not yet available as to the extent of the cooperative movement among American farmers, it is probably safe to say that, despite all the handicaps of the past, cooperative agricultural organizations in this country are doing over a billion dollars' worth of business a year. Manifestly, this is only a beginning, as the movement in the United States is still in its infancy; but I think it will be generally recognized that it is a lusty infant, possibly an infant Hercules.

In the past, farmers have regarded cooperation as merely a means of protection from the wiles of the middleman, but it is destined to be something of vastly greater moment than that. By means of cooperative effort the farmer not only can protect himself from the superior business ability of sinister business organizations but, what is of greater importance, can increase his own efficiency enormously both as a scientific farmer and as a business manager, to the ultimate benefit of everyone concerned.

Moreover, before the farmers in the country or the businessmen in the towns can obtain the maximum benefit from our improved agricultural methods, farmers and businessmen must learn to cooperate for their mutual advantage. There are some farmers to whom this will sound like advising the lamb to lie down with the lion. They will have a fear that in case it is done it will not be long before the lamb will be inside the lion. Indeed, for a long time there has been a widespread suspicion on the part of the farmer that the city businessman regarded the farmers very much as the farmers regard their sheep, as creatures to be sheared, and occasionally even to be skinned. In the past this suspicion has not been without foundation, but the more enlightened among our businessmen are coming to see that their future welfare is indissolubly bound up with the welfare of the farmer, and that it is not only good morals but good business to help the farmer, not only to make a scientific success of crop production but to make as well a business success of crop disposition.

2.

WARREN H. WILSON: The Interaction of Country and City

Warren Wilson, whose Quaker Hill *appeared in 1908, was one of the first to apply rigorous scientific canons to the study of rural communities. Wilson was leery of reformers who promised to bring about rural well-being without first gathering the facts about how the country and city were interacting. His work, along with the report of Theodore Roosevelt's Country Life Commission in 1909, sparked the growing interest in rural planning and education. Wilson's paper, "Country Versus City," which was read at a meeting of the American Sociological Society in 1916, is reprinted in part below.*

Source: *Papers and Proceedings, Eleventh Annual Meeting American Sociological Society Held at Columbus, Ohio, December 27-29, 1916,* Vol. XI, Chicago, 1917, pp. 12-20.

THE POPULATION OF THE CITIES is now, for the nation as a whole, about equal to that of the country. In 1910, 53 percent of the people of the United States lived in communities of 2,500 or less. The communities of 2,500 or over, which are called cities, were growing at such a rate then, and have so increased since that time in growth and in proportionate growth, that we may recognize the division of the people between city and country communities as equal. The division of the population at communities of 2,500, while arbitrary, is on the whole satisfactory. It marks the line of social, educational, and religious differences which are vital and fundamental.

The basis of this difference is the fact that there are two layers of people in this country, the rural and the urban. The rural are predominantly of the older colonial stock; among them are few of the immigrants of recent years. Irish, German, and Scandinavian immigrants used to go to the country; but Poles, Lithuanians, Slavs, Bulgarians, Serbs, Greeks, Syrians, and Jews do not go to farms in any such numbers as to require notice here. They go to the cities. The cities reflect their character and activities. The farming and the village populations, on the other hand, are strongholds of older American conservatism.

It is contended by some authorities that there is a movement of the country population, not to the cities but from farm to farm, from farm to village, and from one agricultural state to another. There are some country people moving into the cities, as is demonstrated by the slow growth of cities in the Southern states where immigrants are few. But that this cityward migration is relatively small is indicated by the predominantly rural character of these states to which little of the more recent immigration has gone. The cities in the South constitute only a small part of the entire population, and they exhibit in this fact the lesser inclination of the older Americans to go into city life.

The contrast between city and country is expressed also in certain social habits. The compacted social forms under which people live in the congested cities are unknown in the country. They are not idealized by country people. Farmers live in homesteads far apart from one another. The village residence of some European tillers of the soil has not been translated to this country,

though similar conditions appear in Utah.

The masterful and independent character of the American countryman explains his country residence and the lonely homestead in which he lives. Eloquent tribute is paid to this chief motive of country life in Bailey's *The Holy Earth*, p. 37:

> As you say, too many people confound farming with that sordid, selfish, money-getting game called "business," whereas the farmer's position is administrative, being in a way a dispenser of the "Mysteries of God," for they are mysteries. Every apple is a mystery, and every potato is a mystery, and every ear of corn is a mystery, and every pound of butter is a mystery, and when a farmer is not able to understand these things he is out of place.
> The farmer uses the soil and the rains and the snows and the frosts and the winds and the sun: these are also the implements of the Almighty, the only tools He uses. . . .

Strangely contrasted to this industrial independence of country people is the variety of minds one finds in the city. Every type of mind that is highly specialized, every industrial character, every mechanical gift that is highly rewarded, every business faculty that inclines its possessor to acquire and to use capital goes to the city. Into the city are thus brought the mechanical, the executive, the acquisitive, the musical, the literary, the humorous.

There are left in the country by this very drastic selection the possessors of an entirely different social mind. The characters entering into its makeup are fewer than in the city. The country lacks the variety and is without the original inventive elements of which the city has a surplusage. A somewhat uniform type of mind after a while characterizes country populations that are under city influence. Wilbert L. Anderson has described this severe conformity of country people to one type as a result of the removal of those who have characters of greater variation to the cities. The effect of this selection is to give the country and city populations an appearance of strong unlikeness each to the other.

Economic forms of the country differ from those of the city, where the joint-stock corporation prevails. Country people cannot endure to work together under joint-stock organization. They have invented in Europe and America, out of the necessity of collective action, a cooperative type of organization based upon the natural partnership of the country neighborhood. Farmers in every land of the earth are said by Sir Horace Plunkett to organize effectively in this form alone, which preserves the individual estate while securing collective action on a basis of personal acquaintance.

The schools of the country are very different from those of the city. The disposition to improve and adapt the city schools, and the degree of that educational progress, are not found in the country, where conservatism affects the school perhaps more than any other institution. The schoolmaster class may have exaggerated the antagonism between city and country because of this retardation of country schools. This class has certainly not belittled it, and the more because the future of the country school is believed to lie in a different direction from that of the city schools. To this the books of Kern, Foght, Carney, Bruere, Eggleston, and Cubberley all testify.

The science of agriculture occupies a great place in national education. Professing to be a whole and adequate training for country life, it greatly influences rural thought. The more it is developed as a formal statement of rural knowledge and practice, so much the more does country life differ from city life. The whole influence of the agricultural college and of the state and national departments of agriculture is exerted in the direction of a different society in the country from that in the city.

To this conviction of a dual organization of society further evidence is added by the country church. Between the city church and that in the country there is a wide divergence. So marked is this contrast that one brilliant observer has called the country church a form of "heathen Christianity."

There is a different personnel in the country ministry and different professional habits, especially in the open country churches. There is a strong tendency among country churches to conform to a common mode and both in liturgy and in relation to social life to resemble one another closely. This occurs, moreover, without abatement of denominational ardor. The same thing may be said of city churches of the Protestant sort: they tend to conform to a city type. But city and country church modes are far apart. Two rural churches of different denominations are more like one another than either of them is like a city congregation of its own communion. The country church generally has an absentee minister. Its affairs are treated as of less importance than individual concerns. It is not an approved channel of benevolence as the city church is. And over-churching, especially in villages, seems to be a cherished expression of the rural religious spirit rather than an evil recognized or deplored.

The widest divergence between city and country is a spiritual one; by this I mean a contrast in the general attitude of either population toward life as a whole. The countryman has the attitude of one who produces his own living. The city man is characterized by the recognition that the sources of his income are invisible. That is, country men think of themselves as producers, while dwellers in cities act the part of consumers. It is true that each farmer is now a consumer of other men's goods; but his mental posture — what Professor Carver calls his "make-believe" — is that of a self-sufficing social life. He still sees before his eyes the most of his consumer's goods produced on the land which he owns or rents, and even manufactured on his own premises. This fact gives him an independence of the city and a resulting contempt for city people and antagonism for all urban concerns.

The relation between city and country may be understood in any one of three ways: first, it may be believed — as many do believe upon the evidence we have just mentioned — that rural society and urban have no connection whatever: that the one is independent of the other; or second, one may conceivably think of them as antagonistic and competitive — as the title of this paper implies; or third, we may believe that urban society and rural society are closely interrelated, causes of either being found in the other.

The prevailing implication of social opinion among students of urban conditions is of the first of these three; that is, urban social students write and speak as if the city were self-sufficing. Rural students usually adhere to the second theory, that city and country compete. Their proposals often imply that the prosperity of the country is to be secured only from rural sources by rural leaders, independently or at the expense of the city. It is the contention of this paper that the third opinion is the true one — that city and country are dynamically one. Studies which ignore progress may regard them as separate and complete each in itself; but the consideration of growth and progress discovers sources of change for the city to be in the country and sources of rural progress in the city.

This is not to say that we are going to "urbanize" the country. So long as farmers persist in living in lonely homesteads, to speak of rural social life as "urban" because of better plumbing or screens on the door of the farm kitchen is simply to confess a poverty of words. But so long as the harvester machinery is made in Chicago and the price of butter is fixed in Elgin and the sale of citrus fruit is made in Los Angeles, just so long will the city be the center of country life. And until typhoid is abolished, the country and the city will require a unified health service.

One reason why we are slow to recognize the interaction of city and country is the fact that we have little knowledge of the dynamic relations of either. We have studied static sociology in city and country, but we in the rural field have only lately begun to study farm management, farm accounting, or the marketing of farm products. We have only the beginnings of a knowledge of rural health; but what we have shows an immediate relation between city and country. The study of suburban life may have surprises in store, as it is on the border line between city and country. The study of the gentleman farmer's way of life, like that of the suburban community, has yet to be made. But the chief confession we have to make is the fact that there is no history of agriculture. The encyclopaedia article is until today the best authority upon the record of country living. . . .

Public health is another field in which rural and urban societies meet. Here we have a beginning, not so much in the books published under that title — which but demonstrate our lack of knowledge of rural health conditions — but in the few field surveys made with a view to the measurement of the effect of well-known pathological forces upon rural populations. The house-to-house study of five rural counties of Indiana by Dr. Hurty, health commissioner of the state, exhibited the typical American homestead as a center of ill-health and insanitary neglect. The survey of rural immorality in Green and Clermont counties, Ohio, by Professor Paul L. Vogt, measured the prevalence of venereal diseases among country people. The State Department of Health of Virginia, Dr. Williams, commissioner, has systematically studied the health conditions in Orange and other rural counties.

The United States Public Health Service is now making rural surveys. Professor T.

D. Wood of Columbia has published in two brief but accurate pamphlets the summaries of these findings, showing the evidence which indicates in the large that the city is the center of dynamic health and pointing to the intolerably bad conditions in the country, which, being unremedied, affect the health of the whole people. The investigations and the subsequent health campaigns with reference to the mosquito and the hookworm are now chapters of the history of national public health in which the city and the country are equally concerned.

The investigation of rural populations with a view to the measurement of the numbers and proportions of subnormal, defective, idiotic, and insane will be particularly important in this connection. The Committee on Provision for the Feebleminded has made a beginning in this investigation. When it is completed we shall know whether those who go to the cities from the country are its best breeding stock, and whether generally the country community has a greater or a less proportion of the insane, idiotic, defective, or subnormal than the city. . . .

In American history the growth of cities corresponds to the growth of the organized idealism of husbandry and the specialized education for agriculture. In our time the cities constrain all men to produce ethically. The city organizes its influence through the state and the commonwealth by books, by literature, by newspapers, and through legislative enactments in such a way as to require from people living in the country that they produce what the community as a whole needs.

Everybody knows how the city governs the great rural industries which center in it. The countryman contributes relatively little by his direct discussion or by his direct proposal in the regulation of the milk trade, of the meat industry, of the speculation in wheat, of the standardization of fruit products, of the storage and shipment of refrigerated products, meat, or fruit. These regulations are usually imposed by the state at the behest of masses of consumers whose centers of influence and authority are in the big cities. These cities themselves are often the organization by which the masses of consumers impose their will upon country producers.

This influence of the city is positive and constructive. It tends to organize country life. For instance, the American farmer has by the demand of the city been obliged to milk his cows at intervals of twelve hours — 4 A.M. and 4 P.M. The farmer in East India is not accustomed to milk the cows at an early hour. A report of cooperative societies in the state of Baroda describes the difficulties encountered by those cooperative societies which handle milk products in that state in inducing farmers to milk their cows at the intervals which tend toward the highest efficiency. These cooperative societies might be called ganglia of social control. The nerve centers in this social control, however, are in the big cities in India.

In this country, in some of the states without cooperative societies, the milk business is regulated from the big cities. Anyone who lives in a dairy country realizes that the farmer rises and goes to bed, eats his meals, and regulates the labor of the day and of the year according to the behest which, directly and indirectly, is laid upon him by the market authorities in the big city to which his milk is shipped. The city is thus a factor in making the farmer think. It lays a bondage upon him which organizes his labor and makes him more industrious.

The effect of this is seen in the higher proportion of regularly industrious persons in the country populations of states like New York, Pennsylvania, or Ohio, than in the states like North Carolina or Tennessee, in which the proportion of cities is less. The number of idle persons and the number of hours of idleness which prevail among a population in rural Arkansas is much greater than in an Ohio rural population. The reason is that the cities of Ohio have regulated the industrial procedure of the country. They have organized the life of the country, whereas in Arkansas or rural Tennessee, or in the inaccessible mountain region, there is no ethical market standard laid upon the people, and they have not, therefore, the discipline of the city's domination.

The contention of this paper is, first, that the sociology of city and country relations should develop by inductive study rather than by speculation; secondly, that the study of rural versus urban society offers a field of most fruitful study in which we may learn much about the nature of social life in general; and, third, that the study of those interrelations which exhibit the city as a center of rural forces and the country as a leverage or a brake upon the social machine will be among the most fruitful of all social investigations in the days before us. In the classroom and seminar in social science this method offers the highest return, and the material thus secured rewards collective study as much as any available for the teacher and the student.

3.

J. J. Carty: Pure Science and Industrial Research

In his presidential address to the American Institute of Electrical Engineers in 1916, J. J. Carty took as his subject the relationship between pure and applied science. At a time when the World War was attracting everyone's attention to efficient production, Carty pointed out the value of research that had no utilitarian aim in mind. He believed, however, that "pure research" would ultimately be of industrial use. His address is reprinted in part below.

Source: *Science*, October 13, 1916: "The Relation of Pure Science to Industrial Research."

Because of the stupendous upheaval of the European war, with its startling agencies of destruction — the product of both science and the industries — and because of the deplorable unpreparedness of our own country to defend itself against attack, there has begun a great awakening of our people. By bringing to their minds the brilliant achievements of the membership of this institute in electric lighting and power and communications and by calling their attention to the manifold achievements of the members of our sister societies in mechanical and mining and civil engineering, and the accomplishments of our fellow workers, the industrial chemists, they are being aroused to the vital importance of the products of science in the national defense.

Arising out of this agitation comes a growing appreciation of the importance of industrial scientific research, not only as an aid to military defense but as an essential part of every industry in time of peace.

Industrial research, conducted in accordance with the principles of science, is no new thing in America. The department which is under my charge, founded nearly forty years ago to develop, with the aid of scientific men, the telephone art, has grown from small beginnings, with but a few workers, to a great institution employing hundreds of scientists and engineers; and it is generally acknowledged that it is largely owing to the industrial research thus conducted that the telephone achievements and developments in America have so greatly exceeded those of other countries.

With the development of electric lighting and electric power and electric traction which came after the invention of the telephone, industrial scientific research laboratories were founded by some of the larger electrical manufacturing concerns, and these have attained a worldwide reputation. While vast sums are spent annually upon industrial research in these laboratories, I can say with authority that they return to the industries each year improvements in the art which, taken all together, have a value many times greater than the total cost of their production. Money expended in properly directed industrial research, conducted on scientific principles, is sure to bring to the industries a most generous return.

While many concerns in America now have well-organized industrial research laboratories, particularly those engaged in metallurgy and dependent upon chemical processes, the manufacturers of our country as a whole have not yet learned of the benefits of industrial scientific research and how to avail themselves of it.

I consider that it is the high duty of our institute and of every member composing it, and that a similar duty rests upon all other engineering and scientific bodies in America, to impress upon the manufacturers of the United States the wonderful possibilities of economies in their processes and improvements in their products which are opened up by the discoveries in science. The way to realize these possibilities is through the medium of industrial research conducted in ac-

cordance with scientific principles. Once it is made clear to our manufacturers that industrial research pays, they will be sure to call to their aid men of scientific training to investigate their technical problems and to improve their processes. Those who are the first to avail themselves of the benefits of industrial research will obtain such a lead over their competitors that we may look forward to the time when the advantages of industrial research will be recognized by all.

Industrial scientific research departments can reach their highest development in those concerns doing the largest amount of business. While instances are not wanting where the large growth of the institution is the direct result of the care which is bestowed upon industrial research at a time when it was but a small concern, nevertheless conditions today are such that without cooperation among themselves the small concerns cannot have the full benefits of industrial research, for no one among them is sufficiently strong to maintain the necessary staff and laboratories.

Once the vital importance of this subject is appreciated by the small manufacturers, many solutions of the problem will promptly appear. One of these is for the manufacturer to take his problem to one of the industrial research laboratories already established for the purpose of serving those who cannot afford a laboratory of their own. Other manufacturers doing the same, the financial encouragement received would enable the laboratories to extend and improve their facilities so that each of the small manufacturers who patronizes them would in course of time have the benefit of an institution similar to those maintained by our largest industrial concerns.

Thus, in accordance with the law of supply and demand, the small manufacturer may obtain the benefits of industrial research in the highest degree and the burden upon each manufacturer would be only in accordance with the use he made of it, and the entire cost of the laboratories would thus be borne by the industries as a whole, where the charge properly belongs. Many other projects are now being considered for the establishment of industrial research laboratories for those concerns which cannot afford laboratories of their own, and in some of these cases the possible relation of these laboratories to our technical and engineering schools is being earnestly studied.

Until the manufacturers themselves are aroused to the necessity of action in the matter of industrial research, there is no plan which can be devised that will result in the general establishment of research laboratories for the industries. But once their need is felt and their value appreciated and the demand for research facilities is put forth by the manufacturers themselves, research laboratories will spring up in all our great centers of industrial activity. Their number and character and size, and their method of operation and their relation to the technical and engineering schools, and the method of their working with the different industries are all matters which involve many interesting problems — problems which I am sure will be solved as they present themselves and when their nature has been clearly apprehended.

In the present state of the world's development, there is nothing which can do more to advance American industries than the adoption by our manufacturers generally of industrial research conducted on scientific principles. I am sure that if they can be made to appreciate the force of this statement, our manufacturers will rise to the occasion with all that energy and enterprise so characteristic of America.

So much has already been said and so much remains to be said urging upon us the importance of scientific research conducted for the sake of utility and for increasing the convenience and comfort of mankind that there is danger of losing sight of another form of research which has for its primary object none of these things. I refer to pure scientific research.

In the minds of many there is confusion between industrial scientific research and this purely scientific research, particularly as the industrial research involves the use of advanced scientific methods and calls for the highest degree of scientific attainment. The confusion is worse because the same scientific principles and methods of investigation are frequently employed in each case and even the subject matter under investigation may sometimes be identical. The misunderstanding arises from considering only the subject matter of the two classes of research. The distinction is to be found, not in the subject matter of the research but in the motive.

The electrical engineer, let us say, finding a new and unexplained difficulty in the working of electric lamps, subjects the phenomenon observed to a process of inquiry employing scientific methods, with a view to removing from the lamps an objectionable characteristic. The pure scientist at the same time investigates in precisely the same manner the same phenomenon, but with the purpose of obtaining an explanation of a physical occurrence, the nature of which cannot be explained by known facts. Although these two researches are conducted in exactly the same manner, the one nevertheless comes under the head of industrial research and the other belongs to the domain of pure science. In the last analysis the distinction between pure scientific research and industrial scientific research is one of motive. Industrial research is always conducted with the purpose of accomplishing some utilitarian end. Pure scientific research is conducted with a philosophic purpose, for the discovery of truth and for the advancement of the boundaries of human knowledge.

The investigator in pure science may be likened to the explorer who discovers new continents or islands or hitherto unknown territory. He is continually seeking to extend the boundaries of knowledge. The investigator in industrial research may be compared to the pioneers who survey the newly discovered territory in the endeavor to locate its mineral resources, determine the extent of its forests, and the location of its arable land, and who in other ways precede the settlers and prepare for their occupation of the new country. . . .

But who is to support the researches of the pure scientist, and who is to furnish him with encouragement and assistance to pursue his self-sacrificing and arduous quest for that truth which is certain, as time goes on, to bring in its train so many blessings to mankind? Who is to furnish the laboratories, the funds for apparatus, and for traveling and for foreign study?

Because of the extraordinary practical results which have been attained by scientifically trained men working in the industrial laboratories and because of the limited and narrow conditions under which many scientific investigators have sometimes been compelled to work in universities, it has been suggested that perhaps the theater of scientific research might be shifted from the university to the great industrial laboratories which have already grown up or to the even greater ones which the future is bound to bring forth. But we can dismiss this suggestion as being unworthy.

Organizations and institutions of many kinds are engaged in pure scientific research and they should receive every encouragement, but the natural home of pure science and of pure scientific research is to be found in the university, from which it cannot pass. It is a high function of the universities to make advances in science, to test new scientific discoveries, and to place their stamp of truth upon those which are found to be pure. In this way only can they determine what shall be taught as scientific truth to those who, relying upon their authority, come to them for knowledge and believe what they teach.

Instead of abdicating in their favor, may not our universities, stimulated by the wonderful achievements of these industrial laboratories, find a way to advance the conduct of their own pure scientific research, the grand responsibility for which rests upon them? This responsibility should now be felt more heavily than ever by our American universities, not only because the tragedy of the great war has caused the destruction of European institutions of learning but because even a worse thing has happened. So great have been the fatalities of the war that the universities of the Old World hardly dare to count their dead.

But what can the American universities do, for they, like the pure scientists, are not engaged in a lucrative occupation. Universities are not moneymaking institutions, and what can be done without money? . . . While there are many things — and most important things — which the universities can do to aid pure science without the employment of large sums of money, there are nevertheless a great many things required in the conduct of pure scientific research which can be done only with the aid of money.

The first of these I think is this: When a master scientist does appear and has made himself known by his discoveries, then he should be provided with all of the resources and facilities and assistants that he can effectively employ, so that the range of his genius will in no way be restricted for the want of anything which money can provide.

Every reasonable and even generous provision should be made for all workers in pure science, even though their reputations have not yet become great by their discoveries, for it should be remembered that the road to great discoveries is long and discouraging and that for one great achievement in science we must expect numberless failures.

I would not restrict these workers in pure science to our great universities, for I believe that they should be located also at our technical schools, even at those with the most practical aims. In such schools the influence of a discoverer in science would serve as a balance to the practical curriculum and familiarize the student with the high ideals of the pure scientist and with his rigorous methods of investigation. Furthermore, the time has come when our technical schools must supply in largely increasing numbers men thoroughly grounded in the scientific method of investigation for the work of industrial research.

Even the engineering student, who has no thoughts of industrial research, will profit by his association with the work of the pure scientist, for if he expects ever to tread the higher walks of the engineering profession he must be qualified to investigate new problems in engineering and devise methods for their solution; and for such work a knowledge of the logical processes of the pure scientist and his rigorous methods of analyzing and weighing evidence in his scrupulous search for the truth will be of the greatest value.

Furthermore, the engineering student should be taught to appreciate the ultimate great practical importance of the results of pure scientific investigation and to realize that pure science furnishes to engineering the raw material, so to speak, which he must work into useful forms. He should be taught that after graduation it will be most helpful to him, and even necessary if he is to be a leader, to watch with care the work of the pure scientist and to scrutinize the reports of new scientific discoveries to see what they may contain that can be applied to useful purposes and more particularly to problems of his own which require solution. There are many unsolved problems in applied science, today, which are insoluble in the present state of our knowledge, but I am sure that in the future, as has so often happened in the past, these problems will find a ready solution in the light of pure scientific discoveries yet to be made.

When thus regarded, the work of the pure scientist should be followed with most intense interest by all of those engaged in the application of science to industrial purposes. Acquaintance, therefore, with the pure scientist, with his methods and results, is of great importance to the student of applied science. I believe that there is need of a better understanding of the relations between the pure scientist and the applied scientist and that this understanding would be greatly helped by a closer association between the pure scientist and the students in the technical schools.

While I have drawn a valid distinction between the work of the two, they nevertheless have much in common. Both are concerned with the truth of things, one to discover new truths and the other to apply these truths to the uses of man. While the object of the engineer is to produce from scientific discoveries useful results, these results are for the benefit of others. They are dedicated to the use of mankind and, as is the case with the pure scientist, they should not be confused with the pecuniary compensation which the engineer himself may receive; for his work for this compensation is slight, often infinitesimally so, compared with the great benefits received by others. Like the worker in pure science, the engineer finds inspiration in the desire for achievement, and his real reward is found in the knowledge of the benefits which others receive from his work.

There are many other things which might be discussed concerning the conduct of pure scientific research in our universities and technical schools, but enough has been said to make it plain that I believe such work should be greatly extended in all of our American universities and technical institutions.

But where are the universities to obtain the money necessary for the carrying out of a grand scheme of scientific research? It should come from those generous and public-spirited men and women who desire to dispose of their wealth in a manner well calculated to advance the welfare of mankind; and it should come from the industries themselves, which owe such a heavy debt to science. While it cannot be shown that the contribution of any one manufacturer or corporation to a particular, purely scientific research will bring any return to the contributor or to others, it is certain that contributions by the manufacturers, in general, and by the industrial corporations to pure scientific research, as a whole, will in the long run bring manifold returns through the medium of industrial research conducted in the rich and virgin territory discovered by the scientific explorer.

4.

Howard E. Coffin: Industrial Organization for National Defense

President Wilson did not join the military preparedness camp until late in 1915, when, in a speech delivered on November 4, he gave notice of his change in viewpoint by quoting Ezekiel 33:6: "But if the watchman see the sword come, and blow not the trumpet, and the people be not warned . . . his blood will I require at the watchman's hand." Wilson proposed, and the next year Congress passed, legislation providing for an increase in the Army, a massive naval building program, and the creation of a coordinating board to take an inventory of the nation's industrial capacity to wage war. "Organizing Industry for National Defense," an article that appeared in May 1916 and is reprinted here, was written by Howard E. Coffin, chairman of the Committee on Industrial Preparedness of the Naval Consulting Board.

Source: *World's Work*, May 1916.

THE EUROPEAN WAR SITUATION of the last year and a half has entirely upset our preconceived notions of a war. We had an idea that an Army and a Navy meant preparedness. We had an idea that the Army and the Navy would take the brunt of any attack upon this country; that the battles should be fought and the naval engagements should take place, and that the winner would be master of the field.

Now, in Europe today, everyone knows that it is not any more a question of a navy nor the question of any particular army. The test has gotten down to which country can fastest and longest supply the munitions of war to the men on the fighting line. It has gotten down to the question of what country can fastest and in the greatest quantity supply shells to the guns; and it has gotten down, not to the point of professional fighting men but to the question of whether every man, woman, and child of the nation has been engaged and is engaged in the production of some kind of materials for the armies at the front. It has even gotten to the point where the women of the leisure classes are going into the mills and the factories at Saturday noon and working in seven-hour shifts until midnight of Sunday in order that the mills may not be closed down during the time that organized labor stops work for its period of rest.

When the problem of warfare comes down to this basis, it is no longer a question of the ability of the departmental heads of the Army and Navy, but it is a question of the ability of every bit of industrial brains in this country.

It is vitally necessary that the civilian end of our whole American defense situation be instructed in the part which it must play in any true plan of national defense. Our departmental heads in Washington are largely, of course, graduates of the very best technical schools in the country. They are from Annapolis and West Point, and have been taught the profession of fighting and of military practice at every angle, and are masters of their profession. Civilians are unable to give to those men any instructions or directions in their particular line of the work.

But from the very nature of their training, the men who head the departments of the Army and Navy have lived and eaten and slept with military problems all their lives. Civilian engineers, on the other hand, have lived and eaten and slept with the industrial problems of the country. The two problems are entirely distinct, and the masters of one cannot possibly, within the human conception, be the masters of the other.

We must organize behind the men of the Army and Navy. We must make them realize that they have the support of the country; and in order to do this we must work in time of peace and not wait until trouble comes upon us suddenly.

There are three steps to be taken to get industry organized behind the Army and the Navy. Our first step is to find out what we can do in this country in the manufacture of munitions. The second step is to apply that knowledge in a practical way which will put the plants of this country into the service of the government behind our Army and Navy. And the third step is to create such an organization of the skilled labor of this country that that skilled labor will not get off the job in the event of war, as it did in England and France, and get to the front and have to be pulled back later

and reorganized for the work in hand, but will stay where it belongs, at work, under governmental supervision, which will actually prevent the men from enlisting in the regular service.

The Role of Labor in National Defense

I do not know whether or not it has occurred to many people that the old cry of labor that it was obliged to fight the wars into which the governments might plunge the country has been pretty thoroughly exploded, and that the wars are being fought by the bankers and the statesmen and the artists and the tradesmen, etc.; while the skilled mechanic is being kept at home and guarded most carefully by the European governments, because they realize that in the preservation of their skilled mechanics they have the answer to the question of whether or not they will win or lose the war.

Now it is the skilled mechanic of the future who is going to win the wars of this country, because he is the man who is going to produce those munitions in such quantities as will be used by the fighting line, whereas the banker, if you like, and the lawyer is merely a man who carries a gun at the front — as they put it abroad, is cannon fodder.

In any problem as big as the question of industrial organization of this country for the service of the government, in any problem as big as the analysis of the industrial resources of the country, we cannot, of course, depend upon any small corps of men or board which may be created for the purpose. Such work must be done by the men who themselves have developed the industries of the country. Therefore, early in the effort of the Naval Consulting Board to organize industry for national defense, we were convinced that in order to do this work as it should be done and in order to place behind the government the true industrial strength of this country, it was necessary that the engineers themselves of the United States take up this work. In the event of war, it will be the engineers who will have to direct the munition industries and who will have to cooperate on the closest possible terms so that the government may accomplish results. Therefore, we felt immediately that we must organize the engineers of the country in this service.

At our suggestion President Wilson wrote a letter to the presidents of the five national technical organizations of this country, which are the Mining Engineers, the Civil Engineers, the Mechanical Engineers, the Electrical Engineers, and the Chemical Engineers, asking them to cooperate with the Naval Consulting Board in the initiation of this work, and further requesting that their method of cooperation with this board should be through the selection of one of the leading businessmen, business engineers, a member of each society of every state in the Union; those five men to be formed into a Board of Directors, to which would be turned over all official action of the technical organizations, all the combined membership of this organization within that state. This gives us a Board of Directors of five men organized in every state of the Union, and under them they have 30,000 of the most highly trained engineers of the country.

The Plan of the Naval Consulting Board

Out of about 240 or 250 men nominated for this work by their societies, I believe that there have been only 2 failures to respond to the affirmative, 1 due to a death and the other due to some insurmountable obstacle. The engineers are entering the work in the most serious frame of mind; and the method of procedure which I shall outline briefly to you is that, under the direction of the Naval Consulting Board, in accordance with the procedure and the practice of the United States Census Office, we are having prepared the necessary forms for the collection of the data on the industries of this country.

There are about 30,000 concerns in which, in the first instance, we are interested. We want to make those concerns a business inventory embodying knowledge such as any businessman would want to have concerning a company with which he expected to enter into serious business relations.

On these forms is filled in the name of the concern on which the report is to be made. The state directors pass them on to the man in the field — a trained engineer who will understand that he is to get a full and accurate report on the business to which he is assigned; and it is our hope that this first step in true preparedness will go through as any other big business goes through in this country. We want to put the thing through in such a manner that it will serve notice upon our friends on the other side of the water that, when it is necessary for the United States to move rapidly in any question of preparedness, we have the old Yankee ability to do it.

Behind us, too, in all this work is the weight of the chambers of commerce of the country. The Chamber of Commerce of the United States has framed as a referendum to its voting members — comprising chambers of commerce, boards of trade, and national organizations throughout the United States — resolutions which are exactly in accordance with our proposed program; and, therefore, we shall have not only the engineering ability and the engineering talent of the country engaged in the actual performance of the work but we shall have the business weight of the country as well.

But when we shall have taken an inventory of our resources, we shall not have gotten very far toward preparedness; because no matter how much data we may acquire as to what the manufacturers of this country may be able to do, the vitally important thing, of course, is to see that those industries are in shape actually to do the work when it is put up to them. This is the second step. There is not a manufacturer in this country who can start on quantity production of shells within one year after the receipt of an order from the United States government unless he has in time of peace, and previously to the receipt of that order, done shellwork in his plant. Consequently, we are going to have to educate the manufacturers of this country in the production of munitions, and we are going to have to show through these educational methods of procedure in this country how to serve the Army and the Navy in time of need.

It does not make any difference what our individual political ideas may be concerning government ownership and government operation of munitions plants. We must remember that from 80 to 90 percent of the total manufacturing and producing resources of the foreign nations today are engaged in the production of materials for the armies and navies, but principally for the fighting lines of the armies. The navies have used practically nothing as yet; so that nearly everything that is being made may be said to be for the armies.

The Necessity of Private Industrial Cooperation

No one can conceive of a government, whether it be our own or any other, which can, through taxation or otherwise, construct and maintain in time of peace a plant which will be qualified to turn out enough munitions to supply the fighting line in time of war. This means that even though we have government-owned plants — and the ideal thing would be to have several of them scattered through the Middle West — but even though we have them to act as educational institutions and to act as clearing houses for specifications and blueprints, in the last equation, in any future war in which this country is engaged, it is going to

be the privately owned manufacturing plants of this country which must feed the guns that will save the nation. If we can have government-owned plants, they will come in as assembling plants and as clearinghouses for specifications, tools, and skilled munition workers.

But we must not overlook the fact that congressional action toward the establishment of government-owned plants may be on a false basis. As I see it, one of the greatest dangers of this country at the present time is that, through the passage by the houses in Washington of bills creating a larger Army, an increased Navy, and a few munitions plants, the country may sit down and fold its hands, and say, "We are prepared."

As a practical working-out of industrial organization for national defense, we purpose to give the private plants of this country small annual orders for munitions. To take a case in point, suppose that we went to a motorcar company with an order for a limited number of three-inch shell casings per year, to be produced at any time during the year, during the slack time or otherwise, with the idea that those casings must be delivered every year. Even an insignificant step like that will insure certain things.

The purchasing department of the motorcar company will learn how and where to buy materials; the manufacturing department of the motorcar company will learn how to handle those materials; the company will learn what jig and tool equipment is necessary, and it will learn the heat treatment; the inspection department will learn the government standard of inspection; the engineering department will have the blueprints and specifications covering that work, and all the arguments that arise on new work will be gotten out of the way during the time of peace; the shipping department will learn how to crate and ship the material after it is finished; and the business end of the motorcar company will learn something of governmental methods of business.

Our Lesson from the War Orders

And this is a very important point. Of the great number of rejections which the European inspectors have made of American munitions, many have been reasonable and many unreasonable. We have no reason to assume that the specifications and drawings and details of our American departments in munitions works are any more nearly accurate than are those similar specifications of foreign governments. And in this country there have been a tremendous number of changes made in those specifications since the placing of orders.

And just so surely as there is a wide distribution of the munitions orders of this country in this educational campaign, just that surely are we going to center upon those specifications the hardheaded business considerations of the quantity producer throughout the country, and we are going to work a tremendous lot of changes in our own specifications; because a large percentage of the manufacture of munitions for the government, of course, has been given in the past to concerns which made it a business, and they are much more willing to put up with, if you like, foolish notions and almost impossible specifications than would be the majority of the quantity producers of the country.

The peace practice of munition manufacture would smooth out the very difficult task of adjusting government specifications and inspection and the exigencies of quantity production in private plants. And the private plants will have covered in the production of small orders a great deal of the necessary fundamental work through which any manufacturing concern must go before it can learn how to produce munitions of war.

If we take that one case of the motorcar company and multiply it by 10,000 or 15,000 and consider those plants set down in every corner of this country, we shall be approaching a state where we can reasonably say that within a very few months we shall be in position to turn out war materials of that kind.

Let us look for a minute at the labor attitude toward a step of this kind. By such a plan we are insuring against the closing of plants throughout this country, even in time of war. We are insuring employment to the maximum number of workmen even under war conditions. And we are laying once for all the bugaboo of the munitions lobby at Washington. We are giving to the government a thousand strings to its bow where it now has a few, and we are bringing home to the American laboring man throughout this country the realization that he has some further obligations to the government than he has felt that he has had to date.

Now the third step, of course, is to gain the support of skilled labor, and there we have of necessity to deal with organized labor. Just as certainly as we insure a governmental regulation of price upon munitions and just as certainly as we insure to the skilled mechanic of this country that he, without going to the front and carrying a musket, is yet going to be placed in the same relative position, so far as honor is concerned, as though he were carrying a gun in the trenches, just that certainly are we going to enlist the support of the skilled laborers behind any move of this kind. And that is the attitude of such leaders in the organized labor field with whom we have been in touch. The cooperation of labor is one of the most vital elements in any campaign for the introduction of such sound methods of preparedness.

I wonder if many people have a real conception of the intricate problem of the thing about which I am writing. I doubt if anyone can have who has never been actively interested in the quantity manufacture of materials. Perhaps one or two little instances will make the difficulties clearer.

*The Industrial Unpreparedness of
the United States*

There are three concerns in this country today that make practically all the gauges and inspection tools for this country, and ship much of that same material to Europe. Those concerns are all in New England — incidentally, two are in seacoast cities. They have gotten together and have compiled certain figures more or less for their own information. Those figures show that to produce 200,000 shells a day in this country of the sizes required by the Army and Navy would require an equipment in measuring tools and gauges and inspection gauges alone of from 17 million to 20 million tools, and would take the combined capacity of their plants five years to produce them; and the lack of these tools is one of the main reasons today why American manufacturers are unable to fill orders from Europe.

Not long ago testimony concerning rifle manufacture to the following effect was given in Washington:

It has taken substantially a year for American manufacturers, with every incentive and under the most favorable circumstances, to manufacture their first rifle for European use. In the manufacture of this rifle, 120 separate and distinct operations are required in order to finish the receiver alone. The receiver is that part of the rifle which contains the bolt and firing mechanism. In other words, 120 gauges of the utmost accuracy must be prepared before this essential part of the rifle can be made. So with the gauges for various other parts in order to manufacture the rifle in quantities. After one complete set is made, additional sets can be made somewhat more rapidly and cheaply, but each must be made independently and separately.

And in that connection here are some figures which have been compiled as to the life of the gauging mechanism. These gauges, after they are once completed, are to be used only for from 8,000 to 10,000 gaugings and then scrapped. The surfaces become so abraded that the gauge is no longer sufficiently accurate for the work, and new gauges must be substituted.

In the manufacture of munitions themselves, I do not know what the average time has been that has been taken in beginning production on foreign orders, by concerns in this country, that have been quantity producers of various kinds of machinery and tools, but there are many of the best concerns in the United States that have been taking a year on the problem and have not yet produced and delivered enough stuff that has passed inspection to be worthwhile. One of the representatives of the English government told me not long ago that if the Allies were whipped in the present war in Europe it would be because the United States had not made specified deliveries of rifles for which we have orders in this country.

We hear a good many statements here about our munitions production. The British, however, point out that although we have concerns in this country which have gone on for fifty years in the manufacture of firearms, anything that those concerns have done after a year or a year and a half of effort upon orders which were placed with them has been practically negligible. And this naturally leads one to wonder if all this munitions work which has come to this country is merely a ripple around the edge of the pool and if we cannot take care of a ripple in any better shape than we are taking care of it, what in heaven's name would we do if we were one of the principals engaged?

*The Plan for Industrial
Preparedness*

It is not that many concerns in this country have not met new conditions quickly and successfully. They have. But these special concerns have manufactured only particular things. Many other items equally necessary for war use we cannot now manufacture at all. As a nation we are not at all ready to supply an army with all its wants. So much of specialized skill is required in the production of munitions of war that it may be truly said to be a new art; and in order that the facilities of this country may be placed in position to combat the difficulties of the taking up of a new art of this kind, it means that we must start the most thorough preparedness now in advance of any time of real trouble.

The plan of the Naval Consulting Board is first to get an accurate census of manufacturing plants; second, to have them equip themselves with the necessary tools and train themselves by making a small amount of munitions each year; and third, to enlist skilled labor in the service of the government to make munitions in time of war rather than to go to the front. Without some such cooperation of industry, if a war come, we shall send our soldiers, be they regulars, militia, or volunteers, to the front to slaughter and defeat.

5.

R. F. PETTIGREW: Public Utilities and the People's Property

Conservationists were put on the defensive during President Wilson's first term by several measures, then pending before Congress, that seemed to threaten the future of the public domain. The longest struggle centered around the increasingly powerful private utilities industry. Its plans to develop hydroelectric power in the West were supported and seconded by U.S. senators and congressmen from the area, who were eager to advance the interests of their states and were thus willing to grant virtually perpetual leases to private companies on rivers and streams in the public domain. Oil and lumber companies also sought legislation in their favor. The following article by R. F. Pettigrew, criticizing several pieces of pending legislation, was typical of the frequent appeals in the press. Despite support from Wilson and Secretary of the Interior Franklin K. Lane, conservationists were defeated in every encounter until 1920, when the Water Power Act was passed under their aegis.

Source: *The Public*, December 8, 1916: "Congress Should Stop Giving Away the People's Property."

DÍAZ ROBBED MEXICO, despoiled her people of the land, and gave away to foreign corporations the mineral and forest lands for a personal consideration, which caused the revolution now in progress in that country and made Díaz a fugitive. Is the Congress of the United States engaged in the same business? Are the representatives of the people of the United States selling the remaining property of the people for a personal consideration? Read the following:

There are four measures now pending in Congress that should be defeated. They are measures masquerading as conservation bills. They constitute the last great raid by the exploiters of the people of the United States upon what is left that is valuable of the public domain.

I appeal to the President to prevent the passage of these bills.

The first bill is the Shields Water Power Bill — Senate Bill 3331. This bill has passed the Senate. It gives away all the remaining waterpower upon all the navigable streams of the United States forever. It is absolutely indefensible. It gives away waterpower enough for the needs of 200 million people — more waterpower, several times over, than is now in use in the United States. It is practically a perpetual grant, although this bill pretends that it is a grant for fifty years; for the fifty-year limit is set, not upon the grant but upon the right of the United States or other public agency to condemn the property; and if this bill becomes a law, the remaining waterpower of the United States is gone forever into the hands of speculators, to be used to exploit the people of this country.

The second bill is the Myers Water Power Bill — H. R. 408. As this bill passed the House of Representatives, it was a very bad measure and utterly indefensible; but the Senate reported a substitute on March 14 last, which makes the Myers Bill one of the most infamous of measures.

The trouble with the Senate of the United States is that it is composed of lawyers, good, bad and indifferent, and a lawyer, owing to his training, is unfit to be a member of any legislative body; for he believes that the rights of property, no matter how acquired, are sacred, and that the rights of man or the rights of the people are matters of utter indifference.

The Myers Bill gives away all the waterpower on all the public domain except national parks and military reservations; and, by its terms, without any reservation whatever, provides for the unlimited exploitation of the national forests and national monuments and what is left of the public domain. It makes the granting of a lease mandatory and provides for no rental until the plant is in operation.

If this second waterpower bill goes through, a monopoly will be created of the waterpower of the United States. The owners can hold it forever, charge what they please for the use of it, and exploit the people.

Great combinations have already acquired the waterpower heretofore improved, and combinations with capital as great as $5 billion have been organized which own the public utilities, such as electric light, street railroads, and gas plants. If they can corral all the remaining waterpower of the United States and tie it up so that no one else can improve it, they can charge what they please for that which they have already improved. One company, Byllesby's Company of Chicago, with its various subsidiary companies, is capitalized for $5 billion, which is over twice, or double, the assessed valuation of all the property in the state of Illinois in 1914.

The fact of the matter is that this waterpower should all be reserved by the government and should be ultimately conveyed to the states where it is located, never to be sold or leased, but to be improved by the states. It should be changed to the form of electricity to be used for the benefit of the whole people. It is power and heat for every purpose. It is power and heat to run machinery and to warm our homes.

On the Missouri River, alone, in South Dakota there are hundreds of thousands of horsepower that ought to be owned by the state of South Dakota; and it is incumbent upon our members of Congress and senators to see that it is not given away to a combination of exploiters and used to plunder the people of this commonwealth.

The scientists now declare that electricity and light are known to travel at the same speed of 186,000 miles per second; they both travel in undulating waves; they both originate and come from the sun, and are alike. Really, they are one and the same thing. Beyond the earth's atmosphere, through the hundred million miles of space from the sun to the earth, the rays of light pass without producing any heat whatever. It is only when the rays of light strike the atmosphere of the earth that heat is produced, and this heat is in proportion to the density of the atmosphere. In fact, if there were no carbonic acid gas in the atmosphere, there would be no heat upon the earth; and without heat there would be no life.

Now, the waterpower which belongs to the government can be changed into heat and light and supply those necessities to the people of the United States at almost no cost. This power should never be sold but should be developed by the people for the public good.

The third measure is the Phelan Oil Land Bill. The government had reserved a few hundred million dollars' worth of oil lands for naval and other purposes, and this bill proposes to dispose of 3 million acres of government oil lands in California and Wyoming. After these lands were withdrawn, claimants went upon the land in great numbers — dummies placed there by the Standard Oil Company — and began developing these properties in spite of the law and in defiance of the rights of the government.

This Phelan Bill proposes to give these claimants the preference. The chief beneficiaries will be the Standard Oil Co. and the Santa Fe Railroad interests. These oil lands should never be sold but should be developed by the people for the general welfare.

The fourth bill is Senate Bill 1065, and is entitled the "Summer Homestead Bill." This is a most vicious and dangerous measure, affecting the national forests. The national forests of 168 million acres were set apart and reserved through legislation which was secured by the writer in 1890. It was enacted to preserve the timber, and also as an outing place for the people.

This Summer Homestead Bill provides that any citizen of the United States can file upon ten acres within the national forests, and get title by paying $1.25 per acre; provided that they have spent $300 for improvements, and provided also that the claimant has spent two months for three consecutive summers upon the land. In other words, people who are able to have two homes can get title to the waterpower and timber embraced within these ten acres; and the rich men can put dummy claimants upon any tract which is valuable and acquire as much of it as they please.

It seems to me that it is about time we quit giving away the public domain; about time to hold it all for the benefit of the people, lease it on short leases to those who want to use it, and lease to one person not more than he can personally use.

In fact, all the public domain, all of the mineral, agricultural, oil and forest and coal lands should, by act of Congress, be immediately withdrawn from disposal and turned over to the various states with the provision that they shall never be sold or leased for a long time, or leased in excess of the amount that the person leasing them can individually use; and such development as is necessary should be done by the public.

Records of old wars mean nothing to me. History is more or less bunk. It's tradition.

HENRY FORD, newspaper interview, May 1916

6.

John D. Rockefeller, Jr.: The Partnership of Labor and Capital

The 1913-1914 strike against the Rockefeller-owned Colorado Fuel and Iron Company drew national attention when the state militia burned and machine-gunned the tent colony where the strikers lived. In spite of pressure from President Wilson and an inflamed public opinion, John D. Rockefeller, Jr., ignored the strikers' demands, and in 1915 imposed a company-devised settlement. Against this background an article by Rockefeller titled "Labor and Capital — Partners" appeared in the Atlantic Monthly *at the beginning of 1916. Part of the article is reprinted here.*

Source: *Atlantic Monthly*, January 1916.

LABOR AND CAPITAL are rather abstract words with which to describe those vital forces which working together become productively useful to mankind. Reduced to their simplest terms, Labor and Capital are men with muscle and men with money — human beings, imbued with the same weaknesses and virtues, the same cravings and aspirations.

It follows, therefore, that the relations of men engaged in industry are human relations. Men do not live merely to toil; they also live to play, to mingle with their fellows, to love, to worship. The test of the success of our social organization is the extent to which every man is free to realize his highest and best self; and in considering any economic or political problem, that fundamental fact should be recognized.

If in the conduct of industry, therefore, the manager ever keeps in mind that in dealing with employees he is dealing with human beings, with flesh and blood, with hearts and souls; and if, likewise, the workmen realize that managers and investors are themselves also human beings, how much bitterness will be avoided!

Are the interests of these human beings with labor to sell and with capital to employ necessarily antagonistic or necessarily mutual? Must the advance of one retard the progress of the other? Should their attitude toward each other be that of enemies or of partners? The answer one makes to these fundamental questions must constitute the basis for any consideration of the relationship of Labor and Capital.

Our difficulty in dealings with the industrial problem is due too often to a failure to understand the true interests of Labor and Capital. And I suspect this lack of understanding is just as prevalent among representatives of Capital as among representatives of Labor. In any event the conception one has of the fundamental nature of these interests will naturally determine one's attitude toward every phase of their relationship.

Much of the reasoning on this subject proceeds upon the theory that the wealth of the world is absolutely limited, and that if one man gets more, another necessarily gets less. Hence there are those who hold that if Labor's wages are increased or its working conditions improved, Capital suffers because it must deprive itself of the money needed to pay the bill. Some employers go so far as to justify themselves in appropriating from the product of industry all that remains after Labor has received the smallest amount which it can be induced or forced to accept; while, on the other hand, there are men who hold that Labor is the producer of all wealth, hence is entitled to the entire product, and that whatever is taken by Capital is stolen from Labor.

If this theory is sound, it might be maintained that the relation between Labor and Capital is fundamentally one of antagonism, and that each should consolidate and arm its forces, dividing the products of industry between them in proportion as their selfishness is enforced by their power.

But all such counsel loses sight of the fact that the riches available to man are practically without limit, that the world's wealth is constantly being developed and undergoing mutation, and that to promote this process both Labor and Capital are indispensable. If these great forces cooperate, the products of industry are steadily increased; whereas, if they fight, the production of wealth is certain to be either retarded or stopped altogether and the wellsprings of material progress choked.

The problem of promoting the cooperation of Labor and Capital may well be regarded, therefore, as the most vital problem of modern civilization. Peace may be established among the nations of the world; but if the underlying factors of material growth within each nation are themselves at war, the foundations of all progress are undermined.

CAPITAL CANNOT MOVE A WHEEL without Labor nor Labor advance beyond a mere primitive existence without Capital. But with Labor and Capital as partners, wealth is created and ever greater productivity made possible. In the development of this partnership, the greatest social service is rendered by that man who so cooperates in the organization of industry as to afford to the largest number of men the greatest opportunity for self-development and the enjoyment by every man of those benefits which his own work adds to the wealth of civilization. . . .

We are all coming to see that there should be no stifling of Labor by Capital or of Capital by Labor; and also that there should be no stifling of Labor by Labor or of Capital by Capital. While it is true that the organization of Labor has quite as important a function to perform as the organization of Capital, it cannot be gainsaid that evils are liable to develop in either of these forms of association. . . .

Because evils have developed and may develop as a result of these increasing complexities in industrial conditions, shall we deny ourselves the maximum benefit which may be derived from using the new devices of progress? We cannot give up the corporation and industry on a large scale; no more can we give up the organization of labor; human progress depends too much upon them. Surely there must be some avenue of approach to the solution of a problem on the ultimate working out of which depends the very existence of industrial society.

To say that there is no way out except through constant warfare between Labor and Capital is an unthinkable counsel of despair; to say that progress lies in eventual surrender of everything by one factor or the other is contrary not only to the teachings of economic history but also to our knowledge of human nature. . . .

ASSUMING THAT LABOR AND CAPITAL are partners and that the fruits of industry are their joint product to be divided fairly, there remains the question: What is a fair division? The answer is not simple — the division can never be absolutely just — and if it were just today, changed conditions would make it unjust tomorrow; but certain it is that the injustice of that division will always be greater in proportion as it is made in a spirit of selfishness and short-sightedness.

Indeed, because of the kaleidoscopic changes which the factors entering into the production of wealth are always undergoing, it is unlikely that any final solution of the problem of the fair distribution of wealth will ever be reached. But the effort to devise a continually more perfect medium of approach toward an ever fairer distribution must be no less energetic and unceasing.

For many years my father and his advisers had been increasingly impressed with the importance of these and other economic problems and, with a view to making a contribution toward their solution, had under consideration the development of an institute for social and economic research.

While this general subject was being studied, the industrial disturbances in Colorado became acute. Their many distressing features gave me the deepest concern. I frankly confess that I felt there was something fundamentally wrong in a condition of affairs which made possible the loss of human lives, engendered hatred and bitterness, and brought suffering and privation upon hundreds of human beings. I determined, therefore, that insofar as it lay within my power I would seek some means of avoiding the possibility of similar conflicts arising elsewhere or in the same industry in the future. It was in this way that I came to recommend to my colleagues in the Rockefeller Foundation the instituting of a series of studies into the fundamental problems arising out of industrial relations. Many others were exploring the same field, but it was felt that these were problems affecting human welfare so vitally that an institution such as the Rockefeller Foundation, whose purpose, as stated in its charter, is "to promote the well-being of mankind throughout the world," could not neglect either its duty or its opportunity.

This resulted in securing the services of Mr. W. L. Mackenzie King, formerly minister of labor in Canada, to conduct an investigation "with a special view to quote the language of an official letter, "to the discovery of some mutual relationship between Labor and Capital which would afford to Labor the protection it needs against oppression and exploitation, while at the same time promoting its efficiency as an instrument of economic production."

In no sense was this inquiry to be local or restricted; the problem was recognized to be a world problem, and in the study of it the experience of the several countries of the world was to be drawn upon. The purpose was neither to apportion blame in existing or past misunderstandings nor to justify any particular point of view; but solely to be constructively helpful, the final and only test of success to be the degree to which the practical suggestions growing out of the investigation actually improved the relations between Labor and Capital.

WITH REFERENCE TO THE SITUATION which had unfortunately developed in Colorado, it became evident to those responsible for the management of one of the large coal companies there — the Colorado Fuel and Iron Company, in which my father and I are interested — that matters could not be allowed to remain as they were. Any situation, no matter what its cause, out of which so much bitterness could grow, clearly required amelioration.

It has always been the desire and purpose of the management of the Colorado Fuel and Iron Company that its employees should be treated liberally and fairly. However, it became clear that there was need of some more efficient method whereby the petty frictions of daily work might be dealt with promptly and justly and of some machinery which, without imposing financial burdens upon the workers, would protect the rights and encourage the expression of the wants and aspirations of the men — not merely of those men who were members of some organization but of every man on the company's payroll.

The problem was how to promote the

well-being of each employee; more than that, how to foster, at the same time, the interest of both the stockholders and the employees through bringing them to realize the fact of their real partnership.

Long before the Colorado strike ended, I sought advice with respect to possible methods of preventing and adjusting such a situation as that which had arisen; and in December 1914, as soon as the strike was terminated and normal conditions were restored, the officers of the Colorado Fuel and Iron Company undertook the practical development of plans which had been under consideration. The men in each mining camp were invited to choose, by secret ballot, representatives to meet with the executive officers of the company to discuss matters of mutual concern and consider means of more effective cooperation in maintaining fair and friendly relations.

That was the beginning, merely the germ, of a plan which has now been developed into a comprehensive "Industrial Constitution." The scheme embodies practical operating experience, the advice and study of experts, and an earnest effort to provide a workable method of friendly consideration, by all concerned, of the daily problems which arise in the mutual relations between employer and employees.

The plan was submitted to a referendum of the employees in all the company's coal and iron mines and adopted by an overwhelming vote. Before this general vote was taken, it had been considered and unanimously approved by a meeting of the employees' elected representatives. At that meeting I outlined the plan, which is described below, as well as the theory underlying it, which theory is in brief as follows:

Every corporation is composed of four parties: the stockholders, who supply the money with which to build the plant, pay the wages, and operate the business; the directors, whose duty it is to select executive officers carefully and wisely, plan the larger and more important policies, and generally see to it that the company is prudently administered; the officers, who conduct the current operations; and the employees, who contribute their skill and their work.

The interest of these four parties is a common interest, although perhaps not an equal one; and if the result of their combined work is to be most successful, each must do its share. An effort on the part of anyone to advance its own interest without regard to the rights of the others, means, eventually, loss to all. The problem which confronts every company is so to interrelate its different elements that the best interests of all will be conserved. . . .

MUCH UNREST AMONG EMPLOYEES is due to the nursing of real or fancied grievances arising out of the daily relations between the workmen and the petty boss. Such grievances should receive attention at once, and this plan provides that they shall. Just as in the case of bodily wounds, so with industrial wounds, it is of prime importance to establish a method of prompt disinfection, lest the germs of distrust and hatred have opportunity to multiply.

This plan is not hostile to labor organizations; there is nothing in it, either expressed or implied, which can rightly be so construed; neither membership in a union nor independence of a union will bring a man either preference or reproach so far as the attitude of the company is concerned.

The fact is that the Colorado Fuel and Iron Company Constitution does not restrict in any way the right of the employees to regulate their own lives, nor does it abridge their right to join any organization they please. At the same time it does insure the men fair treatment and an opportunity to make their voice heard in determining the conditions under which they shall work and live.

The plan does not deny to the representatives the right to act in concert; it does not deny to the men the right to employ counselors or advisers to assist them in formulating their views as to any situation. Indeed, the door is left wide open for the natural exercise of any right or privilege to which the men are entitled. There is nothing in the plan to prevent the men holding open or secret meetings as often as they like, either in the separate camps, the districts, or as representing the whole industry. Such meetings are not specifically provided for because all those who are connected with the corporations are considered to be partners in the enterprise, and their interests common interests.

The plan provides a channel through which not only may the men confer with the management but through which also the officers may lay their purposes, problems, and difficulties before the employees. It provides a medium of adjustment, as between employer and employees, of the problems which constantly arise in the conduct of business, while in regard to the relations of both, it recognizes that the voice of public opinion is entitled to be heard.

The acts of bodies of men in their relations with other men should always be illuminated by publicity, for when the people see clearly what the facts are, they will, in the long run, encourage what is good and condemn what is selfish.

Some may think that the form which the organization of labor takes must necessarily be originated and developed by Labor. If, however, a workable method of cooperation between managers and men is actually developed which is satisfactory to both, is its authorship of consequence, provided only its provisions are adequate and just and it proves to be an effective instrument through which real democracy may have free play?

The Colorado Plan has been devised for the employees of the Colorado Fuel and Iron Company and without reference to the employees, or organizations of employees, in other companies. Some people will maintain that the men's interests cannot be adequately protected or their rights at all times enforced without the support of their

fellows in similar industries. This may be true where Labor and Capital do not generally recognize that their interests are one. But when men and managers grasp that vital point, as I believe this plan will help them to do, and are really awake to the fact that when either takes an unfair advantage of the other the ultimate interests of both are bound to suffer, they will have an incentive to fair dealing of the most compelling kind.

It is clear that a plan of this kind must not overlook the interests of the stockholders, for no plan which disregards their rights can be permanently successful. The interests of Capital can no more be neglected than those of Labor.

At the same time I feel that a prime consideration in the carrying on of industry should be the well-being of the men and women engaged in it, and that the soundest industrial policy is that which has constantly in mind the welfare of the employees as well as the making of profits, and which, when the necessity arises, subordinates profits to welfare.

In order to live, the wage earner must sell his labor from day to day. Unless he can do this, the earnings of that day's labor are gone forever. Capital can defer its returns temporarily in the expectation of future profits, but Labor cannot. If, therefore, fair wages and reasonable living conditions cannot otherwise be provided, dividends must be deferred or the industry abandoned.

On the other hand, a business, to be successful, must not only provide for Labor remunerative employment under proper working conditions but it must also render useful service to the community and earn a fair return on the money invested. The adoption of any policy toward Labor, however favorable it may seem, which results in the bankruptcy of the corporation and the discontinuance of its work is as injurious to Labor, which is thrown out of employment, as it is to the public, which loses the services of the enterprise, and to the stock-holders whose capital is impaired.

This plan is not a panacea; it is necessarily far from perfect, and yet I believe it to be a step in the right direction. Carefully as it has been worked out, experience will undoubtedly develop ways of improving it. While the plan provides elaborate machinery which of itself ought to make impossible many abuses and introduce much that is constructively helpful, too strong emphasis cannot be put upon the fact that its success or failure will be largely determined by the spirit in which it is carried out.

The problem of the equitable division of the fruits of industry will be always with us. The nature of the problem changes and will continue to change with the development of transportation, of invention, and the organization of commerce. The ultimate test of the rightness of any particular method of division must be the extent to which it stimulates initiative, encourages the further production of wealth, and promotes the spiritual development of men.

The Colorado Plan is of possible value in that state and may prove useful elsewhere, because it seeks to serve continually as a means of adjusting the daily difficulties incident to the industrial relationship. It brings men and managers together, it facilitates the study of their common problems, and it should promote an understanding of their mutual interests. Assuming, as we must, the fundamental fairness of men's purposes, we have here possibly a medium through which the always changing conditions of industry may be from time to time more closely adapted to the needs, the desires, and the aspirations of men.

7.

D. W. GRIFFITH: The Rise and Fall of Free Speech in America

D. W. Griffith's classic film The Birth of a Nation *(1915) was the longest movie made up to that time and the screen's first large spectacle. Based on Thomas Dixon's novel* The Clansman, *it depicted the Reconstruction era in American history. But the film's Southern aristocratic point of view elicited protests from nearly all parts of the country and in some areas the film was not shown at all. In response to the many attacks made on the film, Griffith wrote and published in 1916 a booklet in which he included quotations from various sources supporting his right to show the film. His own remarks are reprinted below.*

Source: *The Rise and Fall of Free Speech in America,* Los Angeles, 1916.

FREEDOM OF SPEECH and publication is guaranteed in the Constitution of the United States and in the constitutions of practically all the states. Unjustifiable speech or publication may be punished, but cannot be forbidden in advance. Mayor Gaynor, that great jurist, who stood out from the ordinary gallery-playing, hypocritical type of politician as a white rose stands out from a field of sewer-fed weeds, said in vetoing a moving-picture censorship ordinance in the city of New York:

Ours is a government of free speech and a free press. That is the cornerstone of free government. The phrase "The Press" includes all methods of expression by writing or pictures. . . . If this (moving picture) ordinance be legal, then a similar ordinance in respect to the newspapers and the theaters generally would be legal.

Today the censorship of moving pictures throughout the entire country is seriously hampering the growth of the art. Had intelligent opposition to censorship been employed when it first made itself manifest, it could easily have been overcome. But the Pygmy child of that day has grown to be, not merely a man but a giant, and I tell you who read this, whether you will or no, he is a giant whose forces of evil are so strong that he threatens that priceless heritage of our nation — freedom of expression.

The right of free speech has cost centuries upon centuries of untold sufferings and agonies; it has cost rivers of blood; it has taken as its toll uncounted fields littered with the carcasses of human beings — all this that there might come to live and survive that wonderful thing, the power of free speech. In our country it has taken some of the best blood of our forefathers. The Revolution itself was a fight in this direction — for the God-given, beautiful idea of free speech.

Afterwards the first assault on the right of free speech, guaranteed by the Constitution, occurred in 1798, when Congress passed the Sedition Law, *which made it a crime for any newspaper or other printed publication to criticize the government.* Partisan *prosecution of editors and publishers took place at the instance of the party in power,* and popular indignation was aroused against this abridgment of liberty to such an extent that Thomas Jefferson, the candidate of the opposition party for President, was triumphantly elected. And after that, nothing more was heard of the Sedition Law, which expired by limitation in 1801.

The integrity of free speech and publication was *not again attacked* seriously in this country until the arrival of the motion picture, when this new art was seized by the powers of intolerance as an excuse for an assault on our liberties.

The motion picture is a medium of expression as clean and decent as any mankind has ever discovered. A people that would allow the suppression of this form of speech would unquestionably submit to the suppression of that which we all consider so highly, the printing press. And yet we find all through the country, among all classes of people, the idea that the motion picture should be censored.

When the first small Board of Censorship was established six years ago, we who took it seriously then expected exactly what has come to pass — that a man of the mental caliber of the captain of police of Chicago can tell 2 million American people what they shall and shall not go to see in the way of a moving picture.

They tell us we must not show crime in a motion picture. We cannot listen to such nonsense. These people would not have us show the glories and beauties of the most wonderful moral lesson the world has ever known — the life of Christ — because in that story we must show the vice of the traitor Judas Iscariot. Had the modern censors existed in past ages and followed out their theories to a logical conclusion, there would have been written no *Iliad* of Homer; there would not have been written for the glory of the human race that grand cadence of uplift called the Bible; there would have been no Goethe. There would have been no thrilling, beautiful dramas given us as the grandest heritage of the English-speaking race — the plays of Shakespeare. And even today, none of these creations would these worthy censors leave in our possession had they their way.

All new things in the world, including the Christian religion and the printing press, at their beginnings have been considered as instruments of evil and subject to suspicion. The motion picture has had to undergo the same ordeal that seems to be directed at all new things.

In some communities they do not allow the showing of crime in any form in any motion picture. This, followed to its logical conclusion, would make absolutely impossible the motion picture as an entertainment or as an art.

How is it possible to portray virtue without portraying its opposite — the thing of vice?

Friedrich Schiller, the great German dramatist speaking of the moral of the drama said:

It is the course of mortal things that the good should be shadowed by the bad and virtue shine the brightest when contrasted with vice. Whoever proposes to discourage vice and to vindicate religion, morality, and social order against their enemies must unveil crime in all its deformity and place it before the eyes of men in its colossal magnitude; he must diligently explore its dark mazes and make himself familiar with sentiments at the wickedness of which his soul revolts.

Search your minds for any story worth telling or any play that is worth seeing that does not in some way show vice in some form. The policy of the generally accepted censorship is to approve of pictures which offend no one. That is one way of saying, "We will have nothing in the pictures but milk and water," ridiculous, insipid mediocrity that could not possibly interest anyone. A motion picture of this class would be as interesting and efficient as a newspaper that never steps on anyone's toes, and you can imagine how people would be interested in that kind of a newspaper.

We believe that we have as much right to present the facts of history, as we see them, on the motion-picture screen, as a Guizot, a Bancroft, a Ferrari, or a Woodrow Wilson has to write these facts in his history. We believe it as a right under the Constitution of the United States, and we are supported in this belief by wise judicial decisions in cases where the matter has been presented to the courts in the right way.

Speaking on *The Clansman,* Judge Cooper said:

Every night in every fair-sized community in this broad land where the stage instructs or entertains, each and every play has its good characters and its bad characters portrayed, both of which are essential to a play in the rounding out of the moral of the play, and without which moral a play is of no educational value. If all the plays in which a villain had played were stopped, the theater as an educator and entertainer of the people would become a memory.

The foremost educators of the country have urged upon us moving picture producers to put away the slapstick comedies, the ridiculous, sentimental "mush" stories, the imitation of the cheap magazines, and go to the fields of history for our subjects. They have told us repeatedly that the motion picture can impress upon a people as much of the truth of history in an evening as many months of study will accomplish. As one eminent divine has said to the masses, "It teaches history by lightning." We would like very much to do this.

The reason for the slapstick and the worst that is in pictures is censorship. Let those who tell us to uplift our art invest money in the production of an historic play of the time of Christ. They will find this cannot be staged without incurring the wrath of a certain part of our people. The Massacre of St. Bartholomew, if produced, will tread upon the toes of another part of our people. I was considering the production of the history of the American people only this last year. It got into the papers. From all over the country I was strongly advised that this was not the time for a play on the American Revolution because the

English and their sympathizers would not take kindly, during these emotional war-times, the part the English played in the wars of the American Revolution, and that the pro-Germans would not care to see the Hessians play the part they would play in the story of our freedom.

In other words, so long as censorship holds the motion picture under its thumb, it is in every way enslaved. It dares not speak the truth on any subject and therefore must confine itself to ridiculous, injurious, and childish slapstick and absurd and weak dramatology. The moral reformers plead with us to put on pictures which speak editorially against certain evils of the day. How does any man dare to invest his money in any picture that speaks against any certain class or condition of people, however evil and open to condemnation their works may be, when he knows how easy it is for a few individuals to go to any one of the many hundreds of censorship boards in the country and influence them to destroy the property which the producer has gone to great pains and care to build up?

However alluring the theory of censorship may be to certain well-meaning people, in its practical working-out, experience has taught us that whatever section or class of the people may feel offended by a particular production, their objection is found to have a vote value to the politicians, who in turn are very often influential in the actual work of the censors.

I have already quoted a passage from the veto message of the late Mayor Gaynor of New York, but Mr. Gaynor went even further than this in his expression of legal opinion. He declared in so many words that the censorship of moving pictures is a direct violation of the United States Constitution because it is an abridgment of the freedom of publication.

So long as this matter of censorship is allowed, so long as in a city the size of Chicago, for example, one or more men may tell 2 million persons what they shall or shall not see in a motion picture in the theaters of Chicago — so long as this is allowed — so long as even one man is given the privilege over another of deciding for him the thing he shall or shall not see in the way of even the simplest of motion pictures — then there is no such thing as entire freedom of speech in that community.

The press of the country can awaken the people to the truth of these conditions. Already some of the greatest journalists of the country have been brought to see the light. I quote here from Mr. Louis Sherwin, the eminent dramatic critic of the *New York Globe*, who, upon hearing of the efforts to suppress *The Birth of a Nation*, wrote:

> This is absolutely against public policy, against the spirit of the Constitution, against the very life and essence of what should be true American and democratic ideas. The mere fact of the races constituting the population of the United States being shown in an unpleasant light is no argument whatever. If this factor is to be seriously considered, there is hardly any limit to which censorship may not go.

Again, Bernard Shaw, the brilliant Irish dramatist, speaking on the morals of the cinema in England, says:

> The danger of the cinema is not the danger of immorality, but of morality. . . . People who, like myself, frequent the cinemas testify to their desolating romantic morality. . . . There is no comedy, no wit, no criticism of morals by ridicule or otherwise, no exposure of the unpleasant consequences of romantic sentimentality and reckless tomfoolery in real life, nothing that could give a disagreeable shock to the stupid or shake the self-complacency of the smug. . . . The leveling-down has been thoroughly accomplished.

I thoroughly believe that the principal reason for the popularity of the motion picture is that it softens the hard life of the plain people with beauty and sweetness. It keeps men away from saloons and drink because it gives them a place of recreation in pleasant surroundings; it brings to the poor, who are unable to travel away from their own dingy surroundings, the beauty and poetry of living foreign scenes, of people, of flowers, and waving grasses.

One thing, remember, however unimportant or however crude may happen to be the mannikins [mannequins] that tell the story in our foreground, beneath their feet are green grasses and flowers. Behind this is a backdrop of beauty, of waving seas, curving hills, or crested mountaintops, and this backdrop must express a message of pure and sweet beauty; for if we believe, we must confess that this was done by the hand of God Himself.

"The most beautiful picture ever put on canvas, the finest statue ever carved, is a ridiculous caricature of real life compared with the flickering shadow of a tattered film in a backwoods nickelodeon," says Dr. E. E. Slossen of the Columbia University in an article entitled "The Birth of a New Art," and published in the *Independent* on April 6, 1914.

Nations of today are the result of the experiences of nations of the past. Every human being is made up of his own past experiences. If all the people of today were really educated and knew the history of the world since the beginning of time, there would be no wars, there would be no capital punishment — there would be much less evil from America's favorite sins of hate, hypocrisy, and intolerance. It is ignorance that makes possible the terrible waves of hatred that have caused our many wars and murders, inspired by politics, religion, and all the various other causes. This is the reason for the teaching of history.

We force our children to spend many years in school. At least a few months of this time in an average education are spent in the study of history. Six moving pictures would give these students more knowledge of the history of the world than they have obtained from their entire study. Besides these, the vast majority who cannot spare the time for this study could in a few hours get an excellent idea of the history of the world since its beginning *from moving pictures.* History is valuable, since through the experiences and mistakes of the past we are able to guide our footsteps into the future.

But how is the moving-picture art to express these great lessons of history and convey the morals of the present day contrasted with their attendant vices, if it is to be muzzled by a petty and narrow-minded censorship, a censorship which can see no valuable message in vice punished, a censorship which refuses to have life portrayed in its actuality, with its sins and virtues, its joys and sadness, that we may learn the better way.

According to the theory of the censors, the moving picture producers must slavishly avoid the truth for fear of treading on the toes of races, politicians, and individuals. With a censorship board dictating what pictures are to be produced and displayed, truth is not to be pictured, but a sugar-coated, virtuously garbed version alone can be presented in order to satisfy the public mentors of our so-called morals.

For example, the moving pictures dare not even hint the possibility of wrong conduct of the Democrats in Atlanta; of the Republicans in a Northern state; of the "wets" in another vicinity; of the police in Chicago; of the Germans in Milwaukee; of the Irish in another community. Every time you enter a moving-picture theater where films are subject to censorship, you are forced to accept such pictures as some self-constituted or otherwise appointed board may allow you to see, and your inalienable right of freely selecting your photodrama, your literature, your philosophy, your knowledge of life has been slyly taken away from you.

Now, what is the moving-picture film? Ordinarily, it consists either of a pictorial chronicle of current events, illustrated and explained by written text, or of historical happenings, or of stories, comic features, or some comedy or tragedy of human life. In every essential feature the moving-picture film is a publication within the meaning of the constitutional guarantee. The moving pictures are, in fact, a pictorial press, performing in a modern and entertaining and instructive manner all the functions of the printed press.

Now, the same reasons which make a censorship of the printed press unconstitutional and intolerable to Americans make a censorship of the pictorial press unconstitutional and intolerable.

The theory of the constitutional guarantee, in brief, is this: Every American citizen has a constitutional right to publish anything he pleases, either by speech, or in writing, or in print, or in pictures, subject to his personal liability *after publication* to the penalties of violating any law such as the law forbidding obscenity, libel, and other matter legally unfit for publication.

But the distinction between this theory and a censorship is that a censorship passes upon and forbids printing a picture *before*

publication, and so directly controverts the most valuable of all our liberties under the Constitution which our fathers established for our guidance and our protection.

If the pictorial press can be subjected to censorship by a mere act of Congress, then so can the printed press. And, of course, there would be an end, at once, to the freedom of *writing and printing.*

The constitutional and rightful manner in which to keep the moving pictures within proper bounds is simply to make and to enforce laws which will severely punish those persons who exhibit improper pictures.

As a matter of fact, there are laws now on the statute books which are ample to punish all who deserve punishment. It is simply a question of enforcement. So that the creation of federal censorship is absolutely unnecessary.

It is said the motion picture tells its story more vividly than any other art. In other words, we are to be blamed for efficiency, for completeness. Is this justice? Is this common sense? We do not think so.

We have no wish to offend with indecencies or obscenities, but we do demand, as a right, the liberty to show the dark side of wrong that we may illuminate the bright side of virtue — the same liberty that is conceded to the art of the written word — that art to which we owe the Bible and the works of Shakespeare.

———◆———

All dressed up, with nowhere to go.
WILLIAM ALLEN WHITE, of the Progressive Party in 1916, after Theodore Roosevelt retired from presidential competition

8.

The "New Manner" in Poetry

The new poetry described by Amy Lowell in the following selection is usually associated with Poetry *magazine, founded in Chicago by Harriet Monroe in 1912.* Poetry *was the most respected of "the little magazines" and a leader of the resurgence of the 1920s that brought to the attention of the public figures such as Pound, Eliot, Sandburg, Frost, Lindsay, Masters, Cummings, Robinson, and Miss Lowell herself. Miss Lowell's main point in her recommendation of the new manner was that poetry had fortunately put behind it the falseness in sentiment and diction that had marked the previous age; but in so doing she perhaps went a little too far, and suggested that poets no longer wrote about themselves but about "external" things. Walter Lippmann, an editor of the* New Republic, *in which Miss Lowell's article first appeared, took the occasion to counter her suggestion and to point out that all poets, modern or not, must be "subjective" in some sense of the term. However, he probably agreed with Miss Lowell that the new poetry was better than the old.*

Source: *New Republic,* March 4, 18, 1916.

I.

AMY LOWELL: The New Manner in Modern Poetry

WE HEAR SO MUCH about "the new poetry" today, and see it so injudiciously lauded in publishers' catalogues, and so nonunderstandingly reviled and jeered at in the daily press, that it is no wonder if most people think it a mere advertising term, with no basis in fact.

This is most unfair and uncritical, for there is a "new manner" in the poetry of today which sets it quite apart from the poetry immediately preceding it. I am not referring to the extreme fads so prevalent in Europe before the war, such as Futurism, headed by Marinetti, with its pronunciamento that verbs should only be used in the infinitive, and its algebraic signs of "plus" and "minus," etc., to eke out a language it had intentionally impoverished; or "Fantais-

isme," with Guillaume Appolinaire as chief priest, who wrote so-called ideographic poetry, or poems printed so as to represent a picture of a railroad train with puffing smoke, or some other thing of the sort. That these "notions" (to borrow a phrase from the country shopkeeper) will survive the war is inconceivable, but that the real, sane "new manner" will persist cannot admit of a doubt. For the new manner is not a dress assumed at will, it is the result of changed surroundings, of a changed attitude toward life.

The "new manner" is made up of so many elements that to give all these elements one specific name is a little difficult, but elsewhere I have called it "externality," and that name will quite suffice to show its antagonism to the "internality" which is the most marked quality in the poetry of the '90s.

There is not space in a brief paper to show the steps by which poetry arrived at the introspective state against which the "new manner" is a protest. That the poets of the late Victorian epoch were extraordinarily subjective, no one will deny. And this subjectivity led to a refining and ever refining upon their emotions, until the emotions themselves became somewhat tenuous. With this, growing all the time, went a most beautiful technique. There seems to have been something a little faded about these men; perhaps jaded would be a better term. Were they really so melancholy, or was it just a fashion? Some of them were pensively sad, some were despairingly enraged; they looked at gray and old-rose landscapes and sighed a languid appreciation, or they whipped up their jaded mental appetites with minute descriptions of artificial, insinuated suggestions of quite ordinary vulgarities. But whatever they did they made beautiful, literary backgrounds for a gigantic ego. Each man's ego was swollen to a quite abnormal size, and he was worshiped by his other self, the author, with every conceivable literary device and subtlety.

Egoism may be a crime in the world of morals, but in the world of the arts it is perfectly permissible. It makes very good and very interesting poetry. In mentioning it I am not condemning it, I am only labeling it. It was the manner of the '90s; it is not the manner of today.

Now, by "externality" I mean the attitude of being interested in things for themselves and not because of the effect they have upon oneself. The poet of the "new manner" paints landscapes because landscapes are beautiful, not because they chime with his mood. He tells stories because stories are interesting and not to prove a thesis. He writes narrative poems because his range embraces the world and is not confined to himself. He is ironic, grotesque, ugly at times, because he has the feeling of the universality of life.

Some critics are forever measuring the modernity of poetry by what they call its "social consciousness." When a poet really writes in the "modern manner," social consciousness becomes one facet of his feeling of universality. The greater includes the less, and "externality" includes the universe and everything in it. But Milton and Dante were universal, it may be said, were they therefore modern? Certainly not. They were universal, but they were not "external." Man stuck out in high relief all over their work. Man and his destiny — man completely out of focus, in short — was their theme. The "new manner" attempts to put man in his proper place in the picture; that is why it is so at variance with the method of the so-called "cosmic" poet.

Now "externality" shows itself in two ways: in choice of subject matter, and in treatment; and this last again may be subdivided into general arrangement and ordering of particulars, and style.

First, as to subject matter. "Externality" is the main trend of the "new manner," but of course that does not mean that no poet ever writes subjective verses. He could hardly be universal if he excluded himself. It is a fact, however, that modern poetry of the new kind does not concern itself primarily with introspection.

Another characteristic of the "new manner" is humor. Pensive melancholy is no longer inevitably to be worn, like a badge of office. It has gone, with many other obvious fripperies, such as leonine hair and visioning eyes. Is it because poets are more sincere today that they have less "side"? I do not know, but certainly in the '90s, in England, at least, they were a very carefully put-together lot. It is this sincerity, I believe, which has brought back humor. To many poets of the preceding generation, melancholy must have been a fashion. I really think that if there is a fashion today, it is sincerity.

Another striking tendency of the "new manner" is its insistence upon the poetry in unpoetic things. The new poet is never tired of finding colors in a dustheap and shouting about them. Sometimes the colors so occupy him that he takes them separately, unrelated to the dustheap, as it were. This taking colors, and light and shade, in planes and cubes, with practically no insistence on the substances which produce them, be they men or houses or trees or water, is often called Futurism by the ignorant. Probably because the real Futurists, Marinetti and his followers, never employ it.

The poets of the "new manner" have another distinguishing mark. They endeavor to write poetry in the syntax of prose. Inversions are abhorrent to them, except when used purposely for accent. They try to write in the ordinary phrase construction of everyday speech and make it poetry just the same. How difficult this is, only those who have tried it know. When at a loss for a rhyme they do not permit themselves to drop suddenly into a simile for three lines — a cunning simile, neatly devised to give the necessary rhyme. They use colloquial language; "poetic diction" has sunk into ill repute, only newspaper poets and their ilk employ it. Poets no longer "fain" to do anything, nor "ope" their eyes to the "ethiope splendor of the spangled night," when "they themselves have lain upon a couch to woo reluctant slumber."

Still a third characteristic is the presentation of facts and images without comment. If there is one thing which the "new manner" is more against than another, it is preaching in a poem. And this care not to point a moral is one of the most pronounced features of the "new manner." It is this very thing which leads so many poetry lovers of the older generation to find it cold. An old-fashioned editor once said to me that what he missed in·modern poetry was its lack of noble thoughts. The poetry which is a pepsin to weak intellects to whom crude life is indigestible has nothing in common with the "new manner." "Noble thoughts," neat little uplift labels

wrapped in the tinfoil of pretty verse, has its place in the scheme of existence, no doubt, but to the modern poet it is anathema. He seeks to give life, the world, as it is, as he sees it, at any rate; and the lesson of his poem, if there be one, must be inherent in the poem itself. He takes the intelligence of his readers for granted and trusts to their getting the meaning of the poem as it unfolds, refusing to bellow it at them through a megaphone in impertinent asides.

Why do people refuse to take art as organic and insist upon considering it as merely explanatory? When these same people walk in the garden on a fine morning, do they feel chilled and depressed because the little flower buds are not tagged with texts? But there! We shall never agree, and for people who like to be drugged with fine, conventional sentiments there is no cure in heaven or earth, that I am aware of

Now as to form. It is the belief of most people that interest in metrical experiments is a distinguishing feature of the "new manner." But do you suppose that there has ever been a time when real poets were not interested in metrical experiments? Poets have been widening and deepening and freeing their prosody ever since there was a prosody to tinker with. In experimenting, the modern poet is merely following tradition.

As the word "new" has been "wished on" to contemporary poetry, so are its metrical experiments dubbed and condemned as "new." *Vers libre* in particular is constantly called "new" and hooted at; or poets who employ it are told that they think it is new, and it is not. Of course it is not, only the paragraph writers in the newspapers ever supposed it was. So far as I know, the only metrical experiment which is in the least new is "polyphonic prose," and that had its beginnings in France, in the work of Gustave Kahn and Saint-Pol-Roux and Paul Fort. I believe I am the first poet who has ever employed it in English, and it had to be so adapted in bringing it over from one language to another that it only retains a partial resemblance to the French form.

Now the "new manner" does not consist solely in any one of these characteristics; it consists in all. Some poets have one of them, some another; it may be subject, it may be form. The "new manner" is as characteristic as the manner of differing peoples. All Americans are not alike, but all Americans have something which sets them together, and apart from other nationalities. So the change in poetry is easily distinguished. And it is an inevitable change, reflecting the evolution of life.

II.

WALTER LIPPMANN:
Miss Lowell and Things

EVER SINCE MISS AMY LOWELL explained the "new manner" in poetry, I have been trying to imagine life lived as she describes it. For she says that there has been a changed attitude toward life which compels a poet to paint landscapes because they are beautiful and not because they suit his mood, to tell stories because they are interesting and not because they prove a thesis. I don't understand this "externality"; I don't know what it means to be interested in "things for themselves."

Let Miss Lowell try it some morning and see what happens. I pass over all the things that might catch her poetic attention between the first sound of the alarm clock and her appearance at the breakfast table. I assume that her human interest in breakfast carries her past them and prevents her from lingering immeasurably over their color and form and polyphony. So she arrives at breakfast and beholds a sliced orange. It fascinates her. She "never tires of finding colors in it," and sometimes the colors so occupy her that she takes them separately, unrelated to the sliced orange, as it were. She goes on gazing at "colors, and light and shade, in planes and cubes with practically no insistence on the substance which produces them." Says someone at the table, disconcerted: "Eat your orange, Miss Lowell." "Impossible," is the unhesitating reply. "I am interested in things for themselves. It is an inevitable change, my dear, reflecting the evolution of life."

My guess is that Miss Lowell does not live at this pitch of externality. I imagine that among the thousand objects which might attract her attention — oranges, eggs, umbrellas, dustheaps — she chooses some one about which to write a poem. And I imagine that she chooses it because it interests her for the particular mood she happens to be in. And I imagine that she feels she has written a good poem when her mood has got itself expressed about the object. I imagine she is external when it interests her to be external. To be sure, if she doesn't choose to be interested in her own feelings about the object she selects, that is her affair. But she shouldn't ask us to believe that she has transcended them and is now contemplating the world with the detachment of Aristotle's God. Nobody has ever yet succeeded in being external to himself, and I doubt whether Miss Lowell will succeed.

She speaks in her article about the universality of life, and then tells us that "noble thoughts" are anathema to the modern poet. Of course they are, if you put them in quotation marks. But there are noble thoughts which poets have not always ruled out of the universality of life, and those thoughts expressing the depth and variety of human desire are the elements which Miss Lowell's school somehow seems to avoid.

Much of their work often reminds me of the art collections which museums put in the basement — Persian pottery, a choice array of Egyptian beetles, 650 specimens of Roman drinking cups, and a fascinating group of curious watches made at Nuremberg in the 16th century. All interesting enough if you have the time to look at them, and, if properly distributed, amusing and delightful. A few specialists may be seen poring over the showcases, and an occasional party of tourists comes through bent on seeing all there is to see. But upstairs there is a crowd in front of the "Madonna and Child," the famous "Venus," and somebody's battle picture. Those are the artworks the people remember and hang photographs of in the parlor. It is the art with which they live.

And I wonder whether they're not more right than Miss Lowell when they ask the artist to express human responses to the central issues of life and death. If art is a solace and a stimulus to men, are they such utter Philistines in saying that the significant artist is not he who deals with things for themselves but with things in relation to human need? I grant Miss Lowell that there are colors in the dustheaps, but what I'm afraid of is that her horror of noble thoughts has frightened her away from the effort to find color and significance in those more difficult objects about which human life revolves. I'm afraid that Miss Lowell calls a preoccupation with incidentals a brave attempt to be external and universal.

9.

CARL SANDBURG: Poems for the People

These two angry, early poems of Carl Sandburg appeared in 1916 and added to his reputation as an eloquent upstart, an iconoclast as determined to make the world better as to forge new ways in poetry. The subject of "To a Contemporary Bunkshooter" has been said to be Billy Sunday, the famous revivalist who flourished in the years before and after World War I. Sunday was despised by most of the literary figures of the time, but he was a great success and was loved by thousands of people. Sandburg thought they were being bilked, and in the second poem reprinted here, "I Am the People, the Mob," he expressed his feeling that although the people had often been bilked in the past and often would be in the future, eventually they would rise up and claim the right to control their own destinies. The theme presented in capsule form in this poem was elaborated in The People, Yes (1936).

Source: *Complete Poems,* New York, 1950.

TO A CONTEMPORARY BUNKSHOOTER

You come along . . . tearing your shirt . . . yelling about Jesus.
 Where do you get that stuff?
 What do you know about Jesus?
Jesus had a way of talking soft and outside of a few bankers and higher-
 ups among the con men of Jerusalem everybody liked to have this
 Jesus around because he never made any fake passes and everything
 he said went and he helped the sick and gave the people hope.

You come along squirting words at us, shaking your fist and calling us
all dam fools so fierce the froth slobbers over your lips . . . always
blabbing we're all going to hell straight off and you know all
about it.

I've read Jesus' words. I know what he said. You don't throw any scare
into me. I've got your number. I know how much you know about
Jesus.
He never came near clean people or dirty people but they felt cleaner
because he came along. It was your crowd of bankers and business
men and lawyers hired the sluggers and murderers who put Jesus out
of the running.

I say the same bunch backing you nailed the nails into the hands of this
Jesus of Nazareth. He had lined up against him the same crooks and
strong-arm men now lined up with you paying your way.

This Jesus was good to look at, smelled good, listened good. He threw
out something fresh and beautiful from the skin of his body and the
touch of his hands wherever he passed along.
You slimy bunkshooter, you put a smut on every human blossom in reach
of your rotten breath belching about hell-fire and hiccupping about
this Man who lived a clean life in Galilee.

When are you going to quit making the carpenters build emergency
hospitals for women and girls driven crazy with wrecked nerves from
your gibberish about Jesus — I put it to you again: Where do you get
that stuff; what do you know about Jesus?

Go ahead and bust all the chairs you want to. Smash a whole wagon
load of furniture at every performance. Turn sixty somersaults and
stand on your nutty head. If it wasn't for the way you scare the
women and kids I'd feel sorry for you and pass the hat.
I like to watch a good four-flusher work, but not when he starts people
puking and calling for the doctors.
I like a man that's got nerve and can pull off a great original performance,
but you — you're only a bug-house peddler of second-hand gospel —
you're only shoving out a phoney imitation of the goods this Jesus
wanted free as air and sunlight.

You tell people living in shanties Jesus is going to fix it up all right with
them by giving them mansions in the skies after they're dead and the
worms have eaten 'em.
You tell $6 a week department store girls all they need is Jesus; you take
a steel trust wop, dead without having lived, gray and shrunken at
forty years of age, and you tell him to look at Jesus on the cross and
he'll be all right.

You tell poor people they don't need any more money on payday and even if it's fierce to be out of a job, Jesus'll fix that up all right, all right — all they gotta do is take Jesus the way you say.

I'm telling you Jesus wouldn't stand for the stuff you're handing out. Jesus played it different. The bankers and lawyers of Jerusalem got their sluggers and murderers to go after Jesus just because Jesus wouldn't play their game. He didn't sit in with the big thieves.

I don't want a lot of gab from a bunkshooter in my religion.

I won't take my religion from any man who never works except with his mouth and never cherishes any memory except the face of the woman on the American silver dollar.

I ask you to come through and show me where you're pouring out the blood of your life.

I've been to this suburb of Jerusalem they call Golgotha, where they nailed Him, and I know if the story is straight it was real blood ran from His hands and the nail-holes, and it was real blood spurted in red drops where the spear of the Roman soldier rammed in between the ribs of this Jesus of Nazareth.

❀ I AM THE PEOPLE, THE MOB

I am the people — the mob — the crowd — the mass.

Do you know that all the great work of the world is done through me?

I am the workingman, the inventor, the maker of the world's food and clothes.

I am the audience that witnesses history. The Napoleons come from me and the Lincolns. They die. And then I send forth more Napoleons and Lincolns.

I am the seed ground. I am a prairie that will stand for much plowing. Terrible storms pass over me. I forget. The best of me is sucked out and wasted. I forget. Everything but Death comes to me and makes me work and give up what I have. And I forget.

Sometimes I growl, shake myself and spatter a few red drops for history to remember. Then — I forget.

When I, the People, learn to remember, when I, the People, use the lessons of yesterday and no longer forget who robbed me last year, who played me for a fool — then there will be no speaker in all the world say the name: "The People," with any fleck of a sneer in his voice or any far-off smile of derision.

The mob — the crowd — the mass — will arrive then.

10.

William Howard Taft: Limited Presidential Power

Theodore Roosevelt, in his Autobiography *(1913), discussed the presidential office in terms of what he called Buchanan Presidents and Lincoln Presidents. The former category included those whose strict constitutional view led them to exercise power with undue restraint. Lincoln Presidents, on the other hand, had used the office to its fullest extent, yet within the authority of the Constitution. Roosevelt, who no doubt put himself in the Lincoln camp, regarded his successor (whose nomination Roosevelt had dictated) as a Buchanan President, and strongly criticized Taft's conduct in office. In a series of lectures delivered at Columbia University in 1915 and 1916, former President Taft answered Roosevelt's arguments with his own view of the office.*

Source: *Our Chief Magistrate and His Powers*, New York, 1916, Ch. 6.

THE TRUE VIEW OF THE EXECUTIVE functions is, as I conceive it, that the President can exercise no power which cannot be fairly and reasonably traced to some specific grant of power or justly implied and included within such express grant as proper and necessary to its exercise. Such specific grant must be either in the federal Constitution or in an act of Congress passed in pursuance thereof. There is no undefined residuum of power which he can exercise because it seems to him to be in the public interest. . . . The grants of executive power are necessarily in general terms in order not to embarrass the executive within the field of action plainly marked for him, but his jurisdiction must be justified and vindicated by affirmative constitutional or statutory provision, or it does not exist.

There have not been wanting, however, eminent men in high public office holding a different view and who have insisted upon the necessity for an undefined residuum of executive power in the public interest. They have not been confined to the present generation. We may learn this from the complaint of a Virginia statesman, Abel P. Upshur, a strict constructionist of the old school, who succeeded Daniel Webster as secretary of state under President Tyler. He was aroused by Story's commentaries on the Constitution to write a monograph answering and criticizing them, and in the course of this he comments as follows on the executive power under the Constitution:

> The most defective part of the Constitution beyond all question, is that which related to the Executive Department. It is impossible to read that instrument without being struck with the loose and unguarded terms in which the powers and duties of the President are pointed out. So far as the legislature is concerned, the limitations of the Constitution are, perhaps, as precise and strict as they could safely have been made; but in regard to the executive, the convention appears to have studiously selected such loose and general expressions as would enable the President, by implication and construction, either to neglect his duties or to enlarge his powers.

William Howard Taft, Kent professor of constitutional law at Yale between 1913 and 1921

We have heard it gravely asserted in Congress that whatever power is neither legislative nor judiciary is, of course, executive, and, as such, belongs to the President under the Constitution. How far a majority of that body would have sustained a doctrine so monstrous and so utterly at war with the whole genius of our government it is impossible to say, but this, at least, we know, that it met with no rebuke from those who supported the particular act of executive power, in defense of which it was urged. Be this as it may, it is a reproach to the Constitution that the executive trust is so ill-defined as to leave any plausible pretense even to the insane zeal of party devotion for attributing to the President of the United States the powers of a despot, powers which are wholly unknown in any limited monarchy in the world.

The view that he takes as a result of the loose language defining the executive powers seems exaggerated. But one must agree with him in his condemnation of the view of the executive power which he says was advanced in Congress. In recent years there has been put forward a similar view by executive officials and to some extent acted on. Men who are not such strict constructionists of the Constitution as Mr. Upshur may well feel real concern if such views are to receive the general acquiescence. Mr. Garfield, when secretary of the interior under Mr. Roosevelt, in his final report to Congress in reference to the power of the executive over the public domain, said:

> Full power under the Constitution was vested in the executive branch of the government and the extent to which that power may be exercised is governed wholly by the discretion of the executive unless any specific act has been prohibited either by the Constitution or by legislation.

In pursuance of this principle, Mr. Garfield, under an act for the reclamation of arid land by irrigation which authorized him to make contracts for irrigation works and incur liability equal to the amount on deposit in the Reclamation Fund, made contracts with associations of settlers by which it was agreed that if these settlers would advance money and work, they might receive certificates from the government engineers of the labor and money furnished by them, and that such certificates might be received in the future in the discharge of their legal obligations to the government for water rent and other things under the statute. It became necessary for the succeeding administration to pass on the validity of these government certificates.

They were held by Attorney General Wickersham to be illegal on the ground that no authority existed for their issuance. He relied on the Floyd acceptances in 7th Wallace, in which recovery was sought in the Court of Claims on commercial paper in the form of acceptances signed by Mr. Floyd when secretary of war and delivered to certain contractors. The Court held that they were void because the secretary of war had no statutory authority to issue them. Mr. Justice Miller, in deciding the case, said:

> The answer which at once suggests itself to one familiar with the structure of our government, in which all power is delegated, and is defined by law, constitutional or statutory, is that to one or both of these sources we must resort in every instance. We have no officers in this government, from the President down to the most subordinate agent, who does not hold office under the law, with prescribed duties and limited authority. And while some of these, as the President, the legislature, and the judiciary, exercise powers in some sense left to the more general definitions necessarily incident to fundamental law found in the Constitution, the larger portion of them are the creation of statutory law, with duties and powers prescribed and limited by that law.

In the light of this view of the Supreme Court, it is interesting to compare the language of Mr. Roosevelt in his *Notes for a Possible Autobiography* on the subject of "Executive Powers," in which he says:

> The most important factor in getting the right spirit in my administration, next to insistence upon courage, honesty, and a genuine democracy of desire to serve the plain people, was my insistence upon the theory that the executive power was limited only by specific restrictions and prohibitions appearing in the Constitution or imposed by Congress under its constitutional powers. My view was that every executive officer and, above all, every executive officer in high position was a steward of the people, bound actively and affirmatively to do all he could for the people and not to content himself with the negative merit of keeping his talents undamaged in a napkin. I declined to adopt this view that what was imperatively necessary for the nation could not be done by the President unless he could find some specific authorization to do it.

> My belief was that it was not only his right but his duty to do anything that the needs of the nation demanded unless such action was forbidden by the Constitution or by the laws. Under this interpretation of executive power I did and caused to be done many things not previously done by the President and the heads of the departments. I did not usurp power but I did greatly broaden the use of executive power. In other words, I acted for the common well-being of all our people whenever and in whatever measure was necessary, unless prevented by direct constitutional or legislative prohibition.

I may add that Mr. Roosevelt, by way of illustrating his meaning as to the differing usefulness of Presidents, divides the Presidents into two classes and designates them as "Lincoln Presidents" and "Buchanan Presidents." In order more fully to illustrate his division of Presidents on their merits, he places himself in the Lincoln class of Presidents and me in the Buchanan class. The identification of Mr. Roosevelt with Mr. Lincoln might otherwise have escaped notice, because there are many differences between the two, presumably superficial, which would give the impartial student of history a different impression.

It suggests a story which a friend of mine told of his little daughter Mary. As he came walking home after a business day, she ran out from the house to greet him, all aglow with the importance of what she wished to tell him. She said, "Papa, I am the best scholar in the class." The father's heart throbbed with pleasure as he inquired, "Why, Mary, you surprise me. When did the teacher tell you? This afternoon?" "Oh, no," Mary's reply was, "the teacher didn't tell me — I just noticed it myself."

My judgment is that the view of Mr. Garfield and Mr. Roosevelt, ascribing an undefined residuum of power to the President, is an unsafe doctrine and that it might lead under emergencies to results of an arbitrary character, doing irremediable injustice to private right. The mainspring of such a view is that the executive is charged with responsibility for the welfare of all the people in a general way, that he is to play the part of a universal Providence and set all things right, and that anything that in his judgment will help the people he ought to do, unless he is expressly forbidden not to do it. The wide field of action that this would give to the executive, one can hardly limit. . . .

There is little danger to the public weal from the tyranny or reckless character of a President who is not sustained by the people. The absence of popular support will certainly in the course of two years withdraw from him the sympathetic action of at least one House of Congress, and by the control that that House has over appropriations, the executive arm can be paralyzed, unless he resorts to a coup d'état, which means impeachment, conviction, and deposition. The only danger in the action of the executive under the present limitations and lack of limitation of his powers is when his popularity is such that he can be sure of the support of the electorate and therefore of Congress, and when the majority in the legislative halls respond with alacrity and sycophancy to his will.

This condition cannot probably be long continued. We have had Presidents who felt the public pulse with accuracy, who played their parts upon the political stage with histrionic genius and commanded the people almost as if they were an army and the President their commander in chief. Yet, in all these cases, the good sense of the people has ultimately prevailed and no danger has been done to our political structure and the reign of law has continued. In such times when the executive power seems to be all prevailing, there have always been men in this free and intelligent people of ours who, apparently courting political humiliation and disaster, have registered protest against this undue executive domination and this use of the executive power and popular support to perpetuate itself.

The cry of executive domination is often entirely unjustified, as when the President's commanding influence only grows out of a proper cohesion of a party and its recognition of the necessity for political leadership; but the fact that executive domination is regarded as a useful ground for attack upon a successful administration, even when there is no ground for it, is itself proof of the dependence we may properly place upon the sanity and clear perceptions of the people in avoiding its baneful effects when there is real danger. Even if a vicious precedent is set by the Executive and injustice done, it does not have the same bad effect that an improper precedent of a court may have; for one President does not consider himself bound by the policies or constitutional views of his predecessors.

———————◆———————

One of our defects as a nation is a tendency to use what have been called "weasel words." When a weasel sucks an egg, the meat is sucked out of the egg; and if you use a "weasel word" after another there is nothing left of the other.
THEODORE ROOSEVELT, speech in St. Louis, May 1916

11.

John M. Work: The Gold Brick Twins

The 1916 presidential campaign presented the American voters with three choices: the Democrat Woodrow Wilson, running for reelection; Charles Evans Hughes, the candidate of the Republican Party; and Allen L. Benson, the Socialist. "He Kept Us Out of War" became the Democrats' slogan, while the Republicans criticized Wilson's domestic program and the nation's lack of military strength. The Socialists, arguing that both the Democrats and Republicans were dominated by capitalists and therefore oblivious to the welfare of the general public, labeled them the "gold brick twins." The following campaign tract denouncing the major parties set forth the Socialist program. The Socialist Party polled 585,000 votes in the election.

Source: *The Gold Brick Twins* (A Socialist Party Leaflet), Chicago, 1916.

DID YOU EVER BUY A GOLD BRICK?

Now, don't get indignant. Maybe you have bought gold bricks a good many times without knowing it. If so, it will be well to get your eyes open so you will know a gold brick when you see it.

In case you have at any time in the past voted against your own best interest, this means that you fell for a political confidence game. If you vote against your own best interest this year, it will be proof positive that you are still in the harmless nut stage of development.

No, not so harmless after all, for a few million nuts voting against their own best interest can and do thereby keep the people surrounded by many social evils.

Two of the political parties — the Republican and Democratic parties — are each trying to put over a gold brick on the people.

Let's take a look at them and size them up.

The Republican platform stands for exaggerated nationalism. The baleful jingo spirit pervades it throughout.

Such scanty labor planks as it contains, on child labor and workmen's compensation, were scared out of the party by the rising Socialist vote. The credit for these planks is therefore due to the Socialist Party, not to the Republican Party.

The suffrage plank, such as it is, was scared out of it by the suffrage organization and the rising Socialist vote. The fact that the women now have the ballot in a number of states was an important factor. When suffrage was unpopular, the Republican Party couldn't see it at all. The plank, however, is a compromise, for it leaves the matter to the states and sidesteps the question of granting suffrage by amendment of the federal Constitution.

But these labor and suffrage planks are, to the Republican Party, minor matters thrown in for the purpose of catching votes. They will do just as little as possible in the way of living up to them, as their record abundantly shows.

The great bulk of the platform is given up to that which the party really stands for — the interests of the capitalist class. Of course they do not say this in so many words. Perish the thought! They are too smooth for that. But it is all there just the same. A strong foreign policy. Horror and indignation concerning the Mexican situation. Hang on to the Philippines. Special privileges to the merchant marine. Encouragement for big business. Protective tariff. A big army and a big navy.

The shameless greed of capitalism smirches the whole platform.

The Democratic platform does not differ from the Republican platform fundamentally at all. Of course, the Democratic convention was held a week later than the Republican, and this gave the Democrats a chance to see what the Republicans had done. Naturally they decided to go the Republicans one better in bidding for the labor vote. Like the Republican Party, the Democratic Party stands for the interests of the capitalist class, and it will do just as little for the working class as it can and get by. The labor planks were frightened out of the Democratic Party by the rising Socialist vote. Therefore the Socialist Party, not the Democratic Party, is entitled to the credit for them.

They also straddle the suffrage question, leaving it to the states. Like the Republicans, they dodged this issue altogether until it became popular.

These scanty labor and suffrage planks are minor matters to the Democratic Party. Their purpose is merely to catch votes.

The great body of the platform is devoted to boasting about the alleged achievements of the Democratic administration, and boosting for nationalism, so-called preparedness, and foreign markets.

The platform says that the life, health, and strength of the men, women, and children of the nation are its greatest asset.

This is true.

If the platform stood for principles which would give the utmost life, health, and strength to the men, women, and children of the nation, it would be all right.

But it does not.

On the contrary, after boasting about the achievements of the administration — of which all the good ones were frightened out of it by the rising Socialist vote — they proceed to say that they must now remove, as far as possible, every remaining element of unrest and uncertainty from the path of the business of America and secure for them a continued period of quiet, assured, and confident prosperity.

Do you get that?

If the Democratic Party had ever been anything else than a political representative of capitalism, one could say that this plank is a complete surrender to the capitalist class. But how can a party surrender to those who already own and control it?

This plank merely shows distinctly who does own and control the party. It shows that the party is body and soul the property of the capitalist class. It stands for the continuation of capitalism, with its long and hideous train of woes.

In order to abolish evils, it is entirely necessary to cause unrest and uncertainty among the big businessmen who profit by the continuance of these evils.

But the Democratic Party says we must not disturb their serenity. In other words, it stands for the continuation of the great existing social evils.

The Republican and Democratic platforms are more remarkable for what they do not say than for what they do say.

The Republicans and Democrats are fully aware of the fact that hundreds of Americans die of starvation each year. They know that millions of Americans are underfed all the time. They know that hundreds of thousands of Americans are compelled to accept degrading charity. They know that every little while millions of Americans tramp the streets in a vain attempt to find an opportunity to earn a living. They know that thousands of Americans are killed and hundreds of thousands injured by preventable accidents. They know that thousands of Americans are driven to suicide. They know that thousands of Americans are driven to insanity. They know that hundreds of thousands of Americans are driven to crime. They know that hundreds of thousands of American women and girls are driven to prostitution. They know that the masses of the American people are in poverty. They know that the masses of the people are compelled to starve themselves mentally, morally, and spiritually in order to keep from starving physically. They know that the private ownership of the industries enables a comparatively few capitalists to get for themselves the bulk of the earnings of the rest of the people.

Do the Republican and Democratic parties propose to abolish these evils?

Not on your life.

Why?

Because it is against the interest of the capitalist class to do so — and these parties represent the interest of the capitalist class.

There is no way to abolish these evils except by means of Socialism — and that would abolish the capitalist graft. Therefore the Republican and Democratic parties are against it.

Furthermore, they seize every pretext to get the people interested in something else for fear they will flock to the Socialist Party and do away with the capitalist graft. They are willing to make a big noise about fake preparedness, which both of them are in favor of, or any other old humbug, just so they can keep the wool pulled over the eyes of the voters and keep them from voting for their own interests.

For, if the masses of the people vote for their own interests, they will vote the Socialist ticket.

Please get that thoroughly soaked into your head.

If the masses of the people vote for their own interests, they will vote the Socialist ticket.

The private ownership of the exploiting industries gives the capitalists the whip hand over the rest of the people. It enables the capitalists to deliberately appropriate to their own use most of the earnings of the rest of the people — through profits, dividends, interest, and rent. This keeps the masses of the people impoverished and results in all the wretched and unnecessary evils which I enumerated above.

The Socialist Party stands for the collective ownership and control of the exploiting industries.

They will then be run for the benefit of all the people, instead of being run for the benefit of a few, as they are now.

Socialism will also guarantee to every willing worker, male and female, an opportunity to earn a living and to receive his or her full earnings.

This will cause the above-mentioned evils to disappear like mist before the morning sun.

The Socialist Party is the party of the working masses. It stands for the genuine interests of those who do the necessary and useful mental and manual work. It stands for their ultimate interests and also for their immediate interests. Our platform states this very plainly. Read it. You will find that it stands for the collective ownership and control of the exploiting industries. You will also find that it stands for a long list of minor measures, all of which are in the interest of the useful masses of the people. Among them is equal suffrage. We stand for an amendment to the national Constitution extending suffrage to women. Our platform has carried an equal-suffrage plank ever since the party was organized. We did not wait until it became popular before espousing it. We helped to work it up to the point where it achieved popularity.

Socialism is not hard to understand. Just consider a moment. It is easy to see, is it not, that the benefit of an industry goes to those who own and control it? Practically all the industries are now owned and controlled by capitalists. Therefore the capitalists get the benefit. Socialism will make these industries collectively owned and controlled. Owned by the public. Owned by all the people. Therefore, all the people will get the benefit. The billions of dollars which now go to the useless capitalists will then go to the useful masses.

That is clear, isn't it?

Then vote for it.

Vote the Socialist ticket.

The Republican and Democratic parties are each trying to put over a gold brick on you.

Are you going to fall for it?

12.

Oswald Garrison Villard: Preparedness Is Militarism

Already strained relations between Germany and the United States were aggravated during 1916 by repeated U-boat attacks claiming American lives. Not wanting to provoke Germany, President Wilson nevertheless wished to protect American shipping and in November 1915 had proposed expenditures to create a much larger Navy. For the next several months the proposals were debated throughout the country and in Congress. Many objected; pacifists, progressives, and socialists all opposed any increase in military expenditures, and they were joined by pro-German elements who, realizing that the United States could not be brought into the war on Germany's side, at least hoped to keep America neutral. Oswald Garrison Villard, publisher of the New York Evening Post, *wrote the following article expressing his pacifist views for a special issue of the* Annals of the American Academy of Political and Social Sciences *in July 1916.*

Source: *Annals* of the American Academy of Political and Social Science, July 1916.

THE SIGNIFICANCE OF PREPAREDNESS, we are told, lies merely in the fact that Americans believe that our experiment in democracy is the most precious thing on earth; that it is of greater moment to all the world than any other experiment in human government, and that, for it, Americans are as ready and as willing to die as were their fathers in 1861 and their forefathers in the Revolution.

"Life," remarked to me the other day one who sits in the seats of the mighty, "is but a beautiful adventure, to be flung away for an ideal whenever the hour calls." So we must be ready to count no cost should the enemy be at the door, particularly if that enemy should be one who typifies the greatest military efficiency the world has ever seen, who believes its experiment in monarchical socialism of far greater value to humanity than our own brand of democracy, but combines within itself a military autocracy we hold to be the greatest menace to mankind in modern times.

And so we are counseled to take from our possible enemy the very things that have made him efficient and dangerous and become efficient and dangerous ourselves.

Not that we shall ever make war — *pace* 1846 and 1898 — on anybody; merely that we shall follow in the footsteps of those who believe that the earth is ruled by fear, and that there is no other way to preserve peace than by being so armed that no one shall venture to attack us. And so we have gone about getting a "preparedness" which we are strenuously but falsely pretending will be ours when the legislation now before Congress passes, and so protect us at the close of the war in Europe, and even safeguard us should the present difficulties with Germany result in hostilities. As a matter of fact, the Army reorganization proposed will not be consummated for five years, nor the naval program until 1925 or 1927, by which time the present war will be fading into the background like the earthquakes at St. Pierre and Messina and San Francisco and other great and horrible convulsions of nature, and new world problems will be upon us.

Now, the real significance of this is that we have all at once, in the midst of a terrifying cataclysm, abjured our faith in many things American. We no longer believe, as for 140 years, in the moral power of an America unarmed and unafraid; we believe suddenly that the influence of the United States is to be measured only by the number of our soldiery and our dreadnoughts — our whole history to the contrary notwithstanding. The ardent efforts of both sides in the present European struggle at the outbreak of the war to win for their cause the enormous prestige of the sympathy and moral support of the United States — although "unprepared" — we overlook as if it were not the most outstanding fact of the year from Aug. 1, 1914, to Aug. 1, 1915.

We are to deprive the world of the one great beacon light of a nation unarmed and unafraid, free from the admitted evils of militarism. We are to complete the vicious military circle of the world so that, if we do not desist, if the oppressed of the nations do not rise in revolt against the whole accursed military system, the United States will be doing more than any other nation to intensify the race between peoples as to which will be armed most and at the greatest cost, and it will be one of the most hated and dreaded. As Lord Rosebery has said, nothing since the beginning of the war has been as discouraging, for in Mr. Wilson's advocacy of our new policy there has not been up to this hour one single phrase to the effect that the United States will be ready and eager to lead the way to disarmament at the close of the war, and our five-year naval program, as its terms signify, is a program for preparedness years hence.

Next, the preparedness policy signifies an entire change in our attitude toward the military as to whom we inherited from our forefathers suspicion and distrust. A cardinal principle of our polity has always been the subordination of the military to the civil authority as a necessary safeguard for the republic, particularly in our national councils, and as to all matters affecting national policy. Today, in our sudden worship of the expert in uniform, we are told that what we need is a national council of defense comprising, as one rear admiral suggests and some of our new-born leagues of safety advise, fifteen military and naval officers with only seven civilians graciously given places at the council board.

These men, it appears, sitting in secret session and responsible only to themselves, are to formulate the policies of the nation, congressmen to have no other function than to vote the necessary money, ships, and men, it not being theirs to reason why. In other words, the council is to be our Great General Staff, and, like its German prototype, it is to make our Congress vote first like the Reichstag and ask questions afterwards — the questions to be answered only if the council deems it wise. Its members are not to be elected but are to be designated by act of Congress, once for all.

Already it is openly stated in the press

that the power of the secretary of the Navy is to be curtailed by the present Congress, so that he shall not be able to overrule the naval men, thus putting the military directly above the civil. For this purpose the undeserved unpopularity of the present secretary of the Navy is being cleverly exploited, while the public is kept in ignorance of the fact that England, the greatest and most efficient naval power on earth, has never, not even in its direst hour, yielded to the navalists, but has kept the control of the fleets in the hands of its civilian Lords of the Admiralty. Simultaneously we hear demands that only our future admirals and generals, and no civilians, shall be permitted to be our secretaries of the Navy and of war.

But our sudden worship of the military does not end here. In New York the legislature has just established military drill in all the boys' schools, while all boys between the ages of fifteen and nineteen not at work are to go to camp as soldiers in the summer. There was no public demand for this bill, but the militia wished it, and through it went. Not even in Germany has such a step been advocated, for there, in the home of militarism, gymnastic exercises have been recognized as better preparation for life and military service than military drill. It goes without saying that the smattering of military knowledge the boys will acquire will be of the slightest value, since it is not planned to let them live in trenches, handle bombs, or distribute liquid fire and poisonous gases, and the instruction is bound to be highly superficial.

The bill was not debated and is in its form a model of how not to legislate. It strikes deliberately at one of the most sacred American liberties — the right of freedom of thought, of action, and of conscience — since it excepts not even Quakers, as even England excepts them today. It goes without saying that, we of New York, owe this favor entirely to the German General Staff. Yet are we told that militarism has and can have no foothold among us! As

a matter of fact, we are assured not only that the soldier and the sailor are as infallible as the pope at Rome but similarly beyond criticism. Let a civilian refer to the immorality of our Army, which has been officially denounced by a Republican secretary of war as worse than that of any other army in the world, and the military men in his audience rise and break up the meeting — precisely as British soldiers in England have discredited their uniforms by refusing to allow orderly meetings held to discuss peace to exercise the historic Anglo-Saxon right of free speech.

The publication of a statement, erroneously attributed to a well-known socialist, reflecting so grossly and unjustly upon the Army as to defeat its own purpose, results in an appeal by military officers to the postmaster general for its exclusion from the mail, which action is taken. The German General Staff would have done no less and would but have accomplished the same.

There is a deep significance in the demand by the *New York Times,* now one of the most ultra-conservative class organs in the world, that protestants against preparedness should not be allowed to speak in public after the President made his first public utterance for preparedness. It is of the utmost significance as also showing that, as in Europe, free speech is in danger when it comes to the criticizing of the military class and its program. So the *Seven Seas,* the organ of the Navy League, has recently demanded that Congressman Kitchin be not allowed to speak on the floor of the House because of his opposition to a vast navy, which navy, a contributor to this same journal says, shall have no higher aim than to seize for us the lands of weaker peoples wherever they may be found.

Already some of our Tory newspapers have begun to admit that there is a military party in this country — a military party suddenly raised up to add one more to the innumerable problems of race, of labor, of capital, of church, and all the rest with which the country is afflicted. If further proof were needed that we are well along the road toward militarism, it surely lies in the recent demand for the dismissal of the assistant secretary of labor because he thinks soldiers a feudal anachronism. Further instances could be multiplied; it is only necessary to recall the fierce outburst of indignation at the labor leader who dared to say that the working people in this country were not sufficiently well-governed to make them care to fight for their government and their country.

Now, if our military and naval experts were the shining lights they pretend to be, why is it that by their own admissions they have made ducks and drakes of their own Army and Navy? The maladministration of our submarines cannot, for instance, be laid at the doors of the civilian control of the Navy Department or those of Congress; nor can the inefficiency of our regiments be attributed to the fact that the secretary of war is not a military man. That an American cavalry regiment can have its own machine guns stolen from it through the culpable neglect of its officers, and that this same regiment can, a couple of years later, be surprised in its camp, lose 100 horses, and be unable to shoot off its machine guns because of the dark or to protect the lives of its own men and neighboring citizens, might surely give pause to some of the War College strategists who are so certain of their competency in their own trade as to believe that they are better qualified to advise the nation as to its national and international policies than anybody else who has never studied the art of war.

The truth is that there are no experts the world over so utterly discredited as the military ones. It was the all-wise German General Staff that urged the greatest political blunder of modern times, the invasion of Belgium, as it was the German Navy Staff which ordered the sinking of the *Lusitania* and thereby horrified the world by this unparalleled act of barbarism. The generals

who began this war to the world — where are most of them? Where are the Austrian and Russian generalissimos? Joffre survives as yet, and so does Von Hindenburg. Kitchener hangs by a thread. Sir John French, like many another, is in retirement, while the frightful slaughter at the Dardanelles, like that at Verdun, spells the shattering of many another reputation that deemed itself wise enough to lay down the law to civilians. The German General Staff — what has become of its certainty that it could take Paris in a month, that the raw levies of Kitchener would not fight, that Zeppelin raids over London would terrify the hearts of brave Englishmen? And what soldier truly foresaw trench warfare or the rise of the submarine or the invincibility of coast defenses?

Yet in this very hour, when the military the world over ought to be in the dust, we Americans are told that we must as blindly accept their decrees as did the poor, deluded German people in the years leading up to its present catastrophe. Critics are warned, moreover, not to point out that every military or naval officer is a biased expert, since he never fails to urge more men and more ships to his own personal profit, for this is already beginning to smack of high treason. We are, of course, wholly certain that we can never be quite like the Germans; therefore, a military caste is quite unthinkable among us — and yet we have the word of the secretary of the Navy that one high officer has told him that the only persons who are properly equipped to judge of the needs and conditions of the Navy are officers whose fathers and grandfathers served in our fleet before them! Who is there who has come into contact with our Navy life on its family and social side who has not been struck by its tendencies to snobbishness and aristocracy?

The air has been full of charges during the passage of the Army Bill by the Senate of the existence of two lobbies, that of the National Guard and that of those favoring a

Continental Army. Both sides seem to the outsider to have proved their charges as to the existence of those lobbies, in addition to the existence of the regular army one, which a Cabinet officer once described to me as "the ablest, the most dangerous, and the most successful" lobby that ever came to Washington. We are creating in the National Guard a political machine of such power that already regular Army officers are asking whether Congress has not created a Frankenstein to destroy them.

It is stated that every private in the Virginia militia wrote to Congressman Hay, and got others to, in favor of the militia plan, and particularly of the Federal Pay for the Militia Bill. When we recall that this Army Bill contains a clause undoing a half century of reform by throwing open the civil service to all soldiers who can obtain the signatures of three officers to their certificate of good conduct, when we remember the influence exerted in the matter of earned and unearned pensions by the Grand Army of the Republic, we ought surely to ponder well the significance of what is going on under our eyes.

What it all means is that we are putting the emphasis upon the wrong things in life, on the old *de*structive military policy that holds out no hope for a better world, instead of on the *con*structive policy of facing squarely toward a world federation, or at least the freeing of the world from the old fear of one nation by another, a world whose militarism is the most successful device yet invented by tyrants, like the czar of Russia, for keeping their subjects despotically enslaved. It is a militarism which eats up such vast treasures in wood and iron and steel as to make ridiculous even in our unprepared country any campaign for the preservation of national resources. What will that avail if our defense bill next year is to be more than half a billion of dollars?

Surely so intelligent a people as our own is not long thus to be deceived as to the significance of the new use of the old en-slaving cries of patriotism, of national safety, of rallying about the flag. Nebraska and Michigan have just bid us believe that others will soon see how for us, too, the paths of military glory "lead but to the grave" — to the despair that wrings the hearts of Europe and of England for all who stop to think of the losses to the world from a war which could never have come but for the armies and navies built up for defensive purposes and the war parties born of them, the real reason for which war no man knoweth. American sanity and intelligence will speedily see that the outcry from more soldiers and ships comes not from the masses of the people, but from the fortunate classes in life, and particularly from the very classes that have heretofore battened upon every special privilege. The coming of "preparedness" spells but a new phase of the old battle of democracy against privilege.

American sanity and intelligence and wisdom ought to see to it, when the war excitement is over and news of preparedness is no longer featured in the press as once were the free-silver fallacy and the battles against the trusts and the railroads, that their government face the other way. Indeed, for right-thinking people this is the time to let the time-serving and compromising administration in Washington know that they expect of it the highest "preparedness" in the form of a readiness to take the lead at the peace conference in proposing international disarmament or in calling a conference for this purpose simultaneously with the peace conference. As Mr. Lansing and Mr. Wilson rise to this opportunity, so will their final standing be at the bar of history.

It is idle to say that there are international problems beyond solution; that there is no way out of the present low estate of the world; that its animal passions cannot be checked. Behold in Paris there are now sitting the representatives of eight nations who are legislating, not merely as to measures for carrying on the war against the Central Powers but as to such questions as a joint-tariff system, low telephone and telegraph tolls, an international statute as to the licensing of corporations, as to bankruptcies, yes, even as to the losses resulting from the theft of bonds, and as to the false designation of merchandise.

Now, if these great nations can take time and thought in the middle of a war they believe to be one of life and death to legislate together as to these things, who shall say that after this frightful bloodshed they cannot be led by the great American republic to legislate on other far more vital themes? He who doubts belongs in the class with those who despair of humanity; who see nothing to be gained by tackling world-old evils because they are old; who bow down before brute passion and would touch neither the social evil, nor any social evil, nor smallpox, nor cancer, nor crime, nor ignorance, nor poverty, because of their age.

Against the god of might; against the god of force; against the policy of murder of millions by millions, there will be American citizens to protest as long as there are stars in their courses. Against every preparation for war men henceforth will rise to say *no*, even with their backs to the wall and rifles in front of them. For there is no slavery in the world like this to arms, none that today so checks the growth of liberty, of democracy, of the coming of the kingdom of heaven on earth. They will bear readily and willingly imputations of fanciful, unpractical idealism, of lack of patriotism; only it must never be said of them that they were unfaithful to their faith or that they were ever at peace with militarism, or that they were afraid to die for their ideals, or that they were traitors to the Prince of Peace in thought or deed.

13.

SIMEON STRUNSKY: Armaments and Social Class

The continued and ever more savage and costly fighting in Europe caused widespread and heated debate over preparedness during 1916, the more so because it was an election year. President Wilson had proposed additional military spending in November 1915, and Congress had acted the following spring. Simeon Strunsky, a New York newspaperman and a Marxian Socialist, attacked the President's program in an article titled "Armaments and Caste," published in July 1916 and reprinted here in part. Socialist opposition to military preparedness was based on the belief that the arms buildup was a device of the capitalist class for higher profits.

Source: *Annals* of the American Academy of Political and Social Science, July 1916.

IT IS MY BELIEF that the differences of opinion which undoubtedly exist in this country, both as to the necessity and meaning of large armaments, are to be explained principally by a difference of class-feeling. In many of the arguments for thorough preparedness and in the state of mind which these arguments reveal, I detect an attitude and an outlook which among the older nations would be described as a manifestation of the spirit of caste.

I am aware that other reasons have been

"Ammunition"; drawing by Maurice Baker from "The Masses," June 1914

advanced for the prevailing division of sentiment. One explanation is geographical. The distinction has been drawn between public opinion on the two seaboards and public opinion in the interior of the country. The difference certainly exists. It is usually accounted for by saying that the people of the Middle West either do not realize the serious position of this country in the face of international developments or that they selfishly refuse to bear the trouble and expense involved in a great system of national defense.

Secure behind the Alleghenies and the Sierras, the people of the interior either cannot visualize the menace that confronts the people of the two coasts or refuse to recognize their obligations to the general welfare. Whether the fault be a lack of patriotism or a lack of intelligence, localism is supposed to be one of the principal reasons why the people of Kansas and Iowa do not think like the people of New York and Boston.

The second explanation is one that is more often implied than expressed in the usual plea for armaments. The sentiment is widespread that indifference or outright opposition to national defense arises from a general weakening of national sentiment and that this is due to the presence among us of a large population of foreign birth or of foreign descent. It is true that responsible political leaders, in discussing Americanism, have been careful to make the point that Americanism is not a question of birth or origin; Mr. Roosevelt has asserted repeatedly that hyphenism is psychological and not ethnographic. Yet, in everyday conversation, in much that has been written and said about Americanism, there runs this undercurrent of conviction, that if today we are not as resolutely national as we once were, it is because of the heavy dilution of our citizenship by immigration.

How else shall we explain the widespread concern about facilitating the process of naturalization among our aliens? It is not a logical state of mind. The only element that has fallen under suspicion is the German element. It seems rather absurd, every time we suspect a German-American, to go out and naturalize an Italian, a Slav, a Russian Jew, or an Armenian, who by no stretch of the imagination can be conceived as siding with their native country against our own, even if the international situation admitted of such a divided allegiance. The reason, rather, is what I have indicated it to be. It is simply the general feeling that if we were more purely native today, we would be more emphatically American.

Neither explanation, the parochialism of the Middle West and South or the influence of the foreign element in our population, will adequately account for the existing opposition to a policy of large armaments. This will appear if we look a little more carefully into the variations of popular opinion, both in those sections where the preparedness sentiment is weakest and where it is strongest. If Kansas and Iowa were indifferent because they feel secure from invasion, the feeling ought to prevail among all sections of the population. Whether you are a banker in Des Moines or a streetcar conductor in Des Moines or a farmer in the interior, you would be equally secure against an invading army from Germany or Japan.

Actually there is a notable difference in sentiment, and it is determined by class conditions. Trained newspaper observers who followed in the path of President Wilson to study the effect of his missionary journey to the West found this to be the fact. When they canvassed preparedness sentiment in Des Moines, they found that the bankers and big businessmen were in favor of armament and that the working population was against it. The big army sentiment was strong in the clubs and weak in the cheap restaurants.

For the country as a whole, there is sufficient evidence that the labor unions and the farmers are opposed to militarist expansion.

Debates on the subject in the labor federations have shown an overwhelming sentiment for our traditional policies. Two million farmers, through their Grange representatives at Washington, have gone on record against preparedness in the hearings before the congressional committees. We have the lesson of the Michigan and Nebraska primaries. And there is significance in the attitude of the Socialist Party with its record of nearly a million votes in the last presidential election. That party has nominated an anti-armament man for the presidency and is conducting its campaign on the issue.

So much for the West. If we turn to that part of the country where the sentiment for militarist expansion is strongest, we find the same subdivision of opinion based on class. I speak of New York because I am best acquainted with conditions there, but what I say of New York is true of Boston and, I imagine, of all large cities on the Atlantic Coast as far south as Baltimore.

If two years ago we had approached this problem *a priori;* if we had said, "Suppose a wave of Americanism sweeps over the country, expressing itself in no matter what form, where will this new patriotism manifest itself most strongly?" how many people would have prophesied New York? Recall New York's traditional reputation. It lies almost outside of the United States geographically and quite outside of the United States spiritually. It is the city of the Gay White Way, the tango palaces and the un-American Sunday. It is the city where fortunes made outside of New York, in America, are spent, and where ideals made outside of New York, in America, are rejected and frustrated. It is the home of that foreign incubus on American life — Wall Street.

It is the city, and New York is the state where the great social and political movements that have stirred American life during the last decade have elicited the least response. Recall what the historians have written of the West as the dynamic center of the national life and of the East with New York as its capital, as the dead mass upon which the Western ferment must work. And then consider the situation we face today of New York as the citadel of the New Americanism which is measured by armament!

Put aside this traditional vaudeville interpretation of New York which I have just outlined. There yet remains a solid body of fact why we should expect a reawakened nationalism not to show itself at its strongest in New York City. In 1910 the foreign-born population of the United States was 14 percent of the entire population; in New York State it was 30 percent, or more than twice as great. In 1910 the native population of foreign or mixed parentage in the United States was 21 percent. In New York state it was 33 percent. If we were still reasoning *a priori*, what showing in the matter of Americanism could we predict for New York state, with only 37 percent of its people of native parentage as against Kansas with 72 percent? Or for Massachusetts with only 30 percent of its people of native parentage as against Iowa with 58 percent? Two years ago, looking forward into the future, we should have said that if a President of the United States found it necessary to undertake a missionary journey in behalf of Americanism, he would set out for foreign New York amid the frenzied cheers of the people of Kansas City, and he would proceed to the redemption of foreign Boston at the behest of the excited population of Topeka.

But while New York, as a whole, is in favor of army increase, there are gradations of sentiment. Of our press, for example, the *World*, the largest in circulation among morning newspapers, is moderately in favor of increased armaments; the *Sun* is emphatically in favor; the *Times* and the *Herald* are feverishly in favor; the *Tribune* is deliriously in favor. The Hearst papers are imperialist when it is a question of Mexico or Japan,

but are strangely pacifist when it is a question of Europe.

Thus, while New York as a whole is favorable toward armaments, the emphasis varies with class considerations. The tone of the individual newspapers is plain evidence. Recall that the Hearst newspapers in New York, as in every city where they are established, appeal to our lowest social stratum when measured by the income-tax scale. It is therefore significant that the Hearst papers should be cooler toward armaments as a reflex of European conditions than any other New York newspaper.

Go up one step further and we find that the Pulitzer papers, and especially the *Morning World*, appeal predominantly to the small businessman, to the retail shopkeeper, the more prosperous of the skilled workers, and the moderately prosperous suburban class. And the *World* is more outspoken for armaments than the Hearst papers. But the *World* shows moderation, and that I attribute to the fact I have just mentioned, that its public is among the smaller businessmen and the moderately prosperous sections of the community. It is only when you reach the solid business class and beyond that, the realm of big business and established social position — when you reach the public covered by the *Times*, by the *Sun*, by the *Herald*, and the *Tribune* — that you find the militaristic agitation in its most violent form. I believe it is plain that whether in Kansas or in New York, whether sentiment is predominantly against armaments or in favor, class lines cut across the prevailing drift of opinion.

In speaking of big armaments as an upper-class policy, I am not using "class" quite in the dignified sense of an economic group in the community. I am thinking of class rather as the word is used in the society columns. When the Socialists speak of preparedness as a class issue, they will tell you that it is a movement fostered by the capitalist class with a view to war profits and foreign-trade exploitation. And if we find it difficult to understand why New York state, with a native population of native origin of 37 percent, and Massachusetts, with a like population of only 30 percent, should be hotter for national defense than Kansas or Iowa, the Socialist will say that New York and Massachusetts pay 48 percent of the income tax for the whole country, while Kansas and Iowa together pay 0.9 percent. And of course there are a great many people who are not Socialists, who do not speak of the "capitalist" class as the fomenters of militarism, but who nevertheless do speak of special classes, the munition makers, the armor manufacturers, and the shipbuilders.

But what I have in mind is not only the influence of the wealthy munition maker but the influence of his son at the university and his wife in society. I am not thinking merely of the well-to-do classes as consciously favoring war for the sake of profits, but as favoring the growth of military establishments out of that spirit of caste which among all aristocracies the world over finds in the business of fighting the most congenial of occupations.

Armament is fashionable. I must confess that I am not greatly impressed by the zest with which "society" has gone in for national defense. This business of establishing hospital depots, organizing ambulance units, drilling high-school girls in uniform with rifle strikes me as akin to the zeal with which one goes in for flower shows and barefoot dancing or whatever may be the fashionable preoccupation of the moment. Lenten amusements nowadays have a way of attaching themselves to a great social purpose. In some measure we are confronted today with the same spirit which, at the beginning of the war in Europe, let loose a deluge of duchesses upon British headquarters in Flanders.

But beyond such comparatively harmless excursions into new realms of sensation, I think there is to be found among our well-to-do classes a real approximation to the spirit of *noblesse oblige*. I find a sense of anxious responsibility, of that call to duty, which across the water is every little while addressed to the "Gentlemen of England." There is a very distinct appeal now being addressed to the "Gentlemen of America." Our prosperous citizenship has hitherto refused to render service to the community by doing its share for the political life of the country. Men of wealth have preferred to work upon congressmen and legislatures instead of working in Congress and the legislatures; and their sons have preferred polo and speedboats.

But military service has its own glamor. I cannot help thinking that a great many young men of wealth, who hitherto have seen no field open to them in the service of the nation, now think they have such an opportunity opening up for them. The Army and the Navy as a high-class occupation for the rich unemployed is a factor which enters into the movement toward a heightened military policy.

This growing sense of responsibility has been affected by the wild talk about our declining sense of patriotism, to which I have referred. Continuous insistence on the perils of hyphenism has undoubtedly created the apprehension that a divided allegiance is threatening the honor and safety of these United States. From its specific application to German sympathizers, the reproach has been widened so as to include the whole mass of foreign-born and the descendants of the foreign-born. The melting pot has proven a ghastly failure, and the feeling is widespread that if we are ever plunged into difficulties with other nations such as we have encountered with Germany, we must expect the same disloyalty.

Once that distrust of the great masses of our people becomes widespread, you can see how it would call forth a reassertion of Americanism among the people of the old stock. And that sentiment would be strongest precisely where the foreign element is most numerous. To the extent that in New York or Boston the old native element is threatened with engulfment it would tend to become self-conscious and class-conscious. The natural sense of social exclusiveness of the well-to-do is heightened by the consciousness that they are a saving remnant for true Americanism. Amidst a hyphenated population it is incumbent upon Americans of ancient origin to assert their fidelity to America as a protest against the disloyal and as an example to the wavering or the ignorant. And the most concrete way in which this demonstration can be made is through a wholehearted acceptance of militarism, both as a patriotic service in itself and as a school for patriotism.

It is in this sense that I have been speaking of the present movement for preparedness as appreciably a caste movement, actuated by a certain spirit of aloofness from the mass of indifferent citizenship. It is in this sense that I believe the creation of a large military and naval establishment will react in turn upon caste spirit. If our traditional policy were to be changed under the stress of a universal demand from the citizenship of the country, if the United States went in for militarism on the German scale and navalism on the British scale to the abandonment of traditions as old as the republic, there would yet be some compensation, if that change were the will of the *whole* people. From a nation in peace and industry we would become a nation in arms; but, after all, France after 1789 was a nation in arms and remained democratic.

But if the militarization of the United States should be brought about by the economically and socially superior classes exercising an influence beyond their numerical strength, militarism would come to us as a class policy. Among our farmers and workers the feeling would arise that the policy of

armament has been forced upon the country by the moneyed classes for their own interests, whether financial or social. Among the rich, in turn, the feeling would maintain itself that this country has been saved *in spite* of a large part of the nation, and that the future welfare of the country must depend upon the patriotic and enlightened devotion of a small class in the face of a great mass of ignorant, or imperfect, or disloyal Americanism. That, I believe, is caste.

You may proceed to pile up institutions which in form are democracy; but if the ruling spirit of the nation is what I have outlined it, you will have only a Tory democracy. The voice of the Tory is making itself heard. You hear it in Mr. George W. Perkins' desire for the presence of a commander in chief in the White House. You hear it in the demand for a General Naval Staff independent of civilian control. You hear it in a remarkable editorial published only the other day in one of our New York papers, from which I wish to read a few sentences. The article is called "The Warning," and has for its text the insurrection in Ireland. Our writer says:

> The incidents which have taken place in Dublin may be repeated in Chicago, in Milwaukee, in New York City at any moment. They may occur because with precisely the same warning that the British government has had the American has neglected, dodged, skulked away from the obvious duty and the unmistakable facts. . . . We have lived in this country of ours amidst disorder, violence, outrage, organized from without. . . . There never has been a time when the American peril could not have been disposed of had our rulers dared, had they possessed the courage, the will, the strength to face the situation. . . . The whole world is filled with terrible lessons that are being taught to the selfish, the cowardly, the blind. . . . This is the price Britain is paying for the Asquiths and the Greys and all the rest of the "wait and see" — Gallipoli, Mons, Mes-

opotamia. . . . We have treason and anarchy here. Unless they be dealt with now we shall have insurrection and machine guns hereafter.

I will not enter into a detailed analysis of this argument. I will not attempt to examine how close the parallel is between 21 months of the German-American question in America and 500 years of the Irish question. I need not dwell on the fact that of the three horrid mistakes of the "wait and see" policy — Mons, Gallipoli, and Mesopotamia — Gallipoli was the work of a strong young man named Winston Churchill who had the courage, the will, and the strength to send off 100,000 men to die at Gallipoli on his own hook; and Mesopotamia was the work of another strong man named General Nixon who, as stated in the House of Commons, set out for Baghdad on his own initiative.

But what I do wish you to see is that in the writer of the article I have quoted we have produced a very fair example of Tory mind and the Tory outlook. The civil process of the courts by which German plotters have been seized and sent to prison is not enough for this Junker of Park Row. What we need is the mailed fist; Bethlehem mailed or Krupp mailed does not matter. When you think of several hundred casualties in the streets of Dublin as the result of weak-kneed sentimentalism and compare it with the splendid state of peace and contentment which 500 years of the other sort of thing have produced in Ireland, can you blame this writer for lashing out at the folly and cowardice of the "wait and see" crowd? And if you gave this young man a nice, large army, can you see what he would do with it?

Two thousand miles from Park Row, the spirit of Tory democracy breaks out in a softer, more poetic strain; but the spirit is there. Mr. William Allen White, somewhat uneasy at an alliance that he foresees between Mr. Roosevelt and the "plutes" of Wall Street, as Mr. White calls them, on a militarist platform, finds comfort in the thought that Mr. Roosevelt, while working with the "plutes," will yet compel them to pay "tribute." This tribute, says Mr. White,

> will be paid in larger wages for men, for unemployment insurance, for abolition of child labor, for shorter hours of women in industry, for workingmen's compensation, for old-age pensions, and state insurance. This means that the rich will have to divide.

But which of these things has the Kaiser failed to provide for his people? And how does this social program differ from the Junker state philosophy of a well-fed, safe-guarded, simple-hearted and simple-minded people contentedly taking orders from a small ruling class, which alone has the intelligence to realize national destiny and the vigor to shape it? There is no perceptible difference between the ideal state of William of Potsdam and the ideal state of William of Emporia.

The rich will indeed be glad to divide; for the masses of the people there will be comfort and safety under the form of democratic institutions; for the rich, the power to shape the policies of the nation and to apply the democratic machinery to the uses of imperialism. That vision of social justice which only a few years ago was to be attained through the efforts of a democracy inspired by an ideal and conscious of its power is to be realized. But it is to come, not as the prize of a triumphant democracy but as a profit-sharing bonus declared by the "plutes."

14.

Charles W. Eliot: Shall We Adopt Universal Military Service?

The audacity of the German submarines and the stalemate on the Western front alarmed many Americans in 1916, who feared that an unprepared America would succumb to German aggressiveness. Among the articulate, influential men who became preparedness advocates was Charles W. Eliot, president emeritus of Harvard University. In an article published in November 1916, Eliot explained why universal military service was essential to the well-being of the nation. A portion of his article is reprinted below.

Source: *World's Work,* November 1916.

THERE IS ENDLESS TALK in these days about "preparedness." Both political parties and both candidates for the presidency advocate a larger Navy and a larger Army. On preparedness and Americanism the Republican platform uses the braver words; but the Democratic Party has voted — with more or less reluctance — the largest appropriations for the Navy and Army that have ever been voted and also made the most earnest attempt ever made to convert the state militias into a national force. As to the defunct Progressive Party and its leaders, it shouted louder than either of the others for warlike preparation, and, indeed, appeared to advocate war against piteous little Mexico; but its principal doctrines related to social and industrial improvements at home, and it has had no chance to put those doctrines into practice through legislation. Under these political conditions at home and in the present fearful state of Europe, it is important that the American people, and particularly the public men who undertake to lead the people, should consider, first, for what uses the United States needs a navy and an army; and second, the sort of navy and army which the United States should prepare.

To undertake the maintenance of a great modern navy and a great modern army, always prepared for immediate action, involves the abandonment of a deeply rooted American policy — the ancient reliance for safety on the physical isolation of the country between two great oceans. The maintenance of a larger navy will not require much new legislation or much change of customs; but the maintenance of a great land force which can be mobilized in a few days — all ready for service in the field — will require much new legislation, great new expenditures, and many changes in the habits and customs of the people. The policy of maintaining only a small professional army, and even that imperfectly equipped, will have to be abandoned.

Why should the American people make this formidable change in their national habits and their international policy? First, because the industrial and commercial interests of the nation have completely changed since the Civil War, and can no longer be preserved and promoted in isolation. The country cannot keep its existing machinery running or sell its surplus foods and raw materials unless the foreign markets are open to it and are freely developed. The

United States, having become an industrial and commercial world power, needs to have all the seas and oceans of the world open for its foreign trade in times of peace, and so far as is practicable in times of war also — open for both its imports and its exports of foods, drinks, drugs, raw materials, and manufactured articles.

So long as the British Navy ruled the seas, freedom for American trade with all nations was secure in peaceful times, and with Great Britain and her allies in war times; but the war has demonstrated that Great Britain can no longer secure the freedom of the seas for herself and other nations without assistance. During the present war the combined navies of Great Britain, France, Italy, and Russia have not succeeded in maintaining an effectual blockade of all German, Austrian, Bulgarian, and Turkish ports or in preventing the destruction of an immense tonnage of merchantmen, belonging to the Entente Allies, with their cargoes.

Although many German and Austrian submarines have been destroyed and a few short lines of transportation by water have been made safe against submarines, it cannot be said today that adequate means of defending commercial vessels and fishermen against destruction by hostile submarines have been discovered, or that the full power of the submarine to destroy enemies' property or to maintain some foreign commerce in spite of a blockade has as yet been developed and exhibited. The world still has much to learn about the functions of the submarine.

Hence it follows that the task of keeping the oceans safe for the commerce of the free, manufacturing nations — to which foreign commerce is indispensable — is one in which the United States may reasonably be expected to take its fair part. It is not doing so now. If the United States expects to share the benefits of the resistance the Entente Allies are making to the domination of seas and lands by Germany, should

it not also prepare to share the terrible sacrifices that resistance costs?

Second, steam and electricity have done away with the physical isolation of the United States. The oceans are not barriers but highways which invite the passage of fleets, pacific or hostile. The security of America can no longer be trusted to the width of the Atlantic and the Pacific.

If anyone says that the risk of an invasion of the United States by a strong naval and military power is very small, particularly within twenty years of the close of the present terrifying and exhausting war, the answer is that, since the war in Europe has demonstrated how horrible a catastrophe an invasion would be, the American people may wisely insure themselves against even a small risk of invasion. The only available insurance is a navy powerful in every respect and an army in reserve visibly strong in numbers and visibly prepared for immediate service.

If the principle of universal military service should be accepted and acted on in the United States, several important consequences would immediately follow:

1. The country would always have on call a trained force for all the duties and services which the regular Army now performs, and this force could be increased by telegraph and telephone to any desired extent up to the limit of the reserves. Within ten years these reserves would be formidable in number. It would probably be desirable to maintain a special force for a service of two years in the Philippines, the Panama Zone, and other outlying regions; but this force should consist of young men who volunteered for that special service after they had received the universal training at home, or the better part of it.

2. It would no longer be necessary to maintain any state militia; provided the governors were authorized to call on the national War Department for any troops they might need for local service. But if any state preferred to do so, it might maintain a

local volunteer force made up of young men who had already served their first period (sixty to ninety days) in the national army.

3. The nation would be always prepared for defensive combat with any military power which might assail it for purposes of conquest or ransom and, being prepared, would probably be safe from such attempts.

4. In case of rebellion or outbreak of any sort within the country itself, a national force could be promptly put into the field to subdue it.

5. All the able-bodied young men in the country would receive a training in the hard work of a soldier, which would be of some service to them in any industry in which they might afterward engage. They would have become accustomed to a discipline under which many men cooperate strenuously in the pursuit of common objectives. They would have mastered the use of some instruments of precision and would have learned much about personal and public hygiene, and the means of preserving bodily vigor and utilizing it to advantage.

6. The defense of the country would be always in charge of a navy and army, neither feudal nor mercenary, neither drafted "for the war" nor professional in the sense that its members mean to spend their active lives in the service but, on the contrary, composed of all the able-bodied youth of the nation, acting under a universal sense of obligation or duty, but also willing to serve the country in a hearty, cooperative spirit out of love of freedom, justice, and all that makes "home."

7. In case of war, large or small, long or short, the great waste of lives and money which has taken place at the beginning of every war in which the United States has been engaged since the government was organized would be avoided; because the country would have at call any desired number of competent officers and well-trained men. In case of war alarms, the country would not be obliged to summon untrained militia or to resort to such crude and unsound methods as Plattsburg camps and college regiments. . . .

To protect this country and its productive industries and to exalt the patriotic sentiments of its people are, however, not the only or the strongest motives for abandoning the precious traditional policies of the United States in respect to isolation and the avoidance of foreign entanglements. Durable peace can be maintained after the present war only by a dominant force too strong for Germany, Austria-Hungary, Turkey, and Bulgaria, separately or in any possible combination or with any imaginable allies, to attack or to resist. A limited alliance of competent nations — three, four, or five — can promptly provide such a force already trained to concurrent, cooperative action. Federations and parliaments of the world could not do it. They would be too complicated, vast, slow, and unstable. The "Concert of Europe" is utterly discredited, because it has too often brought about, or permitted, concerted injustice and perpetuated poisonous wrongs.

There is no hope of establishing lasting peace through any treaty making which should include the central monarchies. Their acts since July 1914 prove beyond a doubt that no reliance is to be placed on any pledges or treaties signed by them. No verbal or written evidence of a change of heart on the part of the German people could be depended on. If such a change shall happily occur, the rest of the world will not trust it until its reality is proved by a long course of rational and honorable conduct.

What would be the best group of nations for supplying this dominant force? There might well be two distinct alliances; one for the oceans, the other for the lands. For the oceans, Great Britain, France, and the United States would suffice; but Russia, Italy, Brazil, Argentina, Chile, and Japan would be convenient additions. For continental Europe and the Near East, Great Britain, France, Italy, and Russia would be indispensable, and Spain, Portugal, Belgium, Holland, and Scandinavia would be acceptable additions. . . .

The enlarged American Navy should in times of peace be an active school of practice for scouting, blockading, shooting, and maneuvering. The term of enlistment should be short, not exceeding in length whatever period will suffice to give an average young man a sufficient training. The officers would be, in times of peace, chiefly teachers; for the new men would be joining the Navy in large numbers at frequent intervals. These officers would be, as now, graduates of the Naval Academy, the cadets of the Academy, however, not being nominated by Congressmen but being selected by their officers on board ship from the successive quotas of young men coming into the Navy. The Swiss rule that nobody shall be an officer in the army who has not served as a private and noncommissioned officer would be of high value in securing an American Navy of proper democratic spirit. The utmost pains should be taken to make the term of service in the Navy valuable to the enlisted man in respect to personal hygiene, manual skill, good mental habits, and character. Every man who serves in the Navy should come out of it a man more useful in the national industries than he would have been without that service, and also a better citizen.

The United States has found uses since the war with Spain for a fairly equipped Army of something less than 100,000 men; and a minority of the states have seen reason to maintain a volunteer militia, in the organizing of which no attention has been paid to the married or single state of the volunteers and but little to their physical fitness for the duties of a soldier. The militia has also been poorly equipped or sometimes hardly equipped at all for real work.

The troubles between the United States and Mexico have revealed the fact that the regular Army is in numbers insufficient to guard effectively the long border between the two countries — in addition to its other duties — and that the militia of the states is not only too imperfectly equipped to be rapidly mobilized but also contains a large proportion of men whom it is not expedient to call upon for military service at a distance from their homes.

The militia in all the states which maintain any militia was intended, so far as it had any function beyond parades and vacation camps, to keep the peace and give aid during brief periods of local disturbance, like riots and the disorders which attend great catastrophes by earthquake, fire, or flood. A state militia as a rule elects its officers, the privates electing the company officers, the company officers electing the regimental officers, the regimental officers electing the general. The qualities which win votes in such elections are not identical with those which make a good commander in camp, on the march, and on the battlefield. As a national force to be used in any part of the country or beyond its borders, and for long periods during which the men are detached from their homes and their employments, the state militias are inappropriate. In war with a strong military power, the militia would not be available for several months, or until all the units had been converted into national units and reofficered in large part. The present Democratic administration and Congress have rendered a considerable service to the country by giving a clear demonstration to this effect.

Although the regular Army of the United States is an efficient body of men, well-selected, well-officered, and possessing a fine esprit de corps, it is not a modern army in the European sense; and it is not the kind of army that a democratic people ought to maintain, having been essentially copied from the English Army, which has always been — until "Kitchener's Army" was created — an army officered from the upper classes and recruited by voluntary enlistment from the lower. It has never been a popular or national army in the sense of continental Europe, where conscription or universal military service has long prevailed.

If the United States sees reason for maintaining any army at all, it will be wise for it to maintain a democratic army, in which all able-bodied young Americans should serve for several short periods, and then be held in reserve for a long period; its officers being selected from the ranks by their instructors and commanders during the prescribed periods of service and educated, as now, at the Military Academy, to serve for life as teachers of the successive levies of raw recruits, or held in reserve with liberty to follow civil occupations. A few thousand noncommissioned officers would also be kept in the service permanently, or for considerable periods, to serve as instructors to the raw levies and as noncommissioned officers of any force the country might need for sudden and sustained service. . . .

The answer, then, to the question at the head of this article is — the United States needs a navy modeled on the British Navy, and an army modeled on the Swiss Army; and in order to procure both it needs to adopt the principle of brief universal service in the Army or the Navy. The time lost by the young men from the productive industries and the service of the family will be a trifling loss compared with the gain from an increased feeling of devotion to the country in the hearts of multitudes and a quickened sense of responsibility for its welfare. The slight loss of individual liberty will be more than compensated by experience of a strict, cooperative discipline and by an enlarged sense of comradeship and community interest among the people.

It is a grave conclusion to come to, that a great democracy whose primary object is the promotion of the public welfare and happiness must arm itself to fight and must teach all its young men how to fight — which means how to kill and wound other men with whom individually they have no quarrel, to destroy public and private property, to disrupt homes and extinguish families, to interrupt commerce, and to waste on a prodigious scale the accumulated savings of generations.

What forces this republic to so awful a conclusion? The same experience which has compelled civilized society in general to defend itself by force against lunatics and criminals, and the demonstration given during the last two years that the existing governmental and ecclesiastical institutions of the civilized world afford no adequate protection from a sudden but long-prepared outbreak of primitive savagery which has compelled nearly half the population of the earth to set to work with all their energy and ingenuity to kill each other and to destroy each other's property, and to use, in that killing and destruction, not only all the new instruments with which modern physics, chemistry, and mechanics have supplied it but all the old instruments of hand-to-hand fighting, such as the spear — now bayonet — the short sword, and the hand grenade. . . .

Despite the heterogeneous character of the people of the United States as respects race or stock, the masses of the people worship the same precious ideals of liberty, law, and public happiness. At heart they know that these ideals, so dear to them, will have to be protected and furthered by force for many a year to come, the world being what it is. Everybody hopes that the world is going to be very different hereafter from what it is in these grievous days of return to primitive savagery; but the conduct of the liberty-loving nations today and tomorrow must be determined by the hard, actual facts. They cannot organize now the perpetual defense of liberty under law; but they can provide promptly, through practicable alliances, securities which will last at least for one generation.

1917

15.

WOODROW WILSON: Peace Without Victory

Following his reelection in the fall of 1916 President Wilson renewed his efforts to bring about a negotiated settlement of the war in Europe. On January 22, 1917, less than two weeks after the British had refused a German peace offer on the grounds that it was too vague, the President went before the Senate to try to clarify the American position in the proposed negotiations. Many people rejoiced at his statement that the war's end must bring a "peace without victory." Social worker Lillian Wald wrote the President that this speech alone would make him famous and predicted that "liberals of every faith . . . will be proud as long as men write and speak of these times in which we live."

Source: 64 Congress, 2 Session, Senate Document No. 685: "A League for Peace."

ON THE 18TH OF DECEMBER LAST, I addressed an identic note to the governments of the nations now at war requesting them to state, more definitely than they had yet been stated by either group of belligerents, the terms upon which they would deem it possible to make peace. I spoke on behalf of humanity and of the rights of all neutral nations like our own, many of whose most vital interests the war puts in constant jeopardy.

The Central Powers united in a reply which stated merely that they were ready to meet their antagonists in conference to discuss terms of peace. The Entente Powers have replied much more definitely and have stated, in general terms, indeed, but with sufficient definiteness to imply details, the arrangements, guarantees, and acts of reparation which they deem to be the indispensable conditions of a satisfactory settlement. We are that much nearer a definite discussion of the peace which shall end the present war. We are that much nearer the discussion of the international concert which must thereafter hold the world at peace.

In every discussion of the peace that must end this war, it is taken for granted that that peace must be followed by some definite concert of power which will make it virtually impossible that any such catastrophe should ever overwhelm us again. Every lover of mankind, every sane and thoughtful man must take that for granted.

I have sought this opportunity to address you because I thought that I owed it to you, as the council associated with me in the final determination of our international obligations, to disclose to you without reserve the thought and purpose that have

President Woodrow Wilson marching in a Liberty Loan parade in Washington, D.C., 1918

been taking form in my mind in regard to the duty of our government in the days to come, when it will be necessary to lay afresh and upon a new plan the foundations of peace among the nations.

It is inconceivable that the people of the United States should play no part in that great enterprise. To take part in such a service will be the opportunity for which they have sought to prepare themselves by the very principles and purposes of their polity and the approved practices of their government ever since the days when they set up a new nation in the high and honorable hope that it might, in all that it was and did, show mankind the way to liberty.

They cannot in honor withhold the service to which they are now about to be challenged. They do not wish to withhold it. But they owe it to themselves and to the other nations of the world to state the conditions under which they will feel free to render it.

That service is nothing less than this, to add their authority and their power to the authority and force of other nations to guarantee peace and justice throughout the world. Such a settlement cannot now be long postponed. It is right that before it comes, this government should frankly formulate the conditions upon which it would feel justified in asking our people to approve its formal and solemn adherence to a League for Peace. I am here to attempt to state those conditions.

The present war must first be ended; but we owe it to candor and to a just regard for the opinion of mankind to say that, so far as our participation in guarantees of future peace is concerned, it makes a great deal of difference in what way and upon what terms it is ended. The treaties and agreements which bring it to an end must embody terms which will create a peace that is worth guaranteeing and preserving, a peace that will win the approval of mankind, not merely a peace that will serve the several interests and immediate aims of the nations engaged. We shall have no voice in determining what those terms shall be, but we shall, I feel sure, have a voice in determining whether they shall be made lasting or not by the guarantes of a universal covenant; and our judgment upon what is fundamental and essential as a condition precedent to permanency should be spoken now, not afterwards when it may be too late.

No covenant of cooperative peace that does not include the peoples of the New World can suffice to keep the future safe against war; and yet there is only one sort of peace that the peoples of America could join in guaranteeing. The elements of that peace must be elements that engage the confidence and satisfy the principles of the American governments, elements consistent with their political faith and with the practical convictions which the peoples of America have once for all embraced and undertaken to defend.

I do not mean to say that any American government would throw any obstacle in the way of any terms of peace the governments now at war might agree upon or seek to upset them when made, whatever they might be. I only take it for granted that mere terms of peace between the belligerents will not satisfy even the belligerents themselves. Mere agreements may not make peace secure. It will be absolutely necessary that a force be created as a guarantor of the permanency of the settlement so much greater than the force of any nation now engaged, or any alliance hitherto formed or projected, that no nation, no probable combination of nations, could face or withstand it. If the peace presently to be made is to endure, it must be a peace made secure by the organized major force of mankind.

The terms of the immediate peace agreed upon will determine whether it is a peace for which such a guarantee can be secured. The question upon which the whole future peace and policy of the world depends is

this: Is the present war a struggle for a just and secure peace, or only for a new balance of power? If it be only a struggle for a new balance of power, who will guarantee, who can guarantee the stable equilibrium of the new arrangement? Only a tranquil Europe can be a stable Europe. There must be, not a balance of power but a community of power; not organized rivalries but an organized, common peace.

Fortunately we have received very explicit assurances on this point. The statesmen of both of the groups of nations now arrayed against one another have said, in terms that could not be misinterpreted, that it was no part of the purpose they had in mind to crush their antagonists. But the implications of these assurances may not be equally clear to all — may not be the same on both sides of the water. I think it will be serviceable if I attempt to set forth what we understand them to be.

They imply, first of all, that it must be a peace without victory. It is not pleasant to say this. I beg that I may be permitted to put my own interpretation upon it and that it may be understood that no other interpretation was in my thought. I am seeking only to face realities and to face them without soft concealments. Victory would mean peace forced upon the loser, a victor's terms imposed upon the vanquished. It would be accepted in humiliation, under duress, at an intolerable sacrifice, and would leave a sting, a resentment, a bitter memory upon which terms of peace would rest, not permanently but only as upon quicksand. Only a peace between equals can last. Only a peace the very principle of which is equality and a common participation in a common benefit. The right state of mind, the right feeling between nations, is as necessary for a lasting peace as is the just settlement of vexed questions of territory or of racial and national allegiance.

The equality of nations upon which peace must be founded if it is to last must be an equality of rights; the guarantees exchanged must neither recognize nor imply a difference between big nations and small, between those that are powerful and those that are weak. Right must be based upon the common strength, not upon the individual strength, of the nations upon whose concert peace will depend. Equality of territory or of resources there of course cannot be; nor any other sort of equality not gained in the ordinary peaceful and legitimate development of the peoples themselves. But no one asks or expects anything more than an equality of rights. Mankind is looking now for freedom of life, not for equipoises of power.

And there is a deeper thing involved than even equality of right among organized nations. No peace can last, or ought to last, which does not recognize and accept the principle that governments derive all their just powers from the consent of the governed, and that no right anywhere exists to hand peoples about from sovereignty to sovereignty as if they were property. I take it for granted, for instance, if I may venture upon a single example, that statesmen everywhere are agreed that there should be a united, independent, and autonomous Poland, and that, henceforth, inviolable security of life, of worship, and of industrial and social development should be guaranteed to all peoples who have lived hitherto under the power of governments devoted to a faith and purpose hostile to their own.

I speak of this, not because of any desire to exalt an abstract political principle which has always been held very dear by those who have sought to build up liberty in America but for the same reason that I have spoken of the other conditions of peace which seem to me clearly indispensable — because I wish frankly to uncover realities. Any peace which does not recognize and accept this principle will inevitably be upset. It will not rest upon the affections or the convictions of mankind. The ferment of spirit of whole populations will fight subtly and constantly against it, and all the world will sympathize. The world can be at peace only if its life is stable, and there can be no stability where the will is in rebellion, where there is not tranquillity of spirit and a sense of justice, of freedom, and of right.

So far as practicable, moreover, every great people now struggling toward a full development of its resources and of its powers should be assured a direct outlet to the great highways of the sea. Where this cannot be done by the cession of territory, it can no doubt be done by the neutralization of direct rights of way under the general guarantee which will assure the peace itself. With a right comity of arrangement, no nation need be shut away from free access to the open paths of the world's commerce.

And the paths of the sea must alike in law and in fact be free. The freedom of the seas is the *sine qua non* of peace, equality, and cooperation. No doubt a somewhat radical reconsideration of many of the rules of international practice hitherto thought to be established may be necessary in order to make the seas indeed free and common in practically all circumstances for the use of mankind, but the motive for such changes is convincing and compelling. There can be no trust or intimacy between the peoples of the world without them. The free, constant, unthreatened intercourse of nations is an essential part of the process of peace and of development. It need not be difficult either to define or to secure the freedom of the seas if the governments of the world sincerely desire to come to an agreement concerning it.

It is a problem closely connected with the limitation of naval armaments and the cooperation of the navies of the world in keeping the seas at once free and safe. And the question of limiting naval armaments opens the wider and perhaps more difficult question of the limitation of armies and of all programs of military preparation. Difficult and delicate as these questions are, they must be faced with the utmost candor and decided in a spirit of real accommodation if peace is to come with healing in its wings, and come to stay.

Peace cannot be had without concession and sacrifice. There can be no sense of safety and equality among the nations if great preponderating armaments are henceforth to continue here and there to be built up and maintained. The statesmen of the world must plan for peace, and nations must adjust and accommodate their policy to it as they have planned for war and made ready for pitiless contest and rivalry. The question of armaments, whether on land or sea, is the most immediately and intensely practical question connected with the future fortunes of nations and of mankind.

I have spoken upon these great matters without reserve and with the utmost explicitness because it has seemed to me to be necessary if the world's yearning desire for peace was anywhere to find free voice and utterance. Perhaps I am the only person in high authority among all the peoples of the world who is at liberty to speak and hold nothing back. I am speaking as an individual, and yet I am speaking also, of course, as the responsible head of a great government, and I feel confident that I have said what the people of the United States would wish me to say.

May I not add that I hope and believe that I am in effect speaking for liberals and friends of humanity in every nation and of every program of liberty? I would fain believe that I am speaking for the silent mass of mankind everywhere who have as yet had no place or opportunity to speak their real hearts out concerning the death and ruin they see to have come already upon the persons and the homes they hold most dear.

And in holding out the expectation that the people and government of the United States will join the other civilized nations of the world in guaranteeing the permanence of peace upon such terms as I have named I speak with the greater boldness and confidence because it is clear to every man who can think that there is in this promise no breach in either our traditions or our policy as a nation, but a fulfillment, rather, of all that we have professed or striven for.

I am proposing, as it were, that the nations should with one accord adopt the doctrine of President Monroe as the doctrine of the world: that no nation should seek to extend its polity over any other nation or people, but that every people should be left free to determine its own polity, its own way of development — unhindered, unthreatened, unafraid, the little along with the great and powerful.

I am proposing that all nations henceforth avoid entangling alliances which would draw them into competitions of power, catch them in a net of intrigue and selfish rivalry, and disturb their own affairs with influences intruded from without. There is no entangling alliance in a concert of power. When all unite to act in the same sense and with the same purpose, all act in the common interest and are free to live their own lives under a common protection.

I am proposing government by the consent of the governed; that freedom of the seas which in international conference after conference representatives of the United States have urged with the eloquence of those who are the convinced disciples of liberty; and that moderation of armaments which makes of armies and navies a power for order merely, not an instrument of aggression or of selfish violence.

These are American principles, American policies. We could stand for no others. And they are also the principles and policies of forward-looking men and women everywhere, of every modern nation, of every enlightened community. They are the principles of mankind and must prevail.

16.

ELIHU ROOT: The European War and the Preservation of America's Ideals

Although Woodrow Wilson's "peace without victory" speech of January 22, 1917, made him a hero among liberals, it received its share of criticism from conservative politicians such as the venerable Republican Elihu Root. In a speech three days later Root pointed to what he considered the unrealistic features of Wilson's address. In so doing, Root anticipated some of the problems that Wilson would face after the war in his attempt to form the League of Nations. A portion of Root's speech appears below.

Source: *The United States and the War, The Mission to Russia, Political Addresses,* Robert Bacon and James B. Scott, eds., Cambridge, 1918: "America's Present Needs."

THE PRESENT WAR which is raging in Europe was begun upon an avowal of principles of national action that no reasonable and thoughtful neutral ought to ignore. The central principle was that a state exigency, state interest, is superior to those rules of morality which control individuals. Now, that was not an expedient, an excuse, seized upon to justify the beginning of the war; it is fundamental. The theory of the modern republic is that right begins with the individual. It was stated in the Declaration of Independence, that instrument which it was the fashion to sneer at a few years ago, but which states the fundamental principle upon which alone a free republic can live. It was that individual men have unalienable rights, among which are life, liberty, and the pursuit of happiness, and that governments are instituted to secure those rights.

The ancient theory — the theory alike of monarchies and of the ancient republics upon which they went down to their ruin — was that the state in the beginning was the foundation of right, and that individuals

derive their rights from the state and, therefore, the exigencies of the state are superior to all individual rights. It was upon the continuance and assertion of that principle that this war in Europe was begun. And upon that principle it was declared that there was no obligation upon a nation to keep the faith of a treaty if it did not suit its interests. It was declared that there was no obligation upon a nation to observe the rules of that law of nations upon which all civilized states have agreed, if it did not suit its interest. Now mark, I am not discussing the right or wrong, I am stating the principle of action which was followed and which was asserted to be right.

Upon that principle little Serbia received an ultimatum that demanded the surrender of her independence; and upon her failure to comply to the uttermost, she was overwhelmed. Upon that principle little Belgium, that had no quarrel with anybody, was served with a demand that she surrender her independent rights as a neutral and violate her solemn agreements to preserve her neutrality; and upon her refusal to surrender her rights and violate her faith, she was overwhelmed. And that principle is still maintained and asserted to be right. I repeat that I am not referring to this for the purpose of discussing it; I am referring to it because it bears directly upon our business here today.

It does not matter much what you and I think about these things; it does not matter that I think they were immoral and criminal, as I do; it does not matter that I think that if that principle of national conduct is to be maintained and approved in this world then liberty and civilization must die. What does matter is that approximately one-half the entire military power of this world supports that proposition. And I say to you, and I wish I could say it to every American, if that principle of national conduct be approved in the struggle that is pending, be approved by the free people of America, be approved by the conscience of the civilized world, then our American freedom will surely die, and die while we live.

The German note proposing a peace conference used a phrase which aptly describes the concrete application of the principle about which I am talking. It said, "We were forced to take the sword for justice and for liberty of national evolution." Liberty of national evolution! It was national evolution that overran Serbia. It was national evolution that crushed Belgium. And national evolution has not confined itself to the pathway to the Channel or to the pathway to the Bosporus; it has extended over Asia and Africa, all over the world, except America, North and South, eager and grasping and resolute, gathering in under its flag, under domination, under national control, the territory of the earth.

All nations have been at fault during this last half century. Many crimes have been committed; no nations that I know have been guiltless — none. Neither England,

nor France, nor Russia, nor Germany, nor Austria, nor the United States. For we still have to answer for Mexico. But the world is partitioned — Asia, Africa, Australasia, the islands of the sea, all taken up — except America. And we stand here with the Monroe Doctrine; we stand here with the Monroe Doctrine against the push and sweep of that mighty world tendency of national evolution and its progress under the principle that neither faith of treaties nor obligation of law nor rule of morality should stand in the way of a state that finds its interest to take what it wants for its national interest.

How long will the Monroe Doctrine be worth the paper it was written on in 1823 if that condition is to go on? That doctrine is that the safety of the United States forbids any foreign military power to obtain a foothold upon this continent from which it may readily make war upon the United States — that is the Monroe Doctrine — it is a declaration of what, in the opinion of the United States, is necessary for the safety of the United States.

Now that doctrine is not international law. It has been maintained by three things. In the first place, the men of Monroe's time never thought of such a thing as not being ready to fight for their rights. They were Belgians, those people. The second has been that the balance of power in Europe has been so even, so close, and everybody has been so doubtful about what the other fellows were going to do, that nobody found it worthwhile to take on a row with the United States. And third, England's fleet.

Now I ask what that Monroe Doctrine will be worth if we are not ready to protect it? Suppose the result of this war is such that these foreign influences that have helped preserve the Monroe Doctrine disappear, and we are not ready to defend it? Worthless! What will it mean if a foreign naval power, a real naval power, a real military power obtains a naval base in the Caribbean or in those islands of the Pacific off Panama? Our interests in the Panama Canal will be as worthless to us as the Bosporus is to Russia today. And instead of having what we have spent $400 million to accomplish, the means of transferring our Navy from ocean to ocean, our Navy will be shut up again on one side or the other of the continent.

And then we will have to live as poor, peaceable France has lived for the last forty years, with a sentinel always on the lookout for an approaching foe. Then the fancied security and sweet, comfortable ease of our people will be replaced by alarms and rumors of war and attack upon occasion. For the Monroe Doctrine was based upon sound wisdom, and the abandonment of it or the destruction of it will be the end of our security.

It seems to me that we have reached a point now where we can say that a prudent man, a man competent to be a trustee of property, will see that it is necessary for us to prepare to defend our rights. For why should not this principle of national aggression be applied to us? Why should it not be applied to South and Central America and the West Indies? Here we all are, rich, undefended, supine — fair game for anybody who wants national evolution. Can anybody tell why it should not? Interest and principle and habit all will conspire to a treatment of America like the treatment of China. And there is only one way possible for us to defend or be ready to defend our rights, and that is by going back to the old principle of universal preparation for service.

We have found, beyond the possibility of question, that volunteering, however ready the people may be, will not answer the purpose, because nobody volunteers until war; and when the war comes it is too late for him to learn to do his duty. Nobody is volunteering now, nobody volunteers for the National Guard or the regular Army, and

nobody will until the war. It is a matter of demonstration that you cannot get together a volunteer force in time of peace so as to prepare them to render their service in time of war.

Now, going back to the matters which should lead a reasonable person to consider that there is a possibility of our being attacked, I want to call your attention to the way in which war comes. It does not come ordinarily by some country starting out a great fleet and a million men to go and invade another. It comes by a process of gradual aggression.

What is going to happen to us if we do not get ready to defend our rights will be that first there will be one little aggression upon our rights — we will submit; there will be another little aggression, going a little farther, upon our rights, and we will submit; there will be another, and another, and another, and finally the patience of this great democracy will be worn out, and they will clamor for war, and they will rush into war, unprepared for war. That is what is going to happen if we do not get ready.

You cannot consider what men are going to do as if they were angels. Men are men, and greed and injustice and covetousness, and a desire to overrun the rights of others stalk through the earth today as they did 2,000 years ago. He who does not defend his liberty is foolish and simple and unworthy of liberty.

Another thing: the President has recently made a speech in the Senate, which we have all been reading, and I wish you to observe that the only way he sees out of the war that is devastating Europe is by preparation for war. There is much noble idealism in that speech of the President. With its purpose I fully sympathize. The kind of peace he describes is the peace that I long for. But the way he sees to preserve that peace is by preparation for war. Now, if some of our friends among the cornfields and the cotton fields and the mines and the citrus-fruit orchards will sit up and read this clause of the President's speech, telling how we may prevent further wars, they may have reason to wonder whether they have not forgotten something. Here it is:

> Mere agreements may not make peace secure. It will be absolutely necessary that a force be created as a guarantor of the permanency of the settlement so much greater than the force of any nation now engaged, or any alliance hitherto formed or projected, that no nation, no probable combinations of nations, could face or withstand it. If the peace presently to be made is to endure, it must be a peace made secure by the organized major force of mankind.

Now, I hope that paragraph means what I hope it does. I do not understand it as intended to commit the United States to enter into a convention or treaty with the other civilized countries of the world which will bind the United States to go to war on the continent of Europe or of Asia or in any other part of the world without the people of the United States having an opportunity at the time to say whether they will go to war or not. There would be serious difficulties, I think insurmountable obstacles, to the making of any such agreement. One is, that agreement or no agreement, when the time comes, the people of the United States will not go into any war, and nobody can get them into any war unless they then are in favor of fighting for something. And nothing can be so bad as to make a treaty and then break it. What I understand by it is that a convention shall be made by which all the civilized nations shall agree with all their power to stand behind the maintenance of the peace thus agreed upon; and, if that peace be infringed upon, then each nation shall determine what it is its duty to do under the obligation of that agreement toward the maintenance of that peace.

But observe that that is worthless, meaningless, unless the nations that enter into it keep the power behind it. It will be worthless agreement on our part if we have not a ship or a soldier that we can contribute to the war, if war there ought to be, for the maintenance of that peace. And it absolutely requires that we shall build up a force, a potential power of arms, commensurate with our size, our numbers, our wealth, our dignity, our part among the nations of the earth.

There is just one other sentence of this speech about which I wish to say a word, and that is the declaration that the peace must be a peace without victory. Now, I sympathize with that. But the peace that the President describes involves the absolute destruction and abandonment of the principles upon which this war was begun. It does not say "Serbia," it does not say "Belgium," but there the chosen head of the American people has declared the principles of the American democracy in unmistakable terms; has declared for the independence and equal rights of all small and weak nations; has declared for a Monroe Doctrine of the whole world precluding all nations from interfering with the independent control of its own affairs by every small nation, from taking away the territory of other nations, from attempting to exercise the coercion of superior power over other nations, for disarmament, for the reduction of these mighty armies and navies. And every word of that declaration, which I believe truly represents the conscience and judgment of the American people, denounces the sacrifice of Belgium and of Serbia and the principles upon which they were made.

Now, one side of that is the declaration that peace must be without victory. Suppose that such a peace cannot be made without victory; which is the superior? Which is to obtain? Of course, the great end and the choice of means becomes infinitely subordinate. If that peace — the peace that enthrones in the world principles of individual liberty and national right —

and national subjection to the laws of morals can be obtained without any further military pressure, then, thank God for it. But if it cannot be obtained without such further military pressure as to end in victory, then let us pray for the victory.

It is one of the best qualities of human nature that makes us, as we enjoy the blessings of freedom of intellect, freedom of religion, freedom of action, look back with gratitude to the men who sacrificed themselves in the long struggle of the ages for these things. Whether they be martyrs at the stake, or Cameronians in the Highlands of Scotland, or Huguenots in the Cévennes, or lawyers pleading for justice against popular clamor and disapproval, or brave men fighting in the defense of their country's liberty, we are all grateful to them because our blessings came from their noble sacrifice.

My friends, so sure am I that liberty and security in this land of ours depend upon the destruction and abandonment of the hated principle of national aggrandizement and immorality, and the enthronement of the principles of national responsibility and morality, that for all the countless generations to come after us in our dear land, I am grateful with all my heart to those men who are fighting in the trenches in France and Belgium and Russia and Italy and the Balkans today for the liberty and peace of my children's children.

17.

FRANZ BOAS: Patriotism

Woodrow Wilson had grave misgivings about the effects that war would have on America. "Conformity," he declared, would be "the only virtue . . . . Every man who refused to conform" would "pay the penalty." His fears were borne out even before the United States officially entered the war. The rising war fever after Germany resumed submarine attacks in February 1917 had its effect even in the usually inviolable academic community. Professors who criticized the war often did so at the risk of losing their positions. The president and board of trustees of Columbia University, for example, exerted pressure on the faculty either to be discreet in their political utterances or to resign. After appointment of a committee to investigate the loyalty of the faculty, the distinguished anthropologist Franz Boas made a public protest. A condensation of his statement, read at Columbia University on March 7, 1917, is reprinted here.

Source: *Race and Democratic Society*, New York, 1945, pp. 156-159.

MY OPINIONS ARE FOUNDED to a great extent on the truths taught by the retrospect upon the history of mankind, the study of which is the business of my life. We see in primitive society the feeling of solidarity confined to the small horde, while every outsider is considered a being specifically distinct, and therefore as a dangerous enemy who must be hunted down. With the advance of civilization, we see the groups which have common interests, and in which the bonds of human brotherhood are considered binding, expand until we reach the concept that all men are created with equal rights. Socrates, Buddha, and Christ are the milestones which indicate the birth of this great idea.

The 2,000 or more years which have elapsed since their time have not sufficed, however, to bring about the realization of these ideals. Based on this knowledge, it is my opinion that our first duties are to humanity as a whole, and that, in a conflict of duties, our obligations to humanity are of higher value than those toward the nation; in other words, that patriotism must be subordinated to humanism.

A second principle to which I hold is also based on anthropological knowledge. We see everywhere that the form of thought of man is determined by the prevailing emotions which are intimately connected with the traditional mode of thought. The fact that certain ideas are held sacred in a community and that they are upheld by intelligent thought is no proof of their truth; for we know that in every society the development of thought is shaped more or less by traditional attitudes; that men are more likely to justify their way of feeling and acting by reasoning than to shape their actions and to remodel their emotions on the basis of reasoning. Only the greatest minds can free themselves of this tendency, and they are the ones who in course of time revolutionize the course of our civilization. We should bear in mind all the time the difficulty of developing such strength of character and of reasoning power as to free ourselves of the prejudices that are the foundation of our whole life.

I consider it of fundamental importance to bear in mind all the time these conditions of human thought, and to watch that in the education of the young the respect and love for ideals be tempered by a rational understanding of the principles on which these ideals are based.

For this reason I believe that the purely emotional basis on which, the world over, patriotic feelings are instilled into the minds of children is one of the most serious faults in our educational systems, particularly

Professor Franz Boas

when we compare these methods with the lukewarm attention that is given to the common interests of humanity. I dare say that if all nations cultivated the ideals of equal rights of all members of mankind by emotional means such as are now used to develop passionate patriotism, much of the mutual hatred, distrust, and disrespect would disappear.

The kind of patriotism that we inculcate is intended to develop the notion that the members of each nation, and that the institutions of each nation, are superior to those of all others. Under this stimulus the fact that in each country, normally, people live comparatively comfortably under the conditions in which they have grown up is too often translated by the citizens of that country into the idea that others who live under different conditions have a civilization or institutions of inferior value, and must feel unhappy until the benefits of his own mode of feeling, thinking, and living have been imposed upon them. I consider it one of the great objects worth striving for to counteract this faulty tendency.

If it is not sufficient to train children to an intelligent understanding of the institutions and habits of their country, if these have to be strengthened emotionally by waving of flags and by singing of patriotic songs, then this emotional tendency should be supplemented by equally strong emotional means intended to cultivate respect for the love that foreigners have for their country, and designed to instill into the minds of the young respect for the common interests of humanity. I should prefer, however, to inculcate intelligent love and respect for all human endeavor, wherever found, without trying to destroy the possibility of clear, intelligent thought by emphasizing the emotional side of patriotism.

These opinions bring it about that I am uncompromisingly opposed to all legislation, such as protective tariffs, that is intended to advance the interests of citizens at the expense of foreigners. I recognize that there are certain conditions under which the resources of a limited district may be developed by protective measures; but I should always consider these ill-applied if the local development is secured at an avoidable serious loss to other communities. The natural course of industrial development brings about a sufficient amount of suffering, owing to the depreciation of the resources of some areas when new kinds of products come into demand, or when ampler, newly discovered resources are made available; and we should try to alleviate hardships of this type rather than to accentuate them.

Neither can I share in the feeling that it is necessary to protect one race against others. I can imagine myself much more at home in a company of sympathetic Chinese, Malay, Negroes, and whites who have interests and ideals in common than in a bigoted or presumptuous company of whites who might grate on my feelings by every word and action. As long as a foreign race respects the individuality of a nation, I cannot see any reason why it should be discriminated against. From an anthropological point of view, I consider the laws forbidding intermarriages between whites and Mongols and Negroes as absolutely untenable, and therefore as vicious, because they accentuate antagonisms for which, however strongly they may be felt, there is no valid reason.

I ought to add that these views do not necessarily imply that I consider absolutely unrestricted immigration as right, because the very respect that I have for the individuality of each nation implies that each has the right to maintain its individuality if it seems threatened by the course of human migration.

The kind of patriotism in which most of our fellowmen believe honestly and out of the fullness of their hearts is clearly antagonistic to the points of view that I hold. Nevertheless, I should consider myself entirely wrong if I should take the position that those whose actions are dictated by loyal patriotism, and who elevate the self-interest of their fellow citizens over that of the whole rest of mankind, are wrong. If a minority — to which I belong and which I believe to be in advance of the thoughts of the majority of mankind — hold ideals contrary to those of our times, we have not the right to stamp everything as heinous crime that for well-nigh 3,000 years has been counted as the highest virtue. Patriots are morally wrong just as little as the persecutors of witchcraft, who merely followed out their honest convictions; and, much as we may like to convert them, there is no justice in impugning their moral character.

This leads me to the last and perhaps most important point in our considerations. As I grant that the patriot who cannot free himself from the prejudices of exalting his own environment may be morally as righteous as the cosmopolitan, so I grant to each nation that in a conflict of opinions we have no right to interpret their mode of thought that differs from our own as due to moral depravity, but that we must try to understand it from the point of view of their national life and the exigencies of their situation.

18.

WOODROW WILSON: War Message

Germany's resumption of unrestricted submarine warfare on February 1, 1917, led the United States to break diplomatic relations on February 3. President Wilson continued to hope for peace, but events seemed to make American involvement more and more inevitable. The publication of the secret "Zimmermann Note" from the German foreign secretary to his representative in Mexico proposing a Mexican-Japanese-German alliance against the United States seemed to push the President closer than ever to war. American merchant ships were armed but losses to the German submarine increased sharply. On April 2 Wilson, fully aware of the terrible consequences of his decision, went before Congress with the following message calling for a declaration of war. Congress declared war on Germany four days later.

Source: 65 Congress, 1 Session, Senate Document No. 5.

I HAVE CALLED THE CONGRESS into extraordinary session because there are serious, very serious, choices of policy to be made, and made immediately, which it was neither right nor constitutionally permissible that I should assume the responsibility of making.

On the 3rd of February last, I officially laid before you the extraordinary announcement of the Imperial German government that on and after the 1st day of February it was its purpose to put aside all restraints of law or of humanity and use its submarines to sink every vessel that sought to approach either the ports of Great Britain and Ireland or the western coasts of Europe or any of the ports controlled by the enemies of Germany within the Mediterranean.

That had seemed to be the object of the German submarine warfare earlier in the war, but since April of last year the Imperial government had somewhat restrained the commanders of its undersea craft in conformity with its promise then given to us that passenger boats should not be sunk and that due warning would be given to all other vessels which its submarines might seek to destroy, when no resistance was offered or

escape attempted, and care taken that their crews were given at least a fair chance to save their lives in their open boats. The precautions taken were meager and haphazard enough, as was proved in distressing instance after instance in the progress of the cruel and unmanly business, but a certain degree of restraint was observed.

The new policy has swept every restriction aside. Vessels of every kind, whatever their flag, their character, their cargo, their destination, their errand, have been ruthlessly sent to the bottom without warning and without thought of help or mercy for those on board, the vessels of friendly neutrals along with those of belligerents. Even hospital ships and ships carrying relief to the sorely bereaved and stricken people of Belgium, though the latter were provided with safe conduct through the proscribed areas by the German government itself and were distinguished by unmistakable marks of identity, have been sunk with the same reckless lack of compassion or of principle.

I was for a little while unable to believe that such things would in fact be done by any government that had hitherto subscribed to the humane practices of civilized nations. International law had its origin in the attempt to set up some law which would be respected and observed upon the seas, where no nation had right of dominion and where lay the free highways of the world. By painful stage after stage has that law been built up, with meager enough results, indeed, after all was accomplished that could be accomplished, but always with a clear view, at least, of what the heart and conscience of mankind demanded.

This minimum of right the German government has swept aside under the plea of retaliation and necessity and because it had no weapons which it could use at sea except these which it is impossible to employ as it is employing them without throwing to the winds all scruples of humanity or of respect for the understandings that were supposed to underlie the intercourse of the world. I am not now thinking of the loss of property involved, immense and serious as that is, but only of the wanton and wholesale destruction of the lives of noncombatants, men, women, and children, engaged in pursuits which have always, even in the darkest periods of modern history, been deemed innocent and legitimate. Property can be paid for; the lives of peaceful and innocent people cannot be.

The present German submarine warfare against commerce is a warfare against mankind. It is a war against all nations. American ships have been sunk, American lives taken in ways which it has stirred us very deeply to learn of; but the ships and people of other neutral and friendly nations have been sunk and overwhelmed in the waters in the same way. There has been no discrimination. The challenge is to all mankind.

Each nation must decide for itself how it will meet it. The choice we make for ourselves must be made with a moderation of counsel and a temperateness of judgment befitting our character and our motives as a nation. We must put excited feeling away. Our motive will not be revenge or the victorious assertion of the physical might of the nation, but only the vindication of right, of human right, of which we are only a single champion.

When I addressed the Congress on the 26th of February last, I thought that it would suffice to assert our neutral rights with arms, our right to use the seas against unlawful interference, our right to keep our people safe against unlawful violence. But armed neutrality, it now appears, is impracticable. Because submarines are in effect outlaws when used as the German submarines have been used against merchant shipping, it is impossible to defend ships against their attacks as the law of nations has assumed that merchantmen would defend themselves against privateers or cruisers, visible craft giving chase upon the open sea.

It is common prudence in such circumstances, grim necessity indeed, to endeavor to destroy them before they have shown their own intention. They must be dealt with upon sight, if dealt with at all. The German government denies the right of neutrals to use arms at all within the areas of the sea which it has proscribed, even in the defense of rights which no modern publicist has ever before questioned their right to defend. The intimation is conveyed that the armed guards which we have placed on our merchant ships will be treated as beyond the pale of law and subject to be dealt with as pirates would be.

Armed neutrality is ineffectual enough at best; in such circumstances and in the face of such pretensions it is worse than ineffectual: it is likely only to produce what it was meant to prevent; it is practically certain to draw us into the war without either the rights or the effectiveness of belligerents. There is one choice we cannot make, we are incapable of making: we will not choose the path of submission and suffer the most sacred rights of our nation and our people to be ignored or violated. The wrongs against which we now array ourselves are no common wrongs; they cut to the very roots of human life.

With a profound sense of the solemn and even tragical character of the step I am taking and of the grave responsibilities which it involves, but in unhesitating obedience to what I deem my constitutional duty, I advise that the Congress declare the recent course of the Imperial German government to be in fact nothing less than war against the government and people of the United States; that it formally accept the status of belligerent which has thus been thrust upon it; and that it take immediate steps, not only to put the country in a more thorough state of defense but also to exert all its power and employ all its resources to bring the government of the German Empire to terms and end the war.

What this will involve is clear. It will involve the utmost practicable cooperation in counsel and action with the governments now at war with Germany and, as incident to that, the extension to those governments of the most liberal financial credits, in order that our resources may so far as possible be added to theirs. It will involve the organization and mobilization of all the material resources of the country to supply the materials of war and serve the incidental needs of the nation in the most abundant and yet the most economical and efficient way possible. It will involve the immediate full equipment of the Navy in all respects but particularly in supplying it with the best means of dealing with the enemy's submarines. It will involve the immediate addition to the armed forces of the United States already provided for by law in case of war at least 500,000 men, who should, in my opinion, be chosen upon the principle of universal liability to service, and also the authorization of subsequent additional increments of equal force so soon as they may be needed and can be handled in training.

It will involve also, of course, the granting of adequate credits to the government, sustained, I hope, so far as they can equitably be sustained by the present generation, by well-conceived taxation. I say sustained so far as may be equitable by taxation because it seems to me that it would be most unwise to base the credits which will now be necessary entirely on money borrowed. It is our duty, I most respectfully urge, to protect our people so far as we may against the very serious hardships and evils which would be likely to arise out of the inflation which would be produced by vast loans.

In carrying out the measures by which these things are to be accomplished, we should keep constantly in mind the wisdom of interfering as little as possible in our own preparation and in the equipment of our own military forces with the duty — for it will be a very practical duty — of supplying the nations already at war with Germany with the materials which they can obtain only from us or by our assistance. They are in the field and we should help them in every way to be effective there.

I shall take the liberty of suggesting, through the several executive departments of the government, for the consideration of your committees, measures for the accomplishment of the several objects I have mentioned. I hope that it will be your pleasure to deal with them as having been framed after very careful thought by the branch of the government upon which the responsibility of conducting the war and safeguarding the nation will most directly fall.

While we do these things, these deeply momentous things, let us be very clear, and make very clear to all the world, what our motives and our objects are. My own thought has not been driven from its habitual and normal course by the unhappy events of the last two months, and I do not believe that the thought of the nation has been altered or clouded by them. I have exactly the same things in mind now that I had in mind when I addressed the Senate on the 22nd of January last; the same that I had in mind when I addressed the Congress on the 3rd of February and on the 26th of February.

Our object now, as then, is to vindicate the principles of peace and justice in the life of the world as against selfish and autocratic power and to set up among the really free and self-governed peoples of the world such a concert of purpose and of action as will henceforth ensure the observance of those principles. Neutrality is no longer feasible or desirable where the peace of the world is involved and the freedom of its peoples, and the menace to that peace and freedom lies in the existence of autocratic governments backed by organized force which is controlled wholly by their will, not by the will of their people. We have seen the last of neutrality in such circumstances. We are at the beginning of an age in which it will be insisted that the same standards of conduct and of responsibility for wrong done shall be observed among nations and their governments that are observed among the individual citizens of civilized states.

We have no quarrel with the German people. We have no feeling toward them but one of sympathy and friendship. It was not upon their impulse that their government acted in entering this war. It was not with their previous knowledge or approval. It was a war determined upon as wars used to be determined upon in the old, unhappy days when peoples were nowhere consulted by their rulers and wars were provoked and waged in the interest of dynasties or of little groups of ambitious men who were accustomed to use their fellowmen as pawns and tools.

Self-governed nations do not fill their neighbor states with spies or set the course of intrigue to bring about some critical posture of affairs which will give them an opportunity to strike and make conquest. Such designs can be successfully worked out only under cover and where no one has the right to ask questions. Cunningly contrived plans of deception or aggression, carried, it may be, from generation to generation, can be worked out and kept from the light only within the privacy of courts or behind the carefully guarded confidences of a narrow and privileged class. They are happily impossible where public opinion commands and insists upon full information concerning all the nation's affairs.

A steadfast concert for peace can never be maintained except by a partnership of democratic nations. No autocratic government could be trusted to keep faith within it or observe its covenants. It must be a league of honor, a partnership of opinion. Intrigue would eat its vitals away; the plottings of inner circles who could plan what they would and render account to no one would be a corruption seated at its very heart. Only free peoples can hold their purpose and their honor steady to a common end and prefer the interests of mankind to any narrow interest of their own.

Does not every American feel that assurance has been added to our hope for the future peace of the world by the wonderful and heartening things that have been happening within the last few weeks in Russia? Russia was known by those who knew it best to have been always in fact democratic at heart, in all the vital habits of her thought, in all the intimate relationships of her people that spoke their natural instinct, their habitual attitude toward life. The autocracy that crowned the summit of her political structure, long as it had stood and terrible as was the reality of its power, was not in fact Russian in origin, character, or purpose; and now it has been shaken off and the great, generous Russian people have been added in all their naive majesty and might to the forces that are fighting for freedom in the world, for justice, and for peace. Here is a fit partner for a League of Honor.

One of the things that has served to convince us that the Prussian autocracy was not and could never be our friend is that from the very outset of the present war it has filled our unsuspecting communities and even our offices of government with spies and set criminal intrigues everywhere afoot against our national unity of counsel, our peace within and without, our industries and our commerce. Indeed, it is now evident that its spies were here even before the war began; and it is unhappily not a matter of conjecture but a fact proved in our courts of justice that the intrigues which have more than once come perilously near to disturbing the peace and dislocating the industries of the country have been carried on at the instigation, with the support, and even under the personal direction of official agents of the Imperial government accredited to the government of the United States.

Even in checking these things and trying to extirpate them, we have sought to put the most generous interpretation possible upon them because we knew that their source lay, not in any hostile feeling or purpose of the German people toward us (who were no doubt as ignorant of them as we ourselves were) but only in the selfish designs of a government that did what it pleased and told its people nothing. But they have played their part in serving to convince us at last that that government entertains no real friendship for us and means to act against our peace and security at its convenience. That it means to stir up enemies against us at our very doors the intercepted note to the German minister at Mexico City is eloquent evidence.

We are accepting this challenge of hostile purpose because we know that in such a government, following such methods, we can never have a friend; and that in the presence of its organized power, always lying in wait to accomplish we know not what purpose, there can be no assured security for the democratic governments of the world. We are now about to accept gage of battle with this natural foe to liberty and

shall, if necessary, spend the whole force of the nation to check and nullify its pretensions and its power. We are glad, now that we see the facts with no veil of false pretense about them, to fight thus for the ultimate peace of the world and for the liberation of its peoples, the German peoples included: for the rights of nations great and small and the privilege of men everywhere to choose their way of life and of obedience.

The world must be made safe for democracy. Its peace must be planted upon the tested foundations of political liberty. We have no selfish ends to serve. We desire no conquest, no dominion. We seek no indemnities for ourselves, no material compensation for the sacrifices we shall freely make. We are but one of the champions of the rights of mankind. We shall be satisfied when those rights have been made as secure as the faith and the freedom of nations can make them.

Just because we fight without rancor and without selfish object, seeking nothing for ourselves but what we shall wish to share with all free peoples, we shall, I feel confident, conduct our operations as belligerents without passion and ourselves observe with proud punctilio the principles of right and of fair play we profess to be fighting for.

I have said nothing of the governments allied with the Imperial government of Germany because they have not made war upon us or challenged us to defend our right and our honor. The Austro-Hungarian government has, indeed, avowed its unqualified endorsement and acceptance of the reckless and lawless submarine warfare adopted now without disguise by the Imperial German government, and it has therefore not been possible for this government to receive Count Tarnowski, the ambassador recently accredited to this government by the Imperial and Royal government of Austria-Hungary; but that government has not actually engaged in warfare against citizens of the United States on the seas, and I take the liberty, for the present at least, of postponing a discussion of our relations with the authorities at Vienna. We enter this war only where we are clearly forced into it because there are no other means of defending our rights.

It will be all the easier for us to conduct ourselves as belligerents in a high spirit of right and fairness because we act without animus, not in enmity toward a people or with the desire to bring any injury or disadvantage upon them, but only in armed opposition to an irresponsible government which has thrown aside all considerations of humanity and of right and is running amuck. We are, let me say again, the sincere friends of the German people, and shall desire nothing so much as the early reestablishment of intimate relations of mutual advantage between us — however hard it may be for them, for the time being, to believe that this is spoken from our hearts.

We have borne with their present government through all these bitter months because of that friendship — exercising a patience and forbearance which would otherwise have been impossible. We shall, happily, still have an opportunity to prove that friendship in our daily attitude and actions toward the millions of men and women of German birth and native sympathy who live among us and share our life, and we shall be proud to prove it toward all who are in fact loyal to their neighbors and to the government in the hour of test. They are, most of them, as true and loyal Americans as if they had never known any other fealty or allegiance. They will be prompt to stand with us in rebuking and restraining the few who may be of a different mind and purpose. If there should be disloyalty, it will be dealt with with a firm hand of stern repression; but, if it lifts its head at all, it will lift it only here and there and without countenance except from a lawless and malignant few.

It is a distressing and oppressive duty, gentlemen of the Congress, which I have performed in thus addressing you. There are, it may be, many months of fiery trial and sacrifice ahead of us. It is a fearful thing to lead this great peaceful people into war, into the most terrible and disastrous of all wars, civilization itself seeming to be in the balance. But the right is more precious than peace, and we shall fight for the things which we have always carried nearest our hearts — for democracy, for the right of those who submit to authority to have a voice in their own governments, for the rights and liberties of small nations, for a universal dominion of right by such a concert of free peoples as shall bring peace and safety to all nations and make the world itself at last free.

To such a task we can dedicate our lives and our fortunes, everything that we are and everything that we have, with the pride of those who know that the day has come when America is privileged to spend her blood and her might for the principles that gave her birth and happiness and the peace which she has treasured. God helping her, she can do no other.

America has joined forces with the Allied Powers, and what we have of blood and treasure are yours. Therefore it is that with loving pride we drape the colors in tribute of respect to this citizen of your great republic. And here and now in the presence of the illustrious dead we pledge our hearts and our honor in carrying this war to a successful issue. Lafayette, we are here.

CHARLES E. STANTON, address at the tomb of Lafayette, Picpus Cemetery, Paris, July 4, 1917. Stanton was chief disbursing officer of the A.E.F. in France, and had been deputed by General Pershing to speak on this occasion.

German forces advancing at Villiers Bretonneux move past a dead English soldier

THE GREAT WAR

Woodrow Wilson was elected as a Progressive, as an idealist who symbolized the hopes America had for its own future. He little expected the tragedy of World War I in 1912; when war came, it was a profound shock to him no less than to the country. His first response to European war was one of neutrality through moral superiority. The idealist approach to foreign affairs had already foundered and backfired in the Mexican situation when America's neutrality began to wear thin. Yet the highly moral stance was maintained as long as possible. Incapable of believing that international law and the rules of war changed along with the techniques of war, Wilson set a firm policy that in its very rigidity amounted to a slow drift into war. Undaunted, Wilson proclaimed the war the tool with which to "make the world safe for democracy." That the war had failed to do anything of the kind was made excruciatingly clear in the vindictive peace terms insisted upon by the victorious governments at Versailles. Their sole concession to Wilson, the League of Nations, was defeated in the U.S. Senate. It is perhaps the final irony of Wilson's administration that he, a Progressive Democrat, was forced to resort to new and unprecedented undemocratic means in prosecuting war that, at best, was a diversion from his primary goals as President.

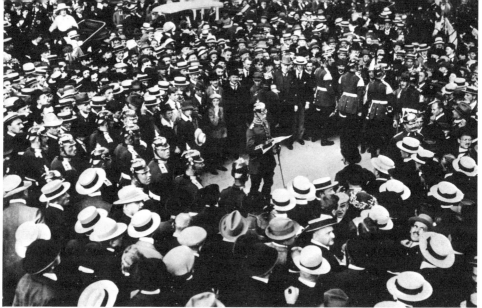

Most Americans were unaware of the structure of European alliances and rivalries in 1914; thus, when war came, it came with a speed and seeming enthusiasm that was stunning. Most confusing was the apparent lack of connection between the ostensible cause — the assassination of an Austrian archduke in Serbia — and the conduct of the war. Germany's war plan called first for the defeat of France; the violation of Belgian neutrality brought England into the war, and Serbia, whatever its actual guilt, was largely forgotten.

(Top) German officer announcing general mobilization in Berlin, 1914; (right) German soldier leaving Berlin, 1914, following the mobilization; (bottom) English troops marching through London enroute to embarkation to the front

(Above) Fort Loncin near Liege, Belgium, destroyed by German mortars in 1914

(Right) Official British photo taken in France showing refugees fleeing German-held territory, 1914; (below) transport troops struck by shrapnel during Battle of the Marne, 1914

(Above) Dead Rumanians on the road near Kronstadt (Brasso), 1916

(Right) The German emperor and his brother, Prince Henry of Prussia, observing the movements of some of the German forces at the Eastern front; (below) ruined market square of Ortelsburg, East Prussia, 1914

Pro-war and antiwar sentiment in the U.S. split along several planes: ethnic groups tended naturally to follow traditional attitudes toward the belligerent nations; pacifist, Socialist, and other radical groups generally opposed the war on moral grounds; the established cultures of the East and the South, largely British in ancestry and pro-French in sympathy, tended to favor the Allies, though not, perhaps, to the point of war. Rooseveltian activists, of course, reacted along the path of greatest strenuousness: a voluntary summer officer-training program was begun in 1915 as a first step to preparedness.

(Top) Peace parade in New York, 1914; (left) marchers in a "Wake Up" parade, 1917; (below) Theodore Roosevelt addressing volunteer officers at summer training in Plattsburg, N.Y., 1915

(Top and bottom) German photographs of sinking Allied "armed" transports enroute to England

(Left) "The American Peace Angel" captures German view of U.S. neutrality, while British view (right) shows Wilson calling for "a copy of our usual No. 1 note to Germany, Humanity Series"

The official neutrality of the U.S. was never any more genuine than was that of the people. By sympathy, by habit, and by convenience, American aid was concentrated on the Allies. As England's blockade of Germany took hold, the shipment of war materiel to the Central Powers dwindled away. Neutrality violations, though committed on both sides, became a danger to American lives and property only on the part of Germany. In light of the inefficacy of stern diplomatic protests, America was clearly destined for war with the Alliance nations.

(Top) New York Preparedness Parade; (left) Senator Robert La Follette of Wisconsin, a leader of Congressional opposition to Wilson's moves toward involvement in the war; (bottom) anachronistic charge by cavalry officers in training

Carrying wounded through knee-deep mud following the Battle of Pilckem Ridge in 1917

(Above) Moving ammunition along Lesboeufs Road, outside Flers, during Battle of the Somme, 1916; (below) British officer moving his men out of the sap with shells bursting around them

The Bettmann Archive

(Top) Aerial view of troops crossing battlefield; (center) Allied soldier standing guard in a trench along the Somme River; (bottom) destruction at Veux, France

United Press International

European Picture Service

(Above) Outbreak of hostilities on the streets of Moscow following Leninist siege of the Duma, 1917

With the overthrow of the tsar in March 1917 and the consequent confusion of the power struggle in Petrograd, the participation of Russia in the war began slowly to deteriorate. Political agitation was carried on even among the troops as a multitude of factions maneuvered for influence. The Russian war officially ended with the Treaty of Brest-Litovsk in March 1918. The Eastern front had lasted long enough to divert German troops from a crumbling France, but the war was now entirely in the West.

(Left) Gen. Kornilov urging Russian soldiers to stay and fight; (below) motor car with Bolshevik banners canvassing for the Constituent Assembly, 1917

(Above) Captain Eddie Rickenbacker (center) and American fliers were the first to arrive in France; (below) troop transport leaving New York for Europe

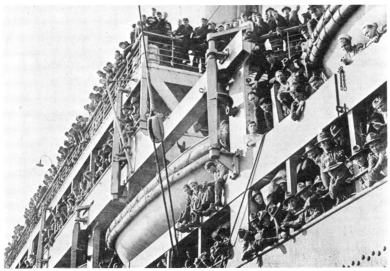

Culver Pictures, Inc.

American troops passing under Arch of Triumph, Paris, 1917

United Press International

The Granger Collection

After Wilson's futile attempt to bring about peace negotiations in the winter of 1916-17, and Germany's resumption of unrestricted U-boat operations, the U.S. finally declared war in April 1917. Although public enthusiasm was slight, the resources of the country were mobilized with tremendous efficiency. Liberty Bond sales, Selective Service, and government control of all vital segments of the economy enabled the nation to provide a vastly greater war force than had been expected in Europe.

(Top) President Wilson participating in a Liberty Bond parade in Washington, 1918; (right) American women's patriotic demonstration; (bottom) sign on a building. OPPOSITE PAGE: (Top) Manufacturing torpedo primers; (center) U.S. preparing food for shipment abroad; (bottom) women filling shells with gunpowder

The Bettmann Archive

European Picture Service

(Above) Americans registering for the draft

(Right) President Wilson blindfolded to select the first names for the draft for military service, 1917; (below) training recruits at Camp Pike, Ark., 1918

American artillery moving to the front in France

(Above) French troops advance over the remains of a bridge destroyed by the retreating Germans; (below) American raiding party in the Marne sector

The elimination of the Russian front released a great number of German troops and made possible the launching of a major offensive in March 1918. The Allies, bolstered by the arrival of the AEF, finally checked the German advance in July. From then until the Armistice, the Allies maintained the initiative.

(Top) Mark V tanks equipped with cribs enabling them to cross the Hindenburg Line during the Battle of the St. Quentin Canal, Bellicourt, 1918; (bottom left) flier's view of a German gas attack on the Eastern front; (bottom right) French soldiers in trenches wearing gas masks

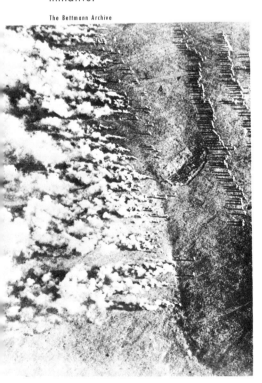

(Above) American infantry unit entering a small village in the Argonne region of France; (below left) Ypres Cathedral in ruins. A British lorry stands in the foreground; (below right) bomb damage in Paris

The Allied offensive begun in July was a series of successes; by September Germany saw the end imminent. Peace was asked by Germany in October and the Armistice was signed November 11. The Allied armies were victorious; but the idealism of Wilson's "war to end war" and his Fourteen Points for peace were about to suffer total defeat.

(**Top left**) Jubilant American soldier at end of the war; (**top right**) Marshall Foch outside the carriage where Armistice was signed; (**bottom**) Allied forces cheer victory

19.

Opposition to Wilson's War Message

After four days of debate over President Wilson's message of April 2, 1917, six senators voted against declaring war on Germany (a seventh senator abstained). Among those voting against were George W. Norris of Nebraska and Robert M. La Follette of Wisconsin, whose speeches of April 4 are reprinted here in part. Both Norris and La Follette represented agricultural communities with a large German population, and both were Republicans devoted to Progressive domestic reforms. La Follette was also a keen isolationist who later opposed America's entry into the League of Nations. Although their votes made them heroes in the Socialist camp, the Wisconsin legislature censured La Follette, and his old Progressive allies at the University of Wisconsin — Charles Van Hise, John R. Commons, Richard T. Ely, and Edward A. Ross — charged him with disloyalty. Ely wrote that La Follette had been "of more help to the Kaiser than a quarter of a million troops."

Source: Record, 65 Cong., 1 Sess., pp. 212-214, 223-236.

I.

Speech by GEORGE W. NORRIS

WHILE I AM MOST EMPHATICALLY and sincerely opposed to taking any step that will force our country into the useless and senseless war now being waged in Europe, yet, if this resolution passes, I shall not permit my feeling of opposition to its passage to interfere in any way with my duty either as a senator or as a citizen in bringing success and victory to American arms. I am bitterly opposed to my country entering the war, but if, notwithstanding my opposition, we do enter it, all of my energy and all of my power will be behind our flag in carrying it on to victory.

The resolution now before the Senate is a declaration of war. Before taking this momentous step, and while standing on the brink of this terrible vortex, we ought to pause and calmly and judiciously consider the terrible consequences of the step we are about to take. We ought to consider like-

wise the route we have recently traveled and ascertain whether we have reached our present position in a way that is compatible with the neutral position which we claimed to occupy at the beginning and through the various stages of this unholy and unrighteous war.

No close student of recent history will deny that both Great Britain and Germany have, on numerous occasions since the beginning of the war, flagrantly violated in the most serious manner the rights of neutral vessels and neutral nations under existing international law, as recognized up to the beginning of this war by the civilized world.

The reason given by the President in asking Congress to declare war against Germany is that the German government has declared certain war zones, within which, by the use of submarines, she sinks, without notice, American ships and destroys American lives. . . . The first war zone was declared by Great Britain. She gave us and the world notice of it on the 4th day of

November, 1914. The zone became effective Nov. 5, 1914. . . . This zone so declared by Great Britain covered the whole of the North Sea. . . . The first German war zone was declared on the 4th day of February, 1915, just three months after the British war zone was declared. Germany gave fifteen days' notice of the establishment of her zone, which became effective on the 18th day of February, 1915. The German war zone covered the English Channel and the high seawaters around the British Isles. . . .

It is unnecessary to cite authority to show that both of these orders declaring military zones were illegal and contrary to international law. It is sufficient to say that our government has officially declared both of them to be illegal and has officially protested against both of them. The only difference is that in the case of Germany we have persisted in our protest, while in the case of England we have submitted.

What was our duty as a government and what were our rights when we were confronted with these extraordinary orders declaring these military zones? First, we could have defied both of them and could have gone to war against both of these nations for this violation of international law and interference with our neutral rights. Second, we had the technical right to defy one and to acquiesce in the other. Third, we could, while denouncing them both as illegal, have acquiesced in them both and thus remained neutral with both sides, although not agreeing with either as to the righteousness of their respective orders. We could have said to American shipowners that, while these orders are both contrary to international law and are both unjust, we do not believe that the provocation is sufficient to cause us to go to war for the defense of our rights as a neutral nation, and, therefore, American ships and American citizens will go into these zones at their own peril and risk.

Fourth, we might have declared an embargo against the shipping from American

Brown Brothers

Sen. George W. Norris, photographed in 1913

ports of any merchandise to either one of these governments that persisted in maintaining its military zone. We might have refused to permit the sailing of any ship from any American port to either of these military zones. In my judgment, if we had pursued this course, the zones would have been of short duration. England would have been compelled to take her mines out of the North Sea in order to get any supplies from our country. When her mines were taken out of the North Sea then the German ports upon the North Sea would have been accessible to American shipping and Germany would have been compelled to cease her submarine warfare in order to get any supplies from our nation into German North Sea ports.

There are a great many American citizens who feel that we owe it as a duty to humanity to take part in this war. Many instances of cruelty and inhumanity can be found on both sides. Men are often biased in their judgment on account of their sympathy and their interests. To my mind, what we ought to have maintained from the beginning was the strictest neutrality. If we had done this, I do not believe we would have been on the verge of war at the present time. We had a right as a nation, if we desired, to cease at any time to be neutral. We had a technical right to respect the English war zone and to disregard the German war zone, but we could not do that and be neutral.

I have no quarrel to find with the man who does not desire our country to remain neutral. While many such people are moved by selfish motives and hopes of gain, I have no doubt but that in a great many instances, through what I believe to be a misunderstanding of the real condition, there are many honest, patriotic citizens who think we ought to engage in this war and who are behind the President in his demand that we should declare war against Germany. I think such people err in judgment and to a great extent have been misled as to the real history and the true facts by the almost unanimous demand of the great combination of wealth that has a direct financial interest in our participation in the war.

We have loaned many hundreds of millions of dollars to the Allies in this controversy. While such action was legal and countenanced by international law, there is no doubt in my mind but the enormous amount of money loaned to the Allies in this country has been instrumental in bringing about a public sentiment in favor of our country taking a course that would make every bond worth a hundred cents on the dollar and making the payment of every debt certain and sure. Through this instrumentality and also through the instrumentality of others who have not only made millions out of the war in the manufacture of munitions, etc., and who would expect to make millions more if our country can be drawn into the catastrophe, a large number of the great newspapers and news agencies of the country have been controlled and enlisted in the greatest propaganda that the world has ever known to manufacture sentiment in favor of war.

It is now demanded that the American citizens shall be used as insurance policies to guarantee the safe delivery of munitions of war to belligerent nations. The enormous profits of munition manufacturers, stockbrokers, and bond dealers must be still further increased by our entrance into the war. This has brought us to the present moment, when Congress, urged by the President and backed by the artificial sentiment, is about to declare war and engulf our country in the greatest holocaust that the world has ever known.

In showing the position of the bondholder and the stockbroker, I desire to read an extract from a letter written by a member of the New York Stock Exchange to his customers. This writer says:

> Regarding the war as inevitable, Wall Street believes that it would be preferable to this uncertainty about the actual date of its commencement. Canada and Japan are at war and are more prosperous than ever before. The popular view is that stocks would have a quick, clear, sharp reaction immediately upon outbreak of hostilities, and that then they would enjoy an old-fashioned bull market such as followed the outbreak of war with Spain in 1898. The advent of peace would force a readjustment of commodity prices and would probably mean a postponement of new enterprises. As peace negotiations would be long drawn out, the period of waiting and uncertainty for business would be long. If the United States does not go to war, it is nevertheless good opinion that the preparedness program will compensate in good measure for the loss of the stimulus of actual war.

Here we have the Wall Street view. Here we have the man representing the class of people who will be made prosperous should we become entangled in the present war, who have already made millions of dollars, and who will make many hundreds of millions more if we get into the war. Here we have the cold-blooded proposition that war brings prosperity to that class of people who are within the viewpoint of this writer.

He expresses the view, undoubtedly, of Wall Street, and of thousands of men elsewhere who see only dollars coming to them through the handling of stocks and bonds that will be necessary in case of war. "Canada and Japan," he says, "are at war, and are more prosperous than ever before."

To whom does war bring prosperity? Not to the soldier who for the munificent compensation of $16 per month shoulders his musket and goes into the trench, there to shed his blood and to die if necessary; not to the brokenhearted widow who waits for the return of the mangled body of her husband; not to the mother who weeps at the death of her brave boy; not to the little children who shiver with cold; not to the babe who suffers from hunger; nor to the millions of mothers and daughters who carry broken hearts to their graves. War brings no prosperity to the great mass of common and patriotic citizens. It increases the cost of living of those who toil and those who already must strain every effort to keep soul and body together. War brings prosperity to the stock gambler on Wall Street — to those who are already in possession of more wealth than can be realized or enjoyed.

Again this writer says that if we cannot get war, "it is nevertheless good opinion that the preparedness program will compensate in good measure for the loss of the stimulus of actual war." That is, if we cannot get war, let us go as far in that direction as possible. If we cannot get war, let us cry for additional ships, additional guns, additional munitions, and everything else that will have a tendency to bring us as near as possible to the verge of war. And if war comes, do such men as these shoulder the musket and go into the trenches?

Their object in having war and in preparing for war is to make money. Human suffering and the sacrifice of human life are necessary, but Wall Street considers only the dollars and the cents. The men who do the fighting, the people who make the sacrifices are the ones who will not be counted

in the measure of this great prosperity that he depicts. The stockbrokers would not, of course, go to war because the very object they have in bringing on the war is profit, and therefore they must remain in their Wall Street offices in order to share in that great prosperity which they say war will bring. The volunteer officer, even the drafting officer, will not find them. They will be concealed in their palatial offices on Wall Street, sitting behind mahogany desks, covered up with clipped coupons — coupons soiled with the sweat of honest toil, coupons stained with mothers' tears, coupons dyed in the lifeblood of their fellowmen.

We are taking a step today that is fraught with untold danger. We are going into war upon the command of gold. We are going to run the risk of sacrificing millions of our countrymen's lives in order that other countrymen may coin their lifeblood into money. And even if we do not cross the Atlantic and go into the trenches, we are going to pile up a debt that the toiling masses that shall come many generations after us will have to pay. Unborn millions will bend their backs in toil in order to pay for the terrible step we are now about to take.

We are about to do the bidding of wealth's terrible mandate. By our act we will make millions of our countrymen suffer, and the consequences of it may well be that millions of our brethren must shed their lifeblood, millions of brokenhearted women must weep, millions of children must suffer with cold, and millions of babes must die from hunger, and all because we want to preserve the commercial right of American citizens to deliver munitions of war to belligerent nations.

II.

Speech by ROBERT M. LA FOLLETTE

I HAD SUPPOSED UNTIL RECENTLY that it was the duty of senators and representatives in Congress to vote and act according to their convictions on all public matters that came before them for consideration and decision. Quite another doctrine has recently been promulgated by certain newspapers, which unfortunately seems to have found considerable support elsewhere, and that is the doctrine of "standing back of the President" without inquiring whether the President is right or wrong.

For myself, I have never subscribed to that doctrine and never shall. I shall support the President in the measures he proposes when I believe them to be right. I shall oppose measures proposed by the President when I believe them to be wrong. The fact that the matter which the President submits for consideration is of the greatest importance is only an additional reason why we should be sure that we are right and not to be swerved from that conviction or intimidated in its expression by any influence of power whatsoever.

If it is important for us to speak and vote our convictions in matters of internal policy, though we may unfortunately be in disagreement with the President, it is infinitely more important for us to speak and vote our convictions when the question is one of peace or war, certain to involve the lives and fortunes of many of our people and, it may be, the destiny of all of them and of the civilized world as well. If, unhappily, on such momentous questions the most patient research and conscientious consideration we could give to them leave us in disagreement with the President, I know of no course to take except to oppose, regretfully but not the less firmly, the demands of the Executive. . . .

Mr. President, many of my colleagues on both sides of this floor have from day to day offered for publication in the *Record* messages and letters received from their constituents. I have received some 15,000 letters and telegrams. They have come from forty-four states in the Union. They have been assorted according to whether they speak in criticism or commendation of my course in opposing war. Assorting the 15,000 letters and telegrams by states in that way, 9 out of 10 are an unqualified endorsement of my course in opposing war with Germany on the issue presented. . . .

A wire from Chicago received this afternoon from Grace Abbott, of Hull House, says that in City Council election held yesterday, John Kennedy received the largest plurality of any of the city councilmen elected. His plurality was 6,157 votes in his ward. On account of his stand against war, every newspaper in Chicago opposed him bitterly throughout the campaign. Mr. Kennedy made his campaign on the war issue, and in every speech he took occasion to declare himself as against war.

There was received in Washington today a petition against war with over 6,120 bona-fide signers, which were secured in the city of Minneapolis in one day; and a wire late this afternoon states that 11,000 more names have been secured to that petition. In New Ulm, Minn., at an election, according to a telegram received this afternoon, 485 votes were cast against war to 19 for war. . . .

Do not these messages indicate on the part of the people a deep-seated conviction that the United States should not enter the European war? . . .

It is unfortunately true that a portion of the irresponsible and war-crazed press, feeling secure in the authority of the President's condemnation of the senators who opposed the armed-ship bill, have published the most infamous and scurrilous libels on the honor of the senators who opposed that bill. It was particularly unfortunate that such malicious falsehoods should fill the public press of the country at a time when every consideration for our country required that a spirit of fairness should be observed in the discussions of the momentous questions under consideration. . . .

Mr. President, let me make a . . . suggestion. It is this: that a minority in one Congress — mayhap a small minority in

Lightfoot Collection

Sen. Robert M. La Follette of Wisconsin

one Congress — protesting, exercising the rights which the Constitution confers upon a minority, may really be representing the majority opinion of the country, and if, exercising the right that the Constitution gives them, they succeed in defeating for the time being the will of the majority, they are but carrying out what was in the mind of the framers of the Constitution; that you may have from time to time in a legislative body a majority in numbers that really does not represent the principle of democracy; and that if the question could be deferred and carried to the people it would be found that a minority was the real representative of the public opinion. So, Mr. President, it was that they wrote into the Constitution that a President — that one man — may put his judgment against the will of a majority not only in one branch of the Congress but in both branches of the Congress; that he may defeat the measure that they have agreed upon and may set his one single judgment above the majority judgment of the Congress. That seems, when you look at it nakedly, to be in violation of the principle that the majority shall rule; and so it is. Why is that power given? It is one of those checks provided by the wisdom of the fathers to prevent the majority from abusing the power that they chance to have, when they do not reflect the real judgment, the opinion, the will of the majority of the people that constitute the sovereign power of the democracy. . . .

The poor, sir, who are the ones called upon to rot in the trenches, have no organized power, have no press to voice their will upon this question of peace or war; but, oh, Mr. President, at some time they will be heard. I hope and I believe they will be heard in an orderly and a peaceful way. I think they may be heard from before long. I think, sir, if we take this step, when the people today who are staggering under the burden of supporting families at the present prices of the necessaries of life find those prices multiplied, when they are raised 100 percent, or 200 percent, as they will be quickly, aye, sir, when beyond that those who pay taxes come to have their taxes doubled and again doubled to pay the interest on the nontaxable bonds held by Morgan and his combinations, which have been issued to meet this war, there will come an awakening; they will have their day and they will be heard. It will be as certain and as inevitable as the return of the tides, and as resistless, too. . . .

In his message of April 2, the President said:

> We have no quarrel with the German people — it was not upon their impulse that their government acted in entering this war; it was not with their previous knowledge or approval.

Again he says:

> We are, let me say again, sincere friends of the German people and shall desire nothing so much as the early reestablishment of intimate relations of mutual advantage between us.

At least, the German people, then, are not outlaws.

What is the thing the President asks us to do to these German people of whom he speaks so highly and whose sincere friend he declares us to be? Here is what he declares we shall do in this war. We shall undertake, he says —

> The utmost practicable cooperation in council and action with the governments now at war with Germany, and as an incident to that, the extension to those governments of the most liberal financial credits in order that our resources may, so far as possible, be added to theirs.

"Practicable cooperation!" Practicable cooperation with England and her allies in starving to death the old men and women, the children, the sick and the maimed of Germany. The thing we are asked to do is the thing I have stated. It is idle to talk of a war upon a government only. We are leagued in this war, or it is the President's proposition that we shall be so leagued, with the hereditary enemies of Germany. Any war with Germany, or any other country for that matter, would be bad enough, but there are not words strong enough to voice my protest against the proposed combination with the Entente Allies.

When we cooperate with those governments, we endorse their methods; we endorse the violations of international law by Great Britain; we endorse the shameful methods of warfare against which we have again and again protested in this war; we endorse her purpose to wreak upon the German people the animosities which for years her people have been taught to cherish against Germany; finally, when the end comes, whatever it may be, we find ourselves in cooperation with our ally, Great Britain, and if we cannot resist now the pressure she is exerting to carry us into the war, how can we hope to resist, then, the thousandfold greater pressure she will exert to bend us to her purposes and compel compliance with her demands?

We do not know what they are. We do not know what is in the minds of those who have made the compact, but we are to subscribe to it. We are irrevocably, by our votes here, to marry ourselves to a nondi-

vorceable proposition veiled from us now. Once enlisted, once in the copartnership, we will be carried through with the purposes, whatever they may be, of which we now know nothing.

Sir, if we are to enter upon this war in the manner the President demands, let us throw pretense to the winds, let us be honest, let us admit that this is a ruthless war against not only Germany's Army and her Navy but against her civilian population as well, and frankly state that the purpose of Germany's hereditary European enemies has become our purpose.

Again, the President says "we are about to accept the gage of battle with this natural foe of liberty and shall, if necessary, spend the whole force of the nation to check and nullify its pretensions and its power." That much, at least, is clear; that program is definite. The whole force and power of this nation, if necessary, is to be used to bring victory to the Entente Allies, and to us as their ally in this war. Remember, that not yet has the "whole force" of one of the warring nations been used.

Countless millions are suffering from want and privation; countless other millions are dead and rotting on foreign battlefields; countless other millions are crippled and maimed, blinded, and dismembered; upon all and upon their children's children for generations to come has been laid a burden of debt which must be worked out in poverty and suffering, but the "whole force" of no one of the warring nations has yet been expended; but our "whole force" shall be expended, so says the President. We are pledged by the President, so far as he can pledge us, to make this fair, free, and happy land of ours the same shambles and bottomless pit of horror that we see in Europe today.

Just a word of comment more upon one of the points in the President's address. He says that this is a war "for the things which we have always carried nearest to our hearts — for democracy, for the right of those who submit to authority to have a voice in their own government." In many places throughout the address is this exalted sentiment given expression.

It is a sentiment peculiarly calculated to appeal to American hearts and, when accompanied by acts consistent with it, is certain to receive our support; but in this same connection, and strangely enough, the President says that we have become convinced that the German government as it now exists — "Prussian autocracy" he calls it — can never again maintain friendly relations with us. His expression is that "Prussian autocracy was not and could never be our friend," and repeatedly throughout the address the suggestion is made that if the German people would overturn their government, it would probably be the way to peace. So true is this that the dispatches from London all hailed the message of the President as sounding the death knell of Germany's government.

But the President proposes alliance with Great Britain, which, however liberty-loving its people, is a hereditary monarchy, with a hereditary ruler, with a hereditary House of Lords, with a hereditary landed system, with a limited and restricted suffrage for one class and a multiplied suffrage power for another, and with grinding industrial conditions for all the wageworkers. The President has not suggested that we make our support of Great Britain conditional to her granting home rule to Ireland, or Egypt, or India. We rejoice in the establishment of a democracy in Russia, but it will hardly be contended that if Russia was still an autocratic government, we would not be asked to enter this alliance with her just the same.

Italy and the lesser powers of Europe, Japan in the Orient; in fact, all the countries with whom we are to enter into alliance, except France and newly revolutionized Russia, are still of the old order — and it will be generally conceded that no one of them has done as much for its people in the solution of municipal problems and in securing social and industrial reforms as Germany.

Is it not a remarkable democracy which leagues itself with allies already far overmatching in strength the German nation and holds out to such beleaguered nation the hope of peace only at the price of giving up their government? I am not talking now of the merits or demerits of any government, but I am speaking of a profession of democracy that is linked in action with the most brutal and domineering use of autocratic power. Are the people of this country being so well-represented in this war movement that we need to go abroad to give other people control of their governments?

Will the President and the supporters of this war bill submit it to a vote of the people before the declaration of war goes into effect? Until we are willing to do that, it illy becomes us to offer as an excuse for our entry into the war the unsupported claim that this war was forced upon the German people by their government "without their previous knowledge or approval."

Who has registered the knowledge or approval of the American people of the course this Congress is called upon to take in declaring war upon Germany? Submit the question to the people, you who support it. You who support it dare not do it, for you know that by a vote of more than ten to one the American people as a body would register their declaration against it.

In the sense that this war is being forced upon our people without their knowing why and without their approval, and that wars are usually forced upon all peoples in the same way, there is some truth in the statement; but I venture to say that the response which the German people have made to the demands of this war shows that it has a degree of popular support which the war upon which we are entering has not and never will have among our people. The espionage bills, the conscription bills, and other forcible military measures which we understand are being ground out of the war machine in this country is the complete proof that those responsible for this war fear that it has no popular support and that armies sufficient to satisfy the demand of the Entente Allies cannot be recruited by voluntary enlistments. . . .

Now, I want to repeat: It was our absolute right as a neutral to ship food to the people of Germany. That is a position that we have fought for through all of our history. The correspondence of every secretary of state in the history of our government who has been called upon to deal with the rights of our neutral commerce as to foodstuffs is the position stated by Lord Salisbury. . . . He was in line with all of the precedents that we had originated and established for the maintenance of neutral rights upon this subject.

In the first days of the war with Germany, Great Britain set aside, so far as her own conduct was concerned, all these rules of civilized naval warfare.

According to the Declaration of London, as well as the rules of international law, there could have been no interference in trade between the United States and Holland or Scandinavia and other countries, except in the case of ships which could be proven to carry absolute contraband, like arms and ammunition, with ultimate German destination. There could have been no interference with the importation into Germany of any goods on the free list, such as cotton, rubber, and hides. There could have properly been no interference with our export to Germany of anything on the conditional contraband list, like flour, grain, and provisions, unless it could be proven by England that such shipments were intended for the use of the German Army. There could be no lawful interference with foodstuffs intended for the civilian population of Germany, and if those foodstuffs were shipped to other countries to be reshipped to Germany, no question could be raised that they

were not intended for the use of the civilian population.

It is well to recall at this point our rights as declared by the Declaration of London and as declared without the Declaration of London by settled principles of international law, for we have during the present war become so used to having Great Britain utterly disregard our rights on the high seas that we have really forgotten that we have any, as far as Great Britain and her allies are concerned.

Great Britain, by what she called her modifications of the Declaration of London, shifted goods from the free list to the conditional contraband and contraband lists, reversed the presumption of destination for civilian population, and abolished the principle that a blockade to exist at all must be effective. . . .

It is not my purpose to go into detail into the violations of our neutrality by any of the belligerents. While Germany has again and again yielded to our protests, I do not recall a single instance in which a protest we have made to Great Britain has won for us the slightest consideration, except for a short time in the case of cotton. I will not stop to dwell upon the multitude of minor violations of our neutral rights, such as seizing our mails, violations of the neutral flag, seizing and appropriating our goods without the least warrant or authority in law, and impressing, seizing, and taking possession of our vessels and putting them into her own service.

I have constituents, American citizens, who organized a company and invested large sums of money in the purchase of ships to engage in foreign carrying. Several of their vessels plying between the United States and South America were captured almost in our own territorial waters, taken possession of by the British Government, practically confiscated, and put into her service or the service of her Admiralty. They are there today, and that company is helpless. When they appealed to our Department of State, they were advised that they might "file" their papers; and were given the further suggestion that they could hire an attorney and prosecute their case in the English Prize Court. The company did hire an attorney and sent him to England, and he is there now, and has been there for almost a year, trying to get some redress, some relief, some adjustment of those rights.

But those are individual cases. There are many others. All these violations have come from Great Britain and her allies, and are in perfect harmony with Briton's traditional policy as absolute master of the seas. . . .

The only reason why we have not suffered the sacrifice of just as many ships and just as many lives from the violation of our rights by the war zone and the submarine mines of Great Britain as we have through the unlawful acts of Germany in making her war zone in violation of our neutral rights is simply because we have submitted to Great Britain's dictation. If our ships had been sent into her forbidden high-sea war zone as they have into the proscribed area Germany marked out on the high seas as a war zone, we would have had the same loss of life and property in the one case as in the other; but because we avoided doing that, in the case of England, and acquiesced in her violation of law, we have not only a legal but a moral responsibility for the position in which Germany has been placed by our collusion and cooperation with Great Britain. By suspending the rule with respect to neutral rights in Great Britain's case, we have been actively aiding her in starving the civil population of Germany. We have helped to drive Germany into a corner, her back to the wall, to fight with what weapons she can lay her hands on to prevent the starving of her women and children, her old men and babes.

The flimsy claim which has sometimes been put forth that possibly the havoc in the North Sea was caused by German mines is too absurd for consideration. . . .

I find all the correspondence about the submarines of Germany; I find them arrayed; I find the note warning Germany that she would be held to a "strict accountability" for violation of our neutral rights; but you will search in vain these volumes for a copy of the British order in council mining the North Sea.

I am talking now about principles. You cannot distinguish between the principles which allowed England to mine a large area of the Atlantic Ocean and the North Sea in order to shut in Germany, and the principle on which Germany by her submarines seeks to destroy all shipping which enters the war zone which she has laid out around the British Isles.

The English mines are intended to destroy without warning every ship that enters the war zone she has proscribed, killing or drowning every passenger that cannot find some means of escape. It is neither more nor less than that which Germany tries to do with her submarines in her war zone. We acquiesced in England's action without protest. It is proposed that we now go to war with Germany for identically the same action upon her part. . . .

I say again that when two nations are at war any neutral nation, in order to preserve its character as a neutral nation, must exact the same conduct from both warring nations; both must equally obey the principles of international law. If a neutral nation fails in that, then its rights upon the high seas — to adopt the President's phrase — are relative and not absolute. There can be no greater violation of our neutrality than the requirement that one of two belligerents shall adhere to the settled principles of law and that the other shall have the advantage of not doing so. The respect that German naval authorities were required to pay to the rights of our people upon the high seas would depend upon the question whether we had exacted the same rights from Germany's enemies. If we had not done so, we lost our character as a neutral nation and our people unfortunately had lost the protection that belongs to neutrals. Our responsibility was joint in the sense that we must exact the same conduct from both belligerents. . . .

The failure to treat the belligerent nations of Europe alike, the failure to reject the unlawful "war zones" of both Germany and Great Britain is wholly accountable for our present dilemma. We should not seek to hide our blunder behind the smoke of battle, to inflame the mind of our people by half truths into the frenzy of war in order that they may never appreciate the real cause of it until it is too late. I do not believe that our national honor is served by

such a course. The right way is the honorable way.

One alternative is to admit our initial blunder to enforce our rights against Great Britain as we have enforced our rights against Germany; demand that both those nations shall respect our neutral rights upon the high seas to the letter; and give notice that we will enforce those rights from that time forth against both belligerents and then live up to that notice.

The other alternative is to withdraw our commerce from both. The mere suggestion that food supplies would be withheld from both sides impartially would compel belligerents to observe the principle of freedom of the seas for neutral commerce.

20.

Norman Thomas *et al.:* Tolerance for the Conscientious Objector

War hysteria swept America after its declaration of war on April 6, 1917. Sauerkraut was renamed "liberty cabbage" and hamburger became "Salisbury steak"; and anyone who objected to the war in any way was viewed as a traitor to his country. Conscientious objectors were mistreated by the police, thrown in jail, and regarded as criminals. This climate of opinion prompted a group of prominent pacifists to compose a public plea for tolerance. Norman Thomas, a leading Socialist and pacifist, representing a group of thirteen persons, wrote a letter to the New Republic *in which he listed the reasons why the government as well as the American public should respect the conscientious objector. The letter was published on May 26, 1917, and is reprinted below.*

Source: *New Republic*, May 26, 1917: "The Religion of Free Men."

As conscientious objectors we turn to your journal because, more powerfully than any other, it has expressed in subtle analyses our abiding faith in humane wisdom. You have never countenanced the evil doctrine of the brute coercion of the human will.

You have preached and practised the virtue of tolerance, the kind of tolerance for the lack of which the state grows mechanized and conscienceless.

You know something of the machinery of unfair play. You understand the tyranny of

Norman Thomas, Presbyterian minister who became a pacifist in World War I

sham shibboleths. You appreciate the menace of military psychology. We appeal to you, strategically situated as you are, to assist the cause of the conscientious objectors. We beg you to note the following facts:

In the evolution of the human mind we discover a gradually widening hiatus between physical competence and intellectual moral competence. So deeply imbedded in our life values is this distinction that we feel rather ashamed of being too expert physically. The man of blood and iron does not appeal to our finer perceptions as a being altogether worthy of our worshipful attention. (The God whom we worship is neither a jingo nor a militarist.) But Voltaire — he of the skinny shanks and the anemic face — what exuberant pride wells up in the greatest and in the least of us at the sound of that marvelous name! And soft-spoken Jesus — what fitting tribute can the reeling world lay at the feet of him who died that goodwill and loving kindness might assuage the hearts of inimical men.

The complexity and richness of life have permitted, and increasingly so, the more or less free play of *all modes* of energy. There are many men best adapted by training and temperament to the performance of physical acts of heroism; there are some men more naturally suited to the performance of intellectual deeds of courage, while yet some others shine in deeds of moral bravery. Why sanction the inhuman device of forcing all manner of men into the narrowly specific kind of devotion for which so many of them are hopelessly unfit? Tolerance arises from the existence of varying types of doers, all willing to respect one another's special competence. It is not too extreme to assert that in wartime (as in peacetime) some of the most heroic deeds are performed by those who do not (and, if called upon, would not) take up arms in defense of the cause. There are other forms of bravery than the purely military one. Let us be reasonable.

The one ineradicable fact which no amount of official intimidation can pulverize out of existence is that there is a type of man to whom (military) participation in war is tantamount to committing murder. He cannot, he will not commit murder. There is no human power on God's earth that can coerce him into committing (what *he* knows to be) the act of murder. You may call him sentimentalist, fool, slacker, mollycoddle, woman — anything "disreputable" you please. But there he is, a tremendous fact. Shall he be maltreated for his scruples? Or shall he be respected (as his deriders are) for his conscientiousness? We cannot leave so momentous an issue to chance or to the cold machinery of administration. Men of sensitive insight must help prepare a social setting within America sufficiently hospitable to all conscientious objectors.

It is good to remind ourselves of our instinctive respect for conscientious objectors. When a man is called to serve on a jury empaneled in a murder case, he may be honorably excused from duty if he has conscientious objections to the death penalty. When we think sanely we are not averse to honoring the man of conscience provided he be an active friend of mankind and not a mere ease-taker. The test of manhood lies in service; *not* in one particular kind of service (suitable to one particular type of mind and body) but genuine service genuinely rendered to humanity.

Hence the philosophic value of tolerance. To keep alive genuine tolerance in wartime is the greatest single achievement to which rationalists can dedicate themselves. America is caught in this insidious entanglement; obsessed with the tradition — the mere outward form and symbol — of liberty of conscience, she has failed to realize the living need of a real grant and a substantial practice of our vaunted freedom of conscience. It is not the tradition we lack; only a vital *belief* in that tradition.

In times of precarious peace, when the social classes wage an almost relentless warfare and the daily grind of poverty and distress lays armies of the proletariat low, life for the disadvantaged groups is made more or less livable only by the thought that between them and their official superiors certain constitutional and humane guarantees of tolerance exist as safeguards of mutual understanding. There is room for difference of opinion. There is a breathing space for discussion.

How desperate must the social situation have become if large numbers of conscientious and law-abiding citizens have begun to feel an appalling sense of uneasiness in the presence of huge inscrutable forces, far beyond their power of control or sympathetic understanding. Why this amazing disquietude? The answer is simple and straightforward. There is no longer the sense — so natural and dear to free men — of being able to appeal from manifestly unfair decisions. Too many subordinate officials are being vested with a tremendous authority over impotent human beings.

The situation is complicated and made more sinister by the suspicion that many of the powerful gentlemen who in the days of ampler opportunity for social service and social justice failed and most lamentably to respond to the public's needs are now the unchallenged controllers of the social destiny. What we must not overlook in this perilous situation is this disquieting fact: An excess of power permits certain antisocial men to wield with utter unscrupulousness the whole machinery of antihumanism, of which by the sheer accident of circumstance they happen to be gaining possession at this critical time.

Then consider this: Sooner or later war must cease. The tremendous enterprise of re-creating out of bloody chaos some new, reinspired internationalism will be the order of the day. Who is better fitted for that reconstructive task than those humanists now in imminent danger of being bullied out of existence because their visions and their faiths extend beyond the time of bloody chaos? It would be folly for a groping democracy to permit the degradation, the torture, and the slow annihilation of conscientious citizens. Whose duty shall it be to bring into permanent realization those humanist values (for which all men in their saner moods proudly contend) in behalf of which our war for democracy is said to be waged?

If the reigning editorial intolerance, directed and sanctioned by official autocrats, is permitted to assassinate the greater promises held in trust by the workers for a world democracy, the outlook for a greater humanity is indeed mournful. Whom can we, in this period of panic and pain, rely upon? Humanitarians, workers in the social service, child-welfare devotees, Tolstoians, radical educators — these constitute the vanguard of a revised and spiritually humanized world state. If civilization were to plan the utter wreckage of its most precious (because most consecrated) values, it could do no better than empower the mechanized state with the authority to brutalize and degrade all its visionaries.

Hasn't our evolving democracy any use

for the student, the reflective man, the lonely thinker, the gentle philosopher, the socialist, the disciple of Jesus, the vision-haunted educator, the pity-racked lover of the human kind? Isn't sheer humanity itself a marvelous force for good? Is there no world recompense in having nurtured, honored, and immortalized Ralph Emerson, Henry Thoreau, Leo Tolstoi, Bertrand Russell, Norman Angell, and Romain Rolland? Is there no duty the conscientious thinker owes to the unborn world, the finer world of tomorrow, regenerated and re-created under the inspiration of the humanitarians? Can't we honestly respect the peculiar rights of those who have given their sincerest devotion to advocating the institution among men of that kind of livable regime by the very nature of which the present world calamity would have been rendered well-nigh unthinkable? Shall the dreamers of a true federation of mankind be sacrificed because they have not yet been permitted to realize their dream?

We desire to contribute our intellectual and moral energies to the creation of that humaner world in which conscience and tolerance and personality and philosophy will count as mightily as do their fierce negations now. We gladly accept the heartening summons pronounced in behalf of our democracy against an overweening autocracy by our own Woodrow Wilson:

> But the right is more precious than peace, and we shall fight for the things we have always carried nearest our hearts — for democracy, for the right of those who submit to authority to have a voice in their own government.

In bringing the gift of freedom to the distant unemancipated, shall we betray so precious a cause by brute denial of freedom to those of our own blood and tradition, to our own freedom lovers within the gate? What a sorry, tragical miscarriage of wisdom!

Our immediate problem is to persuade President Wilson to authorize the appointment to the Exemption Boards of men and women conspicuous for their social service. For example: settlement workers, publicists, educators, social service devotees. We must not repeat the crime of our English cousins who, in a paroxysm of patriotism, fell to the low level of sheer brute inhumanity. The members of the tribunals, as the distinguished Englishman Henry W. Nevinson reports, "nearly all agreed in regarding conscience as an unpatriotic offense which must be visited by penalties!" Even Treitschke, the apostle of state domination, set it down as his belief that "the state is not the whole life of man or of society. It does not and should not touch his conscience or his religion. There is an inner life which is a man's own."

Shall we in America out-Treitschke Treitschke?

We have not been schooled by life to play the military role. We have never found it necessary or desirable to inflict our philosophies with a rod. We have been able and willing to instruct a recreant mankind by force of example, by the persuasions of wisdom, by the practice of fair play. We have found our existence tolerable precisely because we·have known how to substitute for the rigors of coercion the rigors of persuasion. We have no military competence. We possess only intellectual and moral competence. We would serve gladly, generously, high-heartedly — but we cannot serve except it be honestly, conscientiously, morally.

We ask you to bear in mind the inspiring assurance vouched for to a listening world on the eve of our great championship of universal democracy. President Woodrow Wilson asserted as of fundamental importance to the creation and survival of democracy "the privilege of men everywhere to *choose their way of life and of obedience.*" Everywhere, gentlemen!

21.

The Press in Wartime

After war was declared against Germany in April 1917, numerous agencies sprang up whose task was to "sell" Americans on the war. President Wilson himself established the Committee on Public Information, whose efforts were paralleled by several nongovernment agencies, most notably the National Security League. Columbia University, whose administration strongly backed the war, produced a series of "War Papers" promoting everything from universal military service to "victory gardens." An appeal to the nation's press, which later voluntarily censored its news stories, is reprinted below.

Source: *Columbia War Papers*, Series 1, No. 4, New York, 1917, pp. 3-7: "Our Headline Policy."

TEAMWORK AND TEAMWORK ONLY can win this war.

We shall be at war, bearing all the sacrifices that war entails, until the war is won.

To win the war is our one aim — our one supreme duty — to which all our national resources and powers must be directed.

Our greatest national power — that which, in every democracy, must direct and set in motion all the rest — is our public press; and upon you, who direct that press, rests a supreme responsibility.

This war is not an individual duel. It is a stupendous conflict between teams — not of individuals but of nations. No conflict between such enormous forces has ever been waged before, but it will be won or lost upon those age-old principles that have determined the success or failure of all organized contests since the beginning of time.

The first requisite for success is unity. The American people are by nature independent. They tend to think for themselves as individuals and to act upon their individual initiative.

But, also, if they understand the need, they are capable of team play. They do not tolerate upon the baseball field or upon the gridiron those grandstand, spectacular, individual plays that throw the game away in order to obtain personal prominence and applause. The American people understand a *sacrifice hit*. They know that only that team can win in which each player plays for all, with a single eye to the victory of the team as a whole.

It is upon this knowledge that the American people must now act. It is the editors of the public press who have it in their power to lead them to this action, by keeping the necessity for it — the ideal of it — constantly before the people; by making them realize that victory can be won only through unity.

How is this to be done? Editorials, repeated editorials are both desirable and necessary. But to one reader who is influenced once by a given editorial, many hundreds are influenced, day by day, by the headlines of the paper and by the wording and form of presentation of the news. It is, therefore, to a considered and continuous policy of news presentation that we must look primarily for the keeping before the American people of the importance of team play and of the fact that we are today a member of a great team of nations whose success is ours and whose failure would alike be ours.

Team play, sacrifice hits, assists — not grandstand performances, lone hands, and refusal to play the game.

In this policy of news presentation, the following is important:

1. Do not use the phrases "The Allies," "the Entente Powers," etc. Say: "our Allies," "our gallant Allies," "the French," etc. Say "we" whenever possible. Write of "our Allies' advance upon St. Quentin," "our Allies take Le Fer." Speak of "the enemy" in alluding to Germany. Germany is *our* enemy.

In this, it makes no manner of difference whether we have a formal alliance, established by senatorial action, or not. We have a *de facto* and pragmatic alliance in that we are fighting a common enemy. And only as this is iterated and reiterated can it be made to sink into the public consciousness.

2. Keep the news of the actual fighting, so far as possible, upon the front page. It is *our* fighting. It is the reason why all our local activities — the raising of troops, the training of men here or there, the manufacture of munitions, and the issuance of billions of credit — are conducted. These activities can be understood only in their relation to the end for which they are undertaken. Keep that end in evidence.

3. Keep the Americans now with our Allies, before the public as Americans. There are at the present time 25,000 men from the United States fighting in France with the French and English. Prior to our declaration of war, we could not with propriety emphasize this fact; but now that war is declared, it is necessary to recognize it. It is a larger number of American soldiers than were present at the Battle of Santiago. Treat it as such. We do not have to wait to send troops to the battlefields of Europe —

though many additional hundreds of thousands must be sent there before this war is won. Our soldiers are there now. Help the country to realize this and never to forget it. It is, in literal fact, *our* advance upon St. Quentin, *our* mastery of the air.

Berlin recognizes this explicitly in the following dispatch, printed on the eighth page of the *New York Times* for April 9:

> Our opponents, including Americans who were in the French aerial service long prior to the American declaration of war, lost in the month of March, in the west, east, and the Balkans, 161 airplanes and 19 captive balloons by our attacks and antiaircraft devices. Of these, 143 airplanes and 19 balloons were shot down by fire from the ground. The German losses amounted to 45 airplanes. No captive balloons were lost.

If our country, as a whole, had recognized this, this testimony from the enemy of the part we have played and are playing in obtaining the mastery of the air would not be relegated to an eighth-page paragraph without heading.

Keep the news of *our* battles, *our* advances, *our* triumphs, or *our* reverses on the front page. The troops in the trenches are *our* troops. They are ours in a double sense. Thousands of them are our fellow citizens; the rest are fighting in our cause. Only by thus presenting our efforts will our preparations for still greater efforts be seen in their true perspective. The means, to be understood, must be seen as means in relation to their end. That end is the defeat of *Germany,* a defeat that is being accomplished and can only be accomplished on the battlefields of Europe and on the high seas.

The pro-German activity in this country will not cease. It will become only more hidden and more insidious. It will be directed to spreading disunity between ourselves and our Allies, to preventing close cooperation and unity of action, to making us, if possible, play a lone hand. To play a lone hand at such a time, in such a conflict, is to play for certain defeat. The President's message recognizes this explicitly. Yet, unless it be kept constantly before the mind of the American people, our national isolation and our national prejudices may easily make us the victim of insidious pro-German propaganda and duplicity. It is to the press of the country that we must look to keep this necessity of unity, this clear vision of our single aim, constantly before us; and it is in the headlines of the papers, in the placing of the news, and in the words that are used in making that news public that this must be done.

22.

George M. Cohan: "Over There"

"Over There" was actor and songwriter George M. Cohan's main contribution to the U.S. war effort — and no mean contribution it was. Enrico Caruso sang it on the steps of the New York Public Library and sold thousands of dollars worth of Liberty Bonds, and it was adopted by the men of the American Expeditionary Force as their favorite marching song. Congress authorized Cohan a special medal for the song in 1940, and it was sung by a new generation of American soldiers in World War II.

Source: *Legion Airs: Songs of the Armed Forces*, Lee O. Smith, ed., New York, 1960.

♫ OVER THERE

Johnnie get your gun, get your gun, get your gun,
Take it on the run, on the run, on the run;
Hear them calling you and me;
Every son of liberty.
Hurry right away, no delay, go today,
Make your daddy glad, to have had such a lad,
Tell your sweetheart not to pine,
To be proud her boy's in line.

Chorus:
Over there, over there,
Send the word, send the word over there,
That the Yanks are coming, the Yanks are coming,
The drums rum-tumming everywhere.
So prepare, say a prayer,
Send the word, send the word to beware,
We'll be over, we're coming over,
And we won't come back till it's over over there.

Johnnie get your gun, get your gun, get your gun,
Johnnie show the Hun, you're a son-of-a-gun,
Hoist the flag and let her fly,
Like true heroes do or die.
Pack your little kit, show your grit, do your bit,
Soldiers to the ranks from the towns and the tanks,
Make your mother proud of you,
And to liberty be true.

23.

H. L. MENCKEN: Puritanism as a Literary Force

During 1917 and 1918 Henry Louis Mencken served as a war correspondent in Europe for the Baltimore Evening Sun. *His* Book of Prefaces *(1917), from which the following selection is taken, anticipated the intellectual rebellion of the Twenties, when his savage iconoclasm was widely influential. Puritanism, for Mencken, symbolized all that was wrong with American literature and with American life. In his view, the overconcern with sin that marked the Puritan mentality had disturbed if not destroyed the talents even of America's greatest writers.*

Source: *A Book of Prefaces*, New York, 1917, pp. 197-252.

"CALVINISM," says Dr. Leon Kellner, in his excellent little history of American literature, "is the natural theology of the disinherited; it never flourished, therefore, anywhere as it did in the barren hills of Scotland and in the wilds of North America." The learned doctor is here speaking of theology in what may be called its narrow technical sense — that is, as a theory of God. Under Calvinism, in the New World as well as in the Old, it became no more than a luxuriant demonology; even God Himself was transformed into a superior sort of devil, ever wary and wholly merciless. That primitive demonology still survives in the barbaric doctrines of the Methodists and Baptists, particularly in the South; but it has been ameliorated, even there, by a growing sense of the divine grace, and so the old God of Plymouth Rock, as practically conceived, is now scarcely worse than the average jail warden or Italian padrone.

On the ethical side, however, Calvinism is dying a much harder death, and we are still a long way from the enlightenment. Save where Continental influences have measurably corrupted the Puritan idea — *e.g.,* in such cities as New York, San Francisco, and New Orleans — the prevailing American view of the world and its mysteries is still a moral one, and no other human concern gets half the attention that is endlessly lavished upon the problem of conduct, particularly of the other fellow. It needed no official announcement to define the function and office of the republic as that of an international expert in morals, and the mentor and exemplar of the more backward nations. Within, as well as without, the eternal rapping of knuckles and proclaiming of new austerities goes on.

The American, save in moments of conscious and swiftly lamented deviltry, casts up all ponderable values, including even the values of beauty, in terms of right and wrong. He is beyond all things else, a judge and a policeman; he believes firmly that there is a mysterious power in law; he supports and embellishes its operation with a fanatical vigilance.

Naturally enough, this moral obsession has given a strong color to American literature. In truth, it has colored it so brilliantly that American literature is set off sharply from all other literatures. In none other will you find so wholesale and ecstatic a sacrifice of aesthetic ideas, of all the fine gusto of passion and beauty, to notions of what is meet, proper, and nice. From the books of grisly sermons that were the first American contribution to letters down to that amazing literature of "inspiration" which now flowers so prodigiously, with two literary ex-presidents among its chief virtuosi, one observes no relaxation of the moral pressure.

In the history of every other literature there have been periods of what might be called moral innocence — periods in which a naive *joie de vivre* has broken through all concepts of duty and responsibility, and the wonder and glory of the universe have been hymned with unashamed zest. The age of Shakespeare comes to mind at once; the violence of the Puritan reaction offers a measure of the pendulum's wild swing. But in America no such general rising of the blood has ever been seen. The literature of the nation, even the literature of the enlightened minority, has been under harsh Puritan restraints from the beginning, and despite a few stealthy efforts at revolt — usually quite without artistic value or even common honesty, as in the case of the cheap fiction magazines and that of smutty plays on Broadway, and always very short-lived — it shows not the slightest sign of emancipating itself today. The American, try as he will, can never imagine any work of the imagination as wholly devoid of moral content. It must either tend toward the promotion of virtue, or be suspect and abominable.

If any doubt of this is in your mind, turn to the critical articles in the newspapers and literary weeklies; you will encounter enough proofs in a month's explorations to convince you forever. A novel or a play is judged among us, not by its dignity of conception, its artistic honesty, its perfection of workmanship, but almost entirely by its orthodoxy of doctrine, its platitudinousness, its usefulness as a moral tract. A digest of the reviews of such a book as David Graham Phillips' *Susan Lenox* or of such a play as Ibsen's *Hedda Gabler* would make astounding reading for a continental European. Not only the childish incompetents who write for the daily press but also most of our critics of experience and reputation seem quite unable to estimate a piece of writing as a piece of writing, a work of art as a work of art; they almost inevitably drag in irrelevant gabble as to whether this or that personage in it is respectable, or this or that situation in accordance with the national notions of what is edifying and nice.

Fully nine-tenths of the reviews of Dreiser's *The Titan*, without question the best American novel of its year, were devoted chiefly to indignant denunciations of the morals of Frank Cowperwood, its central character. That the man was superbly imagined and magnificently depicted, that he stood out from the book in all the flashing vigor of life, that his creation was an artistic achievement of a very high and difficult order — these facts seem to have made no impression upon the reviewers whatever. They were Puritans writing for Puritans, and all they could see in Cowperwood was an anti-Puritan, and in his creator another. It will remain for Europeans, I daresay, to discover the true stature of *The Titan*, as it remained for Europeans to discover the true stature of *Sister Carrie*.

Just how deeply this corrective knife has

cut you may find plainly displayed in Dr. Kellner's little book. He sees the throttling influence of an ever alert and bellicose Puritanism, not only in our grand literature but also in our petite literature, our minor poetry, even in our humor. The Puritan's utter lack of aesthetic sense, his distrust of all romantic emotion, his unmatchable intolerance of opposition, his unbreakable belief in his own bleak and narrow views, his savage cruelty of attack, his lust for relentless and barbarous persecution — these things have put an almost unbearable burden upon the exchange of ideas in the United States, and particularly upon that form of it which involves playing with them for the mere game's sake. On the one hand, the writer who would deal seriously and honestly with the larger problems of life, particularly in the rigidly partitioned ethical field, is restrained by laws that would have kept a Balzac or a Zola in prison from year's end to year's end; and, on the other hand, the writer who would proceed against the reigning superstitions by mockery has been silenced by taboos that are quite as stringent, and by an indifference that is even worse.

For all our professed delight in and capacity for jocosity, we have produced so far but one genuine wit — Ambrose Bierce — and, save to a small circle, he remains unknown today. Our great humorists, including even Mark Twain, have had to take protective coloration, whether willingly or unwillingly, from the prevailing ethical foliage, and so one finds them leveling their darts, not at the stupidities of the Puritan majority but at the evidences of lessening stupidity in the anti-Puritan minority. In other words, they have done battle, not against but *for* Philistinism — and Philistinism is no more than another name for Puritanism. Both wage a ceaseless warfare upon beauty in its every form, from painting to religious ritual, and from the drama to the dance — the first because it holds beauty to be a mean and stupid thing, and the second because it holds beauty to be distracting and corrupting.

Mark Twain, without question, was a great artist; there was in him something of that prodigality of imagination, that aloof engrossment in the human comedy, that penetrating cynicism which one associates with the great artists of the Renaissance. But his nationality hung around his neck like a millstone; he could never throw off his native Philistinism. One ploughs through *The Innocents Abroad* and through parts of *A Tramp Abroad* with incredulous amazement. Is such coarse and ignorant clowning to be accepted as humor, as great humor, as the best humor that the most humorous of peoples has produced? Is it really the mark of a smart fellow to lift a peasant's cackle over *Lohengrin?* Is Titian's chromo of Moses in the bulrushes seriously to be regarded as the noblest picture in Europe? Is there nothing in Latin Christianity, after all, save petty grafting, monastic scandals, and the worship of the knuckles and shinbones of dubious saints? May not a civilized man, disbelieving in it, still find himself profoundly moved by its dazzling history, the lingering remnants of its old magnificence, the charm of its gorgeous and melancholy loveliness?

In the presence of all beauty of man's creation — in brief, of what we roughly call art, whatever its form — the voice of Mark Twain was the voice of the Philistine. A literary artist of very high rank himself, with instinctive gifts that lifted him, in *Huckleberry Finn*, to kinship with Cervantes and Aristophanes, he was yet so far the victim of his nationality that he seems to have had no capacity for distinguishing between the good and the bad in the work of other men of his own craft. The literary criticism that one occasionally finds in his writings is chiefly trivial and ignorant; his private inclination appears to have been toward such romantic sentimentality as entrances schoolboys; the thing that interested him in Shakespeare was not the man's colossal genius but the absurd theory that Bacon wrote his plays. Had he been born in France (the country of his chief abomination!) instead of in a Puritan village of the American hinterland, I venture that he would have conquered the world. But try as he would, being what he was, he could not get rid of the Puritan smugness and cocksureness, the Puritan distrust of new ideas, the Puritan incapacity for seeing beauty as a thing in itself, and the full peer of the true and the good.

It is, indeed, precisely in the works of such men as Mark Twain that one finds the best proofs of the Puritan influence in American letters, for it is there that it is least expected and hence most significant. Our native critics, unanimously Puritans themselves, are anaesthetic to the flavor, but to Dr. Kellner, with his half-European, half-Oriental culture, it is always distinctly perceptible. He senses it, not only in the harsh Calvinistic fables of Hawthorne and the pious gurglings of Longfellow but also in the poetry of Bryant, the tea-party niceness of Howells, the "maiden-like reserve" of James Lane Allen, and even in the work of Joel Chandler Harris. What! A Southern Puritan? Well, why not? What could be more erroneous than the common assumption that Puritanism is exclusively a Northern, a New England madness? The truth is that it is as thoroughly national as the kindred belief in the devil, and runs almost unobstructed from Portland to Portland and from the Lakes to the Gulf. It is in the South, indeed, and not in the North that it takes on its most bellicose and extravagant forms.

Between the upper tier of New England and the Potomac River there was not a single Prohibition state — but thereafter, alas, they came in huge blocks! And behind that infinitely prosperous Puritanism there is a long and unbroken tradition. Berkeley, the last of the Cavaliers, was kicked out of power in Virginia so long ago as 1650. Lord Baltimore, the Proprietor of Maryland, was brought to terms by the Puritans of the Severn in 1657. The Scotch Covenanter, the most uncompromising and unenlightened of all Puritans, flourished in the Carolinas from the start, and in 1698, or thereabout, he was reinforced from New England. In 1757 a band of Puritans invaded what is now Georgia — and Georgia has been a Puritan barbarism ever since. Even while the early (and half-mythical) Cavaliers were still in nominal control of all these Southern plantations, they clung to the seacoast. The population that moved down the chain of the Appalachians during the latter part of the 18th century, and then swept over them into the Mississippi Valley, was composed almost entirely of Puritans — chiefly intransigents from New England (where Unitarianism was getting on its legs), kirk-crazy Scotch, and that plupious and beauty-hating folk, the Scotch-Irish.

"In the South today," said John Fiske a generation ago, "there is more Puritanism surviving than in New England." In that whole region, an area three times as large as France or Germany, there is not a single orchestra capable of playing Beethoven's C minor symphony, or a single painting worth looking at, or a single public building or monument of any genuine distinction, or a single factory devoted to the making of beautiful things, or a single poet, novelist, historian, musician, painter, or sculptor whose reputation extends beyond his own country. Between the Mason and Dixon Line and the mouth of the Mississippi there is but one opera house, and that one was built by a Frenchman, and is now, I believe, closed. The only domestic art this huge and opulent empire knows is in the hands of Mexican "greasers"; its only native music it owes to the despised Negro; its only genuine poet was permitted to die up an alley like a stray dog.

THE ORIGINAL PURITANS had at least been men of a certain education, and even of a certain austere culture. They were inordinately hostile to beauty in all its forms, but one somehow suspects that much of their hostility was due to a sense of their weakness before it, a realization of its disarming psychical pull. But the American of the new republic was of a different kidney. He was not so much hostile to beauty as devoid of any consciousness of it; he stood as unmoved before its phenomena as a savage before a table of logarithms. What he had set up on this continent, in brief, was a commonwealth of peasants and small traders, a paradise of the third-rate, and its national philosophy, almost wholly unchecked by the more sophisticated and civilized ideas of an aristocracy, was precisely the philosophy that one finds among peasants and small traders at all times and everywhere.

The difference between the United States and any other nation did not lie in any essential difference between American peasants and other peasants, but simply in the fact that here, alone, the voice of the peasant was the single voice of the nation — that here, alone, the only way to eminence and public influence was the way of acquiescence in the opinions and prejudices of the untutored and Philistine mob. Jackson was the *Stammvater* of the new statesmen and philosophers; he carried the mob's distrust of good taste even into the field of conduct; he was the first to put the rewards of conformity above the dictates of common decency; he founded a whole hierarchy of Philistine messiahs, the roaring of which still belabors the ear.

Once established, this culture of the intellectually disinherited tended to defend and perpetuate itself. On the one hand, there was no appearance of a challenge from within, for the exigent problems of existence in a country that was yet but half-settled and organized left its people with no energy for questioning what at least satisfied their gross needs, and so met the pragmatic test. And on the other hand, there was no criti-

cal pressure from without, for the English culture which alone reached over the sea was itself entering upon its Victorian decline, and the influence of the native aristocracy — the degenerating Junkers of the great estates and the boorish magnates of the city *bourgeoisie* — was quite without any cultural direction at all.

The chief concern of the American people, even above the bread-and-butter question, was politics. They were incessantly hag-ridden by political difficulties, both internal and external, of an inordinate complexity, and these occupied all the leisure they could steal from the sordid work of everyday. More, their new and troubled political ideas tended to absorb all the rancorous certainty of their fading religious ideas, so that devotion to a theory or a candidate became translated into devotion to a revelation, and the game of politics turned itself into a holy war. The custom of connecting purely political doctrines with pietistic concepts of an inflammable nature, then firmly set up by skillful persuaders of the mob, has never quite died out in the United States. There has not been a presidential contest since Jackson's day without its Armageddons, its marching of Christian soldiers, its crosses of gold, its crowns of thorns. The most successful American politicians, beginning with the antislavery agitators, have been those most adept at twisting the ancient gauds and shibboleths of Puritanism to partisan uses. Every campaign that we have seen for eighty years has been, on each side, a pursuit of bugaboos, a denunciation of heresies, a snouting up of immoralities. . . .

THIS IS THE ESSENTIAL FACT of the new Puritanism; its recognition of the moral expert, the professional sinhound, the virtuoso of virtue. Under the original Puritan theocracy, as in Scotland, for example, the chase and punishment of sinners was a purely ecclesiastical function, and during the slow disintegration of the theocracy, the only change introduced was the extension of that function to lay helpers, and finally to the whole body of laymen. This change, however, did not materially corrupt the ecclesiastical quality of the enterprise: the leader in the so-called militant field still remained the same man who led in the spiritual field. But with the capitalization of Puritan effort there came a radical overhauling of method. The secular arm, as it were, conquered as it helped. That is to say, the special business of forcing sinners to be good was taken away from the preachers and put into the hands of laymen trained in its technique and mystery, and there it remains.

The new Puritanism has created an army of gladiators who are not only distinct from the hierarchy but who, in many instances, actually command and intimidate the hierarchy. This is conspicuously evident in the case of the Anti-Saloon League, an enormously effective fighting organization, with a large staff of highly accomplished experts in its service. These experts do not wait for ecclesiastical support, nor even ask for it; they force it. The clergyman who presumes to protest against their war upon the saloon, even upon the quite virtuous ground that it is not effective enough, runs a risk of condign and merciless punishment. So plainly is this understood, indeed, that in more than one state the clergy of the Puritan denominations openly take orders from these specialists in excoriation and court their favor without shame. Here, a single moral enterprise, heavily capitalized and carefully officered, has engulfed the entire Puritan movement, and a part has become more than the whole.

In a dozen other directions this tendency to transform a religious business into a purely secular business, with lay backers and lay officers, is plainly visible. The increasing wealth of Puritanism has not only augmented its scope and its daring but it has also had the effect of attracting clever men, of no particular spiritual enthusiasm, to its service. Moral endeavor, in brief, has become a recognized trade, or rather a profession, and there have appeared men who pretend to a special and enormous knowledge of it; and who show enough truth in their pretension to gain the unlimited support of Puritan capitalists. The vice crusade, to mention one example, has produced a large crop of such self-constituted experts, and some of them are in such demand that they are overwhelmed with engagements.

The majority of these men have wholly lost the flavor of sacerdotalism. They are not pastors but detectives, statisticians, and mob orators, and not infrequently their secularity becomes distressingly evident. Their aim, as they say, is to do things. Assuming that "moral sentiment" is behind them, they override all criticism and opposition without argument, and proceed to the business of dispersing prostitutes, of browbeating and terrorizing weak officials, and of forcing legislation of their own invention through city councils and state legislatures. Their very cocksureness is their chief source of strength. They combat objection with such violence and with such a devastating cynicism that it quickly fades away.

The more astute politicians, in the face of so ruthless a fire, commonly profess conversion and join the colors, just as their brethren went over to Prohibition in the "dry" states, and the newspapers seldom hold out much longer. The result is that the "investigation" of the social evil becomes an orgy, and that the ensuing "report" of the inevitable "vice commission" is made up of two parts sensational fiction and three parts platitude. Of all the vice commissions that have sat of late in the United States, not one has done its work without the aid of these singularly confident experts, and not one has contributed an original and sagacious idea, nor even an idea of ordinary common sense, to the solution of the problem.

I need not go on piling up examples of

this new form of Puritan activity, with its definite departure from a religious foundation and its elaborate development as an everyday business. The impulse behind it I have called a *Wille zur Macht*, a will to power. In terms more homely, it was described by John Fiske as "the disposition to domineer," and, in his usual unerring way, he saw its dependence on the gratuitous assumption of infallibility. But even stronger than the Puritan's belief in his own inspiration is his yearning to make someone jump. In other words, he has an ineradicable liking for cruelty in him; he is a sportsman even before he is a moralist, and very often his blood-lust leads him into lamentable excesses.

The various vice crusades afford innumerable cases in point. In one city, if the press dispatches are to be believed, the proscribed women of the Tenderloin were pursued with such ferocity that seven of them were driven to suicide. And in another city, after a campaign of repression so unfortunate in its effects that there were actually protests against it by clergymen elsewhere, a distinguished (and very friendly) connoisseur of such affairs referred to it ingenuously as more fun "than a fleet of aeroplanes." Such disorderly combats with evil, of course, produce no permanent good. It is a commonplace, indeed, that a city is usually in worse condition after it has been "cleaned up" than it was before, and I need not point to New York, Los Angeles, and Des Moines for the evidence as to the social evil, and to any large city, East, West, North, South, for the evidence as to the saloon.

But the Puritans who finance such enterprises get their thrills, not out of any possible obliteration of vice but out of the galloping pursuit of the vicious. The new Puritan gives no more serious thought to the rights and feelings of his quarry than the gunner gives to the rights and feelings of his birds. From the beginning of the Prohibition campaign, for example, the principle

of compensation has been violently opposed, despite its obvious justice, and a complaisant judiciary has ratified the Puritan position. In England and on the continent that principle is safeguarded by the fundamental laws, and during the early days of the antislavery agitation in this country it was accepted as incontrovertible; but if any American statesman were to propose today that it be applied to the license holder whose lawful franchise has been taken away from him arbitrarily, or to the brewer or distiller whose costly plant has been rendered useless and valueless, he would see the days of his statesmanship brought to a quick and violent close.

But does all this argue a total lack of justice in the American character, or even a lack of common decency? I doubt that it would be well to go so far in accusation. What it does argue is a tendency to put moral considerations above all other considerations and to define morality in the narrow Puritan sense. The American, in other words, thinks that the sinner has no rights that anyone is bound to respect, and he is prone to mistake an unsupported charge of sinning, provided it be made violently enough, for actual proof and confession. What is more, he takes an intense joy in the mere chase: he has the true Puritan taste for an *auto da fé* in him. "I am ag'inst capital punishment," said Mr. Dooley, "but we won't get rid av it so long as the people enjic it so much." But though he is thus an eager spectator, and may even be lured into taking part in the pursuit, the average American is not disposed to initiate it, nor to pay for it. The larger Puritan enterprises of today are not popular in the sense of originating in the bleachers, but only in the sense of being applauded from the bleachers. The burdens of the fray, both of toil and of expense, are always upon a relatively small number of men.

In a state rocked and racked by a war upon the saloon, it was recently shown, for example, that but five percent of the members of the Puritan denominations contributed to the war chest. And yet the Anti-Saloon League of that state was so sure of support from below that it presumed to stand as the spokesman of the whole Christian community, and even ventured to launch excommunications upon contumacious Christians, both lay and clerical, who objected to its methods. Moreover, the great majority of the persons included in the contributing five percent gave no more than a few cents a year. The whole support of the League devolved upon a dozen men, all of them rich and all of them Puritans of purest ray serene. These men supported a costly organization for their private entertainment and stimulation. It was their means of recreation, their sporting club. They were willing to spend a lot of money to procure good sport for themselves — *i.e.,* to procure the best crusading talent available — and they were so successful in that endeavor that they enchanted the populace too, and so shook the state.

Naturally enough, this organization of Puritanism upon a business and sporting basis has had a tendency to attract and create a type of "expert" crusader whose determination to give his employers a good show is uncontaminated by any consideration for the public welfare. The result has been a steady increase of scandals, a constant collapse of moral organizations, a frequent unveiling of whited sepulchers. Various observers have sought to direct the public attention to this significant corruption of the new Puritanism. The *New York Sun*, for example, in the course of a protest against the appointment of a vice commission for New York, has denounced the paid agents of private reform organizations as "notoriously corrupt, undependable, and dishonest," and the Rev. Dr. W. S. Rainsford, supporting the charge, has borne testimony out of his own wide experience to their lawlessness, their absurd pretensions to

special knowledge, their habit of manufacturing evidence, and their devious methods of shutting off criticism. But so far, at all events, no organized war upon them has been undertaken, and they seem to flourish more luxuriantly year after year.

The individual whose common rights are invaded by such persons has little chance of getting justice, and less of getting redress. When he attempts to defend himself he finds that he is opposed, not only by a financial power that is ample for all purposes of the combat and that does not shrink at intimidating juries, prosecuting officers, and judges but also by a shrewdness which shapes the laws to its own uses and takes full advantage of the miserable cowardice of legislatures. The moral gladiators, in brief, know the game. They come before a legislature with a bill ostensibly designed to cure some great and admitted evil, they procure its enactment by scarcely veiled insinuations that all who stand against it must be apologists for the evil itself, and then they proceed to extend its aims by bold inferences, and to dragoon the courts into ratifying those inferences, and to employ it as a means of persecution, terrorism, and blackmail.

The history of the Mann Act offers a shining example of this purpose. It was carried through Congress, over the veto of President Taft, who discerned its extravagance, on the plea that it was needed to put down the traffic in prostitutes; it is enforced today against men who are no more engaged in the traffic in prostitutes than you or I. Naturally enough, the effect of this extension of its purposes, against which its author has publicly protested, has been to make it a truly deadly weapon in the hands of professional Puritans and of denouncers of delinquency even less honest. "Blackmailers of both sexes have arisen," says Mr. Justice McKenna, "using the terrors of the construction now sanctioned by the [Supreme] Court as a help — indeed, the means — for their brigandage. The result is grave and should give us pause."

But that is as far as objection has yet gone; the majority of the learned jurist's colleagues swallowed both the statute and its consequences. There is, indeed, no sign as yet of any organized war upon the alliance between the blackmailing Puritan and the pseudo-Puritan blackmailer. It must wait until a sense of reason and justice shows itself in the American people, strong enough to overcome their prejudice in favor of the moralist, on the one hand, and their delight in barbarous pursuits and punishments, on the other. I see but faint promise of that change today.

24.

Ezra Pound: Two Poems from Exile

Ezra Pound was born in Idaho in 1885. Both of his parents were descended from early New England settlers, the family having undertaken the typical American journey during the nineteenth century, moving ever westward in search of expanding horizons. But the young Pound reversed the trend, as a number of his compatriots were to do during the third decade of the twentieth century. After receiving a master's degree in Romance languages, he traveled in 1906-1907 through Spain, Italy, and Provence, settled for awhile in Venice, and then moved to London, where he began the self-exile that was to endure through the two world wars and beyond. His first important collection of poems, Personae, *appeared in London in 1909;* Lustra with Earlier Poems, *from which the two poems reprinted below are taken, was published in 1917.*

Source: *Lustra with Earlier Poems,* New York, 1917.

ঞ THE REST

O helpless few in my country,
O remnant enslaved!

Artists broken against her,
A-stray, lost in the villages,
Mistrusted, spoken-against,

Lovers of beauty, starved,
Thwarted with systems,
Helpless against the control;

You who cannot wear yourselves out
By persisting to successes,

You who can only speak,
Who cannot steel yourselves into
        reiteration;

You of the finer sense,
Broken against false knowledge,
You who can know at first hand,
Hated, shut in, mistrusted:

Take thought:
I have weathered the storm,
I have beaten out my exile.

⅋ SALUTATION

O generation of the thoroughly smug and thoroughly uncomfortable,
I have seen fishermen picnicking in the sun,
I have seen them with untidy families,
I have seen their smiles full of teeth and heard ungainly laughter.
And I am happier than you are,
And they were happier than I am;
And the fish swim in the lake and do not even own clothing.

25.

Doris Stevens: Suffragettes — Criminals or Political Prisoners?

Several states west of the Mississippi had adopted woman suffrage amendments by 1917, but in the East the movement had been less successful. President Wilson was opposed to women voting, but sidestepped the issue by saying it was a problem for the states. The suffragettes in national and local organizations campaigned, paraded, and picketed, especially in Washington, D.C. Occasionally the pickets were arrested as a public nuisance and put in jail. When this happened, they demanded not to be regarded as ordinary lawbreakers but as political prisoners. The following selection by Doris Stevens, describing the attitudes of some jailed suffragettes in 1917, includes a letter of protest to the commissioners of the District of Columbia.

Source: *Jailed for Freedom,* New York, 1920, pp. 175-178.

FINDING THAT A SUFFRAGE COMMITTEE in the House and a report in the Senate had not silenced our banners, the administration cast about for another plan by which to stop the picketing. This time they turned desperately to longer terms of imprisonment. They were, indeed, hard pressed when they could choose such a cruel and stupid course.

Our answer to this policy was more women on the picket line on the outside, and a protest on the inside of prison.

We decided, in the face of extended imprisonment, to demand to be treated as political prisoners. We felt that, as a matter of principle, this was the dignified and self-respecting thing to do, since we had offended politically, not criminally. We believed further that a determined, organized effort to make clear to a wider public the political nature of the offense would intensify the administration's embarrassment and so accelerate their final surrender.

It fell to Lucy Burns, vice-chairman of the organization, to be the leader of the new protest. Miss Burns is in appearance the very symbol of woman in revolt. Her abundant and glorious red hair burns and is not consumed — a flaming torch. Her body is strong and vital. It is said that Lucy

Stone had the "voice" of the pioneers. Lucy Burns without doubt possessed the "voice" of the modern suffrage movement. Musical, appealing, persuading — she could move the most resistant person. Her talent as an orator is of the kind that makes for instant intimacy with her audience. Her emotional quality is so powerful that her intellectual capacity, which is quite as great, is not always at once perceived. . . .

She had no sooner begun to organize her comrades for protest than the officials sensed a "plot" and removed her at once to solitary confinement. But they were too late. Taking the leader only hastened the rebellion. A forlorn piece of paper was discovered on which was written their initial demand. It was then passed from prisoner to prisoner through holes in the wall surrounding leaden pipes, until a finished document had been perfected and signed by all the prisoners.

This historic document — historic because it represents the first organized group action ever made in America to establish the status of political prisoners — said:

To the Commissioners of the District of Columbia:

As political prisoners, we, the undersigned, refuse to work while in prison. We have taken this stand as a matter of principle after careful consideration, and from it we shall not recede.

This action is a necessary protest against an unjust sentence: In reminding President Wilson of his preelection promises toward woman suffrage, we were exercising the right of peaceful petition, guaranteed by the Constitution of the United States, which declares peaceful picketing is legal in the District of Columbia. That we are unjustly sentenced has been well recognized — when President Wilson pardoned the first group of suffragists who had been given sixty days in the workhouse, and again when Judge Mullowny suspended sentence for the last group of picketers. We wish to point out the inconsistency and injustice of our sentences — some of us have been given sixty days, a later group, thirty days, and another group given a suspended sentence for exactly the same action.

Conscious, therefore, of having acted in accordance with the highest standards of citizenship, we ask the commissioners of the District to grant us the rights due political prisoners. We ask that we no longer be segregated and confined under locks and bars in small groups, but permitted to see each other, and that Miss Lucy Burns, who is in full sympathy with this letter, be released from solitary confinement in another building and given back to us.

We ask exemption from prison work, that our legal right to consult counsel be recognized, to have food sent to us from outside, to supply ourselves with writing material for as much correspondence as we may need, to receive books, letters, newspapers, our relatives and friends.

Our united demand for political treatment has been delayed, because, on entering the workhouse, we found conditions so very bad that, before we could ask that the suffragists be treated as political prisoners, it was necessary to make a stand for the ordinary rights of human beings for all the inmates. Although this has not been accomplished, we now wish to bring the important question of the status of political prisoners to the attention of the commissioners, who, we are informed, have full authority to make what regulations they please for the District prison and workhouse.

The commissioners are requested to send us a written reply so that we may be sure this protest has reached them. . . .

The commissioners' only answer to this was a hasty transfer of the signers and the leader, Miss Burns, to the District jail, where they were put in solitary confinement. The women were not only refused the privileges asked but were denied some of the usual privileges allowed to ordinary criminals.

26.

Theodore Roosevelt: The Children of the Crucible

Hours before Woodrow Wilson delivered his war message to Congress he confided to a friend his fear that war would bring "illiberalism at home." He was right: war hysteria had attained serious proportions even before the end of 1917. Anyone with a German-sounding name was suspected of disloyalty, and radical journals that made any kind of sympathetic reference to a negotiated settlement along the lines recommended by the Bolsheviks in Russia were likely to have their presses confiscated and their offices closed. For a time Theodore Roosevelt joined in the hue and cry. He drafted the statement reprinted below on September 11, 1917. It was signed by prominent persons of foreign descent who took this opportunity to declare their undying allegiance to the United States, and to renounce all ties to their country of origin.

Source: *America at War*, Albert B. Hart, ed., New York, 1918, pp. 314-316.

We Americans are the children of the crucible. It has been our boast that out of the crucible, the melting pot of life in this free land, all the men and women of all the nations who come hither emerge as Americans and as nothing else; Americans who proudly challenge as a right, not as a favor, that they "belong" just exactly as much as any other Americans and that they stand on a full and complete equality with them. Americans, therefore, who must even more strongly insist that they have renounced completely and without reserve all allegiance to the lands from which they or their forefathers came, and that it is a binding duty on every citizen of this country in every important crisis to act solidly with all his fellow Americans, having regard only to the honor and interest of America and treating every other nation purely on its conduct in that crisis, without reference to his ancestral predilections or antipathies. If he does not so act, he is false to the teachings and the lives of Washington and Lincoln; he is not entitled to any part or lot in our country; and he should be sent out of

it. If he does not act purely as an American, he shows that in his case the crucible has failed to do its work.

The crucible must melt all who are cast in it; it must turn them out in one American mold; and this must be the mold shaped 140 years ago by the men who under Washington founded this as a free nation, separate from all others. Even at that time, true Americans were of many different race strains; Paul Revere and Charles Carroll, Marion, Herkimer, Sullivan, Schuyler, and Muhlenberg stood on an equality of service and achieved respect with "Lighthorse Harry" Lee and Israel Putnam. But the majority of the leaders and of their followers were of English blood. They did not, because of this, hesitate to resist and antagonize Great Britain when Great Britain wronged this nation; they stood for liberty and for the eternal rule of right and justice and they stood as Americans and as nothing else.

All Americans of other race origin must act toward the countries from which their ancestors severally sprang as Washington and his associates in their day acted. Otherwise they are traitors to America. This applies especially today to all Americans of German blood who directly or indirectly in any manner support Germany as against the United States and the allies of the United States; it applies no less specifically to all American citizens of Irish blood who are led into following the same course, not by their love of Germany but by their hatred of England. One motive is as inexcusable as the other; and in each case the action is treasonable to the United States.

The professional pacifists have, during the last three years, proved themselves the evil enemies of their country. They now advocate an inconclusive peace. In so doing they have shown themselves to be the spiritual heirs of the Tories who in the name of peace opposed Washington, and of the "Copperheads" who in the name of peace opposed Lincoln. We regard these men and women as traitors to the republic; we regard them as traitors to the great cause of justice and humanity. This war is a war for the vital interests of America. When we fight for America abroad we save our children from fighting for America at home beside their own ruined hearthstones.

We believe that the large majority of Americans are proudly ready to fight to the last for the overthrow of the brutal German militarism which threatens America no less than every other civilized nation. We believe that it would be an act of baseness and infamy, an act of unworthy cowardice, and a betrayal of this country and of mankind to accept any peace except the peace of overwhelming victory, a peace based on the complete overthrow of the Prussianized Germany of the Hohenzollerns.

We hold that the true test of loyal Americanism today is effective service against Germany. We should exert as speedily as possible every particle of our vast lazy strength to win the triumph over Germany. Therefore we should demand that the government act at once with unrelenting severity against the traitors here at home, whether their treasonable activity take the form of editing and publishing newspapers, of uttering speeches, or of intrigue and conspiracy.

We must have but one flag. We must also have but one language. That must be the language of the Declaration of Independence, of Washington's Farewell Address, of Lincoln's Gettysburg Speech and Second Inaugural. We cannot tolerate any attempt to oppose or supplant the language and culture that has come down to us from the builders of this republic with the language and culture of any European country. The greatness of this nation depends on the swift assimilation of the aliens she welcomes to her shores. Any force which attempts to retard that assimilative process is a force hostile to the highest interests of our country. It is a force, which, if allowed to develop, will, for the benefit of this group or that, undermine our national institutions and pervert our national ideals.

Whatever may have been our judgment in normal times, we are convinced that today our most dangerous foe is the foreign-language press and every similar agency, such as the German-American Alliance, which holds the alien to his former associations and through them to his former allegiance. We call upon all loyal and unadulterated Americans to man the trenches against the enemy within our gates.

We ask that good Americans . . . uphold the hands of the government at every point efficiently and resolutely against our foreign and domestic foes, and that they constantly spur the government to speedier and more effective action. Furthermore, we ask that, where governmental action cannot be taken, they arouse an effective and indignant public opinion against the enemies of our country, whether these enemies masquerade as pacifists, or proclaim themselves the enemies of our allies, or act through organizations such as the I. W. W. and the Socialist Party machine, or appear nakedly as the champions of Germany. Above all, we ask that they teach our people to spurn any peace save the peace of overwhelming victory in the war to which we have set our hands.

Of us who sign, some are Protestants, some are Catholics, some are Jews. Most of us were born in this country of parents born in various countries of the Old World — in Germany, France, England, Ireland, Italy, the Slavonic and the Scandinavian lands; some of us were born abroad; some of us are of Revolutionary stock. All of us are Americans, and nothing but Americans.

27.

CHARLES A. BEARD: Reasons for His Resignation from Columbia University

The patriotic hysteria that swept the nation after war was declared in 1917 demanded unquestioned support of government policies from all segments of the community, on pain of ostracism and, in some cases, even loss of a job. Perhaps because of the long tradition of academic freedom in America, university faculties reacted to such demands with singular bitterness. When Henry W. L. Dana, an avowed pacifist who worked for the peace movement, was asked to leave Columbia University because of his political beliefs, Professor Charles A. Beard, whose Economic Interpretation of the Constitution *(1913) had brought him national recognition, resigned in protest. His statement was published in the* New Republic *and is reprinted here.*

Source: *New Republic*, December 29, 1917.

IT HAS BEEN INSINUATED by certain authorities of Columbia University that I resigned in a fit of unjustified petulance, and I therefore beg to submit the following statement:

1. My first real experience with the inner administration of the university came with the retirement of Prof. John W. Burgess. For some time before his withdrawal, his work in American constitutional law had been carried by Professor X and it was the desire of the members of the faculty that the latter should be appointed Ruggles Professor to succeed Mr. Burgess. But Mr. X had published a book in which he justified criticism of the Supreme Court as a means of bringing our constitutional law into harmony with our changing social and economic life. He was therefore excluded from the Ruggles professorship. It was given to

Mr. W. D. Guthrie, a successful corporation lawyer, and a partner of one of the trustees of the university.

It was understood that Mr. Guthrie should give one lecture a week for one semester each year in return for the high honor. Mr. Butler is constantly saying that all matters relating to appointment, fitness, and tenure are left to the appropriate faculties, or words to this effect. As a matter of plain fact, the Faculty of Political Science as such was not consulted in advance in the selection of the Ruggles Professor. The whole affair was settled by backstairs negotiation, and it was understood by all of us who had any part in the business that no person with progressive or liberal views would be acceptable.

Mr. Guthrie was duly appointed. Of his

contributions to learning I shall not speak, but I can say that he did not attend faculty meetings, help in conducting doctors' examinations, or assume the burdens imposed upon other professors. This was the way in which the first important vacancy in the Faculty of Political Science was filled after my connection with 'the institution.

2. My second experience with the administration of the university came in 1916. On April 21 of that year I delivered an address before the National Conference of Community Centers in which I advocated the use of the schools as the centers for the discussion of public questions. A few weeks before, a speaker at one of the school forums was alleged to have said, "To hell with the flag," and for that reason a number of persons had urged the closing of school centers altogether. Indeed, some of the speakers at the above-mentioned conference advocated a sort of censorship for all school forums.

In my address I merely took the reasonable and moderate view that the intemperance of one man should not drive us into closing the schools to others. The reports in the newspapers, with one exception, were fairly accurate. But one sensational sheet accused me of approving the sentiment, "To hell with the flag." Dr. Butler, who had had large experience with frenzied journalism, quite rightly took the view that I had been the victim of the headline writer and advised me to do my best to correct the wrong impression and then forget it. I immediately wrote to all of the papers and sought to remove the misunderstanding that had arisen.

Nevertheless, I was summoned before the Committee on Education of the Board of Trustees. I complied because I wanted to clear up any wrong impressions which the members entertained concerning the nature of my address before the Community Center Conference.

As soon as the committee of the trustees opened the inquiry, I speedily disposed of the "flag incident" by showing that I had said nothing that could be construed as endorsing in any way the objectionable language in question. No one doubted my word. Indeed, I had available abundant testimony from reliable men and women who had heard the address. The record was thus soon set straight.

The inquiry as to the flag incident being at an end I prepared to leave the room when I was utterly astonished to have Mr. Bangs and Mr. Coudert launch into an inquisition into my views and teachings. For half an hour I was "grilled" by these gentlemen. Dr. Butler and certain colleagues from the Faculty of Political Science (who were present at the inquisition) made no attempt to stop the proceedings. Mr. Coudert, who had once privately commended my book on the Constitution as "admirably well done," and opening up "a most fertile field," denounced my teachings in vigorous language, in which he was strongly seconded by Mr. Bangs.

I realize now that I should have refused to remain in the room, but I was taken unaware and stunned by the procedure. When the inquisitors satisfied themselves, the chairman of the committee ordered me to warn all other men in my department against teachings "likely to inculcate disrespect for American institutions." I repeated my order to my colleagues, who received it with a shout of derision, one of them asking me whether Tammany Hall and the pork barrel were not American institutions!

I reported to my colleagues in the Faculty of Political Science that I had been subjected by the committee of the trustees to a "general doctrinal inquisition," and urged them, at an informal meeting, to establish a rule that a professor should be examined in matters of opinion only by his peers, namely, men of standing in his profession. Several caucuses of the faculty were held and it was generally agreed that the proceedings of the trustees were highly reprehensible. Action doubtless should have been taken by the faculty at the time if we had not been told by Dean Woodbridge that "the trustees had learned their lesson and that such an inquisition would never happen again."

We were also informed that some of the trustees were "after" President Butler for his pacifist writings and affiliations, and that if the faculty took a firm stand in matters of doctrinal inquisition an open conflict might ensue. In a long conversation President Butler urged me to drop the whole "miserable business" and go on about my work. For the sake of "peace" I consented.

I should not forget, however, the cases of Professor Kendrick and Dr. Fraser, who had been haled before the committee of the trustees on the trivial charge that they had criticized Plattsburg and military discipline at a student meeting some time early in 1916. Their cases I regarded as peculiarly open to objection because they were not even accused of saying anything that was indecent or vulgar or unpatriotic. Nevertheless, I dropped the whole matter on the assurance that such an inquisition would not happen again and that the trustees "had learned their lesson."

3. Though I did not agree with some of my exuberant colleagues that a "great battle for academic freedom had been won," I was ready to abide by their decision. Then, to our utter astonishment, the trustees at their March meeting in 1917 gave to the press a set of resolutions instructing a committee "to inquire and ascertain" whether certain doctrines were being taught in the university. President Butler, in whose name we had been assured that no such inquisition would ever happen again, avoided the issue by taking a vacation and leaving the faculties to deal with the situation.

The action of the Faculty of Political Science was prompt. An informal meeting was held at which a resolution in the following tenor was unanimously adopted:

Whereas the resolution of the trustees by its very terms implies a general doctrinal inquisition, insults the members of the faculty by questioning their loyalty to their country, violates every principle of academic freedom, and betrays a profound misconception of the true function of the university in the advancement of learning, *Be it resolved* that we will not individually or collectively lend any countenance to such an inquiry.

The trustees were forced to abandon their plan for a general inquisition. Indeed, when they learned of the spirit of the Faculty of Political Science and other faculties, they hastily disclaimed any intention of making a "doctrinal inquiry" — as their resolution of March 1917 clearly implied.

It was agreed that such matters should be handled in cooperation with a committee of nine representing the faculties.

4. Notwithstanding this promise of cooperation on the part of the trustees and the committee of nine representing the teaching force, the trustees ignored the recommendations of that committee in the cases of Professors Dana and Cattell and dismissed these gentlemen summarily in the autumn of 1917, after wrongfully charging them with treason and sedition. Prof. John Dewey resigned from the committee of nine, and the body which was to safeguard the interests of the professors collapsed in ignominy.

5. Some time before Professors Cattell and Dana were expelled, another professor was summarily thrown out of the university without warning or trial. No reasons for his expulsion were advanced, and a polite inquiry addressed by his colleagues to President Butler asking for information remained unanswered.

6. Dr. Leon Fraser was an instructor in politics in Columbia College. With this office he combined that of assistant to Dean Keppel and Dr. Butler in the Association for International Conciliation. Dr. Fraser was assigned the task of organizing forces in colleges throughout the country on pacifism and international conciliation. In other words, he was paid by these gentlemen to engage in pacifist propaganda. In a moment of youthful enthusiasm, early in 1916, Dr.

Fraser made some critical remark about the military camp at Plattsburg. For this he was haled before a committee of the trustees.

A year later, namely in the spring of 1917, my department was warned not to renominate Dr. Fraser for reappointment because he was not acceptable to Mr. Bangs, one of the trustees. In spite of our orders we did renominate Dr. Fraser, but before action could be taken by the trustees, he, along with other instructors, was dropped on the assumption that the war would reduce materially the number of students in the college. But not content with dropping him, Mr. Butler informed the college authorities that in case the attendance in the college in the autumn warranted the appointment of additional instructors, under no circumstances should Dr. Fraser be renominated.

In truth, therefore, if not in theory, Dr. Fraser was expelled from the college without notice or hearing. In view of the fact that Mr. Fraser had been inspired by Mr. Butler and Mr. Keppel to engage in pacifist propaganda and had been paid by them for doing it, it seemed to me that they should at least have demanded and insisted upon having a full and fair hearing of the charges against their youthful adherent, especially as those charges grew out of his "pacifist teachings."

7. We are informed by Dr. Butler that nominations for appointment and promotions come from the faculties. Such may be the theory but it is the practice for the trustees and president to warn the committee in charge of appointments and promotions against recommending "unacceptable" persons. For example, when the committee on instruction of the Faculty of Political Science, of which I was a member, was considering promotions last spring, it was informed at the outset by "the committee of one on rumor from the president's office" that "certain of the trustees" would not approve the promotion of Professor Y because he had used "disrespectful language" in speaking of the Supreme Court. Professor Y was not recommended for promotion and the trustees could proudly say that they had not rejected a faculty recommendation!

Mr. Butler cannot conceive of a scholar's entertaining progressive ideas. Once, in asking me to recommend an instructor to a neighboring college, he distinctly pointed out that a man of "Bull Moose" proclivities would not be acceptable.

8. Early in October 1917, I was positively and clearly informed by two responsible officers of the university that another doctrinal inquisition was definitely scheduled for an early date. It was the evident purpose of a small group of the trustees (unhindered, if not aided, by Mr. Butler) to take advantage of the state of war to drive out or humiliate or terrorize every man who held progressive, liberal, or unconventional views on political matters in no way connected with the war. The institution was to be reduced below the level of a department store or factory, and I therefore tendered my resignation.

I make no claims in behalf of academic freedom, though I think they are worthy of consideration: I have merely held that teachers should not be expelled without a full and fair hearing by their peers, surrounded by all of the safeguards of judicial process. Professors in Columbia University have been subjected to humiliating doctrinal inquisitions by the trustees, they have been expelled without notice or hearing, and their appointment and promotion depend upon securing, in advance, the favor of certain trustees. Without that favor, scholarship and learning avail nothing.

These facts I submit to the candid and impartial reader. I believe that they constitute a full and unanswerable indictment of the prevailing method at Columbia University under the administration of Dr. Nicholas Murray Butler.

1918

28.

RANDOLPH BOURNE: War as the Health of the State

Randolph Bourne, whose pacifist writings were published posthumously in Untimely
Papers *(1919), was one of the most persistent critics of U.S. participation in
the First World War. While many intellectuals, most notably Bourne's mentor
John Dewey, acknowledged the need for U.S. involvement, Bourne never reconciled
himself to engaging in war for any reason. In the following essay, begun in the winter
of 1918 but never completed, Bourne sardonically described the role that war played
in maintaining the health of a state. The human traits that were maximally utilized
during wartime were, to Bourne, the worst traits of the species. In the portion of the
essay reprinted here, Bourne's biting criticism reflects a lonely intellectual's appeal
for sanity during a period of excessive and intolerant patriotism.*

Source: *Untimely Papers,* James Oppenheim, ed., New York, 1919:
"Unfinished Fragment on the State."

GOVERNMENT IS SYNONYMOUS with neither
State nor Nation. It is the machinery by
which the nation, organized as a State, carries out its State functions. Government is a
framework of the administration of laws
and the carrying out of the public force.
Government is the idea of the State put
into practical operation in the hands of definite, concrete, fallible men. It is the visible
sign of the invisible grace. It is the word
made flesh. And it has necessarily the limitations inherent in all practicality. Government is the only form in which we can en-
visage the State, but it is by no means identical with it. That the State is a mystical
conception is something that must never be
forgotten. Its glamor and its significance lin-

ger behind the framework of Government
and direct its activities.

Wartime brings the ideal of the State out
into very clear relief, and reveals attitudes
and tendencies that were hidden. In times
of peace the sense of the State flags in a
republic that is not militarized. For war is
essentially the health of the State. The ideal
of the State is that within its territory its
power and influence should be universal. As
the Church is the medium for the spiritual
salvation of man, so the State is thought of
as the medium for his political salvation. Its
idealism is a rich blood flowing to all the
members of the body politic. And it is precisely in war that the urgency for union

seems greatest and the necessity for universality seems most unquestioned.

The State is the organization of the herd to act offensively or defensively against another herd similarly organized. The more terrifying the occasion for defense, the closer will become the organization and the more coercive the influence upon each member of the herd. War sends the current of purpose and activity flowing down to the lowest level of the herd and to its most remote branches. All the activities of society are linked together as fast as possible to this central purpose of making a military offensive or a military defense, and the State becomes what in peacetimes it has vainly struggled to become — the inexorable arbiter and determinant of men's businesses and attitudes and opinions. . . .

The classes which are able to play an active and not merely a passive role in the organization for war get a tremendous liberation of activity and energy. Individuals are jolted out of their old routine; many of them are given new positions of responsibility; new techniques must be learned. Wearing home ties are broken and women who would have remained attached with infantile bonds are liberated for service overseas. A vast sense of rejuvenescence pervades the significant classes, a sense of new importance in the world. Old national ideals are taken out, readapted to the purpose, and used as universal touchstones or molds into which all thought is poured.

Every individual citizen who in peacetimes had no function to perform by which he could imagine himself an expression or living fragment of the State becomes an active amateur agent of the Government in reporting spies and disloyalists, in raising Government funds, or in propagating such measures as are considered necessary by officialdom. Minority opinion, which in times of peace, was only irritating and could not be dealt with by law unless it was conjoined with actual crime, becomes, with the outbreak of war, a case for outlawry. Criticism of the State, objections to war, lukewarm opinions concerning the necessity or the beauty of conscription are made subject to ferocious penalties, far exceeding in severity those affixed to actual pragmatic crimes. Public opinion, as expressed in the newspapers and the pulpits and the schools becomes one solid block.

"Loyalty," or rather war orthodoxy, becomes the sole test for all professions, techniques, occupations. Particularly is this true in the sphere of the intellectual life. There the smallest taint is held to spread over the whole soul, so that a professor of physics is *ipso facto* disqualified to teach physics or to hold honorable place in a university — the republic of learning — if he is at all unsound on the war. Even mere association with persons thus tainted is considered to disqualify a teacher. Anything pertaining to the enemy becomes taboo. His books are suppressed wherever possible, his language is forbidden. His artistic products are considered to convey in the subtlest spiritual way taints of vast poison to the soul that permits itself to enjoy them. So enemy music is suppressed, and energetic measures of opprobrium taken against those whose artistic consciences are not ready to perform such an act of self-sacrifice.

The rage for loyal conformity works impartially, and often in diametric opposition to other orthodoxies and traditional conformities, or even ideals. The triumphant orthodoxy of the State is shown at its apex perhaps when Christian preachers lose their pulpits for taking in more or less literal terms the Sermon on the Mount, and Christian zealots are sent to prison for twenty years for distributing tracts which argue that war is unscriptural.

War is the health of the State. It automatically sets in motion throughout society those irresistible forces for uniformity, for passionate cooperation with the Government in coercing into obedience the minority groups and individuals which lack the larger herd sense. The machinery of government sets and enforces the drastic penalties, the minorities are either intimidated into silence, or brought slowly around by a subtle process of persuasion which may seem to them really to be converting them. Of course the ideal of perfect loyalty, perfect uniformity is never really attained. The classes upon whom the amateur work of coercion falls are unwearied in their zeal, but often their agitation instead of converting merely serves to stiffen their resistance.

Minorities are rendered sullen, and some intellectual opinion bitter and satirical. But in general, the nation in wartime attains a uniformity of feeling, a hierarchy of values culminating at the undisputed apex of the State ideal, which could not possibly be produced through any other agency than war. Other values such as artistic creation, knowledge, reason, beauty, the enhancement of life are instantly and almost unanimously sacrificed, and the significant classes who have constituted themselves the amateur agents of the State are engaged not only in sacrificing these values for themselves but in coercing all other persons into sacrificing them.

War — or at least modern war waged by a democratic republic against a powerful enemy — seems to achieve for a nation almost all that the most inflamed political idealist could desire. Citizens are no longer indifferent to their Government, but each cell of the body politic is brimming with life and activity. We are at last on the way to full realization of that collective community in which each individual somehow contains the virtue of the whole. In a nation at war, every citizen identifies himself with the whole, and feels immensely strengthened in that identification. The purpose and desire of the collective community lives in each person who throws himself wholeheartedly into the cause of war. The impeding distinction between society and the individual is almost blotted out.

At war, the individual becomes almost identical with his society. He achieves a su-perb self-assurance, an intuition of the rightness of all his ideas and emotions, so that in the suppression of opponents or heretics he is invincibly strong; he feels behind him all the power of the collective community. The individual as social being in war seems to have achieved almost his apotheosis. Not for any religious impulse could the American nation have been expected to show such devotion en masse, such sacrifice and labor. Certainly not for any secular good, such as universal education or the subjugation of nature, would it have poured forth its treasure and its life, or would it have permitted such stern coercive measures to be taken against it, such as conscripting its money and its men. But for the sake of a war of offensive self-defense, undertaken to support a difficult cause to the slogan of "democracy," it would reach the highest level ever known of collective effort.

For these secular goods, connected with the enhancement of life, the education of man and the use of the intelligence to realize reason and beauty in the nation's communal living are alien to our traditional ideal of the State. The State is intimately connected with war, for it is the organization of the collective community when it acts in a political manner, and to act in a political manner toward a rival group has meant, throughout all history — war.

There is nothing invidious in the use of the term "herd" in connection with the State. It is merely an attempt to reduce closer to first principles the nature of this institution in the shadow of which we all live, move, and have our being. Ethnologists are generally agreed that human society made its first appearance as the human pack and not as a collection of individuals or of couples. The herd is in fact the original unit, and only as it was differentiated did personal individuality develop. All the most primitive surviving tribes of men are shown to live in a very complex but very rigid social organization where opportunity for individuation is scarcely given. These tribes remain strictly organized herds, and the difference between them and the modern State is one of degree of sophistication and variety of organization, and not of kind. . . . This gregarious impulse is the tendency to imitate, to conform, to coalesce together, and is most powerful when the herd believes itself threatened. . . .

It would be quite enough if we were gregarious enough to enjoy the companionship of others, to be able to cooperate with them, and to feel a slight malaise at solitude. Unfortunately, however, this impulse is not content with these reasonable and healthful demands, but insists that likemindedness shall prevail everywhere, in all departments of life. So that all human progress, all novelty, and nonconformity must be carried against the resistance of this tyrannical herd-instinct which drives the individual into obedience and conformity with the majority. Even in the most modern and enlightened societies this impulse shows little sign of abating. As it is driven by inexorable economic demand out of the sphere of utility, it seems to fasten itself ever more fiercely in the realm of feeling and opinion, so that conformity comes to be a thing aggressively desired and demanded. . . .

Joining as it does to these very vigorous tendencies of the individual — the pleasure in power and the pleasure in obedience — this gregarious impulse becomes irresistible in society. War stimulates it to the highest possible degree, sending the influences of its mysterious herd-current with its inflations of power and obedience to the farthest reaches of the society, to every individual and little group that can possibly be affected. And it is these impulses which the State — the organization of the entire herd, the entire collectivity — is founded on and makes use of. . . .

The members of the working classes, that portion at least which does not identify itself with the significant classes and seek to imitate it and rise to it, are notoriously less affected by the symbolism of the State, or, in other words, are less patriotic than the significant classes. For theirs is neither the power nor the glory. The State in wartime does not offer them the opportunity to regress, for, never having acquired social adulthood, they cannot lose it. If they have been drilled and regimented, as by the industrial regime of the last century, they go out docilely enough to do battle for their State, but they are almost entirely without that filial sense and even without that herd-intellect sense which operates so powerfully among their "betters."

They live habitually in an industrial serfdom, by which, though nominally free, they are in practice as a class bound to a system of machine production, the implements of which they do not own, and in the distribution of whose product they have not the slightest voice, except what they can occasionally exert by a veiled intimidation which draws slightly more of the product in their direction. From such serfdom, military conscription is not so great a change. But into the military enterprise they go, not with those hurrahs of the significant classes whose instincts war so powerfully feeds but with the same apathy with which they enter and continue in the industrial enterprise.

From this point of view, war can be called almost an upper-class sport. The novel interests and excitements it provides, the inflations of power, the satisfaction it gives to those very tenacious human impulses — gregariousness and parent-regression — endow it with all the qualities of a luxurious collective game which is felt intensely just in proportion to the sense of significant rule the person has in the class division of his society. A country at war — particularly our own country at war — does not act as a purely homogeneous herd. The significant classes have all the herd-feeling in all its primitive intensity, but there are barriers, or at least differentials of intensity, so that this feeling does not flow freely without impediment throughout the entire nation. A modern country represents a long historical and social process of disaggregation of the herd. . . .

War, which should be the health of the State, unifies all the bourgeois elements and the common people, and outlaws the rest. [That] the revolutionary proletariat shows more resistance to this unification, is, as we have seen, psychically out of the current. Its vanguard, as the I.W.W., is remorselessly pursued, in spite of the proof that it is a symptom, not a cause, and its prosecution increases the disaffection of labor and intensifies the friction instead of lessening it.

But the emotions that play around the defense of the State do not take into consideration the pragmatic results. A nation at war, led by its significant classes, is engaged in liberating certain of its impulses which have had all too little exercise in the past. It is getting certain satisfactions and the actual conduct of the war or the condition of the country are really incidental to the enjoyment of new forms of virtue and power and aggressiveness. If it could be shown conclusively that the persecution of slightly disaffected elements actually increased enormously the difficulties of production and the organization of the war technique, it would be found that public policy would scarcely change. The significant classes must have their pleasure in hunting down and chastising everything that they feel instinctively to be not imbued with the current State-enthusiasm, though the State itself be actually impeded in its efforts to carry out those objects for which they are passionately contending.

The best proof of this is that with a pursuit of plotters that has continued with ceaseless vigilance ever since the beginning of the war in Europe, the concrete crimes unearthed and punished have been fewer than those prosecutions for the mere crime of opinion or the expression of sentiments critical of the State or the national policy. The punishment for opinion has been far more ferocious and unintermittent than the punishment of pragmatic crime. Unim-

peachable Anglo-Saxon Americans, who were freer of pacifist or socialist utterance than the State-obsessed ruling public opinion, received heavier penalties and even greater opprobrium, in many instances, than the definitely hostile German plotter. A public opinion which, almost without protest, accepts as just, adequate, beautiful, deserved and in fitting harmony with ideals of liberty and freedom of speech, a sentence of twenty years in prison for mere utterances, no matter what they may be, shows itself to be suffering from a kind of social derangement of values, a sort of social neurosis, that deserves analysis and comprehension. . . .

The moment war is declared . . . the mass of the people, through some spiritual alchemy, become convinced that they have willed and executed the deed themselves. They then, with the exception of a few malcontents, proceed to allow themselves to be regimented, coerced, deranged in all the environments of their lives, and turned into a solid manufactory of destruction toward whatever other people may have, in the appointed scheme of things, come within the range of the Government's disapprobation. The citizen throws off his contempt and indifference to Government, identifies himself with its purposes, revives all his military memories and symbols, and the State once more walks, an august presence, through the imaginations of men. Patriotism becomes the dominant feeling, and produces immediately that intense and hopeless confusion between the relations which the individual bears and should bear toward the society of which he is a part.

The patriot loses all sense of the distinction between State, nation, and government. In our quieter moments, the Nation or Country forms the basic idea of society. We think vaguely of a loose population spreading over a certain geographical portion of the earth's surface, speaking a common language, and living in a homogeneous civilization. Our idea of Country concerns itself with the nonpolitical aspects of a people, its ways of living, its personal traits, its literature and art, its characteristic attitudes toward life. We are Americans because we live in a certain bounded territory, because our ancestors have carried on a great enterprise of pioneering and colonization, because we live in certain kinds of communities which have a certain look and express their aspirations in certain ways.

We can see that our civilization is different from contiguous civilizations like the Indian and Mexican. The institutions of our country form a certain network which affects us vitally and intrigues our thoughts in a way that these other civilizations do not. We are a part of Country, for better or for worse. We have arrived in it through the operation of physiological laws, and not in any way through our own choice. By the time we have reached what are called years of discretion, its influences have molded our habits, our values, our ways of thinking, so that however aware we may become, we never really lose the stamp of our civilization, or could be mistaken for the child of any other country.

Our feeling for our fellow countrymen is one of similarity or of mere acquaintance. We may be intensely proud of and congenial to our particular network of civilization, or we may detest most of its qualities and rage at its defects. This does not alter the fact that we are inextricably bound up in it. The Country, as an inescapable group into which we are born, and which makes us its particular kind of a citizen of the world, seems to be a fundamental fact of our consciousness, an irreducible minimum of social feeling.

29.

Songs of World War I

It has been said that every war produces its songs that reflect the feelings of the participants, but, if so, it is hard — at least on the basis of these three famous songs of World War I — to determine just what Americans really felt about the conflict. "Hinky Dinky Parlay-Voo" was probably American in origin, but it was sung with equal enthusiasm by British troops. "Would You Rather Be a Colonel with an Eagle on Your Shoulder, Or a Private with a Chicken on Your Knee?" (it may be the longest title that any song ever had) can be compared to the Civil War song "The Brass-Mounted Army." Both extoll the freedom of the man at the beginning, not the end, of the chain of command. "K-K-K-Katy" is sheer nonsense — but nevertheless fun.

HINKY DINKY PARLAY-VOO

Mademoiselle from Armentiers, parlay-voo,
Mademoiselle from Armentiers, parlay-voo,
Mademoiselle from Armentiers,
She hasn't been kissed in forty years.
  Hinky dinky parlay-voo.

Farmer, have you a daughter fair,
  parlay-voo,
Farmer, have you a daughter fair,
  parlay-voo,
Farmer, have you a daughter fair
To wash a poor soldier's underwear?
  Hinky dinky parlay-voo.

Mademoiselle from Armentiers, parlay-voo,
Mademoiselle from Armentiers, parlay-voo,
Mademoiselle from Armentiers,
She never did hear of underwear.
   Hinky dinky parlay-voo.

Officers came across the Rhine, parlay-voo,
Officers came across the Rhine, parlay-voo,
Officers came across the Rhine
To kiss all the girls and drink the wine.
   Hinky dinky parlay-voo.

One night I had some "beaucoup" jack,
  parlay-voo,
One night I had some "beaucoup" jack,
  parlay-voo,

One night I had some "beaucoup" jack,
Till mademoiselle got on my track.
   Hinky dinky parlay-voo.

You may forget the gas and shells, parlay-voo,
You may forget the gas and shells, parlay-voo,
You may forget the gas and shells —
You'll never forget the mad'moiselles.
   Hinky dinky parlay-voo.

Mademoiselle heard cannon roar, parlay-voo,
Mademoiselle heard cannon roar, parlay-voo,
Mademoiselle heard cannon roar,
But all that we heard was "je t'adore."
   Hinky dinky parlay-voo.

WOULD YOU RATHER BE A COLONEL WITH AN EAGLE ON YOUR SHOULDER, OR A PRIVATE WITH A CHICKEN ON YOUR KNEE?

Once I heard a father ask his soldier son,
"Why can't you advance like other boys have done?
You've been a private mighty long,
Won't you tell me what is wrong?"
And then the soldier lad said, "Listen to me, Dad:

"I'd rather be a private than a colonel in the army.
A private has more fun
When his day's work is done.
And when he goes on hikes,
In every town he strikes,
Girls discover him, and just smother him
With things he likes.
But girlies act so shy when colonel passes by,
He holds his head so high with dignity,
So would you rather be a colonel with an eagle on your shoulder,
    Or a private with a chicken on your knee?

"Every night you find some private in the park,
Spooning on a bench where it is nice and dark.
He's just as happy as can be,
With his girlie on his knee,
But colonel never dares to mix in such affairs.

"I'd rather be a private than a colonel in the army,
A colonel out in France
Can never take a chance.

For though his job is great,
He dare not make a date,
All that he can do is just 'Parley Voo,' then hesitate,
But privates meet the Ma, and then they treat the Pa,
And then they 'Oo la-la' with 'Wee Marie.'
So would you rather be a colonel with an eagle on your shoulder,
   Or a private with a chicken on your knee?"

SIDNEY D. MITCHELL

K-K-K-KATY

Jimmy was a soldier brave and bold,
Katy was a maid with hair of gold,
Like an act of fate,
Kate was standing at the gate,
Watching all the boys on dress parade.
Jimmy with the girls was just a gawk,
Stuttered every time he tried to talk,
Still that night at eight
He was there at Katy's gate,
Stuttering to her this lovesick cry:

  "K-K-K-Katy, beautiful Katy,
  You're the only g-g-g-girl that I adore;
  When the m-moon shines over the cowshed,
  I'll be waiting at the k-k-k-kitchen door."

No one ever looked so nice and neat,
No one could be just as cute and sweet.
That's what Jimmy thought,
When the wedding ring was bought;
Now he's off to France, the foe to meet.
Jimmy thought he'd like to take a chance,
See if he could make the Kaiser dance,
Stepping to a tune,
All about a silvery moon —
This is what they hear in far-off France:

  "K-K-K-Katy, beautiful Katy,
  You're the only g-g-g-girl that I adore;
  When the m-moon shines over the cowshed,
  I'll be waiting at the k-k-k-kitchen door."

GEOFFREY O'HARA

30.

JAMES THURBER: University Days and Draft Board Nights

My Life and Hard Times *was the story of James Thurber's early years in Columbus, Ohio, a city that he made famous as the seat of irrelevant and absurd happenstance. The book was an instant success and launched Thurber on a successful career as a short story writer, playwright, and author of children's books. The selection below, comprising Chapters Eight and Nine of this somewhat fanciful autobiography, describes Thurber's experiences at Ohio State University before and during World War I, and his extraordinary relations with his draft board.* My Life and Hard Times *was published in 1933.*

Source: *My Life and Hard Times*, New York, 1933, pp. 110-144.

UNIVERSITY DAYS

I PASSED ALL THE OTHER COURSES that I took at my university, but I could never pass botany. This was because all botany students had to spend several hours a week in a laboratory looking through a microscope at plant cells, and I could never see through a microscope. I never once saw a cell through a microscope. This used to enrage my instructor. He would wander around the laboratory pleased with the progress all the students were making in drawing the involved and, so I am told, interesting structure of flower cells, until he came to me. I would just be standing there.

"I can't see anything," I would say. He would begin patiently enough, explaining how anybody can see through a microscope, but he would always end up in a fury, claiming that I could *too* see through a microscope but just pretended that I couldn't. "It takes away from the beauty of flowers anyway," I used to tell him. "We are not concerned with beauty in this course," he

would say. "We are concerned solely with what I may call the *mechanics* of flars." "Well," I'd say, "I can't see anything." "Try it just once again," he'd say, and I would put my eye to the microscope and see nothing at all, except now and again a nebulous milky substance — a phenomenon of maladjustment.

You were supposed to see a vivid, restless clockwork of sharply defined plant cells. "I see what looks like a lot of milk," I would tell him. This, he claimed, was the result of my not having adjusted the microscope properly, so he would readjust it for me, or rather, for himself. And I would look again and see milk.

I finally took a deferred pass, as they called it, and waited a year and tried again. (You had to pass one of the biological sciences or you couldn't graduate.) The professor had come back from vacation brown as a berry, bright-eyed, and eager to explain cell structure again to his classes. "Well," he said to me, cheerily, when we met in the first laboratory hour of the semester, "we're going to see cells this time, aren't we?" "Yes, sir," I said. Students to right of me and to left of me and in front of me were seeing cells; what's more, they were quietly drawing pictures of them in their notebooks. Of course, I didn't see anything.

"We'll try it," the professor said to me, grimly, "with every adjustment of the microscope known to man. As God is my witness, I'll arrange this glass so that you see cells through it or I'll give up teaching. In twenty-two years of botany, I —" He cut off abruptly for he was beginning to quiver all over, like Lionel Barrymore, and he genuinely wished to hold onto his temper; his scenes with me had taken a great deal out of him.

So we tried it with every adjustment of the microscope known to man. With only one of them did I see anything but blackness or the familiar lacteal opacity, and that time I saw, to my pleasure and amazement, a variegated constellation of flecks, specks, and dots. These I hastily drew. The instructor, noting my activity, came back from an adjoining desk, a smile on his lips and eyebrows high in hope. He looked at my cell drawing. "What's that?" he demanded, with a hint of a squeal in his voice. "That's what I saw," I said. "You didn't, you didn't, you *did*n't!" he screamed, losing control of his temper instantly, and he bent over and squinted into the microscope. His head snapped up. "That's your eye!" he shouted. "You've fixed the lens so that it reflects! You've drawn your eye!"

Another course that I didn't like, but somehow managed to pass, was economics. I went to that class straight from the botany class, which didn't help me any in understanding either subject. I used to get them mixed up. But not as mixed up as another student in my economics class who came there direct from a physics laboratory. He was a tackle on the football team, named Bolenciecwcz. At that time Ohio

State University had one of the best football teams in the country, and Bolenciecwcz was one of its outstanding stars. In order to be eligible to play it was necessary for him to keep up in his studies, a very difficult matter, for while he was not dumber than an ox he was not any smarter. Most of his professors were lenient and helped him along. None gave him more hints, in answering questions, or asked him simpler ones than the economics professor, a thin, timid man named Bassum.

One day when we were on the subject of transportation and distribution, it came Bolenciecwcz's turn to answer a question. "Name one means of transportation," the professor said to him. No light came into the big tackle's eyes. "Just any means of transportation," said the professor. Bolenciecwcz sat staring at him. "That is," pursued the professor, "any medium, agency, or method of going from one place to another." Bolenciecwcz had the look of a man who is being led into a trap. "You may choose among steam, horse-drawn, or electrically propelled vehicles," said the instructor. "I might suggest the one which we commonly take in making long journeys across land." There was a profound silence in which everybody stirred uneasily, including Bolenciecwcz and Mr. Bassum.

Mr. Bassum abruptly broke this silence in an amazing manner. "Choo-choo-choo," he said, in a low voice, and turned instantly scarlet. He glanced appealingly around the room. All of us, of course, shared Mr. Bassum's desire that Bolenciecwcz should stay abreast of the class in economics, for the Illinois game, one of the hardest and most important of the season, was only a week off. "Toot, toot, too-toooooooot!" some student with a deep voice moaned, and we all looked encouragingly at Bolenciecwcz. Somebody else gave a fine imitation of a locomotive letting off steam. Mr. Bassum himself rounded off the little show. "Ding,

dong, ding, dong," he said, hopefully. Bolenciecwcz was staring at the floor now,
trying to think, his great brow furrowed, his
huge hands rubbing together, his face red.

"How did you come to college this year,
Mr. Bolenciecwcz?" asked the professor.
"*Chuf*fa chuffa, *chuf*fa chuffa."

"M'father sent me," said the football
player.

"What on?" asked Bassum.

"I git an 'lowance," said the tackle, in a
low, husky voice, obviously embarrassed.

"No, no," said Bassum. "Name a means
of transportation. What did you *ride* here
on?"

"Train," said Bolenciecwcz.

"Quite right," said the professor. "Now,
Mr. Nugent, will you tell us —"

If I went through anguish in botany and
economics — for different reasons — gymnasium work was even worse. I don't even
like to think about it. They wouldn't let
you play games or join in the exercises with
your glasses on and I couldn't see with
mine off. I bumped into professors, horizontal bars, agricultural students, and swinging iron rings. Not being able to see, I
could take it but I couldn't dish it out.
Also, in order to pass gymnasium (and you
had to pass it to graduate) you had to learn
to swim if you didn't know how. I didn't
like the swimming pool, I didn't like swimming, and I didn't like the swimming instructor, and after all these years I still
don't. I never swam but I passed my gym
work anyway by having another student
give my gymnasium number (978) and
swim across the pool in my place. He was a
quiet, amiable blond youth, number 473,
and he would have seen through a microscope for me if we could have got away
with it, but we couldn't get away with it.

Another thing I didn't like about gymnasium work was that they made you strip
the day you registered. It is impossible for
me to be happy when I am stripped and

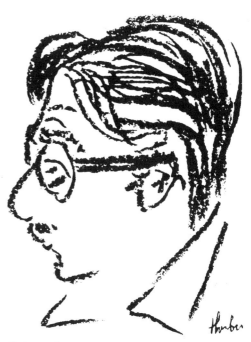

Drawing of himself by James Thurber

being asked a lot of questions. Still, I did
better than a lanky agricultural student who
was cross-examined just before I was. They
asked each student what college he was in
— that is, whether Arts, Engineering, Commerce or Agriculture. "What college are
you in?" the instructor snapped at the
youth in front of me. "Ohio State University," he said promptly.

It wasn't that agricultural student but it
was another a whole lot like him who decided to take up journalism, possibly on the
ground that when farming went to hell he
could fall back on newspaper work. He
didn't realize, of course, that that would be
very much like falling back full-length on a
kit of carpenter's tools. Haskins didn't seem
cut out for journalism, being too embarrassed to talk to anybody and unable to use
a typewriter, but the editor of the college
paper assigned him to the cow barns, the
sheep house, the horse pavilion, and the an-

imal husbandry department generally. This was a genuinely big "beat," for it took up five times as much ground and got ten times as great a legislative appropriation as the College of Liberal Arts.

The agricultural student knew animals, but nevertheless his stories were dull and colorlessly written. He took all afternoon on each of them, on account of having to hunt for each letter on the typewriter. Once in a while he had to ask somebody to help him hunt. "C" and "L," in particular, were hard letters for him to find. His editor finally got pretty much annoyed at the farmer-journalist because his pieces were so uninteresting. "See here, Haskins," he snapped at him one day, "Why is it we never have anything hot from you on the horse pavilion? Here we have two hundred head of horses on this campus — more than any other university in the Western Conference except Purdue — and yet you never get any real lowdown on them. Now shoot over to the horse barns and dig up something lively."

Haskins shambled out and came back in about an hour; he said he had something. "Well, start it off snappily," said the editor. "Something people will read." Haskins set to work and in a couple of hours brought a sheet of typewritten paper to the desk; it was a two-hundred-word story about some disease that had broken out among the horses. Its opening sentence was simple but arresting. It read: "Who has noticed the sores on the tops of the horses in the animal husbandry building?"

Ohio State was a land grant university and therefore two years of military drill was compulsory. We drilled with old Springfield rifles and studied the tactics of the Civil War even though the World War was going on at the time. At 11 o'clock each morning thousands of freshmen and sophomores used to deploy over the campus, moodily creeping up on the old chemistry building. It was good training for the kind of warfare that was waged at Shiloh but it had no connection with what was going on in Europe. Some people used to think there was German money behind it, but they didn't dare say so or they would have been thrown in jail as German spies. It was a period of muddy thought and marked, I believe, the decline of higher education in the Middle West.

As a soldier I was never any good at all. Most of the cadets were glumly indifferent soldiers, but I was no good at all. Once General Littlefield, who was commandant of the cadet corps, popped up in front of me during regimental drill and snapped, "You are the main trouble with this university!" I think he meant that my type was the main trouble with the university but he may have meant me individually. I was mediocre at drill, certainly — that is, until my senior year. By that time I had drilled longer than anybody else in the Western Conference, having failed at military at the end of each preceding year so that I had to do it all over again. I was the only senior still in uniform. The uniform which, when new, had made me look like an interurban railway conductor, now that it had become faded and too tight made me look like Bert Williams in his bellboy act. This had a definitely bad effect on my morale. Even so, I had become by sheer practice little short of wonderful at squad maneuvers.

One day General Littlefield picked our company out of the whole regiment and tried to get it mixed up by putting it through one movement after another as fast as we could execute them: squads right, squads left, squads on right into line, squads right about, squads left front into line, etc. In about three minutes one hundred and nine men were marching in one direction and I was marching away from them at an angle of forty degrees, all alone. "Company, halt!" shouted General Littlefield, "That man is the only man who has it right!" I was made a corporal for my achievement.

The next day General Littlefield summoned me to his office. He was swatting flies when I went in. I was silent and he was silent too, for a long time. I don't think he remembered me or why he had sent for me, but he didn't want to admit it. He swatted some more flies, keeping his eyes on them narrowly before he let go with the swatter. "Button up your coat!" he snapped. Looking back on it now I can see that he meant me although he was looking at a fly, but I just stood there. Another fly came to rest on a paper in front of the general and began rubbing its hind legs together. The general lifted the swatter cautiously. I moved restlessly and the fly flew away. "You startled him!" barked General Littlefield, looking at me severely. I said I was sorry. "That won't help the situation!" snapped the general, with cold military logic. I didn't see what I could do except offer to chase some more flies toward his desk, but I didn't say anything.

He stared out the window at the faraway figures of coeds crossing the campus toward the library. Finally, he told me I could go. So I went. He either didn't know which cadet I was or else he forgot what he wanted to see me about. It may have been that he wished to apologize for having called me the main trouble with the university; or maybe he had decided to compliment me on my brilliant drilling of the day before and then at the last minute decided not to. I don't know. I don't think about it much any more.

DRAFT BOARD NIGHTS

I left the university in June 1918, but I couldn't get into the Army on account of my sight, just as grandfather couldn't get in on account of his age. He applied several times and each time he took off his coat and threatened to whip the men who said he was too old. The disappointment of not getting to Germany (he saw no sense in everybody going to France) and the strain of running around town seeing influential officials finally got him down in bed. He had wanted to lead a division and his chagrin at not even being able to enlist as a private was too much for him. His brother Jake, some fifteen years younger than he was, sat up at night with him after he took to bed because we were afraid he might leave the house without even putting on his clothes. Grandfather was against the idea of Jake watching over him — he thought it was a lot of tomfoolery — but Jake hadn't been able to sleep at night for twenty-eight years, so he was the perfect person for such a vigil.

On the third night, grandfather was wakeful. He would open his eyes, look at Jake, and close them again, frowning. He never answered any question Jake asked him. About 4 o'clock that morning, he caught his brother sound asleep in the big leather chair beside the bed. When once Jake did fall asleep he slept deeply, so that grandfather was able to get up, dress himself, undress Jake, and put him in bed without waking him. When my Aunt Florence came into the room at 7 o'clock, grandfather was sitting in the chair reading the *Memoirs of U.S. Grant* and Jake was sleeping in the bed. "He watched while I slept," said grandfather, "so now I'm watchin' while he sleeps." It seemed fair enough.

One reason we didn't want grandfather to roam around at night was that he had said something once or twice about going over to Lancaster, his old hometown, and putting his problem up to "Cump" — that is, General William Tecumseh Sherman, also an old Lancaster boy. We knew that his inability to find Sherman would be bad for him and we were afraid that he might try to get there in the little electric runabout that had been bought for my grandmother. She had become, surprisingly enough, quite skillful at getting around town in it. Grandfather was astonished and a little indignant when he saw her get into the contraption and drive off smoothly and easily. It was her first vehicular triumph over him in almost fifty years of married life and he determined to learn to drive the thing himself.

A famous old horseman, he approached it as he might have approached a wild colt. His brow would darken and he would begin to curse. He always leaped into it quickly, as if it might pull out from under him if he didn't get into the seat fast enough. The first few times he tried to run the electric, he went swiftly around in a small circle, drove over the curb, across the sidewalk, and up onto the lawn. We all tried to persuade him to give up, but his spirit was aroused. "Git that goddam buggy back in the road!" he would say, imperiously. So we would maneuver it back into the street and he would try again. Pulling too savagely on the guiding-bar — to teach the electric a lesson — was what took him around in a circle, and it was difficult to make him understand that it was best to relax and not get mad. He had the notion that if you didn't hold her, she would throw you. And a man who (or so he often told us) had driven a four-horse McCormick reaper when he was five years old did not intend to be thrown by an electric runabout.

Since there was no way of getting him to give up learning to operate the electric, we would take him out to Franklin Park, where the roadways were wide and unfrequented, and spend an hour or so trying to explain the differences between driving a horse and carriage and driving an electric. He would keep muttering all the time; he never got it out of his head that when he took the driver's seat the machine flattened its ears on him, so to speak. After a few

weeks, nevertheless, he got so he could run the electric for a hundred yards or so along a fairly straight line. But whenever he took a curve, he invariably pulled or pushed the bar too quickly and too hard and headed for a tree or a flower bed. Someone was always with him and we would never let him take the car out of the park.

One morning when grandmother was all ready to go to market, she called the garage and told them to send the electric around. They said that grandfather had already been there and taken it out. There was a tremendous to-do. We telephoned Uncle Will and he got out his Lozier and we started off to hunt for grandfather. It was not yet 7 o'clock and there was fortunately little traffic. We headed for Franklin Park, figuring that he might have gone out there to try to break the car's spirit. One or two early pedestrians had seen a tall old gentleman with a white beard driving a little electric and cussing as he drove. We followed a tortuous trail and found them finally on Nelson Road, about four miles from the town of Shepard. Grandfather was standing in the road shouting, and the back wheels of the electric were deeply entangled in a barbed-wire fence. Two workmen and a farmhand were trying to get the thing loose. Grandfather was in a state of high wrath about the electric. "The ————— backed up on me!" he told us.

But to get back to the war. The Columbus draft board never called grandfather for service, which was a lucky thing for them because they would have had to take him. There were stories that several old men of eighty or ninety had been summoned in the confusion, but somehow or other grandfather was missed. He waited every day for the call, but it never came. My own experience was quite different. I was called almost every week, even though I had been exempted from service the first time I went before the medical examiners. Either they were never convinced that it was me or else there was some clerical error in the records which was never cleared up. Anyway, there was usually a letter for me on Monday ordering me to report for examination on the second floor of Memorial Hall the following Wednesday at 9 P.M. The second time I went up, I tried to explain to one of the doctors that I had already been exempted. "You're just a blur to me," I said, taking off my glass. "You're absolutely nothing to me," he snapped, sharply.

I had to take off all my clothes each time and jog around the hall with a lot of porters and bank presidents' sons and clerks and poets. Our hearts and lungs would be examined, and then our feet; and finally our eyes. That always came last. When the eye specialist got around to me, he would always say, "Why, you couldn't get into the service with sight like that!" "I know," I would say. Then a week or two later I would be summoned again and go through the same rigmarole. The ninth or tenth time I was called, I happened to pick up one of several stethoscopes that were lying on a table and suddenly, instead of finding myself in the line of draft men, I found myself in the line of examiners. "Hello, doctor," said one of them, nodding. "Hello," I said. That, of course, was before I took my clothes off; I might have managed it naked, but I doubt it. I was assigned, or rather drifted, to the chest-and-lung section, where I began to examine every other man, thus cutting old Dr. Ridgeway's work in two. "I'm glad to have you here, doctor," he said.

I passed most of the men that came to me, but now and then I would exempt one just to be on the safe side. I began by making each of them hold his breath and then say "mi, mi, mi, mi," until I noticed Ridgeway looking at me curiously. He, I discovered, simply made them say "ah," and sometimes he didn't make them say anything. Once I got hold of a man who, it came out later, had swallowed a watch —

to make the doctors believe there was something wrong with him inside (it was a common subterfuge: men swallowed nails, hairpins, ink, etc., in an effort to be let out). Since I didn't know what you were supposed to hear through a stethoscope, the ticking of the watch at first didn't surprise me, but I decided to call Dr. Ridgeway into consultation, because nobody else had ticked. "This man seems to tick," I said to him. He looked at me in surprise but didn't say anything. Then he thumped the man, laid his ear to his chest, and finally tried the stethoscope. "Sound as a dollar," he said. "Listen lower down," I told him. The man indicated his stomach. Ridgeway gave him a haughty, indignant look. "That is for the abdominal men to worry about," he said, and moved off. A few minutes later, Dr Blythe Ballomy got around to the man and listened, but he didn't blink an eye; his grim expression never changed. "You have swallowed a watch, my man," he said crisply. The draftee reddened in embarrassment and uncertainty. "On *purpose?*" he asked. "That I can't say," the doctor told him, and went on.

I served with the draft board for about four months. Until the summonses ceased. I couldn't leave town and as long as I stayed and appeared promptly for examination, even though I did the examining, I felt that technically I could not be convicted of evasion. During the daytime, I worked as publicity agent for an amusement park, the manager of which was a tall, unexpected young man named Byron Landis. Some years before, he had dynamited the men's lounge in the statehouse annex for a prank; he enjoyed pouring buckets of water on sleeping persons, and once he had barely escaped arrest by jumping off the top of the old Columbus Transfer Company building with a homemade parachute.

He asked me one morning if I would like to take a ride in the new Scarlet Tornado, a steep and wavy roller coaster. I didn't want to but I was afraid he would think I was afraid, so I went along. It was about 10 o'clock and there was nobody at the park except workmen and attendants and concessionaires in their shirtsleeves. We climbed into one of the long gondolas of the roller coaster and while I was looking around for the man who was going to run it, we began to move off. Landis, I discovered, was running it himself. But it was too late to get out; we had begun to climb, clickety-clockety, up the first steep incline, down the other side of which we careened at eighty miles an hour. "I didn't know you could run this thing!" I bawled at my companion, as we catapulted up a sixty-degree arch and looped headlong into space. "I didn't either!" he bawled back.

The racket and the rush of air were terrific as we roared into the pitch-black Cave of Darkness and came out and down Monohan's Leap, so called because a workman named Monohan had been forced to jump from it when caught between two approaching experimental cars while it was being completed. That trip, although it ended safely, made a lasting impression on me. It is not too much to say that it has flavored my life. It is the reason I shout in my sleep, refuse to ride on the elevated, keep jerking the emergency brake in cars other people are driving, have the sensation of flying like a bird when I first lie down, and in certain months can't keep anything on my stomach.

During my last few trips to the draft board, I went again as a draft prospect, having grown tired of being an examiner. None of the doctors who had been my colleagues for so long recognized me, not even Dr. Ridgeway. When he examined my chest for the last time, I asked him if there hadn't been another doctor helping him. He said there had been. "Did he look anything like me?" I asked. Dr. Ridgeway looked at me. "I don't think so," he said, "he was taller." (I had my shoes off while he was examining me.) "A good pulmonary man," added Ridgeway. "Relative of yours?" I said yes. He sent me on to Dr. Quimby, the specialist who had examined my eyes twelve or fifteen times before. He gave me some simple reading tests. "You could never get into the Army with eyes like that," he said. "I know," I told him.

Late one morning, shortly after my last examination, I was awakened by the sound of bells ringing and whistles blowing. It grew louder and more insistent and wilder. It was the Armistice.

Patriotism: A variety of hallucination which, if it seized a bacteriologist in his laboratory, would cause him to report the streptococcus purogenes to be as large as a Newfoundland dog, as intelligent as Socrates, as beautiful as Mont Blanc, and as respectable as a Yale professor.

H. L. MENCKEN

It seems like the less a statesman amounts to, the more he loves the flag.

KIN HUBBARD

31.

Interpretation of President Wilson's Fourteen Points

As early as May 1916, President Wilson had harbored the idea of a postwar international organization to maintain and insure peace. His specific proposals, however, were not announced until January 8, 1918, in a message to Congress. By that time the Bolshevik regime in Russia was negotiating a separate peace with Germany and denouncing the war aims of the Allies. Wilson's speech, outlining what he felt the Allied peace settlement should be, enumerated fourteen points, the last of which was a proposal for a League of Nations to implement the other thirteen. Colonel Edward House, Wilson's closest adviser, was in Paris in October 1918 as the war was drawing to a close and armistice negotiations were getting under way. Prior to the beginning of the actual negotiations, House asked two American newspapermen who were also in Paris, Frank I. Cobb, editor in chief of the New York World, *and Walter Lippmann, serving at the time as a staff member on the* World, *to draw up a memorandum indicating the American government's interpretation of the President's Fourteen Points, as outlined the previous January. House may or may not have edited the document drafted by Cobb and Lippmann; in any event, he forwarded it to Wilson on October 29 for his approval. It achieved semi-official status and was often referred to during the discussion of peace terms at Versailles. It was later published by the State Department in the version reprinted here.*

Source: PRFA, 1918, Supplement 1: *The World War*, Vol. 1, pp. 405-413.

AT MY REQUEST Cobb and Lippmann have compiled the following respecting your fourteen points. I shall be grateful to you if you will cable me whether it meets with your general approval. Here follows memorandum:

1. Open covenants of peace, openly arrived at, after which there shall be no private international understandings of any kind, but diplomacy shall proceed always frankly and in the public view.

The purpose is clearly to prohibit treaties, sections of treaties or understandings that are secret, such as the [Triple Alliance], etc.

The phrase "openly arrived at" need not cause difficulty. In fact, the President explained to the Senate last winter that the phrase was not meant to exclude confidential diplomatic negotiations involving delicate matters. The intention is that nothing which occurs in the course of such confidential negotiations shall be binding unless it appears in the final covenant made public to the world.

The matter may perhaps be put this way: It is proposed that in future every treaty be part of the public law of the world and that every nation assume a certain obligation in regard to its enforcement. Obviously, nations cannot assume obligations in matters of which they are ignorant; and therefore any secret treaty tends to undermine the solidity of the whole structure of international covenants which it is proposed to erect.

2. Absolute freedom of navigation upon the seas, outside territorial waters, alike in peace and in war, except as the seas may be closed in whole or in part by international action for the enforcement of international covenants.

This proposition must be read in connection with number 14 which proposes a league of nations. It refers to navigation under the three following conditions: (1) general peace; (2) a general war, entered into by the League of Nations for the purpose of enforcing international covenants; (3) limited war, involving no breach of international covenants.

Under "(1) general peace," no serious dispute exists. There is implied freedom to come and go [on the high seas].

No serious dispute exists as to the intention under "(2) a general war entered into by the League of Nations to enforce international covenants." Obviously such a war is conducted against an outlaw nation and complete nonintercourse with that nation is intended.

"(3) A limited war, involving no breach of international covenants" is the crux of the whole difficulty. The question is, what are to be the rights of neutral shipping and private property on the high seas during a war between a limited number of nations when that war involves no issue upon which the League of Nations cares to take sides; in other words, a war in which the League of Nations remains neutral. Clearly, it is the intention of the proposal that in such a war the rights of neutrals shall be maintained against the belligerents, the rights of both to be clearly and precisely defined in the law of nations.

3. The removal, so far as possible, of all economic barriers and the establishment of an equality of trade conditions among all the nations consenting to the peace and associating themselves for its maintenance.

The proposal applies only to those nations which accept the responsibilities of membership in the League of Nations. It means the destruction of all special commercial agreements, each putting the trade of every other nation in the League on the same basis, the most-favored-nation clause applying automatically to all members of the League of Nations. Thus a nation could legally maintain a tariff or a special railroad rate or a port restriction against the whole world, or against all the signatory powers. It could maintain any kind of restriction which it chose against a nation not in the League. But it could not discriminate as between its partners in the League.

This clause naturally contemplates fair and equitable understanding as to the distribution of raw materials.

4. Adequate guarantees given and taken that national armaments will be reduced to the lowest points consistent with domestic safety.

"Domestic safety" clearly implies not only internal policing, but the protection of territory against invasion. The accumulation of armaments above this level would be a violation of the intention of the proposal.

What guarantees should be given and taken, or what are to be the standards of judgment have never been determined. It will be necessary to adopt the general principle and then institute some kind [of international commission of investigation] to prepare detailed projects for its execution.

5. A free, open-minded and absolutely impartial adjustment of all colonial claims based upon a strict observance of the principle that in determining all such questions of sovereignty, the interests of the populations concerned must have equal weight with the equitable claims of the government whose title is to be determined.

Some fear is expressed in France [and England] that this involves reopening of all colonial questions. Obviously it is not so intended. It applies clearly [to those] colonial claims which have been created by the war.

That means the German colonies and any other colonies which may come under international consideration as a result of the war.

The stipulation is that in the case of the German colonies the title is to be determined after the conclusion of the war by "impartial adjustment" based on certain principles. These are of two kinds: (1) "equitable" claims; (2) the interests of the populations concerned.

What are the "equitable" claims put forth by Great Britain and Japan, the two chief heirs of the German colonial empire, that the colonies cannot be returned to Germany? Because she will use them as submarine bases, because she will arm the blacks, because she uses the colonies as bases of intrigue, because she oppresses the natives. What are the "equitable" claims put forth by Germany? That she needs access to tropical raw material, that she needs a field for the expansion of her population, that under the principles of the peace proposed, conquest gives her enemies no title to her colonies.

What are the "interests of the populations?" That they should not be militarized, that exploitation should be conducted on the principle of the "open door," and under the strictest regulation as to labor conditions, profits, and taxes, that a sanitary regime be maintained, that permanent improvements in the way of roads, etc., be made, that native organization and custom be respected, that the protecting authority be stable and experienced enough to thwart intrigue and corruption, that the [protecting] power have adequate resources in money and competent administrators to act successfully.

It would seem as if the principle involved in this proposition is that a colonial power acts not as owner of its colonies but as trustee for the natives and for the interests of the society of nations, that the terms on which the colonial administration is conducted are a matter of international concern and may legitimately be the subject of in-ternational inquiry, and that the peace conference may, therefore, write a code of colonial conduct binding upon [all] colonial powers.

6. The evacuation of all Russian territory and such a settlement of all questions affecting Russia as will secure the best and freest cooperation of the other nations of the world in obtaining for her an unhampered and unembarrassed opportunity for the independent determination of her own political development and national policy and assure her of a sincere welcome into the society of free nations under institutions of her own choosing; and, more than a welcome, assistance also of every kind that she may need and may herself desire. The treatment accorded Russia by her sister nations in the months to come will be the acid test of their goodwill, of their comprehension of her needs as distinguished from their own interests, and of their intelligent and unselfish sympathy.

The first question is whether Russian territory is synonymous with territory belonging to the former Russian Empire. This is clearly not so because proposition 13 stipulates an independent Poland, a proposal which excludes the territorial reestablishment of the Empire. What is recognized as valid for the Poles will certainly have to be recognized for the Finns, the Lithuanians, the Letts, and perhaps also for the Ukrainians. Since the formulating of this condition, these subject nationalities have emerged, and there can be no doubt that they will have to be granted an opportunity of free development.

The problem of these nationalities is complicated by two facts: (1) that they have conflicting claims; (2) that the evacuation called for in the proposal may be followed by Bolshevist revolutions in all of them.

The chief conflicts are: (a) between the Letts and Germans in Courland; (b) between the Poles and the Lithuanians on the northeast; (c) between the Poles and the White Ruthenians on the east; (d) between the Poles and the Ukrainians on the southeast (and in eastern Galicia).

In this whole borderland the relations of the German Poles [sic] to the other nationalities is roughly speaking that of landlord to peasant. Therefore the evacuating of the territory, if it resulted in class war, would very probably also take the form of a conflict of nationalities. It is clearly to the interests of a good settlement that the real nation in each territory should be consulted rather than the ruling and possessing class.

This can mean nothing less than the [recognition] by the peace conference of a series of [de facto] governments representing Finns, Esths, Lithuanians, Ukrainians. This primary [act] of recognition should be conditional upon the calling of national assemblies for the creation of de facto governments as soon as the peace conference has drawn frontiers for these new states. The frontiers should be drawn so far as possible on ethnic lines, but in [every] case the right of unhampered economic [transit] should be reserved. No dynastic ties with German [or] Austrian or Romanov princes should be permitted, and every inducement should be [given] to encourage federal [relations] between these new states. Under proposition 3 the economic sections of the treaty of Brest-Litovsk are obliterated, but this proposition should not be construed as forbidding a customs union, a monetary union, a railroad union, etc., of these states. Provision should also be made by which Great Russia can federate with these states on the same terms.

As for Great Russia and Siberia, the peace conference might well send a message asking for the creation of a government sufficiently [representative] to speak for these territories. It should be understood that economic rehabilitation is offered provided a government carrying sufficient credentials can appear at the peace conference.

The Allies should offer this provisional government any form of assistance it may need. The possibility of extending this will exist when the Dardanelles are opened.

The essence of the Russian problem then in the immediate future would seem to be: (1) the recognition of provisional governments; (2) assistance extended to and through these governments.

The Caucasus should probably be treated as part of the problem of the Turkish Empire. No information exists justifying an opinion on the proper policy in regard to Mohammedan Russia — that is, briefly, Central Asia. It may well be that some power will have to be given a limited mandate to act as protector.

In any case the treaties of Brest-Litovsk and Bucharest must be cancelled as palpably fraudulent. Provision must be made for the withdrawal of all German troops in Russia and the peace conference [will] have a clean slate on which to write a policy for all the Russian peoples.

7. Belgium, the whole world will agree, must be evacuated and restored without any attempt to limit the sovereignty which she enjoys in common with all other free nations. No other single act will serve as this will serve to restore confidence among the nations in the laws which they have themselves set and determined for the government of their relations with one another. Without this healing act the whole structure and validity of international law is forever impaired.

The only problem raised here is in the word "restored." Whether restoration is to be in kind or how the amount of the indemnity is to be determined is a matter of detail, not of principle. The principle that should be established is that in the case of Belgium there exists no distinction between "legitimate" and "illegitimate" destruction. The initial act of invasion was illegitimate and therefore all the consequences of that act are of the same character. Among the consequences may be put the war debt of

Belgium. The recognition of this principle would constitute "the healing act" of which the President speaks.

8. All French territory should be freed and the invaded portions restored, and the wrong done to France by Prussia in 1871 in the matter of Alsace-Lorraine, which has unsettled the peace of the world for nearly fifty years, should be righted in order that peace may once more be made secure in the interest of all.

In regard to the restoration of French territory it might well be argued that the invasion of northern France, being the result of the illegal act as regards Belgium, was in itself illegal. But the case is not perfect. As the world stood in 1914, war between France and Germany was not in itself a violation of international law, and great insistence should be put upon keeping the Belgian case distinct and symbolic. Thus Belgium might well, as indicated above, claim reimbursement, not only for destruction but for the cost of carrying on the war. France could not claim payment, it would seem, for more than the damage done to her northeastern departments.

The status of Alsace-Lorraine was settled by the official statement issued a few days ago. It is to be restored completely to French sovereignty.

Attention is called to the strong current of French opinion which claims "the boundaries of 1914 [1814]" rather than of 1871. The territory claimed is the valley of the Saar with its coalfields. No claim on grounds of nationality can be established, but the argument leans on the possibility of taking this territory in lieu of indemnity; it would seem to be a clear violation of the President's proposal.

Attention is called also to the fact that no reference is made to status of Luxembourg. The best solution would seem to be a free choice by the [people of] Luxembourg themselves.

9. A readjustment of the frontiers of Italy should be effected along clearly recognizable lines of nationality.

This proposal is less than the Italian claim; less, of course, than the territory allotted by the treaty of London; less than the arrangement made between the Italian government and the Yugoslav state.

In the region of Trent the Italians claim a strategic rather than ethnic frontier. It should be noted in this connection that [Italy] and Germany will become neighbors if German Austria joins the German Empire. And if Italy obtains the best geographical frontier she will assume sovereignty over a large number of Germans. This is a violation of principle. But it may be argued that by drawing a sharp line along the crest of the Alps, Italy's security will be enormously enhanced and the necessity of heavy armaments reduced. It might, therefore, be provided that Italy should have her claim in the Trentino, but that the northern part, inhabited by Germans, should be completely autonomous and that the population should not be liable to military service in the Italian Army. Italy could thus occupy the uninhabited Alpine peaks for military purposes, but would not govern the cultural life of the alien population to the south of her frontier.

The other problems of the frontier are questions between Italy and Yugoslavia, Italy and the Balkans, Italy and Greece.

The agreement reached with Yugoslavs may well be allowed to stand, although it should be insisted for [the protection of] the hinterland that both Trieste and Fiume be free ports. This is [essential] to Bohemia, German Austria, Hungary, as well as to prosperity of the cities themselves.

Italy appears in Balkan politics through her claim to a protectorate over Albania and the possession of Valona. There is no serious objection raised to this [although the] terms of the protectorate need to be vigorously controlled. If Italy is protector of

Albania [the local] life of Albania should be guaranteed by the League of Nations.

A conflict with Greece appears through the Greek claim to northern Epirus, or what is now southern Albania. This would bring Greece closer to Valona than Italy desires. A second conflict with Greece occurs over the Aegean Islands of the Dodecanese, but it is understood that a solution favorable to Greece is being worked out.

Italy's claims in Turkey belong to the problem of the Turkish Empire.

> 10. The people of Austria-Hungary, whose place among the nations we wish to see safeguarded and assured, should be accorded the freest opportunity of autonomous development.

This proposition no longer holds. Instead we have [today] the following elements:

(1) *Czechoslovakia.* Its territories include at least a million Germans for whom some provision must be made.

The independence of Slovakia means the dismemberment of the northwestern countries of Hungary.

(2) *Galicia.* Western Galicia is clearly Polish. Eastern Galicia is in large measure Ukrainian (or Ruthenian) and does not of right belong to Poland.

There also are several hundred thousand Ukrainians along the north and northeastern borders of Hungary and in parts of Bukovina (which belonged to Austria).

(3) *German Austria.* This territory should of right be permitted to join Germany, but there is strong objection in [France] because of the increase of [population] involved.

(4) *Yugoslavia.* It faces the following problems: *(a)* frontier questions with Italy in Istria and the Dalmatian coast; with Rumania in the Banat; *(b)* an international problem arises out of the refusal of the Croats to accept the domination of the Serbs of the Serbian Kingdom; *(c)* a problem of the Mohammedan Serbs of Bosnia who are said to be loyal to the Hapsburgs.

They constitute a little less than one-third of the population.

(5) *Transylvania.* Will undoubtedly join Rumania, but provision must be made for the protection of the Magyars, Szeklers, and Germans who constitute a large minority.

(6) *Hungary.* Now independent and very democratic in form, but governed by Magyars whose aim is to prevent the detachment of territory of nationalities on the fringe.

The United States is clearly committed to the program of national unity and independence. It must stipulate, however, for the protection of national minorities, for freedom of access to the Adriatic and the Black Sea, and it supports a program aiming at a confederation of southeastern Europe.

> 11. Rumania, [Serbia], and Montenegro should be evacuated; occupied territories restored; Serbia accorded free and secure access to the sea; and the relations of the several Balkan states to one another determined by friendly counsel along historically established lines of allegiance and nationality; and international guarantees of the political and economic independence and territorial integrity of the several Balkan states should be entered into.

This proposal is also altered by events. Serbia will appear as Yugoslavia with access to the Adriatic. Rumania will have acquired the Dobrudja, Bessarabia, and probably Transylvania. These two states will have 11 or 12 million inhabitants and will be far greater and stronger than Bulgaria.

Bulgaria should clearly have her frontier in the southern Dobrudja as it stood before the second Balkan War. She should also have Thrace up to the Enos-Midia line and perhaps even to the Midia-Rodosto line.

Macedonia should be allotted after an impartial investigation. The line which might be taken as a basis of investigation is the southern line of the "contested zone" agreed upon by Serbia and Bulgaria before the first Balkan War.

Albania could be under a protectorate, no doubt of Italy, and its frontiers in the north might be essentially those of the London conference.

12. The Turkish portions of the present Ottoman Empire should be assured a secure sovereignty, but the other nationalities which are now under Turkish rule should be assured an undoubted security of life and an absolutely unmolested opportunity of autonomous development; and the Dardanelles should be permanently opened as a free passage to the ships and commerce of all nations under international guarantees.

The same difficulty arises here as in the case of Austria-Hungary concerning the word "autonomous."

It is clear that the Straits and Constantinople, while they may remain nominally Turkish, should be under international control. This control may be collective or be in the hands of one power as mandatory of the League.

Anatolia should be reserved for the Turks. The coastlands, where Greeks predominate, should be under special international control, perhaps with Greece as mandatory.

Armenia must be [given] a port on the Mediterranean, and a protecting power established. France may claim it, but the Armenians would prefer Great Britain.

Syria has already been allotted to France by agreement with Great Britain.

Great Britain is clearly the best mandatory for Palestine, Mesopotamia, and Arabia.

A general code of guarantees binding upon all mandatories in Asia Minor should be written into the Treaty of Peace.

This should contain provisions for minorities and the "open door." The trunk railroad lines should be internationalized.

13. An independent Polish state should be erected which should include the territories inhabited by indisputably Polish populations, which should be assured a free and secure access to the sea, and whose political and economic independence and territorial integrity should be guaranteed by international covenants.

The chief problem is whether Poland is to obtain territory west of the Vistula, which would cut off the Germans of East Prussia from the empire, or whether Danzig can be made a free port and the Vistula internationalized.

On the east, Poland should receive no territory in which Lithuanians or Ukrainians predominate.

If Posen and Silesia go to Poland, rigid protection must be afforded the minorities of Germans and Jews living there, as well as in other parts of the Polish state.

The principle on which frontiers will be [delimited] is contained in the President's word "indisputably." This may imply the taking of an impartial census before frontiers are marked.

14. A general association of nations must be formed under specific covenants for the purpose of affording mutual guarantees of political independence and territorial integrity to great and small [states] alike.

The principle of a league of nations as the primary essential of a permanent peace has been so clearly presented by President Wilson in his speech of Sept. 27, 1918, that no further elucidation is required. It is the foundation of the whole diplomatic structure of a permanent peace.

The good Lord had only ten! (Le bon Dieu n'avait que dix!)
GEORGES CLEMENCEAU, on hearing that President Wilson had Fourteen Points

32.

The Archangel Expedition

After the overthrow of the Kerensky regime by the Bolsheviks in the October 1917 revolution, the new rulers of Russia immediately set about ending their country's involvement in the World War. Public opinion in western Europe and in America had been sympathetic to the revolution at first, but sentiment changed when the Lenin-Trotsky regime sued for a separate peace with Germany in March 1918. For a time there was hope that the White, or anti-Bolshevik, Russians would be able to reinstate the "legitimate" government of the country, and to this end several detachments of American troops were sent to join Allied forces already in Archangel. The following aide-mémoire, *sent by Secretary of State Robert Lansing to the Allied ambassadors on July 17, 1918, explained American policy with regard to Russia.*

Source: PRFA, 1918, Supplement on Russia, Vol. II, pp. 287-290.

THE WHOLE HEART OF THE PEOPLE of the United States is in the winning of this war. The controlling purpose of the government of the United States is to do everything that is necessary and effective to win it. It wishes to cooperate in every practicable way with the Allied governments, and to cooperate ungrudgingly; for it has no ends of its own to serve and believes that the war can be won only by common counsel and intimate concert of action.

It has sought to study every proposed policy or action in which its cooperation has been asked in this spirit, and states the following conclusions in the confidence that, if it finds itself obliged to decline participation in any undertaking or course of action, it will be understood that it does so only because it deems itself precluded from participating by imperative considerations either of policy or of fact.

In full agreement with the Allied governments and upon the unanimous advice of the Supreme War Council, the government of the United States adopted, upon its entrance into the war, a plan for taking part in the fighting on the Western front into which all its resources of men and material were to be put, and put as rapidly as possible; and it has carried out that plan with energy and success, pressing its execution more and more rapidly forward and literally putting into it the entire energy and executive force of the nation. This was its response, its very willing and hearty response, to what was the unhesitating judgment alike of its own military advisers and of the advisers of the Allied governments.

It is now considering, at the suggestion of the Supreme War Council, the possibility of making very considerable additions even to this immense program which, if they should prove feasible at all, will tax the industrial processes of the United States and the shipping facilities of the whole group of associated nations to the utmost. It has thus concentrated all its plans and all its resources upon this single absolutely necessary object.

In such circumstances it feels it to be its duty to say that it cannot, so long as the military situation on the Western front remains critical, consent to break or slacken the force of its present effort by diverting any part of its military force to other points or objectives. The United States is at a great distance from the field of action on the Western front; it is at a much greater distance from any other field of action. The instrumentalities by which it is to handle its armies and its stores have at great cost and with great difficulty been created in France. They do not exist elsewhere. It is practicable for her to do a great deal in France; it is not practicable for her to do anything of importance or on a large scale upon any other field. The American government, therefore, very respectfully requests its associates to accept its deliberate judgment that it should not dissipate its force by attempting important operations elsewhere.

It regards the Italian front as closely coordinated with the Western front, however, and is willing to divert a portion of its military forces from France to Italy if it is the judgment and wish of the Supreme Command that it should do so. It wishes to defer to the decision of the commander in chief in this matter, as it would wish to defer in all others, particularly because it considers these two fronts so closely related as to be practically but separate parts of a single line and because it would be necessary that any American troops sent to Italy should be subtracted from the number used in France and be actually transported across French territory from the ports now used by the armies of the United States.

It is the clear and fixed judgment of the government of the United States, arrived at after repeated and very searching reconsiderations of the whole situation in Russia,

that military intervention there would add to the present sad confusion in Russia rather than cure it, injure her rather than help her, and that it would be of no advantage in the prosecution of our main design — to win the war against Germany. It cannot, therefore, take part in such intervention or sanction it in principle.

Military intervention would, in its judgment, even supposing it to be efficacious in its immediate avowed object of delivering an attack upon Germany from the east, be merely a method of making use of Russia, not a method of serving her. Her people could not profit by it, if they profited by it at all, in time to save them from their present distresses, and their substance would be used to maintain foreign armies, not to reconstitute their own.

Military action is admissible in Russia, as the government of the United States sees the circumstances, only to help the Czechoslovaks consolidate their forces and get into successful cooperation with their Slavic kinsmen and to steady any efforts at self-government or self-defense in which the Russians themselves may be willing to accept assistance. Whether from Vladivostok or from Murmansk and Archangel, the only legitimate object for which American or Allied troops can be employed, it submits, is to guard military stores which may subsequently be needed by Russian forces and to render such aid as may be acceptable to the Russians in the organization of their own self-defense. For helping the Czechoslovaks there is immediate necessity and sufficient justification. Recent developments have made it evident that that is in the interest of what the Russian people themselves desire, and the government of the United States is glad to contribute the small force at its disposal for that purpose.

It yields, also, to the judgment of the Supreme Command in the matter of establishing a small force at Murmansk, to guard the military stores at Kola, and to make it safe for Russian forces to come together in organized bodies in the north. But it owes it to frank counsel to say that it can go no further than these modest and experimental plans. It is not in a position, and has no expectation of being in a position, to take part in organized intervention in adequate force from either Vladivostok or Murmansk and Archangel.

It feels that it ought to add, also, that it will feel at liberty to use the few troops it can spare only for the purposes here stated and shall feel obliged to withdraw those forces in order to add them to the forces at the Western front if the plans in whose execution it is now intended that they should cooperate should develop into others inconsistent with the policy to which the government of the United States feels constrained to restrict itself.

At the same time the government of the United States wishes to say with the utmost cordiality and goodwill that none of the conclusions here stated is meant to wear the least color of criticism of what the other governments associated against Germany may think it wise to undertake. It wishes in no way to embarrass their choices of policy. All that is intended here is a perfectly frank and definite statement of the policy which the United States feels obliged to adopt for herself and in the use of her own military forces. The government of the United States does not wish it to be understood that in so restricting its own activities it is seeking, even by implication, to set limits to the action or to define the policies of its associates.

It hopes to carry out the plans for safeguarding the rear of the Czechoslovaks operating from Vladivostok in a way that will place it and keep it in close cooperation with a small military force like its own from Japan and, if necessary, from the other Allies, and that will assure it of the cordial accord of all the Allied powers; and it proposes to ask all associated in this course of action to unite in assuring the people of Russia in the most public and solemn manner that none of the governments uniting in action either in Siberia or in northern Russia contemplates any interference of any kind with the political sovereignty of Russia, any intervention in her internal affairs, or any impairment of her territorial integrity either now or hereafter, but that each of the associated powers has the single object of affording such aid as shall be acceptable, and only such aid as shall be acceptable, to the Russian people in their endeavor to regain control of their own affairs, their own territory, and their own destiny.

It is the hope and purpose of the government of the United States to take advantage of the earliest opportunity to send to Siberia a commission of merchants, agricultural experts, labor advisers, Red Cross representatives, and agents of the Young Men's Christian Association accustomed to organizing the best methods of spreading useful information and rendering educational help of a modest sort, in order in some systematic manner to relieve the immediate economic necessities of the people there in every way for which opportunity may open. The execution of this plan will follow and will not be permitted to embarrass the military assistance rendered in the rear of the westward-moving forces of the Czechoslovaks.

Providence labors with quaint instruments, dilapidating Troy by means of a wooden rocking-horse, and loosing sin into the Universe through a half-eaten apple.

JAMES BRANCH CABELL, *Cream of the Jest*

33.

Lenin: An Open Letter to American Workers

Vladimir Ilyich Ulyanov, or Lenin, as he is known to history, was the guiding spirit of the Bolsheviks and the driving force behind the Soviet revolution of October-November 1917. In March 1918, overriding opposition within his government, he signed the humiliating treaty of Brest-Litovsk, thus taking Russia out of the war with Germany and preserving, as he later said, the new Soviet state for the sake of the ultimate victory of international communism. In a letter addressed to American workers on August 20, 1918, which is reprinted here in part, Lenin revealed his faith in the eventual triumph of the world proletarian revolution.

Source: *Collected Works,* translated by Jim Riordan, Vol. XXVIII, Moscow, 1965, pp. 62-75.

COMRADES! A RUSSIAN BOLSHEVIK who took part in the 1905 Revolution, and who lived in your country for many years afterward, has offered to convey my letter to you. I have accepted his proposal all the more gladly because just at the present time the American revolutionary workers have to play an exceptionally important role as uncompromising enemies of American imperialism — the freshest, strongest, and latest in joining in the worldwide slaughter of nations for the division of capitalist profits. At this very moment the American multimillionaires, these modern slaveowners, have turned an exceptionally tragic page in the bloody history of bloody imperialism by giving their approval — whether direct or indirect, open or hypocritically concealed, makes no difference — to the armed expedition launched by the brutal Anglo-Japanese imperialists for the purpose of throttling the first socialist republic.

The history of modern, civilized America opened with one of those great, really liberating, really revolutionary wars of which there have been so few compared to the vast number of wars of conquest which, like the present imperialist war, were caused by squabbles among kings, landowners, or capitalists over the division of usurped lands or ill-gotten gains. That was the war the American people waged against the British robbers who oppressed America and held her in colonial slavery, in the same way as these "civilized" bloodsuckers are still oppressing and holding in colonial slavery hundreds of millions of people in India, Egypt, and all parts of the world.

About 150 years have passed since then. Bourgeois civilization has borne all its luxurious fruits. America has taken first place among the free and educated nations in level of development of the productive forces of collective human endeavor, in the utilization of machinery and of all the wonders of modern engineering. At the same time, America has become one of the foremost countries in regard to the depth of the abyss which lies between the handful of arrogant multimillionaires who wallow in filth and luxury, and the millions of working people who constantly live on the verge of pauperism.

The American people, who set the world an example in waging a revolutionary war against feudal slavery, now find themselves in the latest, capitalist stage of wage slavery to a handful of multimillionaires, and find themselves playing the role of hired thugs who, for the benefit of wealthy scoundrels, throttled the Philippines in 1898 on the pretext of "liberating" them, and are throttling the Russian Socialist Republic in 1918 on the pretext of "protecting" it from the Germans.

The four years of the imperialist slaughter of nations, however, have not passed in vain. The deception of the people by the scoundrels of both robber groups, the British and the German, has been utterly exposed by indisputable and obvious facts. The results of the four years of war have revealed the general law of capitalism as applied to war between robbers for the division of spoils: the richest and strongest profited and grabbed most, while the weakest were utterly robbed, tormented, crushed, and strangled.

The British imperialist robbers were the strongest in number of "colonial slaves." The British capitalists have not lost an inch of "their" territory (*i.e.*, territory they have grabbed over the centuries), but they have grabbed all the German colonies in Africa, they have grabbed Mesopotamia and Palestine, they have throttled Greece, and have begun to plunder Russia.

The German imperialist robbers were the strongest in organization and discipline of "their" armies, but weaker in regard to colonies. They have lost all their colonies, but plundered half of Europe and throttled the largest number of small countries and weak nations. What a great war of "liberation" on both sides! How well the robbers of both groups, the Anglo-French and the German capitalists, together with their lack-

eys, the social-chauvinists, *i.e.*, the socialists who went over to the side of *"their own"* bourgeoisie, have "defended their country!"

The American multimillionaires were, perhaps, richest of all, and geographically the most secure. They have profited more than all the rest. They have converted all, even the richest, countries into their tributaries. They have grabbed hundreds of billions of dollars. And every dollar is sullied with filth: the filth of the secret treaties between Britain and her "allies," between Germany and her vassals, treaties for the division of the spoils, treaties of mutual "aid" for oppressing the workers and persecuting the internationalist socialists.

Every dollar is sullied with the filth of "profitable" war contracts, which in every country made the rich richer and the poor poorer. And every dollar is stained with blood — from that ocean of blood that has been shed by the 10 million killed and 20 million maimed in the great, noble, liberating, and holy war to decide whether the British or the German robbers are to get most of the spoils, whether the British or the German thugs are to be *foremost* in throttling the weak nations all over the world.

While the German robbers broke all records in war atrocities, the British have broken all records, not only in the number of colonies they have grabbed but also in the subtlety of their disgusting hypocrisy. This very day, the Anglo-French and American bourgeois newspapers are spreading, in millions and millions of copies, lies and slander about Russia, and are hypocritically justifying their predatory expedition against her on the plea that they want to "protect" Russia from the Germans!

It does not require many words to refute this despicable and hideous lie; it is sufficient to point to one well-known fact. In October 1917 after the Russian workers had overthrown their imperialist government, the Soviet government, the government of the revolutionary workers and peasants, openly proposed a just peace, a peace without annexations or indemnities, a peace that fully guaranteed equal rights to all nations — and it proposed such a peace to *all* the belligerent countries.

It was the Anglo-French and the American *bourgeoisie* who refused to accept our proposal; it was they who even refused to talk to us about a general peace! It was *they* who betrayed the interests of all nations; it was they who prolonged the imperialist slaughter! It was they who, banking on the possibility of dragging Russia back into the imperialist war, refused to take part in the peace negotiations and thereby gave a free hand to the no less predatory German capitalists who imposed the annexationist and harsh Brest Peace upon Russia!

It is difficult to imagine anything more disgusting than the hypocrisy with which the Anglo-French and American *bourgeoisie* are now "blaming" us *for* the Brest Peace Treaty. The very capitalists of those countries which could have turned the Brest negotiations into general negotiations for a general peace are now our "accusers!" The Anglo-French imperialist vultures, who have profited from the plunder of colonies and the slaughter of nations, have prolonged the war for nearly a whole year after Brest, and yet they "accuse" *us*, the Bolsheviks, who proposed a just peace to all countries, they accuse *us*, who tore up, published and exposed to public disgrace the secret, criminal treaties concluded between the ex-tsar and the Anglo-French capitalists.

The workers of the whole world, no matter in what country they live, greet us, sympathize with us, applaud us for breaking the iron ring of imperialist ties, of sordid imperialist treaties, of imperialist chains — for breaking through to freedom, and making the heaviest sacrifices in doing so — for, as a socialist republic, although torn and plundered by the imperialists, keeping *out* of the imperialist war and raising the banner of

peace, the banner of socialism for the whole world to see.

Small wonder that the international imperialist gang hates us for this, that it "accuses" us, that all the lackeys of the imperialists, including our Right Socialist-Revolutionaries and Mensheviks, also "accuse" us. The hatred these watchdogs of imperialism express for the Bolsheviks, and the sympathy of the class-conscious workers of the world, convince us more than ever of the justice of our cause.

A real socialist would not fail to understand that for the sake of achieving victory over the *bourgeoisie*, for the sake of power passing to the workers, for the sake of *starting* the world proletarian revolution, we *cannot* and must *not* hesitate to make the heaviest sacrifices, including the sacrifice of part of our territory, the sacrifice of heavy defeats at the hands of imperialism. A real socialist would have proved by *deeds* his willingness for "his" country to make the greatest sacrifice to give a real push forward to the cause of the socialist revolution.

For the sake of "their" cause, that is, for the sake of winning world hegemony, the imperialists of Britain and Germany have not hesitated to utterly ruin and throttle a whole number of countries, from Belgium and Serbia to Palestine and Mesopotamia. But must socialists wait with "their" cause, the cause of liberating the working people of the whole world from the yoke of capital, of winning universal and lasting peace, until a path without sacrifice is found? Must they fear to open the battle until an easy victory is "guaranteed"? Must they place the integrity and security of "their" bourgeois-created "fatherland" above the interests of the world socialist revolution? The scoundrels in the international socialist movement who think this way, those lackeys who grovel to bourgeois morality, thrice stand condemned.

The Anglo-French and American imperialist vultures "accuse" us of concluding an "agreement" with German imperialism. What hypocrites, what scoundrels they are to slander the workers' government while trembling because of the sympathy displayed toward us by the workers of "their own" countries! But their hypocrisy will be exposed. They pretend not to see the difference between an agreement entered into by "socialists" with the *bourgeoisie* (their own or foreign) *against the workers*, against the working people, and an agreement entered into *for the protection* of the workers who have defeated their *bourgeoisie*, with the *bourgeoisie* of one national color *against the bourgeoisie* of another color in order that the proletariat may take advantage of the antagonisms between the different groups of *bourgeoisie*. . . .

The American people have a revolutionary tradition which has been adopted by the best representatives of the American proletariat, who have repeatedly expressed their complete solidarity with us Bolsheviks. That tradition is the war of liberation against the British in the 18th century and the Civil War in the 19th century. In some respects, if we only take into consideration the "destruction" of some branches of industry and of the national economy, America in 1870 was *behind* 1860. But what a pedant, what an idiot would anyone be to deny on *these* grounds the immense, world-historic, progressive, and revolutionary significance of the American Civil War of 1863-65!

The representatives of the *bourgeoisie* understand that for the sake of overthrowing Negro slavery, of overthrowing the rule of the slaveowners, it was worth letting the country go through long years of civil war, through the abysmal ruin, destruction, and terror that accompany every war. But now, when we are confronted with the vastly greater task of overthrowing capitalist *wage* slavery, of overthrowing the rule of the *bourgeoisie* — now, the representatives and defenders of the *bourgeoisie*, and also the re-

formist socialists who have been frightened by the *bourgeoisie* and are shunning the revolution, cannot and do not want to understand that civil war is necessary and legitimate.

The American workers will not follow the *bourgeoisie*. They will be with us, for civil war against the *bourgeoisie*. The whole history of the world and of the American labor movement strengthens my conviction that this is so. I also recall the words of one of the most beloved leaders of the American proletariat, Eugene Debs, who wrote in the *Appeal to Reason*, I believe toward the end of 1915, in the article "What Shall I Fight For" (I quoted this article at the beginning of 1916 at a public meeting of workers in Bern, Switzerland) — that he, Debs, would rather be shot than vote credits for the present criminal and reactionary war; that he, Debs, knows of only one holy and, from the proletarian standpoint, legitimate war, namely: the war against the capitalists, the war to liberate mankind from wage slavery.

I am not surprised that Wilson, the head of the American multimillionaires and servant of the capitalist sharks, has thrown Debs into prison. Let the *bourgeoisie* be brutal to the true internationalists, to the true representatives of the revolutionary proletariat! The more fierce and brutal they are, the nearer the day of the victorious proletarian revolution. . . .

The international imperialist *bourgeoisie* have slaughtered 10 million men and maimed 20 million in "their" war, the war to decide whether the British or the German vultures are to rule the world.

If *our* war, the war of the oppressed and exploited against the oppressors and the exploiters, results in half a million or a million casualties in all countries, the *bourgeoisie* will say that the former casualties are justified, while the latter are criminal.

The proletariat will have something entirely different to say.

Now, amidst the horrors of the imperialist war, the proletariat is receiving a most vivid and striking illustration of the great truth taught by all revolutions and bequeathed to the workers by their best teachers, the founders of modern socialism. This truth is that no revolution can be successful unless *the resistance of the exploiters is crushed*. When we, the workers and toiling peasants, captured state power, it became our duty to crush the resistance of the exploiters. We are proud we have been doing this. We regret we are not doing it with sufficient firmness and determination.

We know that fierce resistance to the socialist revolution on the part of the *bourgeoisie* is inevitable in all countries, and that this resistance will *grow* with the growth of this revolution. The proletariat will crush this resistance; during the struggle against the resisting *bourgeoisie* it will finally mature for victory and for power.

Let the corrupt bourgeois press shout to the whole world about every mistake our revolution makes. We are not daunted by our mistakes. People have not become saints because the revolution has begun. The toiling classes who for centuries have been oppressed, downtrodden, and forcibly held in the vice of poverty, brutality, and ignorance cannot avoid mistakes when making a revolution. And, as I pointed out once before, the corpse of bourgeois society cannot be nailed in a coffin and buried. The corpse of capitalism is decaying and disintegrating in our midst, polluting the air and poisoning our lives, enmeshing that which is new, fresh, young, and virile in thousands of threads and bonds of that which is old, moribund, and decaying. . . .

The old bourgeois-democratic constitutions waxed eloquent about formal equality and right of assembly; but our proletarian and peasant Soviet constitution casts aside the hypocrisy of formal equality. When the bourgeois republicans overturned thrones, they did not worry about formal equality between monarchists and republicans. When it is a matter of overthrowing the *bourgeoisie*, only traitors or idiots can demand formal equality of rights for the *bourgeoisie*.

"Freedom of assembly" for workers and peasants is not worth a farthing when the best buildings belong to the *bourgeoisie*. Our Soviets have *confiscated* all the good buildings in town and country from the rich and have *transferred all* of them to the workers and peasants for *their* unions and meetings. This is *our* freedom of assembly — for the working people! This is the meaning and content of our Soviet, our socialist constitution!

That is why we are all so firmly convinced that no matter what misfortunes may still be in store for it, our republic of Soviets is *invincible*. It is invincible because every blow struck by frenzied imperialism, every defeat the international *bourgeoisie* inflict on us, rouses more and more sections of the workers and peasants to the struggle, teaches them at the cost of enormous sacrifice, steels them and engenders new heroism on a mass scale.

We know that help from you will probably not come soon, comrade American workers, for the revolution is developing in different countries in different forms and at different tempos (and it cannot be otherwise). We know that although the European proletarian revolution has been maturing very rapidly lately, it may, after all, not flare up within the next few weeks. We are banking on the inevitability of the world revolution, but this does not mean that we are such fools as to bank on the revolution inevitably coming on a *definite* and early date.

We have seen two great revolutions in our country, 1905 and 1917, and we know revolutions are not made to order or by agreement. We know that circumstances brought *our* Russian detachment of the socialist proletariat to the fore, not because of our merits but because of the exceptional backwardness of Russia, and that *before* the world revolution breaks out a number of separate revolutions may be defeated.

In spite of this, we are firmly convinced that we are invincible, because the spirit of mankind will not be broken by the imperialist slaughter. Mankind will vanquish it. And the first country to *break* the convict chains of the imperialist war was *our* country. We sustained enormously heavy casualties in the struggle to break these chains, but we *broke* them. We are *free from* imperialist dependence, we have raised the banner of struggle for the complete overthrow of imperialism for the whole world to see.

We are now, as it were, in a besieged fortress, waiting for the other detachments of the world socialist revolution to come to our relief. These detachments *exist,* they are *more numerous* than ours, they are maturing, growing, gaining more strength the longer the brutalities of imperialism continue. The workers are breaking away from their social-traitors — the Gomperses, Hendersons, Renaudels, Scheidemanns, and Renners. Slowly but surely the workers are adopting Communist, Bolshevik tactics and are marching toward the proletarian revolution, which alone is capable of saving dying culture and dying mankind.

In short, we are invincible because the world proletarian revolution is invincible.

34.

Woodrow Wilson: Appeal to the Voters to Return a Democratic Congress

Hoping to go to the Paris peace conference with a popular mandate, President Wilson on October 25, 1918, appealed to the voters to return a Democratic Congress in the fall elections. The maneuver probably would have been a tactical error even if Wilson had been successful, for it seemed to make his cherished dream of a League of Nations a partisan issue; but in fact he was repudiated by the voters and his prestige was lowered during the Versailles negotiations. From that time until the Senate rejection of the Treaty in late 1919 bipartisan support for the President's peace settlement was much more difficult.

Source: *Record,* 65 Cong., 2 Sess., p. 11494.

THE CONGRESSIONAL ELECTIONS are at hand. They occur in the most critical period our country has ever faced or is likely to face in our time. If you have approved of my leadership and wish me to continue to be your unembarrassed spokesman in affairs at home and abroad, I earnestly beg that you will express yourselves unmistakably to that effect by returning a Democratic majority to both the Senate and the House of Representatives.

I am your servant and will accept your judgment without cavil. But my power to administer the great trust assigned me by the Constitution would be seriously impaired should your judgment be adverse, and I must frankly tell you so because so many critical issues depend upon your verdict. No scruple or taste must in grim times like these be allowed to stand in the way of speaking the plain truth.

I have no thought of suggesting that any political party is paramount in matters of patriotism. I feel too deeply the sacrifices which have been made in this war by all our citizens, irrespective of party affiliations, to harbor such an idea. I mean only that the difficulties and delicacies of our present task are of a sort that makes it imperatively necessary that the nation should give its undivided support to the government under a unified leadership, and that a Republican Congress would divide the leadership.

The leaders of the minority in the present Congress have unquestionably been pro-war, but they have been anti-administration. At almost every turn since we entered the war they have sought to take the choice of policy and the conduct of the war out of my hands and put it under the control of instrumentalities of their own choosing.

This is no time either for divided counsel or for divided leadership. Unity of command is as necessary now in civil action as it is upon the field of battle. If the control of the House and Senate should be taken away from the party now in power, an opposing majority could assume control of legislation and oblige all action to be taken amid contest and obstruction.

The return of a Republican majority to either house of the Congress would, moreover, certainly be interpreted on the other side of the water as a repudiation of my leadership. Spokesmen of the Republican Party are urging you to elect a Republican Congress in order to back up and support the President; but, even if they should in this way impose upon some credulous voters on this side of the water, they would impose on no one on the other side. It is well understood there as well as here that Republican leaders desire not so much to support the President as to control him.

The peoples of the Allied countries with whom we are associated against Germany are quite familiar with the significance of elections. They would find it very difficult to believe that the voters of the United States had chosen to support their President by electing to the Congress a majority controlled by those who are not in fact in sympathy with the attitude and action of the administration.

I need not tell you, my fellow countrymen, that I am asking your support, not for my own sake or for the sake of a political party but for the sake of the nation itself in order that its inward unity of purpose may be evident to all the world. In ordinary times I would not feel at liberty to make such an appeal to you. In ordinary times divided counsels can be endured without permanent hurt to the country. But these are not ordinary times.

If in these critical days it is your wish to sustain me with undivided minds, I beg that you will say so in the way which it will not be possible to misunderstand, either here at home or among our associates on the other side of the sea. I submit my difficulties and my hopes to you.

My boy, about seventy-five years ago I learned I was not God. And so, when the people of the various states want to do something and I can't find anything in the Constitution expressly forbidding them to do it, I say, whether I like it or not: "Damn it, let 'em do it!"

OLIVER WENDELL HOLMES, JR.

35.

John B. Densmore: The Mooney-Billings Case

San Francisco labor leaders Thomas J. Mooney and Warren K. Billings were charged with having thrown a bomb into the midst of a "preparedness" parade on July 22, 1916. After a notorious trial in which the prosecution argued that the defendants were anarchists, Mooney was sentenced to death (the sentence was commuted to life imprisonment on November 29, 1918, by the governor under pressure from President Wilson) and Billings received a life sentence. From the beginning the case aroused international attention, especially among those who felt that interests hostile to the labor movement in the United States had interfered. In September 1917, the President appointed a mediation commission to look into the disturbed industrial situation of the Pacific Coast. As chairman of the commission, Secretary of Labor W. B. Wilson delegated Director of General Employment J. B. Densmore to investigate the Mooney case. By secretly installing a Dictograph in the office of the district attorney of San Francisco, Densmore was able to show that Mooney and Billings had probably been framed. His report, reprinted here in part, was submitted on November 1, 1918. However, it was not until January 1939 that Mooney was released from prison after having been pardoned by Governor Olson of California. Billings was released from prison in October 1939, although an official pardon was not granted by Governor Brown until December 1961.

Source: 66 Congress, 1 Session, House Document No. 157, pp. 3-7, 73-76.

Sir:

Pursuant to instructions received from time to time during the past six months, I have the honor to report that I have conducted a secret and altogether informal inquiry into the Mooney case, and beg leave to submit herewith the results of my investigation. Before entering into a recital of the various steps pursued in carrying out the operation, it might be well to call attention to a number of peculiar features which have characterized this case from the beginning, in order that there may be no misconception, either as to the issues involved or as to the necessity which arose for the employment on the part of the investigators, of somewhat unusual methods of obtaining information.

On the surface, and in its narrowest aspect, the Mooney case may be defined as the case of the people of the state of California against Thomas J. Mooney and certain other defendants, four in number, charged with perpetrating a bomb outrage in the city of San Francisco during the Preparedness Day parade, on July 22, 1916, thereby causing the deaths of nine or ten persons and the injury of numerous others. Of the five defendants, four have been tried. Two of these, Mooney and Warren K. Billings, were found guilty, Mooney now being under sentence of death and Billings serving a life term in the penitentiary; the other two, Mrs. Thomas J. Mooney and Israel Weinberg, were acquitted. The case against the fifth defendant, Edward D. Nolan, has virtually been dropped for lack of evidence. All five of these persons have been more or less prominently identified with the union-labor movement in San Francisco.

It was charged by the prosecution that these five defendants were animated by anarchistic motives and that the bomb explosion which they were alleged to have planned and consummated was the climax of a carefully laid plot to strike a blow at existing social and political institutions and intimidate all those who were in any way concerned with placing the country in a state of military preparedness.

This is one view of the case. On the other hand, it has been urged in favor of these defendants that they are the victims of a monstrous frame-up; that the evidence against them has been manufactured out of whole cloth and cut to measure in accordance with a predetermined pattern; and that the district attorney of the city and county of San Francisco, backed by certain sinister influences antagonistic to the cause of union labor, has resolved to accomplish their ruin if it is at all possible to do so.

This, stated briefly, is the Mooney case. The full record is voluminous. As one reads the testimony and studies the way in which the cases were conducted one is apt to wonder at many things — at the apparent failure of the district attorney's office to conduct a real investigation at the scene of the crime; at the easy adaptability of some of the star witnesses; at the irregular methods pursued by the prosecution in identifying the various defendants; at the sorry type of men and women brought forward to prove essential matters of fact in a case of the gravest importance; at the seeming inefficacy of even a well-established alibi; at the sangfroid with which the prosecution occasionally discarded an untenable theory to adopt another not quite so preposterous; at the refusal of the public prosecutor to call as witnesses people who *actually saw the*

falling of the bomb; in short, at the general flimsiness and improbability of the testimony adduced, together with a total absence of anything that looks like a genuine effort to arrive at the facts in the case.

These things, as one reads and studies the complete record, are calculated to cause in the minds of even the most blasé a decided mental rebellion. The plain truth is, there is nothing about the cases to produce a feeling of confidence that the dignity and majesty of the law have been upheld. There is nowhere anything even remotely resembling consistency, the effect being that of patchwork, of incongruous makeshift, of clumsy and often desperate expediency.

It is not the purpose of this report to enter into a detailed analysis of the evidence presented in these cases — evidence which, in its general outlines at least, is already familiar to you in your capacity as president, *ex officio,* of the Mediation Commission. It will be enough to remind you that Billings was tried first; that in September 1916, he was found guilty, owing largely to the testimony of Estelle Smith, John McDonald, Mellie and Sadie Edeau, and Louis Rominger, all of whom have long since been thoroughly discredited; that when Mooney was placed on trial, in January of the year following, the prosecution decided, for reasons which were obvious, not to use Rominger or Estelle Smith, but to add to the list of witnesses a certain Frank C. Oxman, whose testimony, corroborative of the testimony of the two Edeau women, formed the strongest link in the chain of evidence against the defendant; that on the strength of this testimony Mooney was found guilty; that on February 24, 1917, he was sentenced to death; and that subsequently, to wit, in April of the same year, it was demonstrated beyond the shadow of a doubt that Oxman, the prosecution's star witness, had attempted to suborn perjury and had thus in effect destroyed his own credibility.

The exposure of Oxman's perfidy, involving as it did the district attorney's office, seemed at first to promise that Mooney would be granted a new trial. The district attorney himself, Mr. Charles M. Fickert, when confronted with the facts, acknowledged in the presence of reputable witnesses that he would agree to a new trial. His principal assistant, Mr. Edward A. Cunha, made a virtual confession of guilty knowledge of the facts relating to Oxman, and promised, in a spirit of contrition, to see that justice should be done the man who had been convicted through Oxman's testimony. The trial judge, Hon. Franklin A. Griffin, one of the first to recognize the terrible significance of the exposé, and keenly jealous of his own honor, lost no time in officially suggesting the propriety of a new trial. The attorney general of the state, Hon. Ulysses S. Webb, urged similar action in a request filed with the Supreme Court of California.

Matters thus seemed in a fair way to be rectified, when two things occurred to upset the hopes of the defense. The first was a sudden change of front on the part of Fickert, who now denied that he had ever agreed to a new trial, and whose efforts henceforth were devoted to a clumsy attempt to whitewash Oxman and justify his own motives and conduct throughout. The second was a decision of the Supreme Court to the effect that it could not go outside the record in the case — in other words, that judgment could not be set aside merely for the reason that it was predicated upon perjured testimony.

There are excellent grounds for believing that Fickert's sudden change of attitude was prompted by emissaries from some of the local corporate interests most bitterly opposed to union labor. It was charged by the Mooney defendants, with considerable plausibility, that Fickert was the creature and tool of these powerful interests, chief among which are the Chamber of Commerce and the principal public-service utilities of the city of San Francisco. In this connection it is of the utmost significance that Fickert should have entrusted the major portion of the investigating work necessary in these cases to Martin Swanson, a corporation detective, who for some time prior to the bomb explosion had been vainly attempting to connect these same defendants with other crimes of violence.

Since the Oxman exposure, the district attorney's case has melted steadily away until there is little left but an unsavory record of manipulation and perjury, further revelations having impeached the credibility of practically all the principal witnesses for the prosecution. And if any additional confirmation were needed of the inherent weakness of the cases against these codefendants, the acquittal of Mrs. Mooney on July 26, 1917, and of Israel Weinberg on the 27th of the following October would seem to supply it.

These acquittals were followed by the investigation of the Mediation Commission and its report to the President under date of January 16, 1918. The Commission's report, while disregarding entirely the question of the guilt or innocence of the accused, nevertheless found in the attendant circumstances sufficient grounds for uneasiness and doubt as to whether the two men convicted had received fair and impartial trials.

This was the condition of things when I asked for and received official permission to make a further investigation of the case along certain lines which I hoped would develop information of the first importance. By this time the fate of the Mooney defendants had aroused international interest and solicitude. The Netherlands Federation of Labor, the British Trades Union Congress, the General Federation of Labor of Milan, and other similar organizations all over the world had taken official cognizance of the methods used in securing the conviction of Billings and Mooney and had entered their solemn protests against what they considered a gigantic frame-up on the part of unscrupulous capitalistic interests to discredit the whole cause of union labor. The liberal sentiment of Russia was aroused because the circumstances of Mooney's prosecution, in the language of the Mediation Commission, "led to the belief that the terrible and sacred instruments of criminal justice were, consciously or unconsciously, made use of against labor by its enemies in an industrial conflict."

This widespread feeling of suspicion on the part of organized labor throughout the world has in time of war a deep and peculiar significance, in order to understand which it is only necessary to point out that under the authority conferred by various legislative measures passed by Congress since the beginning of the war, supplemented by numerous proclamations of the chief executive, the government itself has become the direct employer of millions of men, while the country's principal economic activities have been subordinated to the public interest in every line of endeavor connected in any way with the war. Never before in the history of the country has this partnership of government and industry been so close or so necessary.

With every resource of the country engaged in the one supreme effort; with cooperation among laborers and between labor and capital the keynote of success; and with the government engaged in working out a labor program designed to promote the efficiency and morale of the vast army of artisans and laborers who are supplying the sinews of war, it is of the utmost importance that mutual respect should characterize the relations of all the parties concerned — that cooperation between capital and labor should be a reality and not a mere dream; that distrust and suspicion should have no place in their councils; and that in

peace and harmony they should strive wholeheartedly for the one common aim — the winning of the war.

In my investigation of the Mooney case I have kept these facts well in mind and proceeded on the theory that an unwarranted attack upon labor leaders, with a premeditated and deliberate intention to injure and discredit union labor generally, and thus in effect to curtail the production of essential war materials, would constitute a virtual violation of the act of Congress approved May 16, 1918, commonly known as the Espionage Act, which makes it a crime punishable by fine and imprisonment to "utter, print, write, or publish any language intended to promote the cause of its (the country's) enemies . . . or advocate any curtailment of production in this country of any thing or things, product or products, necessary or essential to the prosecution of the war." This was not an idle resolution of Congress, but was a serious attempt on the part of the national legislative body to reduce to a minimum the handicap of sedition, perfidy, and the various crimes growing out of a lukewarm or misguided allegiance. . . .

The record establishes three sets of facts, each one of which has a bearing upon the question at issue, namely, whether Mooney and his fellow defendants received fair trials at the hands of the district attorney. These three sets of facts are:

First, that Fickert is in constant association with men and interests of such a nature as to render it incredible that he should be either impartial or honest in the conduct of a case of this nature; that he is and has been for some time past cooperating with notorious jury and case fixers; that, for instance, he is equally guilty with Pete McDonough in conspiring to free a wealthy man charged with crimes of degeneracy; and that he has also been working with the same notoriously corrupt McDonough and

Ben Selig to save from conviction Dave Blaine, an automobile-tire thief. These cases are mentioned simply to illustrate his common practice, of which abundant evidence is furnished by this report.

Second, that Fickert and his associates have within the past month framed, and conspired to frame, cases with which it was his sworn duty to deal impartially.

Third, that Fickert and his associates, within the past month, have conspired to fabricate evidence with which to convict Mrs. Mooney; and that to this end they have attempted, in the grossest manner, to intimidate and blackmail a prospective woman witness.

It will be apparent that these facts, which are all brought out exhaustively in the present report, tend to supplement the revelations already made in the Oxman letters, and that they confirm the impression, made unavoidably by the weak and conflicting nature of the testimony in the bomb cases, that practically the whole of Fickert's case against Mooney, Billings, and Mrs. Mooney was made to order.

Let us, in conclusion, touch once more on the general outline of the "evidence":

Billings, it will be remembered, was convicted on testimony that he had been seen to emerge with a companion from a saloon at the scene of the explosion, put down a suitcase, and walk away through the crowd.

Mooney was convicted on testimony that he had been seen to drive an automobile to the scene of the explosion in company with Billings, Mrs. Mooney, and Israel Weinberg, and that he had afterward driven away in the same vehicle. Other testimony required the entire party to be near Third and Market Streets within a few minutes of the explosion, and then to reach Steuart and Market (nearly a mile away) without attracting the attention of the traffic police at a time when the streets were cleared for the Preparedness Day parade. Photographs and testimony introduced by the defense showed that Mr. and Mrs. Mooney were on the roof of the Eilers Building, a mile from the scene of the explosion, at the moment that they were represented by the prosecution as being in Weinberg's automobile in lower Market Street.

Two witnesses, Mrs. Mellie Edeau and her daughter, who testified in two of the trials, altered their testimony between the two, and were shown, by the police records, to have been at first unable to identify either Billings or Mooney.

It was the theory of the prosecution that the defendants had at first intended to throw the bomb from the roof of a building at 721 Market Street; that they changed their minds when it became apparent that the United Railroads division would not pass before the bomb was due to explode; that they had then proceeded down Market Street to Steuart, where they deposited the bomb (concealed in a suitcase) and fled. This whole theory was not only inherently inconsistent in its several parts, but was discredited by the exposure of every important witness, chief among them being Oxman and the Edeaus.

The methods used by Fickert in framing up the cases were revealed by the publication of the Oxman letters, by the admissions of the Edeaus, and by the exposed attempt to intimidate Estelle Smith, the dental nurse who was induced to testify to the fictitious happenings at 721 Market Street. These methods were identical with the ones still in use, as shown in detail in other parts of this report. So thoroughly were they understood by court, jury, and prosecutor that in the trials of Mrs. Mooney and Israel Weinberg, Oxman was not introduced and swift acquittals resulted. In other words, the testimony which before the Oxman exposure convinced two juries that Mooney, Mrs. Mooney, Billings, and Weinberg were in an automobile at the scene of the crime was too weak, after the exposure, to convince anybody that either Mrs. Mooney or Weinberg were in the automobile or had a part in the crime.

Thus the cases against these defendants had already fallen to pieces before the present investigation began. It only remained to demonstrate that the weakness and dishonesty of the prosecution's testimony was not an accident, but was the result of a consistent policy of conspiracy and corruption. Fickert is seen throughout this report to be prostituting his office in other cases precisely as he prostituted it in the bomb cases, and if there was previously any doubt as to whether a prisoner whom powerful interests desired to convict would receive a fair trial at the hands of Fickert there is now no doubt about the matter whatever. The San Francisco district attorney's office, thrown wide open by this investigation, reveals the public prosecutor, not as an officer of justice but as a conspirator against justice. Fickert is shown setting the guilty free and persecuting the innocent.

Fickert's desperate daily attempts to bolster up a cause which cannot for a moment stand an unprejudiced examination; his affinity for a man who is both a discredited judge and an unblushing representative of dishonest interests; his constant association with, and dependence upon, a corrupt corporation detective; his passionate personal hatred of the various defendants, and his determination to ruin them, despite the fact that he, better than anyone else, knows that they are innocent; his openly expressed contempt, in the midst of a great war, for the President of the United States; his total disregard for law; his affiliation with, and servile truckling to, the most bitterly partisan antilabor element of the Chamber of Commerce; his close personal friendship for Pete McDonough, notorious briber of juries; his illegal quashing of the David Blaine indictment for Bennie Selig; his attempted frame-up of Mrs. Judd to testify against Mrs. Mooney — these and similar questionable activities apparently represent the chief business and ordinary daily routine of the present district attorney of the city and county of San Francisco. In the strictest and most literal meaning of the word, anarchy reigns in the office which is supposed to be dedicated to law and order.

Ordinarily the relentless persecution of four or five defendants, even though it resulted in unmerited punishment for them all, would conceivably have but a local effect, which would soon be obliterated and forgotten. But in the Mooney case, which is nothing but a phase of the old war between capital and organized labor, a miscarriage of justice would inflame the passions of laboring men everywhere and add to a conviction, already too widespread, that workingmen can expect no justice from an orderly appeal to the established courts.

Yet this miscarriage of justice is in process of rapid consummation. One man is about to be hanged; another is in prison for life; the remaining defendants are still in peril of their liberty or lives, one or the other of which they will surely lose if some check is not given to the activities of this most amazing of district attorneys.

The issue involved is immeasurably larger than the city and county of San Francisco. On the day that the state Supreme Court confessed that it was without power in the premises the issue became larger even than the sovereign state of California. The fact is that in its true proportions it is an issue not unworthy to be ranked with the other great problems arising out of the war now being waged for the rights of man and the liberation of peoples.

With these facts uppermost in mind, it seems but logical, in bringing this report to a close, to suggest that it would be well within the province and privilege of the federal government to devise some means by which, without giving offense to the duly constituted and honestly functioning authorities of the city and county of San Francisco, these several defendants would be assured of those rights before the law which are guaranteed by the federal Constitution.

36.

CARL SANDBURG: "Memoir of a Proud Boy"

The hero of this lyrical biography was Don Magregor, a coal miner who participated in the Ludlow, Colorado, strike of the United Mine Workers against the Rockefeller-owned Colorado Fuel and Iron Company. After the strike came to its ambiguous conclusion, Magregor fled the country and took on some of the characteristics of a Robin Hood figure. "Memoir of a Proud Boy" illustrates Sandburg's simple, dramatic style as well as his deep and never-ending concern with social problems. The poem was first published in 1918.

Source: *Complete Poems*, New York, 1950.

MEMOIR OF A PROUD BOY

He lived on the wings of storm.
The ashes are in Chihuahua.

Out of Ludlow and coal towns in Colorado
Sprang a vengeance of Slav miners, Italians, Scots,
     Cornishmen, Yanks.
Killings ran under the spoken commands of this boy
With eighty men and rifles on a hogback mountain.

They killed swearing to remember
The shot and charred wives and children
In the burnt camp of Ludlow,
And Louis Tikas, the laughing Greek,
Plugged with a bullet, clubbed with a gun butt.

As a home war
It held the nation a week
And one or two million men stood together
And swore by the retribution of steel.

It was all accidental.
He lived flecking lint off coat lapels
Of men he talked with.
He kissed the miners' babies
And wrote a Denver paper
Of picket silhouettes on a mountain line.

He had no mother but Mother Jones
Crying from a jail window of Trinidad:
"All I want is room enough to stand
And shake my fist at the enemies of the human race."

Named by a grand jury as a murderer
He went to Chihuahua, forgot his old Scotch name,
Smoked cheroots with Pancho Villa
And wrote letters of Villa as a rock of the people.

How can I tell how Don Magregor went?

Three riders emptied lead into him.
He lay on the main street of an inland town.
A boy sat near all day throwing stones
To keep pigs away.

The Villa men buried him in a pit
With twenty Carranzistas.

There is drama in that point . . .
. . . the boy and the pigs.
Griffith would make a movie of it to fetch sobs.
Victor Herbert would have the drums whirr
In a weave with a high fiddle-string's single clamor.

"And the muchacho sat there all day throwing stones
To keep the pigs away," wrote Gibbons to the *Tribune*.

Somewhere in Chihuahua or Colorado
Is a leather bag of poems and short stories.

37.

THORSTEIN VEBLEN: Business and the Higher Learning

Thorstein Veblen, author of the classic economic study The Theory of the Leisure
Class *(1899), was a bitterly ironic critic of what he saw as the predatory
commercialism of his age. He left no stone unturned and found worms under every
one; but his assertion, in* The Theory of the Leisure Class, *that even the higher
learning was marked by "conspicuous consumption" aroused the hostility of the
academic world, a fact that contributed to Veblen's checkered academic career.
The following selection, taken from the summary chapter of* The Higher Learning
in America *(1918), reflects Veblen's view of the operation of business principles in
university life.*

Source: *The Higher Learning in America*, New York, 1918, pp. 219-227.

As IN EARLIER PASSAGES, so here in speaking
of profit and loss, the point of view taken is
neither that of material advantage, whether
of the individuals concerned or of the community at large, nor that of expediency for
the common good in respect of prosperity
or of morals; nor is the appraisal here ventured upon to be taken as an expression of
praise or dispraise at large, touching this incursion of business principles into the affairs
of learning.

By and large, the intrusion of businesslike
ideals, aims, and methods into this field,
with all the consequences that follow, may
be commendable or the reverse. All that is
matter for attention and advisement at the
hands of such as aim to alter, improve,
amend, or conserve the run of institutional
phenomena that goes to make up the current situation. The present inquiry bears on
the higher learning as it comes into this
current situation and on the effect of this
recourse to business principles upon the
pursuit of learning.

Not that this learning is therefore to be
taken as necessarily of higher and more substantial value than that traffic in competitive
gain and competitive spending upon which
business principles converge, and in which
they find their consummate expression —
even though it is broadly to be recognized
and taken account of that such is the deliberate appraisal awarded by the common
sense of civilized mankind. The profit and
loss here spoken for is not profit and loss to
mankind or to any given community, in respect of that inclusive complex of interests
that makes up the balanced total of good
and ill; it is profit and loss for the cause of
learning, simply; and there is here no aspiration to pass on ulterior questions.

As required by the exigencies of such an
argument, it is therefore assumed, *pro forma*, that profit and loss for the pursuit of
learning is profit and loss without reservation; very much as a corporation accountant
will audit income and outlay within the affairs of the corporation, whereas, *qua* accountant, he will perforce have nothing to
say as to the ulterior expediency of the cor-

poration and its affairs in any other bearing.

Business principles take effect in academic affairs most simply, obviously and avowably in the way of a businesslike administration of the scholastic routine; where they lead immediately to a bureaucratic organization and a system of scholastic accountancy. In one form or another, some such administrative machinery is a necessity in any large school that is to be managed on a centralized plan; as the American schools commonly are, and as, more particularly, they aim to be. This necessity is all the more urgent in a school that takes over the discipline of a large body of pupils that have not reached years of discretion, as is also commonly the case with those American schools that claim rank as universities; and the necessity is all the more evident to men whose ideal of efficiency is the centralized control exercised through a system of accountancy in the modern, large business concerns.

The larger American schools are primarily undergraduate establishments — with negligible exceptions; and under these current American conditions, of excessive numbers, such a centralized and bureaucratic administration appears to be indispensable for the adequate control of immature and reluctant students; at the same time, such an organization conduces to an excessive size. The immediate and visible effect of such a large and centralized administrative machinery is, on the whole, detrimental to scholarship, even in the undergraduate work; though it need not be so in all respects and unequivocally so far as regards that routine training that is embodied in the undergraduate curriculum. But it is at least a necessary evil in any school that is of so considerable a size as to preclude substantially all close or cordial personal relations between the teachers and each of these immature pupils under their charge, as, again, is commonly the case with these American undergraduate establishments.

Such a system of authoritative control, standardization, gradation, accountancy, classification, credits, and penalties will necessarily be drawn on stricter lines the more the school takes on the character of a house of correction or a penal settlement, in which the irresponsible inmates are to be held to a round of distasteful tasks and restrained from (conventionally) excessive irregularities of conduct. At the same time this recourse to such coercive control and standardization of tasks has unavoidably given the schools something of the character of a penal settlement.

As intimated above, the ideal of efficiency by force of which a large-scale centralized organization commends itself in these premises is that pattern of shrewd management whereby a large business concern makes money. The underlying businesslike presumption accordingly appears to be that learning is a merchantable commodity, to be produced on a piece-rate plan, rated, bought, and sold by standard units, measured, counted, and reduced to staple equivalence by impersonal, mechanical tests. In all its bearings the work is hereby reduced to a mechanistic, statistical consistency, with numerical standards and units; which conduces to perfunctory and mediocre work throughout, and acts to deter both students and teachers from a free pursuit of knowledge, as contrasted with the pursuit of academic credits. So far as this mechanistic system goes freely into effect it leads to a substitution of salesmanlike proficiency — a balancing of bargains in staple credits — in the place of scientific capacity and addiction to study.

The salesmanlike abilities and the men of affairs that so are drawn into the academic personnel are, presumably, somewhat undergrade in their kind; since the pecuniary inducement offered by the schools is rather low as compared with the remuneration for office work of a similar character in the common run of business occupations, and since businesslike employees of this kind may fairly be presumed to go unreservedly to the highest bidder. Yet these more unscholarly members of the staff will necessarily be assigned the more responsible and discretionary positions in the academic organization; since under such a scheme of standardization, accountancy and control, the school becomes primarily a bureaucratic organization, and the first and unremitting duties of the staff are those of official management and accountancy. The further qualifications requisite in the members of the academic staff will be such as make for vendibility — volubility, tactful effrontery, conspicuous conformity to the popular taste in all matters of opinion, usage, and conventions.

The need of such a businesslike organization asserts itself in somewhat the same degree in which the academic policy is guided by considerations of magnitude and statistical renown; and this in turn is somewhat closely correlated with the extent of discretionary power exercised by the captain of erudition placed in control. At the same time, by provocation of the facilities which it offers for making an impressive demonstration, such bureaucratic organization will lead the university management to bend its energies with somewhat more singleness to the parade of magnitude and statistical gains. It also, and in the same connection, provokes to a persistent and detailed surveillance and direction of the work and manner of life of the academic staff, and so it acts to shut off initiative of any kind in the work done.

Intimately bound up with this bureaucratic officialism and accountancy, and working consistently to a similar outcome, is the predilection for "practical efficiency" — that is to say, for pecuniary success — prevalent in the American community. This predilection is a matter of settled habit, due, no doubt, to the fact that preoccupation with business interests characterizes this community in an exceptional degree, and

that pecuniary habits of thought consequently rule popular thinking in a peculiarly uncritical and prescriptive fashion. This pecuniary animus falls in with and reinforces the movement for academic accountancy and combines with it to further a so-called "practical" bias in all the work of the schools.

It appears, then, that the intrusion of business principles in the universities goes to weaken and retard the pursuit of learning and therefore to defeat the ends for which a university is maintained. This result follows, primarily, from the substitution of impersonal, mechanical relations, standards and tests, in the place of personal conference, guidance, and association between teachers and students; as also from the imposition of a mechanically standardized routine upon the members of the staff, whereby any disinterested preoccupation with scholarly or scientific inquiry is thrown into the background and falls into abeyance. Few if any who are competent to speak in these premises will question that such has been the outcome.

To offset against this work of mutilation and retardation there are certain gains in expedition and in the volume of traffic that can be carried by any given equipment and corps of employees. Particularly will there be a gain in the statistical showing, both as regards the volume of instruction offered and probably also as regards the enrollment; since accountancy creates statistics and its absence does not.

Such increased enrollment as may be due to businesslike management and methods is an increase of undergraduate enrollment. The net effect as regards the graduate enrollment — apart from any vocational instruction that may euphemistically be scheduled as "graduate" — is in all probability rather a decrease than an increase. Through indoctrination with utilitarian (pecuniary) ideals of earning and spending, as well as by engendering spendthrift and sportsmanlike habits, such a businesslike management diverts the undergraduate students from going in for the disinterested pursuit of knowledge and so from entering on what is properly university work; as witness the relatively slight proportion of graduate students — outside of the professional schools — who come up from the excessively large undergraduate departments of the more expansive universities, as contrasted with the number of those who come into university work from the smaller and less businesslike colleges.

The ulterior consequences that follow from such businesslike standardization and bureaucratic efficiency are evident in the current state of the public schools; especially as seen in the larger towns, where the principles of business management have had time and scope to work out in a fair degree of consistency. The resulting abomination of desolation is sufficiently notorious. And there appears to be no reason why a similarly stale routine of futility should not overtake the universities and give similarly foolish results as fast as the system of standardization, accountancy, and piecework goes consistently into effect — except only for the continued enforced employment of a modicum of impracticable scholars and scientists on the academic staff, whose unbusinesslike scholarly proclivities and inability to keep the miner's-inch of scholastic credit always in mind, must in some measure always defeat the perfect working of standardization and accountancy.

As might be expected, this regime of graduated sterility has already made fair headway in the undergraduate work, especially in the larger undergraduate schools; and this in spite of any efforts on the part of the administration to hedge against such an outcome by recourse to an intricate system of electives and a wide diversification of the standard units of erudition so offered.

In the graduate work the like effect is only less visible, because the measures leading to it have come into bearing more recently and hitherto less unreservedly. But the like results should follow here also, just so fast and so far as the same range of business principles come to be worked into the texture of the university organization in the same efficacious manner as they have already taken effect in the public schools. And, pushed on as it is by the progressive substitution of men imbued with the tastes and habits of practical affairs, in the place of unpractical scholarly ideals, the movement toward a perfunctory routine of mediocrity should logically be expected to go forward at a progressively accelerated rate.

The visible drift of things in this respect in the academic pursuit of the social sciences, so-called, is an argument as to what may be hoped for in the domain of academic science at large. It is only that the executive is actuated by a sharper solicitude to keep the academic establishment blameless of anything like innovation or iconoclasm at this point; which reinforces the drift toward a mechanistic routine and a curtailment of inquiry in this field; it is not that these sciences that deal with the phenomena of human life lend themselves more readily to mechanical description and enumeration than the material sciences do, nor is their subject matter intrinsically more inert or less provocative of questions.

A good listener is not only popular everywhere, but after a while he knows something.
When you take stuff from one writer, it's plagiarism; but when you take it from many writers, it's research.

WILSON MIZNER

1919

38.

WOODROW WILSON: The League of Nations

The agreements arrived at during the Versailles Peace Conference of 1919 dealt, among other things, with territorial adjustments, colonial claims, war reparations, and arms control. President Wilson, who headed the American delegation, was convinced that no lasting peace was possible unless, in addition to those, an international organization came into existence. On January 25 he accepted the post of chairman of the commission that drew up the Covenant of the League of Nations and that submitted it to a plenary session of the Conference on February 14. Reprinted here is Wilson's explanatory speech made immediately after the Covenant was read to the delegates.

Source: 65 Congress, 3 Session, Senate Document No. 389, pp. 12-15.

IT GIVES ME PLEASURE to add to this formal reading of the result of our labors that the character of the discussion which occurred at the sittings of the commission was not only of the most constructive but of the most encouraging sort. It was obvious throughout our discussions that, although there were subjects upon which there were individual differences of judgment with regard to the method by which our objects should be obtained, there was practically at no point any serious differences of opinion or motive as to the objects which we were seeking.

Indeed, while these debates were not made the opportunity for the expression of enthusiasm and sentiments, I think the other members of the commission will agree with me that there was an undertone of high respect and of enthusiasm for the thing we were trying to do which was heartening throughout everything.

Because we felt that in a way this conference did entrust into us the expression of one of its highest and most important purposes, to see to it that the concord of the world in the future with regard to the objects of justice should not be subject to doubt or uncertainty; that the cooperation of the great body of nations should be assured in the maintenance of peace upon terms of honor and of international obligations.

The compulsion of that task was constantly upon us, and at no point was there shown the slightest desire to do anything but suggest the best means to accomplish that great object. There is very great significance, therefore, in the fact that the result was reached unanimously.

Fourteen nations were represented, among them all of those powers which for convenience we have called the Great Powers, and among the rest a representation of the greatest variety of circumstances and interests. So that I think we are justified in saying that the significance of the result, therefore, has the deepest of all meanings, the union of wills in a common purpose, a union of wills which cannot be resisted and which, I dare say, no nation will run the risk of attempting to resist.

Now, as to the character of the document. While it has consumed some time to read this document, I think you will see at once that it is very simple, and in nothing so simple as in the structure which it suggests for a league of nations, a body of delegates, an executive council, and a permanent secretariat.

When it came to the question of determining the character of the representation in the Body of Delegates, we were all aware of a feeling which is current throughout the world.

Inasmuch as I am stating it in the presence of the official representatives of the various governments here present, including myself, I may say that there is a universal feeling that the world cannot rest satisfied with merely official guidance. There has reached us through many channels the feeling that if the deliberating body of the League of Nations was merely to be a body of officials representing the various governments, the peoples of the world would not be sure that some of the mistakes which preoccupied officials had admittedly made might not be repeated.

It was impossible to conceive a method or an assembly so large and various as to be really representative of the great body of the peoples of the world, because, as I roughly reckon it, we represent as we sit

The Granger Collection

Clemenceau, Wilson, and Lloyd George leaving the Palace of Versailles after signing the peace treaty in June 1919

around this table more than 1.2 billion people.

You cannot have a representative assembly of 1.2 billion people, but if you leave it to each government to have, if it pleases, one or two or three representatives, though only with a single vote, it may vary its representation from time to time, not only, but it may (originate) the choice of its several representatives [wireless here unintelligible].

Therefore we thought that this was a proper and a very prudent concession to the practically universal opinion of plain men everywhere that they wanted the door left open to a variety of representation, instead of being confined to a single official body with which they could or might not find themselves in sympathy.

And you will notice that this body has unlimited rights of discussion. I mean of discussion of anything that falls within the field of international relations — and that it is especially agreed that war or international misunderstandings or anything that may lead to friction or trouble is everybody's business, because it may affect the peace of the world.

And in order to safeguard the popular power so far as we could of this representative body, it is provided, you will notice, that when a subject is submitted it is not to arbitration but to discussion by the Executive Council; it can, upon the initiative of either of the parties to the dispute, be drawn out of the Executive Council on the larger form of the general Body of Delegates, because through this instrument we are depending primarily and chiefly upon one great force, and this is the moral force of the public opinion of the world — the pleasing and clarifying and compelling influences of publicity — so that intrigues can no longer have their coverts; so that designs that are sinister can at anytime be drawn into the open; so that those things that are destroyed by the light may be promptly destroyed by the overwhelming light of the universal expression of the condemnation of the world.

Armed force is in the background in this program; but it is in the background, and, if the moral force of the world will not suffice, the physical force of the world shall. But that is the last resort, because this is intended as a constitution of peace, not as a league of war.

The simplicity of the document seems to me to be one of its chief virtues, because, speaking for myself, I was unable to see the variety of circumstances with which this League would have to deal. I was unable, therefore, to plan all the machinery that might be necessary to meet the differing and unexpected contingencies. Therefore, I should say of this document that it is not a straitjacket but a vehicle of life.

A living thing is born, and we must see to it what clothes we put on it. It is not a vehicle of power, but a vehicle in which power may be varied at the discretion of those who exercise it and in accordance with the changing circumstances of the time. And yet, while it is elastic, while it is general in its terms, it is definite in the one thing that we were called upon to make definite.

It is a definite guaranty of peace. It is a definite guaranty by word against aggression. It is a definite guaranty against the things which have just come near bringing the whole structure of civilization into ruin.

Its purposes do not for a moment lie vague. Its purposes are declared, and its powers are unmistakable. It is not in contemplation that this should be merely a league to secure the peace of the world. It is a league which can be used for cooperation in any international matter.

That is the significance of the provision introduced concerning labor. There are many ameliorations of labor conditions which can be effected by conference and discussion. I anticipate that there will be a very great usefulness in the Bureau of Labor which it is contemplated shall be set up by the League.

Men and women and children who work have been in the background through long ages and sometimes seemed to be forgotten, while governments have had their watchful and suspicious eyes upon the maneuvers of one another, while the thought of statesmen has been about structural action and the larger transactions of commerce and of finance.

Now, if I may believe the picture which I see, there comes into the foreground the great body of the laboring people of the world, the men and women and children upon whom the great burden of sustaining the world must from day to day fall, whether we wish it to do so or not; people who go to bed tired and wake up without the stimulation of lively hope. These people will be drawn into the field of international consultation and help, and will be among the wards of the combined governments of the world. This is, I take leave to say, a very great step in advance in the mere conception of that.

Then, as you will notice, there is an imperative article concerning the publicity of all international agreements. Henceforth no member of the League can call any agreement valid which it has not registered with the secretary general, in whose office, of course, it will be subject to the examination of any body representing a member of the League. And the duty is laid upon the secretary general to earliest possible time.

I suppose most persons who have not been conversant with the business of foreign affairs do not realize how many hundreds of these agreements are made in a single year, and how difficult it might be to publish the more unimportant of them immediately. How uninteresting it would be to most of the world to publish them immediately, but even they must be published just as soon as it is possible for the secretary general to publish them.

There has been no greater advance than this, gentlemen. If you look back upon the history of the world you will see how helpless peoples have too often been a prey to powers that had no conscience in the matter. It has been one of the many distressing revelations of recent years that the great power which has just been, happily, defeated put intolerable burdens and injustices upon the helpless people of some of the colonies which it annexed to itself; that its interest was rather their extermination than their development; that the desire was to possess their land for European purposes, and not to enjoy their confidence in order that mankind might be lifted in these places to the next higher level.

Now, the world, expressing its conscience in law, says there is an end of that, that our consciences shall be settled to this thing. States will be picked out which have already shown that they can exercise a conscience in this matter, and under their tutelage the helpless peoples of the world will come into a new light and into a new hope.

39.

Peace At Any Price

Even before President Wilson finally left Paris in June 1919, the fight for the Versailles Treaty had begun at home. Opposition came not only from partisan Republicans and isolationists but also from liberals who felt that the treaty did as much to provide a basis for future global conflicts as it did to insure peace, despite the safeguard of a League of Nations. The following editorial from the New Republic, *which shortly before had endorsed Wilson, criticized the peacemakers for doing too little and making too many compromises.*

Source: *New Republic,* May 24, 1919.

IN THEIR COMMENTS on the Treaty of Versailles, the newspapers published in the Allied countries confine themselves chiefly to the expression of two sharply contrasted verdicts. Those which have vigorously supported the war praise the Treaty as a document, which, however harsh its terms may appear to be, is defensible as a stern but just attempt to make the punishment of Germany fit her crimes. Those which did not support the war or conditioned their support on the fulfillment of definite political objects are equally uncompromising in their rejection of the Treaty. They consider it a flagrant and perfidious repudiation of all the more generous, humane, and constructive objects in the name of which the people in the Allied countries were induced to shed their blood and sacrifice their lives.

These hostile verdicts attract to themselves the limelight of public attention, but particularly in this country we should not overlook the third state of mind about the Treaty which is obtaining expression in some of the Western journals. There are many of our fellow countrymen, both in the East and in the West, whose sense of justice and fair-dealing is outraged by the Treaty, but who cannot quite decide to place themselves in open and uncompromising opposition to it. Their state of mind is analogous to that of those Americans in August 1914 whose consciences were troubled by the wanton violence of the German invasion of Belgium, but who did not know how, as American citizens, they could assume effective responsibility for defeating the monster of militant imperialism.

To Americans who share this third state of mind, we should like to address an appeal. They are in danger now of committing a mistake similar to that which their fellow countrymen committed in the fall of 1914. During the early months of the war the majority of uneasy Americans compromised with their consciences. They usually became definitely pro-Ally in opinion, but they were mentally unprepared for war, and they considered it unnecessary to consider any method, short of an actual declaration of war, which would bring American political influence and economic power to the support of democratic Europe. In an analogous spirit, Americans who are deeply troubled by the proposed treaty of peace are feeling for a way out which does not imply outspoken and uncompromising opposition. Just as four and one-half years ago they shrank from breaking down the traditional aloofness of this country from European political and military controversies, so now

they shrink from parting company with their recent companions in arms. The bonds forged by their fight against a common enemy are hard to break. If they reject the Treaty they are afraid of looking to themselves and to their European friends like quitters. They are longing for peace and are tempted to accept it at any price.

Yet if they connive at this Treaty they will, as liberal and humane American democrats who seek by social experiment and education to render their country more worthy of its still unredeemed national promise, be delivering themselves into the hands of their enemies, the reactionaries and the revolutionists. The future of liberal Americanism depends upon a moral union between democracy and nationalism. Such a union is compromised so long as nationalism remains competitive in policy, exclusive in spirit, and complacently capitalist in organization. Liberals all over the world have hoped that a war, which was so clearly the fruit of competition and imperialist and class-bound nationalism, would end in a peace which would moralize nationalism by releasing it from class bondage and exclusive ambitions.

The Treaty of Versailles does not even try to satisfy these aspirations. Instead of expressing a great recuperative effort of the conscience of a civilization, which for its own sins has sweated so much blood, it does much to intensify and nothing to heal the old and ugly dissensions between political nationalism and social democracy. Insofar as its terms are actually carried out, it is bound to provoke the ultimate explosion of irreconcilable warfare. It weaves international animosities and the class conflict into the very fabric of the proposed new system of public law. The European politicians, who with American complicity have hatched this inhuman monster, have acted either cynically, hypocritically, or vindictively, and their handwork will breed cynicism, hypocrisy, or vindictiveness in the minds of future generations. The moral source of the political life of modern nations remains polluted.

The authors of the Treaty of Versailles are the victims of the blind interests and the imperious determinism of an inhumane class economy. They admit in private conversation the diseased nature of their own offspring. "Even conservative opinion in Europe," says William Allen White, "is frankly cynical about Germany's fulfillment of the terms imposed. They are too severe for Germany to live under for a generation. . . . They practically exterminate her as a nation." Why, then, did they do it? Why do they propose to terminate a war, fought in part to vindicate the sacredness of public treaties, by compelling the vanquished enemy to sign a bond which they know he cannot fulfill? The answer is not pleasant. They do this thing because they themselves are the unconscious servants of the cupidity and the vindictiveness which infect the psychology of an inhumane and complacent capitalist society.

They crave at any cost the emotional triumph of imposing on the German nation the ultimate humiliation of solemnly consenting to its own abdication as a self-governing and self-respecting community. To satisfy this craving they are so far as possible depriving the German people by public law of the status of economic citizens with rights which other nations are bound to respect. Thus they are deliberately raising the question of working class solidarity. They are defying the community of interest and the feeling of brotherhood which unites the socially alert workers of all the European peoples. They are subsidizing the growth of class-conscious and class-bound proletarian internationalism dominated by the conviction of the incorrigible inhumanity of a capitalist national economy. They are demonstrating by example what a perfidious protectorate nationalism exercises over the common human interests of all peoples.

The Socialists are fully alive to this deep-er and less obvious meaning of the Treaty. They will flourish it as a complete vindication of the Marxian dogma that, as long as capitalism prevails, war necessarily operates as the instrument of class aggrandizement and popular exploitation. The Treaty proposes the exploitation of the German people only, but an international organization whose chief object it is to profit by the exploitation of a subject people can survive only through the exploitation and deception of its own workers. The Treaty is, consequently, greeted as a declaration of a class war by organized society against the proletariat of all nations. It is condemned as a final exposure of the hypocrisy and inhumanity of a national economy.

Hitherto, in spite of all their propaganda and of the grievances of the wage-earning class, the Socialists have never persuaded the workers to believe in the need of a class war, or to undermine the popular confidence in nationalism. Now, as they believe, their class enemies have provided them with an unanswerable demonstration, and they are looking forward jubilantly to the inevitable revolution. The New York *Nation* announces confidently that all recent political and social convulsions are only "the preliminaries of the great revolution to whose support the friends of freedom must now rally everywhere."

In our opinion the Treaty of Versailles subjects all liberalism, and particularly that kind of liberalism which breathes the Christian spirit, to a decisive test. Its very life depends upon the ability of the modern national state to avoid the irreconcilable class conflict to which, as the Socialists claim, capitalism condemns the future of society. In the event of such a conflict, liberalism is ground, as it is being ground in Russia, between the upper and lower millstones of reaction and revolution. The Treaty, insofar as it commits the national democracies to a permanent policy of inhumane violence, does weave this conflict into the fabric of international law. It is the most shameless and, we hope, the last of those treaties which, while they pretend to bring peace to a mortified world, merely write the specifications for future revolution and war. It presents liberalism with a perfect opportunity of proving whether or not it is actually founded in positive moral and religious conviction.

If a war which was supposed to put an end to war culminates without strenuous protest by humane men and women in a treaty of peace which renders peace impossible, the liberalism which preached this meaning for the war will have committed suicide. That such a protest on the part of national liberals may not have much immediate success in defeating the ratification of the Treaty is not essential. The Treaty of Versailles, no matter under what kind of compulsion it is ratified by the nations, is impossible of execution and will defeat itself.

But it is essential that the ratification should not take place with the connivance of the sincerely liberal and Christian forces in public opinion. For in that event national liberalism in the Allied countries will be following the example and inviting the fate of national liberalism in imperial Germany. It will become the dishonored accomplice of its own downfall. It will abandon society to an irresistible conflict between the immoral and intransigeant forces of Junkerism and revolutionary socialism.

The calamity of the war descended on the Western nations because of the existence of one crying weakness in Western civilization. The organized Christian nations could never agree upon an effective method of subordinating the exercise of political and economic power to moral and humane purposes. Many liberals have hoped that at the end of the war the enlightened conscience of the Western people would arise and exert itself to cure this weakness. The Treaty of Versailles is damned because it does

nothing to moralize the future exercise of political and economic power. On the contrary, it conceives the victors who exercise the power as possessing only rights and the vanquished who have lost the power as possessing only duties. The powerful are permitted to abuse it as much as they please, and, in their relations to the defeated Hungary, Austria, Russia, and Germany, they are encouraged and licensed to abuse it.

The past sins of the Hungarian and German ruling classes afford no justification for such a convenient and drastic system of future discrimination. Those who will not subordinate the exercise of power to rules of impartial justice sacrifice their moral right to inflict punishment. The Treaty does not embody either the spirit or method even of punitive justice. What it does embody and strain to the breaking point is the pagan doctrine and spirit of retaliation. What it treats with utter ignorance is the Christian doctrine of atonement and redemption. At a crisis in the history of civilization, the rulers of the victorious Christian states conclusively demonstrate their own contemptuous disbelief in the practical value of Christian moral economy.

Just as the acceptance of the Treaty of Versailles without protest will undermine the moral foundation of nationalism and menace civilization with an uncontrollable class conflict, so its defeat or discredit will clearly and emphatically testify to a formative connection between religion and morals and economics and politics. It would begin the cure of the spiritual anarchy in Western civilization which the recent war and the proposed peace both exemplify. It would constitute the first step in the moral preparation of the Western democracies for a League of Nations.

For the possibility of any vital League of Nations does not depend, as so many liberals seem to suppose, on the ratification of the Treaty. It depends on the rejection of the Treaty. The League is not powerful enough to redeem the Treaty. But the Treaty is vicious enough to incriminate the League. It would convert the League into the instrument of competitive imperialist nationalism whose more disinterested members would labor in vain to mold it into a cooperative society. Liberal democrats cannot honestly consent to peace on the proposed terms. If it was wrong when confronted by the imperialist aggression of Germany to tolerate peace by conniving at such an attack, it is equally wrong when confronted by a treaty which organizes competitive imperialism into an international system to pay so high a price for the ending of the war. This above all others is the time and the occasion to repudiate the idea of peace at any price, to reject immediate peace at the price of permanent moral and economic warfare.

40.

Woodrow Wilson: Appeal for Support of the League of Nations

President Wilson was convinced that the great majority of Americans were in favor of the Versailles Treaty and the League of Nations. Thirty-three governors and thirty-two state legislatures had gone on record approving the League; but in the face of growing congressional opposition the President decided to undertake an 8,000-mile speaking tour to arouse public support that Congress could not ignore. The trip, through the Middle and Far West, permanently impaired Wilson's health and virtually took him out of the fight for the League. He gave thirty-seven addresses in all, and by September 25, after speaking in Pueblo, Colorado, the remaining speeches had to be canceled because of physical exhaustion. Reprinted here is the text of his address at Omaha, Nebraska, on September 8, 1919.

Source: *The Public Papers of Woodrow Wilson*, Ray S. Baker and William E. Dodd, eds., Authorized Edition, Vol. I, New York, 1924, pp. 30-44.

I NEVER FEEL MORE COMFORTABLE in facing my fellow citizens than when I can realize that I am not representing a peculiar cause, that I am not speaking for a single group of my fellow citizens, that I am not the representative of a party but the representative of the people of the United States. I went across the water with that happy consciousness, and in all the work that was done on the other side of the sea, where I was associated with distinguished Americans of both political parties, we all of us constantly kept at our heart the feeling that we were expressing the thoughts of America, that we were working for the things that America believed in. I have come here to testify that this treaty contains the things that America believes in.

I brought a copy of the treaty along with me, for I fancy that, in view of the criticisms you have heard of it, you thought it consisted of only four or five clauses.

Only four or five clauses out of this volume are picked out for criticism. Only four or five phrases in it are called to your attention by some of the distinguished orators who oppose its adoption. Why, my fellow citizens, this is one of the great charters of human liberty, and the man who picks flaws in it — or, rather, picks out the flaws that are in it, for there are flaws in it — forgets the magnitude of the thing, forgets the majesty of the thing, forgets that the counsels of more than twenty nations combined and were rendered unanimous in the adoption of this great instrument.

Let me remind you of what everybody admits who has read the document. Everybody admits that it is a complete settlement of the matters which led to this war, and that it contains the complete machinery which provides that they shall stay settled.

You know that one of the greatest difficulties in our own domestic affairs is unsettled land titles. Suppose that somebody were mischievously to tamper with the land records of the state of Nebraska, and that there should be a doubt as to the line of every farm. You know what would happen in six months. All the farmers would be sitting on their fences with shotguns. Litigation would penetrate every community, hot feeling would be generated, contests not only of lawyers but contests of force would ensue. Very well, one of the interesting things that this treaty does is to settle the land titles of Europe, and to settle them in this way, on the principle that every land belongs to the people that live on it.

This is actually the first time in human history that that principle was ever recognized in a similar document, and yet that is the fundamental American principle. The fundamental American principle is the right of the people that live in the country to say what shall be done with that country. We have gone so far in our assertions of popular right that we not only say that the people have a right to have a government

that suits them but that they have a right to change it in any respect at any time. Very well, that principle lies at the heart of this treaty.

There are peoples in Europe who never before could say that the land they lived in was their own, and the choice that they were to make of their lives was their own choice. I know there are men in Nebraska who come from that country of tragical history, the now restored Republic of Poland, and I want to call your attention to the fact that Poland is here given her complete restitution; and not only is she given the land that formerly belonged to the Poles, but she is given the lands which are now occupied by Poles but had been permitted to remain under other sovereignties. She is given those lands on a principle that all our hearts approve of.

Take what in Europe they call High Silesia, the mountainous, the upper, portions of the district of Silesia. The very great majority of the people in High Silesia are Poles, but the Germans contested the statement that most of them were Poles. We said: "Very well, then, it is none of our business; we will let them decide. We will put sufficient armed forces into High Silesia to see that nobody tampers with the processes of the election, and then we will hold a referendum there, and those people can belong either to Germany or to Poland, as they prefer, and not as we prefer."

And, wherever there was a doubtful district, we applied the same principle, that the people should decide and not the men sitting around the peace table at Paris. When these referenda are completed the land titles of Europe will be settled, and every country will belong to the people that live on it to do with what they please. You seldom hear of this aspect of this treaty, my fellow citizens.

You have heard of the council that the newspaper men call the "Big Four." We had a very much bigger name for ourselves than that. We called ourselves the "Supreme Council of the Principal Allied and Associated Powers," but we had no official title, and sometimes there were five of us instead of four. Those five represented, with the exception of Germany, of course, the great fighting nations of the world. They could have done anything with this treaty that they chose to do, because they had the power to do it, and they chose to do what had never been chosen before, to renounce every right of sovereignty in that settlement to which the people concerned did not assent. That is the great settlement which is represented in this volume.

And it contains, among other things, a great charter of liberty for the workingmen of the world. For the first time in history the counsels of mankind are to be drawn together and concerted for the purpose of defending the rights and improving the conditions of working people — men, women, and children — all over the world. Such a thing as that was never dreamed of before, and what you are asked to discuss in discussing the League of Nations is the matter of seeing that this thing is not interfered with. There is no other way to do it than by a universal league of nations, and what is proposed is a universal league of nations.

Only two nations are for the time being left out. One of them is Germany, because we did not think that Germany was ready to come in, because we felt that she ought to go through a period of probation. She says that she made a mistake. We now want her to prove it by not trying it again. She says that she has abolished all the old forms of government by which little secret councils of men, sitting nobody knew exactly where, determined the fortunes of that great nation and, incidentally, tried to determine the fortunes of mankind; but we want her to prove that her constitution is changed and that it is going to stay changed; and then who can, after those proofs are produced, say "No" to a great people, 60 million strong, if they want to come in on equal terms with the rest of us and do justice in international affairs?

I want to say that I did not find any of my colleagues in Paris disinclined to do justice to Germany. But I hear that this treaty is very hard on Germany. When an individual has committed a criminal act, the punishment is hard, but the punishment is not unjust. This nation permitted itself, through unscrupulous governors to commit a criminal act against mankind, and it is to undergo the punishment, not more than it can endure but up to the point where it can pay it must pay for the wrong that it has done.

But the things prescribed in this treaty will not be fully carried out if any one of the great influences that brought that result about is withheld from its consummation. Every great fighting nation in the world is on the list of those who are to constitute the League of Nations. I say every great nation, because America is going to be included among them, and the only choice my fellow citizens is whether we will go in now or come in later with Germany; whether we will go in as founders of this covenant of freedom or go in as those who are admitted after they have made a mistake and repented.

I wish I could do what is impossible in a great company like this. I wish I could read that Covenant to you, because I do not believe, if you have not read it yourself and have only listened to certain speeches that I have read, that you know anything that is in it. Why, my fellow citizens, the heart of the Covenant is that there shall be no war. To listen to some of the speeches that you may have listened to or read, you would think that the heart of it was that it was an arrangement for war. On the contrary, this is the heart of that treaty.

The bulk of it is concerned with arrangements under which all the members of the League — that means everybody but Germany and dismembered Turkey — agree that they never will go to war without first having done one or other of two things — either submitted the question at issue to arbitration, in which case they agree absolutely to abide by the verdict, or, if they do not care to submit it to arbitration, submitted it to discussion by the council of the League of Nations, in which case they must give six months for the discussion and wait three months after the rendering of the decision, whether they like it or not, before they go to war. They agree to cool off for nine months before they yield to the heat of passion, which might otherwise have hurried them into war.

If they do not do that, it is not war that ensues; it is something that will interest them and engage them very much more than war; it is an absolute boycott of the nation that disregards the Covenant. The boycott is automatic, and just as soon as it applies, then this happens: No goods can be shipped out of that country; no goods can be shipped into it. No telegraphic message may pass either way across its borders. No package of postal matter — no letter — can cross its borders either way. No citizen of any member of the League can have any transactions of any kind with any citizen of that nation. It is the most complete isolation and boycott ever conceived, and there is not a nation in Europe that can live for six months without importing goods out of other countries. After they have thought about the matter for six months, I predict that they will have no stomach for war.

All that you are told about in this Covenant, so far as I can learn, is that there is an Article X. I will repeat Article X to you; I think I can repeat it verbatim, the heart of it at any rate. Every member of the League promises to respect and preserve as against external aggression — not as against internal revolution — the territorial integrity and existing political independence of every other member of the League; and if it is necessary to enforce this promise — I

mean, for the nations to act in concert with arms in their hands to enforce it — then the council of the League shall advise what action is necessary. Some gentlemen who doubt the meaning of English words have thought that advice did not mean advice, but I do not know anything else that it does mean, and I have studied English most of my life and speak it with reasonable correctness.

The point is this: The council cannot give that advice without the vote of the United States, unless it is a party to the dispute; but, my fellow citizens, if you are a party to the dispute you are in the scrap anyhow. If you are a party, then the question is not whether you are going to war or not but merely whether you are going to war against the rest of the world or with the rest of the world, and the object of war in that case will be to defend that central thing that I began by speaking about. That is the guarantee of the land titles of the world which have been established by this treaty. Poland, Czechoslovakia, Rumania, Yugoslavia — all those nations which never had a vision of independent liberty until now — have their liberty and independence guaranteed to them.

If we do not guarantee them, then we have this interesting choice: I hear gentlemen say that we went into the recent war because we were forced into it, and their preference now is to wait to be forced in again. They do not pretend that we can keep out; they merely pretend that we ought to keep out until we are ashamed not to go in.

This is the Covenant of the League of Nations that you hear objected to, the only possible guarantee against war. I would consider myself recreant to every mother and father, every wife and sweetheart in this country, if I consented to the ending of this war without a guarantee that there would be no other. You say, "Is it an absolute guarantee?" No; there is no absolute guarantee against human passion; but even if it were only 10 percent of a guarantee, would not you rather have 10 percent guarantee against war than none? If it only creates a presumption that there will not be war, would you not rather have that presumption than live under the certainty that there will be war? For, I tell you, my fellow citizens, I can predict with absolute certainty that within another generation there will be another world war if the nations of the world do not concert the method by which to prevent it.

But I did not come here this morning, I remind myself, so much to expound the treaty as to talk about these interesting things that we hear about that are called "reservations." A reservation is an assent with a big but. We agree — but. Now, I want to call your attention to some of these buts. I will take them, so far as I can remember the order, in the order in which they deal with clauses of the League itself.

In the 1st Article of the Covenant, it is provided that a nation can withdraw from the League on two years' notice, provided, at the time of its withdrawal, that is to say at the expiration of the two years, it has fulfilled all its international obligations and all its obligations under the Covenant. Some of our friends are very uneasy about that. They want to sit close to the door with their hands on the knob, and they want to say, "We are in this thing but we are in it with infinite timidity; we are in it only because you overpersuaded us and wanted us to come in, and we are going to try this thing every now and then and see if it is locked, and just as soon as we see anything we don't like, we are going to scuttle."

Now, what is the trouble? What are they afraid of? I want you to put this to every man you know who makes this objection, what is he afraid of? Is he afraid that when the United States withdraws it will not have fulfilled its international obligations? Is

he willing to bring that indictment against this beloved country? My fellow citizens, we never did fail to fulfill an international obligation and, God guiding and helping us, we never will. I, for one, am not going to admit in any connection the slightest doubt that, if we ever choose to withdraw, we will then have fulfilled our obligations. If I make reservations, as they are called, about this, what do I do? This Covenant does not set up any tribunal to judge whether we have fulfilled our obligations at that time or not. There is only one thing to restrain us, and that is the opinion of mankind.

Are these gentlemen such poor patriots that they are afraid that the United States will cut a poor figure in the opinion of mankind? And do they think that they can bring this great people to withdraw from that League if at that time their withdrawal would be condemned by the opinion of mankind? We have always been at pains to earn the respect of mankind, and we shall always be at pains to retain it. I for one am too proud as an American to say that any doubt will ever hang around our right to withdraw upon the condition of the fulfillment of our international obligations.

I have already adverted to the difficulties under Article X and will not return to it. That difficulty is merely as I repeated it just now, that some gentlemen do not want to go in as partners; they want to go in as late joiners, because they all admit that in a war which imperils the just arrangements of mankind, America, the greatest, richest, freest people in the world, must take sides. We could not live without taking sides. We devoted ourselves to justice and to liberty when we were born, and we are not going to get senile and forget it.

They do not like the way in which the Monroe Doctrine is mentioned. Well, I would not stop on a question of style. The Monroe Doctrine is adopted. It is swallowed, hook, line, and sinker, and, being carefully digested into the central organism of the whole instrument, I do not care what language they use about it. The language is entirely satisfactory so far as I understand the English language. That puzzles me, my fellow citizens. The English language seems to have got some new meaning since I studied it that bothers these gentlemen. I do not know what dictionaries they resort to. I do not know what manuals of conscience they can possibly resort to. The Monroe Doctrine is expressly authenticated in this document, for the first time in history, by all the great nations of the world, and it was put there at our request.

When I came back to this dear country in March, I brought the first draft, the provisional draft, of the Covenant of the League. I submitted it to the Foreign Relations Committee of the Senate of the United States, and I spent an evening discussing it with them. They made a number of suggestions. I carried every one of those suggestions to Paris, and every one of them was adopted. Now, apparently, they want me to go back to Paris and say, "We are much obliged to you, but we do not like the language." I suggested the other night that if they do not like that language there is another language in here. That page is English [*illustrating*]; this page is French [*illustrating*] — the same thing. If the English does not suit them, let them engage the interest of some French scholar and see if they like the French better. It is the same thing. It is done in perfect good faith. Nobody was trying to fool anybody else. This is the genuine work of honest men.

The fourth matter that they are concerned about is domestic questions, so they want to put in a reservation enumerating certain questions as domestic questions which everybody on both sides of the water admits are domestic questions. That seems to me, to say the least, to be a work of supererogation. It does not seem to me necessary to specify what everybody admits, but they are so careful — I believe the

word used to be "meticulous" — that they want to put in what is clearly implied in the whole instrument.

"Well," you say, "why not?" Well, why not, my fellow citizens? The conference at Paris will still be sitting when the Senate of the United States has acted upon this treaty. Perhaps I ought not to say that so confidently. No man, even in the secrets of Providence, can tell how long it will take the United States Senate to do anything, but I imagine that in the normal course of human fatigue the Senate will have acted upon this treaty before the conference in Paris gets through with the Austrian treaty and the Bulgarian treaty and the Turkish treaty. They will still be there on the job.

Now — every lawyer will follow me in this — if you take a contract and change the words, even though you do not change the sense, you have to get the other parties to accept those words. Is not that true? Therefore, every reservation will have to be taken back to all the signatories of this treaty, and I want you to notice that that includes Germany. We will have to ask Germany's consent to read this treaty the way we understand it. I want to tell you that we did not ask Germany's consent with regard to the meaning of any one of those terms while we were in Paris. We told her what they meant and said, "Sign here." Are there any patriotic Americans who desire the method changed? Do they want me to ask the assembly at Weimar if I may read the treaty the way it means but in words which the United States Senate thinks it ought to have been written in?

You see, reservations come down to this, that they want to change the language of the treaty without changing its meaning and involve all the embarrassments. Because, let me say, there are indications — I am judging not from official dispatches but from the newspapers — that people are not in as good a humor over in Paris now as they were when I was there, and it is going to be more difficult to get agreement from now on than it was then. After dealing with some of those gentlemen, I found that they were as ingenious as any American in attaching unexpected meanings to plain words, and, having gone through the mill on the existing language, I do not want to go through it again on changed language.

I must not turn away from this great subject without adverting to one particular in the treaty itself, and that is the provision with regard to the transfer of certain German rights in the province of Shantung, China, to Japan. I have frankly said to my Japanese colleagues in the conference, and therefore I can without impropriety say it here, that I was very deeply dissatisfied with that part of the treaty. But, my fellow citizens, Japan agreed at that very time, and as part of the understanding upon which those clauses were put into the treaty, that she would relinquish every item of sovereignty that Germany had enjoyed to China, and that she would retain only what other nations have elsewhere in China, certain economic concessions with regard to the railway and the mines, which she was to operate under a corporation and subject to the laws of China. As I say, I wish she could have done more.

But suppose, as some have suggested, that we dissent from that clause in the treaty. You cannot sign all of the treaty but one part, my fellow citizens. It is like the President's veto. He cannot veto provisions in a bill. He has got either to sign the bill or veto the bill. We cannot sign the treaty with the Shantung provision out of it; and, if we could, what sort of service would we be doing to China?

Let us state the facts with brutal frank-

ness. England and France are bound by solemn treaty, entered into before the conference at Paris, before the end of the war, to give Japan what she gets in this treaty in the Province of Shantung. They cannot in honor withdraw from that promise. They cannot consent to a peace treaty which does not contain those provisions with regard to Shantung. England and France, therefore, will stand behind Japan; and if we are not signatories to the treaties and not parties, she will get all that Germany had in Shantung, more than she will get under the promises which she made to us, and the only way we can get it away from her is by going to war with Japan and Great Britain and France.

Does that look like a workable proposition? Is that doing China a service? Whereas, if we do accept this treaty, we are members of the League of Nations, China is a member of the League, and Japan is a member of the League, and, under that much-criticized Article X, Japan promises and we guarantee that the territorial integrity and political independence of China will be respected and preserved. That is the way to serve China. That is the only possible way in the circumstances to serve China.

Therefore, we cannot rewrite this treaty. We must take it or leave it, and gentlemen, after all the rest of the world has signed it, will find it very difficult to make any other kind of treaty. As I took the liberty of saying the other night, it is a case of "put up or shut up." The world cannot breathe in the atmosphere of negations. The world cannot deal with nations who say, "We won't play!" The world cannot have anything to do with an arrangement in which every nation says, "We will take care of ourselves."

Sometimes people call me an idealist. Well, that is the way I know I am an American. America is the only idealistic country in the world.
WOODROW WILSON, address, Sioux Falls, Sept. 8, 1919

41.

The Senate and the League of Nations

The Versailles Treaty, including the proposed League of Nations, was presented to the Senate for ratification on July 10, 1919, and debate continued all through the summer. After a series of maneuvers, Senator Henry Cabot Lodge presented a set of reservations to the Treaty that would have had the effect of circumscribing America's participation in the League. These reservations, presented on November 6, were accepted by the Senate, but two weeks later — on November 18 — President Wilson wrote a letter to Senator Hitchcock of Nebraska urging all loyal Democrats to vote against the Lodge reservations if they wanted to preserve the Treaty. The climax came on November 19, when two important votes were taken. In the first, on the question of ratification with the Lodge reservations, the loyal Democrats joined those who were irreconcilably opposed to the Treaty and defeated it. In the second, on the question of ratification without reservations, the main bulk of the Senators changed sides, with irreconcilables still voting against the Treaty, joined this time by those, like Senator Lodge, who opposed an unqualified American commitment. The following selection is in two parts. The first part comprises Senator Lodge's reservations of November 6. The second part comprises a portion of the debate of November 19. Senator Robinson of Alabama, a strong Wilson supporter, voted against the Lodge reservations but for the Treaty without them. Senator Borah of Idaho voted against the Treaty each time. The struggle for ratification continued through the first months of 1920. On March 19 the Treaty failed once more to receive a two-thirds majority and was returned to the President unconfirmed.

Source: *Record,* 66 Cong., 1 Sess., pp. 8777-8778; 8768-8769, 8781-8784.

I.

Henry Cabot Lodge: Reservations with Regard to the Treaty

Resolved (two-thirds of the senators present concurring therein), that the Senate advise and consent to the ratification of the treaty of peace with Germany concluded at Versailles on the 28th day of June, 1919, subject to the following reservations and understandings, which are hereby made a part and condition of this resolution of ratifica-

tion, which ratification is not to take effect or bind the United States until the said reservations and understandings adopted by the Senate have been accepted by an exchange of notes as a part and a condition of this resolution of ratification by at least three of the four principal allied and associated powers, to wit, Great Britain, France, Italy, and Japan:

1. The United States so understands and construes Article 1 that in case of notice of withdrawal from the League of Nations, as provided in said article, the United States

shall be the sole judge as to whether all its international obligations and all its obligations under the said Covenant have been fulfilled, and notice of withdrawal by the United States may be given by a concurrent resolution of the Congress of the United States.

2. The United States assumes no obligation to preserve the territorial integrity or political independence of any other country or to interfere in controversies between nations — whether members of the League or not — under the provisions of Article 10, or to employ the military or naval forces of the United States under any article of the treaty for any purpose, unless in any particular case the Congress, which, under the Constitution, has the sole power to declare war or authorize the employment of the military or naval forces of the United States, shall by act or joint resolution so provide.

3. No mandate shall be accepted by the United States under Article 22, Part 1, or any other provision of the treaty of peace with Germany, except by action of the Congress of the United States.

4. The United States reserves to itself exclusively the right to decide what questions are within its domestic jurisdiction and declares that all domestic and political questions relating wholly or in part to its internal affairs, including immigration, labor, coastwise traffic, the tariff, commerce, the suppression of traffic in women and children, and in opium and other dangerous drugs, and all other domestic questions, are solely within the jurisdiction of the United States and are not under this treaty to be submitted in any way either to arbitration or to the consideration of the Council or of the Assembly of the League of Nations, or any agency thereof, or to the decision or recommendation of any other power.

5. The United States will not submit to arbitration or to inquiry by the Assembly or by the Council of the League of Nations provided for in said treaty of peace any questions which in the judgment of the United States depend upon or relate to its long-established policy, commonly known as the Monroe Doctrine; said doctrine is to be interpreted by the United States alone and is hereby declared to be wholly outside the jurisdiction of said League of Nations and entirely unaffected by any provision contained in the said treaty of peace with Germany.

6. The United States withholds its assent to Articles 156, 157, and 158, and reserves full liberty of action with respect to any controversy which may arise under said articles between the Republic of China and the Empire of Japan.

7. The Congress of the United States will provide by law for the appointment of the representatives of the United States in the Assembly and the Council of the League of Nations, and may in its discretion provide for the participation of the United States in any commission, committee, tribunal, court, council, or conference, or in the selection of any members thereof, and for the appointment of members of said commissions, committees, tribunals, courts, councils, or conferences, or any other representatives under the treaty of peace, or in carrying out its provisions; and until such participation and appointment have been so provided for and the powers and duties of such representatives have been defined by law, no person shall represent the United States under either said League of Nations or the treaty of peace with Germany or be authorized to perform any act for or on behalf of the United States thereunder; and no citizen of the United States shall be selected or appointed as a member of said commissions, committees, tribunals, courts, councils, or conferences except with the approval of the Senate of the United States.

8. The United States understands that

the Reparation Commission will regulate or interfere with exports from the United States to Germany, or from Germany to the United States, only when the United States by act or joint resolution of Congress approves such regulation or interference.

9. The United States shall not be obligated to contribute to any expenses of the League of Nations, or of the Secretariat, or of any commission, or committee, or conference, or other agency organized under the League of Nations or under the treaty or for the purpose of carrying out the treaty provisions, unless and until an appropriation of funds available for such expenses shall have been made by the Congress of the United States.

10. If the United States shall at any time adopt any plan for the limitation of armaments proposed by the Council of the League of Nations under the provisions of Article 8, it reserves the right to increase such armaments without the consent of the Council whenever the United States is threatened with invasion or engaged in war.

11. The United States reserves the right to permit, in its discretion, the nationals of a Covenant-breaking state, as defined in Article 16 of the Covenant of the League of Nations, residing within the United States or in countries other than that violating said Article 16, to continue their commercial, financial, and personal relations with the nationals of the United States.

12. Nothing in Articles 296, 297, or in any of the annexes thereto or in any other article, section, or annex of the treaty of peace with Germany shall, as against citizens of the United States, be taken to mean any confirmation, ratification, or approval of any act otherwise illegal or in contravention of the rights of citizens of the United States.

13. The United States withholds its assent to Part XIII (Articles 387 to 427, inclusive) unless Congress by act or joint resolution shall hereafter make provision for

representation in the organization established by said Part XIII; and in such event the participation of the United States will be governed and conditioned by the provisions of such act or joint resolution.

14. The United States assumes no obligation to be bound by any election, decision, report, or finding of the Council or Assembly in which any member of the League and its self-governing dominions, colonies, or parts of empire, in the aggregate, have cast more than one vote, and assumes no obligation to be bound by any decision, report, or finding of the Council or Assembly arising out of any dispute between the United States and any member of the League if such member, or any self-governing dominion, colony, empire, or part of empire united with it politically has voted.

II.

Senate Debate

Mr. Lodge. Mr. President, I have received from the press a copy of a letter which has been given out, I understand, and which I think, as the senator from Nebraska [Mr. Hitchcock] has not offered it, should be read at this time before we vote. . . .

The White House,
Washington, 18 November, 1919.

My Dear Senator: You were good enough to bring me word that the Democratic senators supporting the treaty expected to hold a conference before the final vote on the Lodge resolution of ratification and that they would be glad to receive a word of counsel from me.

I should hesitate to offer it in any detail, but I assume that the senators only desire my judgment upon the all-important question of the final vote on the resolution containing the many reservations by Senator Lodge. On that I cannot hesitate, for, in my opinion, the resolution in that form does not provide for ratification but, rather, for the nullification of the treaty. I sincerely hope that the friends and supporters of the treaty will vote against the Lodge resolution of ratification.

I understand that the door will probably then be open for a genuine resolution of ratification.

I trust that all true friends of the treaty will refuse to support the Lodge resolution.

Cordially and sincerely yours,

(Signed) WOODROW WILSON.

Hon. G. M. Hitchcock,
United States Senate.

Mr. President, I think comment is superfluous, and I shall make none. . . .

Mr. Robinson. Mr. President, for reasons very different from those asserted by the senator from Pennsylvania [Mr. Knox], it is my purpose to vote against the pending resolution of ratification incorporating reservations adopted by a majority of Senators.

During several months, to the exclusion of nearly all other important business, the Senate has had under consideration the treaty of peace with Germany. It now seems probable, unless the advocates of unqualified ratification and so-called reservation senators reconcile differences, that the result of our labors may be failure. The Senate is about to vote on an alleged resolution of ratification, a resolution which, it seems to me, does not ratify but which, in fact and in legal effect, constitutes a rejection of this treaty.

All senators recognize the importance of the vote soon to be taken. This vote invites the judgment of the people of this country, and, indeed, the judgment of all mankind, upon the policy implied in the resolution of ratification incorporating reservations agreed to by the majority.

Many of us are convinced that the adoption of the pending resolution, as I have already stated, will accomplish no useful purpose. The senator from Massachusetts [Mr.

The Granger Collection

Henry Cabot Lodge, opponent of the League of Nations

Lodge] has had read into the *Record* a letter issued by the President, in which that officer, representing a part of the treaty-making power, declares that the pending resolution of ratification cannot accomplish ratification; that it is, in fact, rejection of the treaty; and therefore it is futile to adopt the resolution.

The statement that the resolution of ratification will in fact defeat the treaty will occasion no regret to the senators who from the beginning have advocated its rejection. They have apparently succeeded, temporarily at least, in accomplishing indirectly what could not be done openly and frankly. Through alleged reservations, which will not likely be accepted by other parties to the treaty, they seek to exclude the United States from fellowship with her late allies and from membership in the League of Nations. In almost every line of the reservations is implied antagonism of senators toward the President. Suspicion and mistrust of the nations associated with this government in the recent war are reflected by the reservations, sometimes poorly concealed, often clearly evinced.

The avowed purpose is to completely repudiate every obligation of this government to encourage and sustain the new and feeble states separated, by our assistance during the war, from their former sovereignties by withholding from them the moral and military power of the United States.

To me it seems regrettable beyond expression that senators who desire to improve the treaty and who desire also that it shall become effective should lend their assistance to a course in which the avowed enemies of the League of Nations must find unbounded gratification and pleasure. Is it not unpardonable for friends of the treaty to couple with the resolution of ratification conditions designed to deprive the Executive of his constitutional functions? It is worse than idle — it seems to me hypocritical — to impose terms and conditions which make the exchange of ratifications impracticable, if not impossible.

Membership in the League of Nations is treated, in the reservations, with so little dignity and as of such slight importance as to authorize its termination by the passage of a mere concurrent resolution of Congress. This attempt to deny to the President participation in withdrawal by this government from the League and to vest that authority solely in the two houses of Congress in disregard of the plain provision of the Constitution displays a spirit of narrow opposition to the executive unworthy of the subject and unworthy of the Senate of the United States.

The requirement that before ratification by the United States shall become effective the reservations adopted by the Senate must be approved by three of the four principal allied powers is designed to make difficult the exchange of ratifications. Mr. President, it can have no other purpose; it can accomplish no other end.

The reservation respecting Article 10 nul-lifies the most vital provision in the League of Nations contract. It absolves the United States from any obligation to assist in enforcing the terms of peace, an obligation that the leader of the majority in his speech to this body on the 23rd day of August, 1918, and again in December of the same year, asserted as one which the United States cannot without dishonor avoid or escape.

No senator can doubt that the repudiation by the United States of the undertaking in Article 10 to respect and preserve the territorial integrity and political independence of the other members of the League weakens, if it does not destroy, one of the principal agencies or means provided by the League for the prevention of international war.

The reservation withholding the agreement of the United States to the arrangement in the treaty respecting Japanese rights in Shantung, and reserving for this government freedom of action in case of controversy between China and Japan regarding the subject, admittedly will not be accepted by Japan, and probably it will not be accepted by either France or Great Britain. In making this declaration, I repeat the statement made in the Senate a day or two ago by the senator from North Dakota [Mr. McCumber], and I make the inquiry how any friend of the treaty who wants it ratified, and who realizes that under these reservations our ratification cannot become effective unless it is approved by three of the four principal allied powers — I make the inquiry now how a senator who takes that view of the subject and wants the treaty ratified can support the pending resolution?

It may be, Mr. President, that the friends of this treaty have made a mistake. Undoubtedly the friends of the treaty, and not its enemies, should dictate the policy of the Senate concerning ratification. The senators who have opposed ratification from the beginning have imposed upon an overwhelming majority of the Senate, by their power and influence, their views respecting the resolution of ratification.

As the measure now comes before the Senate it comes with the open declaration of the Executive, who is the sole agency through whom this government may exchange ratifications, that that act will not be accomplished. It comes with the recognition of the fact by the Senators who favor the treaty that the reservations are of such a nature that they will not be accepted by other nations.

Make no mistake about it. The Senate should either ratify this treaty unqualifiedly or upon such terms and conditions as will justify the Executive and enable him speedily to conclude peace by an exchange of ratifications.

The resolution of the senator from Massachusetts incorporating the reservations as agreed upon will probably result in the refusal of the Executive to attempt to procure the consent and approval of three of the four principal allied powers. If he should make the attempt, it is plain that our self-respecting allies will not accept the terms and conditions which we seek to impose by these reservations. Why, then, Mr. President, should the resolution proposed by the senator from Massachusetts be agreed to? Every senator knows that it cannot effectuate peace. The senator from Massachusetts himself on last Sunday issued a statement to the press in which he declared that "The treaty is dead."

I call now upon the friends of the treaty to take charge of the corpse. By their action they can revitalize it. The enemies of the treaty, senators who do not favor its ratification, have controlled the proceedings of the Senate heretofore. It is time now that those of us who favor the treaty, and we have the necessary number, should get together and ratify it.

Mr. Borah. Mr. President, I am not misled by the debate across the aisle into the view that this treaty will not be ratified. I entertain little doubt that sooner or later — and entirely too soon — the treaty will be ratified with the League of Nations in it; and I am of the opinion with the reservations in it as they are now written. There may possibly be some change in verbiage in order that there may be a common sharing of parentage, but our friends across the aisle will likely accept the League of Nations with the reservations in substance as now written. I think, therefore, this moment is just as appropriate as any other for me to express my final views with reference to the treaty and the League of Nations. It is perhaps the last opportunity I shall have to state, as briefly as I may, my reasons for opposing the treaty and the League.

Mr. President, after Mr. Lincoln had been elected President, before he assumed the duties of the office and at a time when all indications were to the effect that we would soon be in the midst of civil strife, a friend from the city of Washington wrote him for instructions. Mr. Lincoln wrote back in a single line, "Entertain no compromise; have none of it." That states the position I occupy at this time and which I have, in a humble way, occupied from the first contention in regard to this proposal.

My objections to the League have not been met by the reservations. I desire to state wherein my objections have not been met. Let us see what our attitude will be toward Europe and what our position will be with reference to the other nations of the world after we shall have entered the League with the present reservations written therein. With all due respect to those who think that they have accomplished a different thing and challenging no man's intellectual integrity or patriotism, I do not believe the reservations have met the fundamental propositions which are involved in this contest.

When the League shall have been formed, we shall be a member of what is known as the Council of the League. Our accredited representative will sit in judgment with the accredited representatives of the other members of the League to pass upon the concerns, not only of our country but of all Europe and all Asia and the entire world. Our accredited representatives will be members of the Assembly. They will sit there to represent the judgment of these 110 million people — more then — just as we are accredited here to represent our constituencies.

We cannot send our representatives to sit in council with the representatives of the other great nations of the world with mental reservations as to what we shall do in case their judgment shall not be satisfactory to us. If we go to the Council or to the Assembly with any other purpose than that of complying in good faith and in absolute integrity with all upon which the Council or the Assembly may pass, we shall soon return to our country with our self-respect forfeited and the public opinion of the world condemnatory.

Why need you gentlemen across the aisle worry about a reservation here or there when we are sitting in the Council and in the Assembly and bound by every obligation in morals, which the President said was supreme above that of law, to comply with the judgment which our representative and the other representatives finally form? Shall we go there, Mr. President, to sit in judgment, and in case that judgment works for peace join with our allies, but in case it works for war withdraw our cooperation? How long would we stand as we now stand, a great republic commanding the respect and holding the leadership of the world, if we should adopt any such course?

So, sir, we not only sit in the Council and in the Assembly with our accredited representatives, but bear in mind that Article 11 is untouched by any reservation which has been offered here: and with Article 11 untouched and its integrity complete, Article 10 is perfectly superfluous. If any war or threat of war shall be a matter of consideration for the League, and the

League shall take such action as it deems wise to deal with it, what is the necessity of Article 10? Will not external aggression be regarded as a war or threat of war? If the political independence of some nation in Europe is assailed will it be regarded as a war or threat of war? Is there anything in Article 10 that is not completely covered by Article 11?

It remains complete, and with our representatives sitting in the Council and the Assembly, and with Article 11 complete, and with the Assembly, and the Council having jurisdiction of all matters touching the peace of the world, what more do you need to bind the United States if you assume that the United States is a nation of honor?

We have said, Mr. President, that we would not send our troops abroad without the consent of Congress. Pass by now for a moment the legal proposition. If we create executive functions, the executive will perform those functions without the authority of Congress. Pass that question by and go to the other question. Our members of the Council are there. Our members of the Assembly are there. Article 11 is complete, and it authorizes the League, a member of which is our representative, to deal with matters of peace and war, and the League through its Council and its Assembly, deals with the matter, and our accredited representative joins with the others in deciding upon a certain course which involves a question of sending troops. What will the Congress of the United States do? What right will it have left, except the bare technical right to refuse, which as a moral proposition it will not dare to exercise?

Have we not been told day by day for the last nine months that the Senate of the United States, a coordinate part of the treaty-making power, should accept this league as it was written because the wise men sitting at Versailles had so written it, and has not every possible influence and every source of power in public opinion been organized and directed against the Senate to compel it to do that thing? How much stronger will be the moral compulsion upon the Congress of the United States when we ourselves have endorsed the proposition of sending our accredited representatives there to vote for us?

Ah, but you say that there must be unanimous consent, and that there is vast protection in unanimous consent.

I do not wish to speak disparagingly; but has not every division and dismemberment of every nation which has suffered dismemberment taken place by unanimous consent for the last 300 years? Did not Prussia and Austria and Russia by unanimous consent divide Poland? Did not the United States and Great Britain and Japan and Italy and France divide China and give Shantung to Japan? Was that not a unanimous decision? Close the doors upon the diplomats of Europe, let them sit in secret, give them the material to trade on, and there always will be unanimous consent.

How did Japan get unanimous consent? I want to say here, in my parting words upon this proposition, that I have no doubt the outrage upon China was quite as distasteful to the President of the United States as it is to me. But Japan said: "I will not sign your treaty unless you turn over to me Shantung, to be turned back at my discretion," and you know how Japan's discretion operates with reference to such things. And so, when we are in the League, and our accredited representatives are sitting at Geneva, and a question of great moment arises, Japan, or Russia, or Germany, or Great Britain will say, "Unless this matter is adjusted in this way I will depart from your League." It is the same thing, operating in the same way, only under a different date and under a little different circumstances.

Mr. President, if you have enough territory, if you have enough material, if you have enough subject peoples to trade upon and divide, there will be no difficulty about unanimous consent.

Do our Democratic friends ever expect any man to sit as a member of the Council or as a member of the Assembly equal in intellectual power and in standing before the world with that of our representative at Versailles? Do you expect a man to sit in the Council who will have made more pledges, and I shall assume made them in sincerity, for self-determination and for the rights of small peoples than had been made by our accredited representative? And yet, what became of it? The unanimous consent was obtained nevertheless.

But take another view of it. We are sending to the Council one man. That one man represents 110 million people.

Here, sitting in the Senate, we have two from every state in the Union, and over in the other house we have representatives in accordance with population, and the responsibility is spread out in accordance with our obligations to our constituency. But now we are transferring to one man the stupendous power of representing the sentiment and convictions of 110 million people in tremendous questions which may involve the peace or may involve the war of the world.

However you view the question of unanimous consent, it does not protect us.

What is the result of all this? We are in the midst of all of the affairs of Europe. We have entangled ourselves with all European concerns. We have joined in alliance with all the European nations which have thus far joined the League and all nations which may be admitted to the League. We are sitting there dabbling in their affairs and intermeddling in their concerns. In other words, Mr. President — and this comes to the question which is fundamental with me — we have forfeited and surrendered, once and for all, the great policy of "no entangling alliances" upon which the strength of this republic has been founded for 150 years.

My friends of reservations, tell me where is the reservation in these articles which protects us against entangling alliances with Europe?

Those who are differing over reservations, tell me what one of them protects the doctrine laid down by the Father of his Country. That fundamental proposition is surrendered, and we are a part of the European turmoils and conflicts from the time we enter this League.

Let us not underestimate that. There has never been an hour since the Venezuelan difficulty that there has not been operating in this country, fed by domestic and foreign sources, a powerful propaganda for the destruction of the doctrine of no entangling alliances.

Lloyd George is reported to have said just a few days before the conference met at Versailles that Great Britain could give up much, and would be willing to sacrifice much, to have America withdraw from that policy. That was one of the great objects of the entire conference at Versailles so far as the foreign representatives were concerned. Clemenceau and Lloyd George and others like them were willing to make any reasonable sacrifice which would draw America away from her isolation and into the internal affairs and concerns of Europe. This League of Nations, with or without reservations, whatever else it does or does not do, does surrender and sacrifice that policy; and once having surrendered and become a part of the European concerns, where, my friends, are you going to stop?

You have put in here a reservation upon the Monroe Doctrine. I think that, insofar as language could protect the Monroe Doctrine, it has been protected. But as a practical proposition, as a working proposition, tell me candidly, as men familiar with the history of your country and of other countries, do you think that you can intermeddle in European affairs; and, second, never to permit Europe to [interfere in our affairs].

When Mr. Monroe wrote to Jefferson, he asked him his view upon the Monroe Doctrine, and Mr. Jefferson said, in substance, our first and primary obligation should be never to interfere in European affairs; and, second, never to permit Europe to interfere in our affairs. He understood, as every wise and practical man understands, that if we intermeddle in her affairs, if we help to adjust her conditions, inevitably and remorselessly Europe then will be carried into our affairs, in spite of anything you can write upon paper.

We cannot protect the Monroe Doctrine unless we protect the basic principle upon which it rests, and that is the Washington policy. I do not care how earnestly you may endeavor to do so, as a practical working proposition your League will come to the United States. Will you permit me to digress long enough to read a paragraph from a great French editor upon this particular phase of the matter, Mr. Stephen Lausanne, editor of *Le Matin,* of Paris?

When the Executive Council of the League of Nations fixes "the reasonable limits of the armament of Peru"; when it shall demand information concerning the naval program of Brazil: when it shall tell Argentina what shall be the measure of the "contribution to the armed forces to protect the signatures of the social covenant"; when it shall demand the immediate registration of the treaty between the United States and Canada at the seat of the League, it will control, whether it wills or no, the destinies of America. And when the American states shall be obliged to take a hand in every war or menace of war in Europe (Art. 11), they will necessarily fall afoul of the fundamental principle laid down by Monroe, which was that Americans should never take part in a European war.

If the League takes in the world, then Europe must mix in the affairs of America; if only Europe is included, then America will violate of necessity her own doctrine by intermixing in the affairs of Europe.

If the League includes the affairs of the world, does it not include the affairs of all the world? Is there any limitation of the jurisdiction of the Council or of the Assembly upon the question of peace or war? Does it not have now, under the reservations, the same as it had before, the power to deal with all matters of peace or war throughout the entire world? How shall you keep from meddling in the affairs of Europe or keep Europe from meddling in the affairs of America?

Mr. President, there is another and even a more commanding reason why I shall record my vote against this treaty. It imperils what I conceive to be the underlying, the very first principles of this republic. It is in conflict with the right of our people to govern themselves, free from all restraint, legal or moral, of foreign powers. It challenges every tenet of my political faith. If this faith were one of my own contriving, if I stood here to assert principles of government of my own evolving, I might well be charged with intolerable presumption, for we all recognize the ability of those who urge a different course. But I offer in justification of my course nothing of my own save the deep and abiding reverence I have for those whose policies I humbly but most ardently support. I claim no merit save fidelity to American principles and devotion to American ideals as they were wrought out from time to time by those who built the republic and as they have been extended and maintained throughout these years.

In opposing the treaty I do nothing more than decline to renounce and tear out of my life the sacred traditions which throughout fifty years have been translated into my whole intellectual and moral being. I will not, I cannot, give up my belief that America must, not alone for the happiness of her own people but for the moral guidance and greater contentment of the world, be permitted to live her own life. Next to the tie which binds a man to his God is the tie which binds a man to his country; and all schemes, all plans, however ambitious and fascinating they seem in their proposal, but

which would embarrass or entangle and impede or shackle her sovereign will, which would compromise her freedom of action, I unhesitatingly put behind me.

Sir, since the debate opened months ago, those of us who have stood against this proposition have been taunted many times with being little Americans. Leave us the word American, keep that in your presumptuous impeachment, and no taunt can disturb us, no gibe discompose our purposes. Call us little Americans if you will, but leave us the consolation and the pride which the term American, however modified, still imparts. Take away that term and though you should coin in telling phrase your highest eulogy we would hurl it back as common slander. We have been ridiculed because, forsooth, of our limited vision. Possibly that charge may be true. Who is there here that can read the future?

Time, and time alone, unerring and remorseless, will give us each our proper place in the affections of our countrymen and in the esteem and commendation of those who are to come after us. We neither fear nor court her favor. But if our vision has been circumscribed, it has at all times within its compass been clear and steady. We have sought nothing save the tranquillity of our own people and the honor and independence of our own republic. No foreign flattery, no possible world glory and power have disturbed our poise or come between us and our devotion to the traditions which have made us a people or the policies which have made us a nation, unselfish and commanding.

If we have erred we have erred out of too much love for those things which from childhood you and we together have been taught to revere — yes, to defend, even at the cost of limb and life. If we have erred it is because we have placed too high an estimate upon the wisdom of Washington and Jefferson, too exalted an opinion upon the patriotism of the sainted Lincoln. And blame us not therefore if we have, in our limited vision, seemed sometimes bitter and at all times uncompromising, for the things for which we have spoken, feebly spoken, the things which we have endeavored to defend, have been the things for which your fathers and our fathers were willing to die.

Senators, even in an hour so big with expectancy, we should not close our eyes to the fact that democracy is something more, vastly more, than a mere form of government by which society is restrained into free and orderly life. It is a moral entity, a spiritual force, as well. And these are things which live only and alone in the atmosphere of liberty. The foundation upon which democracy rests is faith in the moral instincts of the people. Its ballot boxes, the franchise, its laws, and constitutions are but the outward manifestations of the deeper and more essential thing — a continuing trust in the moral purposes of the average man and woman. When this is lost or forfeited, your outward forms, however democratic in terms, are a mockery. Force may find expression through institutions democratic in structure equal with the simple and more direct processes of a single supreme ruler. These distinguishing virtues of a real republic you cannot commingle with the discordant and destructive forces of the Old World and still preserve them.

You cannot yoke a government whose fundamental maxim is that of liberty to a government whose first law is that of force and hope to preserve the former. These things are in eternal war, and one must ultimately destroy the other. You may still keep for a time the outward form, you may still delude yourself, as others have done in the past, with appearances and symbols, but when you shall have committed this republic to a scheme of world control based upon force, upon the combined military force of the four great nations of the world, you will have soon destroyed the atmosphere of freedom, of confidence in the self-governing

capacity of the masses, in which alone a democracy may thrive. We may become one of the four dictators of the world, but we shall no longer be master of our own spirit. And what shall it profit us as a nation if we shall go forth to the dominion of the earth and share with others the glory of world control and lose that fine sense of confidence in the people, the soul of democracy?

Look upon the scene as it is now presented. Behold the task we are to assume, and then contemplate the method by which we are to deal with this task. Is the method such as to address itself to a government "conceived in liberty and dedicated to the proposition that all men are created equal"? When this league, this combination, is formed, four great powers representing the dominant people will rule one-half of the inhabitants of the globe as subject peoples — rule by force, and we shall be a party to the rule of force. There is no other way by which you can keep people in subjection. You must either give them independence, recognize their rights as nations to live their own life and to set up their own form of government, or you must deny them these things by force.

That is the scheme, the method proposed by the League. It proposes no other. We will in time become inured to its inhuman precepts and its soulless methods, strange as this doctrine now seems to a free people. If we stay with our contract, we will come in time to declare with our associates that force — force, the creed of the Prussian military oligarchy — is after all the true foundation upon which must rest all stable governments.

Korea, despoiled and bleeding at every pore; India, sweltering in ignorance and burdened with inhuman taxes after more than 100 years of dominant rule; Egypt, trapped and robbed of her birthright; Ireland, with 700 years of sacrifice for independence — this is the task, this is the atmosphere, and this is the creed in and under which we are to keep alive our belief in the moral purposes and self-governing capacity of the people, a belief without which the republic must disintegrate and die. The maxim of liberty will soon give way to the rule of blood and iron.

We have been pleading here for our Constitution. Conform this League, it has been said, to the technical terms of our charter and all will be well. But I declare to you that we must go further and conform to those sentiments and passions for justice and freedom which are essential to the existence of democracy. You must respect not territorial boundaries, not territorial integrity, but you must respect and preserve the sentiments and passions for justice and for freedom which God in His infinite wisdom has planted so deep in the human heart that no form of tyranny however brutal, no persecution however prolonged, can wholly uproot and kill. Respect nationality, respect justice, respect freedom, and you may have some hope of peace; but not so if you make your standard the standard of tyrants and despots, the protection of real estate regardless of how it is obtained.

Sir, we are told that this treaty means peace. Even so, I would not pay the price. Would you purchase peace at the cost of any part of our independence? We could have had peace in 1776 — the price was high, but we could have had it. James Otis, Sam Adams, Hancock, and Warren were surrounded by those who urged peace and British rule. All through that long and trying struggle, particularly when the clouds of adversity lowered upon the cause, there was a cry of peace — let us have peace. We could have had peace in 1860; Lincoln was counseled by men of great influence and accredited wisdom to let our brothers — and, thank heaven, they are brothers — depart in peace. But the tender, loving Lincoln, bending under the fearful weight of impending civil war, an apostle of peace, refused to pay the price, and a reunited coun-

The Granger Collection

"Triumphal Entry into Normalcy"; cartoon by Rollin Kirby from the "New York World" relating to the Senate battle against the League of Nations led by Henry Cabot Lodge and Philander C. Knox

try will praise his name forevermore — bless it because he refused peace at the price of national honor and national integrity. Peace upon any other basis than national independence, peace purchased at the cost of any part of our national integrity is fit only for slaves, and even when purchased at such a price it is a delusion, for it cannot last.

But your treaty does not mean peace — far, very far, from it. If we are to judge the future by the past, it means war. Is there any guarantee of peace other than the guarantee which comes of the control of the war-making power by the people? Yet what great rule of democracy does the treaty leave unassailed? The people in whose keeping alone you can safely lodge the power of peace or war nowhere, at no time and in no place, have any voice in this scheme for world peace. Autocracy which has bathed the world in blood for centuries reigns supreme. Democracy is everywhere excluded. This, you say, means peace.

Can you hope for peace when love of country is disregarded in your scheme, when the spirit of nationality is rejected, even scoffed at? Yet what law of that moving and mysterious force does your treaty not deny? With a ruthlessness unparalleled, your treaty in a dozen instances runs counter to the divine law of nationality. Peoples who speak the same language, kneel at the same ancestral tombs, moved by the same traditions, animated by a common hope are torn asunder, broken in pieces, divided, and parceled out to antagonistic nations. And this you call justice. This, you cry, means peace. Peoples who have dreamed of independence, struggled and been patient, sacrificed and been hopeful, peoples who were told that through this peace conference they should realize the aspirations of centuries, have again had their hopes dashed to earth.

One of the most striking and commanding figures in this war, soldier and statesman, turned away from the peace table at Versailles declaring to the world, "The promise of the new life, the victory of the great humane ideals for which the peoples have shed their blood and their treasure without stint, the fulfillment of their aspirations toward a new international order and a fairer and better world, are not written into the treaty." No; your treaty means injustice. It means slavery. It means war. And to all this you ask this republic to become a party. You ask it to abandon the creed under which it has grown to power and accept the creed of autocracy, the creed of repression and force.

Mr. President, I turn from this scheme based upon force to another scheme, planned 143 years ago in old Independence Hall, in the city of Philadelphia, based upon liberty. I like it better. I have become so accustomed to believe in it that it is difficult for me to reject it out of hand. I have difficulty in subscribing to the new creed of oppression, the creed of dominant and subject peoples. I feel a reluctance to give up the belief that all men are created equal — the eternal principle in government that all

governments derive their just powers from the consent of the governed. I cannot get my consent to exchange the doctrine of George Washington for the doctrine of Frederick the Great translated into mendacious phrases of peace. I go back to that serene and masterful soul who pointed the way to power and glory for the new and then weak republic, and whose teachings and admonitions even in our majesty and dominance we dare not disregard.

I know well the answer to my contention. It has been piped about of late from a thousand sources — venal sources, disloyal sources, sinister sources — that Washington's wisdom was of his day only and that his teachings are out of fashion — things long since sent to the scrap heap of history — that while he was great in character and noble in soul he was untrained in the arts of statecraft and unlearned in the science of government. The puny demagogue, the barren editor, the sterile professor now vie with each other in apologizing for the temporary and commonplace expedients which the Father of his Country felt constrained to adopt in building a republic!

What is the test of statesmanship? Is it the formation of theories, the utterance of abstract and incontrovertible truths, or is it the capacity and the power to give to a people that concrete thing called liberty, that vital and indispensable thing in human happiness called free institutions, and to establish over all and above all the blessed and eternal reign of order and law? If this be the test, where shall we find another whose name is entitled to be written beside the name of Washington? His judgment and poise in the hour of turmoil and peril, his courage and vision in times of adversity, his firm grasp of fundamental principles, his almost inspired power to penetrate the future and read there the result, the effect of policies, have never been excelled, if equaled, by any of the world's commonwealth builders.

Peter the Great, William the Silent, and Cromwell the Protector, these and these alone perhaps are to be associated with his name as the builders of states and the founders of governments. But in exaltation of moral purpose, in the unselfish character of his work, in the durability of his policies, in the permanency of the institutions which he more than anyone else called into effect, his service to mankind stands out separate and apart in a class by itself. The works of these other great builders, where are they now? But the work of Washington is still the most potent influence for the advancement of civilization and the freedom of the race.

Reflect for a moment over his achievements. He led the Revolutionary Army to victory. He was the very first to suggest a union instead of a confederacy. He presided over and counseled with great wisdom the Convention which framed the Constitution. He guided the government through its first perilous years. He gave dignity and stability and honor to that which was looked upon by the world as a passing experiment, and, finally, my friends, as his own peculiar and particular contribution to the happiness of his countrymen and to the cause of the republic, he gave us his great foreign policy under which we have lived and prospered and strengthened for nearly a century and a half. This policy is the most sublime confirmation of his genius as a statesman. It was then, and it now is, an indispensable part of our whole scheme of government. It is today a vital, indispensable element in our entire plan, purpose, and mission as a nation. To abandon it is nothing less than a betrayal of the American people. I say betrayal deliberately, in view of the suffering and the sacrifice which will follow in the wake of such a course.

But under the stress and strain of these extraordinary days, when strong men are being swept down by the onrushing forces of disorder and change, when the most sacred things of life, the most cherished hopes of a Christian world seem to yield to the mad forces of discontent — just such days as Washington passed through when the mobs of Paris, wild with new liberty and drunk with power, challenged the established institutions of all the world, but his steadfast soul was unshaken — under these conditions come again we are about to abandon this policy so essential to our happiness and tranquillity as a people and our stability as a government. No leader with his commanding influence and his unquailing courage stands forth to stem the current. But what no leader can or will do, experience, bitter experience, and the people of this country in whose keeping, after all, thank God, is the republic, will ultimately do.

If we abandon his leadership and teachings, we will go back. We will return to this policy. Americanism shall not, cannot, die. We may go back in sackcloth and ashes, but we will return to the faith of the fathers. America will live her own life. The independence of this republic will have its defenders. Thousands have suffered and died for it, and their sons and daughters are not of the breed who will be betrayed into the hands of foreigners. The noble face of the Father of his Country, so familiar to every boy and girl, looking out from the walls of the Capitol in stern reproach, will call those who come here for public service to a reckoning. The people of our beloved country will finally speak, and we will return to the policy which we now abandon. America disenthralled and free in spite of all these things will continue her mission in the cause of peace, of freedom, and of civilization.

42.

Program of Social Reconstruction

John A. Ryan drafted the following program for the Administrative Committee of the National Catholic War Council in 1919 that became the basis of Catholic policy concerning postwar social reconstruction. Ryan's plan, which came to be known as the Bishops' Program of Social Reconstruction, reflected the belief of liberal Catholics that the church was very much a social institution and that it must act on behalf of parishioners in their daily lives. A portion of the program is reprinted here.

Source: 76 Congress, 1 Session, Senate Document No. 79.

THE ENDING OF THE GREAT WAR has brought peace. But the only safeguard of peace is social justice and a contented people. The deep unrest so emphatically and so widely voiced throughout the world is the most serious menace to the future peace of every nation and of the entire world. Great problems face us. They cannot be put aside; they must be met and solved with justice to all.

In the hope of stating the lines that will best guide us in our right solution, the following pronouncement is issued by the Administrative Committee of the National Catholic War Council. Its practical applications are, of course, subject to discussion, but all its essential declarations are based upon the principles of charity and justice that have always been held and taught by the Catholic Church, while its practical proposals are merely an adaptation of those principles and that traditional teaching to the social and industrial conditions and needs of our own time.

Peter J. Muldoon, *Chairman,*
Bishop of Rockford
Joseph Schrembs,
Bishop of Toledo

Patrick J. Hayes,
Bishop of Tagaste
William T. Russell,
Bishop of Charleston

Washington, D.C.
February 12, 1919

Social Reconstruction

"Reconstruction" has of late been so tiresomely reiterated, not to say violently abused, that it has become to many of us a word of aversion. Politicians, social students, labor leaders, businessmen, charity workers, clergymen, and various other social groups have contributed their quota of spoken words and printed pages to the discussion of the subject; yet the majority of us still find ourselves rather bewildered and helpless. We are unable to say what parts of our social system imperatively need reconstruction; how much of that which is imperatively necessary is likely to be seriously undertaken; or what specific methods and measures are best suited to realize that amount of reconstruction which is at once imperatively necessary and immediately feasible. . . .

No Profound Changes in the United States

It is not to be expected that as many or as great social changes will take place in the United States as in Europe. Neither our habits of thinking nor our ordinary ways of life have undergone a profound disturbance. The hackneyed phrase, "Things will never again be the same after the war," has a much more concrete and deeply felt meaning among the European peoples. Their minds are fully adjusted to the conviction and expectation that these words will come true. In the second place, the devastation, the loss of capital and of men, the changes in individual relations, and the increase in the activities of government have been much greater in Europe than in the United States. Moreover, our superior natural advantages and resources, the better industrial and social condition of our working classes still constitute an obstacle to anything like revolutionary changes. It is significant that no social group in America, not even among the wage earners, has produced such a fundamental and radical program of reconstruction as the Labour Party of Great Britain. . . .

Women War Workers

One of the most important problems of readjustment is that created by the presence in industry of immense numbers of women who have taken the places of men during the war. Mere justice, to say nothing of chivalry, dictates that these women should not be compelled to suffer any greater loss or inconvenience than is absolutely necessary; for their services to the nation have been second only to the services of the men whose places they were called upon to fill. One general principle is clear: No female worker should remain in any occupation that is harmful to health or morals. Women should disappear as quickly as possible from such tasks as conducting and guarding streetcars, cleaning locomotives, and a great number of other activities for which conditions of life and their physique render them unfit.

Another general principle is that the proportion of women in industry ought to be kept within the smallest practical limits. If we have an efficient national employment service, if a goodly number of the returned soldiers and sailors are placed on the land, and if wages and the demand for goods are kept up to the level which is easily attainable, all female workers who are displaced from tasks that they have been performing only since the beginning of the war will be able to find suitable employments in other parts of the industrial field, or in those domestic occupations which sorely need their presence. Those women who are engaged at the same tasks as men should receive equal pay for equal amounts and qualities of work.

National War Labor Board

One of the most beneficial governmental organizations of the war is the National War Labor Board. Upon the basis of a few fundamental principles, unanimously adopted by the representatives of labor, capital, and the public, it has prevented innumerable strikes and raised wages to decent levels in many different industries throughout the country. Its main guiding principles have been a family living wage for all male adult laborers; recognition of the right of labor to organize and to deal with employers through its chosen representatives; and no coercion of nonunion laborers by members of the union. The War Labor Board ought to be continued in existence by Congress and endowed with all the power for effective action that it can possess under the federal Constitution. The principles, methods, machinery, and results of this institution constitute a definite and far-reaching gain for social justice. No part of this advantage should be lost or given up in time of peace.

Present Wage Rates Should Be Sustained

The general level of wages attained during the war should not be lowered. In a few industries, especially some directly and peculiarly connected with the carrying on of war, wages have reached a plane upon which they cannot possibly continue for this grade of occupations. But the number of workers in this situation is an extremely small proportion of the entire wage-earning population. The overwhelming majority should not be compelled or suffered to undergo any reduction in their rates of remuneration for two reasons: first, because the average rate of pay has not increased faster than the cost of living; second, because a considerable majority of the wage earners of the United States, both men and women, were not receiving living wages when prices began to rise in 1915.

In that year, according to Lauck and Sydenstricker, whose work is the most comprehensive on the subject, four-fifths of the heads of families obtained less than $800, while two-thirds of the female wage earners were paid less than $400. Even if the prices of goods should fall to the level on which they were in 1915 — something that cannot be hoped for within five years — the average present rates of wages would not exceed the equivalent of a decent livelihood in the case of the vast majority. The exceptional instances to the contrary are practically all among the skilled workers. Therefore, wages on the whole should not be reduced even when the cost of living recedes from its present high level.

Even if the great majority of workers were now in receipt of more than living wages, there are no good reasons why rates of pay should be lowered. After all, a living wage is not necessarily the full measure of justice. All the Catholic authorities on the subject explicitly declare that this is only the minimum of justice. In a country as rich as ours, there are very few cases in which it is possible to prove that the worker would be getting more than that to which he has a right if he were paid something in excess of this ethical minimum. Why, then, should we assume that this is the normal share of almost the whole laboring population?

Since our industrial resources and instrumentalities are sufficient to provide more than a living wage for a very large proportion of the workers, why should we acquiesce in a theory which denies them this measure of the comforts of life? Such a policy is not only of very questionable morality but is unsound economically. The large demand for goods which is created and maintained by high rates of wages and high purchasing power by the masses is the surest guarantee of a continuous and general operation of industrial establishments. It is the most effective instrument of prosperity for labor and capital alike.

The principal beneficiaries of a general reduction of wages would be the less efficient among the capitalists and the more comfortable sections of the consumers. The wage earners would lose more in remuneration than they would gain from whatever fall in prices occurred as a direct result of the fall in wages. On grounds both of justice and sound economics, we should give our hearty support to all legitimate efforts made by labor to resist general wage reductions.

Housing for Working Classes

Housing projects for war workers which have been completed, or almost completed, by the government of the United States have cost some $40 million, and are found in eleven cities. While the federal government cannot continue this work in time of peace, the example and precedent that it has set, and the experience and knowledge that it has developed, should not be forthwith neglected and lost. The great cities in which congestion and other forms of bad housing are disgracefully apparent ought to take up and continue the work, at least to such an extent as will remove the worst features of a social condition that is a menace at once to industrial efficiency, civic health, good morals, and religion.

Reduction of the Cost of Living

During the war the cost of living has risen at least 75 percent above the level of 1913. Some check has been placed upon the upward trend by government fixing of prices in the case of bread and coal and a few other commodities. Even if we believe it desirable, we cannot ask that the government continue this action after the articles of peace have been signed; for neither public opinion nor Congress is ready for such a revolutionary policy. If the extortionate practices of monopoly were prevented by adequate laws and adequate law enforcement, prices would automatically be kept at as low a level as that to which they might be brought by direct government determination.

Just what laws, in addition to those already on the statute books, are necessary to abolish monopolistic extortion is a question of detail that need not be considered here. In passing, it may be noted that government competition with monopolies that cannot be effectively restrained by the ordinary antitrust laws deserves more serious consideration than it has yet received.

More important and more effective than any government regulation of prices would be the establishment of cooperative stores. The enormous toll taken from industry by the various classes of middlemen is now fully realized. The astonishing difference between the price received by the producer and that paid by the consumer has become a scandal of our industrial system. The obvious and direct means of reducing this discrepancy and abolishing unnecessary

middlemen is the operation of retail and wholesale mercantile concerns under the ownership and management of the consumers. . . .

The Legal Minimum Wage

Turning now from those agencies and laws that have been put in operation during the war to the general subject of labor legislation and problems, we are glad to note that there is no longer any serious objection urged by impartial persons against the legal minimum wage. The several states should enact laws providing for the establishment of wage rates that will be at least sufficient for the decent maintenance of a family, in the case of all male adults, and adequate to the decent individual support of female workers. In the beginning the minimum wages for male workers should suffice only for the present needs of the family, but they should be gradually raised until they are adequate to meet future needs as well. That is, they should be ultimately high enough to make possible that amount of saving which is necessary to protect the worker and his family against sickness, accidents, invalidity, and old age.

Social Insurance

Until this level of legal minimum wages is reached, the worker stands in need of the device of insurance. The state should make comprehensive provision for insurance against illness, invalidity, unemployment, and old age. So far as possible the insurance fund should be raised by a levy on industry, as is now done in the case of accident compensation. The industry in which a man is employed should provide with all that is necessary to meet all the needs of his entire life. Therefore, any contribution to the insurance fund from the general revenues of the state should be only slight and temporary. For the same reason no contribution should be exacted from any worker who is not getting a higher wage than is required to meet the present needs of himself and family. Those who are below that level can make such a contribution only at the expense of their present welfare.

Finally, the administration of the insurance laws should be such as to interfere as little as possible with the individual freedom of the worker and his family. Any insurance scheme, or any administrative method, that tends to separate the workers into a distinct and dependent class, that offends against their domestic privacy and independence, or that threatens individual self-reliance and self-respect, should not be tolerated. The ideal to be kept in mind is a condition in which all the workers would themselves have the income and the responsibility of providing for all the needs and contingencies of life, both present and future. Hence all forms of state insurance should be regarded as merely a lesser evil, and should be so organized and administered as to hasten the coming of the normal condition. . . .

Labor Participation in Industrial Management

The right of labor to organize and to deal with employers through representatives has been asserted above in connection with the discussion of the War Labor Board. It is to be hoped that this right will never again be called in question by any considerable number of employers. In addition to this, labor ought gradually to receive greater representation in what the English group of Quaker employers have called the "industrial" part of business management — "the control of processes and machinery; nature of product; engagement and dismissal of employees; hours of work, rates of pay, bonuses, etc.; welfare work; shop discipline; relations with trade unions." The establishment of shop committees, working wherever possible

with the trade union, is the method suggested by this group of employers for giving the employees the proper share of industrial management. There can be no doubt that a frank adoption of these means and ends by employers would not only promote the welfare of the workers but vastly improve the relations between them and their employers and increase the efficiency and productiveness of each establishment.

There is no need here to emphasize the importance of safety and sanitation in work places, as this is pretty generally recognized by legislation. What is required is an extension and strengthening of many of the existing statutes and a better administration and enforcement of such laws everywhere.

Vocational Training

The need of industrial, or as it has come to be more generally called, vocational training, is now universally acknowledged. In the interest of the nation, as well as in that of the workers themselves, this training should be made substantially universal. While we cannot now discuss the subject in any detail, we do wish to set down two general observations.

First, the vocational training should be offered in such forms and conditions as not to deprive the children of the working classes of at least the elements of a cultural education. A healthy democracy cannot tolerate a purely industrial or trade education for any class of its citizens. We do not want to have the children of the wage earners put into a special class in which they are marked as outside the sphere of opportunities for culture.

The second observation is that the system of vocational training should not operate so as to weaken in any degree our parochial schools or any other class of private schools. Indeed, the opportunities of the system should be extended to all qualified private schools on exactly the same basis as to public schools. We want neither class divisions in education nor a state monopoly of education.

Child Labor

The question of education naturally suggests the subject of child labor. Public opinion in the majority of the states of our country has set its face inflexibly against the continuous employment of children in industry before the age of sixteen years. Within a reasonably short time all of our states, except some of the stagnant ones, will have laws providing for this reasonable standard. The education of public opinion must continue, but inasmuch as the process is slow, the abolition of child labor in certain sections seems unlikely to be brought about by the legislatures of those states, and since the Keating-Owen Act has been declared unconstitutional, there seems to be no device by which this reproach to our country can be removed except that of taxing child labor out of existence. This method is embodied in an amendment to the Federal Revenue Bill which would impose a tax of 10 percent on all goods made by children. . . .

Ultimate and Fundamental Reforms

Despite the practical and immediate character of the present statement, we cannot entirely neglect the question of ultimate aims and a systematic program; for other groups are busy issuing such systematic pronouncements, and we all need something of the kind as a philosophical foundation and as a satisfaction to our natural desire for comprehensive statements.

It seems clear that the present industrial system is destined to last for a long time in its main outlines. That is to say, private ownership of capital is not likely to be supplanted by a collectivist organization of industry at a date sufficiently near to justify any present action based on the hypothesis of its arrival. This forecast we recognize as not only extremely probable but as highly desirable; for, other objections apart, Socialism would mean bureaucracy, political tyranny, the helplessness of the individual as a factor in the ordering of his own life and in general social inefficiency and decadence.

Main Defects of Present System

Nevertheless, the present system stands in grievous need of considerable modifications and improvement. Its main defects are three: enormous inefficiency and waste in the production and distribution of commodities; insufficient incomes for the great majority of wage earners, and unnecessarily large incomes for a small minority of privileged capitalists. Inefficiency in the production and distribution of goods would be in great measure abolished by the reforms that have been outlined in the foregoing pages. Production would be greatly increased by universal living wages, by adequate industrial education, and by harmonious relations between labor and capital on the basis of adequate participation by the former in all the industrial aspects of business management. The wastes of commodity distribution could be practically all eliminated by cooperative mercantile establishments and cooperative selling and marketing associations.

Cooperation and Copartnership

Nevertheless, the full possibilities of increased production will not be realized so long as the majority of the workers remain mere wage earners. The majority must somehow become owners, or at least in part, of the instruments of production. They can be enabled to reach this stage gradually through cooperative productive societies and copartnership arrangements. In the former, the workers own and manage the industries themselves; in the latter, they own a substantial part of the corporate stock and exercise a reasonable share in the management. However slow the attainments of these ends, they will have to be reached before we can have a thoroughly efficient system of production, or an industrial and social order that will be secure from the danger of revolution. It is to be noted that this particular modification of the existing order, though far-reaching and involving to a great extent the abolition of the wage system, would not mean the abolition of private ownership. The instruments of production would still be owned by individuals, not by the state.

Increased Incomes for Labor

The second great evil, that of insufficient income for the majority, can be removed only by providing the workers with more income. This means not only universal living wages but the opportunity of obtaining something more than that amount for all who are willing to work hard and faithfully. All the other measures for labor betterment recommended in the preceding pages would likewise contribute directly or indirectly to a more just distribution of wealth in the interest of the laborer.

Abolition and Control of Monopolies

For the third evil mentioned above, excessive gains by a small minority of privileged capitalists, the main remedies are prevention of monopolistic control of commodities, adequate government regulation of such public-service monopolies as will remain under private operation, and heavy taxation of incomes, excess profits, and inheritances. The precise methods by which genuine competition may be restored and maintained among businesses that are naturally competitive cannot be discussed here; but the principle is clear that human beings cannot be trusted with the immense opportunities for oppression and extortion that go with the possession of monopoly power.

That the owners of public-service monopolies should be restricted by law to a fair or average return on their actual investment has long been a recognized principle of the courts, the legislatures, and public opinion. It is a principle which should be applied to competitive enterprises likewise, with the qualification that something more than the average rate of return should be allowed to men who exhibit exceptional efficiency. However, good public policy, as well as equity, demands that these exceptional businessmen share the fruits of their efficiency with the consumer in the form of lower prices. The man who utilizes his ability to produce cheaper than his competitors for the purpose of exacting from the public as high a price for his product as is necessary for the least efficient businessman is a menace rather than a benefit to industry and society.

Our immense war debt constitutes a particular reason why incomes and excess profits should continue to be heavily taxed. In this way two important ends will be attained: The poor will be relieved of injurious tax burdens, and the small class of specially privileged capitalists will be compelled to return a part of their unearned gains to society.

A New Spirit a Vital Need

"Society," said Pope Leo XIII, "can be healed in no other way than by a return to Christian life and Christian institutions." The truth of these words is more widely perceived today than when they were written more than twenty-seven years ago. Changes in our economic and political systems will have only partial and feeble efficiency if they be not reinforced by the Christian view of work and wealth.

Neither the moderate reforms advocated in this paper nor any other program of betterment or reconstruction will prove reasonably effective without a reform in the spirit of both labor and capital. The laborer must come to realize that he owes his employer and society an honest day's work in return for a fair wage, and that conditions cannot be substantially improved until he roots out the desire to get a maximum of return for a minimum of service. The capitalist must likewise get a new viewpoint. He needs to learn the long-forgotten truth that wealth is stewardship, that profitmaking is not the basic justification of business enterprise, and that there are such things as fair profits, fair interest, and fair prices. Above and before

all, he must cultivate and strengthen within his mind the truth which many of his class have begun to grasp for the first time during the present war; namely, that the laborer is a human being, not merely an instrument of production; and that the laborer's right to a decent livelihood is the first moral charge upon industry.

The employer has a right to get a reasonable living out of his business, but he has no right to interest on his investment until his employees have obtained at least living wages. This is the human and Christian, in contrast to the purely commercial and pagan, ethics of industry.

43.

Government Mills in North Dakota

The Nonpartisan League was founded by North Dakota farmers in 1915 to give agriculture a political voice in the affairs of the state. Their program called for a state-operated industrial system along with state-owned grain elevators and mills, state banks and insurance programs, and easier credit for the farmers. In the 1918 election the league won control of the state legislature and succeeded in putting through its program, of which the law creating the North Dakota Mill and Elevator Association, passed on February 25, 1919, is reprinted here in part.

Source: *Laws Passed at the Sixteenth Session of Legislative Assembly of the State of North Dakota*, Bismarck, 1919, pp. 218-221.

An act declaring the purpose of the State of North Dakota to engage in the business of manufacturing and marketing of farm products, and for establishing a warehouse, elevator, and flour mill system under the name of North Dakota Mill and Elevator Association, operated by the state, and defining the scope and manner of its operation, and the powers and duties of the persons charged with its management; and making an appropriation therefor.

Be it Enacted by the Legislative Assembly of the State of North Dakota:

Section 1. That for the purpose of encouraging and promoting agriculture, commerce, and industry, the state of North Dakota shall engage in the business of manufacturing and marketing farm products, and for that purpose shall establish a system of warehouses, elevators, flour mills, factories, plants, machinery, and equipments, owned, controlled, and operated by it under the name of North Dakota Mill and Elevator Association, hereinafter for convenience called the Association.

Section 2. The Industrial Commission shall operate, manage, and control the Association, locate and maintain its places of business, of which the principal place shall be within the state, and shall make and enforce orders, rules, regulations, and bylaws for the transaction of its business. The business of the Association, in addition to other matters herein specified, may include anything that any private individual or corporation may lawfully do in conducting a similar business except as herein restricted. The Industrial Commission shall meet within twenty days after the passage and approval of this act to begin the organization of the Association.

Section 3. To accomplish the purposes of this act, the Industrial Commission shall acquire by purchase, lease, or by exercise of the right of eminent domain, as provided by Chapter 36 of the Code of Civil Procedure, Compiled Laws of 1913, all necessary property or property rights, and may construct, remodel, or repair all necessary buildings; and may purchase, lease, construct, or otherwise acquire warehouses, elevators, flour mills, factories, offices, plants, machinery, equipments, and all other things necessary, incidental, or convenient in the manufacturing and marketing of all kinds of raw and finished farm products within or without the state and may dispose of the same; and may buy, manufacture, store, mortgage, pledge, sell, exchange, or otherwise acquire or dispose of all kinds of manufactured and raw farm and food products and by-products, and may for such purposes establish and operate exchanges, bureaus, markets, and agencies, within or without the state, including foreign countries, on such terms and conditions, and under such rules and regulation as the commission may determine.

Section 4. The Industrial Commission shall obtain such assistance as in its judgment may be necessary for the establishment, maintenance, and operation of the Association. To that end it shall appoint a manager, and may appoint such subordinate officers and employees as it may judge expedient. It may constitute such manager its general agent in respect to the functions of the Association, but subject, nevertheless in such agency, to the supervision, limitation, and control of the commission.

It shall employ such contractors, architects, builders, attorneys, clerks, accountants, and other experts, agents, and servants as in the judgment of the commission the interests of the state may require; and shall define the duties, designate the titles, and fix the compensation and bonds of all such persons so engaged: *Provided,* however, that subject to the control and regulation of the commission, the manager of the Association shall appoint and employ such deputies and other subordinates, and such contractors, architects, builders, attorneys, clerks, accountants, and other experts, agents, and servants as he shall, in his judgment, deem are required by the interests of the Association.

The total compensation of such appointees and employees, together with other expenditures for the operation and maintenance of the Association, shall remain within the appropriation and earnings lawfully available in each year for such purpose. All officers and employees of the Association engaged upon its financial functions shall, before entering upon their duties, respectively furnish good and sufficient bonds to the state in such amount and upon such conditions as the commission may require and approve; but the bond of the manager shall not be less than $50,000. Such bonds shall be filed with the secretary of state.

Section 5. The Industrial Commission may remove and discharge any and all persons appointed in the exercise of the powers granted by this act, whether by the commission or by the manager of the Association, and any such removal may be made whenever in the judgment of the commission the public interests require it: *Provided, however*, that all appointments and removals contemplated by this act shall be so made as the commission shall deem most fit to promote the efficiency of the public service.

Section 6. The Industrial Commission shall fix the buying price of all things bought and the selling price of all things sold incidental to the operation of the Association, and shall fix all charges for any and all services rendered by the Association; but in fixing these prices — while all services are to be rendered, as near as may be, at cost — there shall be taken into consideration, in addition to other necessary costs, a reasonable charge for depreciation of all property, all overhead expenses and a reasonable surplus, together with all amounts required for the repayment, with interest, of funds received from the state.

44.

Andrew W. Mellon: Industrial Research

Andrew Mellon was an industrialist as well as a banker, and, like other Americans, was deeply impressed by the technological strides America had been able to make under the stress of war mobilization. There were no limits, he felt, to the advances that industry could make if greater attention were given to research and development. In the following selection, "The Value of Industrial Research," Mellon stresses the importance of cooperation between sciences and industry.

Source: *Bulletin of the National Research Council,* October 1919.

THE RECOGNITION of the national essentiality of science, particularly chemistry, to the life of a nation has stimulated the industrialists to such a point that they are seeking at this particular time, as never before, to utilize every idea which makes for the advancement of industry. The aim of all industrial operations is toward perfection, both in process and mechanical equipment, and every development in manufacturing creates new problems. It is only to be expected, therefore, that the industrial investigator is becoming less and less regarded as a burden unwarranted by returns.

Industrialists recognize, in fact, that manufacturing is becoming more and more a system of scientific processes; and probably no science has done so much as chemistry in revealing the hidden possibilities of the wastes and by-products of manufacturers. The present great advances are due entirely to the application of knowledge in the development of new things, which is primarily dependent upon systematic industrial research. The industrialist, however, needs all possible assistance in undertaking and developing research work as a means of enlarging his output and improving its quality. In order to be effective it must increase his independence and initiative, and be so given as to enlist his active support. It has been the cooperation of progressive industry with science which has led to the practical application of the results obtained in the laboratories of scientific men.

But, in this matter of the dissemination of knowledge concerning industrial practice, it must be evident to all that there is not complete cooperation between manufacturers and the technical schools. Manufacturers have been quite naturally opposed to publishing any discoveries made in their plants, since "knowledge is power"; while, on the other hand, the technical schools exist for the diffusion of knowledge, and from their standpoint the great disadvantage of the above policy is this concealment of knowledge. It results in a serious retardation of the general growth and development of service in its broader aspects and renders it much more difficult for the technical schools to train men properly for such industries.

Fortunately, the policy of industrial secrecy is becoming more generally regarded in the light of reason and more liberal views are taken, which is bringing about a closer union between science and industry. It may, therefore, be taken for granted that the great corporations all over the country that have entered into such a scheme of cooperation with science have a vivid and comprehensive realization of the need of the efficiency which the scheme represents, and, incidentally, that the scheme itself is founded on sane and practical considerations.

Industrial research is, in fact, a very specialized business and, naturally, requires specially trained men and an understanding on the part of the industrialists as to its requirements and methods. The fundamental differences between pure research and industrial research are, indeed, traceable to the differences in the poise and personality of the representatives of each type of scientific investigation. Success in genuine industrial research presupposes all the qualities which are applicable to success in pure science and, in addition, other qualities, executive and personal, more or less unessential in the pure research laboratory. At this point enters the real value of a system of cooperation between science and industry; the industrialist is aided by being taught the correct methods to follow and by guidance in

the selection of the proper type of research men to carry on his work.

The individual manufacturer is not the only one to be benefited through well-established central research laboratories; as a general policy, "Service to Industry" is exceedingly well carried out through work for associations, as the one laboratory is thereby enabled to serve practically all the manufacturers in any particular field at a very low cost to each manufacturer, and the benefits are received by some industrialists who otherwise would not feel able to support independent research work.

Manufacturers who have benefited by the application of science to industry have not been content to await chance discoveries but have established well-equipped laboratories and strong research staffs. Moreover, some large industrial corporations have found it expedient to keep before the public the fact that investigations on a large scale ultimately bring considerable benefit to the community generally; that every scientific discovery applied in industry reacts to the public gain; and that, consequently, great industrial organizations are justified in the expenditure of large sums of money to carry on such investigations, since it is only where there are large aggregations of capital that the most extensive and productive research facilities can be obtained.

A spirit of cooperation should be encouraged among all types of research laboratories, as no greater good to society can arise than from a wider distribution of the duties and responsibilities of research. Accordingly, well-established research laboratories should be willing to cooperate and render informative service necessary for the establishment and organization of other research laboratories.

We are now passing through a period which clearly brings to mind the fact that civilization unarmed by science is at a terrible disadvantage in a struggle for existence; and we must realize that this arming cannot be done at short notice.

Woodrow Wilson in 1921; his health broken, he seems to embody the defeat of his dreams

POSTWAR REACTION

America's participation in World War I demonstrated several facts about the nation and its possibilities that had until then remained hidden. Foremost among these was the latent ability for massive economic mobilization, a process as spectacular as it was necessary, and one dependent upon the government's surprising aptitude for organizing and proliferating its bureaucracy. Another discovery, less obvious but rather more important for the nation itself, was a generally unsuspected fragility of law, idealism, and tradition, whether in foreign affairs or domestic civil relations. Real or imagined, the apparent importance of unanimity under the pressure of war led quickly to the stern suppression of innocuous dissent; the laws created for the occasion attempted no real distinction between dissent on basic policy or on administrative details, nor even between disappointment and treason. The propaganda campaigns mounted to create and sustain support for the war effort and hatred for the enemy triggered a spirit of viciousness and violence at home that was, with the discovery of a new threat, the mysterious and diabolical Red, to outlast the war.

By means of the Espionage Act of 1917 and later the Sedition Act of 1918, Congress attempted to prevent activities detrimental to the war effort; it succeeded in seriously eroding the civil liberties that the nation was told it was fighting for. Making the world safe for democracy apparently depended on ignoring the rights of conscience of a great many persons and suppressing periodicals like "The Masses" that deviated from the straight and narrow. Even to protest the injustice of the methods, as the "Nation" did, was to be persecuted in turn.

(Top and left) General Pershing's troops moving into Mexico in 1917; (below) protest demonstration

PRES. WILSON won't stand for BANDIT HUERTA But is willing to stand for BANDIT ROCKEFELLER

(Above) Advertisement on the New York elevated urging purchase of War Savings Stamps

Antiwar cartoons from "The Masses": (left) "The Paths of War Lead but to . . ." by Klein, and "Whom the Gods Would Destroy They First Make Mad" by Maurice Becker

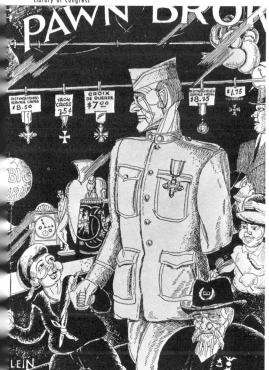

(Above) Col. House, Wilson's chief adviser;
(top) Lloyd George, Orlando, Clemenceau,
and Wilson; (right) Czech President Masaryk,
a principal advocate of Versailles for recognition of former Austrian possessions

VIVE WILSON

(Above) The GOP enjoys election success of the League issue. League was attacked for giving away our prerogatives under the Monroe Doctrine; (below) Wilson sets out smiling to defend the treaty

In spite of Wilson's Fourteen Points and the tremendous popular appeal of the new order of international relations they embodied, the Allies had, by secret treaties predating the end of the war, already virtually finished the actual treaty of peace in the standard victory-with-vengeance form. Wilson's sole victory in the negotiations was the establishment of the League of Nations. In offering the treaty to the Senate, Wilson ran immediately into a resurgent isolationism, based partly in habit, partly in natural postwar reaction, and partly in disappointment with the results of the crusade.

Young volunteers in Petrograd being trained for the Red Army

An Allied expedition, including more than 5,000 American troops, was sent to Archangel and Murmansk in May 1918 to protect those ports from German capture or control. With security assured, the expedition concerned itself for over a year with opposing the Bolshevist forces in the Russian Revolution. Working in support of Admiral Kolchak and as a rear guard for Czech forces supporting White Russia, the Allied expedition represented, for America, a hole in the postwar wall of isolationism. It began to appear, in fact, that intervention would be continued as a policy of the New Freedom.

(Left) Red Army soldiers; (below) Czech troops, who fought with Russia against Austria, took up with the White Russians in the civil war and were supported by aid from Britain and the U.S.

White Russian refugees gathered at Crimean ports for evacuation

(Above) American Relief Administration warehouse in Rayan, Russia; Red Cross hospital serving civil war refugees; (below) clothing distribution in Russia

The depression of the postwar years and the general decline of both wages and the power of labor created considerable unrest. Strikes multiplied, the IWW continued to agitate, and it suddenly appeared to great numbers of semi-hysterical people that there was a Red, perhaps two, under everyone's bed. Under A. Mitchell Palmer, doughty Attorney General, a broad program of radical-hunting and alien-deporting swept the country. The relatively small amount of actually subversive activity going on served only to warrant the allegations of super-patriots and to increase the public clamor for more and more repressive measures.

(Top) White House pickets following the war; (left) "Mary Palmer says good-bye to her daddy, the Attorney General, as he leaves to continue his work against Reds who would wreck the government"; (below) "Big Bill" Haywood in Moscow

(Above) Crowds survey the scene of a bombing, attributed to anarchists, that killed 30 people and injured 400 on Wall Street in 1920

(Left) Sacco and Vanzetti being escorted to the Dedham, Massachusetts, Court House to stand trial for murder; (below) demonstration in New York seeking to stay the execution of Sacco and Vanzetti in 1927

Vast demonstration in front of the Reichstag in Berlin organized by German communists

The possibility of a peaceful postwar Germany was precluded entirely by the terms of the Versailles Treaty and the intransigent hostility of France and England. Stripped of industries and sources of raw materials, and saddled with impossible reparations payments, Germany was split drastically between extremists of left and right. The government at Weimar was held responsible for the political and economic chaos, and its inability to placate internal and external enemies practically assured a radical turn in politics.

(Above) Troops in Berlin during the Junker Revolt; (below) food riot in Berlin market

(Above) Polish partisans gathering in Deszonieach nad Odrz during uprising in Upper Silesia against German rule; (below left) demonstration in Berlin against autonomy for Silesian Poles

(Above right) Adolf Hitler and associates in Landsberg Prison following the abortive Munich putsch; (below) Nazi parade features a banner proclaiming, "Death to Marxism"

Swift & Co. strike, 1904; frequent import of Negro strikebreakers angered labor

Three scenes from the 1919 Chicago race riots: Mob chases a Negro into his back yard and then stones him to death at his own back door; (below) militia policing South Side Negro district

(Above) Polish partisans gathering in Deszonieach nad Odrz during uprising in Upper Silesia against German rule; (below left) demonstration in Berlin against autonomy for Silesian Poles

(Above right) Adolf Hitler and associates in Landsberg Prison following the abortive Munich putsch; (below) Nazi parade features a banner proclaiming, "Death to Marxism"

Swift & Co. strike, 1904; frequent import of Negro strikebreakers angered labor

Three scenes from the 1919 Chicago race riots: Mob chases a Negro into his back yard and then stones him to death at his own back door; (below) militia policing South Side Negro district

"The Awakening," an extravaganza produced for the Beaumont, Texas, Ku Klux Klan in 1924

The growth of the job market in the war economy had attracted large numbers of Negroes to the cities, and the migration continued after the war. Concentrated into overcrowded neighborhoods with high rents and poor facilities, the Negroes who worked in war industry or who fought in France soon realized that democracy was not yet for them. The revived Ku Klux Klan grew rapidly to four million or more by 1924 and carried on their fascist activities throughout the country. The "Red Summer" of 1919 saw 25 race riots, the worst of which was in July in Chicago where 38 persons died. Another record was set that year with the lynching of more than 70 Negroes.

(Right) KKK parade in Washington, 1926; (below) Massachusetts Working Boys' Glee Club and Minstrel

Lightfoot Collection

Culver Pictures, Inc.

Brown Brothers

Library of Congress

For a nation suddenly disillusioned with its own idealism and swept by nostalgia for its lost innocence, the successive administrations of Harding and Coolidge were at once emotionally soothing and totally inadequate to the reality of the postwar world. America returned to the traditions of the Republican Party and protective tariff despite its completely changed economic position in the world. The less hallowed tradition of extensive postwar corruption established by Grant's friends was also vigorously revived by Harding's associates. But scandal was not enough to turn the country from the comfortable and undemanding Republican Party.

(Top) Harding in Kansas; Cox and Roosevelt, Democratic candidates, 1920; (left) Eugene Debs, Socialist candidate running from prison; (below) Washington Conference for Limitation of Arms, 1921

(Top) Coolidge in South Dakota; Andrew Mellon, treasury secretary, 1921-32; (left) Edwin Denby, navy secretary, and oilman Harry Sinclair, both figures in the Teapot Dome case; (below) Attorney General Daugherty was fired for corruption

"Fight LaFollette on every foot of ground in every Northwestern sta
The cry from the Coolidge campaign headquarters.

Calvin Coolidge, quiet, thrifty, and apparently upright, provided a perfect counterpoint to a period remembered primarily for its madcap antics, its scandals, and its jazz. Seeming to embody the virtues that America so revered as to refuse to sully them through practice, Coolidge was in fact capable of little else. The nation and both parties acquiesced, however, in the stand-pat policy, and even the minor opposition of the Progressive Party dissolved with La Follette's death in 1925.

(Top) "New Masses" cover and Rollin Kirby's "The Whirlwind Campaign" show contrasting views of the nation's needs; (right) Progressive Party got four million votes in 1924; (below) Sam Warriner and J. L. Lewis of United Mine Workers

45.

Principles of Progressive Education

The Association for the Advancement of Progressive Education was organized in 1919 to channel the efforts of parents and interested laymen to promote the educational principles of John Dewey. As Stanwood Cobb, one of the founders, said: "We aimed at nothing short of reforming the entire school system in America." Marietta Johnson, a leading progressive educator of the period, participated in the organization, but Dewey himself did not join it at first. Because of this, one historian has called the Association a "partial expression of progressive education circa 1919." The following statement of principles shows the basic aims of the group.

Source: Lawrence A. Cremin, *The Transformation of the School: Progressivism in American Education, 1876-1957*, New York, 1961, pp. 243-245.

1. Freedom to Develop Naturally

THE CONDUCT OF THE PUPIL should be self-governed according to the social needs of his community rather than by arbitrary laws. This does not mean that liberty should be allowed to become license, or that the teacher should not exercise authority when it proves necessary. Full opportunity for initiative and self-expression should be provided, together with an environment rich in interesting material that is available for the free use of every pupil.

2. Interest the Motive of All Work

INTEREST SHOULD BE SATISFIED and developed through: (1) direct and indirect contact with the world and its activities, and use of the experience thus gained; (2) application of knowledge gained, and correlation between different subjects; (3) the consciousness of achievement.

3. The Teacher a Guide, Not a Taskmaster

IT IS ESSENTIAL that teachers believe in the aims and general principles of Progressive Education. They should be thoroughly prepared for the profession of teaching, and should have latitude for the development of initiative and originality. They should be possessed of personality and character, and should be as much at home in all the activities of the school, such as the pupils' play, their dramatic productions, and their social gatherings, as they are in the classroom. Ideal teaching conditions demand that classes be small, especially in the elementary-school years.

Progressive teachers will encourage the use of all the senses, training the pupils in both observation and judgment; and, instead of hearing recitations only, will spend most of the time teaching how to use various sources of information, including life activities as well as books; how to reason about the information thus acquired; and how to express forcefully and logically the conclusions reached. Teachers will inspire a desire for knowledge and will serve as guides in the investigations undertaken, rather than taskmasters.

To be a proper inspiration to their pupils, teachers must have ample opportunity and encouragement for self-improvement and for the development of broad interests.

4. *Scientific Study of Pupil Development*

SCHOOL RECORDS SHOULD NOT be confined to the marks given by the teachers to show the advancement of the pupils in their study of subjects but should also include both objective and subjective reports on those physical, mental, moral, and social characteristics which affect both school and adult life, and which can be influenced by the school and the home.

Such records should be used as a guide for the treatment of each pupil, and should also serve to focus the attention of the teacher on the all-important work of development rather than on simply teaching subject matter.

5. *Greater Attention to All That Affects the Child's Physical Development*

ONE OF THE FIRST CONSIDERATIONS of Progressive Education is the health of the pupils. Much more room in which to move about, better light and air, clean and well-ventilated buildings, easier access to the out-of-doors and greater use of it are all necessary. There should be frequent use of adequate playgrounds.

The teachers should observe closely the physical condition of each pupil in cooperation with a school physician, who should examine the children at stated intervals.

6. *Cooperation Between School and Home to Meet the Needs of Child Life*

THE SCHOOL SHOULD PROVIDE, with the home, as much as is possible of all that the natural interests and activities of the child demand, especially during the elementary-school years. It should give opportunity for manual experience for both boys and girls, for homemaking, and for healthful recreation of various kinds. Most, if not all, of a child's studying should be done at the school and such extra-curriculum studies as a child may take should be at the school or home, so that there will be no unnecessary dissipation of energy.

These conditions can come about only through intelligent cooperation between parents and teachers. It is the duty of the parents to know what the school is doing and why, and to find out the most effective way to cooperate. It is the duty of the school to help the parents to a broader outlook on education and to make available all the resources of the school that can give information or help to the home.

7. *The Progressive School a Leader in Educational Movements*

THE PROGRESSIVE SCHOOL should be a leader in educational movements. It should be a laboratory where new ideas, if worthy, meet encouragement; where tradition alone does not rule, but the best of the past is leavened with the discoveries of today and the result is freely added to the sum of educational knowledge.

46.

VACHEL LINDSAY: "Bryan, Bryan, Bryan, Bryan"

By 1919 the "Great Commoner," William Jennings Bryan, had all but retired from public life — his fervor for great causes a thing of the past, his interests confined to Prohibition, Fundamentalism, and Florida real estate. Only a few remembered what a compelling figure he had made on the national scene, but one of them was the poet Vachel Lindsay, who in the poem reprinted here — perhaps Lindsay's finest — evoked the image of the "silver-tongued orator of the West" as he stampeded the 1896 Democratic convention, demanding reforms that other men would gain and be honored for. Amidst the banalities of the already apparent postwar "return to normalcy," Lindsay's poem was not only a tribute to Bryan but an epitaph for a great era that was gone and that many feared would never come again.

Source: *Collected Poems*, New York, 1923.

❧ BRYAN, BRYAN, BRYAN, BRYAN

*The Campaign of Eighteen Ninety-six, as Viewed at
the Time by a Sixteen-Year-Old, etc.*

I

In a nation of one hundred fine, mob-hearted, lynching,
    relenting, repenting millions,
There are plenty of sweeping, swinging, stinging, gorgeous
    things to shout about,
And knock your old blue devils out.

I brag and chant of Bryan, Bryan, Bryan,
Candidate for president who sketched a silver Zion,
The one American Poet who could sing outdoors,
He brought in tides of wonder, of unprecedented splendor,
Wild roses from the plains, that made hearts tender,
All the funny circus silks
Of politics unfurled,
Bartlett pears of romance that were honey at the cores,
And torchlights down the street, to the end of the world.

There were truths eternal in the gab and tittle-tattle.
There were real heads broken in the fustian and the rattle.

There were real lines drawn:
Not the silver and the gold,
But Nebraska's cry went eastward against the dour and old,
The mean and cold.

It was eighteen ninety-six, and I was just sixteen
And Altgeld ruled in Springfield, Illinois,
When there came from the sunset Nebraska's shout of joy:
In a coat like a deacon, in a black Stetson hat
He scourged the elephant plutocrats
With barbed wire from the Platte.
The scales dropped from their mighty eyes.
They saw that summer's noon
A tribe of wonders coming
To a marching tune.

Oh, the longhorns from Texas,
The jay hawks from Kansas,
The plop-eyed bungaroo and giant giassicus,
The varmint, chipmunk, bugaboo,
The horned-toad, prairie-dog and ballyhoo,
From all the newborn states arow,
Bidding the eagles of the west fly on,
Bidding the eagles of the west fly on.
The fawn, prodactyl and thing-a-ma-jig,
The rakaboor, the hellangone,
The whangdoodle, batfowl and pig,
The coyote, wild-cat and grizzly in a glow,
In a miracle of health and speed, the whole breed abreast,
They leaped the Mississippi, blue border of the West,
From the Gulf to Canada, two thousand miles long: —
Against the towns of Tubal Cain,
Ah, — sharp was their song.
Against the ways of Tubal Cain, too cunning for the young,
The longhorn calf, the buffalo and wampus gave tongue,
These creatures were defending things Mark Hanna never dreamed:
The moods of airy childhood that in desert dews gleamed,
The gossamers and whimsies,
The monkeyshines and didoes
Rank and strange
Of the canyons and the range,
The ultimate fantastics
Of the far western slope,
And of prairie schooner children
Born beneath the stars,
Beneath falling snows,

Of the babies born at midnight
In the sod huts of lost hope,
With no physician there,
Except a Kansas prayer,
With the Indian raid a howling through the air.

And all these in their helpless days
By the dour East oppressed,
Mean paternalism
Making their mistakes for them,
Crucifying half the West,
Till the whole Atlantic coast
Seemed a giant spiders' nest.

And these children and their sons
At last rode through the cactus,
A cliff of mighty cowboys
On the lope,
With gun and rope.
And all the way to frightened Maine the old East heard them call,
And saw our Bryan by a mile lead the wall
Of men and whirling flowers and beasts,
The bard and the prophet of them all.
Prairie avenger, mountain lion,
Bryan, Bryan, Bryan, Bryan,
Gigantic troubadour, speaking like a siege gun,
Smashing Plymouth Rock with his boulders from the West,
And just a hundred miles behind, tornadoes piled across the sky,
Blotting out sun and moon,
A sign on high.

Headlong, dazed and blinking in the weird green light,
The scalawags made moan,
Afraid to fight.

II

When Bryan came to Springfield, and Altgeld gave him greeting,
Rochester was deserted, Divernon was deserted,
Mechanicsburg, Riverton, Chickenbristle, Cotton Hill,
Empty: for all Sangamon drove to the meeting —
In silver-decked racing cart,
Buggy, buckboard, carryall,
Carriage, phaeton, whatever would haul,
And silver-decked farm-wagons gritted, banged and rolled,
With the new tale of Bryan by the iron tires told.

The State House loomed afar,
A speck, a hive, a football,
A captive balloon!
And the town was all one spreading wing of bunting, plumes, and sunshine,
Every rag and flag, and Bryan picture sold,
When the rigs in many a dusty line
Jammed our streets at noon,
And joined the wild parade against the power of gold.

We roamed, we boys from High School
With mankind,
While Springfield gleamed,
Silk-lined.
Oh, Tom Dines, and Art Fitzgerald,
And the gangs that they could get!
I can hear them yelling yet.
Helping the incantation,
Defying aristocracy,
With every bridle gone,
Ridding the world of the low down mean,
Bidding the eagles of the West fly on,
Bidding the eagles of the West fly on,
We were bully, wild and wooly,
Never yet curried below the knees.
We saw flowers in the air,
Fair as the Pleiades, bright as Orion,
— Hopes of all mankind,
Made rare, resistless, thrice refined.
Oh, we bucks from every Springfield ward!
Colts of democracy —
Yet time-winds out of Chaos from the star-fields of the Lord.

The long parade rolled on. I stood by my best girl.
She was a cool young citizen, with wise and laughing eyes.
With my necktie by my ear, I was stepping on my dear,
But she kept like a pattern, without a shaken curl.

She wore in her hair a brave prairie rose.
Her gold chums cut her, for that was not the pose.
No Gibson Girl would wear it in that fresh way.
But we were fairy Democrats, and this was our day.

The earth rocked like the ocean, the sidewalk was a deck.
The houses for the moment were lost in the wide wreck.
And the bands played strange and stranger music as they trailed along.
Against the ways of Tubal Cain,
Ah, sharp was their song!

The demons in the bricks, the demons in the grass,
The demons in the bank-vaults peered out to see us pass,
And the angels in the trees, the angels in the grass,
The angels in the flags, peered out to see us pass.
And the sidewalk was our chariot, and the flowers bloomed higher,
And the street turned to silver and the grass turned to fire,
And then it was but grass, and the town was there again,
A place for women and men.

III

Then we stood where we could see
Every band,
And the speaker's stand.
And Bryan took the platform.
And he was introduced.
And he lifted his hand
And cast a new spell.
Progressive silence fell
In Springfield,
In Illinois,
Around the world.
Then we heard these glacial boulders across the prairie rolled:

"The people have a right to make their own mistakes. . . .
You shall not crucify mankind
Upon a cross of gold."

And everybody heard him —
In the streets and State House yard.
And everybody heard him
In Springfield,
In Illinois,
Around and around and around the world,
That danced upon its axis
And like a darling broncho whirled.

IV

July, August, suspense.
Wall Street lost to sense.
August, September, October,
More suspense,
And the whole East down like a wind-smashed fence.

Then Hanna to the rescue,
Hanna of Ohio,

Rallying the roller-tops,
Rallying the bucket-shops.
Threatening drouth and death,
Promising manna,
Rallying the trusts against the bawling flannelmouth;
Invading misers' cellars,
Tin-cans, socks,
Melting down the rocks,
Pouring out the long green to a million workers,
Spondulix by the mountain-load, to stop each new tornado,
And beat the cheapskate, blatherskite,
Populistic, anarchistic,
Deacon — desperado.

V

Election night at midnight:
Boy Bryan's defeat.
Defeat of western silver.
Defeat of the wheat.
Victory of letterfiles
And plutocrats in miles
With dollar signs upon their coats,
Diamond watchchains on their vests
And spats on their feet.
Victory of custodians,
Plymouth Rock,
And all that inbred landlord stock.
Victory of the neat.
Defeat of the aspen groves of Colorado valleys,
The blue bells of the Rockies,
And blue bonnets of old Texas,
By the Pittsburg alleys.
Defeat of alfalfa and the Mariposa lily.
Defeat of the Pacific and the long Mississippi.
Defeat of the young by the old and silly.
Defeat of tornadoes by the poison vats supreme.
Defeat of my boyhood, defeat of my dream.

VI

Where is McKinley, that respectable McKinley,
The man without an angle or a tangle,
Who soothed down the city man and soothed down the farmer,
The German, the Irish, the Southerner, the Northerner,
Who climbed every greasy pole, and slipped through every crack;

Who soothed down the gambling hall, the bar-room, the church,
The devil vote, the angel vote, the neutral vote,
The desperately wicked, and their victims on the rack,
The gold vote, the silver vote, the brass vote, the lead vote,
Every vote? . . .

Where is McKinley, Mark Hanna's McKinley,
His slave, his echo, his suit of clothes?
Gone to join the shadows, with the pomps of that time,
And the flame of that summer's prairie rose.

Where is Cleveland whom the Democratic platform
Read from the party in a glorious hour,
Gone to join the shadows with pitchfork Tillman,
And sledge-hammer Altgeld who wrecked his power.

Where is Hanna, bulldog Hanna.
Low-browed Hanna, who said: "Stand pat"?
Gone to his place with old Pierpont Morgan.
Gone somewhere . . . with lean rat Platt.

Where is Roosevelt, the young dude cowboy,
Who hated Bryan, then aped his way?
Gone to join the shadows with mighty Cromwell
And tall King Saul, till the Judgment day.

Where is Altgeld, brave as the truth,
Whose name the few still say with tears?
Gone to join the ironies with Old John Brown,
Whose fame rings loud for a thousand years.

Where is that boy, that Heaven-born Bryan,
That Homer Bryan, who sang from the West?
Gone to join the shadows with Altgeld the Eagle,
Where the kings and the slaves and the troubadours rest.

47.

Oliver Wendell Holmes, Jr.: *Abrams et al. v. United States*

Wartime patriotism did not end with the coming of peace but instead changed the object of its fear and hatred from the dreaded Hun to the even more dreadful Bolshevik. The defendants in the famous case of Abrams et al. v. United States had been convicted under the Espionage Act of 1917 of circulating Communist literature critical of America's involvement in the war. The majority opinion of the Supreme Court, handed down on November 10, 1919, upheld the lower court verdict, but Justices Brandeis and Holmes delivered notable dissents. That of Holmes — a classic defense of the right of freedom of speech — is reprinted here.

Source: 250 U.S. 616.

THIS INDICTMENT IS FOUNDED wholly upon the publication of two leaflets which I shall describe in a moment. The first count charges a conspiracy pending the war with Germany to publish abusive language about the form of government of the United States, laying the preparation and publishing of the first leaflet as overt acts. The second count charges a conspiracy pending the war to publish language intended to bring the form of government into contempt, laying the preparation and publishing of the two leaflets as overt acts. The third count alleges a conspiracy to encourage resistance to the United States in the same war and to attempt to effectuate the purpose by publishing the same leaflets. The fourth count lays a conspiracy to incite curtailment of production of things necessary to the prosecution of the war and to attempt to accomplish it by publishing the second leaflet to which I have referred.

The first of these leaflets says that the President's cowardly silence about the intervention in Russia reveals the hypocrisy of the plutocratic gang in Washington. It inti-mates that "German militarism combined with Allied capitalism to crush the Russian Revolution" — goes on that the tyrants of the world fight each other until they see a common enemy — working-class enlightenment, when they combine to crush it; and that now militarism and capitalism combined, though not openly, to crush the Russian Revolution. It says that there is only one enemy of the workers of the world and that is capitalism; that it is a crime for workers of America, etc., to fight the workers' republic of Russia, and ends, "Awake! Awake, you Workers of the World! Revolutionists." A note adds "It is absurd to call us pro-German. We hate and despise German militarism more than do you hypocritical tyrants. We have more reasons for denouncing German militarism than has the coward of the White House."

The other leaflet, headed, "Workers — Wake Up," with abusive language says that America together with the Allies will march for Russia to help the Czechoslovaks in their struggle against the Bolsheviki, and that this time the hypocrites shall not fool the Russian emigrants and friends of Russia in America. It tells the Russian emigrants that they now must spit in the face of the false military propaganda by which their sympathy and help to the prosecution of the war have been called forth and says that with the money they have lent or are going to lend "they will make bullets not only for the Germans but also for the Workers' Soviets of Russia," and, further, "Workers in the ammunition factories, you are producing bullets, bayonets, cannon, to murder not only the Germans but also your dearest, best, who are in Russia and are fighting for freedom." It then appeals to the same Russian emigrants at some length not to consent to the "inquisitionary expedition to Russia," and says that the destruction of the Russian Revolution is "the politics of the march to Russia." The leaflet winds up by saying, "Workers, our reply to this barbaric intervention has to be a general strike!" and after a few words on the spirit of revolution, exhortations not to be afraid, and some usual tall talk ends, "Woe unto those who will be in the way of progress. Let solidarity live! The Rebels."

No argument seems to me necessary to show that these pronunciamentos in no way attack the form of government of the United States, or that they do not support either of the first two counts. What little I have to say about the third count may be postponed until I have considered the fourth. With regard to that it seems too plain to be denied that the suggestion to workers in the ammunition factories that they are producing bullets to murder their dearest, and the further advocacy of a general strike, both in the second leaflet, do urge curtailment of production of things necessary to the prosecution of the war within the meaning of the Act of May 16, 1918. . . . But to make the conduct criminal that statute requires that it should be "with intent by such curtailment to cripple or hinder the United States in the prosecu-

tion of the war." It seems to me that no such intent is proved.

I am aware of course that the word intent as vaguely used in ordinary legal discussion means no more than knowledge at the time of the act that the consequences said to be intended will ensue. Even less than that will satisfy the general principle of civil and criminal liability. A man may have to pay damages, may be sent to prison, at common law might be hanged, if at the time of his act he knew facts from which common experience showed that the consequences would follow, whether he individually could foresee them or not. But, when words are used exactly, a deed is not done with intent to produce a consequence unless that consequence is the aim of the deed. It may be obvious, and obvious to the actor, that the consequence will follow, and he may be liable for it even if he regrets it; but he does not do the act with intent to produce it unless the aim to produce it is the proximate motive of the specific act, although there may be some deeper motive behind.

It seems to me that this statute must be taken to use its words in a strict and accurate sense. They would be absurd in any other. A patriot might think that we were wasting money on airplanes, or making more cannon of a certain kind than we needed, and might advocate curtailment with success, yet even if it turned out that the curtailment hindered and was thought by other minds to have been obviously likely to hinder the United States in the prosecution of the war, no one would hold such conduct a crime. I admit that my illustration does not answer all that might be said but it is enough to show what I think and to let me pass to a more important aspect of the case. I refer to the First Amendment to the Constitution that Congress shall make no law abridging the freedom of speech.

I never have seen any reason to doubt

that the questions of law that alone were before this Court in the cases of *Schenck, Frohwerk,* and *Debs,* 249 U. S. 47, 204, 211, were rightly decided. I do not doubt for a moment that by the same reasoning that would justify punishing persuasion to murder, the United States constitutionally may punish speech that produces or is intended to produce a clear and imminent danger that it will bring about forthwith certain substantive evils that the United States constitutionally may seek to prevent. The power undoubtedly is greater in time of war than in time of peace because war opens dangers that do not exist at other times.

But as against dangers peculiar to war, as against others, the principle of the right to free speech is always the same. It is only the present danger of immediate evil or an intent to bring it about that warrants Congress in setting a limit to the expression of opinion where private rights are not concerned. Congress certainly cannot forbid all effort to change the mind of the country. Now, nobody can suppose that the surreptitious publishing of a silly leaflet by an unknown man, without more, would present any immediate danger that its opinions would hinder the success of the government arms or have any appreciable tendency to do so. Publishing those opinions for the very purpose of obstructing, however, might indicate a greater danger, and, at any rate, would have the quality of an attempt. So I assume that the second leaflet if published for the purposes alleged in the fourth count might be punishable. But it seems pretty clear to me that nothing less than that would bring these papers within the scope of this law.

An actual intent in the sense that I have explained is necessary to constitute an attempt where a further act of the same individual is required to complete the substantive crime, for reasons given in *Swift & Co.* v. *United States,* 196 U.S. 375, 396. It is necessary where the success of the at-

tempt depends upon others, because if that intent is not present the actor's aim may be accomplished without bringing about the evils sought to be checked. An intent to prevent interference with the revolution in Russia might have been satisfied without any hindrance to carrying on the war in which we were engaged.

I do not see how anyone can find the intent required by the statute in any of the defendants' words. The second leaflet is the only one that affords even a foundation for the charge, and there, without invoking the hatred of German militarism expressed in the former one, it is evident from the beginning to the end that the only object of the paper is to help Russia and stop American intervention there against the popular government, not to impede the United States in the war that it was carrying on. To say that two phrases taken literally might import a suggestion of conduct that would have interference with the war as an indirect and probably undesired effect seems to me by no means enough to show an attempt to produce that effect.

I return for a moment to the third count. That charges an intent to provoke resistance to the United States in its war with Germany. Taking the clause in the statute that deals with that in connection with the other elaborate provisions of the act, I think that resistance to the United States means some forcible act of opposition to some proceeding of the United States in pursuance of the war. I think the intent must be the specific intent that I have described, and, for the reasons that I have given, I think that no such intent was proved or existed in fact. I also think that there is no hint at resistance to the United States as I construe the phrase.

In this case, sentences of twenty years imprisonment have been imposed for the publishing of two leaflets that I believe the defendants had as much right to publish as the government has to publish the Constitution of the United States, now vainly invoked by them. Even if I am technically wrong and enough can be squeezed from these poor and puny anonymities to turn the color of legal litmus paper; I will add, even if what I think the necessary intent were shown; the most nominal punishment seems to me all that possibly could be inflicted, unless the defendants are to be made to suffer, not for what the indictment alleges but for the creed that they avow — a creed that I believe to be the creed of ignorance and immaturity when honestly held — as I see no reason to doubt that it was held here, but which, although made the subject of examination at the trial, no one has a right even to consider in dealing with the charges before the Court.

Persecution for the expression of opinions seems to me perfectly logical. If you have no doubt of your premises or your power and want a certain result with all your heart, you naturally express your wishes in law and sweep away all opposition. To allow opposition by speech seems to indicate that you think the speech impotent, as when a man says that he has squared the circle, or that you do not care wholeheartedly for the result, or that you doubt either your power or your premises. But when men have realized that time has upset many fighting faiths, they may come to believe even more than they believe the very foundations of their own conduct that the ultimate good desired is better reached by free trade in ideas — that the best test of truth is the power of the thought to get itself accepted in the competition of the market,

and that truth is the only ground upon which their wishes safely can be carried out. That at any rate is the theory of our Constitution.

It is an experiment, as all life is an experiment. Every year, if not every day, we have to wager our salvation upon some prophecy based upon imperfect knowledge. While that experiment is part of our system, I think that we should be eternally vigilant against attempts to check the expression of opinions that we loathe and believe to be fraught with death, unless they so imminently threaten immediate interference with the lawful and pressing purposes of the law that an immediate check is required to save the country.

I wholly disagree with the argument of the government that the First Amendment left the common law as to seditious libel in force. History seems to me against the notion. I had conceived that the United States through many years had shown its repentance for the Sedition Act of 1798 by repaying fines that it imposed. Only the emergency that makes it immediately dangerous to leave the correction of evil counsels to time warrants making any exception to the sweeping command, "Congress shall make no law . . . abridging the freedom of speech." Of course I am speaking only of expressions of opinion and exhortations, which were all that were uttered here, but I regret that I cannot put into more impressive words my belief that in their conviction upon this indictment the defendants were deprived of their rights under the Constitution of the United States.

The most stringent protection of free speech would not protect a man in falsely shouting fire in a theater and causing a panic.
OLIVER WENDELL HOLMES, JR., *Schenck* v. *U.S.*, 1919

With effervescing opinions, as with the not yet forgotten champagne, the quickest way to let them get flat is to let them get exposed to the air.
OLIVER WENDELL HOLMES, JR., *Letter*, January 1920

48.

Robert Benchley: The Making of a Red

The "Red scare" of 1919-1920 was partly the result of wartime passions as yet unabated, and partly of an intensive propaganda campaign aimed at the Western countries by Russia after the October Revolution. The Justice Department gave the violent but short-lived movement official support, and "Palmer raids" — named after Attorney General A. Mitchell Palmer — occurred from time to time starting in the fall of 1919. These raids, involving countrywide mass arrests of political and labor agitators, came to a head on January 2, 1920, when more than 2,700 people were taken into custody in thirty-three cities. The raids were terminated in May, but not until many aliens had been deported to Russia. Humorist Robert Benchley published some sardonic observations on the "Red Menace" in the Nation *early in 1919. The essay is reprinted here.*

Source: *Nation,* March 15, 1919.

You couldn't have asked for anyone more regular than Peters. He was an eminently safe citizen. Although not rich himself, he never chafed under the realization that there were others who possessed great wealth. In fact, the thought gave him rather a comfortable feeling. Furthermore, he was one of the charter members of the war. Long before President Wilson saw the light, Peters was advocating the abolition of German from the public-school curriculum. There was, therefore, absolutely nothing in his record which would in the slightest degree alter the true blue of a patriotic litmus. And he considered himself a liberal when he admitted that there might be something in this man Gompers, after all. That is how safe he was.

But one night he made a slip. It was ever so tiny a slip, but in comparison with it De Maupassant's famous piece of string was barren of consequences. Shortly before the United States entered the war, Peters made a speech at a meeting of the Civic League in his home town. His subject was: "Interurban Highways: Their Development in the Past and Their Possibilities for the Future." So far, 100 percent American. But, in the course of his talk, he happened to mention the fact that war, as an institution, has almost always had an injurious effect on public improvements of all kinds. In fact (and note this well — the government's sleuth in the audience did) he said that, all other things being equal, if he were given his choice of war or peace in the abstract, he would choose peace as a condition under which to live. Then he went on to discuss the comparative values of macadam and wood blocks for paving.

In the audience was a civilian representative of the Military Intelligence Service. He had a premonition that some sort of attempt was going to be made at this meeting of the Civic League to discredit the war and America's imminent participation therein. And he was not disappointed (no Military Intelligence sleuth ever is), for in the remark of Peters, derogatory to war as an institution, his sharp ear detected the accent of the Wilhelmstrasse.

Time went by. The United States entered the war, and Peters bought Liberty Bonds. He didn't join the Army, it is true, but, then, neither did James M. Beck, and it is an open secret that Mr. Beck was for the war. Peters did what a few slangy persons called "his bit," and not without a certain amount of pride. But he did not hear the slow, grinding noise from that district in which are located the mills of the gods. He did not even know that there was an investigation going on in Washington to determine the uses to which German propaganda money had been put. That is, he didn't know it until he opened his newspaper one morning and, with that uncanny precipitation with which a man's eye lights on his own name, discovered that he had been mentioned in the dispatches. At first he thought that it might be an honor list of Liberty Bond holders, but a glance at the headline chilled that young hope in his breast. It read as follows:

PRO-GERMAN LIST BARED BY ARMY SLEUTH
Prominent Obstructionists
Named at Senate Probe

And then came the list. Peters' eye ran instinctively down to the place where, in what seemed to him to be 24-point Gothic caps, was blazoned the name "Horace W. Peters, Pacifist Lecturer, Matriculated at Germantown (Pa.) Military School." Above his name was that of Emma Goldman, "Anarchist." Below came that of Fritz von Papen, "agent of the Imperial German Government in America," and Jeremiah O'Leary, "Irish and Pro-German Agitator."

Peters was stunned. He telegraphed to his senator at Washington and demanded that the outrageous libel be retracted. He telegraphed to the Military Intelligence office and demanded to know who was the slanderer who had traduced him, and who in h —— l this Captain Whatsisname was who had submitted the report. He telegraphed to Secretary Baker and he cabled to the President. And he was informed, by return stagecoach, that his telegrams had been received and would be brought to the attention of the addressees at the earliest possible moment.

Then he went out to look up some of his friends, to explain that there had been a terrible mistake somewhere. But he was coolly received. No one could afford to be seen talking with him after what had happened. His partner merely said: "Bad business, Horace. Bad business!" The elevator starter pointed him out to a subordinate, and Peters heard him explain: "That's Peters, Horace W. Peters. Did'je see his name in the papers this morning with them other German spies?" At the club, little groups of his friends dissolved awkwardly when they saw him approaching, and, after distant nods, disappeared in an aimless manner. After all, you could hardly blame them.

The next morning the *Tribune* had a double-leaded editorial entitled "Oatmeal," in which it was stated that the disclosures in Washington were revealing the most insidious of all kinds of German propaganda — that disseminated by supposedly respectable American citizens. "It is not a tangible propaganda. It is an emotional propaganda. To the unwary it may resemble real-estate news, or perhaps a patriotic song, but it is the pap of Prussianism. As an example, we need go no further than Horace W. Peters. Mr. Peters' hobby was interurban highways. A very pretty hobby, Mr. Peters, but it won't do. It won't do." The *Times* ran an editorial saying, somewhere in the midst of a solid slab of type, that no doubt it would soon be found that Mr. Peters nourished Bolshevist sentiments, along with his teammate Emma Goldman. Emma Goldman! How Peters hated that woman! He had once written a letter to this very paper about her, advocating her electrocution.

He dashed out again in a search of someone to whom he could explain. But the editorials had done their work. The doorman at the club presented him with a letter from the House Committee saying that, at a special meeting, it had been decided that he had placed himself in a position offensive to the loyal members of the club and that it was with deep regret that they informed him, etc. As he stumbled out into the street, he heard someone whisper to an out-of-town friend, "There goes Emma Goldman's husband."

As the days went by, things grew unbelievably worse. He was referred to in public meetings whenever an example of civic treachery was in order. A signed advertisement in the newspapers protesting, on behalf of the lineal descendants of the Grand Duke Sergius, against the spread of Bolshevism in northern New Jersey, mentioned a few prominent snakes in the grass, such as Trotzky, Victor Berger, Horace W. Peters, and Emma Goldman.

Then something snapped. Peters began to let his hair grow long and neglected his linen. Each time he was snubbed on the street he uttered a queer guttural sound and made a mark in a little book he carried about with him. He bought a copy of "Colloquial Russian at a Glance," and began picking out inflammatory sentences from the *Novy Mir*. His wife packed up and went to stay with her sister when he advocated, one night at dinner, the communization of women. The last prop of respectability having been removed, the descent was easy. Emma Goldman, was it? Very well, then, Emma Goldman it should be! Bolshevist, was he? They had said it! "After all, who is to blame for this?" he mumbled to himself. "Capitalism! Militarism! Those Prussians in the Intelligence Department and the Department of Justice! The damnable *bourgeoisie* who sit back and read their *Times* and their *Tribune* and believe what they read there!" He had tried explanations. He had tried argument. There was only one thing left. He found it on page 112 of a little book of Emma Goldman's that he always carried around with him.

You may have read about Peters the other day. He was arrested, wearing a red shirt over his business cutaway and carrying enough TNT to shift the Palisades back into the Hackensack marshes. He was identified by an old letter in his pocket from Henry Cabot Lodge thanking him for a telegram of congratulation Peters had once sent him on the occasion of a certain speech in the Senate.

The next morning the *Times* said, editorially, that it hoped the authorities now saw that the only way to crush Bolshevism was by the unrelenting use of force.

———◆———

There is no right to strike against the public peace by anybody, anywhere, any time.

> CALVIN COOLIDGE, reply to Samuel Gompers' request that the Boston police commissioner be removed by Coolidge, then governor of Massachusetts, for requesting state troops to break the Boston police strike, 1919

1920

49.

A. LAWRENCE LOWELL: The Management of Universities

The "incursion of business principles into the affairs of higher learning" that Thorstein Veblen pointed to in The Higher Learning in America *(1918) was reflected in the organizational structure of many large universities. Direction of the universities was normally in the hands of boards of trustees made up of businessmen, who, because they held the purse strings, were often able to assume control over academic matters in ways that severely mitigated the traditional freedom of the scholar. The weakness inherent in such an arrangement became apparent when the pressure on faculties for political conformity during the war was very great. In his annual report for 1919-1920, a portion of which is reprinted here, President A. Lawrence Lowell of Harvard sought to clarify the proper relation between faculties and governing boards.*

Source: *At War with Academic Traditions in America,* Cambridge, 1934, pp. 281-291.

IF A UNIVERSITY OR COLLEGE is a society or guild of scholars, why does it need any separate body of trustees at all? Why more than learned societies, which are obviously groups of scholars, and have no such boards recruited outside their own membership? One reason is to be found in the large endowments of our institutions of learning that require for investment a wide knowledge and experience of business affairs. Another reason is that higher educa-

In fact . . . the vast complexity of a modern university has compelled specialization of functions, and one aspect thereof is the separation of the scholarly and business organs. Another reason is that higher educa-

tion has assumed more and more of a public character; its importance has been more fully recognized by the community at large; it must therefore keep in touch with public needs, make the public appreciate its aims and the means essential to attain them; and for this purpose it must possess the influence and obtain the guidance of men conversant with the currents of the outer world.

There is a further reason, more fundamental if less generally understood. Teaching in all its grades is a public service, and the administration of every public service must comprise both expert and lay ele-

Abbott Lawrence Lowell; portrait by John Singer Sargent

ments. Without the former it will be ineffectual; without the latter it will become in time narrow, rigid, or out of harmony with its public object. Each has its own distinctive function, and only confusion and friction result if one of them strives to perform the function of the other. From this flows the cardinal principle, popularly little known but of well-nigh universal application, that experts should not be members of a nonprofessional body that supervises experts. One often hears that men with a practical knowledge of teaching should be elected to school boards, but unless they are persons of singular discretion they are likely to assume that their judgment on technical matters is better than that of the teachers, with effects that are sometimes disastrous. Laymen should not attempt to direct experts about the method of attaining results, but only indicate the results to be attained.

Many years ago the Board of Overseers, after a careful examination, came to the conclusion that the writing of English by Harvard undergraduates was sadly defective. In this they were acting wholly within their proper province, and the result was a very notable improvement in the teaching of English composition. But if they had attempted to direct how the subject should be taught, they would have been hopelessly beyond their province. They would not have known, as the instructing staff did, how it should be done, and they would have exasperated and disheartened the teachers.

But another question may well be asked. Granted that there should be both expert and nonprofessional elements in the management of a university or college, why in a society or guild of scholars should the nonprofessional organ be the final authority? For this there are three reasons. In the first place, so far as the object is public — and where teaching is conducted on a large scale the object cannot fail to concern the public deeply — that object must in the final analysis be determined by public, that is by nonprofessional, judgment. In an endowed university the governing board does not, indeed, represent the public in the sense that it is elected by popular vote, but it is not on that account any less truly a trustee for the public.

In the second place, the nonprofessional board is responsible for the financial administration, and the body that holds the purse must inevitably have the final control.

Third, the nonprofessional board is the only body, or the most satisfactory body, to act as arbiter between the different groups of experts. Everyone knows that in an American university or college there is a ceaseless struggle for the means of development between different departments, and someone must decide upon the relative merits of their claims. In a university with good traditions the professors would be more ready to rely on the fairness and wisdom of a well-constituted board of trustees than on one composed of some of their own number, each affected almost unavoidably by a bias in favor of his particular subject.

Let it be observed, however, that although the governing board is the ultimate authority, it is not in the position of an industrial employer. It is a trustee not to earn dividends for stockholders but for the purposes of the guild. Its sole object is to help the society of scholars to accomplish the object for which they are brought together. They are the essential part of the society; and making their work effective for the intellectual and moral training of youth and for investigation is the sole reason for the existence of trustees, of buildings, of endowments, and of all the elaborate machinery of a modern university. If this conception be fully borne in mind, most of the sources of dissension between professors and governing boards will disappear. At Harvard it has, I believe, been borne in mind as a deep-seated traditional conviction.

The differences between the ordinary industrial employment and the conduct of a society or guild of scholars in a university are wide. In the industrial system of employment the employee is paid according to the value of his services; he can be discharged when no longer wanted; and his duties are prescribed as minutely as may be desired by the employer. In a university there is permanence of tenure; substantial equality of pay within each academic grade; and although the duties in general are well understood, there is great freedom in the method of performing them. It is not difficult to see why each of these conditions prevails, and is in fact dependent upon the others.

Permanence of tenure lies at the base of the difference between a society of scholars in a university and the employees in an industrial concern. In the latter, under prevailing conditions, men are employed in order to promote its earning power. In a university the concern exists to promote the work of the scholars and of the students whom they teach. Therefore, in the industrial concern, an unprofitable employee is discharged; but in the university the usefulness of the scholar depends largely upon his sense of security, upon the fact that he can work for an object that may be remote and whose value may not be easily demonstrated. In a university, barring positive misconduct, permanence of tenure is essential for members who have passed the probationary period.

The equality of pay goes with the permanence of tenure. In an industrial establishment the higher class of officials, those who correspond most nearly to the grade of professors, can be paid what they may be worth to the concern and discharged if they are not worth their salaries. How valuable they are can be fairly estimated, and their compensation can be varied accordingly. But professors, whose tenure is permanent, cannot be discharged if they do not prove so valuable as they were expected to be. Moreover, it is impossible to determine the value of scholars in the same way as that of commercial officials. An attempt to do so would create injustice and endless discontent; and it would offer a temptation to secure high pay, from their own or another institution, by a display wholly inconsistent with the scholarly attitude of mind. The only satisfactory system is that of paying salaries on something very close to a fixed scale, and letting every professor do as good work as he can.

In an industrial concern the prospect of a high salary may be needed to induce the greatest effort; but indolence among professors is seldom found. They may, indeed, prefer a line of work less important than some other; a man may desire to do research who is better fitted for teaching, or he may prefer to teach advanced students when there is a greater need of the strongest men in more elementary instruction; but failure to work hard is rare.

The governing boards of universities having, then, the ultimate legal control in their hands, and yet not being in the position of industrial employers, it is pertinent to inquire what their relation to the professors should be. If we bear in mind the conception of a society or guild of scholars, that relation usually becomes in practice clear. The scholars, both individually and gathered into faculties, are to provide the expert knowledge; the governing board, the financial management, the general coordination, the arbitral determinations, and the preservation of the general direction of public policy. In the words of a former member of the Harvard Corporation, their business is to "serve tables." The relation is not one of employer and employed, of superior and inferior, of master and servant, but one of mutual cooperation for the promotion of the scholars' work.

Unless the professors have confidence in the singleness of purpose and in the wisdom of the governing boards, and unless these in their turn recognize that they exist to promote the work of the society of scholars, the relations will not have the harmony that they should. The relation is one that involves constant seeking of opinion, and in the main the university must be conducted, not by authority but by persuasion. There is no natural antagonism of interests between trustees and professors. To suggest it is to suggest failure in their proper relation to one another; to suppose it is to provoke failure; to assume it is to ensure failure.

The question has often been raised whether nominations for appointments should be made by the faculties or their committees, or by the president. It would seem that the less formal the provisions the better. Any president of a university or college who makes a nomination to the governing board without consulting formally or informally the leading professors in the subject and without making sure that most of them approve of it is taking a grave responsibility that can be justified only by a condition that requires surgery. The objection to a formal nomination by a faculty, or a committee thereof, is that it places the members in an uncomfortable position in regard to their younger colleagues, and that it creates a tendency for the promotion of useful rather than excellent men. A wise president will not make nominations without being sure of the support of the instructing staff, but he may properly, and indeed ought to, decline to make nominations unless convinced that the nominee is of the caliber that ought to be appointed.

Attempts have been made to define, and express in written rules, the relation between the faculties and the governing boards; but the best element in that relation is an intangible, an undefinable, influence. If a husband and wife should attempt to define by regulations their respective rights and duties in the household, that marriage could safely be pronounced a failure. The essence of the relation is mutual confidence and mutual regard; and the respective functions of the faculties and the governing boards — those things that each had better undertake, those it had better leave to the other, and those which require mutual concession — are best learned from experience and best embodied in tradition.

Tradition has great advantages over regulations. It is a more delicate instrument; it accommodates itself to things that are not susceptible of sharp definition; it is more flexible in its application, making exceptions and allowances which it would be difficult to foresee or prescribe. It is also more stable. Regulations can be amended; tradition cannot, for it is not made, but grows, and can be altered only by a gradual change in general opinion, not by a majority vote. In short, it cannot be amended, but only outgrown.

50.

John J. Mahoney: The Schooling of the Immigrant

Americanization and assimilation of the immigrant was a problem for the public schools in any area where large numbers of immigrants tended to congregate. There were basically two theories of what Americanization meant. It was clear to some that an immigrant had to lose all of his ethnic character and values and accept the ideals of Anglo-Saxon, middle-class America, as well as the traditions handed down from the Puritan forefathers. It was clear to others that Americanization was a process in which all ethnic groups made their contribution, adopting new values while retaining many of the old. John J. Mahoney, state supervisor of Americanization for Massachusetts, accepted the second point of view in his Training Teachers for Americanization, *part of which is reprinted here.*

Source: Department of the Interior, Bureau of Education Bulletin, 1920, No. 12, Washington, 1920.

WHY TEACHER TRAINING?

THE SCHOOLING OF THE IMMIGRANT in the past has been, speaking broadly, an unsuccessful performance. The reasons therefor are many and are not to be charged against the schools alone. One of the principal reasons, without a doubt, was the slowness on the part of the public, and not infrequently on the part of school people themselves, to appreciate the fact that the teaching of the adult immigrant is a highly specialized piece of work, requiring not only special aptitude but special training as well.

For years the evening school was but a subordinate part of the educational system, and it was felt that anyone could teach an evening-school class. At first the teaching of English and allied subjects was committed to the hands of nonprofessionals, who not infrequently worked for the night's wage — and for nothing else. Suitable teaching materials were almost wholly lacking. It is not strange, with such conditions, that the schools failed to hold even those who wished to learn. More recently we find the trained day-school teacher working in the immigrant classes. And while this is no unmixed blessing, inasmuch as it means a double burden for teachers already burdened enough, it is an improvement over what has obtained hitherto.

It is quite true that not every good teacher of children proves to be a good teacher of adult immigrants. It is also true that teachers trained in normal-school methods have often made the mistake of trying to use these methods without adaptation in their evening-school instruction. The trained teacher in the evening school nevertheless has marked a step upward in the efficiency of evening-school work.

Since 1915, however, there has come to the American people, and especially to the school administrator, a larger vision as to the solution of the Americanization problem. No longer is the schooling of the immigrant to be an overtime task performed by teachers with only a casual training. Day schools for immigrants, factory classes for immigrants, afternoon classes for immigrant women — these and others are all to find place in the plan of Americanization during the next few years.

And the teachers in these classes must be specifically trained. There is a distinct pedagogy in this work with adult immigrants and a very distinct methodology. The teacher of the immigrant must be acquainted with these. She must have a knowledge of the important aims in her work, namely: (1) what she is to teach; (2) how she is to teach; (3) what standard of achievement she may expect. She must know more specifically also what her aims should be in the task of teaching immigrants to talk English and how this can best be done; to read English and how this can best be done; to write English and how this can best be done. Similarly with the other subjects that are included in the immigrant's program.

Finally, and of greatest importance, she must appreciate that her big task is Americanization — the making of Americans — and must understand just what that means and how it can best be brought about. All this means that the teacher must go to school to learn another lesson in her business of teaching. Colleges, normal schools, state departments of education, large city school systems, all should take it upon themselves to put the work of teacher training in this new field on an established basis. It is very far from being on an established basis now. . . .

FIFTEEN POINTS FOR WORKERS IN AMERICANIZATION

1. Americanization — to give the term its most comprehensive meaning — is the business of making good American citizens, the business of acquainting everyone who inhabits American soil with both physical and spiritual America to the end that this acquaintance may result in a sturdy loyalty to American institutions and American ideals and the habit of living the life of the good American citizen. Really to American-ize America, we must reach the native-born and the immigrant, the adult and the child in school; and, incidentally, our task of Americanizing the newcomer will be rendered comparatively easy if we can but succeed first in Americanizing ourselves.

2. To accomplish this end, we must come to a new realization of what Americanism really is, of the things that the good citizen believes in, swears by, and loves. And these things must be analyzed and interpreted in terms that touch the life of the average man. What is democracy? What are our American ideas, ideals, aspirations, principles of government, and abiding beliefs? We must know these. And, further, we must find out how to teach them so that this teaching may find expression in right conduct. Here is a task we must face and do if our American democracy is to endure.

3. The Americanization of the immigrant has been thought of generally as a matter of schooling alone. It is much more than this. The immigrant is becoming either Americanized or anarchized by every experience which he undergoes, every condition to which he is subjected. Americanization is in a measure the problem of the school. But it is also a matter of prevention of exploitation, of good housing, of clean milk for babies, of adequate wages, of satisfactory industrial conditions, of the spirit of neighborliness between Americans, old and new. Everything that touches the immigrant's life is an instrumentality for his Americanization or the reverse. Hence the need for the entire community through all its organized agencies to take a hand in the induction of our late arrivals into the corporate life of America.

4. The Americanism to be taught is not a static Americanism, belonging exclusively to the native-born. America and the American spirit are dynamic, ever changing concepts. It is not solely the Americanism of the Puritan that we would teach. It is that plus the precious contributions that have come,

and are coming, and will come to us through the spiritual heritages of the many races that seek our shores. The process of Americanization is a reciprocal one. We give — but we receive as well.

The successful worker in Americanization is the one who approaches his task with a healthy feeling of respect for the immigrant, and with some humility of spirit.

5. Americanism cannot be imposed from without. Americanization is best handled when the immigrant becomes assimilated through his own efforts and through his own lively desire. The community should aim to make American citizenship a goal to be prized and should facilitate in every possible way the process of acquiring it. It follows that all schemes for *compulsory* Americanization must fail. It ill becomes the American people, who have long neglected the immigrant, to turn to coercion without first exhausting every encouraging means.

6. Americanization does not imply that the immigrant must give up his cherished spiritual heritages. His language, his religion, his social customs he may retain and yet become a good American. Americanization is a giving, not a taking away. The wise worker in Americanization will adhere to the policy "Hands off."

7. The teaching of a foreign language to school children and the conducting of foreign-language newspapers are matters that should be handled with common sense. The Great War has made a great many people hysterical. The Americanizer, of all people, needs to remain sane.

8. Blanket statements about the immigrant are unsafe and misleading. There is no immigrant. There are immigrants and immigrants, of every nationality and of every degree of repute, just as in the case of native-born. Does the immigrant lend himself readily to the Americanization process? Some nationalities do; some are not so receptive. Is the immigrant a menace? There are undesirables among our newcomers, as

among our native-born. There are also the chosen from many lands. Individuals differ, and races differ also. The person who would deal with immigrants must know racial backgrounds and characteristics. These differ. There is no magic process that can be applied to all national groups with any assurance of the same result. The approach to any group must be based upon the psychology of the folk, their customs, beliefs, and apperceptive bases. One cannot gain the confidence of and help those whom he does not know and those in whom he does not believe.

9. Five things are necessary to make effective the great Americanization movement that is sweeping the country today: (a) the vital interest and support of the public; (b) authoritative leadership; (c) an intelligent coordination of working agencies under public direction; (d) good teachers; (e) adequate public funds.

The Americanization of the immigrant has failed up to date because we have lacked all of these.

10. The schooling of the immigrant is a public function and should be carried on under the supervision of public educational authorities, whether in evening, neighborhood, or industrial classes. To accomplish this task properly, however, public educational authorities must appreciate that the schooling of the immigrant is no "sideshow" to be conducted as before the Great War, when anyone could teach, and when almost anyone did. It is a highly specialized piece of work and must be handled accordingly.

11. Agencies other than the public schools should be encouraged to cooperate in the schooling of the immigrant. Industry has an obligation, and classes in industry may well find place. So, too, with home and mothers' classes, whether conducted in a school, the quarters of a semipublic agency, or in the home itself. But insofar as can be brought about, the responsibility for the

general policy and the character of the teaching in those classes should be lodged in the public schools.

12. Cooperating agencies should work with the idea of carrying out those special functions which they are best equipped to handle. Self-advertisement and an unwillingness to cooperate have too often conspired to do more harm than good in Americanization schemes.

13. The teaching of English is the first step in Americanization. The public must come to realize that this is one of the most difficult pieces of work that any teacher is called upon to do. The public must make it possible to secure for this work teachers who are adequately trained. We have only begun to break ground in this field.

14. After the teaching of English comes education in citizenship. This is very poorly handled today. If we are going to make good American citizens out of the millions who are with us but not of us, it is high time that the whole machinery designed to bring this to pass be thoroughly inspected and overhauled.

15. In the final analysis the major part of the burden of Americanizing the immigrant rests on the shoulders of the teacher. Her task is a meaningful one, and she should approach it as one who engages not for hire. She must be an American 100 percent pure. She must be sane and sympathetic and able to see things whole. She must be ready to give and give, and reckon not the return. But the return will come, if she remembers — as she must remember — that she may not give over giving.

51.

J. McKenna and W. R. Day: *United States* v. *United States Steel Corporation et al.*

According to the famous "rule of reason," promulgated by Chief Justice Edward D. White in the course of the government's prosecution of the Standard Oil Company in 1911, only unreasonable *combinations in restraint of trade were illegal. Applying this rule, the Supreme Court decided on March 1, 1920, that the U.S. Steel Corporation, founded in 1901 by J. P. Morgan as the first "billion dollar" corporation, was not, despite its size, such an illegal combination. While the business community hailed the majority decision in the case as a sign of the Court's growing enlightenment, Progressives tended to see it as a reversion to the "unholy" atmosphere of an earlier day. The selection below includes portions of Justice McKenna's opinion for the majority and of Justice Day's dissent.*

Source: 251 U.S. 417.

Mr. Justice McKenna. Suit against the Steel Corporation and certain other companies which it directs and controls by reason of the ownership of their stock, it and they being separately and collectively charged as violators of the Sherman Antitrust Act.

It is prayed that it and they be dissolved because engaged in illegal restraint of trade and the exercise of monopoly.

Special charges of illegality and monopoly are made and special redresses and remedies are prayed, among others, that there be a prohibition of stock ownership and exercise of rights under such ownership, and that there shall be such orders and distribution of the stock and other properties as shall be in accordance with equity and good conscience and "shall effectuate the purpose of the Antitrust Act." General relief is also prayed.

The Steel Corporation is a holding company only; the other companies are the operating ones, manufacturers in the iron and steel industry, twelve in number. There are, besides, other corporations and individuals more or less connected with the activities of the other defendants that are alleged to be instruments or accomplices in their activities and offendings; and that these activities and offendings (speaking in general terms) extend from 1901 to 1911, when the bill was filed, and have illustrative periods of significant and demonstrated illegality.

Issue is taken upon all these charges, and we see at a glance what detail of circumstances may be demanded, and we may find ourselves puzzled to compress them into an opinion that will not be of fatiguing prolixity.

The case was heard in the District Court by four judges. They agreed that the bill should be dismissed; they disagreed as to the reasons for it. . . . One opinion (written by Judge Buffington and concurred in by Judge McPherson) expressed the view that the Steel Corporation was not formed with the intention or purpose to monopolize or restrain trade, and did not have the motive or effect "to prejudice the public interest by unduly restricting competition or unduly obstructing the course of trade." The corporation, in the view of the opinion, was an evolution, a natural consummation of the tendencies of the industry on account of changing conditions, practically a compulsion from "the metallurgical method of making steel and the physical method of

handling it," this method, and the conditions consequent upon it, tending to combinations of capital and energies rather than diffusion in independent action. And the concentration of powers (we are still representing the opinion) was only such as was deemed necessary, and immediately manifested itself in improved methods and products and in an increase of domestic and foreign trade. Indeed, an important purpose of the organization of the corporation was the building up of the export trade in steel and iron which at that time was sporadic, the mere dumping of the products upon foreign markets.

Not monopoly, therefore, was the purpose of the organization of the corporation but concentration of efforts with resultant economies and benefits.

The tendency of the industry and the purpose of the corporation in yielding to it were expressed in comprehensive condensation by the word "integration," which signifies continuity in the processes of the industry from ore mines to the finished product.

All considerations deemed pertinent were expressed and their influence was attempted to be assigned and, while conceding that the Steel Corporation, after its formation in times of financial disturbance, entered into informal agreements or understandings with its competitors to maintain prices, they terminated with their occasions, and, as they had ceased to exist, the court was not justified in dissolving the corporation.

The other opinion (by Judge Woolley and concurred in by Judge Hunt . . .) was in some particulars in antithesis to Judge Buffington's. The view was expressed that neither the Steel Corporation nor the preceding combinations, which were in a sense its antetypes, had the justification of industrial conditions, nor were they or it impelled by the necessity for integration, or compelled to unite in comprehensive enterprise because such had become a condition of success under the new order of things. On the contrary, that the organizers of the corporation and the preceding companies had illegal purpose from the very beginning, and the corporation became "a combination of combinations, by which, directly or indirectly, approximately 180 independent concerns were brought under one business control," which, measured by the amount of production, extended to 80 or 90 percent of the entire output of the country, and that its purpose was to secure great profits which were thought possible in the light of the history of its constituent combinations, and to accomplish permanently what those combinations had demonstrated could be accomplished temporarily and thereby monopolize and restrain trade.

The organizers, however (we are still representing the opinion), underestimated the opposing conditions and at the very beginning the corporation instead of relying upon its own power sought and obtained the assistance and the cooperation of its competitors (the independent companies). In other words, the view was expressed that the testimony did "not show that the corporation in and of itself ever possessed or exerted sufficient power when acting alone to control prices of the products of the industry." Its power was efficient only when in cooperation with its competitors, and hence it concerted with them in the expedients of pools, associations, trade meetings, and finally in a system of dinners inaugurated in 1907 by the president of the company, E. H. Gary, and called "the Gary Dinners."

The dinners were congregations of producers and "were nothing but trade meetings," successors of the other means of associated action and control through such action. They were instituted first in "stress of panic," but, their potency being demonstrated, they were afterwards called to control prices "in periods of industrial calm." "They were pools without penalties" and more efficient in stabilizing prices. But it was the further declaration that "when joint action was either refused or withdrawn the corporation's prices were controlled by competition."

The corporation, it was said, did not at any time abuse the power or ascendancy it possessed. It resorted to none of the brutalities or tyrannies that the cases illustrate of other combinations. It did not secure freight rebates; it did not increase its profits by reducing the wages of its employees — whatever it did was not at the expense of labor; it did not increase its profits by lowering the quality of its products, nor create an artificial scarcity of them; it did not oppress or coerce its competitors — its competition, though vigorous, was fair; it did not undersell its competitors in some localities by reducing its prices there below those maintained elsewhere, or require its customers to enter into contracts limiting their purchases or restricting them in resale prices; it did not obtain customers by secret rebates or departures from its published prices; there was no evidence that it attempted to crush its competitors or drive them out of the market, nor did it take customers from its competitors by unfair means, and in its competition it seemed to make no difference between large and small competitors.

Indeed it is said in many ways and illustrated that "instead of relying upon its own power to fix and maintain prices, the corporation, at its very beginning sought and obtained the assistance of others." It combined its power with that of its competitors. It did not have power in and of itself, and the control it exerted was only in and by association with its competitors. Its offense, therefore, such as it was, was not different from theirs and was distinguished from theirs "only in the leadership it assumed in promulgating and perfecting the policy." This leadership it gave up, and it had ceased to offend against the law before this suit was brought. It was hence concluded that it should be distinguished from its organizers and that their intent and unsuccessful attempt should not be attributed to it, that it "in and of itself is not now and has never been a monopoly or a combination in restraint of trade," and a decree of dissolution should not be entered against it.

This summary of the opinions, given necessarily in paraphrase, does not adequately represent their ability and strength, but it has value as indicating the contentions of the parties and the ultimate propositions to which the contentions are addressed. The opinions indicate that the evidence admits of different deductions as to the genesis of the corporation and the purpose of its organizers, but only of a single deduction as to the power it attained and could exercise. Both opinions were clear and confident that the power of the corporation never did and does not now reach to monopoly, and their review of the evidence, and our independent examination of it, enable us to elect between their respective estimates of it, and we concur in the main with that of Judges Woolley and Hunt.

And we add no comment except, it may be, that they underestimated the influence of the tendency and movement to integration, the appreciation of the necessity or value of the continuity of manufacture from the ore to the finished product. And there was such a tendency; and though it cannot be asserted it had become a necessity, it had certainly become a facility of industrial progress. There was, therefore, much to urge it and give incentive to conduct that could accomplish it. From the nature and properties of the industry, the processes of production were something more than the stage and setting of the human activities. They determined to an extent those activities, furnished their motives, and gave test of their quality — not, of course, that the activities could get any immunity from size, or resources, or energies, whether exerted in integrated plants or diversified ones.

The contentions of the case, therefore,

must be judged by the requirements of the law, not by accidental or adventitious circumstances. But what are such circumstances? We have seen that it was the view of the District Court that size was such a circumstance and had no accusing or excusing influence. The contention of the government is to the contrary. Its assertion is that the size of the corporation being the result of a "combination of powerful and able competitors" had become "substantially dominant" in the industry and illegal. And that this was determined. The companies combined, is the further assertion, had already reached a high degree of efficiency, and in their independence were factors in production and competition, but ceased to be such when brought under the regulating control of the corporation, which by uniting them offended the law; and that the organizers of the corporation "had in mind the specific purposes of the restraint of trade and the enormous profits resulting from that restraint."

It is the contention of the corporation, opposing those of the government and denying the illegal purposes charged against it, that the industry demanded qualities and an enterprise that lesser industries do not demand and must have a corresponding latitude and facility. Indeed, it is insisted that the industry had practically (to quote the words of Judge Buffington, he quoting those of a witness) "reached the limit, or very nearly so, at which economies from a metallurgical or mechanical standpoint could be made effective," and "that instead, as was then the practice, of having one mill to make ten or twenty or fifty products, the greatest economy would result from having one mill make one product, and make that product continuously."

In other words, that there was a necessity for integration, and rescue from the old conditions — from their improvidence and waste of effort; and that, in redress of the conditions, the corporation was formed, its purpose and effect being "salvage not monopoly," to quote the words of counsel. It was, is the insistence, the conception of ability, "a vision of a great business which should embrace all lines of steel and all processes of manufacture from the ore to the finished product and which by reason of the economies thus to be effected and the diversity of products it would be able to offer, could successfully compete in all the markets of the world." It is urged further that to the discernment of that great possibility was added a courage that dared attempt its accomplishment, and the conception and the courage made the formation of the corporation notable but did not make it illegal. . . .

Our present purpose is not retrospect for itself, however instructive, but practical decision upon existing conditions, that we may not by their disturbance produce, or even risk, consequences of a concern that cannot now be computed. In other words, our consideration should be of not what the corporation had power to do or did, but what it has now power to do and is doing, and what judgment shall be now pronounced — whether its dissolution, as the government prays, or the dismissal of the suit, as the corporation insists? . . .

What then can now be urged against the corporation? Can comparisons in other regards be made with its competitors and by such comparisons guilty or innocent existence be assigned it? It is greater in size and productive power than any of its competitors, equal or nearly equal to them all, but its power over prices was not and is not commensurate with its power to produce. . . .

Besides the circumstances which we have mentioned, there are others of probative strength. The company's officers and, as well, its competitors and customers, testified that its competition was genuine, direct, and vigorous, and was reflected in prices and production. No practical witness was produced by the government in opposition. Its

contention is based on the size and asserted dominance of the corporation — alleged power for evil, not the exertion of the power in evil. Or, as counsel put it, "a combination may be illegal because of its purpose; it may be illegal because it acquires a dominating power, not as a result of normal growth and development but as a result of a combination of competitors." Such composition and its resulting power constitute, in the view of the government, the offense against the law, and yet it is admitted "no competitor came forward and said he had to accept the Steel Corporation's prices."

But this absence of complaint counsel urged against the corporation. Competitors, it is said, followed the corporation's prices because they made money by the imitation. Indeed the imitation is urged as an evidence of the corporation's power. "Universal imitation," counsel assert, is "an evidence of power." In this concord of action, the contention is there is the sinister dominance of the corporation — "its extensive control of the industry is such that the others [independent companies] follow." Counsel, however, admit that there was "occasionally" some competition, but reject the suggestion that it extended practically to a war between the corporation and the independents.

Counsel say, "They [the corporation is made a plural] called a few — they called 200 witnesses out of some 40,000 customers, and they expect with that customer evidence to overcome the whole train of price movement shown since the corporation was formed." And "movement of prices" counsel explained "as shown by the published prices . . . they were the ones that the competitors were maintaining all during the interval." . . .

The suggestion that lurks in the government's contention that the acceptance of the corporation's prices is the submission of impotence to irresistible power is, in view of the testimony of the competitors, untenable. They, as we have seen, deny restraint in any measure or illegal influence of any kind. The government, therefore, is reduced to the assertion that the size of the corporation, the power it may have, not the exertion of the power, is an abhorrence to the law, or, as the government says, "the combination embodied in the corporation unduly restrains competition by its *necessary effect* [the italics are the emphasis of the government] and therefore is unlawful regardless of purpose." "A wrongful purpose," the government adds, is "matter of aggravation."

The illegality is statical, purpose or movement of any kind only its emphasis. To assent to that, to what extremes should we be led? Competition consists of business activities and ability — they make its life; but there may be fatalities in it. Are the activities to be encouraged when militant, and suppressed or regulated when triumphant because of the dominance attained? To such paternalism the government's contention, which regards power rather than its use the determining consideration, seems to conduct. Certainly conducts we may say, for it is the inevitable logic of the government's contention that competition must not only be free but that it must not be pressed to the ascendancy of a competitor, for in ascendancy there is the menace of monopoly.

We have pointed out that there are several of the government's contentions which are difficult to represent or measure and the one we are now considering, that is the power is "unlawful regardless of purpose," is another of them. It seems to us that it has for its ultimate principle and justification that strength in any producer or seller is a menace to the public interest and illegal because there is potency in it for mischief. The regression is extreme, but short of it the government cannot stop. The fallacy it conveys is manifest.

The corporation was formed in 1901, no act of aggression upon its competitors is charged against it, it confederated with them at times in offense against the law,

but abandoned that before this suit was brought, and since 1911 no act in violation of law can be established against it except its existence be such an act. This is urged, as we have seen, and that the interest of the public is involved, and that such interest is paramount to corporation or competitors. Granted — though it is difficult to see how there can be restraint of trade when there is no restraint of competitors in the trade nor complaints by customers — how can it be worked out of the situation and through what proposition of law? Of course it calls for nothing other than a right application of the law and to repeat what we have said above, shall we declare the law to be that size is an offense even though it minds its own business because what it does is imitated?

The corporation is undoubtedly of impressive size and it takes an effort of resolution not to be affected by it or to exaggerate its influence. But we must adhere to the law and the law does not make mere size an offense or the existence of unexerted power an offense. It, we repeat, requires overt acts and trusts to its prohibition of them and its power to repress or punish them. It does not compel competition nor require all that is possible. . . .

In conclusion we are unable to see that the public interest will be served by yielding to the contention of the government respecting the dissolution of the company or the separation from it of some of its subsidiaries; and we do see in a contrary conclusion a risk of injury to the public interest, including a material disturbance of, and, it may be serious detriment to, the foreign trade. And in submission to the policy of the law and its fortifying prohibitions the public interest is of paramount regard.

We think, therefore, that the decree of the District Court should be affirmed.

Mr. Justice Day. This record seems to me to leave no fair room for a doubt that the defendants, the United States Steel Corporation and the several subsidiary corporations which make up that organization, were formed in violation of the Sherman Act. I am unable to accept the conclusion which directs a dismissal of the bill instead of following the well-settled practice, sanctioned by previous decisions of this Court, requiring the dissolution of combinations made in direct violation of the law. . . .

The enormous overcapitalization of companies and the appropriation of $100 million in stock to promotion expenses were represented in the stock issues of the new organizations thus formed and were the basis upon which large dividends have been declared from the profits of the business. This record shows that the power obtained by the corporation brought under its control large competing companies, which were of themselves illegal combinations, and succeeded to their power; that some of the organizers of the Steel Corporation were parties to the preceding combinations, participated in their illegality, and by uniting them under a common direction intended to augment and perpetuate their power. It is the irresistible conclusion from these premises that great profits to be derived from unified control were the object of these organizations.

The contention must be rejected that the combination was an inevitable evolution of industrial tendencies compelling union of endeavor. Nothing could add to the vivid accuracy with which Judge Woolley, speaking for himself and Judge Hunt, has stated the illegality of the organization and its purpose to combine in one great corporation the previous combinations by a direct violation of the purposes and terms of the Sherman Act.

For many years, as the record discloses, this unlawful organization exerted its power to control and maintain prices by pools, associations, trade meetings, and as the result of discussion and agreements at the so-called Gary Dinners, where the assembled trade opponents secured cooperation and joint action through the machinery of special committees of competing concerns, and by prudent prevision took into account the possibility of defection, and the means of controlling and perpetuating that industrial harmony which arose from the control and maintenance of prices.

It inevitably follows that the corporation violated the law in its formation and by its immediate practices. The power thus obtained from the combination of resources, almost unlimited in the aggregation of competing organizations, had within its control the domination of the trade and the ability to fix prices and restrain the free flow of commerce upon a scale heretofore unapproached in the history of corporate organization in this country.

These facts established, as it seems to me they are by the record, it follows that, if the Sherman Act is to be given efficacy, there must be a decree undoing so far as is possible that which has been achieved in open, notorious, and continued violation of its provisions.

I agree that the act offers no objection to the mere size of a corporation nor to the continued exertion of its lawful power when that size and power have been obtained by lawful means and developed by natural growth, although its resources, capital, and strength may give to such corporation a dominating place in the business and industry with which it is concerned. It is entitled to maintain its size and the power that legitimately goes with it provided no law has been transgressed in obtaining it. But I understand the reiterated decisions of this Court construing the Sherman Act to hold that this power may not legally be derived from conspiracies, combinations, or contracts in restraint of trade. To permit this would be to practically annul the Sherman Law by judicial decree. . . .

As I understand the conclusions of the Court affirming the decree directing dismissal of the bill, they amount to this: that these combinations, both the holding company and the subsidiaries which comprise it, although organized in plain violation and bold defiance of the provisions of the act, nevertheless are immune from a decree effectually ending the combinations and putting it out of their power to attain the unlawful purposes sought because of some reasons of public policy requiring such conclusion. I know of no public policy which sanctions a violation of the law, nor of any inconvenience to trade, domestic or foreign, which should have the effect of placing combinations, which have been able thus to organize one of the greatest industries of the country in defiance of law, in an impregnable position above the control of the law forbidding such combinations. Such a conclusion does violence to the policy which the law was intended to enforce, runs counter to the decisions of the Court, and necessarily results in a practical nullification of the act itself.

There is no mistaking the terms of the act as they have hitherto been interpreted by this Court. It was not intended to merely suppress unfair practices, but, as its history and terms amply show, it was intended to make it criminal to form combinations or engage in conspiracies or contracts in restraint of interstate trade. The remedy by injunction, at the instance of the attorney general, was given for the purpose of enabling the courts, as the statute states, to prohibit such conspiracies, combinations and contracts, and this Court interpreting its provisions has held that the proper enforcement of the act requires decrees to end combinations by dissolving them and restoring as far as possible the competitive conditions which the combinations have destroyed. I am unable to see force in the suggestion that public policy, or the as-

sumed disastrous effect upon foreign trade of dissolving the unlawful combination, is sufficient to entitle it to immunity from the enforcement of the statute. . . .

It is said that a complete monopolization of the steel business was never attained by the offending combinations. To insist upon such result would be beyond the requirements of the statute and in most cases practicably impossible. . . .

It is affirmed that to grant the government's request for a remand to the District Court for a decree of dissolution would not result in a change in the conditions of the steel trade. Such is not the theory of the Sherman Act. That act was framed in the belief that attempted or accomplished monopolization, or combinations which suppress free competition, were hurtful to the public interest, and that a restoration of competitive conditions would benefit the public. We have here a combination in control of one-half of the steel business of the country. If the plan were followed, as in the *American Tobacco Case*, of remanding the case to the District Court, a decree might be framed restoring competitive conditions as far as practicable. . . . In that case the subject of reconstruction so as to restore such conditions was elaborated and carefully considered. In my judgment the principles there laid down if followed now would make a very material difference in the steel industry. Instead of one dominating corporation, with scattered competitors, there would be competitive conditions throughout the whole trade which would carry into effect the policy of the law.

It seems to me that if this act is to be given effect, the bill, under the findings of fact made by the Court, should not be dismissed, and the cause should be remanded to the District Court, where a plan of effective and final dissolution of the corporations should be enforced by a decree framed for that purpose.

52.

LOTHROP STODDARD: The Crisis of the Ages

The anti-immigrant views that increasingly prevailed in the early years of the twentieth century were born of the conviction that white Anglo-Saxons were meant to control the destiny as well as the social and political policies of the United States. Such attitudes were strengthened in the postwar years by the "red scare" of 1919-1920, the fear of Japanese power in the Far East, and the overwhelming desire for isolation from world problems. One book that expressed the nativist American's dread of all things foreign was Lothrop Stoddard's The Rising Tide of Color Against White World-Supremacy, *published in 1920. The final chapter is reprinted here.*

Source: *The Rising Tide of Color Against White World-Supremacy,* London, 1920, pp. 299-310.

OURS IS A SOLEMN MOMENT. We stand at a crisis — the supreme crisis of the ages. For unnumbered millenniums man has toiled upward from the dank jungles of savagery toward glorious heights, which his mental and spiritual potentialities give promise that he shall attain. His path has been slow and wavering. Time and again he has lost his way and plunged into deep valleys. . . .

Humanity has thus suffered many a disaster. Yet none of these disasters was fatal because they were merely local. Those wrecked civilizations and blighted peoples were only parts of a larger whole. Always some strong barbarians, endowed with rich, unspoiled heredities, caught the falling torch and bore it onward, flaming high once more.

Out of the prehistoric shadows the white races pressed to the front and proved in myriad ways their fitness for the hegemony of mankind. Gradually they forged a common civilization; then, when vouchsafed their unique opportunity of oceanic mastery four centuries ago, they spread over the earth, filling its empty spaces with their superior breeds and assuring to themselves an unparalleled paramountcy of numbers and dominion.

Three centuries later the whites took a fresh leap forward. The 19th century was a new age of discovery — this time into the realms of science. The hidden powers of nature were unveiled, incalculable energies were tamed to human use, terrestrial distance was abridged, and at last the planet was integrated under the hegemony of a single race with a common civilization.

The prospects were magnificent, the potentialities of progress apparently unlimited. Yet there were commensurate perils. Towering heights mean abysmal depths, while the very possibility of supreme success implies the possibility of supreme failure. All these marvelous achievements were due solely to superior heredity, and the mere maintenance of what had been won depended absolutely upon the prior maintenance of race values. Civilization of itself means nothing. It is merely an effect whose cause is the creative urge of superior germ plasm. Civilization is the body; the race is the soul. Let the soul vanish, and the body molders into the inanimate dust from which it came.

Two things are necessary for the continued existence of a race: it must remain itself, and it must breed its best. Every race is the result of ages of development which evolves specialized capacities that make the race what it is and render it capable of creative achievement. These specialized capacities (which particularly mark the superior races), being relatively recent developments, are highly unstable. They are what biologists call "recessive" characters; that is, they are not nearly so "dominant" as the older, generalized characters which races inherit from remote ages and which have therefore been more firmly stamped upon the germ plasm. Hence, when a highly specialized stock interbreeds with a different stock, the newer, less-stable, specialized characters are bred out, the variation, no matter how great its potential value to human evolution, being *irretrievably lost*. This occurs even in the mating of two superior stocks if these stocks are widely dissimilar in character. The valuable specializations of both breeds cancel out, and the mixed offspring tend strongly to revert to generalized mediocrity.

And, of course, the more primitive a type is, the more prepotent it is. This is why crossings with the Negro are uniformly fatal. Whites, Amerindians, or Asiatics — all are alike vanquished by the invincible prepotency of the more primitive, generalized, and lower Negro blood.

There is no immediate danger of the world being swamped by black blood. But there is a very imminent danger that the white stocks may be swamped by Asiatic blood. The white man's very triumphs have evoked this danger. His virtual abolition of distance has destroyed the protection which nature once conferred. Formerly mankind dwelt in such dispersed isolation that wholesale contact of distant, diverse stocks was practically impossible. But with the development of cheap and rapid transportation, nature's barriers are down. Unless man erects and maintains artificial barriers, the various races will increasingly mingle, and the inevitable result will be the supplanting or absorption of the higher by the lower types.

We can see this process working out in almost every phase of modern migration. The white immigration into Latin America is the exception which proves the rule. That particular migration is, of course, beneficent, since it means the influx of relatively high types into undeveloped lands, sparsely populated by types either no higher or much lower than the new arrivals. But almost everywhere else, whether we consider interwhite migrations or colored encroachments on white lands, the net result is an expansion of lower and a contraction of higher stocks, the process being thus a disgenic one. Even in Asia the evils of modern migration are beginning to show. The Japanese government has been obliged to prohibit the influx of Chinese and Korean "coolies" who were undercutting Japanese labor and thus undermining the economic bases of Japanese life.

Furthermore, modern migration is itself only one aspect of a still more fundamental disgenic trend. The whole course of modern urban and industrial life is disgenic. Over and above immigration, the tendency is toward a replacement of the more valuable by the less valuable elements of the population. All over the civilized world racial values are diminishing, and the logical end of this disgenic process is racial bankruptcy and the collapse of civilization.

Now why is all this? It is primarily because we have not yet adjusted ourselves to the radically new environment into which our epochal scientific discoveries led us a century ago. Such adaptation as we have effected has been almost wholly on the material side. The no less sweeping idealistic adaptations which the situation calls for have not been made. Hence, modern civilization has been one-sided, abnormal, unhealthy — and nature is exacting penalties which will increase in severity until we either fully adapt or *finally perish*.

"Finally perish!" That is the exact alternative which confronts the white race. For white civilization is today conterminous with the white race. The civilizations of the past were local. They were confined to a particular people or group of peoples. If they failed, there were always some unspoiled, well-endowed barbarians to step forward and "carry on." But today *there are no more white barbarians.* The earth has grown small, and men are everywhere in close touch. If white civilization goes down, the white race is irretrievably ruined. It will be swamped by the triumphant colored races, who will obliterate the white man by elimination or absorption. What has taken place in Central Asia, once a white and now a brown or yellow land, will take place in Australasia, Europe, and America. Not today, nor yet tomorrow; perhaps not for generations; but surely in the end. If the present drift be not changed, we whites are all ultimately doomed. Unless we set our house in order, the doom will sooner or later overtake us all.

And that would mean that the race obviously endowed with the greatest creative ability, the race which had achieved most in the past and which gave the richer promise for the future, had passed away, carrying with it to the grave those potencies upon which the realization of man's highest hopes depends. A million years of human evolution might go uncrowned, and earth's supreme life product, man, might never fulfill his potential destiny. This is why we today face "The Crisis of the Ages."

To many minds the mere possibility of such a catastrophe may seem unthinkable. Yet a dispassionate survey of the past shows that it is not only possible but probable if present conditions go on unchanged. The whole history of life, both human and subhuman, teaches us that nature will not condone disobedience; that, as I have already phrased it, "no living being stands above her law, and protozoon or demigod, if they transgress, alike must die."

Now we have transgressed; grievously transgressed — and we are suffering grievous penalties. But pain is really kind. Pain is the importunate tocsin which rouses to dangerous realities and spurs to the seeking of a cure.

As a matter of fact we are confusedly aware of our evil plight, and legion are the remedies today proposed. Some of these are mere quack nostrums. Others contain valuable remedial properties. To be sure, there is probably no *one* curative agent, since our troubles are complex and magic elixirs heal only in the realm of dreams. But one element should be fundamental to all the compoundings of the social pharmacopoeia. That element is *blood.*

It is clean, virile, genius-bearing blood, streaming down the ages through the unerring action of heredity, which, in anything like a favorable environment, will multiply itself, solve our problems, and sweep us on to higher and nobler destinies. What we today need above all else is a changed attitude of mind — a recognition of the supreme importance of heredity, not merely in scientific treatises but in the practical ordering of the world's affairs. We are where we are today primarily because we have neglected this vital principle; because we have concerned ourselves with dead things instead of with living beings.

This disregard of heredity is perhaps not strange. It is barely a generation since its fundamental importance was scientifically established, and the world's conversion to even the most vital truth takes time. In fact, we also have much to unlearn. A little while ago we were taught that all men were equal and that good conditions could, of themselves, quickly perfect mankind. The seductive charm of these dangerous fallacies lingers and makes us loath to put them resolutely aside.

Fortunately, we now know the truth. At last we have been vouchsafed clear insight into the laws of life. We now know that men are not, and never will be, equal. We know that environment and education can develop only what heredity brings. We know that the acquirements of individuals are either not inherited at all or are inherited in so slight a degree as to make no perceptible difference from generation to generation. In other words, we now know that heredity is paramount in human evolution, all other things being secondary factors.

This basic truth is already accepted by large numbers of thinking men and women all over the civilized world, and if it becomes firmly fixed in the popular consciousness it will work nothing short of a revolution in the ordering of the world's affairs.

For race betterment is such an intensely *practical* matter! When peoples come to realize that the *quality* of the population is the source of all their prosperity, progress, security, and even existence; when they realize that a single genius may be worth more in actual dollars than a dozen gold mines, while, conversely, racial decline spells material impoverishment and decay; when such things are really believed, we shall see much-abused "eugenics" actually molding social programs and political policies. Were the white world today really convinced of the supreme importance of race values, how long would it take to stop debasing immigration, reform social abuses that are killing out the fittest strains, and put an end to the feuds which have just sent us through hell and threaten to send us promptly back again?

Well, perhaps our change of heart may come sooner than now appears. The horrors of the war, the disappointment of the peace, the terror of Bolshevism, and the rising tide of color have knocked a good deal of the nonsense out of us, and have given multitudes a hunger for realities who were before content with a diet of phrases. Said wise old Benjamin Franklin: "Dame Experience sets a dear school, but fools will have no other." Our course at the dame's school is already well under way and promises to be exceeding dear.

Only, it is to be hoped our education will be rapid, for time presses and the hour is grave. If certain lessons are not learned and

acted upon shortly, we may be overwhelmed by irreparable disasters and all our dear schooling will go for naught.

What are the things we *must* do promptly if we would avert the worst? This "irreducible minimum" runs about as follows:

First and foremost, the wretched Versailles business will have to be thoroughly revised. As it stands, dragon's teeth have been sown over both Europe and Asia, and unless they be plucked up they will presently grow a crop of cataclysms which will seal the white world's doom.

Second, some sort of provisional understanding must be arrived at between the white world and renascent Asia. We whites will have to abandon our tacit assumption of permanent domination over Asia, while Asiatics will have to forgo their dreams of migration to white lands and penetration of Africa and Latin America. Unless some such understanding is arrived at, the world will drift into a gigantic race war — and genuine race war means war to the knife. Such a hideous catastrophe should be abhorrent to both sides. Nevertheless, Asia should be given clearly to understand that we cannot permit either migration to white lands or penetration of the non-Asiatic tropics, and that for these matters we prefer to fight to a finish rather than yield to a finish — because our "finish" is precisely what surrender on these points would mean.

Third, even within the white world, migrations of lower human types like those which have worked such havoc in the United States must be rigorously curtailed. Such migrations upset standards, sterilize better stocks, increase low types, and compromise national futures more than war, revolutions, or native deterioration.

Such are the things which simply *must* be done if we are to get through the next few decades without convulsions which may render impossible the white world's recovery.

These things will not bring in the millennium. Far from it. Our ills are so deep-seated that in nearly every civilized country racial values would continue to depreciate even if all three were carried into effect. But they will at least give our wounds a chance to heal, and they will give the new biological revelation time to permeate the popular consciousness and transfuse with a new idealism our materialistic age. As the years pass, the supreme importance of heredity and the supreme value of superior stocks will sink into our being, and we will acquire a true *race*-consciousness (as opposed to national or cultural consciousness) which will bridge political gulfs, remedy social abuses, and exorcise the lurking specter of miscegenation.

In those better days, we or the next generation will take in hand the problem of race depreciation, and segregation of defectives and abolition of handicaps penalizing the better stocks will put an end to our present racial decline. By that time biological knowledge will have so increased and the popular philosophy of life will have been so idealized that it will be possible to inaugurate positive measures of race betterment which will unquestionably yield the most wonderful results.

Those splendid tasks are probably not ours. They are for our successors in a happier age. But we have our task, and God knows it is a hard one — the salvage of a shipwrecked world! Ours it is to make possible that happier age, whose full-fruits we shall never see.

Well, what of it? Does not the new idealism teach us that we are links in a vital chain, charged with high duties both to the dead and the unborn? In very truth we are at once sons of sires who sleep in calm assurance that we will not betray the trust they confided to our hands, and sires of sons who in the Beyond wait confident that we shall not cheat them of their birthright.

53.

George Santayana: Materialism and Idealism in the American Character

George Santayana was brought to America in 1872 at the age of nine, spent forty years teaching and writing in this country, and then retired to spend his last years in Europe. Always feeling himself to be in certain respects a foreigner, Santayana published a number of observations on life in his adopted country, some of the most searching of which were collected in Character and Opinion in the United States. *Part of the sixth chapter of this book, "Materialism and Idealism in American Life," is reprinted here.*

Source: *Character and Opinion in the United States*, New York, 1920, pp. 165-191.

I speak of the American in the singular, as if there were not millions of them, north and south, east and west, of both sexes, of all ages, and of various races, professions, and religions. Of course the one American I speak of is mythical; but to speak in parables is inevitable in such a subject, and it is perhaps as well to do so frankly. There is a sort of poetic ineptitude in all human discourse when it tries to deal with natural and existing things. Practical men may not notice it, but in fact human discourse is intrinsically addressed, not to natural existing things but to ideal essences, poetic or logical terms which thought may define and play with. When fortune or necessity diverts our attention from this congenial ideal sport to crude facts and pressing issues, we turn our frail poetic ideas into symbols for those terrible irruptive things. In that paper money of our own stamping, the legal tender of the mind, we are obliged to reckon all the movements and values of the world.

The universal American I speak of is one of these symbols; and I should be still speaking in symbols and creating moral units and a false simplicity if I spoke of classes pedantically subdivided or individuals ideally integrated and defined. As it happens, the symbolic American can be made largely adequate to the facts; because, if there are immense differences between individual Americans — for some Americans are black — yet there is a great uniformity in their environment, customs, temper, and thoughts. They have all been uprooted from their several soils and ancestries and plunged together into one vortex, whirling irresistibly in a space otherwise quite empty. To be an American is of itself almost a moral condition, an education, and a career. Hence a single ideal figment can cover a large part of what each American is in his character, and almost the whole of what most Americans are in their social outlook and political judgements.

The discovery of the New World exercised a sort of selection among the inhabitants of Europe. All the colonists, except the Negroes, were voluntary exiles. The fortunate, the deeply rooted, and the lazy remained at home; the wilder instincts or dissatisfaction of others tempted them beyond the horizon. The American is accordingly the most adventurous, or the descendant of the most adventurous, of Europeans. It is in his blood to be socially a radical, though perhaps not intellectually. What has existed in the past, especially in the remote past, seems to him not only not authoritative but irrelevant, inferior, and outworn. He finds it rather a sorry waste of time to think about the past at all. But his enthusiasm for the future is profound; he can conceive of no more decisive way of recommending an opinion or a practice than to say that it is what everybody is coming to adopt. This expectation of what he approves, or approval of what he expects, makes up his optimism. It is the necessary faith of the pioneer.

Such a temperament is, of course, not maintained in the nation merely by inheritance. Inheritance notoriously tends to restore the average of a race, and plays incidentally many a trick of atavism. What maintains this temperament and makes it national is social contagion or pressure — something immensely strong in democracies. The luckless American who is born a conservative, or who is drawn to poetic subtlety, pious retreats, or gay passions, nevertheless has the categorical excellence of work, growth, enterprise, reform, and prosperity dinned into his ears: every door is open in this direction and shut in the other; so that he either folds up his heart and withers in a corner — in remote places you sometimes find such a solitary gaunt idealist — or else he flies to Oxford or Florence or Montmartre to save his soul — or perhaps not to save it.

The optimism of the pioneer is not limited to his view of himself and his own future: it starts from that; but feeling assured, safe, and cheery within, he looks with smiling and most kindly eyes on everything and everybody about him. Individualism, roughness, and self-trust are supposed to go with selfishness and a cold heart; but I suspect that is a prejudice. It is rather dependence, insecurity, and mutual jostling that poison our placid, gregarious brotherhood; and fanciful, passionate demands upon people's affections, when they are disappointed, as they soon must be, breed ill will and a final meanness. The milk of human kindness is less apt to turn sour if the vessel that holds it stands steady, cool, and separate, and is not too often uncorked.

In his affections the American is seldom passionate, often deep, and always kindly. If it were given me to look into the depths of a man's heart, and I did not find goodwill at the bottom, I should say without any hesitation, You are not an American. But as the American is an individualist his goodwill is not officious. His instinct is to think well of everybody and to wish everybody well, but in a spirit of rough comradeship, expecting every man to stand on his own legs and to be helpful in his turn. When he has given his neighbor a chance, he thinks he has done enough for him; but he feels it is an absolute duty to do that. It will take some hammering to drive a coddling socialism into America.

As self-trust may pass into self-sufficiency, so optimism, kindness, and goodwill may grow into a habit of doting on everything. To the good American many subjects are sacred: sex is sacred, women are sacred, children are sacred, business is sacred, America is sacred, Masonic lodges and college clubs are sacred. This feeling grows out of the good opinion he wishes to have of these things, and serves to maintain it. If he did not regard all these things as sacred, he might come to doubt sometimes if they were wholly good. Of this kind, too, is the idealism of single ladies in reduced circumstances who can see the soul of beauty in ugly things, and are perfectly happy because their old dog has such pathetic eyes, their minister is so eloquent, their garden with its three sunflowers is so pleasant, their dead friends were so devoted, and their distant relations are so rich. . . .

At the same time, the American is imaginative; for where life is intense, imagination is intense also. Were he not imaginative he would not live so much in the future. But his imagination is practical, and the future it forecasts is immediate; it works with the clearest and least ambiguous terms known to his experience, in terms of number, measure, contrivance, economy, and speed. He is an idealist working on matter. Understanding as he does the material potentialities of things, he is successful in invention, conservative in reform, and quick in emergencies. All his life he jumps into the train after it has started and jumps out before it has stopped; and he never once gets left behind, or breaks a leg. There is an enthusiasm in his sympathetic handling of material forces which goes far to cancel the illiberal character which it might otherwise assume.

The good workman hardly distinguishes his artistic intention from the potency in himself and in things which is about to realize that intention. Accordingly his ideals fall into the form of premonitions and prophecies; and his studious prophecies often come true. So do the happy workmanlike ideals of the American. When a poor boy, perhaps, he dreams of an education, and presently he gets an education, or at least a degree; he dreams of growing rich, and he grows rich — only more slowly and modestly, perhaps, than he expected; he dreams of marrying his Rebecca and, even if he marries a Leah instead, he ulitmately finds in Leah his Rebecca after all. He dreams of helping to carry on and to accelerate the movement of a vast, seething, progressive society, and he actually does so. Ideals clinging so close to nature are almost sure of fulfillment; the American beams with a certain self-confidence and sense of mastery; he feels that God and nature are working with him.

Idealism in the American accordingly goes hand in hand with present contentment and with foresight of what the future very likely will actually bring. He is not a revolutionist; he believes he is already on the right track and moving toward an excellent destiny. In revolutionists, on the contrary, idealism is founded on dissatisfaction and expresses it. What exists seems to them an absurd jumble of irrational accidents and bad habits, and they want the future to be based on reason and to be the pellucid embodiment of all their maxims. All their zeal is for something radically different from the actual and (if they only knew it) from the possible; it is ideally simple, and they love it and believe in it because their nature craves it. They think life would be set free by the destruction of all its organs. They are therefore extreme idealists in the region of hope, but not at all, as poets and artists are, in the region of perception and memory.

In the atmosphere of civilized life they miss all the refraction and all the fragrance; so that in their conception of actual things they are apt to be crude realists; and their ignorance and inexperience of the moral world, unless it comes of ill-luck, indicates their incapacity for education. Now incapacity for education, when united with great inner vitality, is one root of idealism. It is what condemns us all, in the region of sense, to substitute perpetually what we are capable of imagining for what things may be in themselves; it is what condemns us, wherever it extends, to think *a priori*; it is what keeps us bravely and incorrigibly pursuing what we call the good — that is, what would fulfill the demands of our nature — however little provision the fates may have made for it.

But the want of insight on the part of revolutionists touching the past and the present infects in an important particular their idealism about the future; it renders their dreams of the future unrealizable. For in human beings — this may not be true of other animals, more perfectly preformed — experience is necessary to pertinent and concrete thinking; even our primitive instincts are blind until they stumble upon some occasion that solicits them; and they can be much transformed or deranged by their first partial satisfactions. Therefore a man who does not idealize his experience, but idealizes *a priori*, is incapable of true

prophecy; when he dreams he raves, and the more he criticizes the less he helps. American idealism, on the contrary, is nothing if not helpful, nothing if not pertinent to practicable transformations; and when the American frets, it is because whatever is useless and impertinent, be it idealism or inertia, irritates him; for it frustrates the good results which he sees might so easily have been obtained.

The American is wonderfully alive; and his vitality, not having often found a suitable outlet, makes him appear agitated on the surface; he is always letting off an unnecessarily loud blast of incidental steam. Yet his vitality is not superficial; it is inwardly prompted and as sensitive and quick as a magnetic needle. He is inquisitive and ready with an answer to any question that he may put to himself of his own accord; but if you try to pour instruction into him, on matters that do not touch his own spontaneous life, he shows the most extraordinary powers of resistance and oblivescence; so that he often is remarkably expert in some directions and surprisingly obtuse in others. He seems to bear lightly the sorrowful burden of human knowledge. In a word, he is young.

What sense is there in this feeling, which we all have, that the American is young? His country is blessed with as many elderly people as any other, and his descent from Adam, or from the Darwinian rival of Adam, cannot be shorter than that of his European cousins. Nor are his ideas always very fresh. Trite and rigid bits of morality and religion, with much seemly and antique political lore, remain axiomatic in him, as in the mind of a child; he may carry all this about with an unquestioning familiarity which does not comport understanding. To keep traditional sentiments in this way insulated and uncriticized is itself a sign of youth. A good young man is naturally conservative and loyal on all those subjects which his experience has not brought to a test; advanced opinions on politics, marriage, or literature are comparatively rare in America; they are left for the ladies to discuss, and usually to condemn, while the men get on with their work.

In spite of what is old-fashioned in his more general ideas, the American is unmistakably young; and this, I should say, for two reasons: one, that he is chiefly occupied with his immediate environment; and the other, that his reactions upon it are inwardly prompted, spontaneous, and full of vivacity and self-trust. His views are not yet lengthened; his will is not yet broken or transformed. The present moment, however, in this, as in other things, may mark a great change in him; he is perhaps now reaching his majority, and all I say may hardly apply today and may not apply at all tomorrow. I speak of him as I have known him; and whatever moral strength may accrue to him later, I am not sorry to have known him in his youth.

The charm of youth, even when it is a little boisterous, lies in nearness to the impulses of nature, in a quicker and more obvious obedience to that pure, seminal principle which, having formed the body and its organs, always directs their movements, unless it is forced by vice or necessity to make them crooked, or to suspend them. Even under the inevitable crust of age, the soul remains young, and, wherever it is able to break through, sprouts into something green and tender. We are all as young at heart as the most youthful American, but the seed in his case has fallen upon virgin soil, where it may spring up more bravely and with less respect for the giants of the wood. Peoples seem older when their perennial natural youth is encumbered with more possessions and prepossessions, and they are mindful of the many things they have lost or missed. The American is not mindful of them.

In America there is a tacit optimistic assumption about existence, to the effect that the more existence the better. The soulless critic might urge that quantity is only a physical category, implying no excellence, but at best an abundance of opportunities both for good and for evil. Yet the young soul, being curious and hungry, views existence *a priori* under the form of the good; its instinct to live implies a faith that most things it can become or see or do will be worthwhile. . . .

The circumstances of his life hitherto have necessarily driven the American into moral materialism; for in his dealings with material things he can hardly stop to enjoy their sensible aspects, which are ideal, nor proceed at once to their ultimate uses, which are ideal too. He is practical as against the poet, and worldly as against the clear philosopher or the saint. The most striking expression of this materialism is usually supposed to be his love of the almighty dollar; but that is a foreign and unintelligent view. The American talks about money because that is the symbol and measure he has at hand for success, intelligence, and power; but, as to money itself, he makes, loses, spends, and gives it away with a very light heart.

To my mind the most striking expression of his materialism is his singular preoccupation with quantity. If, for instance, you visit Niagara Falls, you may expect to hear how many cubic feet or metric tons of water are precipitated per second over the cataract; how many cities and towns (with the number of their inhabitants) derive light and motive power from it; and the annual value of the further industries that might very well be carried on by the same means, without visibly depleting the world's greatest wonder or injuring the tourist trade. That is what I confidently expected to hear on arriving at the adjoining town of Buffalo; but I was deceived. The first thing I heard instead was that there are more miles of asphalt pavement in Buffalo than in any city in the world. Nor is this insistence on quantity confined to men of business. The president of Harvard College, see-

ing me once by chance soon after the beginning of a term, inquired how my classes
were getting on; and when I replied that I
thought they were getting on well, that my
men seemed to be keen and intelligent, he
stopped me as if I was about to waste his
time. "I meant," said he, "*what is the number* of students in your classes."

Here I think we may perceive that this
love of quantity often has a silent partner,
which is diffidence as to quality. The democratic conscience recoils before anything that
savors of privilege; and lest it should concede an unmerited privilege to any pursuit
or person, it reduces all things as far as possible to the common denominator of quantity. Numbers cannot lie; but if it came to
comparing the ideal beauties of philosophy
with those of Anglo-Saxon, who should decide? All studies are good — why else have
universities? — but those must be most encouraged which attract the greatest number
of students. Hence the president's question.
Democratic faith, in its diffidence about
quality, throws the reins of education upon
the pupil's neck, as Don Quixote threw the
reins on the neck of Rocinante, and bids his
divine instinct choose its own way.

The American has never yet had to face
the trials of Job. Great crises, like the Civil
War, he has known how to surmount victoriously; and now that he has surmounted a
second great crisis victoriously, it is possible
that he may relapse, as he did in the other
case, into an apparently complete absorption in material enterprise and prosperity.
But if serious and irremediable tribulation
ever overtook him, what would his attitude
be? It is then that we should be able to
discover whether materialism or idealism
lies at the base of his character.

Meantime his working mind is not without its holiday. He spreads humor pretty
thick and even over the surface of conversation, and humor is one form of moral
emancipation. He loves landscape, he loves
mankind, and he loves knowledge; and in
music at least he finds an art which he un-

feignedly enjoys. In music and landscape, in
humor and kindness, he touches the ideal
more truly, perhaps, than in his ponderous
academic idealisms and busy religions; for it
is astonishing how much even religion in
America (can it possibly be so in England?)
is a matter of meetings, building funds,
schools, charities, clubs, and picnics. To be
poor in order to be simple, to produce less
in order that the product may be more
choice and beautiful, and may leave us less
burdened with unnecessary duties and useless possessions — that is an ideal not articulate in the American mind; yet here and
there I seem to have heard a sigh after it, a
groan at the perpetual incubus of business
and shrill society.

Significant witness to such aspirations is
borne by those new forms of popular religion, not mere variations on tradition,
which have sprung up from the soil — re-
vivalism, spiritualism, Christian Science, the
New Thought. Whether or no we can tap,
through these or other channels, some cosmic or inner energy not hitherto at the disposal of man (and there is nothing incredible in that), we certainly may try to remove
friction and waste in the mere process of
living; we may relax morbid strains, loosen
suppressed instincts, iron out the creases of
the soul, discipline ourselves into simplicity,
sweetness, and peace. These religious movements are efforts toward such physiological
economy and hygiene; and while they are
thoroughly plebeian, with no great lights,
and no idea of raising men from the most
vulgar and humdrum worldly existence, yet
they see the possibility of physical and moral health on that common plane and pursue
it. That is true morality. . . .

When the senses are sharp, as they are in
the American, they are already half liberated, already a joy in themselves; and when
the heart is warm, like his, and eager to be
just, its ideal destiny can hardly be doubtful.
It will not be always merely pumping and
working; time and its own pulses will lend
it wings.

54.

W. L. George: Random Impressions

Of the many Europeans who visited the United States and later published their impressions of the country, few were so sympathetic and generous in their appreciation as the British novelist and feminist Walter Lionel George. He toured the country in 1920, and Hail, Columbia! *was published in the United States the next year. The selection below is taken from the third chapter of the book, "The American Scene."*

Source: *Hail, Columbia!*, London, 1923, pp. 78-115.

It is not superfluous to repeat, before preparing an outline of the American character, that a lifetime would not be too much for such a task, covering so many regions, such various races, temperaments with three centuries of tradition, and new Americans whose fathers were Poles. So what I wish to say is in the nature of impression rather than conclusion, and I am prepared to be corrected by my own experience. But I do feel entitled to call the United States "God's own country." It is true that (according to the American Bankers' Association) 30 percent of Americans aged fifty-five depend on their children or charity; that at the age of sixty-five no less than 54 percent are thus unfortunate; it is true that the ravages of tuberculosis, the enormous divorce rate, compare with the schedule of European miseries. Still, here is a favored land which, owing to its area and to its wealth, can give a chance to every young man, and, if it chooses, even to every young woman.

All benefits have been poured out upon America and America is using them as a cheerful prodigal; America is conscious of her good fortune and that is why she can afford the manifestation of pride which is called democracy. Democracy is the most arrogant of all forms; it is the converse of snobbery, for the snob conceives only superiors and inferiors. The snob is a man who thinks he has no equals, while the democrat is the man who thinks he has only equals. He is often mistaken in his view.

And so a European thinks it picturesque and delightful to go to a bathing hut on a lake, ask for his bathing things, and hear a youth call out to his boss, "Say, where's *this man's* bathing suit?" To have a colored chambermaid stop him on the stairs and bluntly ask, "Where's your wife?" It is amusing, after the bent backs of the English servant class, though I should add that these backs are bending less and less now. It is pleasing because, like most things American, the democratic notion is cut out in sharp lines and painted in bright colors. The American fantasia, if I may so call it, is scarlet and gold. The scarlet of American excess creeps even into the pale blue of American sentimentality. Let not the reader conclude that I claim for England freedom from sentimentality; we, too, suffer greatly from what is mainly emotion gone moldy. But England feels a little ashamed of her sentimentality, while America tends to account it as righteousness.

Of the sentimental attitude toward women, noblest and purest, I will say something of a little farther on. It sometimes takes a strange lyrical form, particularly in the newspapers. And the newspapers matter, for the newspaper exhibition of the national character is the national character seen under a magnifying glass. The newspaper character is the national character — more so. For instance, I read in a newspaper that a certain lady has extraordinary courage, a keen sense of intuition, and a sublime faith in God. A very sagacious diagnosis inside a single interview.

But sentimentality, which so naturally envelops the young bride, the good mother, the little child, takes in America some forms that interest me more. One of them is the sweet and simple life of millionaires. I am continually reading descriptions showing that the financial superman does not live on caviar off diamond-studded plates; that his subtle mind subsists upon the rudest fare and the highest thought; that he likes to set aside the nurture of his millions for a peaceful hour with Artemus Ward; that his true pleasure is serving in the local crèche, teaching the creed that is called, "How to get on and yet be good." I like to think of the millionaire talking freely in the street to someone who owns rather less, and with a green watering can assisting into beauty a little bed of marigolds.

I think that impulse, which is purely American, arises from a desire to humanize the apparently inhuman. American business, shrewd as it is, seems to have a heart; it wants to do for individual men the fair and the generous thing. The whole trend of American civilization is toward stressing the human factor; indeed, the word "human" (in the sense of "friendly") is used in no other part of the English-speaking countries. Also, a certain reverence attaches to power; reverence is always apparent in the American character, curiously combined with irreverence. For instance, the magazine and novel continually present allusions to "the great surgeon" and "the great lawyer." The cynical European suspects that the great surgeon is a scrubby reactionary who does not read the medical journals; he views the great lawyer either as a foxy fee snatcher or as a toothless dodderer on the bench. But the American seems to invest these people with mental robes of ermine and scarlet. He is more easily impressed; his vision is more direct and less often leads him to doubt; where a European would doubt, an American often hates.

You find this seriousness extending even to the most ignoble of occupations, the arts. In civilized countries, the arts are, as a rule, merely the resounding kettles tied to the tails of the hounds that are hunting the great quarry of profit. But in an American newspaper you will see headlines such as this — "Playwright Finds His Inspiration in Lonely Sand Dunes." No European would be interested in the playwright's inspiration, except as an object for jeers. The American takes the arts seriously, just as he takes seriously the funds for the restoration of churches. He is altogether more literal; he uses the words "right" and "wrong," as to the meaning of which many Europeans have become rather shaky.

He takes his tradition more seriously. For instance, in Chicago I observed a headline in the newspaper, "Cotton Exchange Fifty Years Old Today." That has an irresistible charm. One need not, from the false vantage of the Oxford turf, smile at a record of fifty years; one envies, rather, the contentment so aroused. Then, once more, American complexity appears — I contrast this headline with the fact that in nearly every American city I have visited, hotels and office buildings, erected round about 1900, are being pulled down to give place to buildings that shall be up-to-date. America delights in tradition, and destroys it as she goes. She hates the thing she respects, burns the god that she worships. . . .

Lyricism takes all forms. In the United States, one of the strangest from the European point of view is the adulation of business. As if America were reacting against the traditional adoration by England of the professions, she seems to set a peculiar value upon making, buying, and selling things. *The Dignity of Business* was written by an American; *The Romance of Commerce* was invented by another. To an extent this is a defense as well as an evangel, but it is certain that America has enshrined within business a portion of her romantic impulses. She respects the businessman; while ready to give his due to the professional man, and more than his due to the artist, she intimately feels that business is the finest, as well as the most valuable, function of man; she perceives in the businessman the qualities of a hero; in her view, he is doing the best that can be done by man. . . .

The American wants trade, but he also wants to know things, to secure new impressions, and, if you will let him, he wants to like you. This combines with the old pioneer spirit into true hospitality. It may be thought that I am stressing the pioneer spirit, which seems to elucidate the Middle West, but I do believe that America still carries the pioneer habit of giving hospitality to all. I am not deceived by the reasons for this; the pioneer had not a warmer heart than anybody else; he gave hospitality because in pioneer days he had to give hospitality so as to enjoy it himself when in need. For many years in America you had to take hospitality or die on the prairie; that taught all men hospitality, and much of the tradition stays in the American spirit. That is why the stranger finds America so delightful. He is readily admitted into the American home, while he may spend a lifetime in France and be admitted only to a restaurant.

I am perfectly sure that, on an average, the American is warmer hearted than the European. I have had many instances of this, and one of the most noteworthy was in New England. I am fond of country walks, which the American seems to dislike; his view of life is "automobiles to everywhere and violent exercise at the weekend."

Therefore, the Americans who saw me trudging the roads were sorry for me, and only in two cases was I allowed to finish my walk undisturbed; in every other case total strangers in automobiles stopped and offered me a lift. . . .

There is no better friend than an Englishman, if you can get him as a friend; but it is very difficult, and until you succeed he will stay on his guard. On the other hand, an American will take immense trouble over you, waste his time over you, drive you about, get you introductions, secure you privileges. Sometimes this is ostentation, sometimes it is local pride; but human sentiments are always complex, and there runs through it an honest desire to oblige.

You find this particularly in the American of the middle-sized towns. New York is too large for anybody to be proud of; you cannot be town conscious in a city of that size as you can be, for instance, in Cincinnati. The American is almost invariably proud and fond of his hometown. He is always anxious that you should visit it; he will accompany you and show you round; you will offend him if you refuse to go and see the statue of Colonel Judson, who was killed at Saratoga. I am afraid that I have offended many people already by writing a book about America; nearly all those I have met felt that the book ought to be about their city, or at most about their state; I have been told everywhere that "to stay only three days here" was akin to crime. . . .

Kindness is almost universal in America; in my first three months I collected only three deliberate rudenesses, though, doubtless, I deserved many more. I found everywhere assistance and, what the stranger needs so much, information. Sometimes I found a little too much, for the American does not always realize how lost is the stranger in this immense, complicated system, and so burdens him with detail. The American is often quiet, but he never refuses conversation, and, on the whole, it is better that people should talk too much than too little; this contributes to general sociability and ease of intercourse. Also, conversation helps a man to exhibit himself. Very few of us ever attempt to discover what the other man thinks; we talk so as to assert to him what *we* think; this helps us to discover what we really think. I suspect that the American, more than any other kind of man, his mind being filled with a vast number of physical impressions, needs conversation to sort out these impressions. Burdened by certain forms of national pride, local pride, and personal pride, by old puritanic views and new efficiency views, by sentiment and by ruthlessness, he needs conversation as a sort of clearinghouse. He has to formulate. . . .

Nearly all Americans will, to a certain extent, proclaim, if you talk to them about America. I have met a few Americans who criticized America, but they nearly all belonged to the intellectual class, which does nothing but intellectualize. Those people take a queer pleasure in running down America. They vaunt the culture of France and the courtesy of Spain; they read no American books, but criticize them all the same. They are few, while the mass of Americans who openly boost their country is large. Many of them will criticize America in a temperate spirit, and, more and more, I suspect, the educated American is reacting against certain features of American civilization, such as haste and noise.

One thing in him is noteworthy — he is always willing to discuss America. He will state her, explain her, defend her, and the subject never wearies him. That is a profound difference with the Englishman, who, confronted with a foreigner, is more likely to talk to him about the foreign land — that is, if he must. The Englishman would rather stick to safe topics, such as games, or London communications, but if he is dragged into national discussions he will

avoid England. It is not that he lacks national pride, but that pride has become to him a habit of mind. He is really more arrogant than the American, for the American takes the trouble to speak for his country and proclaims as an argument, "I am an American citizen." The Englishman is much worse. He does not trouble to proclaim, "I am a British subject." He expects you to know that, and at bottom does not care whether you know it or not, or what you say about it.

The Englishman's complacency is immense: First, there is the Church-of-England God; then, there is the Englishman; then, there is the Englishman's bulldog; then, there is nothing. So, realizing this, I am not with those who are offended by the occasionally loud American patriotism; I know only too well that its occasional loudness means that America doubts itself. . . .

Citizenship here has lyrical value, whereas, in Europe, it has only practical value. The naturalization method of America suggests that a sort of honor is being conferred upon a man when he is admitted to citizenship. No doubt many jingo Europeans would understand this emotion, which is foreign to me, but it may be that here we find a faint indication of the craving for distinction which is so strong in the United States. It is commonplace to describe the American ambassador at a continental reception, distinguishing himself from among the uniforms and the decorations by the Spartan democracy of his evening suit. America has made a virtue of this evening suit, but I do not think she likes it. Seventeen seventy-six was the hot fit of democracy, and long before 1920, the cold fit came.

For many years Americans have shown how much they missed the satisfactions called "honors" which are given in all other countries. . . . In America, the need has shown itself through the many marriages of American girls to members of various aristocratic European families. It is something to get wealth, but it is not quite enough; the natural vanity of man does not thrive on wealth alone. That is why the Americans have invented a number of social ranks.

Business titles are given in America more readily than in England. Men are distinguished by being called "president" of a corporation. I know one president whose staff consists of two typists. Many firms have four "vice-presidents." Or there is a "press representative," or a "purchasing agent." In the magazines you seldom find merely an editor; the others need their share of honor; so they are "associate" (not "assistant") editors. A dentist is called "doctor." The hotel valet is a "tailor." Magistrates of police courts are "judges," instead of merely Mr. I wandered into a university, knowing nobody, and casually asked for the dean. I was asked, "Which dean?" In that building there were enough deans to stock all the English cathedrals. The master of a secret society is "royal supreme knight commander."

Perhaps I reached the extreme at a theater in Boston, where I wanted something, I forget what, and was told that I must apply to the chief of the ushers. He was a mild little man, who had something to do with people getting into their seats, rather a comedown from the pomp and circumstance of his title. Growing interested, I examined my program, with the following result: It is not a large theater, but it has a press representative, a treasurer (box office clerk), an assistant treasurer (box office junior clerk), an advertising agent, our old friend the chief of the ushers, a stage manager, a head electrician, a master of properties (in England called "props"), a leader of the orchestra (pity this — why not president?), and a matron (occupation unknown).

What does this mean in American psychology? It means that here, as elsewhere, mankind comes to believe in itself only by asserting itself, by decorating itself with high-sounding names. This is the efflorescence of the human ego, the manifestation of the adorable childishness of man, which holds its sway under the pinions of the Bird of Freedom, just as much as before the indifferent eyes of the Lion and the Unicorn. It is an evidence of the innocence, the splendid capacity for taking clear-cut views, which may give young America the leadership, if not the hegemony, of the world. . . .

Most Europeans look upon love as a comparatively simple and temporary reaction, which leaves behind it a certain sediment called affection. According to temperament, they look upon love as a regrettable physical excess, or as a natural desire for intimacy with a person of the other sex; or as a joke; or an act of business; but they very seldom look upon it as a sacrament. In America, I am not so sure of the men. The men do not talk much about love, and I have a suspicion that they do not place it on quite so lofty a plane as their women would desire. It is not in the nature of men to grow rhapsodic over anything; all great rhapsodies, it is true, have come from men, but always from unusual men; the ordinary man has a way of placing love and its consequences among the material facts of life; in Europe the women hold only slightly more refined views.

But in America certain peculiarities appear in the conception of love which the American woman proclaims. (What actual conception she holds, as against the one she proclaims, may be a matter for further discussion.) The things that people proclaim are quite as important as the things they believe, because what people say to you is not always what they think, but what they would like to think, or what they would like you to think they think. The American woman's proclamation of the nature of love may be the proclamation of what she thinks love ought to be.

Now from America came the phrase, "Divinity of Sex." It is a phrase that I cannot understand; I can discover in sex beauty, lyricism, exaltation, all that is delightful, much that leads to generosity — I can discover all that, except "spirituality," or "divinity." I suspect that the words "Divinity of Sex" merely express the fact that the American woman sets upon herself a price higher than does the European. When giving herself in marriage to a man she appears to lay down that she is doing something significant, which honors him by preferment and her by self-sacrifice. Also, she conveys that she is the cradle of the race, forgetting that nature is so arranged as to demand that a masculine hand shall rock this cradle.

It seems to be set up that "love" is wonderful; that "the child" is wonderful; that "the race" is wonderful; in other words, exaltation. Whether this is wholly sincere or wholly insincere does not matter very much; the American man hardly ever echoes the point of view, but he never controverts it; he maintains silence and seems to accept the feminine theory. I wonder. . . . Perhaps he does not care. . . .

The whole of the American civilization seems to me willfully, and often splendidly, excessive. The people seem to find a pleasure in the height of their buildings, in the size of their restaurants. The freak dinner, for instance, where a musical prodigy was concealed in a bush of roses and revealed only when coffee was served, where every guest was presented with a gift worth one thousand dollars, is not only an indication of reckless wealth but also of a deliberate desire to do things largely, magnificently, excessively.

One discovers this in the lavish magnificence of American hospitality. It is delightful, but to a pallid European it sometimes proves exhausting. One rides to too many places in too many automobiles; one meets too many interesting people; visits to the opera, to the theater, to the country club, to the famous view over the valley — all this, so kindly, so generous, is part of the American tendency to do too much, too fast. They do not think that they themselves suffer from it, but I suspect that much of the sensitiveness of American public opinion to newspaper stunts is due to an overstimulated condition of the nerves. Excess brings its penalty in the shape of reaction. The noise of America, the swift movement, the passion for the automobile, a passion so violent that people mortgage their house to buy one — all this is excess.

I have been in American towns of less than twenty thousand inhabitants and found them closely modeled upon the big towns. The big towns provide excess for the millions; the little towns, excess for the thousands. It is merely a matter of proportion. Sometimes one does not know how to behave. The Englishman is not accustomed to the spaciousness of American hospitality. American hospitality will explain the difference between watermelon, honeydew, and casaba, while English hospitality consists in letting the lunch lie about for you to eat if you like. We are not accustomed to being shown a house in detail — the laborsaving appliances at work; told the story of the pieces of furniture, of the pictures. The Americans are never weary of this, because their vitality is enormous.

It is not only nerves which permit them to do so many things in a single day; it is not only their magnificent climate, which is bright and bracing like champagne; it is the rude strength of a race not yet sophisticated; it is the hunger for impressions of a race just entering into possession of its powers. Hunger and innocence, this defines a vast tract of the American mind.

1921

55.

Franz Boas: The Negro Race in America

Franz Boas was one of the first anthropologists to discredit the concept of race as a principle for classifying human beings. At a time when many of his colleagues still believed in the race theory, and moreover proclaimed the superiority of their own Caucasian race, Boas maintained that the only result of discussions of racial differences was race prejudice. On the contrary, he argued, there were no significant biological differences between the various races of the human species. His thesis, expressed in books and other writings, was politely ignored by most people. The selection reprinted here is taken from an article that first appeared in 1921.

Source: *Yale Review*, January 1921: "The Problem of the American Negro."

EVEN IF THERE IS neither a biological nor a psychological justification for the popular belief in the inferiority of the Negro race, the social basis of the race prejudice in America is not difficult to understand. The prejudice is founded essentially on the tendency of the human mind to merge the individual in the class to which he belongs and to ascribe to him all the characteristics of his class. It does not even require a marked difference in type, such as we find when we compare Negro and white, to provoke the spirit that prevents us from recognizing individuals and compels us to see only representatives of a class endowed with imaginary qualities that we ascribe to the group as a whole. We find this spirit at work in anti-Semitism as well as in American nativism, and in the conflict between labor and capitalism. We have recently seen it at its height in the emotions called forth by a world war.

It is not by any means the class consciousness of the segregated group that determines this feeling. It is rather the consciousness of the outsider who combines a large number of individuals in a group and thus assigns to each the same character. The less feeling of unity the heterogeneous members of the group possess, the harder it is for them to bear the discrimination under which they suffer.

This is obviously the psychological basis of the present situation of the American Negro. To the popular mind, the Negro appears as a class, and the impressions made by the life of the poor Negro are generalized by the white man and are combined with dogmatic beliefs regarding the physical and hereditary mental makeup of the race.

The consciousness that the Negro belongs to a class by himself is kept alive by the contrast presented by his physical appearance with that of the whites. For the descendants of the Teutonic peoples of northern Europe, this consciousness has attained a high emotional value.

It is natural that the stronger the individuality of a person who is thus assigned to a class with which he has little in common, the stronger must also be his resentment against those who refuse to take him at his individual worth. Every moment of his life, the self-respecting Negro feels the strain of his inability to overcome the prejudices that merge him in a type. This resentment will grow in extent as individual achievement develops among the Negroes while they are still not valued as individuals.

It is claimed by many that the Negro problem is economic rather than racial, that the fear of Negro competition causes racial opposition. Obviously, this explanation also would not hold good if the tendency did not exist to treat the Negro as a class, not as an individual. I do not wish to deny that the economic conflict may be a contributing cause that accentuates the preexisting feeling of the contrast between whites and Negroes. This feeling may be emphasized in many ways — by economic interests, by questions of social privilege, or by any other social process that brings about conflicts of interest between large groups of whites and Negroes. It would, however, be an error to seek in these sources the fundamental cause for the antagonism; for the economic conflict, as well as the other conflicts, presupposes the social recognition of the classes.

It is easier to point out the causes of conflict between whites and Negroes than to formulate a remedy. If my view is correct, it is clear that the only fundamental remedy for the situation is the recognition that the Negroes have the right to be treated as individuals, not as members of a class. But how can this be brought about in a population that is so deeply saturated with class-consciousness as our own? Even if, in the education of the young, the importance of individual differences were emphasized so that an intelligent understanding could be attained of the irrationality of the assumption that all Negroes are inferior, we should not effectively overcome the general human tendency of forming groups that in the mind of the outsider are held together by his emotional attitude toward them. In other words, the hostile feeling of each individual to foreign social groups would not be eradicated.

Mankind has traveled a long road from the time when every stranger was an enemy. According to our modern theoretical standards, we maintain that justice should be given to the individual, that it should not be meted out to him as to a representative of his class. And still, how very far removed are we from the realization of this ideal! The natural habit of protecting ourselves against a supposedly hostile foreign group determines our life in great matters as well as in small details, and the life of nations as well as the life of the individual and of the family.

For this reason there is no great hope that the Negro problem will find even a half-way satisfactory solution in our day. We may, perhaps, expect that an increasing number of strong minds will free themselves from race prejudice and see in every person a man entitled to be judged on his merits. The weak-minded will not follow their example.

But the greatest hope for the immediate future lies in a lessening of the contrast between Negroes and whites which will bring about a lessening of class-consciousness. As I have already pointed out, under present conditions a penetration of the white race by the Negro does not occur, while the effects of intermixture in which the fathers are white and the mothers Negro will lead in all probability to an increase of the amount of white blood in the Negro population. This should allay the fears of those who believe that the white race might deteriorate by race mixture. On the other hand, intermixture will decrease the contrast between the extreme racial forms, and, in the course of time, this will lead to a lessening of the consciousness of race distinction. If conditions were ever such that it could be doubtful whether a person were of Negro descent or not, the consciousness of race would necessarily be much weakened. In a race of octoroons, living among whites, the color question would probably disappear.

There is absolutely no biological evidence which would countenance the assumption that race mixture of itself would have unfavorable results, that the children of white fathers and of mulatto or quadroon mothers would be inferior to their Negro ancestors.

It would seem, therefore, to be in the interest of society to permit rather than to restrain marriages between white men and Negro women. It would be futile to expect that our people would tolerate intermarriages in the opposite direction, although no scientific reason can be given that would prove them to be detrimental to the individual. Intermixture between white males and Negro females has been common ever since Negroes were brought to our continent, and the efficacy of the modern attempts to repress this intermingling is open to grave doubt.

Thus it would seem that man being what he is, the Negro problem will not disappear in America until the Negro blood has been so much diluted that it will no longer be recognized, just as anti-Semitism will not disappear until the last vestige of the Jew as a Jew has disappeared.

56.

WILLIAM ALLEN WHITE: Criticism of the Ku Klux Klan

After a long period of quiescence, the Ku Klux Klan was reorganized in 1915 at Atlanta, Georgia, under the leadership of William Joseph Simmons. It had little success until 1920, when it was able to trade on the fears that produced, and were in turn generated by, the "Red scare." When control changed hands in 1922, it became prosperous and expanded its activities into a number of states. Membership reached 4,000,000 by 1924. As the Klan grew, so did the opposition to it. William Allen White revealed his own feelings about the organization in this letter of September 17, 1921, to Herbert Bayard Swope, the executive editor of the New York World.

Source: *Selected Letters of William Allen White, 1899-1943,* Walter Johnson, ed., New York, 1947, pp. 220-221.

AN ORGANIZER of the Ku Klux Klan was in Emporia the other day, and the men whom he invited to join his band at $10 per join turned him down. Under the leadership of Dr. J. B. Brickell and following their own judgment after hearing his story, the Empo-

rians told him that they had no time for him. The proposition seems to be:

Anti-foreigners
Anti-Catholics
Anti-Negroes.

There are, of course, bad foreigners and

good ones, good Catholics and bad ones, and all kinds of Negroes. To make a case against a birthplace, a religion, or a race is wickedly un-American and cowardly. The whole trouble with the Ku Klux Klan is that it is based upon such deep foolishness that it is bound to be a menace to good government in any community. Any man fool enough to be Imperial Wizard would have power without responsibility and both without any sense. That is social dynamite.

American institutions, our courts, our legislators, our executive officers are strong enough to keep the peace and promote justice and goodwill in the community. If they are not, then the thing to do is to change these institutions and do it quickly, but always legally. For a self-constituted body of moral idiots, who would substitute the findings of the Ku Klux Klan for the processes of law to try to better conditions, would be a most un-American outrage which every good citizen should resent.

It is to the everlasting credit of Emporia that the organizer found no suckers with $10 each to squander here. Whatever Emporia may be otherwise, it believes in law and order, and absolute freedom under the Constitution for every man, no matter what birth or creed or race, to speak and meet and talk and act as a free, law-abiding citizen. The picayunish cowardice of a man who would substitute Klan rule and mob law for what our American fathers have died to establish and maintain should prove what a cheap screw outfit the Klan is.

57.

JAMES BRYCE: Public Opinion in America

James Bryce's perceptive as well as sympathetic magnum opus, The American Commonwealth *(1888), had won him many admirers both here and in England, and he was a logical choice for ambassador from Britain to the United States, a post that he occupied from 1907 to 1913. In spite of the press of official duties, Bryce kept up his scholarly work, and in 1921 he published his important study* Modern Democracies. *A selection from this work appears below.*

Source: *Modern Democracies*, New York, 1921, Vol. II, pp. 112-122.

THERE IS NO BETTER TEST of the excellence of a popular government than the strength of public opinion as a ruling power. I have sought to explain . . . wherein its rule differs, and differs for the better, from that of a numerical majority acting by votes only. In the United States, though votings are more frequent than in any other country, yet public opinion is, more fully than elsewhere, the ruling power. The founders of the republic expected from the average citizen a keener sense of his duty to vote wisely than he has shown, but in the function of giving, by his opinion, a general direction to public policy he has done well.

The doctrine of popular sovereignty and the structure of the government made it specially necessary that he should respond to the call made upon him of giving such direction, because the functions of government are divided and parceled out between its several organs. There are many checks and balances. Where each organ is watched and restrained by others, where terms of office are short, and changes in the persons who administer are consequently frequent, the watchfulness and directive control of the citizens are essential in order to keep the complicated machinery working and to guide each of its parts to a common aim.

The citizen must feel his constant responsibility, both to form an opinion and to make it known between the periods at which he delivers it by an electoral vote. Though this duty is not perfectly discharged, public opinion is on the whole more alert, more vigilant, and more generally active through every class and section of the nation than in any other great state. The frame of government has by its very complication served to stimulate the body of the people to observe, to think, and to express themselves on public questions.

To explain why this is so and what are the wholesome results it has produced, let us note some features of public opinion as determined by the character of the national mind.

Not even in the United States are politics the first thing in the citizen's thoughts. His own business, his domestic life, his individual tastes, come first, yet more here than elsewhere does one discover a people seriously interested in public affairs. Nobody says, as men so often say in France, Germany, and Italy, "I never trouble myself about politics." Current events are constantly discussed among the ordinary rural folk, and though the country newspaper is chiefly filled by farming topics and "local happenings," still the affairs of the nation figure somewhere in the landscape of nearly every native American.

It is, moreover, the good fortune of the country to possess a real national opinion as well as an ardent national patriotism; that is to say, there exists on most political topics a certain agreement which rises above and softens down the differences between the various sections or types of view. In some countries — France for instance — those differences are so marked that no such general concurrence of opinion can, as regards domestic issues, be discerned. It is usually antagonisms that are conspicuous. But in the United States, vast as the country is, there are many matters on which the great majority seem to be of one mind all the way from one ocean to the other.

During the first two years of the late war, there were diversities of attitude and feeling between the North Atlantic states and the South and the Middle West and the Far West, easily explicable by the fact that the first-named were in much closer touch with Europe and felt themselves more affected by what was passing there. But America's entrance into the conflict effaced these diversities. The same wave of feeling, sweeping over the whole continent, brought its sections into full accord. Considering how dissimilar are the conditions of economic and social life in the East, in the South, and in the West, this similarity of opinion is remarkable. It is qualified only by the feeling, still strong in the South, that, whatever happens, the colored men must not be allowed to regain any considerable voting power.

Racial diversities may be found everywhere, for one-third of the inhabitants were born abroad or of foreign parents, but such diversities affect but slightly the opinion of the nation because the most recent immigrants have neither the education nor the experience needed to enable them to influence others; while those who have been born and bred in the country have already become substantially American in their interests and ways of thought. Though, in some cities, masses of Slavs or Italians remain unabsorbed, the only large minorities which retain an attachment to the country of their origin sufficient to have political importance are a section of the Germans and a section of the Irish. It is, however, only insofar as questions of foreign relations are affected that these two elements stand out of the general stream of opinion.

The solvent and assimilative forces of education, of companionship, of all the things that make up social environment are stronger in America than in any other country. Religious differences also count for very little. In some few matters Roman Catholics may be influenced by respect for the head of their church, and they usually support the demand of their clergy for grants to denominational schools. But there is nothing resembling that strength of ecclesiastical sentiment which used to affect the political attitude of many Nonconformists and many members of the Established Church in England, much less any manifestations of the bitterness which in France arrays in hostile camps the Roman Catholics and the anti-clerical or the non-Christian part of the population.

Class distinctions have during the last hundred years become in continental Europe the forces which chiefly split and rend a people into antagonistic sections of opinion. This tendency has increased with the spread of the revolutionary school which preaches the so-called class war of the "proletariat" against the "bourgeois." It is only within the last three decades that this doctrine, brought from Europe by German and Russo-Jewish immigrants, has been making way, and what support it receives comes almost wholly from the still unassimilated part of the immigrant population. America had been theretofore exempt from class antagonisms because opinion had been divided, not horizontally along the strata of less or greater wealth but vertically, so that each view, each political tenet, was common to men in every social class.

The employer and his workmen, the merchant and his clerks were not led by their different social positions to think differently on politics any more than they would think differently on religion. They have been Republicans or Democrats for reasons unconnected with pecuniary means or station in life, neither of these two parties having any permanent affinity either with the richer or with the poorer, though from time to time one or other might, in some parts of the country, enlist the support of the moneyed class on a particular party issue, like that of free silver in 1896.

This fact suggests another reflection. In many of the largest and gravest questions, public opinion does not move on party lines. This is partly because the tenets, or at least the professions, of the opposite parties sometimes come very near to one another. A famous journalist observed to me in 1908: "Our two parties are like two bottles, both empty but bearing different labels." He spoke truly, for though there were strong currents of opinion discernible, none was flowing in a party channel.

One observes in America that men accustomed to support their party by their votes frequently disapprove both its acts and its promises. Thus the power and cohesiveness of party does not prevent the existence of a common sentiment in the bulk of the nation, often more united than the vehemence of party language leads foreigners to suppose. There are, in fact, only two fairly well-defined types of class opinion. One is that of the small financial class, including the heads of great industrial concerns, the other that of the advanced Socialist Party, largely under the influence of European syndicalistic or even anarchistic ideas. Among the rest there are no sharp and permanent oppositions of political tenets or of social sympathies.

Political opinion is better instructed than in continental Europe because a knowledge of the institutions of the country and their working is more generally diffused here than there through the rank and file of the native population. This is mainly due to the practice of local self-government and to the publicity given by the newspapers to all that passes in the political field.

Something may be attributed to the active part in public affairs that has always been played by members of the legal profession, and even more, in recent times, to the influence of college teaching. The number of men who have graduated in some place of higher instruction is probably ten times as large (in proportion to population) as in any part of continental Europe, and much more than twice as large as in Great Britain. These men have done much to leaven the voting mass. Most of them have not received what Europeans would call a complete university education, and the so-called literary or humanistic studies have been often neglected.

But they have been led into the realms of thought, and their horizons have been widened. They are often the leaders in reform movements, with higher ideas of good citizenship than the average businessman used to possess, and they are less inclined to a blind support of their party. One of the most significant and most hopeful features of American life has been the increase during the last forty years of the number and the influence of the universities, and of the extent to which their alumni, businessmen as well as lawyers, teachers, and clergymen, make themselves felt in the higher forms of political activity.

What, then, of the press, which is in all modern countries the chief factor in forming as well as in diffusing opinion? This is not the place to describe its general features, nor to inquire how far it deserves the censures which many Europeans, repelled by the faults of the worst newspapers, have unfairly bestowed upon it as a whole. These faults are due, not to democracy but to the social and economic conditions of the lower strata in city populations, conditions that produce in all countries results generally similar, but more marked here, because nowhere are there so many newspapers which find their circulation in that vast reading mass which is chiefly interested in records of crime and of events in the field of sport.

The press, including many weekly and some monthly magazines which handle political questions, is a chief agent in forming opinion by letting everybody know what everybody else is saying or is supposed to be thinking. This tells on the minds of undecided or unreflective people. Having neither the time nor the knowledge to think for themselves, they feel safe in thinking with the majority. In this sense the press makes opinion more effectively here than in any other country because the habit of reading is more general, and prominent men, though less given than are the English to writing letters to the newspapers, are more wont to confide their views to an interviewer.

The papers have their defects. The reporting of even the best speeches is full and exact only in a very few of the best journals, the rest confining themselves to abridgments which often miss the really important points. As everything is done in haste, the truth of facts fares ill; but in the general result the whole opinion of the country is mirrored more completely than anywhere in Europe. It is the statements of events and of the opinions of public men that tell. They would tell even more but for the inaccuracies frequent in papers of the second rank and rarely corrected, yet here, as elsewhere, these do not prevent the average man from assuming that what he sees in print is likely to be true.

Editorial articles count for less than in England or France: few people swear by their favorite paper, as many still do in England, and the names of editors and of writers of leading articles are scarcely known to the public. Hardly more than six or seven men have, during the last thirty years, be-

come familiar and personally influential figures in the world of political journalism,
great as is the literary talent which many
have displayed. Thus the profession does
not offer that opening to a public career
which it has often done in France and
sometimes in England, though the proprietor of a widely circulated paper or group
of papers may become a political figure, and
even seek high office by bringing himself
before the public. Scarcely ever has a leading statesman controlled, as in France, a
newspaper which habitually pushed his
views or urged his personal claims, so it
may be assumed that this form of advocacy
or advertisement would prove unprofitable.

Press hostility directed against a statesman, not by mere abuse, which seldom
tells, but by persistently recalling errors he
has committed, or (more rarely) by invent-
ing and repeating gross calumnies, can injure his prospects more than praise, however lavish, can improve them. Men have
been "boomed" into popularity and power
more frequently in England than in America. Does this argue the presence of more
discernment in the public?

Partisanship also, *i.e.,* the indiscriminating
support of a political party, is rather less
marked in American than in European journals, the former holding a more independent attitude and bestowing their censures
on one or other party with reference less to
their professed political principles than to
their action at any particular time or their
attitude on any particular issue. This increases their weight with thoughtful readers
and has a wholesome influence on party
chiefs, who know they must expect criticism
even from the organs to which they usually
look for support. To be wounded in the
house of your friends, though a painful, is
sometimes a profitable experience.

Though the press as a whole is at least as
important a factor in the working of government as it is anywhere else in the world,
no single paper is as powerful as some have
been in England, in France, in Italy, in Australia, and in Argentina. This is due to the
size of the country. The range of a journal
which can be read in the forenoon of its
issue is confined to some few hundreds of
miles, and though the utterances of the very
best papers are widely read and largely
quoted much further off, or may have their
views telegraphed all over the Union, they
have no great hold on a distant public.

The ascendancy of any wealthy proprietor
or group of proprietors influencing a large
proportion of the voters by impressing on
them, day after day and week after week,
one set of views and the same one-sided
statement of facts or alleged facts, is a danger only in the sphere of foreign relations.
In that sphere, plausible falsehoods and persistently malignant misrepresentation of the
character and purposes of another people
may do infinite mischief. One form of such
misrepresentation is to pick out and reprint
any unfriendly utterances that appear in the
newspapers, perhaps contemptible and without influence, of the country which it is desired to injure.

The exposure and denunciation of municipal misgovernment and corruption is
among the greatest services which the
American press — including some religious
and other nonpolitical weeklies — performs. We have seen how largely these evils
sprang from the ignorance or apathy of the
"respectable classes," who constantly need
to be awakened from their torpor and driv-
en to support the too-scanty band of civic
reformers. European observers, offended by
the excesses to which the passion for publicity can run in the United States, sometimes
fail to realize how many evils the incessant
vigilance of the press prevents or helps to
cure. Whether its faults, which were
thought to have been aggravated with the
upspringing of some papers of a low type in
the end of last century, have tended to de-

crease in later years is a quesion which some judicious observers answer by saying that the best papers have grown better and the worst papers worse. On several great occasions, and notably during the course of the recent war, the press rendered conspicuous services to the nation as an exponent of instructed and thoughtful opinion.

Since it was on the average man and his civic virtue that the founders of the republic relied for the working of its institutions, it is well to consider that generalized being, taking a sort of composite photograph from many individuals, and inquiring how far his power of forming a sound opinion has justified the confidence reposed in him. As the characteristic type of the average man, take the native American landowning farmer in the Northern and especially in the Middle Western and North Western States, where he is seen at his best, for in New England he has been largely replaced by the new immigrant not yet thoroughly Americanized. With the farmer, one may couple the storekeeper or artisan of those smaller towns which have a sort of rural color. These two classes, and particularly the former, are specifically American products, the like of whom one finds nowhere else, independent and fairly well-educated. Though sometimes querulous, as are agriculturists generally, accustomed to complain of the weather, they would, but for their resentment at the exploitation they suffer at the hands of financial interests, be as nearly satisfied with their lot as man is ever likely to be.

The normal member of these classes has a great pride in his country and a sense of his own duty to it. He follows the course of national and state politics, not assiduously but with fair intelligence and attention, usually voting at elections, though apt to leave political work to be done by the party organization. He is overprone to vote the party ticket, whatever names are put on it, and needs to be made to feel his own interest affected before he will join in a reforming movement. Shrewd, and critical of the motives and character of politicians, he is rather less suspicious than is the English or French peasant, because he has confidence in his own shrewdness, is socially the equal of the politicians, and quite as well-instructed as most of them.

But his horizon is limited. His thought, like his daily work, moves in a small circle; his imagination fails to grasp conditions unlike those of his own life. Thus he is not well-qualified to form a judgment on the larger questions of policy. Working hard to secure decent comfort for his family, he does not understand the value of special knowledge, thinks one man as good as another for official work, refuses to pay salaries to a judge or an administrator twice or thrice as large as his own net income. Not versed in economic principles, and seldom fitted by education to comprehend them when stated, he may fall a prey to plausible fallacies and be captured by vague promises to redress grievances of which he feels the pinch.

But if he be no good judge of measures, he is no bad judge of men. Here his shrewdness helps him; here his respect for honesty and courage comes in. When he recognizes in any public man uprightness, firmness, and a sincere desire to serve the public, he is ready to trust and to follow, rarely withdrawing a confidence once given. A strong state governor or mayor who fights the politicians of the legislature in the public interest, speaking clearly to the plain people, and above the suspicion of selfish motives, can count upon his vote, even against the party organization. It was by the confidence of average men of this type that Abraham Lincoln was carried to the presidency, and that Governor Hughes of New York was enabled to bend to his will the party machine that had been ruling that great state. These men who till the land they own are solid and intelligent, one of the great assets of the republic.

Of some qualities which the American people as a whole show in their political life, little need be said, because it is hard to determine how far these are due to democratic habits, how far to national character, *i.e.,* to the original English character as modified by physical and economic conditions in a new country, as well as (in a lesser degree) by admixture with other races. Still, as we are considering how American democracy works, it may be observed that they are an impressionable people, among whom excitement rises suddenly and spreads fast, quickened by the contagion of numbers.

Communication is so easy and swift over the continent that the same impulse seems to possess everyone at the same moment, as if all were assembled, like the Athenians, in one huge public meeting. It is then that the cunningly devised divisions of power and other constitutional checks are found serviceable, for at such moments opinion is apt to be intolerant of opposition, and may even resort to extralegal methods of suppressing it. But this seldom happens.

In ordinary times that tyranny of the majority which Tocqueville described and feared as an evil inherent in democracies no longer exists. Independence of mind is respected. Even cranks are borne with, nor does any country produce a richer crop. Americans are, moreover, a kindly and, in normal times, an indulgent people. This was seen half a century ago when after the Civil War an unprecedented clemency was extended towards those who were then talked of as Rebels.

Still less are they, as most Europeans suppose, a materialistic people. The race for wealth, not really greater than in western Europe, is a passion rather for success in making than for pleasure in enjoying a fortune. Nowhere is money so freely given to any charitable or other public purpose. Nowhere, except perhaps in Italy and France, are intellectual attainments so widely honored. These two last-named characteristics may be credited to democracy, which has here instilled a sense of a rich man's duty to return to the community a large part of what individual energy has won, and which respects achievements that reflect credit upon the nation and give it a pride in itself. Both sentiments flourish wherever, as here, class antagonisms are overborne by the sense of a higher common national life.

In saying that public opinion is the real ruler of America, I mean that there exists a judgment and sentiment of the whole nation which is imperfectly expressed through its representative legislatures, is not to be measured by an analysis of votes cast at elections, is not easily gathered from the most diligent study of the press, but is nevertheless a real force, impalpable as the wind, yet a force which all are trying to discover and nearly all to obey.

———————◆———————

Say it ain't so, Joe.
> A little boy who accosted "Shoeless" Joe Jackson on the street after the airing of the "Black Sox" scandal of 1920, and begged him to say that he and other White Sox players had not received money to "throw" the World Series of 1919

58.

WARREN G. HARDING: The Return to Normalcy

The Republican Party in 1920 turned its back on a number of strong contenders and — as his friend Harry Daugherty had predicted as early as February — picked the relatively unknown Warren Gamaliel Harding of Ohio as its presidential candidate. The Republicans, with Congress once more in their hands, desired to reestablish the authority of the legislative branch after eight years of Wilson; and they furthermore sensed a deep longing on the part of the American people for an end to international involvements and a "return to normalcy." Harding was just the man, and he won a resounding victory after a "front porch" campaign similar to McKinley's twenty years before. In a speech to a special session of Congress on April 12, 1921, Harding described the direction in which he thought the country should go in the next four years. Passages from the speech are reprinted here.

Source: *Record,* 67 Cong., 1 Sess., pp. 169-173.

Mr. Speaker, Vice-President, and Members of the Congress:

You have been called in extraordinary session to give your consideration to national problems far too pressing to be long neglected. We face our tasks of legislation and administration amid conditions as difficult as our government has ever contemplated. Under our political system the people of the United States have charged the new Congress and the new administration with the solution — the readjustments, reconstruction, and restoration which must follow in the wake of war.

It may be regretted that we were so illy prepared for war's aftermath, so little made ready to return to the ways of peace, but we are not to be discouraged. Indeed, we must be the more firmly resolved to undertake our work with high hope, and invite every factor in our citizenship to join in the effort to find our normal, onward way again.

The American people have appraised the situation, and, with that tolerance and patience which go with understanding, they will give to us the influence of deliberate public opinion which ultimately becomes the edict of any popular government. They are measuring some of the stern necessities, and will join in the give and take which is so essential to firm reestablishment.

First in mind must be the solution of our problems at home, even though some phases of them are inseparably linked with our foreign relations. The surest procedure in every government is to put its own house in order. I know of no more pressing problem at home than to restrict our national expenditures within the limits of our national income and at the same time measurably lift the burdens of war taxation from the shoulders of the American people.

One cannot be unmindful that economy is a much-employed cry, most frequently stressed in preelection appeals, but it is ours to make it an outstanding and ever impelling purpose in both legislation and administration. The unrestrained tendency to heedless expenditure and the attending growth of public indebtedness, extending from federal authority to that of state and municipality and including the smallest political subdivision, constitute the most dangerous phase of government today. The nation cannot restrain except in its own activities, but it can be exemplar in a wholesome reversal.

The staggering load of war debt must be cared for in orderly funding and gradual liquidation. We shall hasten the solution and aid effectively in lifting the tax burdens if we strike resolutely at expenditure. It is far more easily said than done. In the fever of war our expenditures were so little questioned, the emergency was so impelling, appropriation was so unimpeded that we little noted millions and counted the Treasury inexhaustible. It will strengthen our resolution if we ever keep in mind that a continuation of such a course means inevitable disaster. . . .

The most substantial relief from the tax burden must come for the present from the readjustment of internal taxes, and the revision or repeal of those taxes which have become unproductive and are so artificial and burdensome as to defeat their own purpose. A prompt and thoroughgoing revision of the internal tax laws, made with due regard to the protection of the revenues, is, in my judgment, a requisite to the revival of business activity in this country. It is earnestly hoped, therefore, that the Congress will be able to enact without delay a revision of the revenue laws and such emergency tariff measures as are necessary to protect American trade and industry.

It is of less concern whether internal taxation or tariff revision shall come first than has been popularly imagined because we must do both, but the practical course for earliest accomplishment will readily suggest itself to the Congress. We are committed to the repeal of the excess-profits tax and the abolition of inequities and unjustifiable exasperations in the present system.

The country does not expect and will not approve a shifting of burdens. It is more interested in wiping out the necessity for imposing them and eliminating confusion and cost in the collection.

The urgency for an instant tariff enactment, emergency in character and understood by our people that it is for the emergency only, cannot be too much emphasized. I believe in the protection of American industry, and it is our purpose to prosper America first. The privileges of the American market to the foreign producer are offered too cheaply today, and the effect on much of our own productivity is the destruction of our self-reliance, which is the foundation of the independence and good fortune of our people. Moreover, imports should pay their fair share of our cost of government.

One who values American prosperity and maintained American standards of wage and living can have no sympathy with the proposal that easy entry and the flood of imports will cheapen our costs of living. It is more likely to destroy our capacity to buy. Today, American agriculture is menaced and its products are down to prewar normals, yet we are endangering our fundamental industry through the high cost of transportation from farm to market and through the influx of foreign farm products, because we offer, essentially unprotected, the best market in the world. It would be better to err in protecting our basic food industry than paralyze our farm activities in the world struggle for restored exchanges. . . .

A very important matter is the establishment of the government's business on a business basis. There was toleration of the easy-going, unsystematic method of handling our fiscal affairs, when indirect taxa-

Lightfoot Collection

President Harding reading message announcing election of Lincoln, with Charles Becker, the original Pony Express rider who carried it; Meachem, Oregon

tion held the public unmindful of the federal burden. But there is knowledge of the high cost of government today, and high cost of living is inseparably linked with high cost of government. There can be no complete correction of the high living cost until government's cost is notably reduced.

Let me most heartily commend the enactment of legislation providing for the national budget system. Congress has already recorded its belief in the budget. It will be a very great satisfaction to know of its early enactment, so that it may be employed in establishing the economies and business methods so essential to the minimum of expenditure.

I have said to the people we meant to have less of government in business as well as more business in government. It is well to have it understood that business has a right to pursue its normal, legitimate, and righteous way unimpeded, and it ought have no call to meet government competition where all risk is borne by the public

Treasury. There is no challenge to honest and lawful business success. But government approval of fortunate, untrammeled business does not mean toleration of restraint of trade or of maintained prices by unnatural methods. It is well to have legitimate business understand that a just government, mindful of the interests of all the people, has a right to expect the cooperation of that legitimate business in stamping out the practices which add to unrest and inspire restrictive legislation. Anxious as we are to restore the onward flow of business, it is fair to combine assurance and warning in one utterance. . . .

It is proper to invite your attention to the importance of the question of radio communication and cables. To meet strategic, commercial, and political needs, active encouragement should be given to the extension of American-owned and operated cable and radio services. Between the United States and its possessions there should be ample communication facilities providing direct services at reasonable rates. Between the United States and other countries, not only should there be adequate facilities but these should be, so far as practicable, direct and free from foreign intermediation. Friendly cooperation should be extended to international efforts aimed at encouraging improvement of international communication facilities and designed to further the exchange of messages. Private monopolies tending to prevent the development of needed facilities should be prohibited. Government-owned facilities, wherever possible without unduly interfering with private enterprise or government needs, should be made available for general uses.

Particularly desirable is the provision of ample cable and radio services at reasonable rates for the transmission of press matter, so that the American reader may receive a wide range of news and the foreign reader receive full accounts of American activities. The daily press of all countries may well be put in position to contribute to international understandings by the publication of interesting foreign news.

Practical experience demonstrates the need for effective regulation of both domestic and international radio operation if this newer means of intercommunication is to be fully utilized. Especially needful is the provision of ample radio facilities for those services where radio only can be used, such as communication with ships at sea, with aircraft, and with out-of-the-way places. International communication by cable and radio requires cooperation between the powers concerned. Whatever the degree of control deemed advisable within the United States, government licensing of cable landings and of radio stations transmitting and receiving international traffic seems necessary for the protection of American interests and for the securing of satisfactory reciprocal privileges.

Aviation is inseparable from either the Army or the Navy, and the government must, in the interests of national defense,

encourage its development for military and civil purposes. The encouragement of the civil development of aeronautics is especially desirable as relieving the government largely of the expense of development, and of maintenance of an industry, now almost entirely borne by the government through appropriations for the military, naval, and postal air services. The air mail service is an important initial step in the direction of commercial aviation.

It has become a pressing duty of the federal government to provide for the regulation of air navigation; otherwise, independent and conflicting legislation will be enacted by the various states which will hamper the development of aviation. The National Advisory Committee for Aeronautics, in a special report on this subject, has recommended the establishment of a Bureau of Aeronautics in the Department of Commerce for the federal regulation of air navigation, which recommendation ought to have legislative approval. . . .

During the recent political canvass the proposal was made that a Department of Public Welfare should be created. It was endorsed and commended so strongly that I venture to call it to your attention and to suggest favorable legislative consideration.

Government's obligation affirmatively to encourage development of the highest and most efficient type of citizenship is modernly accepted, almost universally. Government rests upon the body of citizenship; it cannot maintain itself on a level that keeps it out of touch and understanding with the community it serves. Enlightened governments everywhere recognize this and are giving their recognition effect in policies and programs. Certainly no government is more desirous than our own to reflect the human attitude, the purpose of making better citizens — physically, intellectually, spiritually. To this end I am convinced that such a department in the government would be of real value. It could be made to crystallize much of rather vague generalization about social justice into solid accomplishment. Events of recent years have profoundly impressed thinking people with the need to recognize new social forces and evolutions, to equip our citizens for dealing rightly with problems of life and social order.

In the realms of education, public health, sanitation, conditions of workers in industry, child welfare, proper amusement and recreation, the elimination of social vice, and many other subjects, the government has already undertaken a considerable range of activities. . . .

Somewhat related to the foregoing human problems is the race question. Congress ought to wipe the stain of barbaric lynching from the banners of a free and orderly, representative democracy. We face the fact that many millions of people of African descent are numbered among our population, and that in a number of states they constitute a very large proportion of the total population. It is unnecessary to recount the difficulties incident to this condition, nor to emphasize the fact that it is a condition which cannot be removed. There has been suggestion, however, that some of its difficulties might be ameliorated by a humane and enlightened consideration of it, a study of its many aspects, and an effort to formulate, if not a policy, at least a national attitude of mind calculated to bring about the most satisfactory possible adjustment of relations between the races, and of each race to the national life. One proposal is the creation of a commission embracing representatives of both races, to study and report on the entire subject. The proposal has real merit. I am convinced that in mutual tolerance, understanding, charity, recognition of the interdependence of the races, and the maintenance of the rights of citizenship lies the road to righteous adjustment. . . .

Nearly two and a half years ago the World War came to an end, and yet we find ourselves today in the technical state of war, though actually at peace, while Europe is at technical peace, far from tranquillity

and little progressed toward the hoped-for restoration. It ill becomes us to express impatience that the European belligerents are not yet in full agreement, when we ourselves have been unable to bring constituted authority into accord in our own relations to the formally proclaimed peace.

Little avails in reciting the causes of delay in Europe or our own failure to agree. But there is no longer excuse for uncertainties respecting some phases of our foreign relationship. In the existing League of Nations, world-governing with its superpowers, this republic will have no part. There can be no misinterpretation, and there will be no betrayal of the deliberate expression of the American people in the recent election; and, settled in our decision for ourselves, it is only fair to say to the world in general, and to our associates in war in particular, that the League Covenant can have no sanction by us. The aim to associate nations to prevent war, preserve peace, and promote civilization our people most cordially applauded. We yearned for this new instrument of justice, but we can have no part in a committal to an agency of force in unknown contingencies; we can recognize no superauthority.

Manifestly, the highest purpose of the League of Nations was defeated in linking it with the treaty of peace and making it the enforcing agency of the victors of the war. International association for permanent peace must be conceived solely as an instrumentality of justice, unassociated with the passions of yesterday, and not so constituted as to attempt the dual functions of a political instrument of the conquerors and of an agency of peace. There can be no prosperity for the fundamental purposes sought to be achieved by any such association so long as it is an organ of any particular treaty or committed to the attainment of the special aims of any nation or group of nations.

The American aspiration, indeed, the world aspiration, was an association of nations, based upon the application of justice and right, binding us in conference and co-operation for the prevention of war and pointing the way to a higher civilization and international fraternity in which all the world might share. In rejecting the League Covenant and uttering that rejection to our own people and to the world, we make no surrender of our hope and aim for an association to promote peace in which we would most heartily join. We wish it to be conceived in peace and dedicated to peace, and will relinquish no effort to bring the nations of the world into such fellowship, not in the surrender of national sovereignty but rejoicing in a nobler exercise of it in the advancement of human activities, amid the compensations of peaceful achievement. . . .

It would be unwise to undertake to make a statement of future policy with respect to European affairs in such a declaration of a state of peace. In correcting the failure of the executive, in negotiating the most important treaty in the history of the nation, to recognize the constitutional powers of the Senate, we would go to the other extreme, equally objectionable, if Congress or the Senate should assume the function of the executive. Our highest duty is the preservation of the constituted powers of each and the promotion of the spirit of cooperation so essential to our common welfare.

It would be idle to declare for separate treaties of peace with the Central Powers on the assumption that these alone would be adequate, because the situation is so involved that our peace engagements cannot ignore the Old World relationship and the settlements already effected, nor is it desirable to do so in preserving our own rights and contracting our future relationships. The wiser course would seem to be the acceptance of the confirmation of our rights and interests as already provided and to engage under the existing treaty, assuming, of course, that this can be satisfactorily accomplished by such explicit reservations and modifications as will secure our absolute

freedom from inadvisable commitments and safeguard all our essential interests.

Neither Congress nor the people needs my assurance that a request to negotiate needed treaties of peace would be as superfluous and unnecessary as it is technically ineffective, and I know in my own heart there is none who would wish to embarrass the executive in the performance of his duty when we are all so eager to turn disappointment and delay into gratifying accomplishment.

Problems relating to our foreign relations bear upon the present and the future and are of such a nature that the all-important future must be deliberately considered with greater concern than mere immediate relief from unhappy conditions. We have witnessed, yea, we have participated in, the supremely tragic episode of war, but our deeper concern is in the continuing life of nations and the development of civilization.

We must not allow our vision to be impaired by the conflict among ourselves. The weariness at home and the disappointment to the world have been compensated in the proof that this republic will surrender none of the heritage of nationality, but our rights in international relationship have to be asserted; they require establishment in compacts of amity; our part in readjustment and restoration cannot be ignored, and must be defined.

With the supergoverning League definitely rejected and with the world so informed, and with the status of peace proclaimed at home, we may proceed to negotiate the covenanted relationships so essential to the recognition of all the rights everywhere of our own nation and play our full part in joining the peoples of the world in the pursuits of peace once more. Our obligations in effecting European tranquillity, because of war's involvements, are not less impelling than our part in the war itself. This restoration must be wrought before the human procession can go onward again. We can be helpful because we are moved by no hatreds and harbor no fears. Helpfulness does not mean entanglement, and participation in economic adjustments does not mean spon sorship for treaty commitments which do not concern us and in which we will have no part.

In an all-impelling wish to do the most and best for our own republic and maintain its high place among nations and at the same time make the fullest offering of justice to them, I shall invite in the most practical way the advice of the Senate, after acquainting it with all the conditions to be met and obligations to be discharged, along with our own rights to be safeguarded. Prudence in making the program and confident cooperation in making it effective cannot lead us far astray. We can render no effective service to humanity until we prove anew our own capacity for cooperation in the coordination of powers contemplated in the Constitution, and no covenants which ignore our associations in the war can be made for the future. More, no helpful society of nations can be founded on justice and committed to peace until the covenants reestablishing peace are sealed by the nations which were at war.

To such accomplishment — to the complete reestablishment of peace and its contracted relationships, to the realization of our aspirations for nations associated for world helpfulness without world government, for world stability on which humanity's hopes are founded — we shall address ourselves, fully mindful of the high privilege and the paramount duty of the United States in this critical period of the world.

59.

Edward E. Purinton: Business as the Savior of the Community

The Twenties saw unprecedented success for American business. Profits were high; investment grew by leaps and bounds; and consumer credit, advertising, and salesmanship took their places at the center of the American way of life. The businessman, noted Nation's Business *in 1925, is "the most influential person in the nation." "Never before," boasted the* Wall Street Journal, *". . . has a government been so completely fused with business." "This is a business country," declared Vice-President Calvin Coolidge, ". . . and it wants a business government." Reverence for free enterprise came close to being an article of faith, a fact that is made evident by the article reprinted below. Titled "Big Ideas from Big Business," it was written by Edward E. Purinton and published early in 1921.*

Source: *Independent,* April 16, 1921.

Among the nations of the earth today America stands for one idea: *Business.* National opprobrium? National opportunity. For in this fact lies, potentially, the salvation of the world.

Through business, properly conceived, managed, and conducted, the human race is finally to be redeemed. How and why a man works foretells what he will do, think, have, give, and be. And real salvation is in doing, thinking, having, giving, and being — not in sermonizing and theorizing.

I shall base the facts of this article on the personal tours and minute examinations I have recently made of twelve of the world's largest business plants: U.S. Steel Corporation; International Harvester Company; Swift & Company; E. I. du Pont de Nemours & Company; National City Bank; National Cash Register Company; Western Electric Company; Sears, Roebuck & Company; H. J. Heinz Company; Peabody Coal Company; Statler Hotels; Wanamaker Stores.

These organizations are typical, foremost representatives of the commercial group of interests loosely termed "Big Business." A close view of these corporations would reveal to any trained, unprejudiced observer a new conception of modern business activities. Let me draw a few general conclusions regarding the best type of business house and businessman.

What is the finest game? Business. The soundest science? Business. The truest art? Business. The fullest education? Business. The fairest opportunity? Business. The cleanest philanthropy? Business. The sanest religion? Business.

You may not agree. That is because you judge business by the crude, mean, stupid, false imitation of business that happens to be located near you.

The finest game is business. The rewards are for everybody, and all can win. There are no favorites — Providence always crowns the career of the man who is worthy. And in this game there is no "luck" — you have the fun of taking chances but the sobriety of guaranteeing certainties. The speed and size of your winnings are for you alone to determine; you needn't wait for the other fellow in the game — it is always your move. And your slogan is not "Down the Other Fellow!" but rather "Beat Your Own Record!" or "Do It Better Today!" or "Make Every Job a Masterpiece!" The great sportsmen of the world are the great businessmen.

The soundest science is business. All investigation is reduced to action, and by action proved or disproved. The idealistic motive animates the materialistic method. Hearts as well as minds are open to the truth. Capital is furnished for the researches of "pure science"; yet pure science is not regarded pure until practical. Competent scientists are suitably rewarded — as they are not in the scientific schools.

The truest art is business. The art is so fine, so exquisite, that you do not think of it as art. Language, color, form, line, music, drama, discovery, adventure — all the components of art must be used in business to make it of superior character.

The fullest education is business. A proper blend of study, work, and life is essential to advancement. The whole man is educated. Human nature itself is the open book that all businessmen study; and the mastery of a page of this educates you more than the memorizing of a dusty tome from a library shelf. In the school of business, moreover, you teach yourself and learn most from your own mistakes. What you learn here you live out, the only real test.

The fairest opportunity is business. You can find more, better, quicker chances to get ahead in a large business house than anywhere else on earth. The biographies of champion businessmen show how they climbed, and how you can climb. Recognition of better work, of keener and quicker thought, of deeper and finer feeling, is gladly offered by the men higher up, with early promotion the rule for the man who justifies it. There is, and can be, no such thing as buried talent in a modern business organization.

The cleanest philanthropy is business. By "clean" philanthropy I mean that devoid of graft, inefficiency, and professionalism, also of condolence, hysterics, and paternalism. Nearly everything that goes by the name of Charity was born a triplet, the other two members of the trio being Frailty and Cruelty. Not so in the welfare departments of leading corporations. Savings and loan funds; pension and insurance provisions; health precautions, instructions, and safeguards; medical attention and hospital care; libraries, lectures, and classes; musical, athletic, and social features of all kinds; recreational facilities and financial opportunities — these types of "charitable institutions" for employees add to the worker's self-respect, self-knowledge, and self-improvement by making him an active partner in the welfare program, a producer of benefits for his employer and associates quite as much as a recipient of bounty from the company. I wish every "charity" organization would send its officials to school to the heads of the welfare departments of the big corporations; the charity would mostly be transformed into capability, and the minimum of irreducible charity left would not be called by that name.

The sanest religion is business. Any relationship that forces a man to follow the Golden Rule rightfully belongs amid the ceremonials of the church. A great business enterprise includes and presupposes this relationship. I have seen more Christianity to the square inch as a regular part of the office equipment of famous corporation presidents than may ordinarily be found on Sunday in a verbalized but not vitalized church congregation. A man is not wholly religious until he is better on weekdays than he is on Sunday. The only ripened fruits of creeds are deeds. You can fool your preacher with a sickly sprout or a wormy semblance of character, but you can't fool your employer. I would make every business house a consultation bureau for the guidance of the church whose members were employees of the house.

I am aware that some of the preceding statements will be challenged by many readers. I should not myself have made them, or believed them, twenty years ago, when I was a pitiful specimen of a callow youth and cocksure professional man combined. A thorough knowledge of business has implanted a deep respect for business and real businessmen.

The future work of the businessman is to teach the teacher, preach to the preacher, admonish the parent, advise the doctor, justify the lawyer, superintend the statesman, fructify the farmer, stabilize the banker, harness the dreamer, and reform the reformer. Do all these needy persons wish to have these many kind things done to them by the businessman? Alas, no. They rather look down upon him, or askance at him, regarding him as a mental and social inferior — unless he has money or fame enough to tilt their glance upward.

A large variety of everyday lessons of popular interest may be gleaned from a tour of the world's greatest business plants and a study of the lives of their founders. We suggest a few.

1. *The biggest thing about a big success is the price.* It takes a big man to pay the price. You can measure in advance the size of your success by how much you are willing to pay for it. I do not refer to money. I refer to the time, thought, energy, economy, purpose, devotion, study, sacrifice, patience, care that a man must give to his lifework before he can make it amount to anything.

The business world is full of born crusaders. Many of the leaders would be called martyrs if they weren't rich. The founders of the vast corporations have been, so far as I know them, fired with zeal that is supposed to belong only to missionaries. Of all the uncompromising, untiring, unsparing idealists in the world today, none surpass the founders and heads of the business institutions that have made character the cornerstone. The costliest thing on earth is idealism.

2. *Great men are silent about themselves.* Conversely, the more a man talks about his personality, his family, his property, his po-

sition, his past, present or future achievements, the less he usually amounts to or will ever become. We had to spend weeks of hard work to obtain personal interviews with the heads of the International Harvester Company.

They prefer the forge to the limelight. They do not want free "publicity." And they refuse to make oral statements that might be misquoted or misunderstood; they insist that all facts and figures for publication be checked with utmost care, sometimes through a dozen departments, to prevent the least inaccuracy.

The publicity director of E. I. du Pont de Nemours & Company was disturbed, on reading our monograph prior to publication, because he felt we had praised the company too highly! He explained that part of his job was to avoid appearance of exaggeration; and though we stated facts, he detected a slight sound of praise. The president of the National City Bank hasn't had a photograph of himself taken for over ten years, even to give to his friends and relatives. He accorded us a delightful interview, but requested us not to quote him directly or mention his name at all in preparing our essay on the bank.

3. *The best way to keep customers is to make friends.* Of all the assets of a business concern the chief is goodwill. To gain this, you can afford to spend as much as to manufacture or sell your product.

Now a fundamental rule in creating goodwill is to benefit the customer in a way he does not look for, does not pay for. The Western Electric Company offers to teach any woman the principles of household efficiency, mailing on request literature without charge. The science of managing a home indicates the use of electrical appliances, but the company wants to teach the science whether it sells the goods or not. This is "good business" because genuine service.

The Peabody Coal Company gladly tells the customer how to save coal. A short-sighted man would infer that the company lost sales in doing this because the customer, using less coal, would buy less. On the other hand, the customer who follows Peabody rules of trade will buy more regularly, pay more promptly, and cooperate with the company in ways quite as important as the chance of purchasing a few more tons of coal on a single deal.

4. *Only common experiences will unite the laborer and the capitalist.* Each must get the viewpoint of the other by sharing the work, duties, and responsibilities of the other. The sons of the families of Swift, McCormick, Wanamaker, Heinz, du Pont have learned the business from the ground up; they know the trials, difficulties, and needs of workers because they *are* workers; and they don't have to settle agitations and strikes because there aren't any.

Further, by councils and committees of employees, management courses for department heads and foremen, plans of referendum and appeal, offers of stock and voting power to workers, employee representation on the Board of Directors, and other means of sharing authority and responsibility, owners of a business now give the manual workers a chance to think and feel in unison with themselves. All enmity is between strangers. Those who really know each other cannot fight.

5. *Every business needs a woman counselor.* Better, a woman's advisory board. Nearly all manufacturing and merchandising relates somehow to the interests of womankind.

Before E. M. Statler built his latest hotel in his big chain of hostelries, he consulted the housekeeper and matron of his masterpiece house, Hotel Pennsylvania, the world's largest inn. He wanted to know the precise arrangement, equipment, and service that women guests valued most. He knew that no man could tell him.

There could be written a book of business revelations that would astonish the world. Over and over, at critical times in the development of national corporations, the hidden hand of a woman has held the huge concern at balance, or swung it in the right direction. You can no more run a business without a woman's intuition than you can run a boat without a keel.

6. *The great new field for professional men is corporation work.* Teachers, doctors, lawyers, editors, psychologists, chemists, bankers, engineers, even philosophers and ministers now find pleasant, permanent, lucrative employment as heads of departments in famous business houses.

On my tour of the establishment of Swift & Company, I met a former editor of a big Chicago paper, a former professor and noted economist of one of our largest universities, a former engineer and author of national reputation, other professional men of high standing who were doing bigger work, for better pay, in the Swift employ than previous positions had afforded opportunity to develop. More and more, business will demand the knowledge and skill of scientists and artists of many kinds.

7. *The pleasure of money is not in having or spending it.* The pleasure is in getting it — and giving it away. Money rewards the exercise of keen brains and quick wits, but the real fun is in the exercise. I don't know of a single self-made millionaire who puts money first. There is always something bigger and better than money in his mind.

As for his heart, that is where he *gives* the most. The heart of Judge Gary is in the manifold benefits he creates for the employees of U.S. Steel. The heart of John Wanamaker is in the John Wanamaker Foundation, a beneficial organization for Wanamaker workers, and in the international Sunday school forces that he set in motion. The heart of Julius Rosenwald is in the schools he established for poor boys and girls, and the relief work he founded among the Jews. The heart of Harold F. McCormick is in the free education he gives to farmers and the uplifting music he provides for the people of Chicago. The heart of Howard Heinz is in the Sarah Heinz Community House, maintained by him as a living memorial to his mother. The heart of every great man is in some philanthropy made possible only by his money.

8. *A family heritage of wealth alone is the worst kind.* Most parents think they are good to their children if they leave a large bankroll, easily accessible. Others foolishly magnify the bestowal of a college education, or social position, or some other inheritance not earned, and not valued because not earned.

Founders of great business enterprises know better. They bequeath to their sons a personal equipment of aims, principles, and methods which make real men of the scions of wealth. When I asked Howard Heinz, president of the H. J. Heinz Company, to describe the ideal businessman, he answered simply, "My father." When I asked him to outline his own secret of success and purpose in life, he answered, "The fulfillment of my father's plans for industrial and social betterment, by carrying out faithfully the principles he laid down for the conduct of the business."

9. *Age is nothing to a live man.* When a person gets old the calendar is not to blame — he was born dead from the heart out and the neck up.

John H. Patterson was of middle age before he really started the National Cash Register Company. He had no experience in the business either, having been a country storekeeper without personal knowledge of engineering or manufacturing. But he got a purpose — and forgot everything else. Whoever does that is young till he dies. It is never too late to make a fresh start in life.

The men who grow immortal have stopped counting birthdays. J. Pierpont Morgan, James J. Hill, Henry Ford, Elbert Hubbard, Walt Mason, Dr. Frank Crane, many others in places of high renown didn't really get going till past forty.

This is the world-age of young old men. Look at Judge Gary, John Wanamaker, John D. Rockefeller, Chauncey M. Depew, Thomas A. Edison, Bishop Samuel Fallows, Dr. Charles W. Eliot, Dr. J. H. Kellogg, scores of other leaders who, seventy to eighty-five years old, think, feel, and act like men twenty years their juniors.

10. *The most powerful preacher is, or can be, the lay preacher.* The business manager of Gary, Indiana, the world's largest industrial city, preaches nearly every Sunday. He is called upon by the pastors and priests of churches of a dozen different faiths and nationalities whose members are employees of the U.S. Steel Corporation to address the congregations in some helpful, appropriate way. Because he is a fine businessman, with power, skill, and money back of him, the men of the city want to hear what he has to say. And because he is a gentleman — kind, thoughtful, and sympathetic — the women of the church listen gladly to his lay sermons.

I look forward to the day when professional sermonizers will be considered a relic of past incompetence, and in their place will be men who are personal vitalizers and organizers.

11. *Charity must be cleansed of poverty and sentimentality.* You are not kind to the poor when you merely give them food, clothes, or money. You pauperize them when they most need energizing, organizing, and reorganizing.

A leading official of Sears, Roebuck & Company hates "welfare work." He says the company won't do any. Why? Because (1) the company refuses to pose as a philanthropist, socialist, or fairy godfather; (2) a self-respecting employee hates being "welfared" by his employer; (3) charity and business don't go together; (4) the majority of welfare workers are officious, crude, paternalistic, and unscientific, out of place in business; and (5) employers need welfare work, perhaps of a different kind, as much as employees, and a one-sided program of such voluntary philanthropy is unwise and unfair.

This man claims that whatever improves the health, happiness, homelife, or future progress of the worker improves the work and should be considered a straight business proposition. He believes that commercialism should include idealism and fraternalism, but without mention of the fact.

12. *Industry will finally be the savior of the community.* We hear much about a decadence of morality and increase of crime. Now the person who gets into mischief and goes astray was doing nothing, or the wrong thing, or the right thing badly. Put everybody in the work he loves, teach him how to do it well, and treat him and reward him fairly; then you take away the chief components of wrongdoing, which are idleness, irresponsibility, loneliness, and curiosity, aided and abetted by a consciousness of misfitness. Thomas A. Edison remarks that he never had time to break a moral law.

Even now, the brightest and best spot in the community of such corporations as U.S. Steel, National Cash Register Company, National City Bank, Heinz, McCormick, or du Pont is generally the community house or center founded, built, and maintained by the corporation. Happiness for a human being lies in his work, or nowhere. And the way to make people good is to make them know they are good for something.

The victor belongs to the spoils.

F. Scott Fitzgerald, *The Beautiful and the Damned,* 1922

1922

60.

George Sylvester Counts: The Selective Character of American Secondary Education

The American public-school system had become a well-established institution by 1920, but many critics nonetheless felt that the schools, especially the high schools, were catering to the middle and upper classes and ignoring the needs of the poor. In 1922 George Sylvester Counts, an educator and sociologist, published a study of high-school dropouts in which he tried to show that the nation's secondary schools were perpetuating class differences. Portions of the introductory and concluding sections of the study are reprinted below.

Source: *The Selective Character of American Secondary Education*, Chicago, 1922, pp. 1-4, 141-148.

FOR TWO GENERATIONS the public high school in the United States has grown at such a rapid rate as to give it a unique place in the history of educational institutions. Appearing late in the first quarter of the 19th century, it at once entered into a struggle for survival with the dominant secondary school of the time, the private academy. For a half-century the high school maintained itself with more or less success, and was well established by 1870. During the fifty years that have elapsed in the meantime, it has expanded in a manner quite without precedent.

From 1890 to 1918 the number of high schools reporting to the bureau at Washington increased from 2,526 to 13,951; the number of pupils in attendance, from 202,963 to 1,645,171; and the number of teachers, from 9,120 to 81,034. At the same time the population of the United States

increased from 62,622,250 to approximately 105,253,000. Thus, while the high school enrollment increased 711 percent, the total population increased but 68 percent. From year to year this institution has constantly attracted a larger and larger proportion of the children of high-school age in the nation. . . .

From 1870 to 1880, the increase in high school enrollment actually failed to keep pace with the growth of population; during the following decade the two series were parallel; and since 1890 the high school enrollment has been growing at a rate constantly accelerated from period to period without showing any marked dependence on the general increase of population. Truly the American public high school occupies a unique place among educational institutions.

And the end is not yet. . . . In view of the direction it is taking today, apparently there is but one ultimate limitation to the increase in the high school registration and that is to be found in the number of children of high school age in the population. We are already hearing murmurings about universal secondary education. It is pointed out that, in spite of the very rapid increase in high school enrollment in recent years, there are enrolled today in our secondary schools, both public and private, only about 2 million out of a total of approximately 8.3 million children of high school age in the nation. Some of our states are passing compulsory education laws that break with our tradition of compulsory education for the elementary period only, and point toward some measure of compulsory secondary education.

The conception of secondary education as education for the selected few, whether by birth or by talent, appears to be giving ground before the assaults of political democracy and the demands of a society of increasing complexity and wealth. Some are saying that as public elementary education is no longer education for the masses but rather education for childhood, so secondary education is no longer education for the classes but rather education for adolescence. Thus in a statement made by the teachers of the Washington Irving High School for Girls in New York City in 1911 we find these words: "A public high school differs from an elementary school chiefly in the age of its children." Such a statement marks a new era in the history of secondary education. . . .

IT IS CLEAR that we in America have not abandoned in practice the selective principle in secondary education, even though we have established a free public high school in almost every community in the country. It is not strictly in accord with the facts to say that "a public high school differs from an elementary school chiefly in the age of its children." It is true that children in high school are on the average somewhat older

than those in the elementary school, yet, as a matter of fact, there is not very much difference in the ages of pupils enrolled in the eighth grade and those in the first year of the high school. High school students, even today and in spite of the amazing growth of the high school enrollment since 1880, are a highly selected group. And this difference is just as important as the difference in age. Secondary education is not education for adolescence, as elementary education is education for childhood, but rather education for a selected group of adolescents. . . .

Parental Occupation and the Public High School

THERE IS A CLOSE RELATION between parental occupation and the privileges of secondary education. If we examine the entire high school population, we find certain occupational groups very well and others very poorly represented in proportion to their numbers in the general population. Among the former are the five great non-labor groups, with professional service occupying the most advantageous position, followed by the proprietors, commercial service, managerial service, and clerical service. At the other end of the series are the lower grades of labor, with common labor almost unrepresented and personal service, miners, lumber workers, and fishermen, and the miscellaneous trades and machine operatives in the manufacturing and mechanical industries occupying somewhat better positions in the order named.

The other occupational groups are found between these two extremes. Next to the non-labor groups are the printing trades and the public service, followed by the machine trades, transportation service, and the building trades. In general, the order here given reflects the social and economic status of the occupation, its educational and intellectual standards, and the stability of employment.

Not only do these various occupational

classes exhibit different degrees of representation in the high school at the beginning of the course, but those very groups that are under-represented in the freshman year have the smallest ratio of seniors to freshmen. In fact, the representation of an occupation in the first year of the high school is at the same time a fairly accurate measure of its tendency to persist through the fourth year. Consequently, the differences among the groups become more and more pronounced in the successive years of the school.

The student population gradually becomes more and more homogeneous as the source from which it is drawn becomes more narrow, until by the time the senior year of the high school is reached, the student body exhibits a distinctly class character. Here the representatives of the laboring classes are few indeed in proportion to their number in the general population, and the lower grades of labor have practically disappeared. . . .

Evidence in corroboration of these conclusions, drawn from a study of the high school population, is derived from the investigation of groups of children of high school age not in high school in Seattle and Bridgeport. In the former city, a study of 514 children of high school age at work showed a social composition very different from that of the high school population. Here, four great labor groups — the building trades, common labor, machine trades, and transportation service — contribute over 60 percent of the children. The situation is just the reverse of that found in the high school.

In Bridgeport a similar condition is found. In the evening high school of that city, the sons and daughters of the laboring classes constitute the great majority of the enrollment with the machine trades in the lead, followed by the miscellaneous trades, common labor, and the building trades. In the trade school the situation is about the same, except that the representation of the laboring classes is yet larger and common labor forges ahead of the miscellaneous trades to second place.

Apparently the children of the laboring classes are destined to follow in the footsteps of their fathers. This representation of the labor groups is still further increased in that group of educational unfortunates enrolled in the compulsory continuation classes in which common labor holds first place, accounting for over one-fourth of the entire registration.

These differences in the extent of educational opportunity are further accentuated through the choice of curricula. As a rule, those groups which are poorly represented in the high school patronize the more narrow and practical curricula, the curricula which stand as terminal points in the educational system and which prepare for wage earning. And the poorer their representation in high school, the greater is the probability that they will enter these curricula.

The one- and two-year vocational courses, wherever offered, draw their registration particularly from the ranks of labor. This tendency is considerably more pronounced among the girls than among the boys. The former seem to be peculiarly bound by the social class from which they come. One is surprised at the unmistakable class character of the girls' college preparatory course in a high school such as that in Bridgeport. Furthermore, the thesis may be cautiously advanced that these differences appear somewhat more clearly in the East than in the West, but it is hardly safe to generalize on the basis of returns from four cities.

A study of expectations following graduation, as given by the students, indicates that this selective principle continues to operate beyond the period of secondary education. Those classes which are least well represented in the last year of the high school will apparently be yet less well represented in the colleges and universities. And, as in the case of the choice of curricula, this tendency is more marked among the girls than among the boys, in the East than in the West.

The Public High School and the Cultural Level

PARENTAL OCCUPATION, as one index of cultural level, exhibits a close relation to educational opportunity. The same is true of the possession of a telephone in the home, according to the returns from Bridgeport and Mt. Vernon. In the former city, it was found that telephones are two and one-half times as frequent in the homes of high school students as in those of children attending the trade school, and seven times as frequent as in the homes of the children in the compulsory continuation classes. Furthermore, the percentage of telephones increases decidedly from year to year in the high school. Thus we find but 39.7 percent of the students in the freshman year coming from homes with telephones, whereas in the senior year this percentage is 60.3.

There are also wide differences among the curricula in this respect. In the case of the girls, telephones are almost twice as frequent in the homes of those who are enrolled in the college preparatory as in the homes of those taking the commercial course. And these curricular differences are less marked among the boys than among the girls as was observed in the study of the parental occupation. Data from Mt. Vernon, including returns from the sixth grade, support in every particular these conclusions drawn from the Bridgeport study.

The Public High School and Family Influences

ALL THE EVIDENCE brought to light in this study points to the importance of the family as a powerful factor in determining attendance at high school. The mortality of parents of high school students is found to be considerably below the expectation for children of high school age, and does not increase perceptibly from the freshman to the senior year. In fact, according to the returns from Mt. Vernon, the mortality of parents is appreciably higher among sixth grade children than among students in the last year of the high school. An examination of the various groups of children of high school age not in high school shows a much higher mortality of parents here than among high school students. In the case of young people attending the evening high school in Bridgeport, the mortality of parents is extraordinarily high, more than two and one-half times as high as among those attending the day high school. Unquestionably the disorganization of the home through the death of a parent is reflected in the diminution of the opportunities of secondary education.

While the evidence is neither quite so clear nor quite so objective, apparently the engaging in remunerative employment on the part of the mother acts in the same way as the death of a parent. Comparisons made among the groups studied usually hold in the one case as in the other. Yet, it must not be forgotten that the working mother is usually just one element in a complex social situation.

The influence of the size of the family on educational opportunity is not altogether clear. On the average, those elements in the population who do not patronize the high school have larger families than those who do, but there is no evidence to indicate that the size of the family itself is a determining factor; for the number of brothers and sisters is no smaller among seniors than among freshmen, and the very large families have just as high representation in the last as in the first year of the high school. Likewise, the very small families do not apparently increase their representation in the later years of the high school.

The order of birth seems to be a matter of more importance, although the complexity of the situation is hardly compatible with any but the most cautious of statements. Our clearest evidence, drawn from the four groups studied in Bridgeport, indicates that the firstborn has somewhat more limited chances of securing a high school education than the lastborn child. It is on him particularly that the burden of family support is likely to fall, if one or more of the children must help to bear it.

The Public High School and the Immigrant

RETURNS from Bridgeport and Mt. Vernon indicate very clearly that children of native parentage attend the public high school in proportionately much larger numbers than do children of immigrant parentage. There are certain immigrant groups, however, that approximate, if they do not surpass, the native stock in their zeal for secondary education, altogether apart from the social and economic handicaps under which the immigrant labors. Among these, probably the Russian Jews stand at the top, followed by the Irish, the Germans, and the peoples of the British Empire. At the other extreme are the Italians, the Poles, and the races of the old Austro-Hungarian Empire, who patronize the high school in exceedingly small measure. Disregarding the record of the Russian Jews, it may be stated as a general principle that the farther east and south we go in Europe as the source of our immigrants, we find less interest in secondary education.

The well-known tendency among our own people for the girls to patronize the high school in greater numbers than the boys is reversed among certain immigrant stocks. Thus, while in the Bridgeport High School there are but 74 boys of native parentage to every 100 girls, among the Italians this ratio of boys to girls is 154. This social trait, if such it may be called, varies much from group to group. Beginning with the Irish who exhibit the American trait in approximately its native strength of sending girls rather than boys to high school, the proportion of boys steadily increases as we pass east and south into Europe. Among the peoples of the "new" immigration, the right of the girl to a secondary education is not recognized as on a parity with that of the boy.

In choice of curricula the girls of immigrant stock are clearly less inclined toward the college preparatory course than are the girls of native parentage. Curiously enough the reverse is true of the boys, but, since the boys of American parentage are exceptionally well represented in the scientific course, which in reality is a college preparatory course, no large significance should be attached to this difference between the foreign and native stock.

The Public High School and the Negro

WHILE FOR THE COUNTRY as a whole the proportion of Negroes of high school age to be found in our high schools is very small, in the city of St. Louis they do about as well as the whites. A study of the student population in the Negro high school of this city helps us to understand the difficulties that stand in the way of educational achievement on the part of members of this race. The fathers of the students in this high school are for the most part engaged in manual labor, and the lower and less respectable grades of manual labor, particularly personal service and common labor.

The Negro family exhibits a large measure of disorganization, as indicated by such crude and unsatisfactory phenomena as a deceased parent or a working mother. In the high school population of St. Louis the parental mortality for the Negro children is well over twice as high as for the children of white stock, and the frequency of the working mother is between five and six times as great for the students of the one as for those of the other race. All of which makes it safe to conclude that nowhere else in the nation is there a similarly large representation of any other race living on the same social and economic level that is sending as large a proportion of its children to high school as the Negroes of St. Louis.

The Negroes exhibit in a pronounced fashion the American trait of sending a larger proportion of their girls than of their boys to high school. In choice of curricula, the Negro girls differ from their white sisters chiefly in avoidance of the two-year commercial curriculum and in their very frequent selection of the home economics course. The Negro boys avoid the general and concentrate on the manual training course.

Following graduation, the Negro girls expect to attend normal school and enter professional service in much larger numbers than do the whites. And they are not apparently looking forward to clerical service in proportionate numbers. Surprisingly, in the case of the boys, the only important difference between the two races is the much larger expectation of college attendance on the part of the Negroes. It should be kept in mind, however, that these conclusions are based altogether on statements by the students, and consequently require considerable discounting.

The Public High School and Psychological Selection

NOT ONLY is the high school population selected sociologically but it is selected psychologically as well. Children of high school age not in high school, whether they be in the evening high school, the trade school, or the continuation classes, show a lower intelligence rating on the average than do those in high school. But there is much overlapping in the distribution of ability for the two groups. There is much excellence out of, as well as much mediocrity in, the high

school. The trade school population shows a particularly wide distribution of ability.

In the high school itself the traditional academic curricula draw a higher type of ability, on the average, than do the newer and vocational curricula. Here also, however, the overlapping of the distributions is pronounced, and perhaps even more significant than the average difference.

The children from the laboring classes exhibit ability of practically as high grade as do those from the other occupational groups. This is probably due to the much greater elimination of children of labor parentage. Likewise, the children of immigrants do about as well on the tests as do the children of native stock.

Firstborn make records somewhat superior to the records of lastborn children. This is probably to be explained in terms of greater elimination and thus more rigid selection among the former. The intelligence score also varies inversely with the size of the family. The explanation here is apparently to be found in the limitation of births among the more foresighted elements in the population.

The Population of the Private Secondary School

IN THE POPULATION of the private secondary school, which charges a considerable tuition fee and which is fundamentally college preparatory in its function, we probably have as accurate a picture as we can get today of the sources from which the private academy drew its students before the rise of the free public high school. While this picture is certainly not accurate to the details, the general outlines in all probability do not falsify the facts.

Taking the student populations of Exeter Academy and the University of Chicago High School, we find the laboring classes practically absent, in contrast to a representation of 29 percent in the public high school. Furthermore, these two schools draw almost three-fourths of their students from two occupational groups — the proprietors and professional service. Also, almost 90 percent of these students are of native parentage. Thus, while we may say that public secondary education is still highly selective, it is obvious that it has been and might be much more so.

LITTLE NEED BE SAID IN CONCLUSION. The story that has been told in the foregoing pages is not a new one. Misfortune, as well as fortune, passes from generation to generation. The children of unfortunate parentage are unfortunate, assuming here that the current secondary education is worth to the individual some fraction of its cost. The ancient adage, "To them that hath shall be given," is true today as in olden times.

When not preserved through the operation of biological forces, the inequalities among individuals and classes are still perpetuated to a considerable degree in the social inheritance.

While the establishment of the free public high school marked an extraordinary educational advance, it did not by any means equalize educational opportunity; for the cost of tuition is not the entire cost of education, or even the larger part of it. Education means leisure, and leisure is an expensive luxury. In most cases today this leisure must be guaranteed the individual by the family. Thus, secondary education remains largely a matter for family initiative and concern, and reflects the inequalities of family means and ambition.

61.

KIRBY PAGE: Labor Policies of the United States Steel Corporation

The national income, $27 billion in 1909, had risen to $63 billion by 1922, and an era of unprecedented prosperity had been ushered in after the war; yet control of the country's vast wealth remained in the hands of a relatively small number of capitalists. In a study reminiscent of the muckraking era, Kirby Page revealed in 1922 the disproportion between the total income of the United States Steel Corporation and the amount paid out by the company in wages to its workers, and in the process criticized what in his opinion was an unnecessarily penurious attitude on the part of management toward its employees.

Source: *Atlantic Monthly*, May 1922: "The United States Steel Corporation."

WHAT ARE THE SOCIAL consequences of current business policies? To what extent are human values subordinated in the effort to secure large returns on invested capital? Do the workers receive an adequate share of the proceeds of modern industry? How shall we determine an equitable adjustment of profits and wages? Wherein resides the dominant power in the control of modern business?

This study of one of our large corporations is an attempt to shed light upon such questions as these. The United States Steel Corporation was selected for this purpose because of its magnitude and the important part which it plays in one of our basic industries. . . . The officials of the corporation emphatically disagree with the general viewpoint of this article. Perhaps I ought to state that I do not regard the policies of the Steel Corporation as unique, but rather as a fair illustration of practices which are widely prevalent in modern business circles. It seems highly important that a vigorous effort be made to discover the social consequences and ethical implications of these policies.

"A Corporation with a Soul"

THIS IS THE SUBTITLE of a recent book dealing with the United States Steel Corporation. There is much to be said in favor of the contention that this corporation has a soul. Ninety-five million dollars have been spent by the Steel Corporation in various kinds of welfare work for its employees.

It is estimated that safety devices installed and precautionary measures taken have reduced the number of accidents in its plants approximately 55 percent. Much attention has been given to the protection of the health of its workers. Twenty-five base hospitals have been erected and supported.

Large sums have been expended for sanitation, toilet, and locker facilities, lunchrooms, clubrooms, playgrounds, athletic fields, and other recreational features. Fifty schools and twenty-six churches have been built. Many thousands of dollars have been appropriated for the building of houses for its employees.

Employees have been given the opportunity to purchase stock in the corporation, and thousands of them are now small stockholders.

The corporation has been tremendously successful in its business. Its products have found their way into all parts of the world. Regular dividends have been paid and a huge reserve has been built up. Enormous sums have been paid to the federal government in taxes. High wages are paid to its skilled mechanics. The average earnings of all employees during the year 1920 were approximately $7 per day.

Hours of Work

THERE ARE OTHER FACTORS, however, which need to be taken into account. First of all, let us inquire as to hours and working conditions. In his testimony before the United States Senate Investigating Committee, Judge Gary, chairman of the Steel Corporation, said: "Twenty-six and a half percent of all employees work the twelve-hour turn, and the number is 69,284."

Concerning the proportion of those actually employed in the processes of steelmaking who work the twelve-hour day, Mr. Horace B. Drury, after an extensive investigation, says:

> So far as concerns these continuous operation processes which make up the heart of the steel industry, such as the blast furnace, the open-hearth furnace, and most types of rolling mills, together with the various auxiliary departments necessary to keep these processes going and make a complete plant, the bulk of the employees work twelve hours. All the men whose presence is essential to the carrying-on of the processes, from the chemist and boss down to the lowest helper — the technical graduate, the American-born roller, and the unskilled foreigner — all these, with very few exceptions, work twelve hours. Most likely the percentage of twelve-hour workers for the whole plant — which, we are assuming, is entirely, or almost entirely, devoted to the more fundamental steel processes — will be considerably over 50 percent; in some cases two-thirds. . . .

For them and for their families, numbering perhaps a half or three-quarters of a million people, the twelve-hour day has become a fixed industrial habit, firmly entrenched in the traditions of the industry and in human lives and habits.

As to the necessity for the twelve-hour shift, Mr. Drury reminds us that in England, France, Germany, Sweden, Italy, Belgium, and Spain, it has been abandoned, and that twenty steel plants in America are now running on three shifts.

As to the increased cost of steel under an eight-hour day, Mr. Drury says: "If all the departments in a steel plant were to be changed from two to three shifts, the increase in total cost for the finished rail, bar, or plate could not, on the average, be more than about 3 percent."

As to the effects of the twelve-hour day, President Farrell said that the situation is not so bad as it is often pictured. He said that many of the men actually work only half of the time they are on duty. The other side of the case is presented by Mr. John A. Fitch in these words:

Some of the twelve-hour men, such as blooming-mill rollers, for example, are busy practically every minute of the full twelve hours of work. Others work under conditions of such strain, or under such heat, that "spell-hands" are provided. Others, as in the open-hearth furnaces, have periods of idleness between heats. When these men work, however, they work under conditions of terrific strain and in great heat.

Judge Gary said that the corporation is endeavoring to abolish the twelve-hour day, and hopes to succeed within the near future.

It does not require a vivid imagination to picture the consequences of the twelve-hour day. Twelve hours at the mill, one-half hour going to and one-half hour coming from work, one-half hour for breakfast and one-half hour for supper, eight hours sleep — add these up! A scant two hours are left for domestic duties, homelife, social and civic life, reading and study! What sort of a husband, father, and citizen is a twelve-hour worker likely to be? How much energy and interest is such a worker likely to have left for intellectual and spiritual matters?

Wages

LET US NEXT ANALYZE the wages paid by the Steel Corporation. Surely wages must be adequate if the average for all employees in 1920 was approximately $7 per day. There is no doubt that skilled labor is paid well in comparison with other industries. But how about unskilled labor? According to the Interchurch Report on the steel strike of 1919,

The annual earnings of over one-third of all productive iron and steel workers were, and had been for years, below the level set by government experts as the minimum subsistence standard for families of five. The annual earnings of 72 percent of all workers were, and had been for years, below the level set by government experts as the minimum of comfort level for families of five. This second standard being the lowest which scientists are willing to term an "American standard of living," it follows that nearly three-quarters of the steel workers could not earn enough for an American standard of living.

That was the condition in 1919. What are the facts at the present time? Three successive wage cuts during 1921 reduced the wages of unskilled labor in the employ of the Steel Corporation slightly more than 40 percent, the rate now being 30 cents per hour, with no extra pay for overtime. Eight hours a day, six days per week, at this rate amounts to $14.40 per week — $748.80 per year, if no time is lost from sickness or otherwise. Is this a partial explanation of the reluctance of the employees to give up the twelve-hour day, about which we hear so much?

Ten hours a day at this rate amounts to $18 per week, or $936 per year. Twelve hours a day at this rate amounts to $21.60 per week, or $1,123.20 per year.

The numbers of workers in normal times receiving this lowest wage is about 70,000. About 30 percent of the steel workers are unmarried. These figures mean that about 50,000 married men are unable to earn as much as $1,150 per year, even by working twelve hours per day and fifty-two weeks per year. The size of the average American family is five — father, mother, and three children under fourteen years of age. The average family of the foreign steel worker has 6.63 members.

Family Budgets

PERSONS WHO ARE INTERESTED in human and community welfare will pause to inquire as to the standard of life these thousands of families are able to maintain. Extensive investigations have been made by a number of agencies as to minimum health and decency budgets, among which are those of Professor Ogburn, Professor Chapin, the New York Factory Investigation Commission, the New York Board of Estimate. These estimates were made at different periods, but it is possible to reduce them to a common date. At the average prices prevailing in June 1918, they varied from $1,317 to $1,395 per year. According to the National Industrial Conference Board, an organization maintained by employers' associations, the cost of living in June 1918 was 52 percent higher than in July 1914. The high peak was reached in July 1920, when the increase over 1914 amounted to 104 percent. In July 1921, the increase over 1914 was 63 percent, an increase of 7 percent as compared with July 1918.

Reduced to the prices of July 1921, these minimum budgets vary from $1,410 to $1,490, the average being $1,465. In the opinion of these authorities, a family of five cannot maintain a minimum health and decency standard on less than $1,465, at July 1921 prices. During August and September 1921, there was a slight upward trend in the cost of living. At the prices of July 1921, $1,465 was the equivalent of $898 at July 1914 prices. Any reader who has had experience with family budgets during this period of high cost of living will recognize that $1,465 is an exceedingly limited annual budget for father, mother, and three children under fourteen.

Fifty thousand married workers in the employ of the United States Steel Corporation in normal times, by working twelve hours per day, six days per week, and fifty-two weeks per year, can earn only $1,125 — $340 less than this minimum health and decency budget. As a matter of fact, the actual earnings of a large proportion of these men are much less than $1,125 per year, because of lost time and unemployment.

Our next inquiry is, of course, whether or not the Steel Corporation could afford to pay its married workers a living wage. To increase the annual pay of these 50,000 married men $340 each, would require $17 million. In the scale above these men is a group of 60,000 semiskilled workers, of whom approximately 40,000 are married men. To increase the annual pay of this group the modest sum of $200 per year would require $8 million.

If the annual wages of 50,000 married men in the unskilled class were increased $340 each, and those of 40,000 married men in the semiskilled class were increased $200 each, the additional cost to the Steel Corporation would be $25 million a year.

Cost of Abolishing the Twelve-Hour Day

THIS WOULD STILL LEAVE the twelve-hour day undisturbed, however. Can the Steel Corporation afford to pay these wages for an eight-hour day?

To change from two shifts to three shifts

per day would not require a 50 percent increase in the number of employees, because eight-hour workers are more efficient than twelve-hour workers. After investigation, Mr. Drury estimated that the change to three shifts would not require more than a 35 percent increase in the working force.

With regard to the cost of changing to an eight-hour day, Mr. John A. Fitch says in the *Survey*:

> If the Steel Corporation had introduced the three-shift system in 1920 by increasing its force in the departments affected by 35 percent and had paid each man as much for eight hours as he formerly had received for twelve, the addition to the payroll would be something over $61 million. This statement is made without taking into account a probable increase in efficiency that would cut down the cost very materially.

As a matter of fact, however, the actual increase would probably be very much less than $61 million. After his investigation of the twenty steel plants in the United States which have already adopted the three-shift system, Mr. Drury says:

> There seems, in fact, to be substantial reason for believing — in view of results already accomplished in some of the plants — that, when the three-shift system once gets into fair running order, the labor cost need not be to any great degree higher than it has been under two-shift operation; and, indeed, a rather fair argument might be drawn up to show that all of the increase in labor costs might in time be wiped out.

Earnings of the Steel Corporation

Now LET US LOOK into the question of the financial ability of the corporation to stand higher wage costs. The annual report for 1920 shows that the total earnings were slightly more than $185 million, and the net income $130 million.

The first annual report of the corporation was for the year ending Dec. 31, 1902. In the eighteen years following, ending Dec.

31, 1920, the total earnings of all properties, after deducting all expenditures incident to operation, including ordinary repairs and maintenance, also interest on bonds and mortgages of the subsidiary companies, employees' bonus and pension funds, corporation excise tax, federal income tax, and excess-profits tax, amounted to slightly more than $2,817,000,000. Of this amount some $574 million were set aside for depreciation, depletion, sinking and replacement funds, leaving $2,243,000,000 as the net income for nineteen years.

Out of this net income a total of $1,002,000,000 has been paid in dividends. A regular 7 percent dividend on preferred stock has been paid each year. The dividends on common stock have been as follows: two years no dividends were paid on common stock; one year, 1¼ percent; three years, 2 percent; one year, 3 percent; one year, 3½ percent; two years, 4 percent; six years, 5 percent; one year, 8¾ percent; one year, 14 percent; one year, 18 percent — making an average for these years of a fraction less than 5 percent on common stock and 7 percent on preferred stock. Regular 5 percent interest has been paid on bonds.

The total net amount expended for additional property and construction and development work amounts to more than $991 million.

As far back as 1911, Mr. Herbert Knox Smith, United States commissioner of corporations, in referring to the Steel Corporation, said:

> During the period from April 1901 to Dec. 31, 1910, the Corporation has made an additional net investment in its properties of no less than $504,928,653. Of this amount, roughly, $435 million was virtually provided from earnings. These amounts, it should be noted, are over and above the allowance for ordinary maintenance and repairs and for actual net depreciation.

In his recent book, *United States Steel: A Corporation with a Soul* — the library copy of this book which the present writer consulted bears the inscription: "Presented by Elbert H. Gary" — Mr. Arundel Cotter says in this connection: "Practically all this gain in production has been attained by 'ploughing' profits back into additions and improvements. Practically all expenditures for extensions have been from earnings. Approximately $900 million have been expended in this manner."

At the end of 1920, the total undivided surplus of the Steel Corporation amounted to more than $523 million.

Overcapitalization

ANOTHER FACTOR must be considered. At the time of its formation the corporation was heavily overcapitalized. In this connection, Mr. Herbert Knox Smith, United States commissioner of corporations, said:

In 1901 the fair market value of its tangible property was about $700 million, slightly less than one-half of its capitalization. The figures show clearly that the entire issue of approximately $508 million of common stock of the Steel Corporation in 1901 had no physical property back of it; and also a considerable fraction, say from one-fifth to two-fifths, of the preferred stock was likewise unprotected by physical property. Even granting that there may have been a considerable value in intangible considerations, it is reasonably clear that at least the entire issue of common stock, except insofar as what may be termed "merger value" may be considered, represented nothing but "water."

In his book, Mr. Cotter admits that the common stock of the corporation "had nothing behind it but blue sky." He says that this claim "has never been denied and probably cannot be."

In spite of the fact that this issue of $508 million of common stock was all "water," regular dividends have been paid upon it. During the nineteen years the total amount of dividends paid on this "watered" common stock amounts to more than $480 million. We are not attempting to say that this

common stock is heavily watered at the present time. We are merely pointing out the fact that it has value only because more than $900 million of earnings have been "ploughed" back. If the corporation had not been heavily overcapitalized, a large part of this $900 million could have been paid out in increased wages to unskilled workers without jeopardizing the financial position of the corporation.

Summary of Earnings

LET US SUMMARIZE these figures: total earnings in eighteen years, $2,817,000,000; total net income, $2,243,000,000; total dividends, $1,002,000,000 — 7 percent on preferred stock and 5 percent on common stock, including $480 million on common stock, which was originally all "water"; 5 percent on bonds; a total of $574 million set aside for depreciation, depletion, sinking and replacement funds; a total of more than $900 million from earnings "ploughed" back in the form of new property and improvements.

The average net income of the corporation from 1901 to the end of 1920, after deducting all operating expenses, ordinary maintenance and repairs, and generous appropriations for depreciation, depletion, and sinking funds, was approximately $118 million per year. This means that the returns on the $868 million of common and preferred stock have been at the rate of approximately 13½ percent annually — this in spite of the fact that originally more than half of this stock was "pure water."

If the rate of return on capital stock had been reduced to 10 percent, the additional amount available for wages would have been more than $30 million annually; and if the rate had been reduced to 7 percent, the additional amount available for wages would have been more than $56 million annually. Either of these sums would have gone a long way toward making possible the abolition of the twelve-hour day and raising the wages of unskilled workers to a point where they could maintain a decent standard of living.

Causes of Low Wages and Long Hours

WHY, THEN, DOES THE CORPORATION continue to pay its unskilled workers about $340 a year less than a minimum health and decency standard, and in normal times compel approximately 70,000 of its employees to work the twelve-hour day?

The first reason is because it follows the usual procedure of not basing wages upon the needs of the workers but upon the market rate. The market rate is paid for labor as for any material commodity. The size of the corporation enables it to play an important part in determining the market rate. Unskilled workers can now be secured for 30 cents an hour, and therefore it is not necessary to pay a higher wage. Judge Gary told the present writer that he regards it as utterly impracticable to base wages upon family budgets. He said that wages respond to the law of supply and demand.

The second reason is that, from the viewpoint of the management, it is more important to pay regular dividends and to build up a huge reserve than it is to pay workers in excess of the market rate, even though this rate is insufficient for the maintenance of a decent or comfortable standard of life. Judge Gary said that capital invested in manufacturing properties is entitled to a return of 15 percent annually, and pointed out that the earnings of many manufacturing concerns are greatly in excess of this rate. He said that the Steel Corporation could not afford to raise wages since this would reduce the returns on capital below a fair rate, that is, below 13 to 15 percent.

The third reason is that adequate pressure has not been brought to bear upon the Steel Corporation by the workers themselves or by public opinion.

Labor Policy

WHAT IS THE LABOR POLICY of the corporation? On June 17, 1901, six weeks after the corporation was organized, the Executive Committee passed the following resolution:

That we are unalterably opposed to any extension of union labor, and advise subsidiary companies to take a firm position when these questions come up, and say that they are not going to recognize it — that is, any extension of unions in mills where they do not now exist; that great care should be used to prevent trouble, and that they promptly report and confer with this corporation.

This policy has been rigidly adhered to. "Whereas, in 1901, one-third of the corporation's mills dealt with unions, in 1919 these and all other unions had been ousted; no unions were dealt with." Judge Gary, the chairman, refused to confer with representatives of the American Federation of Labor in the face of an imminent strike, even when requested to do so by President Wilson.

On April 18, 1921, Judge Gary thus expressed his attitude toward unions:

As stated and repeated publicly, we do not combat, though we do not contract or deal with, labor unions as such. Personally, I believe they may have been justified in the long past, for I think the workmen were not always treated justly; that because of their lack of experience or otherwise, they were unable to protect themselves and therefore needed the assistance of outsiders in order to secure their rights. But whatever may have been the condition of employment in the long past, and whatever may have been the results of unionism, concerning which there is at least much uncertainty, there is at present, in the opinion of the large majority of both employers and employees, no necessity for labor unions; and that no benefit or advantage through them will accrue to anyone except the union labor leaders.

Some years ago Mr. Andrew Carnegie, in his *Gospel of Wealth,* said:

> Now the poorest laborer in America or in England, or indeed throughout the civilized world, who can handle a pick or shovel stands upon equal terms with the purchaser of his labor. He sells or withholds, as it may seem best to him. He negotiates, and thus rises to the dignity of an independent contractor. Not only has the laborer conquered his political and personal freedom, he has achieved industrial freedom as well.

It will be worthwhile to look into this matter a little further. Does the unskilled worker, with his "pick or shovel," stand upon equal terms with the United States Steel Corporation? Does he "negotiate" and has he "the dignity of an independent contractor"?

Power of the Corporation

IN ATTEMPTING TO ANSWER this question, let us consider the size and strength of the Steel Corporation. Its total assets are listed at $2,430,000,000. Its gross volume of business during 1920 was $1,755,000,000. It owns 145 steel works, approximately 800,000 acres of coal and coke properties, 993 miles of railway, 1,470 locomotives, and 112 steamers.

In addition to these huge holdings, the corporation is represented in many other industries. Some years ago, an investigating committee of the House of Representatives found that

> one or more of the directors of the Steel Corporation are also directors in terminal, steamship, express, and telegraph companies having a total capitalization of $1,271,778,890; in industrial corporations with a combined capitalization of $2,803,509,348; and in banks and trust companies having a capital, surplus, and undivided profits aggregating $3,314,-811,178; of $18,417,132,238 invested in railways of the United States, the direc-

tors of the United States Steel Corporation have a voice in the directorates of, or act as executive officers of, railroad companies with a total capitalization or bonded indebtedness of $10,365,-071,833.

The policies of the corporation are determined by a Board of Directors, composed of thirteen members in 1921, and a Finance Committee of six members. The total number of stockholders is over 100,000, but a majority of the stock is held by less than 2 percent of the stockholders. The vast majority of the stockholders take no active part whatever in determining policies. Actual control is in the hands of the thirteen directors, six of whom are also members of the Finance Committee.

The degree of this control was brought out by Judge Gary in a recent interview with Mr. Whiting Williams:

> Some years ago, in 1912, I believe, Mr. Charles Cabot of Boston arose in a stockholders' meeting and proposed a committee to study the hours of work. I asked him how many shares he had. He replied that he had ten or twenty, I have forgotten which. I reminded him that, as I held the proxies of a majority of the voting shares, I could very easily outvote his motion. Nevertheless I was glad to vote for it, and so the committee was put into action.

This concentration of control is brought out even more vividly in the address of Judge Gary at the annual meeting of the stockholders of the corporation on April 19, 1920, in these words:

> Since the United States Steel Corporation commenced business on April 1, 1901, there have been held, including the present one, nineteen regular and also ten special stockholders' meetings. I have had the honor of presiding at every one, and of voting the major part of all the outstanding capital stock. For the confidence reposed and the uniformly courteous treatment accorded, I am appreciative and grateful.

Consequences of Anti-union Policy

IN THE LIGHT OF THE FACTS obtained, the Commission of Inquiry of the Interchurch World Movement summarized these consequences as follows:

> Maintaining the nonunionism alternative entailed for the employers: (1) discharging workmen for unionism; (2) black lists; (3) espionage and the hiring of "labor detective agencies" operatives; (4) strikebreakers, principally Negroes. Maintaining the nonunionism alternative entailed for communities: (1) the abrogation of the right of assembly, the suppression of free speech, and the violation of personal rights (principally in Pennsylvania); (2) the use of state police, state troops, and (in Indiana) of the United States Army; (3) such activities on the part of constituted authorities and of the press and the pulpit as to make the workers believe that these forces oppose labor. In sum, the actually existent state of the steel industry is a state of latent war over rights of organization conceded by public opinion in other civilized countries.

Concluding Questions

THE PRESENT WRITER DESIRES to state emphatically that this article is not intended as a specific attack upon the officers and directors of the United States Steel Corporation. This discussion deals with policies and not with personalities. The facts set forth herein are used as conspicuous examples of widely accepted policies and practices in modern business life.

Let us conclude this discussion by asking five fundamental questions upon which the people of America will do well to deliberate.

First, should labor be regarded as a commodity to be purchased at the lowest possible rate, or should the cost of maintaining a decent and comfortable standard of life be used as the basis of determining the lower rates of wages?

Second, what are the costs to society of driving mothers and children under sixteen into industry because of the inadequacy of the father's wage?

Third, is invested capital ethically entitled to an annual return of 13 percent, or even 10 percent, if this involves the payment of inadequate wages to unskilled workers?

Fourth, what should be our attitude toward overcapitalization, the "watering" of stock, and the concealing of profits?

Fifth, what should be our attitude toward employers who hold in their hands an enormous concentration of economic power, and who refuse to bargain collectively with their workers through representatives of the workers' own choice?

The material and spiritual well-being of a large proportion of our population, the stability and prosperity of industry, the growth of real democracy, and the progress of mankind depend upon the answers given to such questions as these.

Frenchmen drink wine just like we used to drink water before Prohibition.

If the penalty for selling honest old beer to minors was $100 fine why 2 to 14 years in a meat grinder would be mild for a guy that sells white pop on the theory that it is a drink.

RING LARDNER

62.

Child Labor in the Anthracite Coal Mines

Although many states had child-labor laws by 1920, they were usually easy to evade, and attempts to pass federal legislation prohibiting child labor were vigorously opposed by businessmen. Supporters of such a law, which, it was said, would be destructive of individual and states' rights, were accused of being Communists and atheists. In 1922 the U.S. government published a study of child-labor practices in the anthracite coal mining region of the Shenandoah Valley in 1919; a portion of the study is reprinted here.

Source: *Child Labor and the Welfare of Children in an Anthracite Coal-Mining District,*
U.S. Department of Labor Children's Bureau Publication No. 106, Washington, 1922.

ALTHOUGH UNLIKE IN MANY WAYS, the mining towns throughout the anthracite region bear the mark of the pit, and their general problems are similar. Everywhere the industry has wrought great changes in the face of the landscape. It is a black country dominated by the great breakers which rise above the towns. The streams are black with soot and there are black piles of refuse and culm, and the men returning from work wear masks of coal dust. Trees have been cut down for mine timber, so that only stumps and scrubby bush, saplings, or misshaped trees are left. The earth mixed with the slate and coal dust is for the most part bare, and the few gardens, which demonstrate that the ground can still be cultivated, emphasize the general desolation. Throughout the region are fissures and cave-ins where the props in the mines have given way.

The district selected by the Children's Bureau in 1919 for a study of the problems of adolescent children lies in the central field in Schuylkill County, where the mountains cut the land into valleys and basins, narrow and irregular in outline. It includes the boroughs of Shenandoah, Gilberton, and Frackville and surrounding patches up to the boundary line of Mahanoy City on the east and Girardville on the west. The characteristics of the anthracite region seem especially prominent here.

Shenandoah, the business and educational center of the district, is a congested town shut in by high hills. In its setting of culm heaps there is no touch of color or beauty, but, from the hills above it, long ranges of mountains may be seen, and in the scrubby brush which covers the hills great masses of wild rhododendron blossom in the spring. The air is usually filled with the sulfurous dust which blows from the culm banks and the coal dust which comes from the breakers and the coal cars. The noise of the coal as it rushes down the breakers and of the chugging of the mine fans and other machinery is almost incessant.

For most of its length, Gilberton Borough is a single row of houses along the trolley. Here, much of the land has been undermined — a model mining town of the district. The patches which are located conveniently along the railroad and trolley lines are set amidst great heaps of culm and refuse, while the isolated ones are surrounded by brush, which is green in summer.

In all these communities the life revolves

around the mines. In Shenandoah, at the time the study was made, there were three overall, two cigar, and two shirt factories, and one mining-cap factory. These employed chiefly the wives and daughters of the mine workers. Two branch packing-houses, with their accompanying slaughter-houses and fertilizer plants, bottling works, and two lumber companies, employed a larger proportion of men. As Shenandoah is the business center of the district, there were also retail stores, bakeries, and banks, as well as freight houses and railroad and building operations, which offered some opportunities for employment.

In Frackville there were a nightdress and pajama factory and an overall factory dependent on the women and girls for a labor supply. In the patches and in Gilberton there was no possibility of employment except in the mines or in a few small retail stores. . . .

The mine workers of the United States, as a rule, have been recruited from recently arrived immigrants; and at every period the nationalities which were coming to the country in the largest numbers have tended to displace the older miners. During this process of displacement the population usually is highly complex, with a concentration of particular nationalities in individual mining towns as there has been in individual industrial towns. Thus, Poles have predominated in one, Lithuanians in another, Italians in a third, Slovaks in a fourth, and so on. . . .

By the time this study was begun, the federal child labor tax law was in effect. This act does not prohibit the employment of children but places a 10 percent tax on the net income of any mill, cannery, workshop, factory, or manufacturing establishment employing children under the age of fourteen, or children between fourteen and sixteen years of age more than eight hours a day or six days a week, or before 6 A.M. or after 7 P.M., and on any mine or quarry in which children under the age of sixteen years are employed.

Prior to 1909, Pennsylvania had prohibited the employment of children under sixteen years of age in the mines, but the only kind of certificate or work permit required was the parent's affidavit; and experience proved that in Pennsylvania, as in other states, a law of this sort did not keep children under that age out of the mines. In 1909 this law was amended so as to require documentary proof of the child's age, but it is reported that "through an unfortunate error in drafting the bill," the minimum age was reduced to fourteen years for employment inside the anthracite mines. This was amended in 1915, so that at the time the federal law went into effect no minor under sixteen years of age could be legally employed or permitted to work "in any anthracite or bituminous coal mine or in any other mine."

While the Pennsylvania act provided for the enforcement of this and all other sections of the state child labor law by the commissioner of labor and industry, the inspection of the mines, in practice, was left to the Department of Mines. The breaker boys in the anthracite coal region were not regarded as working in the mine within the meaning of the Pennsylvania law; and regular inspections of the breakers, with a view to the enforcement of the child labor law, were not being made by either department at the time this investigation was made.

Under the interpretation of the state law, followed by the state officials, children between fourteen and sixteen years of age were permitted to work on breakers, but they could not be legally so employed unless regularly issued work permits were on file and not then for more than fifty-one hours in any one week, or more than nine hours in any one day, or before 6 in the morning or after 8 in the evening.

In general the provisions of the Pennsylvania law with reference to the issuance of certificates of age were good. The law required certificates for all children between fourteen and sixteen years of age employed in any occupation except agriculture and domestic service. They were to be issued by the local school superintendent or someone authorized by him. The evidence of age required was: *(a)* transcript of birth certificate; *(b)* baptismal certificate; *(c)* passport showing age; *(d)* any other documentary record of age other than school record; *(e)* physician's certificate of evidence of age.

This system, devised for the protection of young children, did not always function in the Shenandoah district.

Some children reported that they began work with no certificate other than a "work paper" bought from the "Squire" for 50 cents. One child reported he had secured employment on a baptismal certificate when he was twelve. Another boy said that when he first applied for a "working paper," it was refused because he was under fourteen; but one was finally granted him for vacation work, and he started in a newspaper office. Here he learned to set type and liked his work. When school started, however, the newspaper refused to keep him as his employment certificate was for vacation only and he was not yet fourteen. He went to one of the mining companies, however, and was given work, though he still had no regular certificate. . . .

The proportion of children employed was, as would be expected, much larger among the older children than among the younger. . . . Seventy-two percent of the sixteen-year-old children, 58.9 percent of the fifteen-year-old, 31.6 percent of the fourteen-year-old, and 10.8 percent of the thirteen-year-old children had entered regular work. The total number of boys in the age groups studied was slightly less than the total number of girls; still, about twice as many boys as girls had entered regular work. Of the children who had entered regular employment, 896 (66.4 percent) were boys and 453 (33.6 percent) were girls. . . .

The kind of work these children did was largely determined by the industrial character of the district. The life of the district revolves around the mines, and for the boys, more than for their fathers, their place of employment was the mines. The canvass made by the Children's Bureau showed that for the district as a whole, 90.4 percent of the boys doing full-time work were in mining, as compared with 78 percent of their fathers. A larger percent of the boys with native fathers (16.6) than of the boys with foreign-born fathers (6.8 percent) were able to find some place other than the mines in which to begin work.

The fact that the breakers offered opportunities for profitable employment of young boys is the explanation of the large number of boys employed in connection with the mining of anthracite coal. It also accounts for the poorer pay and the current opinion that the breakers should be reserved for the young boys or men who had long since passed their maximum working capacity. Of the 810 boys whose first regular work was in the mines, 723 (89 percent) began as breaker boys; 422 were in this classification at the time the investigation was made.

These breakers which tower above the town of Shenandoah to the east and the south and the west are great barnlike structures filled with chutes, sliding belts, and great crushing and sorting machines. Around these machines a scaffolding was built on which the workers stand or sit. The coal is raised from the mine to the top of the breaker and dumped down the chute into a crushing machine, which breaks it into somewhat smaller lumps. These are carried along a moving belt or gravity incline on each side of which men and boys stand or sit picking out pieces of slate and any coal which has slate mixed with it. The latter is carried into another crusher, where it is broken again and then carried down chutes to be sorted further by slate pickers or by sorting machines. After the coal has been broken and cleaned of slate or other alien materials, it is sorted by being shaken through a series of screens.

The work in the breakers might be described as disagreeable but much less hazardous than underground mining. As it is not heavy and does not require skill, young boys or the older men are employed. "If you don't die, you wind up in the breakers," one man said. Another remarked, "You begin at the breaker and you end at the breaker, broken yourself." These older men and boys worked in the constant roar which the coal makes as it rushes down the chute, is broken in the crushing machines, or sorted in the shakers. Black coal dust is everywhere, covering the windows and filling the air and the lungs of the workers.

The slate is sharp so that the slate pickers often cut or bruise their hands; the coal is carried down the chute in water and this means sore and swollen hands for the pickers. The first few weeks after a boy begins work, his fingers bleed almost continuously and are called red tops by the other boys. Slate picking is not itself dangerous; the slate picker is, however, sometimes set at cleaning-up jobs, which require him to clean out shakers, the chute, or other machinery.

Sixty-three of the breaker boys included in this study were jig runners. In other words, they operated a jig machine, which has a series of sliding pans in which the coal is shaken up and down and back and forth in water so that the lighter slate is gradually shaken to the top and can be cleared from the pan so that only the coal will remain. It is a more dangerous job than slate picking and few boys are assigned to it as a first job. Usually the foreman promotes quick, bright slate pickers to be jig runners.

However, four boys were included in this study who had begun at this work.

There were thirty-three boys employed as scraper line tenders and thirty-three as shaker watchers; none of the boys began at the former and only six at the latter occupation. The shaker watcher tends the sets of screens through which the coal is sorted, and the scraper line tender operates the scrapers which carry the coal from one process to another. Of the others who were at work in the breakers, thirteen were oilers; five were repair boys; eight, known as patchers, worked on the coal cars as coupler, switchman, etc.; twenty-eight were spraggers, a highly dangerous occupation, requiring them to thrust heavy wooden sticks in between the iron spokes of the wheels of the coal cars in order to stop them; twenty-four other boys were known as laborers and were assigned to do various kinds of unskilled work. There were six who worked above ground, although not in the breakers, driving mules where the work of excavating or stripping was being done as well as fifty-nine other boys who were outside workers.

Whatever the hazards and dangers of the breakers are, underground work is much more undesirable for young boys. In addition to isolation and darkness, much more intense than that which the coal dust makes in the breakers, the . . . miner sometimes works in mud and water, sometimes stripped to the waist because of the heat, sometimes in suffocating gas and smoke.

Young boys were working daily underground at the time this investigation was made. Of those employed underground, nine were spraggers, eighteen were patchers, thirty-four were drivers, forty-seven were trapper boys, one was a fan turner, three were oilers, and eighteen were laborers. . . .

Of the 163 boys who had been underground workers, 92 began as trapper boys, which means they sat or stood in darkness or semi-darkness by a door which led from one mine chamber to another and opened

Library of Congress

Boys working in the coal mines of South Pittston, Pa.; photo by Hine

and closed the door to allow the coal cars as they came to pass through. Of the trapper boys, 17 were only thirteen and 3 were only twelve years old when they began to do regular, full-day duty at this work. An automatic contrivance which makes unnecessary the employment of either men or boys for this work is now available and has been introduced in many mines.

The boys who turned by hand the ventilating fans frequently worked on the dangerous robbing sections where the last remaining coal is being cut away from pillars and walls and where, in consequence, the roof sometimes falls in or the section is filled with a waste material known as slush. The men interviewed told of the nervous strain they experienced when they worked at robbing. Turning the fans for these workers was the first underground work for twelve boys included in this study; of that number one began when he was twelve years old, one at thirteen, four at fourteen, and six at fifteen years of age. A few other

boys were employed underground as oilers and as laborers doing a variety of work.

It is unnecessary to point out the dangers of underground work. Where electric cars are operated, where dynamiting is done, where supports give way and cave-ins and squeezes occur, and rock and coal fall, serious accidents and sudden death, more terrible to endure because of the victim's isolation and consequent distance from relief of any kind, are incidents of the occupation.

There are more fatalities in the anthracite than in the bituminous coalfields of Pennsylvania. For the three years preceding the one in which the study was made by the Children's Bureau, fatal accidents in connection with the mining of anthracite coal in Pennsylvania were 551 in 1918, 582 in 1917, and 555 in 1916. The number of serious and minor injuries was of course very much higher. While most of the accidents occur in the mines rather than on the surface where the largest numbers of young children are employed, the surface work is also hazardous. It was therefore to be expected that all kinds of injuries were reported by the boys — to the head, to internal organs, to eyes, to hands, arms, legs, back, hips, and shoulders.

Accidents that had occurred to boys in the breakers as well as underground were recounted to the Children's Bureau agents. One boy told of a friend who had dropped a new cap in the rollers and how, in trying to pull it out, his arm was caught, crushed, and twisted. The older brother of another boy, a jig runner, slipped while at work and his arm was caught in the jig and mashed. One boy told of the death of another while watching the dam beneath the breaker. He and some of the other breaker boys had helped to extricate the mutilated body from the wheels in which their companion was caught; he himself had held the bag into which the recovered parts of the dead body were put.

As reported by the boys, 42 percent of these accidents kept them from work less than two weeks; one boy was incapacitated for a year, eighteen for less than a year but more than ten weeks, while twenty-five accidents were reported to have kept the boys from work six but less than ten weeks. According to the reports made to the Children's Bureau, no compensation was paid forty-four boys who were incapacitated for a period of two weeks or more as the result of injuries received while they were employed in the mines, although the Pennsylvania Compensation Law entitled them to receive it.

Of those who received compensation, eleven boys reported that they were paid in all less than $5; nine that they received from $5 to $10; twenty-three, from $10 to $25; twelve received between $25 and $50; four, between $50 and $75; five, between $75 and $100; while three reported that they received $100 or more.

As these accidents occurred during the working life of the boys and the total number of hours the boys had worked in mining could not be learned, an accident rate could not be computed. The accident rate is, however, not as important in the case of children as in the case of adults. Dangerous work must be done, and the important question in the case of adults is whether progress is being made in reducing the hazards. Children, on the other hand, regardless of the progress that is being made in the prevention of accidents, ought not to do dangerous work at any age when they are too young to assume responsibility for their own acts. Of the 978 boys who at the time of the inquiry had been employed in the mining industry for a longer or shorter time in regular or in vacation or part-time jobs, 178 had suffered accidents.

It would be superfluous to point out that, in view of the hazards of mining, young boys should not be employed in the mines or around the breakers. Public opinion had already prohibited underground work in Pennsylvania and in most other states, and the federal government had imposed a penalty in the form of a tax if children under sixteen were employed in or about a mine. The real problem here, as in many other parts of the country, was how to secure the enforcement of the child labor laws that had been enacted.

In spite of the fact that the evil effects are swifter and more dramatic than in most other occupations in which children are employed, less public attention has been given to the problem of enforcement of child labor laws in mining than in industrial districts. This may perhaps be due to the isolation of the mines, which means that fewer people see the children as they go down in the cage in the morning and come up again at night or hear of accidents and occasional deaths among child workers in or about the mines. The fact that there is in most states divided responsibility in the enforcement of the laws regulating the employment of children in mining is doubtless also a factor.

63.

Harry Emerson Fosdick: The Fundamentalist Controversy

As the American Protestant churches tried desperately to adjust to the rapid social, economic, and political changes of the early twentieth century, a rift developed between those who felt a need for a new "social gospel" and those who would accept only the literal truths of the Bible. In 1909 twelve small pamphlets titled The Fundamentals *laid the groundwork for the movement called Fundamentalism by delineating what was felt to be the necessary beliefs of Christianity, while denouncing such ideas as Darwinism and all forms of evolutionary socialism. By the early 1920s the "modernist-fundamentalist" controversy was well under way. In 1922 the noted preacher Harry Emerson Fosdick analyzed — and criticized — the Fundamentalist position in a sermon from which the following selection is taken.*

Source: *The Christian Work*, CII, June 10, 1922, pp. 716-722: "Shall the Fundamentalists Win?"

THIS MORNING WE ARE TO THINK of the Fundamentalist controversy which threatens to divide the American churches as though already they were not sufficiently split and riven. A scene, suggestive for our thought, is depicted in the fifth chapter of the Book of the Acts, where the Jewish leaders hale before them Peter and other of the apostles because they had been preaching Jesus as the Messiah. Moreover, the Jewish leaders propose to slay them, when in opposition Gamaliel speaks: "Refrain from these men, and let them alone; for if this counsel or this work be of men, it will be overthrown; but if it is of God ye will not be able to overthrow them; lest haply ye be found even to be fighting against God." . . .

Already all of us must have heard about the people who call themselves the Fundamentalists. Their apparent intention is to drive out of the evangelical churches men and women of liberal opinions. I speak of them the more freely because there are no two denominations more affected by them than the Baptist and the Presbyterian. We should not identify the Fundamentalists with the conservatives. All Fundamentalists are conservatives, but not all conservatives are Fundamentalists. The best conservatives can often give lessons to the liberals in true liberality of spirit, but the Fundamentalist program is essentially illiberal and intolerant.

The Fundamentalists see, and they see truly, that in this last generation there have been strange new movements in Christian thought. A great mass of new knowledge has come into man's possession — new knowledge about the physical universe, its origin, its forces, its laws; new knowledge about human history and in particular about the ways in which the ancient peoples used to think in matters of religion and the methods by which they phrased and explained their spiritual experiences; and new knowledge, also, about other religions and the strangely similar ways in which men's faiths and religious practices have developed everywhere.

Now, there are multitudes of reverent Christians who have been unable to keep this new knowledge in one compartment of

Harry Emerson Fosdick during a radio broadcast

their minds and the Christian faith in another. They have been sure that all truth comes from the one God and is His revelation. Not, therefore, from irreverence or caprice or destructive zeal but for the sake of intellectual and spiritual integrity, that they might really love the Lord their God, not only with all their heart and soul and strength but with all their mind, they have been trying to see this new knowledge in terms of the Christian faith and to see the Christian faith in terms of this new knowledge.

Doubtless they have made many mistakes. Doubtless there have been among them reckless radicals gifted with intellectual ingenuity but lacking spiritual depth. Yet the enterprise itself seems to them indispensable to the Christian Church. The new knowledge and the old faith cannot be left antagonistic or even disparate, as though a man on Saturday could use one set of regulative ideas for his life and on Sunday could change gear to another altogether. We must

be able to think our modern life clear through in Christian terms, and to do that we also must be able to think our Christian faith clear through in modern terms.

There is nothing new about the situation. It has happened again and again in history, as, for example, when the stationary earth suddenly began to move and the universe that had been centered in this planet was centered in the sun around which the planets whirled. Whenever such a situation has arisen, there has been only one way out — the new knowledge and the old faith had to be blended in a new combination. Now, the people in this generation who are trying to do this are the liberals, and the Fundamentalists are out on a campaign to shut against them the doors of the Christian fellowship. Shall they be allowed to succeed?

It is interesting to note where the Fundamentalists are driving in their stakes to mark out the deadline of doctrine around the church, across which no one is to pass except on terms of agreement. They insist that we must all believe in the historicity of certain special miracles, preeminently the virgin birth of our Lord; that we must believe in a special theory of inspiration — that the original documents of the Scripture, which of course we no longer possess, were inerrantly dictated to men a good deal as a man might dictate to a stenographer; that we must believe in a special theory of the Atonement — that the blood of our Lord, shed in a substitutionary death, placates an alienated Deity and makes possible welcome for the returning sinner; and that we must believe in the second coming of our Lord upon the clouds of heaven to set up a millennium here, as the only way in which God can bring history to a worthy denouement. Such are some of the stakes which are being driven to mark a deadline of doctrine around the church.

If a man is a genuine liberal, his primary protest is not against holding these opinions, although he may well protest against their being considered the fundamentals of Christianity. This is a free country and anybody has a right to hold these opinions or any others if he is sincerely convinced of them. The question is — Has anybody a right to deny the Christian name to those who differ with him on such points and to shut against them the doors of the Christian fellowship? The Fundamentalists say that this must be done. In this country and on the foreign field they are trying to do it. They have actually endeavored to put on the statute books of a whole state binding laws against teaching modern biology. If they had their way, within the church, they would set up in Protestantism a doctrinal tribunal more rigid than the pope's.

In such an hour, delicate and dangerous, when feelings are bound to run high, I plead this morning the cause of magnanimity and liberality and tolerance of spirit. I would, if I could reach their ears, say to the Fundamentalists about the liberals what Gamaliel said to the Jews, "Refrain from these men and let them alone; for if this counsel or this work be of men, it will be everthrown; but if it is of God ye will not be able to overthrow them; lest haply ye be found even to be fighting against God."

That we may be entirely candid and concrete and may not lose ourselves in any fog of generalities, let us this morning take two or three of these Fundamentalist items and see with reference to them what the situation is in the Christian churches. Too often we preachers have failed to talk frankly enough about the differences of opinion which exist among evangelical Christians, although everybody knows that they are there. Let us face this morning some of the differences of opinion with which somehow we must deal.

We may well begin with the vexed and mooted question of the virgin birth of our Lord. I know people in the Christian churches, ministers, missionaries, laymen, devoted lovers of the Lord and servants of the Gospel, who, alike as they are in their personal devotion to the Master, hold quite different points of view about a matter like the virgin birth. Here, for example, is one point of view: that the virgin birth is to be accepted as historical fact; it actually happened; there was no other way for a personality like the Master to come into this world except by a special biological miracle. That is one point of view, and many are the gracious and beautiful souls who hold it. But side by side with them in the evangelical churches is a group of equally loyal and reverent people who would say that the virgin birth is not to be accepted as an historic fact. . . . So far from thinking that they have given up anything vital in the New Testament's attitude toward Jesus, these Christians remember that the two men who contributed most to the Church's thought of the divine meaning of the Christ were Paul and John, who never even distantly allude to the virgin birth.

Here in the Christian churches are these two groups of people and the question which the Fundamentalists raise is this — Shall one of them throw the other out? Has intolerance any contribution to make to this situation? Will it persuade anybody of anything? Is not the Christian Church large enough to hold within her hospitable fellowship people who differ on points like this and agree to differ until the fuller truth be manifested? The Fundamentalists say not. They say the liberals must go. Well, if the Fundamentalists should succeed, then out of the Christian Church would go some of the best Christian life and consecration of this generation — multitudes of men and women, devout and reverent Christians, who need the church and whom the church needs.

Consider another matter on which there is a sincere difference of opinion between evangelical Christians: the inspiration of the Bible. One point of view is that the original documents of the Scripture were inerrantly dictated by God to men. Whether we deal with the story of creation or the list of the dukes of Edom or the narratives of Solomon's reign or the Sermon on the Mount or the thirteenth chapter of First Corinthians, they all came in the same way, and they all came as no other book ever came. They were inerrantly dictated; everything there — scientific opinions, medical theories, historical judgments, as well as spiritual insight — is infallible. That is one idea of the Bible's inspiration. But side by side with those who hold it, lovers of the Book as much as they, are multitudes of people who never think about the Bible so. Indeed, that static and mechanical theory of inspiration seems to them a positive peril to the spiritual life. . . .

Here in the Christian Church today are these two groups, and the question which the Fundamentalists have raised is this — Shall one of them drive the other out? Do we think the cause of Jesus Christ will be furthered by that? If He should walk through the ranks of his congregation this morning, can we imagine Him claiming as His own those who hold one idea of inspiration and sending from Him into outer darkness those who hold another? You cannot fit the Lord Christ into that Fundamentalist mold. The church would better judge His judgment. For in the Middle West the Fundamentalists have had their way in some communities and a Christian minister tells us the consequences. He says that the educated people are looking for their religion outside the churches.

Consider another matter upon which there is a serious and sincere difference of opinion between evangelical Christians: the second coming of our Lord. The second coming was the early Christian phrasing of hope. No one in the ancient world had ever

thought, as we do, of development, progress, gradual change as God's way of working out His will in human life and institutions. They thought of human history as a series of ages succeeding one another with abrupt suddenness. The Graeco-Roman world gave the names of metals to the ages — gold, silver, bronze, iron. The Hebrews had their ages, too — the original Paradise in which man began, the cursed world in which man now lives, the blessed Messianic kingdom someday suddenly to appear on the clouds of heaven. It was the Hebrew way of expressing hope for the victory of God and righteousness. When the Christians came they took over that phrasing of expectancy and the New Testament is aglow with it. The preaching of the apostles thrills with the glad announcement, "Christ is coming!"

In the evangelical churches today there are differing views of this matter. One view is that Christ is literally coming, externally, on the clouds of heaven, to set up His kingdom here. I never heard that teaching in my youth at all. It has always had a new resurrection when desperate circumstances came and man's only hope seemed to lie in divine intervention. It is not strange, then, that during these chaotic, catastrophic years there has been a fresh rebirth of this old phrasing of expectancy. "Christ is coming!" seems to many Christians the central message of the Gospel. In the strength of it some of them are doing great service for the world. But, unhappily, many so overemphasize it that they outdo anything the ancient Hebrews or the ancient Christians ever did. They sit still and do nothing and expect the world to grow worse and worse until He comes.

Side by side with these to whom the second coming is a literal expectation, another group exists in the evangelical churches. They, too, say, "Christ is coming!" They say it with all their hearts; but they are not thinking of an external arrival on the clouds. They have assimilated as part of the divine revelation the exhilarating insight which these recent generations have given to us, that development is God's way of working out His will. . . .

And these Christians, when they say that Christ is coming, mean that, slowly it may be, but surely, His will and principles will be worked out by God's grace in human life and institutions, until "He shall see of the travail of His soul and shall be satisfied."

These two groups exist in the Christian churches and the question raised by the Fundamentalists is — Shall one of them drive the other out? Will that get us anywhere? Multitudes of young men and women at this season of the year are graduating from our schools of learning, thousands of them Christians who may make us older ones ashamed by the sincerity of their devotion to God's will on earth. They are not thinking in ancient terms that leave ideas of progress out. They cannot think in those terms. There could be no greater tragedy than that the Fundamentalists should shut the door of the Christian fellowship against such.

I do not believe for one moment that the Fundamentalists are going to succeed. Nobody's intolerance can contribute anything to the solution of the situation which we have described. If, then, the Fundamentalists have no solution of the problem, where may we expect to find it? In two concluding comments let us consider our reply to that inquiry.

The first element that is necessary is a spirit of tolerance and Christian liberty. When will the world learn that intolerance solves no problems? This is not a lesson which the Fundamentalists alone need to learn; the liberals also need to learn it. Speaking, as I do, from the viewpoint of liberal opinions, let me say that if some young, fresh mind here this morning is holding new ideas, has fought his way through, it may be by intellectual and spiritual struggle, to novel positions, and is tempted to be intolerant about old opinions, offensively to condescend to those who hold them and to be harsh in judgment on them, he may well remember that people who held those old opinions have given the world some of the noblest character and the most rememberable service that it ever has been blessed with, and that we of the younger generation will prove our case best, not by controversial intolerance, but by producing, with our new opinions, something of the depth and strength, nobility and beauty of character that in other times were associated with other thoughts. It was a wise liberal, the most adventurous man of his day — Paul the Apostle — who said, "Knowledge puffeth up, but love buildeth up."

Nevertheless, it is true that just now the Fundamentalists are giving us one of the worst exhibitions of bitter intolerance that the churches of this country have ever seen. As one watches them and listens to them he remembers the remark of General Armstrong of Hampton Institute, "Cantankerousness is worse than heterodoxy." There are many opinions in the field of modern controversy concerning which I am not sure whether they are right or wrong, but there is one thing I am sure of: courtesy and kindliness and tolerance and humility and fairness are right. Opinions may be mistaken; love never is.

As I plead thus for an intellectually hospitable, tolerant, liberty-loving church, I am, of course, thinking primarily about this new generation. We have boys and girls growing up in our homes and schools, and because we love them we may well wonder about the church which will be waiting to receive them. Now, the worst kind of church that can possibly be offered to the allegiance of the new generation is an intolerant church. Ministers often bewail the fact that young people turn from religion to science for the regulative ideas of their lives. But this is easily explicable.

Science treats a young man's mind as though it were really important. A scientist says to a young man, "Here is the universe challenging our investigation. Here are the truths which we have seen, so far. Come, study with us! See what we already have seen and then look further to see more, for science is an intellectual adventure for the truth." Can you imagine any man who is worthwhile turning from that call to the church if the church seems to him to say, "Come, and we will feed you opinions from a spoon. No thinking is allowed here except such as brings you to certain specified, predetermined conclusions. These prescribed opinions we will give you in advance of your thinking; now think, but only so as to reach these results."

My friends, nothing in all the world is so much worth thinking of as God, Christ, the Bible, sin and salvation, the divine purposes for humankind, life everlasting. But you cannot challenge the dedicated thinking of this generation to these sublime themes upon any such terms as are laid down by an intolerant church.

The second element which is needed if we are to reach a happy solution of this problem is a clear insight into the main issues of modern Christianity and a sense of penitent shame that the Christian Church should be quarreling over little matters when the world is dying of great needs. If,

during the war, when the nations were wrestling upon the very brink of hell and at times all seemed lost, you chanced to hear two men in an altercation about some minor matter of sectarian denominationalism, could you restrain your indignation? You said, "What can you do with folks like this who, in the face of colossal issues, play with the tiddledywinks and peccadillos of religion?" So, now, when from the terrific questions of this generation one is called away by the noise of this Fundamentalist controversy, he thinks it almost unforgivable that men should tithe mint and anise and cummin, and quarrel over them, when the world is perishing for the lack of the weightier matters of the law, justice, and mercy, and faith. . . .

The present world situation smells to heaven! And now, in the presence of colossal problems, which must be solved in Christ's name and for Christ's sake, the Fundamentalists propose to drive out from the Christian churches all the consecrated souls who do not agree with their theory of inspiration. What immeasurable folly!

Well, they are not going to do it; certainly not in this vicinity. I do not even know in this congregation whether anybody has been tempted to be a Fundamentalist. Never in this church have I caught one accent of intolerance. God keep us always so and ever increasing areas of the Christian fellowship; intellectually hospitable, open-minded, liberty-loving, fair, tolerant, not with the tolerance of indifference, as though we did not care about the faith, but because always our major emphasis is upon the weightier matters of the law.

As a career, the business of an orthodox preacher is about as successful as that of a celluloid dog chasing an asbestos cat through Hell.

ELBERT HUBBARD, *Roycroft Dictionary and Book of Epigrams*, 1923

64.

D. H. Lawrence: Benjamin Franklin

D. H. Lawrence's Studies in Classic American Literature *was begun in 1915 but not completed until 1922, the year in which — in September — he came to America to remain, mostly in New Mexico, except for trips of varying length to other parts of the world, until 1925. The work has been highly praised — Edmund Wilson called it "one of the few first-rate books ever to have been written on the subject." Lawrence brought to his task, which was to "read our books for their meaning in the life of the Western world as a whole" (as Wilson put it), an unparalleled energy and the insight of a professional novelist. The selection below comprises portions of the first study in the book, a withering critique of Benjamin Franklin and, by extension, of the prudence combined with prudery that Lawrence felt Americans had inherited from Franklin. Later studies in the book, particularly the one of Walt Whitman, soften the indictment somewhat, but the volume is best known for its iconoclastic view of some of America's best-loved writers.*

Source: *Studies in Classic American Literature,* London, 1924, pp. 15-27.

THE PERFECTIBILITY OF MAN! Ah heaven, what a dreary theme! The perfectibility of the Ford car! The perfectibility of which man? I am many men. Which of them are you going to perfect? I am not a mechanical contrivance.

Education! Which of the various me's do you propose to educate, and which do you propose to suppress?

Anyhow, I defy you. I defy you, oh society, to educate me or to suppress me, according to your dummy standards.

The ideal man! And which is he, if you please? Benjamin Franklin or Abraham Lincoln? The ideal man! Roosevelt or Porfirio Díaz?

There are other men in me, besides this patient ass who sits here in a tweed jacket. What am I doing, playing the patient ass in a tweed jacket? Who am I talking to? Who are you, at the other end of this patience?

Who are you? How many selves have you? And which of these selves do you want to be?

Is Yale College going to educate the self that is in the dark of you, or Harvard College?

The ideal self! Oh, but I have a strange and fugitive self shut out and howling like a wolf or a coyote under the ideal windows. See his red eyes in the dark? This is the self who is coming into his own.

The perfectibility of man, dear God! When every man as long as he remains alive is in himself a multitude of conflicting men. Which of these do you choose to perfect, at the expense of every other?

Old Daddy Franklin will tell you. He'll rig him up for you, the pattern American. Oh, Franklin was the first downright American. He knew what he was about, the sharp little man. He set up the first dummy American.

At the beginning of his career this cunning little Benjamin drew up for himself a creed that should "satisfy the professors of every religion, but shock none."

Now wasn't that a real American thing to do?

"That there is One God, who made all things."

(But Benjamin made Him.)

"That He governs the world by His Providence."

(Benjamin knowing all about Providence.)

"That He ought to be worshiped with adoration, prayer, and thanksgiving."

(Which cost nothing.)

"But ——" But me no buts, Benjamin, saith the Lord.

"But that the most acceptable service of God is doing good to men."

(God having no choice in the matter.)

"That the soul is immortal."

(You'll see why, in the next clause.)

"And that God will certainly reward virtue and punish vice, either here or hereafter."

Now if Mr. Andrew Carnegie, or any other millionaire, had wished to invent a God to suit his ends, he could not have done better. Benjamin did it for him in the 18th century. God is the supreme servant of men who want to get on, to *produce*. Providence. The provider. The heavenly storekeeper. The everlasting Wanamaker.

And this is all the God the grandsons of the Pilgrim Fathers had left. Aloft on a pillar of dollars.

"That the soul is immortal."

The trite way Benjamin says it!

But man has a soul, though you can't locate it either in his purse or his pocketbook or his heart or his stomach or his head. The *wholeness* of a man is his soul. Not merely that nice little comfortable bit which Benjamin marks out.

It's a queer thing is a man's soul. It is the whole of him. Which means it is the unknown him, as well as the known. It seems to me just funny, professors and Benjamins fixing the functions of the soul. Why the

soul of man is a vast forest, and all Benjamin intended was a neat back garden. And we've all got to fit into his kitchen garden scheme of things. Hail Columbia!

The soul of man is a dark forest. The Hercynian Wood that scared the Romans so, and out of which came the white-skinned hordes of the next civilization.

Who knows what will come out of the soul of man? The soul of man is a dark vast forest, with wildlife in it. Think of Benjamin fencing it off!

Oh, but Benjamin fenced a little tract that he called the soul of man, and proceeded to get it into cultivation. Providence, forsooth! And they think that bit of barbed wire is going to keep us in pound for ever? More fools they.

This is Benjamin's barbed wire fence. He made himself a list of virtues, which he trotted inside like a gray nag in a paddock.

1
TEMPERANCE

Eat not to fullness; drink not to elevation.

2
SILENCE

Speak not but what may benefit others or yourself; avoid trifling conversation.

3
ORDER

Let all your things have their places; let each part of your business have its time.

4
RESOLUTION

Resolve to perform what you ought; perform without fail what you resolve.

5
FRUGALITY

Make no expense but to do good to others or yourself — *i.e.*, waste nothing.

6
INDUSTRY

Lose no time, be always employed in something useful; cut off all unnecessary action.

7
SINCERITY

Use no hurtful deceit; think innocently and justly, and, if you speak, speak accordingly.

8
JUSTICE

Wrong none by doing injuries, or omitting the benefits that are your duty.

9
MODERATION

Avoid extremes, forbear resenting injuries as much as you think they deserve.

10
CLEANLINESS

Tolerate no uncleanliness in body, clothes, or habitation.

11
TRANQUILLITY

Be not disturbed at trifles, or at accidents common or unavoidable.

12
CHASTITY

Rarely use venery but for health and offspring, never to dullness, weakness, or the injury of your own or another's peace or reputation.

13
HUMILITY

Imitate Jesus and Socrates.

A Quaker friend told Franklin that he, Benjamin, was generally considered proud, so Benjamin put in the humility touch as an afterthought. The amusing part is the sort of humility it displays. "Imitate Jesus and Socrates," and mind you don't outshine either of these two. One can just imagine Socrates and Alcibiades roaring in their cups over Philadelphian Benjamin, and Jesus looking at him a little puzzled, and murmuring: "Aren't you wise in your own conceit, Ben?"

"Henceforth be masterless," retorts Ben. "Be ye each one his own master unto himself, and don't let even the Lord put His spoke in." "Each man his own master" is but a puffing up of masterlessness.

Well, the first of Americans practised this enticing list with assiduity, setting a national example. He had the virtues in columns, and gave himself good and bad marks according as he thought his behavior deserved. Pity these conduct charts are lost to us. He only remarks that order was his stumbling block. He could not learn to be neat and tidy.

Isn't it nice to have nothing worse to confess?

He was a little model, was Benjamin. Doctor Franklin. Snuff-colored little man! Immortal soul and all!

The immortal soul part was a sort of cheap insurance policy.

Benjamin had no concern, really, with the immortal soul. He was too busy with social man.

1. He swept and lighted the streets of young Philadelphia.

2. He invented electrical appliances.

3. He was the center of a moralizing club in Philadelphia, and he wrote the moral humorisms of Poor Richard.

4. He was a member of all the important councils of Philadelphia, and then of the American colonies.

5. He won the cause of American independence at the French court, and was the economic father of the United States.

Now what more can you want of a man? And yet he is *infra dig.,* even in Philadelphia.

I admire him. I admire his sturdy courage first of all, then his sagacity, then his glimpsing into the thunders of electricity, then his common sense humor. All the qualities of a great man, and never more than a great citizen. Middle-sized, sturdy, snuff-colored Doctor Franklin, one of the soundest citizens that ever trod or "used venery."

I do not like him.

And, by the way, I always thought books of venery were about hunting deer.

There is a certain earnest naïveté about him. Like a child. And like a little old man. He has again become as a little child, always as wise as his grandfather, or wiser.

Perhaps, as I say, the most complete citizen that ever "used venery."

Printer, philosopher, scientist, author, and patriot, impeccable husband and citizen, why isn't he an archetype?

Pioneer, Oh Pioneers! Benjamin was one of the greatest pioneers of the United States. Yet we just can't do with him.

What's wrong with him then? Or what's wrong with us?

I can remember, when I was a little boy, my father used to buy a scrubby yearly almanac with the sun and moon and stars on the cover. And it used to prophesy bloodshed and famine. But also crammed in corners it had little anecdotes and humorisms, with a moral tag. And I used to have my little priggish laugh at the women who counted her chickens before they were hatched and so forth, and I was convinced that honesty was the best policy, also a little priggishly. The author of these bits was Poor Richard, and Poor Richard was Benjamin Franklin, writing in Philadelphia well over a hundred years before.

And probably I haven't got over those Poor Richard tags yet. I rankle still with them. They are thorns in young flesh.

Because, although I still believe that honesty is the best policy, I dislike policy altogether; though it is just as well not to count your chickens before they are hatched, it's still more hateful to count them with gloating when they *are* hatched. It has taken me many years and countless smarts to get out of that barbed wire moral enclosure that Poor Richard rigged up. Here am I now in tatters and scratched to ribbons, sitting in the middle of Benjamin's America looking at the barbed wire, and the fat sheep crawling under the fence to get fat outside, and the watchdogs yelling at the gate lest by chance anyone should get out by the proper exit. Oh America! Oh Benjamin! And I just utter a long loud curse against Benjamin and the American corral.

Moral America! Most moral Benjamin. Sound, satisfied Ben!

He had to go to the frontiers of his state to settle some disturbance among the Indians. On this occasion he writes:

"We found that they had made a great bonfire in the middle of the square; they were all drunk, men and women quarrelling and fighting. Their dark-colored bodies, half-naked, seen only by the gloomy light of the bonfire, running after and beating one another with firebrands, accompanied by their horrid yellings, formed a scene the most resembling our ideas of hell that could well be imagined. There was no appeasing the tumult, and we retired to our lodging. At midnight a number of them came thundering at our door, demanding more rum, of which we took no notice.

"The next day, sensible they had misbehaved in giving us that disturbance, they sent three of their counselors to make their apology. The orator acknowledged the fault, but laid it upon the rum, and then endeavored to excuse the rum by saying: 'The Great Spirit, who made all things, made everything for some use; and whatever he designed anything for, that use it should always be put to. Now, when he had made the rum, he said: "Let this be for the Indians to get drunk with." And it must be so.'

"And, indeed, if it be the design of Providence to extirpate these savages in order to make room for the cultivators of the earth, it seems not improbable that rum may be the appointed means. It has already annihilated all the tribes who formerly inhabited all the seacoast. . . ."

This, from the good doctor with such suave complacency, is a little disenchanting. Almost too good to be true.

But there you are! The barbed wire fence. "Extirpate these savages in order to make room for the cultivators of the earth." Oh, Benjamin Franklin! He even "used venery" as a cultivator of seed.

Cultivate the earth, ye gods! The Indians did that, as much as they needed. And they left off there. Who built Chicago? Who cultivated the earth until it spawned Pittsburgh, Pa.?

The moral issue! Just look at it! Cultivation included. If it's a mere choice of *Kultur* or cultivation, I give it up.

Which brings us right back to our question, what's wrong with Benjamin that we can't stand him? Or else, what's wrong with us that we find fault with such a paragon?

Man is a moral animal. All right. I am a moral animal. And I'm going to remain such. I'm not going to be turned into a virtuous little automaton as Benjamin would have me. "This is good, that is bad. Turn the little handle and let the good tap flow," saith Benjamin, and all America with him. "But first of all extirpate those savages who are always turning on the bad tap."

Here's my creed, against Benjamin's. This is what I believe:

"*That I am I.*"

"*That my soul is a dark forest.*"

"*That my known self will never be more than a little clearing in the forest.*"

"*That gods, strange gods, come forth from the forest into the clearing of my known self, and then go back.*"

"*That I must have the courage to let them come and go.*"

"*That I will never let mankind put anything over me, but that I will try always to recognize and submit to the gods in me and the gods in other men and women.*"

There is my creed. He who runs may read. He who prefers to crawl, or to go by gasoline, can call it rot.

Then for a "list." It is rather fun to play at Benjamin.

1
TEMPERANCE

Eat and carouse with Bacchus, or munch dry bread with Jesus, but don't sit down without one of the gods.

2
SILENCE

Be still when you have nothing to say; when genuine passion moves you, say what you've got to say, and say it hot.

3
ORDER

Know that you are responsible to the gods inside you and to the men in whom the gods are manifest. Recognize your superiors and your inferiors according to the gods. This is the root of all order.

4
RESOLUTION

Resolve to abide by your own deepest promptings and to sacrifice the smaller thing to the greater. Kill when you must, and be killed the same: the *must* coming from the gods inside you or from the men in whom you recognize the Holy Ghost.

5
FRUGALITY

Demand nothing; accept what you see fit. Don't waste your pride or squander your emotion.

6
INDUSTRY

Lose no time with ideals; serve the Holy Ghost; never serve mankind.

7
SINCERITY

To be sincere is to remember that I am I, and that the other man is not me.

8
JUSTICE

The only justice is to follow the sincere intuition of the soul, angry or gentle. Anger is just, and pity is just, but judgment is never just.

9
MODERATION

Beware of absolutes. There are many gods.

10
CLEANLINESS

Don't be too clean. It impoverishes the blood.

11
TRANQUILLITY

The soul has many motions, many gods come and go. Try and find your deepest issue, in every confusion, and abide by that. Obey the man in whom you recognize the Holy Ghost; command when your honor comes to command.

12
CHASTITY

Never "use" venery at all. Follow your passional impulse, if it be answered in the other being; but never have any motive in mind, neither offspring nor health nor even pleasure, nor even service. Only know that "venery" is of the great gods. An offering up of yourself to the very great gods, the dark ones, and nothing else.

13
HUMILITY

See all men and women according to the Holy Ghost that is within them. Never yield before the barren.

There's my list. I have been trying dimly to realize it for a long time, and only America and old Benjamin have at last goaded me into trying to formulate it.

And now I, at least, know why I can't stand Benjamin. He tries to take away my wholeness and my dark forest, my freedom. For how can any man be free without an illimitable background? And Benjamin tries to shove me into a barbed wire paddock and make me grow potatoes or Chicagoes.

And how can I be free, without gods that come and go? But Benjamin won't let anything exist except my useful fellowmen, and I'm sick of them; as for his Godhead, his Providence, He is Head of nothing except a vast heavenly store that keeps every imaginable line of goods, from victrolas to cat-o'-nine-tails.

And how can any man be free without a soul of his own, that he believes in and won't sell at any price? But Benjamin doesn't let me have a soul of my own. He says I am nothing but a servant of mankind — galley slave I call it — and if I don't get my wages here below — that is, if Mr. Pierpont Morgan or Mr. Nosey Hebrew or the grand United States government, the great US, US or SOMEOFUS, manages to scoop in my bit, along with their lump — why, never mind, I shall get my wages HEREAFTER.

Oh Benjamin! Oh Binjum! You do NOT suck me in any longer.

And why, oh why should the snuff-colored little trap have wanted to take us all in? Why did he do it?

Out of sheer human cussedness, in the

first place. We do all like to get things inside a barbed wire corral. Especially our fellowmen. We love to round them up inside the barbed wire enclosure of FREEDOM, and make 'em work. *"Work, you free jewel, Work!"* shouts the liberator, cracking his whip. Benjamin, I will not work. I do not choose to be a free democrat. I am absolutely a servant of my own Holy Ghost.

Sheer cussedness! But there was as well the salt of a subtler purpose. Benjamin was just in his eyeholes — to use an English vulgarism, meaning he was just delighted — when he was at Paris judiciously milking money out of the French monarchy for the overthrow of all monarchy. If you want to ride your horse to somewhere you must put a bit in his mouth. And Benjamin wanted to ride his horse so that it would upset the whole applecart of the old masters. He wanted the whole European applecart upset. So he had to put a strong bit in the mouth of his ass.

"Henceforth be masterless."

That is, he had to break-in the human ass completely, so that much more might be broken, in the long run. For the moment it was the British government that had to have a hole knocked in it. The first real hole it ever had: the breach of the American rebellion.

Benjamin, in his sagacity, knew that the breaking of the Old World was a long process. In the depths of his own under-consciousness he hated England, he hated Europe, he hated the whole corpus of the European being. He wanted to be American. But you can't change your nature and mode of consciousness like changing your shoes. It is a gradual shedding. Years must go by and centuries must elapse before you have finished. Like a son escaping from the domination of his parents. The escape is not just one rupture. It is a long and half-secret process.

So with the American. He was a European when he first went over the Atlantic. He is in the main a recreant European still.

From Benjamin Franklin to Woodrow Wilson may be a long stride, but it is a stride along the same road. There is no new road. The same old road, become dreary and futile. Theoretic and materialistic.

Why then did Benjamin set up this dummy of a perfect citizen as a pattern to America? Of course, he did it in perfect good faith, as far as he knew. He thought it simply was the true ideal. But what we *think* we do is not very important. We never really know what we are doing. Either we are materialistic instruments, like Benjamin, or we move in the gesture of creation, from our deepest self, usually unconscious. We are only the actors, we are never wholly the authors of our own deeds or works. IT is the author, the unknown inside us or outside us. The best we can do is to try to hold ourselves in unison with the deeps which are inside us. And the worst we can do is to try to have things our own way, when we run counter to IT, and in the long run get our knuckles rapped for our presumption.

So Benjamin contriving money out of the court of France. He was contriving the first steps of the overthrow of all Europe, France included. You can never have a new thing without breaking an old. Europe happens to be the old thing. America, unless the people in America assert themselves too much in opposition to the inner gods, should be the new thing. The new thing is the death of the old. But you can't cut the throat of an epoch. You've got to steal the life from it through several centuries.

And Benjamin worked for this both directly and indirectly. Directly, at the court of France, making a small but very dangerous hole in the side of England, through which hole Europe has by now almost bled to death. And indirectly in Philadelphia, setting up this unlovely, snuff-colored little ideal, or automaton, of a pattern American. The pattern American, this dry, moral, utilitarian little democrat, has done more to ruin the old Europe than any Russian nihilist. He has done it by slow attrition, like a son who has stayed at home and obeyed his parents, all the while silently hating their authority, and silently, in his soul, destroying not only their authority but their whole existence. For the American spiritually stayed at home in Europe. The spiritual home of America was, and still is, Europe. This is the galling bondage, in spite of several billions of heaped-up gold. Your heaps of gold are only so many muck-heaps, America, and will remain so till you become a reality to yourselves.

All this Americanizing and mechanizing has been for the purpose of overthrowing the past. And now look at America, tangled in her own barbed wire and mastered by her own machines. Absolutely got down by her own barbed wire of shalt-nots, and shut up fast in her own "productive" machines like millions of squirrels running in millions of cages. It is just a farce.

Now is your chance, Europe. Now let hell loose and get your own back, and paddle your own canoe on a new sea, while clever America lies on her muck-heaps of gold, strangled in her own barbed wire of shalt-not ideals and shalt-not moralisms. While she goes out to work like millions of squirrels in millions of cages. Production!

Let hell loose, and get your own back, Europe!

65.

GEORGE JEAN NATHAN: The Native Theater

George Jean Nathan is probably best known as an editor with H. L. Mencken of the Smart Set *(1914-1923) and of the* American Mercury *(1924-1930), periodicals in which the two iconoclasts printed caustic commentaries by themselves and others on various aspects of the American scene. Nathan was also a drama critic of great importance and influence, publishing more than thirty volumes of lively essays on theatrical and other subjects. The following selection, a chapter in Harold Stearns's slashing indictment of American culture,* Civilization in the United States *(1922), is typical both of the critical attitude of the collection and of Nathan's general view of the subject. His remarks about the banality of the American theater in the early Twenties are particularly interesting in that they antedate by forty years the dire prophecies of doom that were so common in the early Sixties.*

Source: *Civilization in the United States,* Harold E. Stearns, ed., New York, 1922, pp. 243-253.

OF THE PERCEPTIBLE gradual improvement in the American popular taste so far as the arts are concerned, the theater as we currently engage it offers, comparatively, the least evidence. The best selling E. Phillips Oppenheims, Robert W. Chamberses, and Eleanor H. Porters of yesterday have given considerable ground to Wharton and Bennett, to Hergesheimer and Wells. The audiences in support of Stokowski, the Flonzaley Quartette, the Philharmonic, the great piano and violin virtuosos, and the recognized singers are yearly augmented. Fine painting and fine sculpture find an increasing sober appreciation. The circulation of *Munsey's Magazine* falls, and that of the *At-*

lantic Monthly rises. But the best play of an American theatrical season, say a *Beyond the Horizon*, has still to struggle for full breath, while across the street the receipts of some *Ladies' Night, Gold Diggers,* or *Bat,* running on without end, mount to the half-million mark.

If one speaks of the New York theater as the American theater, one speaks with an exaggerated degree of critical charity, for the New York theater — so far as there is any taste in the American theater — is the native theater at its fullest flower. Persons insufficiently acquainted with the theater have a fondness for controverting this, but the bookkeeping departments offer concrete testimony that, if good drama is supported at all, it is supported in the metropolitan theater, not in the so-called road theater. The New York theater supports an American playwright like Booth Tarkington when he does his best in *Clarence*, where the road theater supports him only when he does his worst, as in *Mister Antonio*. The New York theater, these same financial records prove, supports Shaw, O'Neill, Galsworthy, Bahr, and others of their kind, at least in sufficient degree to permit them to pay their way, where the theater of Philadelphia, Boston, Cleveland, Chicago, St. Louis, Baltimore, and Pittsburgh spells failure for them.

Save it be played by an actor or actress of great popular favor, a first-rate piece of dramatic writing has today hardly a chance for success outside of New York. These other cities of America, though they are gradually reading better books and patronizing better music and finer musicians, are almost drama-deaf. "There is, in New York," the experienced Mr. William A. Brady has said to me, "an audience of at least 15,000 for any really good play. That isn't a large audience; it won't turn the play into a profitable theatrical venture; but it is a damned sight larger audience than you'll be able to find in any other American city." Let the native sons of the cities thus cruelly ma-

ligned, before they emit their habitual bellows of protest, consider, once they fared forth from New York, the fate of nine-tenths of the first-rate plays produced in the American theater without the hocus-pocus of fancy box-office "stars" during the last ten years.

The theatrical taste of America at the present time, outside of the metropolis, is demonstrated by the box-office returns to be one that venerates the wall-motto *opera* of Mr. William Hodge and the spectacular imbecilities of Mr. Richard Walton Tully above the finest work of the best of its native dramatists like O'Neill, and above the finest work of the best of the modern Europeans. In the metropolis, an O'Neill's *Beyond the Horizon*, a Galsworthy's *Justice*, a Shaw's *Androcles* at least can live; sometimes, indeed, live and prosper. But for one respectable piece of dramatic writing that succeeds outside of New York, there are twenty that fail miserably. The theatrical culture of the American countryside is in the main of a piece with that of the French countryside, and to the nature of the latter the statistics of the French provincial theaters offer a brilliant and dismaying attestation.

Save a good play first obtain the endorsement of New York, it is today impossible to get a paying audience for it in any American city of size after the first curiosity-provoking performance. These audiences buy, not good drama but notoriety. Were all communication with the city of New York suddenly to be cut off for six months, the only theatrical ventures that could earn their way outside would be the Ziegfeld *Follies*, the Winter Garden shows, *Ben Hur*, and the hack dramatizations of the trashier best sellers like *Pollyanna* and *Daddy Longlegs*.

This is not postured for sensational effect. It is literally true. So true, in fact, that there is today not a single producer in the American theater who can afford to, or who will, risk the loss of a mere four weeks' preliminary "road" trial of a first-class play. If he cannot get a New York theater for his production, he places it in the storehouse temporarily until he can obtain a metropolitan booking rather than hazard the financial loss that, nine times in ten, is certain to come to him.

More and more, the better producing managers — men like Hopkins, William Harris, Jr., Ames *et al* — are coming to open their plays in New York "cold," that is, without the former experimental performances in thitherward cities. And more and more they are coming to realize to their sorrow that, unless New York supports these plays of the better sort, they can look for no support elsewhere. Chicago, boasting of its hospitality to sound artistic endeavor, spent $3,500 on a drama by Eugene O'Neill in the same week that it spent $45,000 on Al Jolson's Winter Garden show. Boston, one of the first cities to rush frantically forward with proofs of its old New England culture, has turned into a prompt and disastrous failure every first-rate play presented in its theaters without a widely advertised star actor during the last five years, and at the same time has made a fortune for the astute Mr. A. H. Woods, who, gauging its culture accurately, has sent it *Up in Mabel's Room, Getting Gertie's Garter*, and similar spicy boudoir and hay-mow farces, together with Miss Theda Bara in *The Blue Flame.*

It is no secret among the theatrical managers that the only way to bring the culture of Boston to the box-office window is through a campaign of raw advertising: the rawer the better. Thus, the Boston Sunday newspaper advertisements of *Up in Mabel's Room* were made to display a girl lying on a bed, with the suggestive catch lines, "10,000 Visitors Weekly" and "Such a Funny Feeling." Thus, the advertisements of another exhibit presented a rear view of a nude female with the title of the show,

Oh, Mommer, printed across the ample buttocks. Thus, the advertisements of a Winter Garden music show, alluding to the runway used in these exhibitions, christened it "The Bridge of Thighs." No play presented in Philadelphia since *The Girl with the Whooping Cough* (subsequently suppressed by the New York police authorities on the ground of indecency) has been patronized to the extent where it has been found necessary to call out the police reserves to maintain order, as was the case when the play in point was produced.

Washington is a cultural wilderness; I have personally attended the premieres of ten highly meritorious dramas in the national capital in the last six years and can report accurately on the quality of the receptions accorded to them. Washington would seem still to be what it was some fifteen years or so ago when, upon the initial revelation of Barrie's *Peter Pan,* it essayed to boo it into permanent discard. Baltimore, Detroit (save during the height of the war prosperity when the poor "bohicks," "wops," and Greeks in the automobile works found themselves suddenly able to buy theater seats regularly), Cleveland, St. Louis, San Francisco — the story is the same. Honorable drama spells ruin; legs, lewdness, and sentimentality spell riches.

In comparison with the taste of the great American cultural prairie whereon these cities are situated, the city of New York, as I have written, looms up an aesthetic Athens. In New York, too, there is prosperity for bare knees, bed humors, and *Peg o' My Heart* bathos, but not alone for these. Side by side with the audiences that crowd into the leg shows, the couch farces, and the uplift sermons are audiences of considerable bulk that make profitable the production of such more estimable things as Shaw's *Heartbreak House,* O'Neill's *Emperor Jones,* the plays of St. John Ervine and Dunsany, of Tolstoy and Hauptmann, of Bahr and Benavente and Guitry. True enough, in order to get to the theaters in which certain of these plays are revealed, one is compelled to travel in a taxicab several miles from Broadway — and at times has to sit with the chauffeur in order to pilot him to far streets and alleyways that are not within his sophisticated ken — but, once one gets to the theaters, one finds them full, and their audiences enthusiastic and responsive.

The culture of the American theater — insofar as it exists — may be said, in fact, to be an alleyway culture. Almost without exception in the last dozen years and more have the best dramatists of Europe and of our own country been driven up alleyways and side streets for their first American hearing. Up these dark alleys and in these remote malls alone have they been able to find a sufficient intelligence for their wares. Hervieu, Shaw, Echegaray, Strindberg, Björnson, Dunsany, Masefield, Ervine, Bergström, Chekhov, Andreyev, Benavente, O'Neill — these and many others of emi-nence owe their New York introduction to the side-street American who, in the majori-ty of cases, is found upon analysis to be of 50 percent foreign blood. And what thus holds true of New York holds equally true in most of the other cities. In most of such cities, that is, as have arrived at a degree of theatrical polish sufficient to boast a little playhouse up an ulterior mews.

The more general American theatrical taste, reflected perhaps most fairly in such things as the idiotic endorsements of the Drama League and the various "white lists" of the different religious organizations, is — for all the undeniable fact that it seems gradually to be improving — still in the playing-blocks and tin choo-choo-car stage. Satire, unless it be of the most obvious sort and approach easily assimilable burlesque, spells failure for a producer. A point of view that does not effect a compromise with sentimentality spells failure for a dram-atist. Sex, save it be presented in terms of a seltzer siphon, "Abendstern," or the *Police*

Gazette, spells failure for both. The leaders in the propagation of this low taste are not the American managers and producers, as is commonly maintained, but the American playwrights.

During the seventeen years of my active critical interest in the theater, I have not en-countered a single honest piece of dramatic writing from an American hand that could not get a hearing — and an intelligent hearing — from one or another of these regularly abused managers and producers. And during these years I have, by virtue of my joint professional duties as critic and coeditor of a sympathetic literary periodical, read perhaps nine-tenths of the dramatic manuscripts which aspiring young America has confected. This young America, loud in its inveighing against the managers and pro-ducers, has, in the space of time indicated, produced very, very little that was worth producing, and that little has promptly found a market.

A bad workman is always indignant. But I know of no good American play that ei-ther has not already been produced, or has not been bought for future production. Any good play by an American will find its pro-ducer readily enough. The first manager who read *Beyond the Horizon* bought it im-mediately he laid the manuscript down, and this, recall, was its professionally unknown author's first three-act play. The American theater has altered in this department; the last fifteen years have wrought a tonic change.

No, the fault is not with the managers and producers but with the playwrights. The latter, where they are not mere parrots, are cowards. Young and old, new and expe-rienced, talented and talentless alike, they are in the mass so many *Saturday Evening Post* souls, alone dreaming of and intent upon achieving a sufficient financial gain to transmute the Ford into a Rolls-Royce and the Hudson Bay seal collar into Russian sa-ble. A baby cannot be nourished and developed physically upon water; a theatrical public, for all its potential willingness, cannot be developed aesthetically upon a diet of snide writing.

In the American theater of the present time there are not more than two, or at most three, playwrights out of all the hundreds who retain in their hearts a determined and uncorrupted purpose. Take away young O'Neill, and give a bit of ground to Miss Rita Wellman (whose accomplishment is still too vague for fixed appraisal), and there is next to nothing left. Flashes of talent, yes, but only flashes. Craven's *Too Many Cooks* and *The First Year* are observant, highly skillful depictions of the American scene, but they are dramatic literature only in the degree that *Main Street* and *This Side of Paradise* are literature. With the extraordinary *Papa*, Miss Zoë Akins gave up and surrendered — at least temporarily — to the box-office skull and crossbones.

Until Tarkington proves that *Clarence* was not a happy accident in the long and unbroken line of *Up from Nowhere, Mister Antonio, The Country Cousin, The Man from Home, Cameo Kirby, Your Humble Servant, Springtime, Getting a Polish, The Gibson Upright,* and *Poldekin,* we shall have to hold up our decision on him. George Ade, the great promise of authentic American drama, is no more; he pulled in his oars, alas, in midstream. Joseph Medill Patterson, an honest dramatist, fell through the bridge while not yet half-way across. The rest? Well, the rest are the Augustus Thomases, leftovers from the last generation, proficient technicians with empty heads, or youngsters still dramatically wet behind the ears. The rest of the rest? Ticket salesmen.

In no civilized country in the world today is there among playwrights so little fervor for sound drama as in the United States. In England, they at least try, in a measure, to write well; in Germany, to experiment bravely in new forms; in France, to philosophize either seriously or lightly upon life as they find it; in Russia, to treat soberly of problems physical and spiritual; in Spain, to depict the Spanish heart and conscience and atmosphere; in Ireland, to reflect the life and thoughts, the humor and tragedy and encompassing aspirations of a people.

And in the United States — what? In the United States, with hardly more than two exceptions, there is at the moment not a playwright who isn't thinking of "success" above honest work. Good and bad craftsmen alike, they all think the same. Gold, silver, copper. And the result is an endless procession of revamped crook plays, detective plays, Cinderella plays, boudoir plays, bucolic plays: fodder for doodles. The cowardice before the golden snake's eye spreads to the highest as well as to the lowest. Integrity is thrown overboard as the ship is steered unswervingly into the Golden Gate. The unquestionable talent of an Avery Hopwood — a George M. Cohan — a George Bronson-Howard — is deliberately self-corrupted.

The American professional theater is today at once the richest theater in the world, and the poorest. Financially, it reaches to the stars; culturally, with exception so small as to be negligible, it reaches to the drains. For both of these reaches, the American newspaper stands largely responsible. The American newspaper, in general, regards the theater with contempt. My early years, upon leaving the university, were spent on the staff of one of them — the leading daily journal of America, it was in those days — and I shall never forget its attitude toward the theater — cheap, hollow, debased.

If a play was produced by a manager who advertised extensively in the paper, it was praised out of all reason. If a play was produced by a manager who happened to be *persona non grata* in the office, it was dismissed with a brief reportorial notice. If a play was produced by a new and enterprising manager on the night of another production in a theater patronized by fashionable audiences — the Empire, say — the former play, however worthy an effort it might be, was let down with a stick or two that there might be room to print the names of the fashionables who were in the Empire seats.

The surface of things has changed somewhat since then, but the situation at bottom is much the same. A talented young reviewer writes honestly of a tawdry play in the *Evening Sun;* the producer of the play, an office favorite, complains; and the young reviewer is promptly discharged. A moving-picture producer takes half-page advertisements of his forthcoming opus in the New York newspapers; and the screen exhibit, a piece of trash, is hailed as a master work. Let a new drama by Gerhart Hauptmann be presented in the Park Theatre tonight and let Mr. John Barrymore also appear at eight-thirty in a play by some obscure hack at the Empire, and there will not be a single newspaper in the whole of New York City that will not review the latter flashy affair at the expense of the former.

It is not that the newspapers, in New York as elsewhere, are dishonest — few of them are actually dishonest; it is that they are suburban, shoddy, cheap. With only four exceptions that I can think of, the American newspaper, wherever you find it, treats the theater as if it were of very much less importance than baseball and of but a shade more importance than a rape in Perth Amboy, New Jersey. Two columns are given freely to the latest development in bootlegging in Harlem, and a begrudged half-column to a play by John Galsworthy. A society woman is accused by her husband of having been guilty of adultery with a half-breed Indian, and the allotment is four columns. On the same day, a Shakespearean production is mounted by the most artistic producer in the American theater and the allotment of space is two-thirds of a column. The reply of the newspapers is, "Well, we give the public what it wants! And it is more greatly interested in scandal than in Shakespeare."

Have not then the theatrical managers the right to reply in the same terms? And when they do, some of them, disgustedly reply in the same terms, what is the hypocritical appraisal of their offerings that the self-same newspapers vouchsafe to them? If the *New York Times* devotes three columns to a dirty divorce case, I fail to see how it can with justice or reason permit its theatrical reviewer indignantly to denounce Mr. A. H. Woods in the same issue for devoting three hours to a dirty farce.

The American drama, like the American audience, lacks repose. This is ever logically true of a new civilization. Time must mellow the mind and heart before drama may achieve depth and richness; time must mellow the mind and heart before an audience may achieve the mood of calm deliberation. Youth is a rare and precious attribute, but youth, for all its fine courage and derring-do, is inclined to be superficial. Its emotions and its reactions are respectively of and to the primary colors; the pastels it is impatient of. The American theater, drama, and audience are the theater, drama, and audience of the metaphysical and emotional primary colors: substantial, vivid, but all too obvious and glaring.

I speak, of course, generally; for there are a few notable exceptions to the rule, and these exceptions portend in the American theater the first signs of the coming dawn. A producer like Arthur Hopkins, perhaps the first American man of the theater gifted with a genuine passion for fine and beautiful things and the talent with which to do — or at least to try to do — them; a dramatist like young O'Neill, permitting no compromise or equivoke in the upward sweep of his dynamic imagination; an actor like Arnold Daly and an actress like Margaret Anglin to whom failure in the service of honest drama means absolutely nothing — these are they who inspire our faith in the future. Nor do they stand alone. Hume and Moeller, Jones, Peters, Simonson, and Bel-Geddes, Glaspell, Wellman, and Puttle such youngsters, too, are dreaming their dreams — some of them, true enough, still silly dreams, but yet dreams. And the dreaming spreads, spreads. . . .

But in its slow and brave ascent, the American theater is still heavily retarded by the insular forces that, as in no other theater save the English, operate in the republic. The fight against outworn convention is a brave and bitter fight, but victory still rests mainly on the banners of the Philistines. The drama that dismisses sentimentality for truth, that seeks to face squarely the tragedy and comedy of love and life, that declines to pigeonhole itself and that hazards to view the American scene with cosmopolitan eyes is confronted at every turn by the native Puritanism (as often shammed as inborn), and by the native parochialism and hypocrisy. The production that derides all stereotype — all the ridiculous and mossy rubber stamps — is in turn derided. The actor or actress who essays to filter a role through the mind of a human being instead of through the mind of a rouged marionette is made mock of. Here, the playgoing public finds its leaders in three-fourths of the newspaper reviewing chairs, chairs influenced, directly or indirectly, by an intrinsic inexperience and ignorance, or by an extrinsic suggestion of "policy."

The American theater and drama have long suffered from being slaves to the national hypocrisy. Only on rare occasions have they been successful in casting off the shackles, and then but momentarily. The pull against them is stubborn, strong. Cracking the black snake across their backs are a hundred padrones; newspapers trembling at the thought of offending their advertisers, religious orders poking their noses into what should not concern them, corrupt moral-uplift organizations and lecherous anti-vice societies itching for the gauds of publicity, meddling college professors augmenting their humble wage by writing $20 articles on subjects they know nothing about for the Sunday supplements, ex-real estate reporters and divorcée interviewers become "dramatic critics," notoriety-seeking clergymen, snide producers trying to protect their snide enterprises from the dangers of the invasion of truth and beauty.

Let a group of drama-loving and theater-loving young men, resourceful, skillful, and successful, come upon the scene, as the Washington Square Players came, let them bring flashes of authentic dramatic art into their native theater, and against them is promptly hurled the jealous irony of the Old Guard that is dead, but never surrenders. Let a young playwright like Zoë Akins write an admirable fantastic comedy (Papa), and against her are brought all the weapons of the morals-in-art mountebanks. Let a producer like Hopkins break away from the mantel-leaning histrionism and palm-pot investiture, and against him is brought up the curt dismissal of freakishness.

The native theater, for all the fact that it is on the way, is not yet ready for such things as demand a degree of civilization for receptive and remunerative appreciation. The Pegs o' My Heart and Pollyannas, the Turn to the Rights and Lightnin's still make millions, while the bulk of finer things languish and perish. I speak, remember, not of the theater of one city but of the theater of the land. This theater, considering it insofar as possible as a unit, is still not much above the Midway Plaisance, the honk-a-tonk, the Sunday school charade. That one, or maybe two, foreign national theaters may not be much better is no apology. Such foreign theaters — the French, say — are less national theaters than one-city theaters, for Paris is France. But the American theater spreads from coast to coast. What it spreads, I have herein tried to suggest.

66.

DEEMS TAYLOR: Music in the United States

*Deems Taylor wrote the critique of American music for Harold Stearns's dour
collection* Civilization in the United States *(1922). In keeping with the
generally sardonic attitude of the work — most of the contributors to it viewed
America's culture with either distrust or disdain — Taylor emphasized the
vulgarity of American musical taste and the innocence and lack of technical
training of American composers. So much was typical of intellectual critics of
the Twenties; but Taylor went on to suggest that such devices as the phonograph,
as well as musical accompaniment of motion pictures, might have an important effect
in uplifting American taste in general. In this he seems to have been a prophet.
He could not have foreseen the recent popularity of classical discs, but it
probably would not have surprised him. Taylor's essay, "Music," is reprinted
here in part.*

Source: *Civilization in the United States*, Harold E. Stearns, ed., New York, 1922, pp. 199-214.

WE SPEND MORE MONEY upon music than does any other nation on earth; some of our orchestras, notably those of Boston, Chicago, and Philadelphia, are worthy to rank among the world's best; in the Metropolitan Opera House we give performances of grand opera that for consistent excellence of playing, singing, and *mise-en-scène* are surpassed probably nowhere. Yet there has never been a successful opera by an American offered at that opera house, and the number of viable American orchestral works is small enough to be counted almost upon one's fingers. We squander millions every year upon an art that we cannot produce.

There are apologists for the American composer who will say that we do produce it, but that it is strangled at birth. According to their stock argument, there are numberless greatly gifted native composers whose works never get a hearing, (*a*) because Americans are prejudiced against American music and in favor of foreign music, and (*b*) because the foreigners who largely control the musical situation in this country jealously refuse to allow American works to be performed.

This would be impressive if it were consistent or true. As far as concerns the Jealous Foreigner myth — he does not dominate the musical situation — I have never noticed that the average European in this country is deficient either in self-interest or tact. He is generally anxious, if only for diplomatic reasons, to find American music that is worth singing or playing. Even when he fails to find any that is worth performing, he often performs some that isn't in order to satisfy local pride. Moreover, Americans are no more prejudiced against American musicians than they are against other kinds. As a matter of fact, if intensive boosting campaigns produced creative artists, the American composer during the past decade should have expanded like a hot-house strawberry.

We have had prize contests of all kinds, offering substantial sums for everything from grand operas to string quartets; we have had societies formed to publish his chamber-music scores; publishers have rushed to print his smaller works; we have had concerts of American compositions; we have had all-American festivals. Meanwhile, the American composer has, with a few lonely exceptions, obstinately refused to produce anything above the level of what it would be flattering to call mediocrity.

No. If he is not heard oftener in concert halls and upon recital platforms, it is because he is not good enough. There is, in the music of even the second-rate continental composers, a surety of touch, a quality of evident confidence in their material and ease in its handling that is rarely present in the work of Americans. Most American symphonic and chamber music lacks structure and clarity. The workmanship is faulty, the utterance stammers and halts. Listening to an average American symphonic poem, you get the impression that the composer was so amazed and delighted at being able to write a symphonic poem at all that the fact that it might be a dull one seemed of minor importance to him. When he isn't being almost entirely formless, he is generally safely conventional, preferring to stick to what a statesman would call the Ways of the Fathers rather than risk some structural innovation that might or might not be effective. Tchaikovsky's variation of the traditional sequence of movements in the *Pathétique* symphony for example — ending with the slow movement instead of the march — would scandalize and terrify the average American.

This feebleness and uncertainty in the handling of material makes American music sound more sterile and commonplace than it really is. The American composer never seems certain just what, if anything, he wants to say. His themes, his fundamental ideas are often of real significance, but he has no control over that very essence of the language of music, mood. He lacks taste. The fact that an American composition may begin in a genuinely impressive mood is no guarantee at all that inside of twenty-four bars it may not fall into the most appalling banalities.

We start with lyric beauty and finish in stickiness. The curse of bathos is upon us. We lack staying power. Just as so many American dramatists can write two good acts of a three-act play, so many American novelists can write superb opening chapters, so do American composers devise eloquent opening themes. But we all fail when it comes to development. The train is laid, the match is applied, and the spectators crowd back in delighted terror amid tremendous hissings and sputterings. But when the awaited detonation comes, it is too often only a pop.

Such failure to make adequate use of his ideas is partially attributable to the American musician's pathetically inadequate technical equipment. Generally speaking, he doesn't know his business. He has been unable, or hasn't bothered, to learn his trade. Imagine if you can a successful dramatist who can neither read nor write, but has to dictate his plays; or a painter who can only draw the outlines of his pictures, hiring someone else to lay in the colors, and you have something analogous to many an American "composer" whose music is taken seriously by Americans, and who cannot write out a playable piano part, arrange a song for choral performance, or transcribe a hymn tune for a string quartet. Such elementary work he has to have done for him, whenever it is necessary, by some hack. This, to say nothing of the more advanced branches of musical science, like counterpoint, fugue, orchestration. Though it is risky to generalize, it is probably safe to say that among Americans who write music, the man who can construct a respectable fugue or canon or score a piece for full orchestra is decidedly the exception. In Europe, of course, any man who did not have these technical resources at his fingertips would have to be a Mussorgsky to be taken seriously as a composer at all.

It is not entirely the American's fault that he is so ill-equipped. Much of his comparative musical illiteracy, true, is the result of his own laziness and his traditional American contempt for theory and passion for results. On the other hand, the young American who honestly desires a good theoretical training in music must either undertake the expensive adventure of journeying to one of the few cities that contain a first-class conservatory, or the equally expensive one of going to Europe. If he can do neither, he must to a great extent educate himself.

Some kinds of training it is nearly impossible for him to obtain here at any price. Orchestration, for instance, a tremendously complex and difficult science, can be mastered only by the time-honored trial and error method, *i.e.*, by writing out scores and hearing them played. How is our young American to manage this? Granted that there is a symphony orchestra near him, how can he get his scores played? The conductor cannot be blamed for refusing. He is hired to play the works of masters, not to try out the apprentice efforts of unskilled aspirants. What we need so badly here are not more first-class orchestras but more second-rate ones, small town orchestras that could afford to give the tyro a chance.

Because of their lack of technical skill, many composers in this country never venture into the broader fields of composition at all. As a class, we write short piano and violin pieces, or songs. We write them because we do earnestly desire to write something and because they do not demand the technical resourcefulness and sustained inspiration that we lack. Parenthetically, I

don't for a moment mean to imply that clumsy workmanship and sterility are unknown in Europe, that we are all mediocrities and they are all *Uebermenschen*. As a matter of fact, we have today probably much more creative musical talent, if less brains, than Europe; but, talent for talent, the European is infinitely better trained. This, at least in part, because he respects theory and has a desire for technical proficiency that we almost totally lack. Then too, the European has some cultural background. There is a curious lack of intercommunication among the arts in this country. The painter seems to feel that literature has nothing direct to give him; the writer, that music and painting are not in his line; and the musician — decidedly the worst of the three in this respect — that his own art has no connection with anything.

The American composer's most complete failure is intellectual. The fact that he writes music seldom warrants the assumption that he has the artist's point of view at all. He is likely to be a much less interesting person than one's iceman. Ten to one, he never visits a picture gallery or a sculpture exhibition, his taste in the theater is probably that of the tired businessman, and what little reading he does is likely to be confined to trade papers, *Snappy Stories,* and best sellers. He takes no interest in politics, economics, or sociology, either national or international (how could they possibly concern him?), and probably cannot discuss even music with pleasure or profit to anybody.

The natural inference that might be drawn from this diatribe — that the composing of music in this country is confined exclusively to the idiot classes — is not strictly true. Plenty of American musicians are intelligent and cultured men as well; but that is not America's fault. She is just as cordial to the stupid ones. And the widespread impotence and technical sloppiness of American music is the inevitable result of the American attitude toward music and to the anomalous position the art occupies in this country. . . .

Instruction, release, or amusement that, in general, is all we want of art. The American's favorite picture is one that tells a story, or shows the features of some famous person, or the topography of some historic spot. Fantastic pictures he likes because they show him people and places far-removed from his own rather tedious environment, but they must be a gaudy, literal, solid sort of fantasy — Maxfield Parrish rather than Aubrey Beardsley. If he can't have these, he wants pretty girls or comics. Purely decorative or frankly meaningless pictures — Hokusai and Whistler (except, of course, the portraits of Carlyle and his mother) — do not exist for him. Sculpture — which he does not understand — probably his favorite art form, for it is tangible, three dimensionable, stable. He doesn't mind poetry, for it, too, gives him release. He likes novels, especially "glad" ones or mystery stories. He even tolerates realism if, as in *Main Street*, it gives him release by showing him a set of consistently contemptible and uncultured characters to whom even he must feel superior. His architecture he likes either ornate to imbecility or utilitarian to hideousness.

In other words, the typical American goes to an art work either frankly to have his senses tickled or for the sake of a definite thing that it says or a series of extraneous images or thoughts that it evokes — never for the *Ding an sich*. Of pure aesthetic emotion he exhibits very little. To him, beauty is emphatically not its own excuse for being. He does not want it for its own sake, and distrusts and fears it when it appears before him unclothed in moral lessons or associated ideas. In such a civilization, music can occupy but a very unimportant place. For music is, morally or intellectually, the most meaningless of arts: it teaches no lesson, it offers no definite escape from life to the literal-minded, and aside from the primitive and obvious associations of patriotic airs and "mother" songs, it evokes no associated images or ideas.

To love music you must be willing to enjoy beauty pretty largely for its own sake, without asking it to mean anything definite in words or pictures. This the American hates to do. Since he cannot be edified, he refuses to be stirred. There is nothing left for him, therefore, in music except such enjoyment as he can get out of a pretty tune or an infectious rhythm.

And that, despite our admirable symphony orchestras and our two superb permanent opera companies (all run at a loss, by the way), is about all that music means to the average American — amusement. He simply does not see how an art that doesn't teach him anything, that is a shameless assault upon his emotions (he makes no distinction between emotions and senses), can possibly play any significant part in his life. So, as a nation, he does what he generally does in other matters of art, delegates its serious cultivation to women. . . .

The total unconsciousness on the part of his fellow countrymen that art is related to life, a sense of futility and unreality is what makes the lot of the musician in America a hard one and is responsible for his failure as an artist. If people get the kind of government they deserve, they most certainly get the kind of art they demand; and if, comparatively speaking, there is no American composer, it is because America doesn't want him, doesn't see where he fits in.

Suppose most American music is trivial and superficial? How many Americans would know the difference if it were profound? The composer here lives in an atmosphere that is, at the worst, good-natured contempt. Contempt, mind you, not for himself — that wouldn't matter — but for his very art. In the minds of many of his compatriots it ranks only as an entertainment and a diversion, slightly above embroidery and unthinkably below baseball. At best, what he gets is unintelligent admiration, not as an artist but as a freak. Blind

Tom, the Negro pianist, is still a remembered and admired figure in American musical history; and Blind Tom was an idiot.

To an American, the process of musical composition is a mysterious and incomprehensible trick — like sword swallowing or levitation — and as such he admires it; but he does not respect it. He cannot understand how any normal he-man can spend his life thinking up tunes and putting them down on paper. Tunes are pleasant things, of course, especially when they make your feet go or take you back to the days when you went straw riding; but as for taking them seriously and calling it work — man's work — to think them up . . . anyone who thinks that can be dismissed as a crank.

If the crank could make money, it might be different. The respect accorded to artists in our country is pretty sharply graded in accordance with their earning power. Novelists and playwrights come first, since literature and the stage are known to furnish a "good living." Sculptors have a certain standing on account of the rumored prices paid for statues and public memorials, though scenario writers are beginning to rank higher. Painters are eyed with a certain suspicion, though there is always the comfortable belief that the painter probably pursues a prosperous career of advertising art on the side. But poets and composers are decidedly men not to be taken seriously.

This system of evaluation is not quite as crass as it sounds. America has so long been the land of opportunity, we have so long gloried in her supremacy as the place to make a living, that we have an instinctive conviction that if a man is really doing a good job he must inevitably make money at it. Only, poetry and music have the bad luck to be arts wherein a man may be both great and successful and still be unable to look the landlord in the eye. Since such trades are so unprofitable, we argue, those who pursue them are presumably incompetent. The one class of composer whom the American does take seriously is the writer of musical comedy and popular songs, not only because he can make money but because he provides honest, understandable entertainment for man and beast. That, perhaps, is why our light music is the best of its kind in the world.

The self-styled music lover in this country too often brings little more genuine comprehension to music. He is likely to be a highbrow (defined as a person educated beyond his intelligence), with all the mental obtuseness and snobbishness of his class. He divides music into "popular" — meaning light — and "classical" — meaning pretentious. Now, there is good music and bad, and the composer's pretensions have little to do with the case. Compare, for example, the first-act finale of Victor Herbert's *Mlle. Modiste* with such vulgar rubbish as *Donna è mobile*. Yet because the latter is sung by tenors at the Metropolitan, the highbrow solemnly catalogues it as "classical," abolishing the work of Herbert, Berlin, and Kern, three greatly gifted men, with the adjective "popular." In general, he is the faithful guardian of the Puritan tradition, always sniffing the air for a definite "message" or moral, seeking sermons in tones, books in running arpeggios. It never occurs to him that just as words are the language of intellect, so is music the language of emotion, that its whole excuse for existence is its perfection in saying what lies just beyond and above words, and that if you can reduce a composer's message to words, you automatically render it meaningless. . . .

Any significant work of art is inevitably based on the artist's relation and reaction to life. But the American composer's relation to the common life is unreal. His activities strike his fellows as unimportant and slightly irrational. He can't lay his finger upon the great, throbbing, common pulse of America because for him there is none. So he tries this, that, and the other, hoping by luck to stumble upon the thing he wants to say. He tries desperately to be American. Knowing that the great national schools of music in other countries are based upon folksong, he tries to find the American folksong so as to base his music upon that. He utilizes Negro tunes, and when they fail to strike the common chord, he devises themes based upon Indian melodies. What he fails to see is that the folksongs of Europe express the common *racial* emotions of a nation, not its geographical accidents.

When a Frenchman hears *Malbrouck,* he is moved by what moved generations of long-dead Frenchmen; when a Russian hears *Dubinushka,* he is stirred by what has stirred Russians for centuries. But even if some melody did stir the pulse of Geronimo, the mere fact that he was a former resident of my country is no proof that it is going to stir mine. If you insist that Negro music is the proper basis for an American school of composition, try telling a Southerner that when he hears *Swing Low, Sweet Chariot,* he is hearkening to the voices of his ancestors!

A curious symptom of this feeling of disinheritance is the tendency of so many Americans to write what might be called the music of escape, music that far from attempting to affirm the composer's relation to his day and age is a deliberate attempt to liberate himself by evoking alien and exotic moods and atmosphere. The publishers' catalogues are full of Arab meditations, Persian dances, Hindu serenades, and countless similar attempts to get "anywhere out of the world." The best work of Charles Griffes, whose untimely death last year robbed us of a true creative talent, was his symphonic poem, *The Pleasure Dome of Kubla Khan,* and his settings of Chinese and Japanese lyrics in Oriental rhythms and timbres. Not that the mere choice of subject is important; it is the actual mood and idiom of so much of this music that is significant evidence of the impulse to give up and forget America, to create a dream world wherein one can find refuge from the land of chewing gum and victrolas.

These same victrolas, by the way, with their cousin the player piano, which so outrage the sensibilities of many a musician of the elder day, are a very real force in helping to civilize this country musically. The American is by no means as unmusical as he thinks he is. His indifference to art is only the result of his purely industrial civilization, and his tendency to mix morals with aesthetics is a habit of thought engendered by his ancestry. The Puritan tradition makes him fearful and suspicious of any sort of sensuous or emotional response, but it has not rendered him incapable of it. Catch him off his guard, get him away from the fear of being bored, and he is far from insensitive to music. He buys victrola records because he is a hero-worshiper, because he wants to hear the expensive Caruso and Kreisler and McCormack; but inevitably he is bound to take some notice of what they play and sing, and to recognize it when he hears it again. In spite of himself he begins to acquire a rudimentary sort of musical background. He begins by buying jazz rolls for his player piano, and is likely, in the long run, if only out of curiosity, to progress from "blues" to Chopin, via Moszkowski and Grainger.

The greatest present-day force for good, musically, in this country, is the large motion-picture house. Music has always been a necessary accompaniment to motion pictures in order to compensate for the uncanny silence in which these photographic wraiths unfold their dramas. Starting with a modest ensemble of piano and glass crash, the motion-picture orchestra has gradually increased in size and quality, the pipe organ has been introduced to augment and alternate it, so that the larger houses today can boast a musical equipment that is amazingly good.

A few years ago S. L. Rothafel devised a glorified type of entertainment that was a sort of combination picture show and "pop" concert. He built a theater, the Rialto, especially to house it, containing a stage that was little more than a picture frame, a large pipe organ, and an orchestra platform large enough to hold seventy or eighty players. He recruited a permanent orchestra large enough to play symphonic works, and put Hugo Riesenfeld, an excellent violinist and conductor, who had been trained under Arthur Nikisch, in charge of the performances. These, besides the usual film presentations, comprised vocal and instrumental solos and detached numbers by the orchestra. All the music played at these entertainments was good — in what is known in this country as "classical." Riesenfeld devised a running accompaniment to the films, assembled from the best orchestral music obtainable — a sort of synthetic symphonic poem that fitted the mood and action of the film presented, and was, of course, much too good for it.

This new entertainment form was instantly successful and is rapidly becoming the standard offering at all the larger picture houses. It is a significant step in our musical life, for it is the first entirely successful attempt in this country to adapt art to popular wants. At last the average man is going of his own accord into a public hall and hearing music — real music — and discovering that he likes it. The picture house allows him to pretend that he is going solely to see the films, and needn't listen unless he wants to. He finds that "classical" music is not nearly so boresome as many of its admirers. Freed from the highbrow's condescension, unconscious of uplift, he listens and responds to music like the prelude to *Tristan*, the *Walkürenritt*, the *New World* symphony, Tchaikovsky's *Fourth*, and the *Eroica*. Theodore Thomas rendered no more valuable service to music in America than have Samuel Rothafel and Hugo Riesenfeld.

67.

FRANK MOORE COLBY: Humor in America

Frank Moore Colby, in the opinion of Clifton Fadiman, "was one of the best informal essayists produced in this country, the negligent master of a style witty, humorous, and urbane." These qualities are evident in the following selection, a chapter in Harold Stearns's collection Civilization in the United States *(1922). On the whole, Colby was not much impressed by American humor; its keynote, exaggeration, seemed to his Horatian mind more than a little vulgar. He was not even impressed by Mark Twain, who, he suggested, spoiled a great talent by overuse. This attitude toward "America's greatest humorist" was, of course, just as shocking two generations ago as it would be today.*

Source: *Civilization in the United States*, Harold E. Stearns, ed., New York, 1922, pp. 463-466.

WITH THE AID of a competent bibliographer for about five days, I believe I could supply the proof to any unreflecting person in need of it that there is no such thing as an American gift of humorous expression; that the sense of humor does not exist among our upper classes, especially our upper literary class; that in many respects almost every other civilized country in the world has more of it; that quiet New England humor is exceedingly loud and does not belong to New England; that British incomprehension of our jokes is as a rule commendable, the sense of humor generally beginning where our jokes leave off. And while you can prove anything about a race or about all races with the aid of a bibliographer for five days, as contemporary sociologists are now showing, I believe these things are true.

Belief in American humor is a superstition that seldom outlasts youth in persons who have been exposed to American practice, and hardly ever if they know anything of the practice elsewhere. Of course I am not speaking of the sad formalism of the usual thing as we see it in newspapers and on movie screens or of the ritual of magazines wholly or in part sanctified to our solemn god of fun. I mean the best of it.

In the books and passages collated by my bibliographer, the American gift of humor would be distributed over areas of time so vast and among peoples so numerous, remote, or savage that no American would have the heart to press his claim. The quaintness, dryness, ultra-solemnity with or without the wink, exaggeration, surprise, contrast, assumption of common misunderstanding, hyperbolical innocence, quiet chuckle, upsetting of dignity, *éclat* of spontaneity with appeals to the everlasting, dislocation of elegance or familiarity, imperturbability, and twinkle — whatever the qualities may be as enumerated by the bacteriologists who alone have ever written on the subject, the most American of them would be shown in my bibliographer's report to be to a far greater degree unAmerican.

Patriotic exultation in their ownership is like patriotic exultation in the possession of the parts of speech. Humor is no more altered by local reference than grammar is altered by being spoken through the nose. And if the bibliography is an ideal one it will not only present American humor at all times and places but will produce almost verbatim long passages of American humorous text dated at any time and place, and will show how by a few simple changes in local terms they may be made wholly verbatim and American. It will show that American humorous writing did in fact begin everywhere but only at certain periods was permitted to continue, and that these periods were by no means the happiest in history. I have time to mention here only the laborious section that it will probably devote to Mark Twain in the Age of Pericles, though for the more active reader the one on Mr. Cobb, Mr. Butler, and others around the walls of Troy might be of greater contemporary interest.

Mark Twain, according to the citations in this section, would seem actually to have begun all of his longer stories, including *Pudd'nhead Wilson,* and most of the shorter ones, essays, and other papers, at Athens or thereabouts during this period, but not to have finished a single one, not even the briefest of them. He started, gave a clear hint as to how the thing would naturally run, and then he stopped. The reason for this was that owing to the trained imagination of the people for whom he wrote, the beginning and the hint were sufficient, and from that point on they could amuse themselves along the line that Mark Twain indicated better than he would have amused them had he continued.

Mark Twain finally saw this and that is why he stopped, realizing that there was no need of his keeping the ball rolling when to their imaginative intelligence the ball would roll of itself. He did at first try to keep on, and being lively and observant and voluble even for a Greek, he held large crowds on street corners by the sheer repetition of a single gesture of the mind throughout long narratives of varied circumstance. In good society this was not tolerated, even after supper, and there was never the slightest chance of publication. But the streets of Athens were full of the suppressed writings of Mark Twain.

Every man of taste in Athens loved Mark Twain for the first push of his fancy, but none could endure the unmitigated constancy of his pushing of it; and as Mark Twain went everywhere and was most persistent, the compression of his narrative flow within the limits of the good breeding of the period was an embarrassing problem to hosts unwilling to be downright rude to him. Finally, he was snubbed in public by his friends and a few of the more intimate explained to him afterwards the reason why.

The gist of their explanation was evidently this: The hypothesis of the best society in town nowadays is that the prolongation of a single posture of the mind is intolerable, no matter how variegated the substance in which the mind reposes. That sort of thing belongs to an earlier day than ours, although, as you have found, it is still much relished in the streets. If all the slaves were writers; if readers bred like rabbits so that the pleasing of them assured great wealth; if the banausic element in our life should absorb all the rest of it, and if, lost in the external labor process, with the mechanism of it running in our minds, we turned only a sleepy eye to pleasure; then we might need the single thought strung with adventures, passions, incidents and need only that — infinitudes of detail easily guessed but inexorably recounted; long lists of sentiments with human countenances doing this and that; physiological acts in millions of pages and unchanging phrase; volumes of imaginary events without a thought among them; invented public documents equaling the real; enormous anecdotes; and all in a strange reiterated gesture, caught from machines, disposing the mind to nod itself to sleep repeating the names of what it saw while awake. But the bedside writer for the men in bed is not desired at the present moment in our best society.

All these things are now carried in ellipsis to the reader's head, if the reader's head de-sires them; they are implied in dots at ends of sentences. We guess long narratives merely from a comma; we do not write them out. In this space left free by us with deliberate aposiopesis, a literature of countless simplicities may someday arise. At present we do not feel the need of it. And in respect to humor the rule of the present day is this: never do for another what he can do for himself. A simple process of the fancy as in contrast, incongruity, exaggeration, impossibility, must be confined in public to one or two displays.

Let us take the simplest of illustrations — a cow in the dining room, for example — and proceed with it as simply as we can. If by a happy stroke of fancy a cow in the dining room is made pleasing to the mind, never argue that the pleasure is doubled by the successive portrayal of two cows in two dining rooms, assuming that the stroke of fancy remains the same. Realize rather that it diminishes, and that with the presentation of nine cows in nine dining rooms it has changed to pain. Now, if for cows in dining rooms be substituted gods in tailor shops, tailors in the houses of gods, cobblers at king's courts, Thebans before masterpieces, one class against another, one age against another, and so on through incalculable details, however bizarre, all in simple combination, all easily gathered, without a shift of thought or wider imagery, the fancy mechanistically placing the objects side by side, picked from the world as from a catalogue — even then the situation to our present thinking is not improved.

"Distiktos," said they, playfully turning the name of the humorist into the argot of the street, "we find you charming just at the turn of the tide, but when the flood comes in, *ne Dia!* you are certainly *de trop.* And in your own private interest, Distiktos, unless you really want to lead a life totally anexetastic and forlorn, how can you go on in that manner?"

68.

H. L. MENCKEN: On Being an American

H. L. Mencken made a career in the Twenties of celebrating the preposterousness of American life. America, with its "homo boobiens" (businessmen) and "gaping primates" (farmers), fascinated him as zoos fascinated others. A self-styled "Tory in politics," he nonetheless rebelled against American Puritanism's "haunting fear that someone somewhere might be happy." In his articles in the Smart Set, *the* American Mercury, *the* Nation, *and other periodicals, he held nothing sacred but individualism. "Doing good" was "in bad taste." He advocated vivisection, war, prostitution, the assassination of public officials, and the abolition of public schools. He announced his candidacy for the U.S. presidency on a platform including compulsory gladiatorial combats between clergymen and the dumping of the Statue of Liberty into the ocean. Mencken's appeal waned during the Depression, but Walter Lippmann called him "the most powerful influence" on the generation of the Twenties. The following selection is taken from* Prejudices: Third Series.

Source: *Prejudices: Third Series,* New York, 1922, pp. 9-64.

APPARENTLY THERE ARE THOSE who begin to find it disagreeable — nay, impossible. Their anguish fills the Liberal weeklies, and every ship that puts out from New York carries a groaning cargo of them, bound for Paris, London, Munich, Rome, and way points — anywhere to escape the great curses and atrocities that make life intolerable for them at home.

Let me say at once that I find little to cavil at in their basic complaints. In more than one direction, indeed, I probably go a great deal further than even the Young Intellectuals. It is, for example, one of my firmest and most sacred beliefs, reached after an inquiry extending over a score of years and supported by incessant prayer and meditation, that the government of the United States, in both its legislative arm and its executive arm, is ignorant, incompetent, corrupt, and disgusting — and from this judgment I except no more than twenty living lawmakers and no more than twenty executioners of their laws. It is a belief no less piously cherished that the administration of justice in the Republic is stupid, dishonest, and against all reason and equity — and from this judgment I except no more than thirty judges, including two upon the bench of the Supreme Court of the United States.

It is another that the foreign policy of the United States — its habitual manner of dealing with other nations, whether friend or foe — is hypocritical, disingenuous, knavish, and dishonorable — and from this judgment I consent to no exceptions whatever, either recent or long past. And it is my fourth (and, to avoid too depressing a bill, final) conviction that the American people, taking one with another, constitute the most timorous, sniveling, poltroonish, ignominious mob of serfs and goose-steppers ever gathered under one flag in Christendom since the end of the Middle Ages, and that they grow more timorous, more sniveling, more poltroonish, more ignominious every day.

So far I go with the fugitive Young Intellectuals — into the Bad Lands beyond. Such, in brief, are the cardinal articles of my political faith, held passionately since my admission to citizenship and now growing stronger and stronger as I gradually disintegrate into my component carbon, oxygen, hydrogen, phosphorus, calcium, sodium, nitrogen, and iron. This is what I believe and preach, *in nomine Domini,* Amen. Yet I remain on the dock, wrapped in the flag, when the Young Intellectuals set sail. Yet here I stand, unshaken and undespairing, a loyal and devoted Americano, even a chauvinist, paying taxes without complaint, obeying all laws that are physiologically obeyable, accepting all the searching duties and responsibilities of citizenship unprotestingly, investing the sparse usufructs of my miserable toil in the obligations of the nation, avoiding all commerce with men sworn to overthrow the government, contributing my mite toward the glory of the national arts and sciences, enriching and embellishing the native language, spurning all lures (and even all invitations) to get out and stay out — here am I, a bachelor of easy means, forty-two years old, unhampered by debts or issue, able to go wherever I please and to stay as long as I please — here am I, contentedly and even smugly basking beneath the Stars and Stripes, a better citizen, I daresay, and certainly a less murmurous and exigent one, than thousands who put the Hon. Warren Gamaliel Harding beside Friedrich Barbarossa and Charlemagne, and hold the Supreme Court to be directly inspired by the Holy Spirit, and belong ardently to every Rotary Club, Ku Klux Klan, and Anti-Saloon League, and choke with emotion when the band plays "The Star-Spangled Banner," and believe with the faith of little children that one of Our Boys, taken at random, could dispose in a fair fight of ten Englishmen, twenty Germans, thirty Frogs, forty Wops, fifty Japs, or a hundred Bolsheviki.

Well, then, why am I still here? Why am I so complacent (perhaps even to the point of offensiveness), so free from bile, so little fretting and indignant, so curiously happy? Why did I answer only with a few academic "Hear, Hears" when Henry James, Ezra Pound, Harold Stearns and the *emigrés* of Greenwich Village issued their successive calls to the corn-fed intelligentsia to flee the shambles, escape to fairer lands, throw off the curse forever? The answer, of course, is to be sought in the nature of happiness, which tempts to metaphysics. But let me keep upon the ground. To me, at least (and I can only follow my own nose), happiness presents itself in an aspect that is tripartite. To be happy (reducing the thing to its elementals) I must be:

a. Well-fed, unhounded by sordid cares, at ease in Zion.

b. Full of a comfortable feeling of superiority to the masses of my fellowmen.

c. Delicately and unceasingly amused according to my taste.

It is my contention that, if this definition be accepted, there is no country on the face of the earth wherein a man roughly constituted as I am — a man of my general weaknesses, vanities, appetites, prejudices, and aversions — can be so happy, or even one-half so happy, as he can be in these free and independent states. Going further, I lay down the proposition that it is a sheer physical impossibility for such a man to live in These States and *not* be happy — that it is as impossible to him as it would be to a schoolboy to weep over the burning down of his schoolhouse. If he says that he isn't happy here, then he either lies or is insane.

Here the business of getting a living, particularly since the war brought the loot of all Europe to the national strongbox, is enormously easier than it is in any other

Christian land — so easy, in fact, that an educated and forehanded man who fails at it must actually make deliberate efforts to that end. Here the general average of intelligence, of knowledge, of competence, of integrity, of self-respect, of honor is so low that any man who knows his trade, does not fear ghosts, has read fifty good books, and practises the common decencies stands out as brilliantly as a wart on a bald head, and is thrown willy-nilly into a meager and exclusive aristocracy. And here, more than anywhere else that I know of or have heard of, the daily panorama of human existence, of private and communal folly — the unending procession of governmental extortions and chicaneries, of commercial brigandages and throat-slittings, of theological buffooneries, of aesthetic ribaldries, of legal swindles and harlotries, of miscellaneous rogueries, villainies, imbecilities, grotesqueries, and extravagances — is so inordinately gross and preposterous, so perfectly brought up to the highest conceivable amperage, so steadily enriched with an almost fabulous daring and originality, that only the man who was born with a petrified diaphragm can fail to laugh himself to sleep every night, and to awake every morning with all the eager, unflagging expectation of a Sunday-school superintendent touring the Paris peep shows.

A certain sough of rhetoric may be here. Perhaps I yield to words as a Chautauqua lecturer yields to them, belaboring and fermenting the hinds with his Message from the New Jerusalem. But fundamentally I am quite as sincere as he is. For example, in the matter of attaining to ease in Zion, of getting a fair share of the national swag, now piled so mountainously high. It seems to me, sunk in my Egyptian night, that the man who fails to do this in the United States today is a man who is somehow stupid — maybe not on the surface, but certainly deep down. Either he is one who cripples himself unduly, say by setting up a family before he can care for it, or by making a bad bargain for the sale of his wares, or by concerning himself too much about the affairs of other men; or he is one who endeavors fatuously to sell something that no normal American wants.

Whenever I hear a professor of philosophy complain that his wife has eloped with some moving-picture actor or bootlegger, who can at least feed and clothe her, my natural sympathy for the man is greatly corrupted by contempt for his lack of sense. Would it be regarded as sane and laudable for a man to travel the Sudan trying to sell fountain pens, or Greenland offering to teach double-entry bookkeeping or counterpoint? Coming closer, would the judicious pity or laugh at a man who opened a shop for the sale of incunabula in Little Rock, Ark., or who demanded a living in McKeesport, Pa., on the ground that he could read Sumerian? In precisely the same way it seems to me to be nonsensical for a man to offer generally some commodity that only a few rare and dubious Americans want, and then weep and beat his breast because he is not patronized.

One seeking to make a living in a country must pay due regard to the needs and tastes of that country. Here in the United States we have no jobs for grand dukes, and none for *Wirkliche Geheimräte,* and none for palace eunuchs, and none for masters of the buckhounds, and none (anymore) for brewery *Todsaufer* — and very few for oboe players, metaphysicians, astrophysicists, Assyriologists, water colorists, stylites, and epic poets. There was a time when the *Todsaufer* served a public need and got an adequate reward, but it is no more. There may come a time when the composer of string quartettes is paid as much as a railway conductor, but it is not yet. Then why practise such trades — that is, as trades? The man of independent means may venture into them prudently; when he does so, he is seldom molested; it may even be argued that he performs a public service by adopting them. But the man who has a living to make is simply silly if he goes into them; he is like a soldier going over the top with a coffin strapped to his back.

Let him abandon such puerile vanities and take to the uplift instead, as, indeed, thousands of other victims of the industrial system have already done. Let him bear in mind that, whatever its neglect of the humanities and their monks, the Republic has never got half enough bond salesmen, quack doctors, ward leaders, phrenologists, Methodist evangelists, circus clowns, magicians, soldiers, farmers, popular song writers, moonshine distillers, forgers of gin labels, mine guards, detectives, spies, snoopers, and *agents provocateurs.*

The rules are set by Omnipotence; the discreet man observes them. Observing them, he is safe beneath the starry bedtick, in fair weather or foul. The *boobus Americanus* is a bird that knows no closed season — and if he won't come down to Texas oil stock, or one-night cancer cures, or building lots in Swampshurst, he will always come down to Inspiration and Optimism, whether political, theological, pedagogical, literary, or economic.

The doctrine that it is *infra dignitatem* for an educated man to take a hand in the snaring of this goose is one in which I see nothing convincing. It is a doctrine chiefly voiced, I believe, by those who have tried the business and failed. They take refuge behind the childish notion that there is something honorable about poverty *per se* — the Greenwich Village complex. This is nonsense. Poverty may be an unescapable misfortune, but that no more makes it honorable than a cocked eye is made honorable by the same cause. Do I advocate, then, the ceaseless, senseless hogging of money? I do not. All I advocate — and praise as virtuous — is the hogging of enough to provide security and ease.

Despite all the romantic superstitions to the contrary, the artist cannot do his best work when he is oppressed by unsatisfied wants. Nor can the philosopher. Nor can the man of science. The best and clearest thinking of the world is done and the finest art is produced, not by men who are hungry, ragged and harassed, but by men who are well-fed, warm, and easy in mind. It is the artist's first duty to his art to achieve that tranquility for himself. Shakespeare tried to achieve it; so did Beethoven, Wagner, Brahms, Ibsen, and Balzac. Goethe, Schopenhauer, Schumann, and Mendelssohn were born to it. Joseph Conrad, Richard Strauss, and Anatole France, have got it for themselves in our own day. In the older countries, where competence is far more general and competition is thus more sharp, the thing is often cruelly difficult, and almost impossible. But in the United States it is absurdly easy, given ordinary luck. Any man with a superior air, the intelligence of a stockbroker, and the resolution of a hatcheck girl — in brief, any man who believes in himself enough, and with sufficient cause, to be called a journeyman — can cadge enough money, in this glorious commonwealth of morons, to make life soft for him.

And if a lining for the purse is thus facilely obtainable, given a reasonable prudence and resourcefulness, then balm for the ego is just as unlaboriously got, given ordinary dignity and decency. Simply to exist, indeed, on the plane of a civilized man is to attain, in the Republic, to a distinction that should be enough for all save the most vain; it is even likely to be too much, as the frequent challenges of the Ku Klux Klan, the American Legion, the Anti-Saloon League, and other such vigilance committees of the majority testify. Here is a country in which all political thought and activity are concentrated upon the scramble for jobs — in which the normal politician, whether he be a President or a village road supervisor, is willing to renounce any principle, however precious to him, and to adopt any lunacy, however offensive to him, in order to keep his place at the trough. Go into politics, then, without seeking or wanting office, and at once you are as conspicuous as a red-haired blackamoor — in fact, a great deal more conspicuous, for red-haired blackamoors have been seen, but who has ever seen or heard of an American politician, Democrat or Republican, Socialist or Liberal, Whig or Tory, who did not itch for a job?

Again, here is a country in which it is an axiom that a businessman shall be a member of a Chamber of Commerce, an admirer of Charles M. Schwab, a reader of the *Saturday Evening Post,* a golfer — in brief, a vegetable. Spend your hours of escape from *Geschäft* reading Remy de Gourmont or practising the violoncello, and the local Sunday newspaper will infallibly find you out and hymn the marvel — nay, your banker will summon you to discuss your notes, and your rivals will spread the report (probably truthful) that you were pro-German during the war. Yet again, here is a land in which women rule and men are slaves. Train your women to get your slippers for you, and your ill fame will match Galileo's or Darwin's. Once more, here is the Paradise of back-slappers, of democrats, of mixers, of go-getters. Maintain ordinary reserve, and you will arrest instant attention — and have your hand kissed by multitudes who, despite democracy, have all the inferior man's unquenchable desire to grovel and admire.

Nowhere else in the world is superiority more easily attained or more eagerly admitted. The chief business of the nation, as a nation, is the setting up of heroes, mainly bogus. It admired the literary style of the late Woodrow; it respects the theological passion of Bryan; it venerates J. Pierpont Morgan; it takes Congress seriously; it would be unutterably shocked by the proposition (with proof) that a majority of its judges are ignoramuses, and that a respectable minority of them are scoundrels. The manufacture of artificial *Durchlauchten, k.k. Hoheiten* and even gods goes on feverishly and incessantly; the will to worship never

flags. Ten ironmolders meet in the backroom of a near-beer saloon, organize a lodge of the Noble and Mystic Order of American Rosicrucians, and elect a wheelwright Supreme Worthy Whimwham; a month later they send a notice to the local newspaper that they have been greatly honored by an official visit from that Whimwham, and that they plan to give him a jeweled fob for his watch chain. The chief national heroes — Lincoln, Lee, and so on — cannot remain mere men. The mysticism of the medieval peasantry gets into the communal view of them, and they begin to sprout haloes and wings. As I say, no intrinsic merit — at least, none commensurate with the mob estimate — is needed to come to such august dignities.

Everything American is a bit amateurish and childish, even the national gods. The most conspicuous and respected American in nearly every field of endeavor, saving only the purely commercial (I exclude even the financial), is a man who would attract little attention in any other country. The leading American critic of literature, after twenty years of diligent exposition of his ideas, has yet to make it clear what he is in favor of, and why. The queen of the *haut monde,* in almost every American city, is a woman who regards Lord Reading as an aristocrat and her superior, and whose grandfather slept in his underclothes. The leading American musical director, if he went to Leipzig, would be put to polishing trombones and copying drum parts. The chief living American military man — the national heir to Frederick, Marlborough, Wellington, Washington, and Prince Eugene — is a member of the Elks, and proud of it. The leading American philosopher (now dead, with no successor known to the average pedagogue) spent a lifetime erecting an epistemological defense for the national aesthetic maxim: "I don't know nothing about music, but I know what I like." The most eminent statesman the United States has produced since Lincoln was fooled by

Arthur James Balfour, and miscalculated his public support by more than 5 million votes. And the current Chief Magistrate of the nation — its defiant substitute for czar and kaiser — is a small-town printer who, when he wishes to enjoy himself in the Executive Mansion, invites in a homeopathic doctor, a Seventh-Day Adventist evangelist, and a couple of moving-picture actresses. . . .

THE AMERICAN REPUBLIC, as nations go, has led a safe and easy life, with no serious enemies to menace it, either within or without, and no grim struggle with want. Getting a living here has always been easier than anywhere else in Christendom; getting a secure foothold has been possible to whole classes of men who would have remained submerged in Europe, as the character of our plutocracy, and no less of our *intelligentsia* so brilliantly shows. The American people have never had to face such titanic assaults as those suffered by the people of Holland, Poland, and half a dozen other little countries; they have not lived with a ring of powerful and unconscionable enemies about them, as the Germans have lived since the Middle Ages; they have not been torn by class wars, as the French, the Spaniards, and the Russians have been torn; they have not thrown their strength into far-flung and exhausting colonial enterprises, like the English. All their foreign wars have been fought with foes either too weak to resist them or too heavily engaged elsewhere to make more than a half-hearted attempt. The combats with Mexico and Spain were not wars; they were simply lynchings. . . .

Coming down to the time of the World War, one finds precious few signs that the American people, facing an antagonist of equal strength and with both hands free, could be relied upon to give a creditable account of themselves. The American share in that great struggle, in fact, was marked by poltroonery almost as conspicuously as it was marked by knavery.

Library of Congress

H. L. Mencken, American social critic and newspaperman from Baltimore, Md.; photo dated 1928

Let us consider briefly what the nation did. For a few months it viewed the struggle idly and unintelligently, as a yokel might stare at a sword swallower at a county fair. Then, seeing a chance to profit, it undertook with sudden alacrity the ghoulish office of *Kriegslieferant*. One of the contestants being debarred, by the chances of war, from buying, it devoted its whole energies, for two years, to purveying to the other. Meanwhile, it made every effort to aid its customer by lending him the cloak of its neutrality — that is, by demanding all the privileges of a neutral and yet carrying on a stupendous wholesale effort to promote the war. On the official side, this neutrality was fraudulent from the start, as the revelations of Mr. Tumulty have since demonstrated; popularly it became more and more fraudulent as the debts of the customer contestant piled up, and it became more and more apparent — a fact diligently made known by his partisans — that they would be worthless if he failed to win.

Then, in the end, covert aid was transformed into overt aid. And under what gallant conditions! In brief, there stood a nation of 65 million people, which, without effective allies, had just closed two and a half years of homeric conflict by completely defeating an enemy state of 135 million and two lesser ones of more than 10 million together, and now stood at bay before a combination of at least 140 million. Upon this battle-scarred and war-weary foe the Republic of 100 million freemen now flung itself, so lifting the odds to 4 to 1. And after a year and a half more of struggle it emerged triumphant — a knightly victor surely!

There is no need to rehearse the astounding and unprecedented swinishness that accompanied this glorious business — the colossal waste of public money, the savage persecution of all opponents and critics of the war, the open bribery of labor, the half-insane reviling of the enemy, the manufacture of false news, the knavish robbery of enemy civilians, the incessant spy hunts, the floating of public loans by a process of blackmail, the degradation of the Red Cross to partisan uses, the complete abandonment of all decency, decorum, and self-respect. The facts must be remembered with shame by every civilized American; lest they be forgotten by the generations of the future I am even now engaged with collaborators upon an exhaustive record of them, in twenty volumes folio. More important to the present purpose are two things that are apt to be overlooked, the first of which is the capital fact that the war was "sold" to the American people, as the phrase has it, not by appealing to their courage but by appealing to their cowardice — in brief, by adopting the assumption that they were not warlike at all, and certainly not gallant and chivalrous, but merely craven and fearful.

The first selling point of the proponents of American participation was the contention that the Germans, with gigantic wars still raging on both fronts, were preparing to invade the United States, burn down all the towns, murder all the men, and carry off all the women — that their victory would bring staggering and irresistible reprisals for the American violation of the duties of a neutral. The second selling point was that the entrance of the United States would end the war almost instantly — that the Germans would be so overwhelmingly outnumbered, in men and guns, that it would be impossible for them to make any effective defense — above all, that it would be impossible for them to inflict any serious damage upon their new foes.

Neither argument, it must be plain, showed the slightest belief in the warlike skill and courage of the American people. Both were grounded upon the frank theory that the only way to make the mob fight was to scare it half to death, and then show it a way to fight without risk, to stab a helpless antagonist in the back. And both were mellowed and reenforced by the hint that such a noble assault, beside being safe, would also be extremely profitable — that it would convert very dubious debts into very good debts, and dispose forever of a diligent and dangerous competitor for trade, especially in Latin America. All the idealist nonsense emitted by Dr. Wilson and company was simply icing on the cake. Most of it was abandoned as soon as the bullets began to fly, and the rest consisted simply of meaningless words — the idiotic babbling of a Presbyterian evangelist turned prophet and seer. . . .

Would men so degraded in gallantry and honor, so completely purged of all the military virtues, so submerged in baseness of spirit — would such pitiful caricatures of soldiers offer the necessary resistance to a public enemy who was equal, or perhaps superior in men and resources, and who came on with confidence, daring, and resolution — say England supported by Germany as *Kriegslieferant* and with her inevitable swarms of Continental allies, or Japan with the Asiatic hordes behind her? Against the best opinion of the Chautauquas, of Congress, and of the patriotic press, I presume to doubt it. It seems to me quite certain, indeed, that an American Army fairly representing the American people, if it ever meets another army of anything remotely resembling like strength, will be defeated, and that defeat will be indistinguishable from rout. I believe that, at any odds less than two to one, even the exhausted German Army of 1918 would have defeated it, and in this view, I think, I am joined by many men whose military judgment is far better than mine — particularly by many French officers.

The changes in the American character since the Civil War, due partly to the wearing out of the old Anglo-Saxon stock, inferior to begin with, and partly to the infusion of the worst elements of other stocks, have surely not made for the fostering of the military virtues. The old cool head is gone, and the old dogged way with difficulties. The typical American of today has lost all the love of liberty that his forefathers had, and all their distrust of emotion, and pride in self-reliance. He is led no longer by Davy Crocketts; he is led by cheer leaders, press agents, wordmongers, uplifters. I do not believe that such a faint-hearted and inflammatory fellow, shoved into a war demanding every resource of courage, ingenuity, and pertinacity, would give a good account of himself. He is fit for lynching bees and heretic hunts, but he is not fit for tight corners and desperate odds. . . .

TURN, NOW, TO POLITICS. Consider, for example, a campaign for the Presidency. Would it be possible to imagine anything more uproariously idiotic — a deafening, nerve-wracking battle to the death between Tweedledum and Tweedledee, Harlequin and Sganarelle, Gobbo and Dr. Cook — the unspeakable, with fearful snorts, gradu-

ally swallowing the inconceivable? I defy anyone to match it elsewhere on this earth. In other lands, at worst, there are at least intelligible issues, coherent ideas, salient personalities. Somebody says something, and somebody replies. But what did Harding say in 1920, and what did Cox reply? Who was Harding, anyhow, and who was Cox? Here, having perfected democracy, we lift the whole combat to symbolism, to transcendentalism, to metaphysics. Here we load a pair of palpably tin cannon with blank cartridges charged with talcum powder, and so let fly. Here one may howl over the show without any uneasy reminder that it is serious, and that someone may be hurt.

I hold that this elevation of politics to the plane of undiluted comedy is peculiarly American, that nowhere else on this disreputable ball has the art of the sham-battle been developed to such fineness. Two experiences are in point. During the Harding-Cox combat of bladders, an article of mine, dealing with some of its more melodramatic phases, was translated into German and reprinted by a Berlin paper. At the head of it the editor was careful to insert a preface explaining to his readers, but recently delivered to democracy, that such contests were not taken seriously by intelligent Americans, and warning them solemnly against getting into sweats over politics. At about the same time I had dinner with an Englishman. From cocktails to Bromo Seltzer he bewailed the political lassitude of the English populace — its growing indifference to the whole partisan harlequinade.

Here were two typical foreign attitudes: the Germans were in danger of making politics too harsh and implacable, and the English were in danger of forgetting politics altogether. Both attitudes, it must be plain, make for bad shows. Observing a German campaign, one is uncomfortably harassed and stirred up; observing an English campaign (at least in times of peace), one falls asleep. In the United States the thing is done better. Here politics is purged of all menace, all sinister quality, all genuine significance, and stuffed with such gorgeous humors, such inordinate farce that one comes to the end of a campaign with one's ribs loose, and ready for "King Lear," or a hanging, or a course of medical journals. . . .

Well, here is the land of mirth, as Germany is the land of metaphysics and France is the land of fornication. Here the buffoonery never stops. What could be more delightful than the endless struggle of the Puritan to make the joy of the minority unlawful and impossible? The effort is itself a greater joy to one standing on the sidelines than any or all of the carnal joys that it combats. Always, when I contemplate an uplifter at his hopeless business, I recall a scene in an old-time burlesque show, witnessed for hire in my days as a dramatic critic. A chorus girl executed a fall upon the stage, and Rudolph Krausemeyer, the Swiss comedian, rushed to her aid. As he stooped painfully to succor her, Irving Rabinovitz, the Zionist comedian, fetched him a fearful clout across the cofferdam with a slap-stick. So the uplifter, the soul-saver, the Americanizer, striving to make the Republic fit for Y.M.C.A. secretaries. He is the eternal American, ever moved by the best of intentions, ever running *a la* Krausemeyer to the rescue of virtue, and ever getting his pantaloons fanned by the Devil.

I am naturally sinful, and such spectacles caress me. If the slap-stick were a sash-weight, the show would be cruel, and I'd probably complain to the *Polizei*. As it is, I know that the uplifter is not really hurt, but simply shocked. The blow, in fact, does him good, for it helps to get him into Heaven, as exegetes prove from Matthew 5:11: *Heureux serez-vous, lorsqu'on vous outragera, qu'on vous persécutera* [Blessed are ye, when men shall revile you and persecute you], and so on. As for me, it makes me a more contented man, and hence a better citizen. One man prefers the Republic because it pays better wages than Bulgaria. Another, because it has laws to keep him sober and his daughter chaste. Another, because the Woolworth Building is higher than the cathedral at Chartres. Another, because, living here, he can read the New York *Evening Journal*. Another, because there is a warrant out for him somewhere else. Me, I like it because it amuses me to my taste. I never get tired of the show. It is worth every cent it costs.

That cost, it seems to me, is very moderate. Taxes in the United States are not actually high. I figure, for example, that my private share of the expense of maintaining the Hon. Mr. Harding in the White House this year will work out to less than 80 cents. Try to think of better sport for the money: in New York it has been estimated that it costs $8 to get comfortably tight, and $17.50, on an average, to pinch a girl's arm. The United States Senate will cost me perhaps $11 for the year, but against that expense set the subscription price of the *Congressional Record*, about $15, which, as a journalist, I receive for nothing. For $4 less than nothing I am thus entertained as Solomon never was by his hooch dancers. Col. George Brinton McClellan Harvey costs me but 25 cents a year; I get Nicholas Murray Butler free.

Finally, there is young Teddy Roosevelt, the naval expert. Teddy costs me, as I work it out, about 11 cents a year, or less than a cent a month. More, he entertains me doubly for the money, first as naval expert, and secondly as a walking *attentat* upon democracy, a devastating proof that there is nothing, after all, in that superstition. We Americans subscribe to the doctrine of human equality — and the Rooseveltii reduce it to an absurdity as brilliantly as the sons of Veit Bach. Where is your equal opportunity now? Here in this Eden of clowns, with the highest rewards of clowning theoretically open to every poor boy — here in the very citadel of democracy we found and cherish a clown *dynasty!*

Women's suffrage parade on Fifth Avenue in New York, 1915

SUFFRAGE AND PROHIBITION

After World War I there seemed to be just enough of the old crusading spirit left to carry through the unfinished business of earlier reform eras. In spite of the militant agitation of the Suffragettes, the issue of women's suffrage was carried largely on inertia. Suffrage had been a goal of early reformers as a necessary step to political influence; Susan B. Anthony and Lucretia Mott had seen it as a prerequisite to other reforms. It is no more than ironic that it was achieved last. Prohibition was a movement of long standing, and in its last stages it represented the final Populist-Progressive alliance. Rural support for Prohibition stemmed from the Protestant ethic and a rapidly growing anti-urban sentiment. Progressive support was grounded in the general reforming zeal associated with Progressives, and particularly in the drive for honest government and civic reform. Enforcement, the great problem of Prohibition, was most effective in rural and small-town areas where the population supported it; in cities, far from the rural, middle-class values of the Populists, enforcement was at best sketchy. As the rural support of Prohibition became identified with the growing rural-nativist reaction, and even with the KKK, Prohibitionist sentiment fell off generally. Eventually, a vigorous anti-Prohibition campaign was mounted.

The drive for women's suffrage grew with and from the large involvement of women in the reform movements dating from the 1840s. Seen first as a means to effect reform and then as an end in itself, full voting citizenship was attained by stages. In 1860, Susan B. Anthony badgered the New York legislature into finally recognizing full rights of property for women.

A deputation of women's suffrage advocates at a hearing before the House Judiciary Committee, 1871; (below left) Susan B. Anthony, early leader of the movement; (below) Lucretia Mott

European Picture Service

Library of Congress

"The Age of Brass or the triumphs of woman's rights," a parody of the Suffragettes

(Left) Women voting in Wyoming, 1888. Suffrage was extended to women from the start in some states; (right) Elizabeth Cady Stanton; (below) executives of the International Council

(Above) Float in a women's suffrage parade in New York, 1915, exhorting men to support the woman's cause; (below) Mrs. Emmeline Pankhurst, aggressive leader of feminists in Britain, photographed on a visit to the U.S.; (right) Dorothea Dix (Mrs. Elizabeth Gilmer)

Influenced by the militant approach adopted by Emmeline Pankhurst in England, the movement for women's suffrage grew rapidly after 1900. The Bull Moose Party endorsed suffrage in 1912, and the economic status that came with the large-scale employment of women during World War I made the step inevitable. After the proclamation of the Nineteenth Amendment in 1920, women first voted in the November presidential election. Contrary to many expectations, both positive and negative, the only noticeable result was the increased electorate.

(Top) Headquarters of an anti-suffrage organization in New York; **(left)** Congress is pictured in terror of the "ghosts" of suffrage and Prohibition rising to haunt it; **(below)** women voting for the first time in a national election

Prohibition, as the extreme wing of the temperance movement, is one of the hallowed reforms from the 1840s. As the wave of state prohibition laws passed in the 1850s began to be repealed, prohibition agitators began to organize formally; the Prohibition Party founded in 1869 and the Women's Christian Temperance Union of 1874 represented the two strategic approaches. When a second wave of state prohibition in the 1880s receded, both were superseded by the Anti-Saloon League, founded in 1893. The League operated as a classic political pressure group, evaluating candidates for office solely on their position on Prohibition.

(Top) Early days of the Temperance Movement: members of the Anti-Saloon League demonstrate in front of a liquor store; (right) 1874 cartoon: women trying to save drunks in a saloon; (below) a poster for the Prohibition Party, 1888

(Left) Carry Nation spent a good deal of time in jail for trying to destroy "demon rum" with direct action tactics: she took an axe to the saloon keeper's supply; (below) Ida B. Wise Smith, president of the Women's Christian Temperance Union, testifying before hearings on Congressman Joseph Bryson's Prohibition Bill; Representative Bryson (right) listens; (bottom) mock-earnest float in an anti-Prohibition parade

Government agents disposing of captured liquor by the easiest means

(Above) Agents confiscating a supply of moonshine in Maryland; (below) destruction of a still

With the passage of the Webb-Kenyon Act of 1913, prohibiting the transportation of intoxicating beverages into dry states, a national prohibition began to seem possible. A temporary Prohibition Act was passed during the war to save grain for food, and state laws were being passed everywhere. By January 1920 when the 18th Amendment took effect, 33 states had prohibition laws. The central problem was then enforcement, and it proved to be of disillusioning difficulty.

"Speakeasies" were numerous but the booze was expensive; (below) jury freed Helen Morgan, a popular singer, after agents raided her club

With the great market potential of the urban centers, where large numbers of people refused to accept Prohibition, there was a sudden rebirth of entrepreneurship in the new bootlegging industry. And, true to the pattern of business, high ambition led to attempts at monopoly by the larger manufacturers. The methods employed, while perhaps more spectacular, were not really so much different from those of the great trusts. Prohibition is generally credited with providing the impetus for the beginning of organized crime in America.

(Top) Crowds at the funeral of gangster Tony Lombardo in Cicero, Illinois; (left) victims of Capone's gunmen in Valentine's Day Massacre; (below) result of failure to pay "protection"

1923

69.

ANONYMOUS: Listening In

Although the invention of the vacuum tube had made the amplification of weak signals possible as early as 1906, commercial broadcasting did not begin in America until the 1920s. By the end of the ensuing decade, rapid improvements had made broadcasting a thriving industry, every third house in the country had a radio receiver, and "listening in" had become a national pastime. The following article, published in January 1923, described the rise of broadcasting stations, not yet connected in national networks, and the tremendous success radio was already enjoying.

Source: *American Review of Reviews*, January 1923.

IT WOULD BE A COMMONPLACE REMARK to say that when wireless telephoning became practical, about the year 1914, no one dreamed that its use would ever be general or popular. Even two years ago few enthusiasts would have dared to assert that they would live to see hundreds of thousands of persons interested in radio-telephony. The rapidity with which the thing has spread has possibly not been equaled in all the centuries of human progress.

Americans are a home-loving people. When the day's work is done and the evening meal is over, the natural desire is to remain at home; one goes out merely to seek entertainment, recreation, and education which could not otherwise be had. There, perhaps, lies the secret of radio; for enterprising "broadcasters" bring to the ear, every hour and every day, wholly without cost to the "listener-in," a most amazing variety of entertainment and instruction.

These broadcasting stations are operated by manufacturers of radio supplies, who are repaid by the creation of a boom market for sets and parts; by newspapers and department stores, which see an advertising value in the new fad; and by amateur enthusiasts or experimenters. No one knows how many thousand persons each night are informed, before and after a musical selection or a talk, that "This is WSB, the Atlanta *Journal*"; or "This is WHB, the Sweeney Automobile School, Kansas City"; or "This is WOO, John Wanamaker, Philadelphia"; or "This is WDAP, the Drake Hotel, Chicago." One station in Iowa mailed printed programs weekly until 30,000 listeners had asked for them; and then it quit issuing printed programs.

Who are these radio fans? Strange to say, they are not mechanics, even though every set requires a certain amount of installation and most sets are either homemade or home-assembled. Among the menfolk at an office with which the writer is familiar, one in every three has a radio outfit. All were more or less homemade, no two are in any way alike, and every one gives satisfaction. Two of them regularly pick up broadcasting stations 1,000 miles away. The most expensive set in the group costs less than $75, including telephone receivers and batteries.

Even an outfit of limited range will bring to one's sitting room or fireside — through the turning of a knob or two, or the sliding of a cylinder — a variety of entertainment and instruction such as he could not himself have planned. Vocal and instrumental selections there are aplenty, as clear as though the artists were in the next room — solos, duets, quartets, whole choruses, symphonies, and even operas. But besides those offerings the radio fan "gets" varsity football or baseball games and professional prizefights, described from field or ringside; he hears church services from beginning to end; he listens to a Shakespeare reading or to a speech. Last month General Pershing spoke

one evening to a radio audience from St. Louis; it is entirely probable that his voice carried to every state in the Union. The musical selections of WJZ, from Newark, N.J., have been heard in England.

There are now more than 500 broadcasting stations scattered all over this country. The amateur listener is unfortunate, indeed, who cannot hear any one that he chooses among half a dozen, while the more patient or skillful person can pick up one after another a score of stations. In and around New York, during any evening, a hundred-foot length of copper wire in one's backyard will receive messages sent out into the air from Boston, Schenectady, Newark, Philadelphia, Pittsburgh, Baltimore, Atlanta, Louisville, Indianapolis, Chicago, Davenport, Kansas City, and St. Louis. And a modest companion outfit indoors will permit the radio fan to select, one at a time, the station or the message he wishes to hear.

Installing a home set is a shortcut to neighborhood fame, a sure way to become known as a mechanical genius. But, in truth, no special knowledge is required. The novice needs to learn only one thing: Seek good advice, and follow it! A week of tinkering, off and on; and then a winter full of pleasant and profitable evenings at home.

———◆———

All I can tell 'em is I pick a good one and sock it. I get back to the dugout and they ask me what it was I hit and I tell 'em I don't know except it looked good.
                                        GEORGE HERMAN ("BABE") RUTH

The House That Ruth Built.
                                        Sobriquet of Yankee Stadium

70.

William Carlos Williams: "The Crowd at the Ball Game"

Baseball attained the apex of its national popularity during the 1920s, when vast crowds turned out to applaud the achievements of players such as Babe Ruth, Ty Cobb, and Walter Johnson. William Carlos Williams, a young poet who was just beginning to be admired for his daring innovations in verse, went to the ball parks along with everyone else, but his study was the spectators and not the players. "The Crowd at the Ball Game" is typical of Williams' austere style and of his democratic sentiments.

Source: *Dial*, August 1923.

THE CROWD AT THE BALL GAME

The crowd at the ball game
    is moved uniformly

by a spirit of uselessness
    which delights them —

all the exciting detail
    of the chase

and the escape, the error
    the flash of genius —

all to no end save beauty
    the eternal —

So in detail they, the crowd,
    are beautiful

for this
    to be warned against

saluted and defied —
    It is alive, venomous

it smiles grimly
    its words cut —

The flashy female with her
    mother, gets it —

The Jew gets it straight — it
    is deadly, terrifying —

It is the Inquisition, the
    Revolution

It is beauty itself
    that lives

day by day in them
    idly —

This is
    the power of their faces

It is summer, it is the solstice
    the crowd is

cheering, the crowd is laughing
    in detail

permanently, seriously
    without thought

71.

Thorstein Veblen: The New Order of Business

Economist Thorstein Veblen's last book, Absentee Ownership and Business Enterprise in Recent Times, *published in 1923, was meant to be a summary of his ideas on the evolution of the modern industrial system and its social and political consequences. Business, as Veblen saw it, tended naturally to develop into the giant corporation, and in the early part of the twentieth century there were the signs of a further development: the separation of ownership and management. The eighth chapter of* Absentee Ownership *is reprinted here.*

Source: *Absentee Ownership and Business Enterprise in Recent Times,* New York, 1923, pp. 205-228.

THE NEW ORDER OF THINGS which now faces the Americans is an outgrowth of a period of unexampled changes. So there has arisen a situation which foots up to a new order of things; although the new order carries over much of the old order out of which it has arisen. The changes that have been going forward have taken effect primarily and most profoundly in the material circumstances which condition the life and work of this people. The material conditions, the ways and means of living and of procuring a livelihood, have been altered in a very substantial degree. At the same time these material and technical changes have also put a strain on the received canons of knowledge and belief and on the established order of law and custom; although the strain to which they have been subjected has not yet brought on any substantial measure of change in these principles of use and merit that govern belief and conduct.

The changes that have been going forward have not affected all parts of the scheme of life in anything like the same measure. The drive of change has not been the same, and the rate of change has therefore not been the same throughout. The driving forces of change have taken direct effect in the industrial arts, and have touched matters of law and custom only at the second remove. Habits of thought have therefore not been displaced and shifted forward to a new footing in law and morals in anything like the same measure in which men have learned to use new ways and means in industry. The principles (habits of thought) which govern knowledge and belief, law and morals, have accordingly lagged behind, as contrasted with the forward drive in industry and in the resulting workday conditions of living.

As is always the case, in the nature of things, so in this case, too, the changes that have taken effect in the material circumstances are the creative factors which have gone into action, as a driving force and a controlling agency, and have set afoot a new line of habituation. And as is always the case, in the nature of things, the new pattern of knowledge and the new elements of belief and conviction which these new habits of workday living are pushing forward are finding acceptance and endorsement only tardily and by way of reluctant concession to the *force majeure* of continued and rigorous habituation. In point of time, these adaptations of knowledge and belief come after the fact. And any departure from ancient precedent in law and morals will come into effect still more tardily, still farther in arrears. So much so that opinionated persons are quite able to believe that no substantial change need take place or can take place in that range of habitual "action patterns" in which law and morals are grounded, at least not in America.

Indeed, it is something of a boast among Americans of the stricter observance that American law and custom have suffered no change, in principle, since the date of the federal Constitution. In principle, that is to say in respect of its underlying habits of thought, the working system of American law and custom is held to be the finished product of a process of growth which came to a ripe conclusion some 150 years ago. This rigorously retrospective position is formally binding on the judiciary and the legal profession. It overlooks the service rendered by legal fiction and constructive precedents, of course; but there is after all a modicum of truth in the contention — so much as will enable the judiciary and the legal profession to rest their arguments on it, *pro forma.*

It results that insofar as the new order of things departs from the old it has not the countenance of law and custom, except by way of legal fiction. Or to turn the proposition about, insofar as the new order of things departs from the old, the American system of law and order as embodied in the federal Constitution is out-of-date, except by way of legal fiction. The federal Constitution was framed by the elder statesmen of the eighteenth century; whereas the new industrial order of things is created by the technicians of the twentieth century. There is accordingly a discrepancy between the run of material facts in the present and the canons of law and order as stabilized in the eighteenth century.

In the same fashion, though in a less formal conflict, the traditional system of knowledge and belief also is holding out against the pressure brought by the revolution in industry. Such is necessarily the case with any stable system of usages and beliefs and with any established order of law and custom; and it holds true with particular cogency in this American case, where the rate and volume of change in the material conditions of life during this interval have been large and swift beyond example.

The established system of knowledge and belief, law and order, came out of the remoter past that lies back of the period of its own stabilization, and it embodies the habits of thought and the frame of mind that were engendered in still earlier generations by habituation and precedent in the course of that past experience. In this sense, then, it is necessarily out-of-date by so much as the material circumstances which condition the present have departed from those past conditions to which it owes its rise and fixation; and, indeed, by so much more as the working scheme of knowledge and belief, law and order, in that past time carried forward and perpetuated habits of thought, preconceptions, principles that are of still older date.

The new order of things has arisen out of the past by a change in degree carried so far as to result in an effectual change in kind. In the American case this change in the material conditions of life has gone so far as to amount to a break with the past; while the system of legal and customary rights, powers, immunities, and privileges stands over on the base given it by the elder statesmen of the past, except for legal fiction.

The changes which have made this break with the past and have set up this discrepancy between the current conditions of life and the received rules which govern the conduct of life — these changes have been, primarily and immediately, changes in the material circumstances of the case due to a progressive change in the state of the industrial arts and to a continued growth of population. And in both of these respects the rate and volume of change have been large, beyond example. And this altered state of their material circumstances has not yet had time to affect the spiritual animus, the frame of mind of the American community, at all seriously or substantially; nor has it all at all seriously affected their outlook on things even in those matters of knowledge and belief that have to do directly with the industrial arts and the material welfare of the community.

It is true, business enterprise and business methods have undergone some measure of reorganization, designed to get the benefit of the new opportunities offered by the new scale of work that has been brought into action by the continued advance of the industrial arts. So that business has been conducted on a larger scale and at a swifter pace, and with a wider sweep of credit relations — all due in great part to improved mechanical facilities; but the spirit in which American business is conducted, as well as the law and custom which formally govern its powers and procedure, are still the same spirit and the same principles of law and morals that have long been familiar to the horse-trading farmer and the collusive retailers of the country towns.

The material circumstances which underlie and enable the new order, which supply its working forces and limit its powers, are the state of the industrial arts and the manpower of the underlying population; and these forces have come up into their present state by an irrepressible growth, and they are still engaged in a sweeping advance which is pushing them farther and farther from their point of departure. But the control of these industrial powers, and the decision as to what, when, and how much work shall be done by them, is vested in the absentee owners of the country's resources. And these owners and their business agents go into this work of directing and restrain-

ing the work in hand with such powers and preconceptions as have been conferred on them according to a scheme of law and custom that was worked out and stabilized in an alien past for purposes that are alien to this latter-day state of the industrial arts and out of touch with the latter-day state of population.

The New Order, therefore, is by way of being a misfit. It is an organization of new ways and means in the way of industrial processes and manpower, subject to irresponsible control at the hands of a superannuated general staff of businessmen moving along lines of an old-fashioned strategy toward obsolete ends.

This new order of things in American business and industry may be said to have arisen so soon as a working majority of the country's industrial resources, including the transportation system, had been brought securely under absentee ownership on a sufficiently large scale, in sufficiently large holdings, to make these national resources and the industries which make use of them amenable to concerted surveillance and control by the vested interests that represent these larger absentee owners. Of course, there is no sharply drawn dateline to mark the beginning of this new dispensation; *de jure* it does not exist. But the *de facto* rise of the new order may be conveniently dated from about the turn of the century. Loosely speaking, that large-scale control of the industrial forces which has made the outcome, dates back to the ten or twelve years overlapping the end of the century. The "era of trust-making," sometimes so called, that ran for some years from, say, 1897 onward, was concerned in this transition to a new footing in American business.

This appears to make the New Order a new order of business. And so it is, in the sense that the New Order is an order of things in which business considerations are paramount. Its distinctive characteristic on this head being that it is an order of things in which Big Business is paramount. But Big Business still is business of the old familiar kind, with the old familiar aims to be worked out in the old familiar spirit.

Big Business is paramount in the New Order. But all the while the conditioning circumstances which underlie this new order of business enterprise are circumstances of a material, tangible, mechanical, technical nature, ways and means of doing tangible work, not merely new and improved ways and means of doing business. Business has to do with the intangibles of ownership and only indirectly with the tangible facts of workmanship. Under the new dispensation as under any other, the whole duty of business enterprise is to come in for as large and secure a net gain as may be, to acquire title, to "make money," and therefore to turn all tangible means and performances to account for this intangible but paramount purpose of acquiring title.

The new expedients that have been brought into action in the conduct of business are contrivances and expedients designed to serve this intangible end; new ways and means of responding to the call of those new opportunities for gain that arise out of tangible changes in the industrial system — for it is out of the tangible performance of this industrial system that the gains of ownership are drawn and it is to these tangibles of industrial work and products that title is to be acquired. And the tangible changes affecting the industrial system have been going forward as an unremitting proliferation, a continuous advance in the scale and articulation of the industrial process at large.

No new order of business and industry has sprung up suddenly and complete at any given date, even though a visible change has taken effect within a reasonably short time. It is only that somewhere about the turn of the century a critical point was reached and passed, without much visible change of circumstances at the time. The new system, in business and in industry, has in fact been maturing into its present working shape through some twenty years past. And it is still feasible for legally-minded persons to believe that no substantial change has taken effect for a longer period than that.

Nor will it do to say that this new growth has now run its course to a finality; although it should perhaps not come as a surprise if the present phase of it turns out to mark something like a station in the course of events, possibly even something of a new point of departure. . . .

The critical pass, the point at which the New Order may be said to have set in, was reached and passed so soon as a working majority of the country's industrial resources had been brought under absentee ownership on a sufficiently large scale for collusive management. But this is not intended to say that at that period anything like a statistical majority of the natural resources had been taken over into large holdings; but only that, loosely about that period, an effectual working majority of those natural resources and industrial plants which are immediately engaged in the so-called key industries had already passed into absentee ownership on so large a scale as to enable an effectual collusive control of these things by the vested interests concerned, such a degree of control as to make a reasonably concerted check on production in these key industries a manageable undertaking.

In effect, whether by intention or not, the country's industrial system as a working whole, as an industrial going concern, was thereby brought under control and became subject to a varying degree of sabotage at the hands of the vested interests in these key industries. That is what is meant by calling them "key industries." The business concerns that have to do with other branches of production and trade necessarily wait on the movement of things in these key industries. That is also a matter of course and of common notoriety.

Not that the businesslike management of one and another of these key industries will aim to administer sabotage to any or all of the underlying and outlying members of the industrial system. That is not the intention; it is only the effect. Indeed, in so curtailing employment and output in the underlying and outlying industries by curtailing the output in the key industries, the business management of these latter unintentionally curtail the fund of wealth from which the owners of the key industries are to draw their run of free income. So that it is, in effect, at a sacrifice of the long run of gain that the management of the key industries "grabs off" an enhanced rate of earnings for the time being, by curtailing its output and advancing its price schedule. But then, business enterprise, particularly American business enterprise, habitually looks to the short run. And there are reasons why Big Business in particular should conduct its operations with a view to the short-time returns.

The working schedule throughout the rest of the industrial system is conditioned from day to day on the rate, volume, and balance of work and output in these key industries; inasmuch as the secondary, underlying, and outlying branches of the system are, in effect, engaged on what may be called continuation work, which draws unremittingly on the output of the key industries for power, raw materials, transportation, and mechanical equipment, and which presently will unavoidably halt when the flow of these indispensable ways and means of production is clogged by obstructive maneuvers and curtailment in the key industries. So also the habitual and deliberate failure of the key industries, for business reasons, to run at their full productive capacity acts, in effect, to set the pace, to adjust the rate and volume of employment

and output throughout the rest of the industrial system at a lower average than would otherwise be the rule. Any degree of concerted control over these natural resources, as it takes effect in the curtailment or speeding-up of these main industries that so lie at the tactical center of the system, will effectually govern the movements of the country's industrial system at large, as a comprehensive going concern.

And this control, and the running balance of sabotage which is its chief method of control and its chief material consequence, all takes effect in an impersonal and dispassionate way, as a matter of business routine. Absentee ownership and absentee management on this grand scale is immune from neighborly personalities and from sentimental considerations and scruples.

It takes effect through the colorless and impersonal channels of corporation management, at the hands of businesslike officials whose discretion and responsibility extend no farther than the procuring of a reasonably large — that is to say the largest obtainable — net gain in terms of price. The absentee owners are removed out of all touch with the working personnel or with the industrial work in hand, except such remote, neutral, and dispassionate contact by proxy as may be implied in the continued receipt of a free income; and very much the same is true for the business agents of the absentee owners, the investment bankers and the staff of responsible corporation officials. Their relation to what is going on, and to the manpower by use of which it is going on, is a fiscal relation.

As industry, as a process of workmanship and a production of the means of life, the work in hand has no meaning for the absentee owners sitting in the fiscal background of these vested interests. Personalities and tangible consequences are eliminated and the business of governing the rate and volume of the output goes forward in terms of funds, prices, and percentages.

But all the while the work in hand goes

forward in terms of mechanical power, fuel, raw materials, mechanical equipment, chemical processes, manpower, and technical design and surveillance — matters hidden, perhaps mercifully, from the absentee owners who come in for that free income on which the strategy of these vested interests converges. Thereby the absentee owners as well as their absentee business managers are spared many distasteful experiences, saved from reflecting on many dreary trivialities of life and death — trivialities on the balance sheet of assets and liabilities, although their material counterfoil in terms of life and death among the underlying population may be grave enough to those on whom their impact falls. But the absentee owners and their business agents are also by the same screen of absentee immunity barred out from knowing what to do, or from doing anything at all to the purpose in case of need, in case these trivialities of life and death head up in a tangle of discord and mutiny such as to jeopardize the orderly run of their free income, after the fashion which is now becoming familiar to all men.

The strategy of business — the strategy of getting a larger net gain in dollars — dictates what is to be done or left undone; and having so dictated, it moves on to the next thing in the same line. There is no place in Big Business for considerations of a more material sort or of a more sentimental sort than net gain within the law. It moves on that particular plane of make-believe on which the net gain in money values is a more convincing reality than productive work or human livelihood. Neither the tenuous things of the human spirit nor the gross material needs of human life can come in contact with this business enterprise in such a way as to deflect its course from the line of least resistance, which is the line of greatest present gain within the law.

This line of least resistance and greatest present gain runs in the main by way of a vigilant sabotage on production. So true is this and so impassively binding is this duty of businesslike sabotage, that even in a crisis of unexampled privation, such as these years since the war, the captains of Big Business have been unable to break away and let the forces of production take their course; and this in spite of their being notably humane persons, imbued with the most benevolent sentiments. With an eye single to the net gain, business strategy still continues impartially to dictate a conscientious withdrawal of efficiency.

The state of things brought on by the war and perpetuated by the businesslike peace which has followed after is complicated enough in detail; but the outline of things so far as regards the main circumstances which govern business and industry is not especially obscure. When relieved of those personalities and moralities that commonly cloud the argument, the case will stand somewhat as follows. There is a very large inflation of credits, both in the set form of loan credits and in fiduciary currency, in all the civilized nations. The inflation in America, taking one thing with another, may perhaps be rated at something like 100 percent, rather over than under. Hence money values have advanced, resulting in an effectual recapitalization of American business concerns, their assets and their presumptive earnings.

At the same time the aggregate wealth of the country, as counted by weight and tale and use value, has fallen off greatly, as has also the manpower available for productive work. Hence there has arisen a discrepancy between the country's material wealth and the business community's capitalized wealth, which may in a manner of speaking be called a divergence between the country's wealth *de facto* and its wealth *de jure*; between the country's wealth in hand considered as a business proposition (which has increased) and its material wealth considered as a proposition in livelihood (which has decreased). The country is richer in money values and poorer in use values.

But capitalization and earnings are a business proposition; livelihood is not. And in any civilized country like America, business controls industry; which means that production must wait on earnings. Under these circumstances it is, as a matter of common honesty, incumbent on the businessmen in charge to keep this — in a sense fictitious — capitalization intact, and to make it good by bringing current earnings up to the mark. And they have been endeavoring to do this by curtailing employment and output to such a point that the resulting smaller volume of output at the resulting increased price per unit will yield the requisite increased total price return. Among the expedients by which it is sought to save the capitalization intact is a concerted effort to reduce wages.

It is evident that in its main lines this precarious situation that has been precipitated by the war, and the peace, does not differ notably, unless in degree, from the orderly run of business and industry during the times of peace immediately preceding the war. The drift of things in that time set visibly in the direction of such an outcome as the war has brought to a head. Then, as since then, overcapitalization was the rule; as a standard practice there has been more or less of a running sabotage on production, that is to say, more or less unemployment of equipment and manpower; there has been intermittent and, on the whole, increasing discord and distrust between the workmen in the larger industries and their corporate employers, rising with increasing frequency into hostilities in the way of strikes and lockouts, while there has also been a rapidly increasing use of strikebreakers, labor spies ("undercover men"), armed guards, hired "deputies," state police, and other armed forces to keep the peace, uphold the rights of property and make good the absentee owners' claim to a reasonable net gain. By and large, the system of civilized business and industry appears to have been moving forward as a whole and in an orderly fashion toward some such state of balanced inaction and suspended hostilities as that which has been precipitated by the war.

At first sight this view seems to be sound, but a closer scrutiny may leave it in doubt. On the face of things, it looks as if the business community which controls the country's industrial forces had for some time past been engaged in a concerted movement of cumulative overcapitalization and sabotage; while the industrial manpower has been increasingly and systematically falling into an attitude of cross-purposes and ill will. There is scarcely a question about the intractable attitude of the industrial manpower and the steadily rising pitch and sweep of it. Nor is there a tenable doubt as regards the increasing resort to overcapitalization and sabotage on the part of the business community. But there is at least a reasonable doubt as to how far the business managers have been moving in concert in this matter. Their dutiful denials have, of course, no significance except as a ground of suspicion. But the circumstantial evidence in the case is not convincing.

The war and the businesslike peace have brought the economic system as a whole to a state of balanced inaction by a general and uniform check, which gives the resulting situation of sabotage on employment and output the appearance of concerted action on a deliberate and comprehensive plan. But there is no good evidence of widely concerted inaction in that businesslike sabotage that prevailed in the prewar period. And there is at least a reasonable doubt whether the present apparently concerted inaction, after the war, is the outcome of deliberate choice arrived at in concert by the business community at large acting in collusion.

Superficially it has the appearance of conspiracy, of course; and the evidence is perhaps reasonably conclusive that the large employers have been working together the past two years on a common understanding to break down the labor unions in the well-known campaign for what is called the "open shop." But there is no good evidence of any similarly wide concert of action on their part in earlier years. They have showed no capacity for concerted action on such a scale in the past. Except for the banking community, who are held under passable control of a coercive kind by the great credit establishments at the financial center, acting under the coercive surveillance of the Federal Reserve, the American business community have showed no great aptitude for such intelligent and sustained concert of action as this would imply.

There has in the past, from time to time, been an effectual concert of action within certain groups, among the business concerns which take care of certain industries; as, *e.g.*, in steel, coal, lumber, oil, copper, electrical and building supplies, and, in a degree, in transportation. But the resulting inaction and curtailment, so far as it has affected the industrial system at large, has been somewhat haphazard. It has had the appearance of being governed by uncoordinated yielding to the pressure of circumstances, tracing back to curtailment of supplies from one or another of the key industries or to measures taken in the centralized credit business.

The industrial business concerns at large have commonly appeared to act in severalty, yielding to a common pressure, rather than moving by a common impulse and looking to a shrewdly balanced sabotage on employment and output as a whole. Of course, in ordinary times there is a routine of sabotage, a restriction of output to meet the market, which goes into the day's work of all sizable concerns that do business in productive industry; but all that has been a matter of routine business within each concern; which is something quite different from such a nationwide campaign of inaction and hostilities as has held up the country's industry since the war.

The question may be put in this way — Is this postbellum state of resolute inaction in business and of unemployment and hostilities in industry the rightful outgrowth of the ordinary agencies that have been at work during the past two decades? Or is it all a transient derangement of things due to transient causes extraneous to that system of absentee ownership and finance that makes the New Order of things? And if the latter appears to be the case, if this postbellum complication of hardships and inaction does not belong in the orderly course of things under the New Order, what should then reasonably be looked for in the calculable future as an outcome of continued growth along the line of the past two decades? What is reasonably to be looked for as the outcome of absentee ownership and control on this large scale as it is working out on the ground of an increasingly large and close-knit industrial system, and an increasingly large and compact underlying population?

It is a question of human behavior under pressure of changing circumstances with a minimum of change in the formal rules which govern this behavior. Apparently it should involve a question of the degree and direction of change to be looked for in the law and the administrative procedure that touches the conduct of industry and business. Which becomes, in effect, a question of what the courts, the legislatures, and the administrative officials are likely to decide in these premises. There should apparently be small ground for doubt on that head, in the light of what has been taking place. So that the answer to this part of the question may be taken for granted, with a fair degree of confidence.

As has been customary in recent times, so also during the past two decades, the courts and legislatures have, on the whole, acted to safeguard and fortify the rights, powers, and immunities of absentee ownership whenever there has been occasion, and the administrative officials have acted in the same sense with celerity and effect, to the best of their knowledge and belief; in all of which the constituted authorities have doubtless acted in good faith and have followed out the logic of law and custom that has been bred in them by precept, example, and tradition. There need be no apprehension of interference with the course of things from that side, so far as the course of things is dictated by the needs of absentee ownership.

It may accordingly be assumed that the case of America as it runs into the calculable future will continue to be ordered on the lines of absentee ownership without much afterthought, governed by business enterprise carried on with an eye single to the largest net gain in terms of price. The law allows it and the court awards it. The changes to be looked for are such changes as are initiated from outside the jurisdiction of law and custom.

There are three somewhat divergent main lines, at least, along which the resulting new growth may move; according as one or another of the country's main business interests comes to dominate the situation, alone or in a combination.

(a). The funded power, the control of credit, in the hands of the associated banking houses and the Federal Reserve may be able to govern the course of business to such effect as to safeguard the interests of absentee ownership at large, maintain a steadily rising overcapitalization of absentee assets, and assure an indefinitely continued increase of net gains on investments and credit commitments. The drift just now appears to set in that direction. These agencies may be able to maintain such a balanced and stable progressive expansion of assets and earnings. In any case, the dominant position of this community of "investment bankers," moving in concert under the steady surveillance of the Federal Reserve, will exercise an influence of this kind and will greatly affect the outcome.

(b). At the same time it is conceivable that the vested interests which own and control the main natural resources and the key industries may take the lead, with the support of the banking community. Ownership of these tangible assets that underlie the country's industrial system, the underlying material resources and equipment, will enable these corporate interests to draw together on a concerted plan of common action and set the pace for the country's industry as a whole by limiting output and service to such a rate and volume as will best serve their own collective net gain. In so doing they will be in a position progressively to draw the industrial system as a whole in under their own absentee ownership, without material reservation, at least to the extent of coming in for the effectual usufruct of the whole — somewhat after the fashion in which the packers, millers, and railways now enjoy the usufruct of the farming community in the Middle West, but with a stricter authority.

In this connection it is to be recalled that there is already a far-reaching identity both of personnel and of corporate interests between the group of corporations who control the key industries on the one side and the banking community on the other, and this coalescence or consolidation of the masters of tangible assets with the masters of credit and solvency is visibly on the increase. So that what should be looked for is quite as likely to be an effectual coalescence and concert of these two powers, the bankers and the key industries, rather than the dominance of either one as against the other.

(c). There is also the possibility that the business concerns which control the natural resources and the great industries will continue to act by groups as in the recent past, each group taking measures for itself in what may be called group severalty, and each group of interests seeking its own immediate advantage by charging what the traffic will bear, at the cost of any other vested interests and of the underlying population. In so doing these collusive groups of industrial concerns will necessarily be working more or less at cross-purposes, and will thereby carry on a haphazard and fluctuating sabotage on employment and output, after the pattern that had become familiar during the years before the war.

Such is the tradition of business enterprise in industry and of that "competitive system" that still lives in American tradition, and there is always the chance that the conservative spirit of the American business may preclude any effectual departure from this familiar plan of mutual distrust and sharp practice. In the background of any such pattern of semidetached group action there is, of course, always the collusive banking community to be counted with;

and there remains therefore the question of how far the banking community will tolerate cross-purposes between groups of industrial business concerns.

There is also the more obscure question of what the industrial manpower and the underlying population will say to it all, if anything. In strict consistency, of course, under the dispassionate logic of established law and custom, neither the industrial manpower nor the underlying population come into the case except as counters in the computation of what the traffic will bear. Anything like reasoned conduct or articulate behavior on their part will scarcely be looked for in this connection. Yet there remains an uneasy doubt as touches the *de facto* limits of tolerance.

72.

FRANK H. KNIGHT: The Ethics of Competition

The Twenties was the decade of business; never before had the country known such prosperity. Moreover, there had been, according to Dr. Julius Klein, "an amazing transformation in the soul of business," which had, he asserted, become "a thing of morals." Business, indeed, came close to being a new religion, in which the factory was the church, work was worship, and advertising was a kind of theology. One thoughtful critic of this novel faith was Frank H. Knight, a professor at the University of Iowa and, later, at the University of Chicago. His essay "The Ethics of Competition" (1923) challenged the spirit of rugged individualism that marked the era. Part of the essay appears here.

Source: *Quarterly Journal of Economics*, August 1923.

DISCUSSION OF THE MERITS of free competition, or "laissez faire," takes on an especial interest in view of the contrast between the enticing plausibility of the case for the "obvious and simple system of natural liberty," and the notoriously disappointing character of the results which it has tended to bring about in practice. In the later eighteenth and early nineteenth centuries, under the influence of the "classical economists," of the Manchester liberals, of the political pressure of the rising bourgeoisie, and the general force of circumstances, rapid progress was made toward the establishment of individual liberty in economic affairs. But long before complete individualism was closely approached, its consequences were recognized to be intolerable, and there set in that countermovement toward social interference and control which has been going on at an accelerating pace ever since.

The argument for individualism, as developed by its advocates from Adam Smith down, may be summarized in a sentence as follows: a freely competitive organization of society tends to place every productive resource in that position in the productive system where it can make the greatest possible addition to the total social dividend as measured in price terms, and tends to reward every participant in production by giving it the increase in the social dividend which its cooperation makes possible. In the writer's opinion, such a proposition is entirely sound; but it is not a statement of a sound ethical social ideal, the specification for a utopia. Discussion of the issue between individual freedom and socialization, however, has largely centered around the truth of the proposition as a statement of the tendencies of competition rather than around its ethical significance if true. Those who do not like the actual tendencies of the system as they appear to work out when it is tried — and that is virtually everybody — attack the scientific analysis.

We propose to argue, in the first place, that the conditions of life do not admit of an approximation to individualism of the sort necessarily assumed by the theory, and, second, that there are in the conditions of actual life no ethical implications of the kind commonly taken for granted as involved in individualism insofar as it is possible of realization. . . .

Thus the competitive system, viewed simply as a want-satisfying mechanism, falls far short of our highest ideals. To the theoretical tendencies of perfect competition must be opposed just as fundamental limitations and countertendencies, of which careful scrutiny discloses a rather lengthy list. Its standards of value for the guidance of the use of resources in production are the prices of goods, which diverge widely from accepted ethical values; and if the existing order were more purely competitive, if social control were reduced in scope, it seems clear that the divergence would be enormously wider still. Moreover, untrammeled individualism would probably tend to lower standards progressively rather than to raise them. "Giving the public what it wants" usually means corrupting popular taste. . . .

We must treat still . . . the question of the ethics of competition as such. Is emulation as a motive ethically good or base? Is success in any sort of *contest*, as such, a noble objective? Are there no values which are real in a higher sense than the fact that people have agreed to strive after them and to measure success in life by the result of their striving? It seems evident that most of the ends which are actually striven after in the daily lives of modern peoples are primarily of this character; they are like the cards and checkermen, worthless (at best) in themselves, but the objects of the game; and to raise questions about the game is to make oneself disagreeable. To "play the game" is the current version of accepting the universe, and protest is blasphemy; the good man has given place to the "good sport."

In America particularly, where competitive business and its concomitant, the sporting view of life, have reached their fullest development, there have come to be two sorts of virtue. The greater virtue is to win; and meticulous questions about the methods are not in the best form provided the methods bring victory. The lesser virtue is to go out and die gracefully after having lost.

We do not mean to beg the question whether the spirit of rivalry is ethically good, but only to state it in a form which raises it sharply. It cannot be denied that appeal to the competitive motive may be a source of interest in activity. The issue raised is in part the old and doubtless scientifically unanswerable one of pleasure versus discipline as the fundamental moral value. The hedonist would say that, as a matter of course, whatever adds to the pleasure adds to the value, and would ask only whether more is added than is taken away.

But here we appear to run into the obverse of Mill's paradox of hedonism, which is perhaps the paradox of life. It is in fact much easier to argue that the introduction of the contest motive into economic life has made it more efficient than that it has made it more pleasurable! Candid observations of industrial operatives at work, and of their frenzied, pathetic quest for recreation when off duty, alike fail to give the impression of particularly happy existence. . . . Economic production has been made a fascinating sport *for the leaders*, but this has been accomplished by reducing it to mechanical drudgery for the rank and file.

In the large, is the competitive urge a lure, or is it rather a goad? Is it positive or negative, especially when we recall that for the masses the competition is in the field of consumption, with production regarded purely as a means? From the standpoint of pleasure, does the normal human being prefer a continuous, unquestioning, and almost deadly competition, or the less strenuous atmosphere of activity undertaken for ends that seem intrinsically worthwhile, with a larger admixture of the spectator attitude of appreciation? Current comment on the rush of life and the movement toward guilds and medievalism indicate a widespread feeling of opposition to the competitive tendency.

If, on the other hand, one adopts the view that the end of life is to get things done, the case for competition becomes much stronger; but even here misgivings arise. It is hard to avoid asking *what things*. If it is thought to be important which things are done, competition may be entirely indifferent and unselective, equally effec-

tive as a drive toward worthy and unworthy ends. If so, the selection of ends must be left to accident or to some other principle. There seems to be a tendency, however, for competition to be selective, and not in a very exalted sense. It is hard to believe that emulation is as effective in the "higher" fields of endeavor as it is in relation to material concerns or mere trivialities.

It is possible to hold that it does not matter what is done, that all activity develops personality equally, or that action and change as such are what make life worth living. From the point of view of mere interested activity, if we are to bring into question neither the character of the result nor that of the interest (beyond the fact that it is an "intelligent" interest, the result a foreseen result), the organization of life on a competitive basis would seem to be abundantly justified. Perhaps the organization tends to foster a philosophic attitude which will justify itself; and if so, we have a sufficient "economic interpretation" of the vogue of pragmatism. Interpreting life in terms of power as such, including "intelligence" as a form of power, there can be little question that competitive business has been an effective agency in bringing the forces of nature under human control and is largely responsible for the material progress of the modern era.

It is in terms of power, then, if at all, that competitive economics and the competitive view of life for which it must be largely accountable are to be justified. Whether we are to regard them as justified at all depends on whether we are willing to accept an ethics of power as the basis of our world view. . . . It is the eternal law of reciprocal cause and effect . . . the system tends to mold men's minds in the channels which will justify the system itself, and in this sense there is a partial truth in the "economic interpretation," which we have gone to such lengths to attack and repudiate.

But the matter does not, cannot, rest

there. The whole question is, are we to accept an "ethics of power" *à la* Nietzsche, or does such an acceptance involve a contradiction in terms and really mean the rejection of any true "ethics" altogether? Most of us have been taught in various connections not only that there is some sort of contrast between ethics and power, between right and might, but that the contrast is fundamental to the nature of morality. In these days it is eminently respectable to hold that all ideas of this sort belong to those childish things which one must put away on becoming a man. It is a part of the modern scientific world view, and a legitimate part. To many of its "tough-minded" advocates, one who calls it in question must class himself as not merely "tender-minded," but "feebleminded" as well.

And "logically" they are inevitably right! A strictly scientific discussion of general world problems leads inexorably to fatalism, to a mere question of power, to the relegation to a land of dreams of any ethics which involves questions of another sort than that as to which of two forces is the greater in magnitude. The question at issue must be clearly recognized to be precisely this: whether the logic of science itself is universally valid; whether there is or is not a realm of reality which is not comprehended in factual categories and describable in terms of definite meaning combined in propositions subject to empirical verification. Or, more accurately, it is the question whether knowledge of any such reality is possible, or whether it can be intelligently discussed.

The tough-minded scientist, if candid, will admit that there *may be* such a reality, but will insist that we cannot talk about it "intelligently." Which of course is true, in the nature of the case, if to talk intelligently means to talk scientifically, which are to him equivalent terms. To the modern mind any attempt to argue such a question is fraught with the greatest difficulty, since the modern mind itself is molded into conformity with the scientific view of what is meant by intelligent discourse. Two facts, however, must apparently be accepted. The first is that one may also find "respectable" company in the belief that the scientific world view not only finds no place for many of the most fundamental data of human experience but that, tested by the canons of its own logic, it is ultimately riddled with contradictions; numerous minds of demonstrated competence in the field of science itself hold this view. The second fact is that people do manage to "understand each other" more or less, in conversation about things which are not matters of scientific fact but of interpretation, as in discussions of art and of character or personality.

Assuming that all ethical standards other than that of quantity of accomplishment, the ideal generated by the institution itself, are not to be dismissed *a priori* as manifestations of incompetence to discuss the question, we may close the discussion by referring briefly to the relation of some historic types of ethical theory to the problem of the evaluation of competition. From the standpoint of hedonism, the question would be simply whether competition has added to the pleasure of living. . . .

In our view the nineteenth-century hedonists were not ethical hedonists anyway. They held, or assumed, the position of psychological hedonism, which involves the question-begging procedure of using pleasure as a synonym for motive in general, and to attack or criticize it at this day would be to slay the slain. They were really utilitarians in the sense in which the term was used by Paulsen, referring to the judgment of human actions by their consequences and not in accordance with formal rules. On the crucial question, how to judge the consequences, they were commonly silent or vague.

But examination will show that nineteenth-century utilitarianism was in essence merely the ethics of power, the "glorified economics." . . . Its outcome was to reduce virtue to prudence, its ideal the achievement of the greatest *quantity of desired results*. It was scientific, intellectual, in the naturalistic, pragmatic conception of knowledge as instrumental to power, that is, as power itself. As to the purposes for which power *ought* to be used, the true problem of ethics, they had nothing to say in any definite or systematic way; the fact of desire was tacitly accepted as the essence of value. Spencer bravely reduced the whole system to an ethical absurdity by explicitly carrying desire back to an ultimate justification in the desire to live, postulating that any species "must" desire what is good for it in a biological sense; and for all the group, survival power was in fact the final measure of rightness.

It seems to the writer almost superfluous to deny the appropriateness of the term "ethics" to any such conception. The conditions of survival are merely the laws of biology. It may well be the part of prudence to act in accordance with them, assuming that one *wants* to survive, but it can hardly be associated with the notions of right or duty, and if these have no meaning beyond prudence, the whole realm of ethics is illusory. Ethics deals with the problem of choosing between different kinds of life and assumes that there is real choice between different kinds, or else there is no such thing as ethics. The ethical character of competition is not decided by the fact that it stimulates a greater amount of activity; this merely raises the question of the ethical quality of what is done or of the motive itself.

With this so-called ethics of scientific naturalism may be contrasted, as general types of ethical thought, true ethical hedonism or eudemonism, the Greek and the Christian views. From the standpoint of the first, the happiness philosophy, little need be added to what has already been said. Competition may form an added source of pleasure in

activity, especially to the winner or, in the progress of the game, to those who stand some chance to win. But it is more likely to become a goad, especially when participation in the contest is compulsory. There is a fairly established consensus that happiness depends more on spiritual resourcefulness and a joyous appreciation of the costless things of life, especially affection for one's fellow creatures, than it does on material satisfaction. A strong argument for cooperation, if it would work, would be its tendency to teach people to like each other in a more positive sense than can ever be bred by participation in a contest — certainly in a contest in which the means of life, or of a decent life, are felt to be at stake. The dominance of salesmanship in the business world, as well as the spirit of economic rivalry, must also tend to work against the appreciation of the "free goods."

It should be observed also that while the principle of "whom the Lord loveth He chasteneth" is hard to apply as a maxim of practical morality, it is generally admitted that human nature is likely to show up morally finer under adversity than in security and ease; also that few people can be trusted with much power without using it to the physical damage of others and their own moral discredit.

Surely no justification of competition as a motive is to be found in the Aristotelian conception of the good as that which is intrinsically worthy of man as man, or the Platonic idea of archetypal goodness. The outstanding characteristic of Greek ethical thought was the conception of the good as objective and of the moral judgment as a cognition. A thing should be done because it is the thing to do, not because it is or is not being done by others. Virtue is knowledge and the good is intellectually conceived, but the meaning of these statements contrasts as widely as possible with the modern reduction of virtue to prudence and of choice to a calculation of advantage. The intellectual quality in Greek ethics is the capacity of discrimination between true and false values, which is a wholly different thing from the ability to foresee changes and adapt means to ends. The one runs in terms of appreciation as the other runs in terms of power. The ideal, in the one case, is perfection; in the other, that of bigness. To be sure, the Greeks were far from indifferent to recognition and glory, and the contest spirit played a large role in the life of the people, as shown in the national games. But the ideal seems always to have been the achievement of perfection and the education of the people to recognize superior merit, not merely to win. Certainly it was not the mere winning of power.

Christianity has been interpreted in so many conflicting ways that one must hesitate to bring it into a scientific discussion; yet even this wide range of uncertainty will not admit competitive values into Christian thought. If there is anything on which divergent interpretations would have to agree, it would be the admission that the Christian conception of goodness is the antithesis of competitive. We are by no means forced to believe that the central figure of the Gospels was an ascetic; he never condemned pleasure as such, and seems to have had his own pleasure in life. But his participation in any sort of competitive sport is not to be imagined. Among his most characteristic utterances were the fervent exhortations that the last should be first and that he who would be chief should be the servant of all.

The Christian ethical ideal contrasts as sharply with the Greek as either does with modern ideas derived from natural science and political economy. We have said that any *ethical* judgment of activity must be based not upon its efficiency, the quantity of results accomplished, but on either the character of those results or the character of the motive which led to the action. The Greek view fixes attention upon the character of the result and gives an essentially aesthetic conception of ethical value; Christianity centers attention upon the motive, and its ideal of life may be summed up in the word "spirituality," as the Greek ideal is summed up in "beauty" or "perfection." As the Greek identified virtue with knowledge, assuming it to be inconceivable that one should recognize true values and not act in accordance with them, Christianity (more explicitly as formulated by Paul — Romans 7:15; Galatians 5:19-23) makes virtue consist in conscientiousness, in doing what one believes to be right; rather than in the correct perception of objective goodness.

It must be admitted that if it is hard to describe or define beauty, it is enormously more difficult to discuss spirituality in terms that seem at all intelligible to a scientific age. Both ideals agree in differing from economic (scientific, pragmatic) ethics in that they are *qualitative* in their ideals, whereas the last is merely quantitative. It seems fairly clear to the writer that it is from Christianity (and from Kant, who merely systematized Christian, or Pauline, principles) that modern common sense derives its conceptions of what is ethical when that point is explicitly under discussion.

The striking fact in modern life is the virtually complete separation between the spiritual ethics which constitutes its accepted theory of conduct and the unethical, uncriticized notion of efficiency which forms its substitute for a practical working ideal, its effective values being accepted unconsciously from tradition or the manipulations of commercial sales managers, with a very slight admixture of aesthetic principles. For "spirituality" is reserved in practice a smaller and smaller fraction of the seventh day, by a smaller and smaller fraction of the population; and even that is more and more transformed by organizations into a mere contest in membership and display, with a larger or smaller admixture of the element of aesthetic diversion and a smaller or larger admixture of pure commercialism.

The spirit of life in the "Christian" nations and the spirit of Christianity offer an interesting study in the contrast between theory and practice. And all the while there are multiplying evidences of a genuine spiritual hunger in the modern peoples. They have got away from the spiritual attitude toward life and do not know how to get back. Science is too strong for old beliefs and competitive commercialism too strong for old ideals of simplicity, humility, and reverence.

Thus we appear to search in vain for any really ethical basis of approval for competition as a basis for an ideal type of human relations, or as a motive to action. It fails to harmonize either with the pagan ideal of society as a community of friends or the Christian ideal of spiritual fellowship. Its only justification is that it is effective in getting things done; but any candid answer to the question, "what things," compels the admission that they leave much to be desired. Whether for good or bad, its aesthetic ideals are not such as command the approval of the most competent judges, and as for spirituality, commercialism is in a fair way to make that term incomprehensible to living men. The motive itself has been generally condemned by the best spirits of the race.

73.

G. Sutherland, W. H. Taft, and O. W. Holmes, Jr.: *Adkins v. Children's Hospital*

During the administrations of Taft and Wilson, the Supreme Court had approved a good deal of progressive legislation; but during the decade that began in 1919, a conservative, even reactionary, trend set in. There was persistent opposition to any federal legislation on behalf of labor, and pro-labor state laws were also reversed. In Adkins v. Children's Hospital *(April 9, 1923), the Court ruled unconstitutional a District of Columbia minimum wage law for women. The selection reprinted below gives portions of Justice Sutherland's decision and of the dissents by Chief Justice Taft and Justice Holmes.*

Source: 261 U.S. 525.

Mr. Justice Sutherland. The judicial duty of passing upon the constitutionality of an act of Congress is one of great gravity and delicacy. The statute here in question has successfully borne the scrutiny of the legislative branch of the government, which, by enacting it, has affirmed its validity; and that determination must be given great weight. This Court, by an unbroken line of decisions from Chief Justice Marshall to the present day, has steadily adhered to the rule that every possible presumption is in favor of the validity of an act of Congress until overcome beyond rational doubt. But if by clear and indubitable demonstration a statute be opposed to the Constitution, we have no choice but to say so.

The Constitution, by its own terms, is

the supreme law of the land, emanating from the people, the repository of ultimate sovereignty under our form of government. A congressional statute, on the other hand, is the act of an agency of this sovereign authority, and, if it conflict with the Constitution, must fall; for that which is not supreme must yield to that which is. To hold it invalid (if it be invalid) is a plain exercise of the judicial power — that power vested in courts to enable them to administer justice according to law.

From the authority to ascertain and determine the law in a given case, there necessarily results, in case of conflict, the duty to declare and enforce the rule of the supreme law and reject that of an inferior act of legislation which, transcending the Constitution, is of no effect and binding on no one. This is not the exercise of a substantive power to review and nullify acts of Congress, for no such substantive power exists. It is simply a necessary concomitant of the power to hear and dispose of a case or controversy properly before the court, to the determination of which must be brought the test and measure of the law.

The statute now under consideration is attacked upon the ground that it authorizes an unconstitutional interference with the freedom of contract included within the guarantees of the due-process clause of the Fifth Amendment. That the right to contract about one's affairs is a part of the liberty of the individual protected by this clause is settled by the decisions of this Court and is no longer open to question. . . .

In the *Muller Case*, the validity of an Oregon statute forbidding the employment of any female in certain industries more than ten hours during any one day was upheld. The decision proceeded upon the theory that the difference between the sexes may justify a different rule respecting hours of labor in the case of women than in the case of men. It is pointed out that these consist in differences of physical structure, especially in respect of the maternal functions, and also in the fact that historically woman has always been dependent upon man, who has established his control by superior physical strength. . . .

In view of the great — not to say revolutionary — changes which have taken place since that utterance, in the contractual, political, and civil status of women, culminating in the Nineteenth Amendment, it is not unreasonable to say that these differences have now come almost, if not quite, to the vanishing point. In this aspect of the matter, while the physical differences must be recognized in appropriate cases, and legislation fixing hours or conditions of work may properly take them into account, we cannot accept the doctrine that women of mature age, *sui juris*, require or may be subjected to restrictions upon their liberty of contract which could not lawfully be imposed in the case of men under similar circumstances. To do so would be to ignore all the implications to be drawn from the present-day trend of legislation, as well as that of common thought and usage, by which woman is accorded emancipation from the old doctrine that she must be given special protection or be subjected to special restraint in her contractual and civil relationships. In passing, it may be noted that the instant statute applies in the case of a woman employer contracting with a woman employee as it does when the former is a man. . . .

A law forbidding work to continue beyond a given number of hours leaves the parties free to contract about wages and thereby equalize whatever additional burdens may be imposed upon the employer as a result of the restrictions as to hours, by an adjustment in respect of the amount of wages. . . . The authority to fix hours of labor cannot be exercised except in respect of those occupations where work of long-continued duration is detrimental to health. This Court has been careful in every case where the question has been raised to place its decision upon this limited authority of the legislature to regulate hours of labor and to disclaim any purpose to uphold the legislation as fixing wages, thus recognizing an essential difference between the two. It seems plain that these decisions afford no real support for any form of law establishing minimum wages.

If now, in the light furnished by the foregoing exceptions to the general rule forbidding legislative interference with freedom of contract, we examine and analyze the statute in question, we shall see that it differs from them in every material respect. It is not a law dealing with any business charged with a public interest or with public work, or to meet and tide over a temporary emergency. It has nothing to do with the character, methods, or periods of wage payments. It does not prescribe hours of labor or conditions under which labor is to be done. It is not for the protection of persons under legal disability or for the prevention of fraud. It is simply and exclusively a price-fixing law, confined to adult women (for we are not now considering the provisions relating to minors), who are legally as capable of contracting for themselves as men.

It forbids two parties having lawful capacity — under penalties as to the employer — to freely contract with one another in respect of the price for which one shall render service to the other in a purely private employment where both are willing, perhaps anxious, to agree, even though the consequence may be to oblige one to surrender a desirable engagement and the other to dispense with the services of a desirable employee. The price fixed by the board need have no relation to the capacity or earning power of the employee, the number of hours which may happen to constitute

the day's work, the character of the place where the work is to be done, or the circumstances or surroundings of the employment; and, while it has no other basis to support its validity than the assumed necessities of the employee, it takes no account of any independent resources she may have. It is based wholly on the opinions of the members of the board and their advisers — perhaps an average of their opinions, if they do not precisely agree — as to what will be necessary to provide a living for a woman, keep her in health, and preserve her morals. It applies to any and every occupation in the District, without regard to its nature or the character of the work.

The standard furnished by the statute for the guidance of the board is so vague as to be impossible of practical application with any reasonable degree of accuracy. What is sufficient to supply the necessary cost of living for a woman worker and maintain her in good health and protect her morals is obviously not a precise or unvarying sum — not even approximately so. The amount will depend upon a variety of circumstances — the individual temperament, habits of thrift, care, ability to buy necessaries intelligently, and whether the woman live alone or with her family. To those who practise economy, a given sum will afford comfort, while to those of contrary habit the same sum will be wholly inadequate. The cooperative economies of the family group are not taken into account, though they constitute an important consideration in estimating the cost of living, for it is obvious that the individual expense will be less in the case of a member of a family than in the case of one living alone.

The relation between earnings and morals is not capable of standardization. It cannot be shown that well-paid women safeguard their morals more carefully than those who are poorly paid. Morality rests upon other considerations than wages; and there is, certainly, no such prevalent connection between the two as to justify a broad attempt to adjust the latter with reference to the former. As a means of safeguarding morals, the attempted classification, in our opinion, is without reasonable basis. No distinction can be made between women who work for others and those who do not; nor is there ground for distinction between women and men, for, certainly, if women require a minimum wage to preserve their morals men require it to preserve their honesty.

For these reasons, and others which might be stated, the inquiry in respect of the necessary cost of living and of the income necessary to preserve health and morals presents an individual and not a composite question, and must be answered for each individual considered by herself and not by a general formula prescribed by a statutory bureau. . . .

The law takes account of the necessities of only one party to the contract. It ignores the necessities of the employer by compelling him to pay not less than a certain sum, not only whether the employee is capable of earning it but irrespective of the ability of his business to sustain the burden, generously leaving him, of course, the privilege of abandoning his business as an alternative for going on at a loss. Within the limits of the minimum sum, he is precluded, under penalty of fine and imprisonment, from adjusting compensation to the differing merits of his employees. It compels him to pay at least the sum fixed in any event, because the employee needs it, but requires no service of equivalent value from the employee. It therefore undertakes to solve but one-half of the problem. The other half is the establishment of a corresponding standard of efficiency, and this forms no part of the policy of the legislation, although in practice the former half without the latter must lead to ultimate failure in accordance with the inexorable law that no one can continue indefinitely to take out more than he puts in without ultimately exhausting the supply.

The law is not confined to the great and powerful employers but embraces those whose bargaining power may be as weak as that of the employee. It takes no account of periods of stress and business depression, of crippling losses, which may leave the employer himself without adequate means of livelihood. To the extent that the sum fixed exceeds the fair value of the services rendered, it amounts to a compulsory exaction from the employer for the support of a partially indigent person, for whose condition there rests upon him no peculiar responsibility, and therefore, in effect, arbitrarily shifts to his shoulders a burden which, if it belongs to anybody, belongs to society as a whole.

The feature of this statute which, perhaps more than any other, puts upon it the stamp of invalidity is that it exacts from the employer an arbitrary payment for a purpose and upon a basis having no causal connection with his business, or the contract or the work the employee engages to do. The declared basis, as already pointed out, is not the value of the service rendered but the extraneous circumstance that the employee needs to get a prescribed sum of money to insure her subsistence, health, and morals.

The ethical right of every worker, man or woman, to a living wage may be conceded. One of the declared and important purposes of trade organizations is to secure it. And with that principle and with every legitimate effort to realize it in fact, no one can quarrel; but the fallacy of the proposed method of attaining it is that it assumes that every employer is bound at all events to furnish it. The moral requirement implicit in every contract of employment, viz., that the amount to be paid and the service to be rendered shall bear to each other some relation of just equivalence, is completely ignored. The necessities of the employee are alone considered and these arise outside of the employment, are the same when there is no employment, and as great in one occupation as in another.

Certainly the employer by paying a fair equivalent for the service rendered, though not sufficient to support the employee, has neither caused nor contributed to her poverty. On the contrary, to the extent of what he pays he has relieved it. In principle, there can be no difference between the case of selling labor and the case of selling goods. If one goes to the butcher, the baker, or grocer to buy food, he is morally entitled to obtain the worth of his money, but he is not entitled to more. If what he gets is worth what he pays, he is not justified in demanding more simply because he needs more; and the shopkeeper, having dealt fairly and honestly in that transaction, is not concerned in any peculiar sense with the question of his customer's necessities. Should a statute undertake to vest in a commission power to determine the quantity of food necessary for individual support and require the shopkeeper, if he sell to the individual at all, to furnish that quantity at not more than a fixed maximum, it would undoubtedly fall before the constitutional test.

The fallacy of any argument in support of the validity of such a statute would be quickly exposed. The argument in support of that now being considered is equally fallacious, though the weakness of it may not be so plain. A statute requiring an employer to pay in money, to pay at prescribed and regular intervals, to pay the value of the services rendered, even to pay with fair relation to the extent of the benefit obtained from the service, would be understandable. But a statute which prescribes payment without regard to any of these things and solely with relation to circumstances apart from the contract of employment, the business affected by it and the work done under it, is so clearly the product of a naked, arbitrary exercise of power that it cannot be allowed to stand under the Constitution of the United States. . . .

It is said that great benefits have resulted from the operation of such statutes, not alone in the District of Columbia but in the several states where they have been in force. A mass of reports, opinions of special observers and students of the subject, and the like, has been brought before us in support of this statement, all of which we have found interesting but only mildly persuasive. That the earnings of women now are greater than they were formerly and that conditions affecting women have become better in other respects may be conceded, but convincing indications of the logical relation of these desirable changes to the law in question are significantly lacking. They may be, and quite probably are, due to other causes.

We cannot close our eyes to the notorious fact that earnings everywhere in all occupations have greatly increased — not alone in states where the minimum wage law obtains but in the country generally — quite as much or more among men as among women and in occupations outside the reach of the law as in those governed by it. No real test of the economic value of the law can be had during periods of maximum employment, when general causes keep wages up to or above the minimum; that will come in periods of depression and struggle for employment when the efficient will be employed at the minimum rate while the less capable may not be employed at all.

Finally, it may be said that if, in the interest of the public welfare, the police power may be invoked to justify the fixing of a minimum wage, it may, when the public welfare is thought to require it, be invoked to justify a maximum wage. The power to fix high wages connotes, by like course of reasoning, the power to fix low wages. If, in the face of the guarantees of the Fifth Amendment, this form of legislation shall be legally justified, the field for the operation of the police power will have been widened to a great and dangerous degree. If, for example, in the opinion of future lawmakers, wages in the building trades shall become so high as to preclude people of ordinary means from building and owning homes, an authority which sustains the minimum wage will be invoked to support a maximum wage for building laborers and artisans, and the same argument which has been here urged to strip the employer of his constitutional liberty of contract in one direction will be utilized to strip the employee of his constitutional liberty of contract in the opposite direction. A wrong decision does not end with itself: it is a precedent, and, with the swing of sentiment, its bad influence may run from one extremity of the arc to the other.

It has been said that legislation of the kind now under review is required in the interest of social justice, for whose ends freedom of contract may lawfully be subjected to restraint. The liberty of the individual to do as he pleases, even in innocent matters, is not absolute. It must frequently yield to the common good, and the line beyond which the power of interference may not be pressed is neither definite nor unalterable but may be made to move, within limits not well-defined, with changing need and circumstance. Any attempt to fix a rigid boundary would be unwise as well as futile. But, nevertheless, there are limits to the power, and when these have been passed, it becomes the plain duty of the courts in the proper exercise of their authority to so declare. To sustain the individual freedom of action contemplated by the Constitution, is not to strike down the common good but to exalt it; for surely the good of society as a whole cannot be better served than by the preservation against arbitrary restraint of the liberties of its constituent members.

It follows from what has been said that the act in question passes the limit prescribed by the Constitution, and, accordingly, the decrees of the court below are *affirmed*.

Mr. Chief Justice Taft. I regret much to differ from the Court in these cases.

The boundary of the police power beyond which its exercise becomes an invasion of the guarantee of liberty under the Fifth and Fourteenth Amendments to the Constitution is not easy to mark. Our Court has been laboriously engaged in pricking out a line in successive cases. We must be careful, it seems to me, to follow that line as well as we can and not to depart from it by suggesting a distinction that is formal rather than real.

Legislatures in limiting freedom of contract between employee and employer by a minimum wage proceed on the assumption that employees, in the class receiving least pay, are not upon a full level of equality of choice with their employer and in their necessitous circumstances are prone to accept pretty much anything that is offered. They are peculiarly subject to the overreaching of the harsh and greedy employer. The evils of the sweating system and of the long hours and low wages which are characteristic of it are well known.

Now, I agree that it is a disputable question in the field of political economy how far a statutory requirement of maximum hours or minimum wages may be a useful remedy for these evils, and whether it may not make the case of the oppressed employee worse than it was before. But it is not the function of this Court to hold congressional acts invalid simply because they are passed to carry out economic views which the Court believes to be unwise or unsound.

Legislatures which adopt a requirement of maximum hours or minimum wages may be presumed to believe that when sweating employers are prevented from paying unduly low wages by positive law, they will continue their business, abating that part of their profits which were wrung from the necessities of their employees, and will concede the better terms required by the law; and that while in individual cases hardships may result, the restriction will enure to the benefit of the general class of employees in whose interest the law is passed and so to that of the community at large.

The right of the legislature under the Fifth and Fourteenth Amendments to limit the hours of employment on the score of the health of the employee, it seems to me, has been firmly established. As to that, one would think, the line had been pricked out so that it has become a well-formulated rule. . . .

If it be said that long hours of labor have a more direct effect upon the health of the employee than the low wage, there is very respectable authority from close observers, disclosed in the record and in the literature on the subject quoted at length in the briefs, that they are equally harmful in this regard. Congress took this view and we cannot say it was not warranted in so doing.

With deference to the very able opinion of the Court and my brethren who concur in it, it appears to me to exaggerate the importance of the wage term of the contract of employment as more inviolate than its other terms. Its conclusion seems influenced by the fear that the concession of the power to impose a minimum wage must carry with it a concession of the power to fix a maximum wage. This, I submit, is a *non sequitur*. A line of distinction like the one under discussion in this case is, as the opinion elsewhere admits, a matter of degree and practical experience and not of pure logic. Certainly the wide difference between prescribing a minimum wage and a maximum wage could as a matter of degree and experience be easily affirmed.

Moreover, there are decisions by this Court which have sustained legislative limitations in respect to the wage term in contracts of employment. . . . While these did not impose a minimum on wages, they did take away from the employee the freedom to agree as to how they should be fixed, in what medium they should be paid, and when they should be paid, all features that might affect the amount or the mode of enjoyment of them. The first two really rested on the advantage the employer had in dealing with the employee. The third was deemed a proper curtailment of a sailor's right of contract in his own interest because of his proneness to squander his wages in port before sailing.

In *Bunting v. Oregon, supra,* employees in a mill, factory, or manufacturing establishment were required, if they worked over ten hours a day, to accept for the three additional hours permitted not less than 50 percent more than their usual wage. This was sustained as a mild penalty imposed on the employer to enforce the limitation as to hours; but it necessarily curtailed the employee's freedom to contract to work for the wages he saw fit to accept during those three hours. I do not feel, therefore, that either on the basis of reason, experience, or authority the boundary of the police power should be drawn to include maximum hours and exclude a minimum wage. . . .

I am not sure from a reading of the opinion whether the Court thinks the authority of *Muller* v. *Oregon* is shaken by the adoption of the Nineteenth Amendment. The Nineteenth Amendment did not change the physical strength or limitations of women upon which the decision in *Muller* v. *Oregon* rests. The amendment did give women political power and makes more certain that legislative provisions for their protection will be in accord with their interests as they see them. But I don't think we are warranted in varying constitutional construction based on physical differences between men and women because of the amendment. . . .

I am authorized to say that Mr. Justice Sanford concurs in this opinion.

Mr. Justice Holmes. The question in this case is the broad one — Whether Congress can establish minimum rates of wages for women in the District of Columbia with due provision for special circumstances, or whether we must say that Congress has no power to meddle with the matter at all. To me, notwithstanding the deference due to the prevailing judgment of the Court, the power of Congress seems absolutely free from doubt. The end, to remove conditions leading to ill health, immorality, and the deterioration of the race, no one would deny to be within the scope of constitutional legislation. The means are means that have the approval of Congress, of many states, and of those governments from which we have learned our greatest lessons.

When so many intelligent persons, who have studied the matter more than any of us can, have thought that the means are effective and are worth the price, it seems to me impossible to deny that the belief reasonably may be held by reasonable men. If the law encountered no other objection than that the means bore no relation to the end or that they cost too much, I do not suppose that anyone would venture to say that it was bad. I agree, of course, that a law answering the foregoing requirements might be invalidated by specific provisions of the Constitution. For instance, it might take private property without just compensation. But in the present instance the only objection that can be urged is found within the vague contours of the Fifth Amendment, prohibiting the depriving any person of liberty or property without due process of law. To that I turn.

The earlier decisions upon the same words in the Fourteenth Amendment began within our memory and went no farther than an unpretentious assertion of the liberty to follow the ordinary callings. Later, that innocuous generality was expanded into the dogma, Liberty of Contract. Contract is not specially mentioned in the text that we have to construe. It is merely an example of doing what you want to do, embodied in the word "liberty." But pretty much all law consists in forbidding men to do some things that they want to do, and contract is no more exempt from law than other acts. . . .

I confess that I do not understand the principle on which the power to fix a minimum for the wages of women can be denied by those who admit the power to fix a maximum for their hours of work. I fully assent to the proposition that here as elsewhere the distinctions of the law are distinctions of degree, but I perceive no difference in the kind or degree of interference with liberty, the only matter with which we have any concern, between the one case and the other. The bargain is equally affected whichever half you regulate. *Muller* v. *Oregon*, I take it, is as good law today as it was in 1908. It will need more than the Nineteenth Amendment to convince me that there are no differences between men and women, or that legislation cannot take those differences into account. . . .

This statute does not compel anybody to pay anything. It simply forbids employment at rates below those fixed as the minimum requirement of health and right living. It is safe to assume that women will not be employed at even the lowest wages allowed unless they earn them, or unless the employer's business can sustain the burden. In short, the law in its character and operation is like hundreds of so-called police laws that have been upheld. I see no greater objection to using a board to apply the standard fixed by the act than there is to the other commissions with which we have become familiar, or than there is to the requirement of a license in other cases. The fact that the statute warrants classification, which like all classifications may bear hard upon some individuals, or in exceptional cases, notwithstanding the power given to the board to issue a special license, is no greater infirmity than is incident to all law. But the ground on which the law is held to fail is fundamental and therefore it is unnecessary to consider matters of detail.

The criterion of constitutionality is not whether we believe the law to be for the public good. We certainly cannot be prepared to deny that a reasonable man reasonably might have that belief in view of the legislation of Great Britain, Victoria, and a number of the states of this Union.

The belief is fortified by a very remarkable collection of documents submitted on behalf of the appellants, material here, I conceive, only as showing that the belief reasonably may be held. . . .

I am of opinion that the statute is valid and that the decree should be reversed.

74.

E. E. Cummings: "the Cambridge ladies"

E. E. Cummings returned from World War I a daring poetic innovator, an iconoclast, and an experimenter with new forms (he insisted on spelling his own name e e cummings). More conventional than some of his poems, "the Cambridge ladies" nevertheless demonstrates his unorthodox style and his satiric treatment of various segments of American society — in this case, the staid ladies of Cambridge, Massachusetts, and, by extension, a whole class of women who lived, according to Cummings, in "furnished souls." The poem was first published in 1923.

Source: *Collected Poems*, New York, 1963.

⅋ THE CAMBRIDGE LADIES

the Cambridge ladies who live in furnished souls
are unbeautiful and have comfortable minds
(also, with the church's protestant blessings
daughters, unscented shapeless spirited)
they believe in Christ and Longfellow, both dead,
are invariably interested in so many things —
at the present writing one still finds
delighted fingers knitting for the is it Poles?
perhaps. While permanent faces coyly bandy
scandal of Mrs. N and Professor D
. . . . the Cambridge ladies do not care, above
Cambridge if sometimes in its box of
sky lavender and cornerless, the
moon rattles like a fragment of angry candy

75.

Louis Sullivan: The *Chicago Tribune* Competition

The early recognition by such architects as Louis Sullivan and Frank Lloyd Wright of the possibilities inherent in steel-frame construction had made Chicago a leading architectural center as early as the 1890s. Apparently in an effort to maintain the city's reputation for innovation in building, the Chicago Tribune *announced a competition to select the design for its new skyscraper to be erected on Michigan Avenue. Entries were received from architects the world over, but although professional opinion favored the design of Finnish architect Eliel Saarinen, the* Tribune *awarded first prize in the competition to a local architect whose entry called for a traditional Gothic tower. (Saarinen's design, nevertheless, was subsequently very influential.) Louis Sullivan, in an article first published in February 1923 and reprinted here, discussed the significance of the choice.*

Source: *Architectural Record,* February 1923.

SOME SEVENTY YEARS AGO, a philosopher, in the course of his studies of the ego, separated men into two classes, distinct, yet reciprocally related, to wit: masters of ideas and those governed by ideas. It was upon ideas as powers for good or ill that he laid the heavy hand; upon ideas as a living force obedient to the mastery of vision, springing forth from imagination's depths, from the inexhaustible reservoir of instinct.

Ego, considered solely as free spirit, stands out visibly as master of ideas. Ego, examined as a spirit benumbed through lack of action, hence inert and unfree, becomes dim of vision and renounces its will. It thus becomes the slave of imposed ideas whose validity it assumes it has not the strength to test, even were the idea of testing to arise. Hence in timidity, it evokes the negative idea of authority as a welcome substitute for its declining volition.

Masters of ideas are masters of courage; the free will of adventure is in them. They stride where others creep. The pride of action is in them. They explore, they test, they seek realities to meet them face to face — knowing well that realities and illusions exist commingled within and without, but also knowing well that ego is its own. Hence they walk erect and fearless in the open, with that certitude which vision brings — while slaves are slaves by choice. They seek shelter in the *shadows* of ideas.

Ever such were the great free spirits of the past, and such are those of our own day.

Masters of ideas of the past and now frequently have sought, and seek, dominion, and have reached it because the idea of dominion coincides precisely with the idea of submission. Other masters of ideas then and now, mostly those of immense compassion, have been, and still are, crucified by those so long in the dark that the idea of spiritual freedom is abhorrent.

A consciousness is now growing and widely spreading in our modern world of thought, among masters, of truly great ideas, that unless we become free spirits casting off the cruel and awakening to the constructive power of beneficence, we shall vanish in decay and self-destruction.

The simple world idea, now in process of becoming in the hearts of men, is the idea of freedom from the domination of feudal ideas. Is there a power that can stop this becoming? There is not.

The eyelids of the world are slowly, surely lifting. The vision of the world of men is slowly, surely clearing. A world idea is sprouting from its seed in the rich soil of world sorrow. Beneath the surface of things as they are, everywhere it is germinating — unconsciously with the many, consciously with the few.

The old idea that man must ever remain the victim of fate will fade as fear fades. The new idea that man may shape his destiny will appear in its place, in a dissolving scene of the world drama, as democracy arises through the humus of the age-long feudal idea. For democracy would remain, as now it is, a senseless word, a vacant shell, a futile sentimentalism, a mere fetish did it not carry in its heart the loftiest of optimistic aspirations, wholly warranted, spite of all appearance to the contrary, and grasp the mastery of ideas wholly beneficent in power to create a world of joy devoid of fear.

The world is growing more compact every day, and every day the day is shortening, while the fleeting hour becomes thereby so much the fuller. The cold rigidity of frontiers is melting away, unnoted by the blind — every day the world becomes increasingly mobile, every day there is a silent interchange, every day communication is more fleet, and humanity, in response, more fluent. Slowly, day by day, with enormous and gathering momentum, the hearts of the world draw together.

The process is silent and gentle as the dewfall. There are those who see this; there are those who do not. There are those who see in the lightnings and the raging storms of the feudal idea, reaching now the climac-

teric of its supreme mania for dominion, the symbol of self-destruction of a race gone wholly mad. But that is not so. The masters of the feudal idea alone have gone mad with hate; the multitudes are sound. They have lost a pathetic faith in the feudal concept of self-preservation which has wooed and betrayed them. They are moving somnambulistically now, upward toward a faith that is new and real, a constructive idea, common to all, because springing from the hearts of all, of which all shall be masters, and about which shall form for the first time beneath the sun, a sane hope and faith in life, a faith in man — an idea which shall banish fear and exalt courage to its seat of power.

This idea will become the luminous, the central idea of all mankind because it is the offspring of that which is deepest down in all. It is and will continue as long as life lasts in the race, the shining symbol of man's resurrection from the dead past, of man's faith in himself and his power to create anew.

There are those who will decry this hope as they view in despair a world writhing in the depths of pessimism, of mendacity and intrigue. Yet are they those who are without faith in mankind, without faith in themselves. For this is the modern affirmation: Man is not born in sin but in glory.

All of this has sharply to do with the *Tribune* Competition, for in that showing was brought into clearest light the deadline that lies between a master of ideas and one governed by ideas. There they came, squarely face to face: the second prize and the first. All the others may be grouped aside, for what is involved here is not a series of distinctions in composition or in detail but the leading forth into the light of day of the profoundest aspiration that animates the hearts of men.

This aspiration has remained inarticulate too long; its utterance at large has been choked by varied emotions of fear; the splendor of its singleness of purpose has been obscured by the host of shadows generated in bewilderment of thought, in a world that has lost its bearings and submits in distress to the government of dying ideas.

In its preliminary advertising, the *Tribune* broadcasted the inspiring idea of a new and great adventure, in which pride, magnanimity, and its honor were to be inseparably unified and voiced in "the most beautiful office building in the world," to be created for it by any man sufficiently imaginative and solid in competence in whatever spot on the surface of the earth such a man might dwell.

Specifically, on the third page of its formal and official program, these statements are made: "To erect the most beautiful and distinctive office building in the world is the desire of the *Tribune,* and in order to obtain the design for such an edifice, this competition has been instituted."

These words are high-minded; they stir imagination.

At the beginning of the paragraph immediately succeeding are found these words: "The competition will be of international scope, qualified architects of established reputation in all parts of the world being eligible."

These words are magnanimous; they stir not only the world of architectural activity but as well that of enlightened laity. Never perhaps, in our day, has such interest in architecture been aroused.

Not yet content in its eagerness, and purposing to make assurance of good faith and loyalty to an ideal triply sure, there is to be found on page 13, the final page of the program, the following statement: "It cannot be reiterated too emphatically that the primary objective of the *Chicago Tribune* in instituting this Competition is to secure the design for a structure distinctive and imposing — the most beautiful office building in the world."

The intensive use of the word "primary"

gives to the full clause the imposing promise of a token, of a covenant with the earth. With that one word "primary," the *Tribune* set its bow in the cloud.

The craving for beauty thus set forth by the *Tribune* is imbued with romance; with that high romance which is the essence, the vital impulse that inheres in all the great works of man in all places and all times, that vibrates in his loftiest thoughts, his heroic deeds, his otherwise inexplicable sacrifices, and which forms the halo of his great compassions and of the tragedy within the depths of his sorrows. So deeply seated, so persistent, so perennial in the heart of humanity is this ineffable presence that, suppressed in us, we decay and die. For man is not born to trouble, as the sparks fly upward; he is born to hope and to achieve.

If a critique of architecture, or any other art, or any activity whatsoever, is to be valid, it must be based upon a reasoned process. It must enter with intelligence into the object or subject at hand, there to seek what signifies, and yet maintain such detachment as to render judgment unconstrained and free. A true critique is not satisfied with the surface of things, it must penetrate that surface to search the animus, the thought; it must go deeply to the roots, it must go to origins, it must seek the elemental, the primitive; it must go to the depths and gauge the status of the work thereby. A true critique must likewise derive of the humanities. It is not its function to deal with cold truths but with living truths.

Viewed in this light, the second and the first prize stand before us side by side. One glance of the trained eye, and instant judgment comes; that judgment which flashes from inner experience in recognition of a masterpiece. The verdict of the Jury of Award is at once reversed, and the second prize is placed first, where it belongs by virtue of its beautifully controlled and virile power. The first prize is demoted to the level of those works evolved of dying ideas, even as it sends forth a frantic cry to escape from the common bondage of those governed by ideas. The apposition is intensely dramatic to the sensitive mind. Yet it is in this very apposition that we find a key wherewith to unlock and swing open wide a door, and reveal to all the vast and unused power resident in the great architectural art when inspired into motion by a master of ideas.

The Finnish master-edifice is not a lonely cry in the wilderness, it is a voice, resonant and rich, ringing amidst the wealth and joy of life. In utterance sublime and melodious, it prophesies a time to come, and not so far away, when the wretched and the yearning, the sordid and the fierce shall escape the bondage and the mania of fixed ideas.

It is wretched psychology to assume that man is by nature selfish. The clear eye of sympathy sees beyond a doubt that this is not so; that, on the contrary, man by nature is a giver; and it is precisely this one discerns in this beauteous edifice; the native quality of manhood giving freely of inherent wealth of power, with hands that overflow, as to say: There is more and more and more in me to give, as also is there in yourselves — if but ye knew — ye of little faith.

Qualifying as it does in every technical regard, and conforming to the mandatory items of the official program of instructions, it goes freely in advance, and, with the steel frame as a thesis, displays a high science of design such as the world up to this day had neither known nor surmised. In its single solidarity of concentrated intention, there is revealed a logic of a new order, the logic of living things; and this inexorable logic of life is most graciously accepted and set forth in fluency of form. Rising from the earth in suspiration as of the earth and as of the universal genius of man, it ascends and ascends in beauty, lofty and serene to the full height limit of the Chicago building ordinance, un-

til its lovely crest seems at one with the sky.

This is not all; there remain, for some, two surprises; first, that a Finlander who, in his prior experience, had not occasion to design a soaring office building, should, as one to the manner born, have grasped the intricate problem of the lofty steel-framed structure, the significance of its origins, and held the solution unwaveringly in mind, in suchwise as no American architect has as yet shown the required depth of thought and steadfastness of purpose to achieve.

Philosophy has been defined by a modern philosopher as the science of substantial grounds. It is the notable absence of substantial grounds, in the ambitious works of our American architects, that so largely invalidates such works and groups them as ephemera. But the design of the Finlander, master of ideas, is *based* upon substantial grounds, and therefore it lives within the domain of the enduring.

Second surprise: That a foreigner should possess the insight required to penetrate to the depths of the sound, strong, kindly and aspiring idealism which lies at the core of the American people — one day to make them truly great sons of earth — and that he should possess the poet's power to interpret and to proclaim in deep sympathy and understanding, incarnate in an edifice rising from earth in response to this faith, an inspiring symbol to endure.

Why did the men behind the *Tribune* throw this priceless pearl away?

Would that one might say words of similar nature, if less fervent, for the unfortunate first prize; but it is the business of this review to make a searching psychological analysis and summary of the two designs, as *types*, in order that the heavy of eye may see revealed the architectural art as a vast beneficent power, lying now in continental sleep, ready, ever ready, to be awakened by masters of ideas, who shall affirm its reality in eloquence of form.

Then shall we become articulate as a people; for to reveal one art is to reveal all arts, all aspirations, all hopes; and the substantial ground of it all shall arise from out our timid faith in man — a faith patient and long suffering under the superstitious tyranny of insane ideas. But once let the beckoning finger of the free spirit be seen in the open, and a voice heard that saith: Arise; come unto me, for I am life — then will that timorous faith come forth inquiringly, and in the glow of the free spirit grow strong. The ego of our land shall thus find its own; for man shall find man. Why, therefore, deal in trivialities? Why inquire, with spectacles on nose, why this or that doodad should be thus or so?

Confronted by the limpid eye of analysis, the first prize trembles and falls, self-confessed, crumbling to the ground. Visibly it is not architecture in the sense herein expounded. Its formula is literary: words, words, words. It is an imaginary structure — not imaginative. Starting with false premise, it was doomed to false conclusion, and it is clear enough, moreover, that the conclusion was the real premise, the mental process in reverse of appearance. The predetermination of a huge mass of imaginary masonry at the top very naturally required the appearance of huge imaginary masonry piers reaching up from the ground to give imaginary support. Such weird process of reasoning is curious. It savors of the nursery where children bet imaginary millions. Is it possible that its author in his heart of hearts, or his head of heads, really believed that bathos and power are synonyms? It looks that way.

It also looks like the output of a mind untrained in the mastery of ideas, in the long discipline of realities and the test of substantial grounds. It looks also like the wandering of a mind unaccustomed to distinguish between architecture and scene painting. This design, this imaginary building, this simulacrum, is so helpless, so defenseless when brought face to face with mastery of ideas and validity of grounds, that it is cruel to go on, for analysis is now becoming vivisection, unless we recognize the palpable effect of self-hypnotism.

This is not to say that the individual who made the first-prize design did not *believe* he had a great idea. Certainly he believed it, otherwise he would not have taken himself so seriously. Such seriousness prevented him from seeing the humor of it, from seeing something funny and confiding. If the monster on top with its great long legs reaching far below to the ground could be gently pried loose, the real building would reveal itself as a rather amiable and delicate affair with a certain grace of fancy. And even so, it could be but as a foundling at the doorstep of the Finn — for it seems they breed *strong* men in Finland.

So much, for the present, concerning the second and the first prize.

Our attention now shall concentrate upon the *Tribune*. By "the *Tribune*" is here meant, not alone printed white paper but incisively the men behind its screen who stand for ownership and control. These men made a solemn promise to the world. Why did they renege? Individually and jointly they made a triple promise — as set forth above — as members of the Jury of Award. A design setting forth the most beautiful conception of a lofty office building that has been evolved by the fertile mind of man, was presented squarely to them at the last moment. Were they frightened? Why did they welch? Did it come upon them as a ghost, an apparition — a revelation most unwelcome at a time when everything seemed nicely settled? Was this vision as trebly disconcerting as the remembered triple promise, arising now also as a confronting ghost — the two ghosts standing side by side — likewise the two designs, in material form, standing side by side?

For no choice can exist without motive. Men are both revealed and betrayed by their acts. For men's acts show forth their inmost thoughts — no matter what their speech may be. Man can create solely in the image of his thought; for thoughts are living things — words may dissemble. In men's acts alone is the reality of their thought to be sought and found — there is no hiding place secure against the tracking searcher. In the same sense the two competing drawings are acts. Each clearly reveals the thought of its responsible author. Each sets forth in the materials of a drawing, presented as a symbol of an edifice to be, the power or the frailty of the thought within.

No manipulation of words or felicity of phrasing can screen from view the act of the Jury of Award, or the dominating will of one or more of its personnel. The final choice is most obviously an act of dominion — of brutal will. For, to cast aside, with the sop of a money prize, the surpassing work of a foreigner of high distinction and thorough discipline in executed works was an act of savagery in private, regardless of how neatly, how sweetly, thereafter, the man may have been shown the door, as a parting and an honored guest, as one whose presence in the house had indeed triply honored his host.

Thus vanished from sight the *Tribune's* bow in the cloud.

Its act has deprived the world of a shining mark, denied it a monument to beauty, to faith, to courage, and to hope. Deprived an expectant world of that romance for which it hungers and had hoped to receive. "It cannot be reiterated too emphatically that the primary objective of the *Chicago Tribune* in instituting this Competition is to secure the design for a structure distinctive and imposing — the most beautiful office building in the world."

76.

WILLIAM E. BORAH: The Release of Political Prisoners

The Espionage Act of June 1917 resulted in the arrest and conviction of a large number of Americans — pacifists, Socialists, union members, and others — whose ideas on the war were not in harmony with the prevailing public opinion. For many citizens the Bill of Rights became a dead letter and was to remain so well into the 1920s. Eugene Debs, the Socialist leader, had been released from prison by President Harding in December 1921. But more than fifty less well-known figures still languished there as late as 1923, when Senator William E. Borah of Idaho gave the address from which the following selection is taken. He spoke at the Lexington Theatre in New York City on March 11.

Source: *Bedrock: Views on Basic National Problems*, Washington, 1936, pp. 148-154.

AND SO, MY FRIENDS this Sunday afternoon, 1923, more than four years after the signing of the Armistice, the people of the great Republic of the West, a government conceived in liberty and dedicated to the proposition that all men are created equal, are still discussing the question of whether or not they should release their political prisoners. I cannot regard such a fact as other than strange and, to my mind, intolerable.

Brown Brothers
Sen. William E. Borah of Idaho

the American people would favor the immediate release of these men.

Let us bear in mind, my friends, that these men are not in prison at the present time by reason of any acts of violence to either person or property. Whatever might have inhered in the case with reference to these matters in the beginning has long since passed out of the case, and these men are in prison today, separated from their families, deprived of an opportunity of earning a livelihood, their health being undermined for the sole and only reason that they expressed their opinions concerning the war and the activities of the government in the prosecution of the war. They are distinctly and unquestionably political prisoners in the true sense of that term. They are not there for the violation of ordinary criminal statutes or for deeds of violence of any kind. . . .

They are, in other words, in prison some four years after the war for expressing an opinion in regard to it. I was thinking today as I was reflecting over this situation that six months before the time we declared war some of the most prominent members of the government at that time would have been guilty of the same offense for which these men are now in prison. Six months before we entered the war it was considered most objectionable in the United States to advocate going into the war. Six months before the war began we were told that this great World War had its roots in causes which we did not understand and with which we were not concerned and that we should keep out of it. It would seem that the gravest offense upon the part of these men, so far as expressing their views was concerned, is that they were late in catching up with the procession. They did not or were unable to adjust their views to the changed condition of affairs as readily as others.

Do not misunderstand me. I am one of those who believe that when my country is

Let us hasten to make our belief as a people known that the time has come when we should without further delay give these men their freedom.

I do not know, and of course therefore I am not permitted to conjecture, just why the government at Washington has hesitated to grant amnesty to these political prisoners. But I believe nevertheless that good can only come from a thorough discussion of these matters in public. I believe, furthermore, that public opinion always has a wholesome effect upon such questions as these. It at least, properly expressed, aids the executive department in coming to a conclusion upon this proposition. After all, we are occasionally a government of the people. There is one power which we all down at Washington respect, and that is the power of public opinion. I have no doubt at all that if the American people were thoroughly informed as to the facts, there would be an undoubted public opinion upon this question; and I have no doubt either that a very large majority of at war, engaged in deadly strife with an enemy, as a matter of policy, we ought to surrender our individual views and get behind the government if we can possibly do so. In such times we ought to reconcile ourselves to our government's successful conduct of the war. But while that is my belief, it is also my contention, grounded in the deepest principles of free government, that if a man thinks a war is unjust or improvident, or that it is being carried on in a corrupt manner, it is his absolute right to say so. Indeed, if it is a question of the method of carrying on the war and he believes it is unwise or unjust, it is his duty to say so. . . .

What, therefore, is the real, the controlling reason for denying these political prisoners their freedom. It is not, in my opinion, the offense for which they were convicted. It is not because the court record condemns them. It is for another offense — unknown to the criminal code and undisclosed in the sentences under which they are now serving. These men it is claimed are members of an organization known as the Industrial Workers of the World — an organization, as many of us believe, antagonistic in its teachings to the good order and happiness of society and to the principles of representative government. I understand they are members of this organization, some of them at least. Let that fact be conceded. Let it be conceded that they are believers in these insupportable doctrines. But these men are not now in prison, under sanction of law, for sabotage, for acts of violence to either persons or property. They are being punished for political offenses — charged with having offered opinions and views upon the war and the activities of the government in the prosecution of the war.

If these men have violated any law touching the character of the organization of which they are members, if they have been guilty of acts of violence defined by any provision of the criminal code, for these offenses let them be charged, and if convicted, be punished in accordance with the established laws and procedure of a government of law. If they have come under the ban of our immigration laws, let them be dealt with in the manner there prescribed. But it is manifestly unjust, it is an act of tyranny, to put men in prison because of political opinions and keep them there because they are members of an unpopular organization.

It is the very essence of despotism to punish men for offense for which they have not been convicted. It is the first essential of justice in a government of law to punish men only and alone for offenses defined by law. It is the dominating tenet of tyranny to punish men for what they think — for what they believe. It is a cardinal rule under free institutions to punish men only and alone for what they do. These men are not only now suffering for offenses of which they have not been convicted but for things of which the criminal law has not yet taken notice. Such procedure, such treatment of our citizens, be they high or low, wise or unwise, correct in their views or wholly erroneous, brings government into disparagement, if not contempt. Such procedure is a prostitution of our courts — a perversion of the first principles of constitutional government. . . .

There is a peculiar doctrine which has come to have recognition in this country to which I must refer. It was said during the late war that as soon as war was declared the Constitution of the United States was in a sense suspended, that the Congress could pass any law it saw fit to pass. At first, that seemed to me to be a subject of amusement, and I still really think it is. But, as a matter of fact, it was seriously advocated by learned and able men, legislators and executive departments. It was upon that theory and apparently upon that principle that many things were done during the war. For myself, I want to repudiate it once and for all. I trust that no such vicious and un-

American doctrine will ever be seriously considered by the people of this country.

There is only one way that you can change the Constitution of the United States or suspend any of its provisions and that is in the same way and by the same power that made it, to wit, the people of the United States themselves in the manner pointed out by the Constitution. Every clause, every line, every paragraph of that great charter obtains in time of war just the same as in time of peace. . . .

There is still another reason why I feel so keenly about this matter. I think this is one of the steps which should be taken to help break this fearful psychology of war which still remains with us, notwithstanding four years have passed since the signing of the Armistice. You will all remember the morning after the signing of the Armistice — what a happy world it seemed at that time. You could not meet anyone that happiness was not written on his or her very countenance. We thought we were passing out of the bitterness, away from the hatreds and the passions which had cursed the world for many, many months. We felt that we were about to escape from that fearful condition of mind which had been expressing itself in so many ugly ways, hoping to get rid of the antipathies, the hatreds, and the vengeance which naturally come with war. We felt that we were turning our backs upon these things and would again be free from them. But while the fighting had ceased upon the battlefield and the armies had surrendered, we know today, as a matter of fact, that we did not get away from the passions which came with the war.

Look over Europe today, torn and distracted from corner to corner and side to side by the same racial antipathies, the same hatreds, the same turmoil, the same strife, the same urge for blood. Where, my friends, is this all going to end? Shall we not make a brave fight to get away from these things? You may talk your leagues and your alliances, your schemes for peace, but if you cannot get rid of this passion, this bitterness, this urge for blood, there can be no peace — there can be no peace until we turn our backs upon the ugly things which came with the war. Let us take one step, at least — release the political prisoners and put that ugly record behind us.

It is a little thing, in one sense, an inconsequential thing, to turn loose 53 men, 53 out of 110 million people; but it is an awful thing, on the other hand, to keep them in prison, an awful thing for the United States to say that even one man shall be restrained in prison four years after the war for expressing his views as to the wisdom of the war. If we can do that, my friends, if America can get rid of these things, if we can put behind us these questions which have torn and distracted us for years, then shall we again become a happy and contented people.

That is Americanism. Americanism is liberty. And what is liberty? It is not a mere right to be free from chains, it is not a mere right to be outside the prison walls — liberty is also the right to express yourself, to entertain your views, to defend your policies, to treat yourself and your neighbors as free and independent agents under a great representative republic.

The business of America is business.

Calvin Coolidge

77.

Calvin Coolidge: The Destiny of America

Calvin Coolidge was a Vermont Yankee, thrifty, conservative, almost puritanical in his zeal for the old-fashioned virtues. Vice-President under Harding, Coolidge gave a Memorial Day Address in 1923, the simple, homespun language of which typified all of his future utterances. In discussing the destiny of America, he reiterated the familiar myths in so persuasive a way that some people believed, one historian has said, that they were hearing them for the first time. A portion of the speech is reprinted here. Within three months Coolidge was to become President on Harding's death.

Source: *The Price of Freedom: Speeches and Addresses,* New York, 1924, pp. 331-353.

PATRIOTISM IS EASY TO UNDERSTAND in America. It means looking out for yourself by looking out for your country. In no other nation on earth does this principle have such complete application. It comes most naturally from the fundamental doctrine of our land that the people are supreme. Lincoln stated the substance of the whole matter in his famous phrase, "government of the people; by the people, and for the people."

The authority of law here is not something which is imposed upon the people; it is the will of the people themselves. The decision of the court here is not something which is apart from the people; it is the judgment of the people themselves. The right of the ownership of property here is not something withheld from the people; it is the privilege of the people themselves. Their sovereignty is absolute and complete. A definition of the relationship between the institutions of our government and the American people entirely justifies the assertion that: "All things were made by *them;* and without *them* was not anything made that was made." It is because the American government is the sole creation and possession of the people that they have always cherished it and defended it, and always will.

There are two fundamental motives which inspire human action. The first and most important, to which all else is subordinate, is that of righteousness. There is that in mankind, stronger than all else, which requires them to do right. When that requirement is satisfied, the next motive is that of gain. These are the moral motive and the material motive. While in some particular instance they might seem to be antagonistic, yet always, when broadly considered or applied to society as a whole, they are in harmony. American institutions meet the test of these two standards. They are founded on righteousness, they are productive of material prosperity. They compel the loyalty and support of the people because such action is right and because it is profitable.

These are the main reasons for the formation of patriotic societies. Desiring to promote the highest welfare of civilization,

Calvin Coolidge photographed at the White House with his wife and sons, 1923

their chief purpose is to preserve and extend American ideals. No matter what others may do, they are determined to serve themselves and their fellowmen by thinking America, believing America, and living America. That faith they are proud to proclaim to all the world.

It is no wonder that the people are attached to America when we consider what it has done and what it represents. It has been called the last great hope of the world. Its simple story is a romance of surpassing interest. Its accomplishments rise above the realm of fable. To live under the privileges of its citizenship is the highest position of opportunity and achievement ever reached by a people.

If there be a destiny, it is of no avail for us unless we work with it. The ways of Providence will be of no advantage to us unless we proceed in the same direction. If we perceive a destiny in America, if we believe that Providence has been the guide, our own success, our own salvation require that we should act and serve in harmony and obedience.

Throughout all the centuries this land remained unknown to civilization. Just at a time when Christianity was at last firmly established, when there was a general advance in learning, when there was a great spiritual awakening, America began to be revealed to the European world. When this new age began, with its new aspirations and its new needs, its new hopes, and its new desires, the shores of our country rose through the mist, disclosing a new hemisphere in which, untrammeled by Old World conventions, new ideals might establish for mankind a new experience and a new life.

Settlers came here from mixed motives, some for pillage and adventure, some for trade and refuge, but those who have set their imperishable mark upon our institutions came from far higher motives. Generally defined, they were seeking a broader freedom. They were intent upon establishing a Christian commonwealth in accordance with the principle of self-government.

They were an inspired body of men. It has been said that God sifted the nations that He might send choice grain into the wilderness. They had a genius for organized society on the foundation of piety, righteousness, liberty, and obedience to law. They brought with them the accumulated wisdom and experience of the ages wherever it contributed to the civilizing power of these great agencies. But the class and caste, the immaterial formalism of the Old World, they left behind. They let slip their grasp upon conventionalities that they might lay a firmer hold upon realities. . . .

The main characteristics of those principles [of government] from which all others are deduced is a government of limited and defined powers, leaving the people supreme. The executive has sole command of the military forces, but he cannot raise a dollar of revenue. The legislature has the sole authority to levy taxes, but it cannot issue a command to a single private soldier. The judiciary interprets and declares the law and the Constitution, but it can neither create nor destroy the right of a single individual. Freedom of action is complete, within moral bounds, under the law which the people themselves have prescribed. The individual is supported in his right to follow his own choice, live his own life, and reap the rewards of his own effort. Justice is administered by impartial courts. It is a maxim of our law that there is no wrong without a remedy. All the power and authority of the whole national government cannot convict the most humble individual of a crime, save on the verdict of an impartial jury composed of twelve of his peers. Opportunity is denied to none, every place is open, and every position yields to the humblest in accordance with ability and application.

The chief repository of power is in the legislature, chosen directly by the people at frequent elections. It is this body, which is particularly responsive to the public will, and yet, as in the Congress, is representative of the whole nation. It does not perform an executive function. It is not, therefore, charged with the necessity of expedition. It is a legislative body and is, therefore, charged with the necessity for deliberation. Sometimes this privilege may be abused, for this great power has been given as the main safeguard of liberty, and wherever power is bestowed it may be used unwisely. But whenever a legislative body ceases to deliberate, then it ceases to act with due consideration.

That fact in itself is conclusive that it has ceased to be independent, has become subservient to a single directing influence or a small group, either without or within itself, and is no longer representative of the people. Such a condition would not be a rule of the people, but a rule of some unconstitutional power. It is my own observation and belief that the American Congress is the most efficient and effective deliberative body, more untrammeled, more independent, more advised, more representative of the will of the people than any body which legislates for any of the great powers. An independent legislature never deprived the people of their liberty.

Such is America, such is the government and civilization which have grown up around the church, the town meeting, and the schoolhouse. It is not perfect, but it surpasses the accomplishments of any other people. Such is the state of society which has been created in this country, which has brought it from the untrodden wilderness of 300 years ago to its present state of development. Who can fail to see in it the hand of destiny? Who can doubt that it has been guided by a Divine Providence? What has it not given to its people in material advantages, educational opportunity, and religious consolation? Our country has not failed, our country has been a success. You are here because you believe in it, because you believe that it is right, and because you know that it has paid. You are determined to defend it, to support it, and, if need be, to fight for it. You know that America is worth fighting for.

But if our republic is to be maintained

and improved it will be through the efforts and character of the individual. It will be, first of all, because of the influences which exist in the home, for it is the ideals which prevail in the homelife which make up the strength of the nation. The homely virtues must continue to be cultivated. The real dignity, the real nobility of work must be cherished. It is only through industry that there is any hope for individual development. The viciousness of waste and the value of thrift must continue to be learned and understood. Civilization rests on conservation. To these there must be added religion, education, and obedience to law. These are the foundation of all character in the individual and all hope in the nation. . . .

A growing tendency has been observed of late years to think too little of what is really the public interest and too much of what is supposed to be class interest. The two great political parties of the nation have existed for the purpose, each in accordance with its own principles, of undertaking to serve the interests of the whole nation. Their members of the Congress are chosen with that great end in view. Patriotism does not mean a regard for some special section or an attachment for some special interest, and a narrow prejudice against other sections and other interests; it means a love of the whole country. This does not mean that any section or any interest is to be disproportionately preferred or disproportionately disregarded, but that the welfare of all is equally to be sought. Agriculture, transportation, manufacturing, and all the other desirable activities should serve in accordance with their strength and should be served in accordance with the benefits they confer.

A division of the people or their representatives in accordance with any other principle or theory is contrary to the public welfare. An organization for the purpose of serving some special interest is perfectly proper and may be exceedingly helpful, but whenever it undertakes to serve that interest by disregarding the welfare of other interests, it becomes harmful alike to the interest which it proposes to serve and to the public welfare in general. Under the modern organization of society there is such a necessary community of interests that all necessarily experience depression or prosperity together.

They cannot be separated. Our country has resources sufficient to provide in abundance for everybody. But it cannot confer a disproportionate share upon anybody. There is work here to keep amply employed every dollar of capital and every hand of honest toil, but there is no place for profiteering, either in high prices or in low, by the organized greed of money or of men. The most pressing requirement of the present day is that we should learn this lesson and be content with a fair share, whether it be the returns from invested capital or the rewards of toil. On that foundation there is a guarantee of continued prosperity, of stable economic conditions, of harmonious social relationships, and of sound and enduring government. On any other theory or action the only prospect is that of wasteful conflict and suffering in our economic life and factional discord and trifling in our political life. No private enterprise can succeed unless the public welfare be held supreme.

Another necessity of the utmost urgency in this day, a necessity which is worldwide, is economy in government expenditures. This may seem the antithesis of military preparation, but, as a matter of fact, our present great debt is due, in a considerable extent, to creating our last military establishment under the condition of war haste and war prices, which added enormously to its cost. There is no end of the things which the government could do, seemingly, in the way of public welfare, if it had the money. Everything we want cannot be had at once. It must be earned by toilsome labor. There is a very decided limit to the amount which can be raised by taxation without ruinously affecting the people of the country by virtual confiscation of a part of their past savings.

The business of the country, as a whole, is transacted on a small margin of profit. The economic structure is one of great delicacy and sensitiveness. When taxes become too burdensome, either the price of commodities has to be raised to a point at which consumption is so diminished as greatly to curtail production, or so much of the returns from industry is required by the government that production becomes unprofitable and ceases for that reason. In either case there is depression, lack of employment, idleness of investment and of wage earner, with the long line of attendant want and suffering on the part of the people. After order and liberty, economy is one of the highest essentials of a free government. It was in no small degree the unendurable burden of taxation which drove Europe into the Great War. Economy is always a guarantee of peace.

It is the great economic question of government finances which is burdening the people of Europe at the present time. How to meet obligations is the chief problem on continental Europe and in the British Isles. It cannot be doubted that high taxes are the chief cause for the extended condition of unemployment which has required millions to subsist on the public treasury in Great Britain for a long period of time, though the number of these unfortunate people has been declining. A government which requires of the people the contribution of the bulk of their substance and rewards cannot be classed as a free government, or long remain as such. It is gratifying to observe, in our own national government, that there has been an enormous decrease in expenditures, a large reduction of the debt, and a revision of taxation affording great relief.

But it is in peace that there lies the greatest opportunity for relief from burdensome taxation. Our country is at peace, not only legal but actual, with all other peoples. We cherish peace and goodwill toward all the earth, with a sentiment of friendship and a desire for universal well-being. If we want peace it is our business to cultivate goodwill. It was for the promotion of peace that the Washington Conference on the Limitation of Armaments and Pacific Questions was called. For the first time in history the great powers of the earth have agreed to a limitation of naval armaments. This was brought about by American initiative in accordance with an American plan, and executed by American statesmanship. Out of regard for a similar principle is the proposal to participate in the establishment of a World Court. These are in accordance with a desire to adjust differences between nations, not by an overpowering display or use of force but by mutual conference and understanding in harmony with the requirement of justice and of honor.

Our country does not want war, it wants peace. It has not decreed this memorial season as an honor to war, with its terrible waste and attendant train of suffering and hardship which reaches onward into the years of peace. Yet war is not the worst of evils, and these days have been set apart to do honor to all those, now gone, who made the cause of America their supreme choice. Some fell with the word of Patrick Henry, "Give me liberty, or give me death," almost ringing in their ears. Some heard that word across the intervening generations and were still obedient to its call. It is to the spirit of those men, exhibited in all our wars, to the spirit that places the devotion to freedom and truth above the devotion to life, that the nation pays its ever enduring mark of reverence and respect.

It is not that principle that leads to conflict but to tranquillity. It is not that principle which is the cause of war but the only foundation for an enduring peace. There can be no peace with the forces of evil.

Peace comes only through the establishment of the supremacy of the forces of good. That way lies only through sacrifice. It was that the people of our country might live in a knowledge of the truth that these, our countrymen, are dead. "Greater love hath no man than this, that a man lay down his life for his friends."

This spirit is not dead, it is the most vital thing in America. It did not flow from any act of government. It is the spirit of the people themselves. It justifies faith in them and faith in their institutions. Remembering all that it has accomplished from the day of the Puritan and Cavalier to the day of the last, least immigrant, who lives by it no less

than they, who shall dare to doubt it, who shall dare to challenge it, who shall venture to rouse it into action? Those who have scoffed at it from the day of the Stuarts and the Bourbons to the day of the Hapsburgs and the Hohenzollerns have seen it rise and prevail over them. Calm, peaceful, puissant, it remains, conscious of its authority, "slow to anger, plenteous in mercy," seeking not to injure but to serve, the safeguard of the republic, still the guarantee of a broader freedom, the supreme moral power of the world. It is in that spirit that we place our trust. It is to that spirit again, with this returning year, we solemnly pledge the devotion of all that we have and are.

78.

Sinclair Lewis: The Norse State

By 1923 Sinclair Lewis, native of Sauk Centre, Minnesota, was well established as a novelist. Main Street and Babbitt were best sellers, and Americans could continue to look forward to more satire from his witty pen. In the early 1920s the Nation ran a series on "These United States" and asked Lewis to write an apologia for his native state. He may have relished the opportunity to dispel some of the illusions of Easterners about the Middle West. Lewis' article "Minnesota: The Norse State" was published in May 1923, the 65th anniversary of statehood.

Source: *Nation*, May 30, 1923.

On May 9, 1922, Mr. Henry Lorenz of Pleasantdale, Saskatchewan, milked the cows and fed the horses and received the calls of his next farm neighbors. Obviously he was still young and lively, though it did happen that on May 9 he was one hundred and seventeen years old. When St. Paul, Mendota, and Marine, the first towns in Minnesota, were established, Henry was a man in his mid-thirties — yes, and President Eliot was seven and Uncle Joe Cannon was five. As for Minneapolis, now a city of

400,000 people, seventy-five years ago it consisted of one cabin. Before 1837, there were less than 300 whites and mixed breeds in all this Minnesotan domain of 80,000 square miles — the size of England and Scotland put together.

It is so incredibly new; it has grown so dizzyingly. Here is a man still under forty, born in a Minnesota village. Twenty-two years before he was born, the village was a stockade with two or three log stores and a company of infantry, a refuge for the settlers when the Sioux came raiding. During a raid in 1863, a settler was scalped within sight of the stockade. Yet so greatly had the state changed in those twenty-three years that not till he was sixteen did the man himself ever see an Indian. That Indian was on a train, bound East to continue the study of Latin which he had begun on the reservation.

On the spot where the settler was scalped in 1863 is a bungalow farmhouse now, with leaded casement windows, with radio and phonograph, and electric lights in house and garage and barns. A hundred blooded cows are milked there by machinery. The farmer goes into town for Kiwanis Club meetings, and last year he drove his Buick to Los Angeles. He is, or was, too prosperous to belong to the Nonpartisan League or to vote the Farmer-Labor ticket.

Minnesota is unknown to the average Easterner, say to a Hartford insurance man or to a New York garment worker, not so much because it is new as because it is neither definitely Western and violent, nor Eastern and crystallized. Factories and shore hotels are inevitably associated with New Jersey, cowpunchers and buttes with Montana; California is apparent, and Florida and Maine. But Minnesota is unplaced. I have heard a Yale junior speculate: "Now you take those Minnesota cities — say take Milwaukee, for instance. Why, it must have a couple of hundred thousand population, hasn't it?"

This would be a composite Eastern impression of Minnesota: a vastness of windbeaten prairie, flat as a parade ground, wholly given up to wheat growing, save for a fringe of pines at the north and a few market towns at the south; these steppes inhabited by a few splendid Yankees — one's own sort of people — and by Swedes who always begin sentences with "Vell, Aye tank," who are farmhands, kitchenmaids, and icemen, and who are invariably humorous.

This popular outline bears examination as well as most popular beliefs; quite as well as the concept that Negroes born in Chicago are less courteous than those born in Alabama. Minnesota is not flat. It is far less flat than the province of Quebec. Most of it is prairie, but the prairie rolls and dips and curves; it lures the motorist like the English roads of Broad Highway fiction. Along the skyline the cumulus clouds forever belly and, with our dry air, nothing is more spectacular than the crimson chaos of our sunsets. But our most obvious beauty is the lakes. There are thousands of them — nine or ten thousand — brilliant among suave grainfields or masked by cool birch and maples. On the dozen mile-wide lakes of the north are summer cottages of the prosperous from Missouri, Illinois, even Texas.

Leagues of the prairie are utterly treeless, except for artificial windbreaks of willows and cottonwoods encircling the farmhouses. Here the German Catholic spire can be seen a dozen miles off, and the smoke of the Soo Line freight two stations away. But from this plains country you come into a northern pine wilderness, "the Big Woods," a land of lumber camps and reservation Indians and lonely toteroads, kingdom of Paul Bunyan, the mythical hero of the lumberjacks.

The second error is to suppose that Minnesota is entirely a wheat state. It was, at one time, and the Minneapolis flour mills are still the largest in the world. Not even Castoria is hymned by more billboards than is Minneapolis flour. But today it is Montana and Saskatchewan and the Dakotas which produce most of the wheat for our mills, while the Minnesota farmers, building tall red silos which adorn their barns like the turrets of Picardy, turn increasingly to dairying. We ship beef to London, butter to Philadelphia. The iron from our Mesaba mines is in Alaskan rails and South African bridges, and as to manufacturing, our refrigerators and heat regulators comfort Park

Sinclair Lewis

Avenue apartment houses, while our chief underwear factory would satisfy a Massachusetts Brahmin or even a Chicago advertising man.

Greatest error of all is to believe that Minnesota is entirely Yankee and Scandinavian, and that the Swedes are helots and somehow ludicrous.

A school principal in New Duluth analyzed his 330 children as Slovene, 49; Italian, 47; Serbian, 39; American, 37; Polish, 30; Austrian and Swedish, 22 each; Croatian, 20; colored, 9 (it is instructive to note that he did not include them among the "Americans"); Finnish, 7; Scotch, 6; Slav, unspecified, 5; German, French, Bohemian, and Jewish, 4 each; Rumanian, Norwegian, and Canadian, 3 each; Scandinavian, unspecified; Lithuanian, Irish, Ukrainian, and Greek, 2 each; Russian and English, 1 each — 60 percent of them from southern and eastern Europe!

Such a Slavification would, of course, be true only of an industrial or mining community, but it does indicate that the whole

Midwestern population may alter as much as has the East. In most of the state there is a predomination of Yankees, Germans, Irish, and all branches of Scandinavians — Icelanders and Danes as well as Swedes and Norwegians. And among all racial misconceptions none is more vigorously absurd than the belief that the Minnesota Scandinavians are, no matter how long they remain here, like the characters of that estimable old stock-company play "Yon Yonson" — a tribe humorous, inferior, and unassimilable. To generalize, any popular generalization about Scandinavians in America is completely and ingeniously and always wrong.

In Minnesota itself one does not hear (from the superior Yankees whom one questions about that sort of thing) that the Scandinavians are a comic people, but rather that they are surly, that they are socialistic, that they "won't Americanize." Manufacturers and employing lumbermen speak of their Swedish employees precisely as wealthy Seattleites speak of the Japs, Bostonians of the Irish, Southwesterners of the Mexicans, New Yorkers of the Jews, Marine officers of the Haitians, and Mr. Rudyard Kipling of nationalist Hindus — or nationalist Americans. Unconsciously, all of them give away the Inferior Race Theory, which is this: An inferior race is one whose members work for me. They are treacherous, ungrateful, ignorant, lazy, and agitator-ridden, because they ask for higher wages and thus seek to rob me of the dollars which I desire for my wife's frocks and for the charities which glorify me. This inferiority is inherent. Never can they become good Americans (or English Gentlemen, or Highwellborn Prussians). I know that this is so because all my university classmates and bridge partners agree with me.

The truth is that the Scandinavians Americanize only too quickly. They Americanize much more quickly than Americans. For generation after generation there is a remnant of stubborn American Abolitionist stock which either supports forlorn causes and in jail sings low ballads in a Harvard accent, or else upholds, like Lodge, an Adams tradition which is as poisonous as communism to a joy in brotherly boosting. So thorough are the Scandinavians about it that in 1963 we shall be hearing Norwegian Trygavasons and Icelandic Gislasons saying of the Montenegrins and Letts: "They're reg'lar hogs about wages but the worst is, they simply won't Americanize. They won't vote either the Rotary or the Ku Klux ticket. They keep hollering about wanting some kind of a doggone Third Party."

Scandinavians take to American commerce and schooling and journalism as do Scotsmen or cockneys. Particularly they take to American politics, the good old politics of Harrison and McKinley and Charley Murphy. Usually, they bring nothing new from their own experimental countries. They permit their traditions to be snatched away. True, many of them have labored for the Nonpartisan League, for woman suffrage, for cooperative societies. The late Governor John Johnson of Minnesota seems to have been a man of destiny; had he lived he would probably have been President, and possibly a President of power and originality. But again — there was Senator Knute Nelson, who made McCumber look like a left-wing syndicalist and Judge Gary like François Villon. There is Congressman Steenerson of Minnesota, chairman of the House Postal Committee. Mr. Steenerson once produced, out of a rich talent matured by a quarter of a century in the House, an immortal sentence. He had been complaining at lunch that the Nonpartisan League had introduced the obscene writings of "this Russian woman, Ellen Key" into the innocent public schools. Some one hinted to the Swedish Mr. Steenerson, "But I thought she was a Swede."

He answered: *"No, the Key woman comes*

from Finland and the rest of Red Russia, where they nationalize the women."

Good and bad, the Scandinavians monopolize Minnesota politics. Of the last nine governors of the state, six have been Scandinavians. So is Dr. Shipstead, who defeated Senator Kellogg in the 1922 election; so is Harold Knutson, Republican whip of the House. Scandinavians make up a large proportion of the Minnesota state legislature, and while in Santa Fe the Mexican legislators speak Spanish, while in Quebec the representatives still debate in French, though for generations they have been citizens of a British dominion, in Minnesota the politicians who were born abroad are zealous to speak nothing but Americanese. So is it in business and the home. Though a man may not have left Scandinavia till he was twenty, his sons will use the same English, good and bad, as the sons of settlers from Maine, and his daughters will go into music clubs or into cocktail sets, into college or into factories, with the same prejudices and ideals and intonations as girls named Smith and Brewster.

The curious newness of Minnesota has been suggested, but the really astonishing thing is not the newness — it is the oldness, the solid, traditionalized, cotton-wrapped oldness. A study of it would be damaging to the Free and Fluid Young America theory. While parts of the state are still so raw that the villages among the furrows or the dusty pines are but frontier camps, in the cities and in a few of the towns there is as firm a financial oligarchy and almost as definite a social system as London, and this power is behind all "sound" politics, in direct or indirect control of all business. It has its Old Families, who tend to marry only within their own set. Anywhere in the world, an Old Family is one which has had wealth for at least thirty years longer than average families of the same neighborhood. In England, it takes (at most) five generations to absorb "parvenus" and "profiteers" into the gentry, whether they were steel profiteers in the Great War or yet untitled land profiteers under William the Conqueror. In New York it takes three generations — often. In the Middle West it takes one and a half.

No fable is more bracing, or more absurd, than that all the sons and grandsons of the pioneers, in Minnesota or in California, in Arizona or Nebraska, are racy and breezy, unmannerly but intoxicatingly free. The grandchildren of the men who in 1862 fought the Minnesota Indians, who dog-trotted a hundred miles over swamp-blurred trails to bear the alarm to the nearest troops — some of them are still clearing the land, but some of them are complaining of the un-English quality of the Orange Pekoe in dainty-painty city tearooms which stand where three generations ago the Red River fur carts rested; their chauffeurs await them in Pierce Arrow limousines (special bodies by Kimball, silver fittings from Tiffany); they present Schnitzler and St. John Ervine at their Little Theaters; between rehearsals they chatter of meeting James Joyce in Paris; and always in high-pitched Mayfair laughter they ridicule the Scandinavians and Finns who are trying to shoulder into their sacred, ancient Yankee caste. A good many of their names are German.

Naturally, beneath this *Junker* class there is a useful, sophisticated, and growing company of doctors, teachers, newspapermen, liberal lawyers, musicians who have given up Munich and Milan for the interest of developing orchestras in the new land. There is a scientific body of farmers. The agricultural school of the huge University of Minnesota is sound and creative. And still more naturally, between Labor and Aristocracy there is an army of the peppy, poker-playing, sales-hustling He-men who are our most characteristic Americans. But even the He-men are not so obvious as they seem. What their future is, no man knows — and no woman dares believe.

It is conceivable that, instead of being a menace, in their naïve boosting and their fear of the unusual, they may pass only too soon; it is possible that their standardized bathrooms and Overlands will change to an equally standardized and formula-bound culture — yearning Culture, arty Art. We have been hurled from tobacco chewing to tea drinking with gasping speed; we may as quickly dash from boosting to a beautiful and languorous death. If it is necessary to be Fabian in politics, to keep the reformers (left-wing or rigid right) from making us perfect too rapidly, it is yet more necessary to be a little doubtful about the ardent souls who would sell Culture; and if the Tired Businessman is unlovely and a little dull, at least he is real, and we shall build only on reality.

The nimbler among our pioneering grandfathers appropriated to their private uses some thousands of square miles in northern Minnesota, and cut off — or cheerfully lost by forest fire — certain billions of feet of such lumber as will never be seen again. When the lumber was gone, the land seemed worthless. It was good for nothing but agriculture, which is an unromantic occupation, incapable of making millionaires in one generation. The owners had few of them acquired more than a million, and now they could scarcely give their holdings away. Suddenly, on parts of this scraggly land, iron was discovered, iron in preposterous quantities, to be mined in the open pit, as easily as hauling out gravel. Here is the chief supply of the Gary and South Chicago mills. The owners of the land do not mine the ore. They have gracefully leased it — though we are but Westerners, we have our subsidiary of the United States Steel Company. The landowners themselves have only to go abroad and sit in beauty like a flower, and every time a steam shovel dips into the ore, a quarter drops into the owner's pocket.

This article is intended to be a secret but

flagrant boost. It is meant to increase civic pride and the value of Minnesota real estate. Yet the writer wonders if he will completely satisfy his chambers of commerce. There is a chance that they would prefer a statement of the value of our dairy products, the number of our admirable new school buildings, the number of motor tourists visiting our lakes, and an account of Senator Nelson's encouraging progress from poverty to magnificence. But a skilled press agent knows that this would not be a boost; it would be an admission of commerce-ruled barrenness.

The interesting thing in Minnesota is the swift evolution of a complex social system and, since in two generations we have changed from wilderness to country clubs, the question is what the next two generations will produce. It defies certain answer; it demands a scrupulous speculation free equally from the bland certitudes of chambers of commerce and the sardonic impatience of professional radicals. To a realistic philosopher, the existence of an aristocracy is not (since it does exist) a thing to be bewailed, but to be examined as a fact.

There is one merit not of Minnesota alone but of all the Middle West which must be considered. The rulers of our new land may to the eye seem altogether like the rulers of the East — of New England, New York, Pennsylvania. Both groups are chiefly reverent toward banking, sound Republicanism, the playing of golf and bridge, and the possession of large motors. But whereas the Easterner is content with these symbols and smugly desires nothing else, the Westerner, however golfocentric he may be, is not altogether satisfied; and raucously though he may snortle at his wife's "fool suffrage ideas" and "all this highbrow junk the lecture hounds spring on you," yet secretly, wistfully he desires a beauty that he does not understand.

As a pendant, to hint that our society has become somewhat involved in the few years since Mr. Henry Lorenz of Saskatchewan was seventy, let me illogically lump a few personal observations of Minnesota:

Here is an ex-professor of history in the State University, an excellent scholar who, retiring after many years of service, cheerfully grows potatoes in a backwoods farm among the northern Minnesota pines, and builds up cooperative selling for all the farmers of his district.

Here is the head of a Minneapolis school for kindergartners, a woman who is summoned all over the country to address teachers' associations. She will not admit candidates for matriculation until she is sure that they have a gift for teaching. She does something of the work of a Montessori, with none of the trumpeting and anguish.

Here is the greatest, or certainly the largest, medical clinic in the world — the Mayo Clinic, with over a hundred medical specialists besides the clerks and nurses. It is the supreme court of diagnosis. Though it is situated in a small town, off the through rail routes, yet it is besieged by patients from Utah and Ontario and New York as much as by Minnesotans. When the famous European doctors come to America, they may look at the Rockefeller Institute, they may stop at Harvard and Rush and Johns Hopkins and the headquarters of the American Medical Association, but certainly they will go on to Rochester. The names of "Charley" and "Will" have something of the familiarity of "R. L. S." and "T. R."

Here is a Chippewa as silent and swart as his grandfather, an active person whom the cavalry used to hunt every open season. The grandson conducts a garage, and he actually understands ignition. His farm among the lowering Norway pines he plows with a tractor.

Here is a new bookshop which is publishing the first English translation of the autobiography of Abelard.

Here are really glorious buildings: the Minneapolis Art Institute, the State Capitol, the St. Paul Public Library, and Ralph Adams Cram's loveliest church. Here, on the shore of Lake of the Isles, is an Italian palace built by a wheat speculator. Here, where five years ago were muddy ruts, are perfect cement roads.

Here is a small town, a "typical prairie town," which has just constructed a competent golf course. From this town came an ambassador to Siam and a professor of history in Columbia.

And here are certain Minnesota authors. You know what Midwestern authors are — rough fellows but vigorous, ignorant of the classics and of Burgundy, yet close to the heart of humanity. They write about farmyards and wear flannel shirts. Let us confirm this portrait by a sketch of nine Minnesota authors, eight of them born in the state:

Charles Flandrau, author of *Harvard Episodes* and *Viva Mexico*, one-time Harvard instructor, now wandering in Spain. Agnes Repplier has called him the swiftest blade among American essayists. Scott Fitzgerald, very much a Minnesotan, yet the father of the Long Island flapper, the prophet of the Ritz, the idol of every Junior League. Alice Ames Winter, president of the General Federation of Women's Clubs. Claude Washburn, author of *The Lonely Warrior* and several other novels which, though they are laid in America, imply a European background. He has lived for years now in France and Italy. Margaret Banning, author of *Spellbinders*. Woodward Boyd, whose first novel, *The Love Legend*, is a raid on the domestic sentimentalists. Carlton Miles, a dramatic critic who gives his Minnesota readers the latest news of the continental stage. He is just back from a European year spent with such men as Shaw, Drinkwater, and the director of La Scala. Brenda Ueland, who lives in Greenwich Village and writes for the *Atlantic Monthly*. Sinclair Lewis, known publicly as a scolding cornbelt realist, but actually (as betrayed by the samite-yclad, Tennyson-and-water verse which he wrote when he was in college) a yearner over what he would doubtless call "quaint ivied cottages."

Seventy-five years ago — a Chippewa-haunted wilderness. Today — a complex civilization with a future which, stirring or dismayed or both, is altogether unknowable. To understand America, it is merely necessary to understand Minnesota. But to understand Minnesota you must be an historian, an ethnologist, a poet, a cynic, and a graduate prophet all in one.

---

1. *Whom the gods would destroy, they first make mad with power.*
2. *The mills of God grind slowly, but they grind exceeding small.*
3. *The bee fertilizes the flower it robs.*
4. *When it is dark enough, you can see the stars.*

CHARLES A. BEARD. Asked if he could summarize the lessons of history in a short book, he replied that he could do it in four sentences.

79.

Robert Frost: "A Brook in the City"

Robert Frost loved brooks; they were symbolic, for him, of the freedom that the country fostered and that cities tended to inhibit. In the poem reprinted here, he tells of a brook that had once run free and was now imprisoned "In fetid darkness still to live and run" — and wonders whether its incarceration is somehow an evil influence on the city's own life. The poem was published in 1923, in the volume called New Hampshire — *a collection that included some of Frost's most famous lyrics, among them the title poem, "Fire and Ice," "To Earthward," "The Need of Being Versed in Country Things," and, most famous of all, "Stopping by Woods on a Snowy Evening."*

Source: *New Hampshire*, New York, 1923.

A BROOK IN THE CITY

The farmhouse lingers, though averse to square
With the new city street it has to wear
A number in. But what about the brook
That held the house as in an elbow-crook?
I ask as one who knew the brook, its strength
And impulse, having dipped a finger length
And made it leap my knuckle, having tossed
A flower to try its currents where they crossed.
The meadow grass could be cemented down
From growing under pavements of a town;
The apple trees be sent to hearth-stone flame.
Is water wood to serve a brook the same?
How else dispose of an immortal force
No longer needed? Staunch it at its source
With cinder loads dumped down? The brook was thrown
Deep in a sewer dungeon under stone
In fetid darkness still to live and run —
And all for nothing it had ever done
Except forget to go in fear perhaps.
No one would know except for ancient maps
That such a brook ran water. But I wonder
If from its being kept forever under
The thoughts may not have risen that so keep
This new-built city from both work and sleep.

1924

80.

Objections to the Child Labor Amendment

Reformers who desired the passage of federal legislation outlawing child labor found their efforts thwarted by the Supreme Court, which, in decisions handed down in 1918 and again in 1922, had declared unconstitutional any federal law regarding child labor. In 1924 a movement got under way to adopt a constitutional amendment to deal with the problem, and groups such as the National League of Women Voters lobbied in its behalf. An example of the opposition to the efforts is reprinted below. The amendment was never ratified.

Source: *Manufacturers Record*, September 4, 1924.

BECAUSE THE CHILD LABOR AMENDMENT in reality is not legislation in the interest of children but legislation which would mean the destruction of manhood and womanhood through the destruction of the boys and girls of the country, the *Manufacturers Record* has been giving much attention to the discussion of the subject, and will continue to do so.

In this week's issue, Mrs. Margaret C. Robinson, president of the Massachusetts Public Interests League, Boston, a woman's organization, presents very strongly the reasons why the men and women of this country should awaken to the seriousness of this proposition.

It is an interesting fact that Massachusetts, which was for so many years noted for its work in behalf of eliminating child workers from factory life, is now aggressively fighting the proposed amendment, re-

alizing that it would endanger the very existence of this government.

Last week we published a strong letter from Mr. Felix Rackemann, a leading attorney of Boston, long known for his humanitarian activities, and now Mrs. Robinson and her associates in the Massachusetts Public Interests League are carrying on an active campaign in many directions to prevent this amendment becoming a part of our Constitution.

This proposed amendment is fathered by Socialists, Communists, and Bolshevists. They are the active workers in its favor. They look forward to its adoption as giving them the power to nationalize the children of the land and bring about in this country the exact conditions which prevail in Russia. These people are the active workers back of this undertaking, but many patriotic men and women, without at all realizing the seriousness of this proposition, thinking only of it as an effort to lessen child labor in factories, are giving countenance to it.

If adopted, this amendment would be the greatest thing ever done in America in behalf of the activities of hell. It would make millions of young people under eighteen years of age idlers in brain and body, and thus make them the devil's best workshop. It would destroy the initiative and self-reliance and manhood and womanhood of all the coming generations.

A solemn responsibility to this country and to all future generations rests upon every man and woman who understands this situation to fight, and fight unceasingly, to make the facts known to their acquaintances everywhere. Aggressive work is needed. It would be worse than folly for people who realize the danger of this situation to rest content under the belief that the amendment cannot become a part of our Constitution. The only thing that can prevent its adoption will be active, untiring work on the part of every man and woman who appreciates its destructive power and who wants to save the young people of all future generations from moral and physical decay under the domination of the devil himself.

81.

Louis Marshall: Against Immigration Restrictions Based on National Origins

Because the emergency Quota Act of 1921 had not proved to be an effective tool for limiting immigration, especially from the countries of southern and eastern Europe, Congress began to consider other devices for restricting the number of immigrants from these countries. In 1924 the legislators were debating the merits and demerits of a bill that would limit annual immigrants from a given country to 2 percent of their numbers in the United States in 1890. By using 1890 as a base, the proposed law would discriminate against immigration from such countries as Italy, Poland, and Russia, whose nationals had come in large numbers to the United States only after that date. In addition, immigration from the countries of the Orient would be prohibited altogether. Louis Marshall, who was chairman of the American Jewish Relief Committee, wrote the following letter on May 22, 1924, to President Coolidge, who was then considering the bill. The National Origins Act, as the bill was called, was passed, and the quota system begun with the act of 1921 remained in force until amendments, in 1965, to the McCarran-Walter Act (1952) abolished national quotas.

Source: *Louis Marshall, Champion of Liberty: Selected Papers and Addresses,* Charles Reznikoff, ed., Philadelphia, 1957, Vol. I, pp. 208-214.

On behalf of many hundred thousands of citizens of the United States, both native-born and naturalized, who feel slighted by the terms of the Immigration Bill now before you for Executive action, and availing ourselves of your permission, we venture to state reasons justifying your disapproval of the measure.

Before proceeding to a consideration of the main objections urged by those for whom we speak, it is fitting to refer, as symptomatic of the atmosphere of racial hostility which permeates this proposed legislation, to the provision which is intended to terminate forthwith the so-called Gentlemen's Agreement with the Empire of Japan and to exclude from the quota privileges conferred by the act all subjects of that Government. At the Disarmament Conference there was complete cooperation, and the desire on the part of Japan for maintaining amicable relations toward us has been consistently sincere. Past experience demonstrates that, however distasteful to Japan discriminatory legislation on the subject of immigration may be, there can be no doubt that, by means of appropriate diplomatic procedure, which would avoid the placing of an affront upon a proud people, a satisfactory arrangement regarding immigration, based on mutual consent, can be arrived at between the two countries.

Instead of permitting such an obviously conciliatory method to be pursued by the treaty-making branch of our Government, this bill, in the most offensive manner and in total disregard of the natural feelings of a sister nation, whom we have regarded as a political equal, inflicts a deep insult upon the national and racial consciousness of a highly civilized and progressive country. Such a wound will never cease to rankle. It will give rise to hostility which, even when not apparent on the surface, will prove most serious. It cannot fail to be reflected upon our commerce, and in days of stress will be likely to occasion unspeakable concern. And what will be the net result upon immigration by the elimination of Japan from the quota provisions? The exclusion of possibly 250 immigrants a year at a time when a large number of Japanese now in this country are emigrating annually.

Coming now to the principal purpose of this communication:

(1) The central provision of this bill is that contained in Section 11, subdivision (a), which limits the annual quota of any nationality to two per centum of the number of foreign-born individuals of such nationality residing in continental United States as determined by the census of 1890, the minimum quota to any nationality being 100.

The present quota law is based on the census of 1910 and fixes a rate of three per cent. That idea was fathered by the late Senator Dillingham, who had given the subject careful study as the Chairman of the Immigration Commission appointed during President Roosevelt's Administration. He proposed a rate of five per cent., but it was reduced while the bill was on its passage. The census of 1910 was chosen because that of 1920 was not then available. The idea was that the proper test was the number of foreign-born individuals of the various nationalities in the country at the time the quota was to become effective. Even that bill gave rise to great hardships. It was, however, fair, in that it did not discriminate among the foreign-born individuals of various nationalities.

The present bill, however, is avowedly discriminatory, as is apparent from the Majority and Minority Reports of the House Committee on Immigration which reported this bill. While under the present law the number of immigrants who come from Northern and Western Europe and of those who come from Southern and Eastern Europe are equal, under this bill the number of immigrants who may come from Northern and Western Europe is largely increased, even on the reduced basis of two per cent., over the number admitted from those countries under the present law; whereas those coming from Southern and Eastern Europe will not exceed one-fifth of those now admitted from that portion of Europe. . . .

This is the first time in the history of American legislation that there has been an attempt to discriminate in respect to European immigration between those who come from different parts of the continent. It is not only a differentiation as to countries of origin, but also of racial stocks and of religious beliefs. Those coming from Northern and Western Europe are supposed to be Anglo-Saxon or mythical Nordics, and to a large extent Protestant. Those coming from Southern and Eastern Europe are of different racial stocks and of a different faith. There are today in this country millions of citizens, both native-born and naturalized, descended from those racial stocks and entertaining those religious beliefs against which this bill deliberately discriminates. There is no mincing of the matter.

To add insult to injury, the effort has been made to justify this class legislation by charging that those who are sought to be excluded are inferior types and not assimilable. There is no justification in fact for such a contention. In common with all other immigrants, those who have come from the countries sought to be tabooed have been industrious and law-abiding and have made valuable contributions to our industrial, commercial and social development. They have done the hard, manual work which is indispensable to normal economic growth. Their children, educated in our public schools, are as American in their outlook as are those of the immigrants of earlier periods. Some of the intellectual leaders of the nation have sprung from this decried origin. During the World War some of these very immigrants and their children fought for the country, thousands of them waiving the exemption to which they would have been entitled.

To say that they are not assimilable argues ignorance. The facts show that they adopt American standards of living and that they are permeated with the spirit of our institutions. It is said that they speak foreign languages, but in those foreign languages they are taught to love our Govern-

ment, and to a very great extent they are acquiring the use of the English language as completely as most Americans would acquire foreign languages were they to migrate to other countries.

Under the existing basic Immigration Act of 1917, which is a highly selective law, ample provision is made for the exclusion of those who are mentally, morally and physically unfit, of those who are likely to become public charges, and of those who entertain views which are opposed to organized government and not consonant with our institutions. It has been the boast of those who have advocated the legislation now under consideration, that the United States has ceased to be an asylum of the oppressed; and one of the projectors of this bill has declared it to be a new Declaration of Independence, forgetting that the old Declaration, in reciting the injuries and usurpations of the British monarch, charged: "He has endeavored to prevent the population of these States, for that purpose obstructing the laws for naturalization of foreigners; refusing to pass others to encourage their migrations hither, and raising the conditions of new appropriations of lands." Let us not forget that what has made ours a noble nation has been the fact that we have received the oppressed and have admitted to our shores men and women who were worthy of sharing the opportunities afforded by our tremendous national resources, which, to an extraordinary extent, still clamor for development.

What we regard as the danger lurking in this legislation is, that it stimulates racial, national and religious hatreds and jealousies, that it encourages one part of our population to arrogate to itself a sense of superiority, and to classify another as one of inferiority. At a time when the welfare of the human race as an entirety depends upon the creation of a brotherly spirit, the restoration of peace, harmony and unity, and the termination of past animosities engendered by the insanity and brutality of war, it should be our purpose, as a nation which has demonstrated that those of diverse racial, national and religious origins can live together and prosper as a united people, to serve as the world's conciliator. Instead of that this bill, if it becomes a law, is destined to become the very Apple of Discord.

(2) Subdivision (b) of Section 11 only adds to the injustice and the confusion of thought which characterize this bill. Instead of dealing with what was claimed by the Dillingham bill to be an emergency and leaving it to future Congresses to take up the subject anew, this section provides that the annual quota of any nationality for the fiscal year beginning July 1, 1927, *and for each fiscal year thereafter,* shall be a number which bears the same ratio to 150,000 as the number of immigrants in continental United States in 1920 having that national origin bears to the number of inhabitants in continental United States in 1920. This attempts to fix indefinitely, beginning three years hence, the number of immigrants to be admitted at 150,000.

Heretofore we have had no difficulty in absorbing a million immigrants a year. From August, 1914, down to 1920, because of the war, there were practically no immigrants into the United States — in fact during that period the emigrants exceeded in number the immigrants; and yet there is an attempt to determine once for all the number of immigrants who are to be admitted into our vast domain to supply our industries and to meet our many other needs.

But here, again, the vice of the legislation is that it is based entirely on national origin, regardless of fitness or usefulness, diligence or energy, or of our country's needs. Moreover, the reference to "national origin" is not to the number of foreign-born individuals of the several nationalities resident in the United States, but it is expected to make a biological, anthropological, ethnological investigation into the birth or ancestry of those resident in the United States in 1920. It is believed that there are no statistics which would make it possible to work out a reliable conclusion as to national origin. The very fact that there have been intermarriages between those of diverse nationalities and that there may be an admixture of the blood of half a dozen nationalities into a single individual, demonstrates the absurdity of such a scheme. There has been no scientific or other investigation indicating that it is practicable to work out such a theory, and yet it is written into our law as a happy thought originating during the heat of argument.

It is evident that three years will be required to make the determination called for, and yet, in advance of any trustworthy investigation, the fundamental theory of our immigration laws, in force for more than a century and by means of which we have progressed as no other nation in the world has during a like period, is to be forever rejected. It will be a sorry day for our Republic when our national legislation shall substitute for the humane, farsighted and statesmanlike theories of the past, the feudal, medieval and inhuman concepts which characterize this bill.

(3) Although it has been the declared public policy of this country not to separate families, under the present bill, with its reduced quotas, where practically every immigrant is to be governed by the quota principle, it will become virtually impossible for a wife and children of a husband and father coming to this country for the purpose of establishing a home for them to join the head of the household. The fact that under Section 6 (a) they are entitled to preference will be of but little avail in the light of the diminished quotas. Nor does Section 4, subdivision (a), remedy the situation, because it deals merely with the unmarried child under the age of 18 years, or the wife, of a citizen of the United States. In such

cases a period of five years may elapse during which the separation would be continued.

(4) Further discrimination is shown by the fact that under Section 4 (c) an immigrant born in the Dominion of Canada, Newfoundland, the Republic of Mexico, the Republic of Cuba, the Republic of Haiti, the Dominican Republic, the Canal Zone, or an independent country of Central or South America, and his wife and his unmarried children under eighteen years of age, are admitted as non-quota immigrants. Can it be seriously contended that Mexicans, Cubans, Haitians, Santo Domingoans, or Central or South Americans, are more desirable or more assimilable than Italians, Poles, Russians, Austrians, Belgians, Hungarians, Roumanians, Greeks, Dutch, Czechoslovakians or Yugoslavians?

(5) Section 24 reverses the rule of evidence which has always hitherto obtained, by seeking to impose the burden of proof upon the alien to establish that he is not subject to exclusion under any provision of the immigration law, and that in any deportation proceeding against any alien the burden of proof shall be upon him to show that he entered the United States lawfully. By the operation of this provision, if an immigrant arrives here and is told that the quota of his nationality had on the day previous been exhausted, it will be necessary for him to prove the contrary, although the records are within the control of the Government and it is utterly impossible for the immigrant to establish by legal evidence the inaccuracy of the statement that he was not admissible.

You will recollect, Mr. President, that in the early part of November, 1923, it was announced by the Department of Labor that the Russian quota for the year had been exhausted, and approximately 1,000 immigrants were excluded and ordered deported. Some of the cases were of excruciating hardship. Two hundred of them were in fact deported, when it was learned that, through erroneous bookkeeping in the Department or otherwise, all of these arrivals were admissible. The facts being called to your attention, those remaining in this country were promptly admitted. Let us suppose that the burden of proof to show that they were entitled to admission rested on these immigrants. It would not have been possible to have met it. If habeas corpus proceedings had been instituted the Government would have stood mute and the writ would necessarily have been dismissed.

Illustrations could be multiplied to show that such a rule of evidence as is now contemplated is not only unjust and inequitable, but contrary to American traditions.

Without dwelling upon other objections, we most respectfully and earnestly submit that if this bill shall become a law it will be a positive misfortune to the country and will mark a sharp departure from those policies which have proven a blessing to mankind as well as to our beloved land.

The official language of the state of Illinois shall be known hereafter as the American language, and not as the English language.
Acts of the Legislature of Illinois, Ch. 127, Sec. 178, 1923

82.

Herbert Hoover: Moral Standards in an Industrial Era

Herbert Hoover, who, according to John Maynard Keynes, was "the only man [to emerge] from the ordeal of Paris with an enhanced reputation," returned to America in 1919 a national political figure. Although courted by the Democrats, Hoover supported Harding in the 1920 campaign and was rewarded with the choice of two different cabinet posts. He chose the Commerce Department, remaining as secretary until 1928, when he was elected President. Hoover's policy was one of respectful cooperation with the business community. Believing that businessmen would regulate themselves, he encouraged voluntary trade associations and developed codes of "fair practice." "We are passing from a period of extremely individualistic action," he declared, "into a period of associational activities." He retained the philosophy developed during his sojourn as secretary of commerce throughout the rest of his public career. The following selection is taken from a speech delivered in Cleveland on May 7, 1924.

Source: *The Hoover Policies*, Ray L. Wilbur and Arthur M. Hyde, eds., New York, 1937, pp. 300-305.

THE ADVANCEMENT OF SCIENCE and our increasing population require constantly new standards of conduct and breed an increasing multitude of new rules and regulations. The basic principles laid down in the Ten Commandments and the Sermon on the Mount are as applicable today as when they were declared, but they require a host of subsidiary clauses. . . .

A whole host of rules and regulations are necessary to maintain human rights with this amazing transformation into an industrial era. Ten people in a whole county, with a plow apiece, did not elbow each other very much. But when we put 7 million people in a county with the tools of electric, steam, thirty-floor buildings, telephones, miscellaneous noises, streetcars, railways, motors, stock exchanges, and what not, then we do jostle each other in a multitude of directions. Thereupon our lawmakers supply the demand by the ceaseless piling up of statutes. . . .

Moreover, with increasing education our senses become more offended and our moral discriminations increase; for all of which we discover new things to remedy. In one of our states over 1,000 laws and ordinances have been added in the last eight months. It is also true that a large part of them will sleep peacefully in the statute book.

The question we need to consider is whether these rules and regulations are to be developed solely by government or whether they cannot be in some large part developed out of voluntary forces in the nation. In other words, can the abuses which give rise to government in business be eliminated by the systematic and voluntary action of commerce and industry itself? . . .

National character cannot be built by law. It is the sum of the moral fiber of its individuals. When abuses which rise from our growing system are cured by live individual conscience, by initiative in the creation of voluntary standards, then is the growth of moral perceptions fertilized in every individual character.

No one disputes the necessity for constantly new standards of conduct in relation to all these tools and inventions. Even our latest great invention — radio — has brought a host of new questions. No one disputes that much of these subsidiary additions to the Ten Commandments must be made by legislation. Our public utilities are wasteful and costly unless we give them a privilege more or less monopolistic. At once when we have business affected with monopoly we must have regulation by law. Much of even this phase might have been unnecessary had there been a higher degree of responsibility to the public, higher standards of business practice among those who dominated these agencies in years gone by. . . .

When legislation penetrates the business world it is because there is abuse somewhere. A great deal of this legislation is due rather to the inability of business hitherto to so organize as to correct abuses than to any lack of desire to have it done. Sometimes the abuses are more apparent than real, but anything is a handle for demagoguery. In the main, however, the public acts only when it has lost confidence in the ability or willingness of business to correct its own abuses.

Legislative action is always clumsy — it is incapable of adjustment to shifting needs. It often enough produces new economic currents more abusive than those intended to be cured. Government too often becomes the persecutor instead of the regulator.

The thing we all need to searchingly consider is the practical question of the method by which the business world can develop and enforce its own standards and thus stem the tide of governmental regulation. The cure does not lie in mere opposition. It lies in the correction of abuse. It lies in an adaptability to changing human outlook.

The problem of business ethics as a prevention of abuse is of two categories: those where the standard must be one of individual moral perceptions, and those where we must have a determination of standards of

Lightfoot Collection

Herbert Hoover, photographed when he was serving as secretary of commerce

conduct for a whole group in order that there may be a basis for ethics.

The standards of honesty, of a sense of mutual obligation, and of service were determined 2,000 years ago. They may require at times to be recalled. And the responsibility for them increases infinitely in high places either in business or government, for there rests the high responsibility for leadership in fineness of moral perception. Their failure is a blow at the repute of business and at confidence in government itself.

The second field, and the one which I am primarily discussing, is the great area of indirect economic wrong and unethical practices that spring up under the pressures of competition and habit. There is also the great field of economic waste through destructive competition, through strikes, booms and slumps, unemployment, through failure of our different industries to synchronize, and a hundred other causes which directly lower our productivity and employment. Waste may be abstractly unethical, but in any event it can only be remedied by economic action.

If we are to find solution to these collective issues outside of government regulation we must meet two practical problems:

First, there must be organization in such form as can establish the standards of conduct in this vast complex of shifting invention, production, and use. There is no existing basis to check the failure of service or the sacrifice of public interest. Someone must determine such standards. They must be determined and held flexibly in tune with the intense technology of trade.

Second, there must be some sort of enforcement. There is the perpetual difficulty of a small minority who will not play the game. They too often bring disrepute upon the vast majority; they drive many others to adopt unfair competitive methods which all deplore; their abuses give rise to public indignation and clamor which breed legislative action.

I believe we now for the first time have the method at hand for voluntarily organized determination of standards and their adoption. I would go further; I believe we are in the presence of a new era in the organization of industry and commerce in which, if properly directed, lie forces pregnant with infinite possibilities of moral progress. I believe that we are, almost unnoticed, in the midst of a great revolution — or perhaps a better word, a transformation in the whole super-organization of our economic life. We are passing from a period of extremely individualistic action into a period of associational activities.

Practically our entire American working world is now organized into some form of economic association. We have trade associations and trade institutes embracing particular industries and occupations. We have chambers of commerce embracing representatives of different industries and commerce. We have the labor unions representing the different crafts. We have associations embracing all the different professions — law, engineering, medicine, banking, real estate, and what not. We have farmers' associa-

tions, and we have the enormous growth of farmers' cooperatives for actual dealing in commodities. Of indirect kin to this is the great increase in ownership of industries by their employees and customers, and again we have a tremendous expansion of mutualized insurance and banking.

Associational activities are, I believe, driving upon a new road where the objectives can be made wholly and vitally of public interest. . . . Three years of study and intimate contact with associations of economic groups, whether in production, distribution, labor, or finance, convince me that there lies within them a great moving impulse toward betterment. If these organizations accept as their primary purpose the lifting of standards, if they will cooperate together for voluntary enforcement of high standards, we shall have proceeded far along the road of the elimination of government from business. . . .

The test of our whole economic and social system is its capacity to cure its own abuses. New abuses and new relationships to the public interest will occur as long as we continue to progress. If we are to be wholly dependent upon government to cure these abuses we shall by this very method have created an enlarged and deadening abuse through the extension of bureaucracy and the clumsy and incapable handling of delicate economic forces. . . .

American business needs a lifting purpose greater than the struggle of materialism. Nor can it lie in some evanescent, emotional, dramatic crusade. It lies in the higher pitch of economic life, in a finer regard for the rights of others, a stronger devotion to obligations of citizenship that will assure an improved leadership in every community and the nation; it lies in the organization of the forces of our economic life so that they may produce happier individual lives, more secure in employment and comfort, wider in the possibilities of enjoyment of nature, larger in its opportunities of intellectual life.

83.

Thomas J. Walsh: Teapot Dome

Of the numerous scandals of the Harding administration none was so notorious as Teapot Dome. In 1921, Albert B. Fall, newly appointed secretary of the interior, obtained jurisdiction for his department over certain oil fields in Wyoming and California that had previously been administered by the Navy Department. Fall made arrangements with two private companies to extract the oil, in return for financial favors for himself. It seems likely that President Harding knew most of the facts of the case before his death in August 1923, for members of Congress had already begun to ask questions and suggestive articles had been printed in newspapers. But the full scope of the scandal — each of the oil companies stood to gain more than $100 million, and Fall could anticipate a fortune for himself — was not made public until an investigation was undertaken by Montana Senator Thomas J. Walsh. In July 1924 Walsh published an article, part of which is reprinted here, outlining the background of the case. The leases were canceled in 1927, and two years later Fall was fined $100,000 and sent to prison.

Source: *Forum*, July 1924: "The True History of Teapot Dome."

OUR GOVERNMENT IS OPERATED on the party system. That system has its vices, but one of its cardinal virtues is that the one party, always standing ready to point out the objections to and the weaknesses of candidates, officials, policies, and measures of the other, better men are advanced as candidates, officials are held to a higher degree of efficiency, and a stricter responsibility and policies demanded by the public interest are pursued. So it is no discredit whatever to either me or my colleagues, if it be the fact, as has been so acrimoniously charged, that no sense of public duty, no detestation of crime, no love of country actuated us, that our activities are and have been, as charged, "pure politics."

With both friends and foes, however, there is an acute curiosity to know the sequence of events which ended in the public disgrace of Fall, by what sinuous and devious route the pursuit which led to his exposure was followed, and to learn of the intellectual processes by which that result was achieved. It is a queer trait of human character that finds gratification in the reading of detective stories. This tale reveals some queer manifestations of the operations of the mass mind.

In the spring of 1922 rumors reached parties interested that a lease had been or was about to be made of Naval Reserve No. 3 in the state of Wyoming, — popularly known, from its local designation, as the Teapot Dome. This was one of three great areas known to contain petroleum in great quantity which had been set aside for the use of the Navy — Naval Reserves No. 1 and No. 2 in California by President Taft in 1912, and No. 3 by President Wilson in 1915. The initial steps toward the creation of these reserves — the land being public, that is, owned by the government — were taken by President Roosevelt, who caused to be instituted a study to ascertain the existence and location of eligible areas, as a result of which President Taft in 1909 withdrew the tracts in question from disposition under the public land laws. These areas were thus set apart with a view to keeping in the ground a great reserve of oil available at some time in the future, more or less remote, when an adequate supply for the Navy could not, by reason of the failure or depletion of the world store, or the exigencies possibly of war, be procured or could be procured only at excessive cost; in other words to ensure the Navy in any exigency the fuel necessary to its efficient operation.

From the time of the original withdrawal order, private interests had persistently endeavored to assert or secure some right to exploit these rich reserves, the effort giving rise to a struggle lasting throughout the Wilson administration. Some feeble attempt was made by parties having no claim to any of the territory to secure a lease of all or a portion of the reserves, but in the main the controversy was waged by claimants asserting rights either legal or equitable in portions of the reserves antedating the withdrawal orders, on the one hand, and the Navy Department on the other. In that struggle Secretary Lane was accused of being unduly friendly to the private claimants, Secretary Daniels being too rigidly insistent on keeping the areas intact. President Wilson apparently supported Daniels in the main in the controversy which became acute and Lane retired from the cabinet, it is said, in consequence of the differences which had thus arisen.

The reserves were created, in the first place, in pursuance of the policy of conservation, the advocates of which, a militant body, active in the Ballinger affair, generally supported the attitude of Secretary Daniels and President Wilson.

They too became keen on the report of the impending lease of Teapot Dome. Failing to get any definite or reliable informa-

tion at the departments, upon diligent inquiry, Senator Kendrick of Wyoming introduced and had passed by the Senate on April 16, 1922, a resolution calling on the secretary of the interior for information as to the existence of the lease which was the subject of the rumors, in response to which a letter was transmitted by the acting secretary of the interior on April 21, disclosing that a lease of the entire Reserve No. 3 was made two weeks before to the Mammoth Oil Company organized by Harry Sinclair, a spectacular oil operator. This was followed by the adoption by the Senate on April 29, 1922, of a resolution introduced by Senator LaFollette directing the Committee on Public Lands and Surveys to investigate the entire subject of leases of the naval oil reserves and calling on the secretary of the interior for all documents and full information in relation to the same.

In the month of June following, a cartload of documents said to have been furnished in compliance with the resolution was dumped in the committee rooms, and a letter from Secretary Fall to the President in justification of the lease of the Teapot Dome and of leases of limited areas on the other reserves was by him sent to the Senate. I was importuned by Senators LaFollette and Kendrick to assume charge of the investigation, the chairman of the committee and other majority members being believed to be unsympathetic, and assented the more readily because the Federal Trade Commission had just reported that, owing to conditions prevailing in the oil fields of Wyoming and Montana, the people of my state were paying prices for gasoline in excess of those prevailing anywhere else in the Union.

In the letter of Secretary Fall the course taken was said to have been required by the fact that wells in the adjacent Salt Creek field were draining the oil from the Teapot Dome area. As this theory was disputed, two geologists were employed by the committee to make a study of the ground during the summer of 1923, and the committee, on the incoming of their report, entered, on October 22, 1923, upon the inquiry with which it was charged. I had meanwhile caused to be made a somewhat careful but by no means complete examination of the mass of documents furnished the committee by the Department of the Interior, and went into a laborious study of the exhaustive reports made by the experts, much of it of a highly technical character. I undertook a critical analysis of the lease itself and of the lengthy letter of Secretary Fall to the President, and prepared to interrogate him on the stand concerning features of both, with the purpose of bringing out what I conceived to be fatal vices in the one and misrepresentations and weaknesses in the other.

Incidental to this part of the preparation it was necessary to make a careful study of the acts of Congress of February 25, 1920, and June 4, 1920, of the so-called Overman Act, and the statutes touching contracts by the executive departments generally and by the Navy Department specifically. A somewhat intimate familiarity with the laws in relation to the disposition of the public domain and the procedure before the Department of the Interior in connection therewith lightened the task of preparation.

Concurrently with the prosecution of the work outlined, I addressed letters to all journals which had exhibited any special interest in the subject either at the time or since publicity was given to the execution of the Teapot Dome lease, asking for such information as they might be able to give me or for the sources of the statements of facts made in articles appearing in their columns on the subject.

The reports of the experts gave not a little support to the contention that drainage to an appreciable, if not a very considerable, extent was taking place from the Teapot Dome into the Salt Creek wells, contrary to the view expressed by some, whose opinions were entitled to respect, that owing to

Brown Brothers

"It's Washday Every Day in Washington"; cartoon by McCutcheon in the Chicago "Tribune" pertaining to the Senate's investigation into the government's leasing of the Teapot Dome oil reserves and related corruption in Harding's administration

the geological conditions such a result could not ensue. This was unfortunate because from the first it was recognized that there would be some migration of oil across the boundary line of Naval Reserve No. 3 which was purposely made to embrace an area beyond what was believed to be the separate Teapot Dome structure, that the oil in it might be safe.

The Geological Survey had reported that some drainage was taking place and had recommended that the situation be met by drilling a row of line wells along the relatively narrow common boundary. The propriety of leasing the whole 9,000 acres should have been mooted rather than the question of whether any drainage was taking place or was to be apprehended. However, the reports of the experts submitted at the first day's session were decidedly favorable to the leasing so far as they went, and, in the popular mind, if one may so speak, when general indifference to the whole subject was the rule, they went the whole length, it being supposed that the only question involved was geological.

The effect of the reports was heightened by the grossest misrepresentation concerning their import, put out by one of the great news agencies, subsequently asserted by it and probably truly, through the error of a careless reporter. A member of the committee gave out the statement that the inquiry would terminate within a day or two. Apathetically, a few reporters listened in the succeeding sessions to the tedious presentation of extracts from official documents and publications setting out the need of an oil reserve, of the wisdom of maintaining a great supply in the ground, and reciting the story of the efforts of private interests to secure a foothold within the reserves.

Secretary Fall being called to the stand, it was disclosed that hardly had the new administration been installed when the determination was arrived at to transfer the administration of the reserves from the Navy Department, to which it had been confided by Congress because it was believed that department was friendly to their preservation, to the Interior Department, suspected of being disposed to tolerate their exploitation, and an order making the transfer bearing date May 30, 1921, over the signature of President Harding was brought to light. No one now seriously contends that the President had any authority to issue such an order, which, however, at the time of its promulgation, notwithstanding that fact and its evil augury, evoked little attention, though the significance of it was not lost on the watchful leaders of the conservation movement, particularly as Secretary Fall was known from his record in the Senate to be far from friendly to the conservation policy.

No one seemed willing to assume any wrong in or even to criticize the acts of the new administration, buttressed by that 7 million majority and guided by the "best minds." Some little dent in the complacent confidence of the public was made at the time the lease was made through the speeches of Senators Kendrick and LaFollette, who called attention to the significant fact that its execution indicated a departure from the settled policy of the government; that it reversed the result of the struggle that had been carried on throughout the preceding administration; that it was made pursuant to negotiations prosecuted in secret and without competitive biddings. But the listlessness of the public was but little disturbed.

Interest flared fitfully later on when Sinclair declared before a Senate Committee that he expected to make $100 million out of the lease, but it was at a low ebb when the hearings began and the reports of the experts chilled whatever there remained. Nevertheless the reversal of the policy to which general adherence had been given, the secrecy which attended the negotiations, the effort to keep from the public information that the lease had been executed, cast about the transaction a suspicion which my study of the facts had heightened until it had passed to conviction. This was strengthened by the examination of Fall and the disclosures made in connection with his testimony. It might be entertaining did time or space permit to specify these in detail. Misstatements of fact in the letter to the President were not infrequent, but more persuasive with me was the total disregard of the plain provisions of the law, and the utterly untenable arguments made to sustain the action that was taken.

To illustrate: Twice in letters to the President upon inquiry from senators, Fall justified the executive order upon the Overman Act and the acts of February 25 and June 4, 1920. Confronted with the Overman Act, he was compelled to admit that by its plain language it had no application. He could find nothing in either of the other acts to justify his reference to them and then fell back on some vague authority arising from the general scheme of our government. He made a futile effort to find some ground for the provision in the contract authorizing the use of the oil to pay the cost of constructing great storage tanks, pursuant to a program of the Navy, which contemplated the construction of public works without authorization by Congress, involving an expenditure mounting up to $102 million.

He took great credit to himself for sagaciously inserting in the lease that the pipeline to be constructed by Sinclair should be a common carrier, which the Interstate Commerce Law made it without any stipulation to that effect. He reiterated the assertion made in his letter to the President that he considered himself the guardian of important military secrets of the government in connection with the leases which he would, under no circumstances, reveal, plainly intimating that those who were trying to pry into the affair were lacking in loyalty and wanting in that fine sense of duty to country by which he was actuated, recalling, to me at least, that cynical saying of Dr. Johnson that patriotism is the last refuge of a scoundrel. He was voluble to a degree.

There followed other witnesses, mainly attachés of the department, who testified about drainage and kindred matters when the committee suspended on November 2 to resume on November 30, the case being made as to the legality of the leases, which no one in either house of Congress rose to defend on the resolution to begin suit to annul them, and as to the policy of abandoning the purpose to keep the oil in the ground which has, except for a feeble voice lately raised in the House, had no defender in either body. The public, however, so far as the press indicated, remained apathetic.

In the interim, stories had reached me, rumors rather, about some significant land deal in New Mexico — sometimes it was Fall who purchased for Sinclair, again Sinclair who purchased for Fall. They were vague in character, and diligent inquiry revealed no details. The statement above as to the press is too general. A few newspapers early sensed the importance of the revelations, notably the St. Louis *Post-Dispatch,* the Omaha *World Herald,* the Raleigh *News and Observer,* and the Washington *Daily News,* a Scripps publication. From the Honorable W. B. Colver, editor of the last named, I learned that the Denver *Post,* which virulently denounced the lease at the outset and then strangely and suddenly quit, had in the summer of 1922 sent a man to New Mexico to investigate the land deal and that he had made a report which, for some reason, the *Post* had omitted to publish. Rumors of why the *Post* had changed its policy fed the suspicion with which I viewed the transaction.

Through Colver and his Denver connections I learned that the reporter was friendly but fearful and that his report, still available, was interesting. I had no funds at my command to bring him to Washington. I had no investigator at my service to interview him or anyone. I went before the Committee and asked for a subpoena to require his attendance. Grudgingly, authority for its issuance was awarded. He came with his report and gave the names and addresses of witnesses in New Mexico who could tell of Fall's sudden rise from financial embarrassment, if not impecuniosity, to comparative affluence. He brought certified copies of the records showing the acquisition by Fall of the Harris ranch, of his delinquencies in the matter of his local taxes extending over a period of ten years, and of his liquidation of them in the summer of 1922, and of the shipment of blooded stock from Sinclair's farm in New Jersey to Fall's ranch in New Mexico.

I then dismissed him and secured subpoenas for the New Mexico witnesses, who told the story of Fall's having paid $91,500 for the ranch mentioned — the initial payment of $10,000 having been made in bills taken from a black tin box — of his subsequent purchase of other lands costing $33,000 more, of the installation of a hydroelectric plant at a cost of from $40,000 to $50,000, and of other expenditures in the aggregate approximating $200,000.

I did not enter into that field of inquiry without misgivings. Seeking advice from a friendly associate on the Committee, I was assured that some plausible story would be told and the effort come to naught. I determined, however, that the duty of the Committee being to investigate, the witnesses should be called, whatever might be the outcome. The significance of their testimony, synchronizing in its details so strangely with Sinclair's visit in his private car to Fall's ranch in the latter part of 1921, an added circumstance of a suspicious character, could not be overlooked and gave rise to obvious consternation among the friends of Fall on the Committee who were, however, reassured by a message from him to the effect that his son-in-law, who was entirely conversant with his business affairs, would come on to explain all.

By this time there was attracted to the committee room an increasing number of representatives of the press, but though the daily reports of the proceedings were reasonably complete, the editorial force seemed oblivious of what was going on. It was at about that stage of the inquiry that I sought through influential friends to arouse the interest of some of the metropolitan papers, which, for one reason or another, might be expected to aid; for I realized that many might be prompted to help should the issue be agitated who would otherwise remain silent. If they made any effort it was fruitless. Doheny coming upon the stand about that time denounced as an "outrage" the bringing of witnesses from New Mexico to besmirch the character of so upright a public official as Albert B. Fall. More recent denunciatory comment on the investigators does not specify Fall or any other particular individual, for that matter. But at that time I was a muckraker, vilifying worthy public servants.

Still it was up to Fall to tell where the money came from. His son-in-law did not appear according to promise. Fall did not. A statement made by him to the press gave the assurance that a full explanation would be made. Later it was reported in a vague way that he was ill — now in Chicago, now in New York. Reporters were unable to locate him, for they were now on the job. In fact he came to Chicago, went from there to New York, thence to Atlantic City, and to Washington, where he had an interview with Senators Smoot and Lenroot, members of the Committee, and with Will Hayes, late chairman of the Republican National Committee, to whom he told, as he did in a letter to the Committee on December 27, 1923, that he had borrowed $100,000 with which to purchase the Harris Ranch from Edward B. McLean, owner and editor of the Washington *Post,* then at Palm Beach, Florida, whither Fall speedily betook himself as McLean's guest.

The same volubility which characterized his testimony was in evidence in his written communication to the Committee. It bore intrinsic evidence of being of doubtful veracity. A month had gone by since the damaging evidence had been heard. An honest man would have hastened to take the stand to refute the inferences to which it naturally gave rise and the doubts that it must inevitably have raised. Had such a man been desperately ill he would have told the story on the stand and not sought refuge from cross-examination by sending a letter from his hotel in the city in which the Committee was sitting. Moreover, the knowing ones smiled incredulously at the idea of Ned McLean's having such a sum of money at hand to loan, though rich in property, or of his loaning it if he had it.

Forthwith that gentleman began to exhibit a feverish anxiety lest he be called as a witness, singularly divining what was coming. He communicated by wire with the Committee; he sent lawyers to represent to it and to me that he was ill, that his wife was ill; that it would be dangerous for him to tempt the rigorous climate of Washington at that season of the year; that he had loaned $100,000 to Fall in November or December 1922; that he knew nothing about the facts otherwise; that he would make a written statement under oath if the Committee desired him to attest to the truth of a statement he would send. He begged not to be called to Washington. I was insistent that he appear; other members of the Committee were disposed to be accommodating, and on a record vote on which I and my supporters were outnumbered, it was agreed to take from him a statement and hold in abeyance until it was received his plea to be excused.

In the discussion Senator Smoot suggested that I go to Palm Beach and take his testimony. That seemed to me impracticable in view of the demands upon my time, but leave was given me to submit interrogatories to be answered in connection with his statement. But on attempting to draft such I became convinced that the effort to get the truth by that method would be unavailing and I signified to the Committee my willingness to go to Palm Beach. The proper authority to take his testimony was given and on the 11th of January he confronted me at "The Breakers."

I made the trip in the expectation that he would say that he had made the loan, intending to interrogate him as to the source from which the money was derived. I proposed to trace it to its source, either to his own private funds, kept in his own private account, or to some account earmarked in a manner that would permit following it to some other origin. I suspected that in some way it came from Sinclair and that I could follow it through various banking transactions to that source. It had not occurred to me that it might have come from Doheny, though it had been disclosed — a fact of which Fall omitted to make any mention when on the stand — that the whole of Naval Reserve No. 1 in California, 32,000 acres in area, estimated to contain 250 million barrels of oil, had been on December 11, 1922, leased to Doheny, who afterward told us that he too expected to make $100 million out of his lease secured from Fall in the same secret manner as had characterized the Sinclair deal.

I was dumbfounded when McLean, evidently appreciating that he would be required to tell the bank upon which he drew to make the loan to Fall, should he adhere to his earlier story, frankly admitted that he never did loan the money to Fall, adding that he gave Fall his checks for that sum, which were returned a few days later and destroyed without being cashed, the recipient asserting that he had arranged to secure the necessary elsewhere.

Now the affair could no longer be kept off the front page. Leading newsgatherers sent representatives to Palm Beach to report the proceedings there; but the country was not fully aroused until on January 21 the Roosevelts went on the stand to relate their lurid story, and the climax was reached when on January 24 Doheny voluntarily appeared to tell that on November 30, 1921, he had loaned $100,000 to Fall without security, moved by old friendship and commiseration for his business misfortunes, negotiations between them then pending eventuating in the contract awarded to Doheny on April 25, following, through which he secured, without competition, a contract giving him a preference right to a lease of a large part of Naval Reserve No. 1, to be followed by the lease of the whole of it, as above recited.

Followed the appearance of Fall, forced by the Committee to come before it, after pleading inability on account of illness, to take refuge under his constitutional immunity, a broken man, the cynosure of the morbidly curious that crowded all approaches to the committee room and packed it to suffocation, vindicating the wisdom of the patriarch who proclaimed centuries ago that the way of the transgressor is hard.

84.

Henri Hauser: Observations on American Farming

Henri Hauser came to the United States in 1923 as a visiting lecturer in history at Harvard University. Like other visitors to this country, he observed a great deal and committed his observations to writing in a volume entitled L'Amérique vivante, *published in 1924. He discussed some of the problems America faced in the "return to normalcy," particularly in the areas of economic, industrial, and agricultural readjustment. The following selection deals with the American farmer — whom the prosperity of the decade tended to bypass.*

Source: TWA, pp. 486-490.

THE AMERICAN FARMERS are landowners, not tenants. Yet they are not peasants; there is nothing analogous here to our type of small proprietors, nor are there any agglomerations which resemble our villages. There are indeed many places called "villages." But, imagine a road: to the right and the left along the road and for some distance back away from it, are little houses, generally of wood, sometimes of brick, dispersed, surrounded by lawns and trees; along a part of the road the cluster is more dense — one or more churches, for the little village may contain members of many denominations; a cemetery with simple stones; the school and, invariably, the public library; a police and a fire station; shops; a gasoline station; almost always a movie; very often a monument to the heroes of the Revolution, of the Civil War, of the World War; statue, cannons, pile of shells or of balls. That is an American village, hardly different from a small city.

I forget the inns, their facades covered with ivy, Virginia creepers, or wisteria, square, shadowy, and beflowered. These are sometimes carefully preserved in the style of the eighteenth century, with the room in which Lafayette slept, or Washington, or both. The farm buildings are out in the fields. And the village blacksmith of Longfellow is long since dead, even in the East.

The American farmer among us would be reckoned a great proprietor. There is very little morcellating of the land except in the very old sections of New England. The Puritan was a true agriculturist. The ancient books which describe primitive New England show us a rural population very like that of England at the time. But these little farms were emptied; their owners drifted in ever greater numbers to the city, to industry. In the northeast the urban population gains increasingly upon the rural, so that many of these abandoned farms are taken up by the French-Canadians. There is, therefore, a drift across the frontier, and certain villages in Massachusetts and Vermont are now given over to the French language.

This situation is peculiar to New England. But the great agricultural lands really begin in northern New York near the Great Lakes. There also has raged the pestilent massacre of the trees. In the vicinity of Buffalo, for instance, only a few isolated clumps, or even just the stumps which no one ever took the trouble to clear, testify to the former splendor of the destroyed forests. It is even worse in the prairie West. Between Chicago and Milwaukee, west of

Lake Michigan, is a true steppe, completely bare. There, there are not even villages; only the great farm buildings scattered through the empty spaces through which the electric tram hurtles at top speed. This is land that calls for cultivation on a large scale, for the machine, for uniform mass production.

The essential features of the landscape that take the place of trees and hills are the elevators in which the grain is stored. Our agricultural life, economically, centers about the market, the fair; here it turns about the railroad junctions where the wagons line up at the foot of those gigantic edifices, or even about the ports where the lake vessels come to take on cargoes of wheat and corn. Or even around the mill! But what is a mill? Put out of your minds all memories of Europe, of Dutch windmills or those of Sans Souci, sails flapping in the wind, bubbling streams where the wheel turns to the song of the miller, black boats moored on the Hungarian or Slovak banks of the Danube.

Imagine instead the banks of the Mississippi, where the pretty queen of the Northwest, the twin city of Minneapolis and Saint Paul, offers a charming sight with its parks, its brooks, its lakes, and cascades. Imagine there domesticated rapids, girdled with iron and stone put to the service of the technician. There, at the falls of Saint Anthony, the old French explorers, Father Marquette, Nicolet, and Radisson, marveled before the beauties of the creation.

Today the father of Waters is only a factory worker; the falls have given way to dams, to inclined planes over which flow waters potent with energy. One must go downstream, descend to the beautiful avenues of which we spoke, maintained by a wise and tasteful municipality, to discover the primitive freshness of the deep gorges which Chateaubriand saw only in his dreams.

At the falls rises the mill, a fortress of eight stories. Directly over the river an enormous pneumatic tube pours the grain out of the elevators into the sides of the mill. The grain descends from top to bottom, from story to story, from mill to mill, becoming a finer and finer flour. No creaky millstones or white powder, only closed chambers of varnished wood with glass windows in which the cylinders turn. There are in this single building 250 of these little mills, and in all 50 "millers" to take care of them. But the term "miller" can scarcely be applied to these mechanics, who follow the movement of the cylinders or of the sorting machines, who check the automatic filling of the paper or cloth sacks, the boxes, and the barrels, and who may be seen in off hours playing football in front of the factory.

The elevators, the mills, the giant abattoirs, the meat factories of Chicago or Kansas City, those are the magnetic poles of the farmer, the molding forces of his economic life, at least in the regions I saw. In the South quite different social classes are categorized as farmers: the tobacco, sugar, and, above all, the cotton planters. But I never ventured into the realm of King Cotton. I have had in mind primarily the farmer of the Middle West in my attempts to understand the position, the mentality, and the tendencies of the agriculturists, who are undoubtedly a fundamental element in the political life of America.

The industrial wealth of the United States must not deceive us. Agriculture is still the greatest American industry. That is why the farmer is the prime element, one might say the backbone of the nation. This is still the first agricultural country of the world.

It is true that this element is on the decline. In New England, of course, one can get an abandoned farm as a country home at a slight cost; but even more generally the land is losing a part of its population. The tillers of the soil were at the last census no longer a majority of the total.

What are the complaints of the farmers

who still make up 30 percent of the active population and who produce about 18 percent of the national income? They charge that they cannot get a sufficiently remunerative return for their products. That is difficult to believe when one sees the prodigious movements of agricultural goods, fruits, vegetables, and bacon in the ports and markets of the great cities. The American stomach is blessed with an enormous capacity. The consumption of sugar, for instance, is amazing, and any falling off in the harvest results in a rise in price. It is useless to propose a boycott. I was in New York in front of City Hall where 3,000 mothers had announced they would come to swear to reduce their consumption of sugar; actually some 200 turned out, about as many as the police there to watch them.

But apart from sugar, the products of agriculture are more dependent than those of industry on foreign, and particularly on European, markets. The United States could, if need be, absorb all the Fords but not all the lard of Chicago, nor the wheat, the corn, the grains of the Mississippi Valley. The question of exports is central here.

If the high tariffs lead, by retaliation, to the closing of certain outlets, if the rise in the value of the dollar loses customers for American products, that does not halt a spindle in the immense cotton factories of New England or Carolina. But the farmer cannot regard these developments with the same tranquillity. The result is that, farther away from Europe, more ignorant of European affairs, he is nevertheless more sensitive to fluctuations in the European markets. Politically, he will be more moved by descriptions of the troubled state of European economy. That explains many of the characteristics of the politics of the Western senators.

The country finds that it is working only for the industrialists. The latter reap the profits of the ultra-protectionist tariff, of credit facilities. The great reform which created the solid system of Federal Reserve

banks is very similar to that which created our Bank of France. Negotiable paper at ninety days is commercial and manufacturing, not farming, paper. Furthermore, this reform, in stabilizing the monetary situation and in making the dollar uniform in value, completely put an end to inflation, in which the farmer, here as everywhere, had an interest. The farmer asserts that his income is lower than that of the miners, of the railroad employees, of the factory workers. The only effect of the tariff on his situation has been to raise the price of articles indispensable to him.

The farmers carried on a lively agitation just before the adjournment of Congress. The administration resisted, taking the position that economic theory forbade a paper currency based on agricultural credit, necessarily long-term. But beyond the theory was that reality of politics, the farm bloc which speaks with authority in Washington and before which the administration had to capitulate.

The Federal Reserve Act of 1913 had already provided for the discount of farm paper for a period of not more than six months. But not all the banks had adhered to that system, and the result was that credit in some regions was too tight. In any case, six months are not much in terms of farm credit. A law of 1916 had also helped the producers of cotton, flax, grains, tobacco, and wool by providing for warehouse receipts negotiable for loans as collateral. In this very year they have even set up twelve federal farm credit banks.

Finally, during the war, the War Finance Corporation aided agricultural exporters as it did others. After the suspension of its operations in May 1920, the corporation was recreated in January 1921, and authorized to make loans to farm banks and to cooperatives. But a wartime institution cannot indefinitely be extended, and a definitive end to its service was provided for by the 30th of June of this year. It was time to act.

It was under these conditions that the

farm bloc last March pushed to a vote the law permanently creating the twelve federal farm banks. The capital of each, $5 million, was to be furnished by the United States Treasury, and the law authorized in addition the creation of corporations with agricultural credit, particularly elevators, with a minimum capital of $250,000. These private corporations could make loans, discount and rediscount on agricultural paper for nine months, on livestock for three years.

There will, therefore, now be a complete separation between the Federal Reserve banks which take only three-month paper and the new banks which receive nine-month or even three-year paper. The latter will play for the farmers the role of credit intermediaries that the Federal Reserve banks play for merchants and industrialists. The new banks are now being organized.

The farmer will, however, not yet be satisfied. He says that the crux of the matter for him is to be able to sell his products at a price that enables him to exist. If he can with his labor earn a profit of only 5 percent on his capital, he would be better off to invest his money passively. Nevertheless, he has received a great satisfaction. He would get an even greater one were he furnished with manpower, which becomes more and more rare.

85.

Lewis Mumford: Mechanical Architecture

If it is true, as Aristotle asserted, that man by nature is a social animal, then it is probably also true that man's greatest invention is the city. Lewis Mumford has devoted a large part of his writing to considerations of the social organization of cities, especially the modern American city — the "megalopolis." One of his early critical works, Sticks and Stones, *published in 1924, was a trenchant critique of the spirit of American architecture. The following selection is from the chapter entitled "The Age of the Machine."*

Source: *Sticks and Stones*, New York, 1924, pp. 177-189.

THE PROVINCES in which mechanical architecture has been genuinely successful are those in which there have been no conventional precedents, and in which the structure has achieved a sense of absolute form by following sympathetically the limitations of material and function. Just as the bridge summed up what was best in early industrialism, so the modern subway station, the modern lunchroom, the modern factory, and its educational counterpart, the modern school, have often been cast in molds which would make them conspicuous aesthetic achievements. In the Aristotelian sense, every purpose contains an inherent form; and it is only natural that a factory or lunchroom or grain elevator, intelligently conceived, should become a structure quite different in every aspect from the precedents that are upheld in the schools.

It would be a piece of brash aesthetic bigotry to deny the aesthetic values that derive from machinery: the clean surfaces, the hard lines, the calibrated perfection that the machine has made possible carry with them a beauty quite different from that of handicraft — but often it is a beauty. Our new sensitiveness to the forms of useful objects and purely utilitarian structures is an excellent sign; and it is not surprising that this sensitiveness has arisen first among artists. Many of our power plants are majestic; many of our modern factories are clean and lithe and smart, designed with unerring logic and skill. Put alongside buildings in which the architect has glorified his own idiosyncrasy or pandered to the ritual of conspicuous waste, our industrial plants at least have honesty and sincerity and an inner harmony of form and function. There is nothing peculiar to machine technology in these virtues, however, for the modern factory shares them with the old New England mill, the modern grain elevator with the Pennsylvania barn, the steamship with the clipper, and the airplane hangar with the castle.

The error with regard to these new forms of building is the attempt to universalize the mere process or form, instead of attempting to universalize the scientific spirit in which they have been conceived. The design for a dwelling house which ignores everything but the physical necessities of the occupants is the product of a limited conception of science which stops short at physics and mechanics and neglects biology, psychology, and sociology. If it was bad aesthetics to design steel frames decorated with iron cornucopias and flowers, it is equally bad aesthetics to design homes as if babies were hatched from incubators and as if wheels, rather than love and hunger, made the world go round. During the first movement of industrialism it was the pathetic fallacy that crippled and warped the new achievements of technology; today we are beset by the plutonic fallacy, which turns all living things it touches into metal.

In strict justice to our better sort of mechanical architecture, I must point out that the error of the mechanolators is precisely the opposite error to that of the academies. The weakness of conventional architecture

in the schools of the 19th century was the fact that it applied only to a limited province. We knew what an orthodox palace or post office would be like, and we had even seen their guilty simulacra in tenement houses and shopfronts; but no one had ever dared to imagine what a Beaux Arts factory would be like; and such approaches to it as the pottery works in Lambeth only made the possibility more dubious. The weakness of our conventional styles of architecture was that they stopped short at a province called building — which meant the province where the ordinary rules of aesthetic decency and politeness were completely abandoned for lack of a precedent.

The modernist is correct in saying that the mass of building ought to speak the same language; it is well for him to attempt to follow Mr. Louis Sullivan in his search for a "rule so broad as to admit of no exceptions." Where the modernist becomes confused, however, is in regarding the *dictionary* of modern forms, whose crude elements are exhibited in our factories and skyscrapers and grain elevators, as in any sense equivalent for their creative expression. So far, our mechanical architecture is a sort of structural Esperanto: it has a vocabulary without a literature, and when it steps beyond the elements of its grammar it can only translate badly into its own tongue the noble poems and epics that the Romans and Greeks and medieval builders left behind them.

The leaders of modernism do not, indeed, make the mistake that some of their admirers have made: Mr. Frank Lloyd Wright's pleasure pavilions and hotels do not resemble either factories or garages or grain elevators; they represent the same tendencies, perhaps, but they do so with respect to an entirely different set of human purposes. In one important characteristic, Mr. Wright's style has turned its back upon the whole world of engineering; whereas the steel cage lends itself to the vertical skyscraper, Mr. Wright's designs are the very products of the prairie, in their low-lying, horizontal lines, in their flat roofs, while at the same time they defy the neutral gray or black or red of the engineering structure by their colors and ornament.

In sum, the best modern work does not merely respect the machine; it respects the people who use it. It is the lesser artists and architects who, unable to control and mold the products of the machine, have glorified it in its nakedness, much as the producer of musical comedies, in a similar mood of helpless adulation, has "glorified" the American girl — as if either the machine or the girl needed it.

It has been a genuine misfortune in America that, as Mr. Sullivan bitterly pointed out in *The Autobiography of an Idea*, the growth of imperialism burked the development of a consonant modern style. In Europe, particularly in Finland, Germany, and the Netherlands, the best American work has been appreciated and followed up, and as so often happens, exaggerated; so that the aesthetic appreciation of the machine has been carried across the Atlantic and back again, very much in the way that Emerson's individualism was transformed by Nietzsche and became the mystic doctrine of the Superman.

Some of the results of this movement are interesting and valid — the work of the Dutch architects, for example, in the garden suburbs around Amsterdam — but what pleases one in these new compositions is not the mechanical rigor of form but the playfulness of spirit — they are good architecture precisely because they are something more than mere engineering. Except for a handful of good precedents, our mechanical work in America does not express this vitality. The machine has stamped us, and we have not reacted.

Moreover, in the building of separate houses in the city and its suburbs, where the demands of mechanical efficiency are not so drastic as they are in the office building, the effect of the machine process has been to narrow the scope of individual taste and personality. The designer, whether he is the architect, the owner, or the working contractor, works within a tradition whose bearing lies beyond him. Outside this mechanical tradition we have had many examples of good individual work, like the stone houses that have been erected around Philadelphia and the more or less native cement and adobe houses in New Mexico and California; but the great mass of modern houses are no longer framed for some definite site and some definite occupants; they are manufactured for a blind market.

The boards are cut to length in the sawmill, the roofing is fabricated in a roofing plant, the window frames are cut in standard sizes and put together in the framing factory, the balustrade is done in a turning mill, the very internal fittings like china closets and chests are made in a distant plant after one of a dozen patterns fixed and exemplified in the catalog. The business of the building worker is reduced to a mere assemblage of parts; and except for the more expensive grades of work, the architect is all but eliminated. The charming designs that the European modernists make testify to the strength of their long architectural tradition even in the face of machinery; the truth is that they fit our modern methods of house production scarcely much better than the thatched cottage of clay and wattle. The nemesis of mechanism is that it inexorably eliminates the architect — even the architect who worships its achievements!

So much of the detail of a building is established by factory standards and patterns that even the patron himself has precious little scope for giving vent to his impulses in the design or execution of the work; for every divergence from a standardized design represents an additional expense. In fact, the only opportunity for expressing his taste and personality is in choosing the mode in which the house is to be built. He must find his requirements in Italy, Colonial America, France, Tudor England, or Spain — woe to him if he wants to find them in 20th-century America! Thus the machine process has created a standardized conception of style; of itself it can no more invent a new style than a mummy can beget children.

If one wishes a house of red brick it will be Georgian or Colonial; that is to say, the trimming will be white, the woodwork will have classic moldings, and the electric-light fixtures will be pseudo-candlesticks in silvered metal. If one builds a stucco house, one is doomed by similar mechanical canons to rather heavy furniture in the early Renaissance forms, properly duplicated by the furniture makers of Grand Rapids — and so on. The notion of an American stucco house is so foreign to the conception of the machine mode that only the very poor and the very rich can afford it. Need I add that Colonial or Italian, when it falls from the mouth of the "realtor," has nothing to do with authentic Colonial or Italian work?

Commercial concentration and the national market waste resources by neglect, as in the case of the Appalachian forests they squandered them by pillage. Standardized materials and patterns and plans and elevations — here are the ingredients of the architecture of the machine age; by escaping it we get our superficially vivacious suburbs; by accepting it, those vast acres of nondescript monotony that, call them West Philadelphia or Long Island City or what you will, are but the anonymous districts of Coketown. The chief thing needful for the full enjoyment of this architecture is a standardized people. Here our various educational institutions, from the advertising columns of the five-cent magazine to the higher centers of learning, from the movie to the radio, have not perhaps altogether failed the architect.

The manufactured house is set in the midst of a manufactured environment. The quality of this environment calls for satire rather than description; and yet a mere catalog of its details, such as Mr. Sinclair Lewis gave in *Babbitt*, is almost satire in itself. In this environment the home tends more and more to take last place. Mr. Henry Wright has in fact humorously suggested that at the present increasing ratio of site costs — roads, sewers, and so forth — to house costs, the house itself will disappear in favor of the first item by 1970. The prophetic symbol of this event is the tendency of the motor car and the temple garage to take precedence over the house. Already these incubi have begun to occupy the last remaining patch of space about the suburban house, where up to a generation ago there was a bit of garden, a swing for the children, a sandpile, and perhaps a few fruit trees.

The end of a civilization that considers buildings as mere machines is that it considers human beings as mere machine tenders; it therefore frustrates or diverts the more vital impulses which would lead to the culture of the earth or the intelligent care of the young. Blindly rebellious, men take revenge upon themselves for their own mistakes; hence the modern mechanized house, with its luminous bathroom, its elegant furnace, its dainty garbage-disposal system, has become more and more a thing to get away from. The real excuse for the omnipresent garage is that, in a mechanized environment of subways and house machines, some avenue of escape and compensation must be left open. Distressing as a Sunday automobile ride may be on the crowded highways that lead out of the great city, it is one degree better than remaining in a neighborhood unsuited to permanent human habitation.

So intense is the demand for some saving grace among all these frigid commercial perfections that handicraft is being patronized once more, in a manner that would have astonished Ruskin; and the more audacious sort of interior decorator is fast restoring the sentimentalities in glass and wax flowers that marked the Victorian Age. This is a pretty comment upon the grand achievements of modern industry and science; but it is better, perhaps, that men should be foolish than that they should be completely dehumanized.

The architecture of other civilizations has sometimes been the brutal emblem of the warrior, like that of the Assyrians. It has remained for the architecture of our own day in America to be fixed and stereotyped and blank, like the mind of a robot. The age of the machine has produced an architecture fit only for lathes and dynamos to dwell in. Incomplete and partial in our applications of science, we have forgotten that there is a science of humanity as well as a science of material things. Buildings which do not answer to this general description are either aristocratic relics of the age of handicraft, enjoyed only by the rich, or they are fugitive attempts to imitate cheaply the ways and gestures of handicraft.

We have attempted to live off machinery, and the host has devoured us. It is time that we ceased to play the parasite; time that we looked about us to see what means we have for once more becoming men. The prospects of architecture are not divorced from the prospects of the community. If man is created, as the legends say, in the image of the gods, his buildings are done in the image of his own mind and institutions.

86.

Andrew W. Mellon: Fundamental Principles of Taxation

Andrew Mellon, secretary of the treasury during the Harding, Coolidge, and Hoover administrations, was a Pittsburgh banker and capitalist who typified Republican economic thinking during the 1920s. "The government is just a business," he maintained, "and can and should be run on business principles." Hailed by fellow industrialists and businessmen as the greatest treasury secretary since Alexander Hamilton, his economic policies greatly influenced President Coolidge. Mellon's main interest was in lowering taxes, especially in the higher brackets, and his reduction of minimum income taxes from 4 to 2 percent, the repeal of the excess profits tax, and the allowance of large tax refunds were viewed by Republican businessmen as wise and intelligent policies. The following selection is taken from Mellon's book Taxation: The People's Business *(1924), which expressed his fundamental beliefs on fiscal policy.*

Source: *Taxation: the People's Business,* New York, 1924: "Fundamental Principles."

THE PROBLEM OF THE GOVERNMENT is to fix rates which will bring in a maximum amount of revenue to the Treasury and at the same time bear not too heavily on the taxpayer or on business enterprises. A sound tax policy must take into consideration three factors. It must produce sufficient revenue for the government; it must lessen, so far as possible, the burden of taxation on those least able to bear it; and it must also remove those influences which might retard the continued steady development of business and industry on which, in the last analysis, so much of our prosperity depends. Furthermore, a permanent tax system should be designed, not merely for one or two years nor for the effect it may have on any given class of taxpayers but should be worked out with regard to conditions over a long period and with a view to its ultimate effect on the prosperity of the country as a whole. These are the principles on which the Treasury's tax policy is based, and any revision of taxes which ignores these fundamental principles will prove merely a makeshift and must eventually be replaced by a system based on economic rather than political considerations.

There is no reason why the question of taxation should not be approached from a nonpartisan and business viewpoint. In recent years, in any discussion of tax revision, the question which has caused most controversy is the proposed reduction of the surtaxes. Yet recommendations for such reductions have not been confined to either Republican or Democratic administrations. My own recommendations on this subject were in line with similar ones made by Secretaries Houston and Glass, both of whom served under a Democratic President. Tax revision should never be made the football either of partisan or class politics but should be worked out by those who have made a careful study of the subject in its larger aspects and are prepared to recommend the course which, in the end, will prove for the country's best interest.

I have never viewed taxation as a means of rewarding one class of taxpayers or punishing another. If such a point of view ever controls our public policy, the traditions of freedom, justice, and equality of opportunity, which are the distinguishing characteristics of our American civilization, will have disappeared and in their place we shall have class legislation with all its attendant evils. The man who seeks to perpetuate prejudice and class hatred is doing America an ill service. In attempting to promote or to defeat legislation by arraying one class of taxpayers against another, he shows a complete misconception of those principles of equality on which the country was founded. Any man

of energy and initiative in this country can get what he wants out of life. But when that initiative is crippled by legislation or by a tax system which denies him the right to receive a reasonable share of his earnings, then he will no longer exert himself and the country will be deprived of the energy on which its continued greatness depends.

This condition has already begun to make itself felt as a result of the present unsound basis of taxation. The existing tax system is an inheritance from the war. During that time the highest taxes ever levied by any country were borne uncomplainingly by the American people for the purpose of defraying the unusual and ever increasing expenses incident to the successful conduct of a great war. Normal tax rates were increased, and a system of surtaxes was evolved in order to make the man of large income pay more proportionately than the smaller taxpayer. If he had twice as much income, he paid not twice but three or four times as much tax. For a short time the surtaxes yielded a large revenue.

But since the close of the war people have come to look upon them as a business expense and have treated them accordingly by avoiding payment as much as possible. The history of taxation shows that taxes which are inherently excessive are not paid. The high rates inevitably put pressure upon the taxpayer to withdraw his capital from productive business and invest it in tax-exempt securities or to find other lawful methods of avoiding the realization of taxable income. The result is that the sources of taxation are drying up; wealth is failing to carry its share of the tax burden; and capital is being diverted into channels which yield neither revenue to the government nor profit to the people.

Before the period of the war, taxes as high as those now in effect would have been thought fantastic and impossible of payment. As a result of the patriotic desire of the people to contribute to the limit to the successful prosecution of the war, high taxes were assessed and ungrudgingly paid. Upon the conclusion of peace and the gradual removal of wartime conditions of business, the opportunity is presented to Congress to make the tax structure of the United States conform more closely to normal conditions and to remove the inequalities in that structure which directly injure our prosperity and cause strains upon our economic fabric. . . .

Adam Smith, in his great work *Wealth of Nations,* laid down as the first maxim of taxation that, "The subjects of every state ought to contribute toward the support of the government, as nearly as possible, in proportion to their respective abilities," and in his fourth and last maxim, that "Every tax ought to be so contrived as both to take out and to keep out of the pockets of the people as little as possible over and above what it brings into the public treasury of the state," citing as one of the ways by which this last maxim is violated a tax which "may obstruct the industry of the people, and discourage them from applying to certain branches of business which might give maintenance and employment to great multitudes. . . . While it obliges the people to pay, it may thus diminish, or perhaps destroy, some of the funds, which might enable them more easily to do so."

The further experience of 150 years since this was written has emphasized the truth of these maxims, but those who argue against a reduction of surtaxes to more nearly peacetime figures cite only the first maxim and ignore the fourth. The principle that a man should pay taxes in accordance with his "ability to pay" is sound but, like all other general statements, has its practical limitations and qualifications, and when, as a result of an excessive or unsound basis of taxation, it becomes evident that the source of taxation is drying up and wealth is being diverted into unproductive channels, yielding neither revenue to the government nor profit to the people, then it is time to read-

Andrew Mellon; photographed in 1921

just our basis of taxation upon sound principles.

It seems difficult for some to understand that high rates of taxation do not necessarily mean large revenue to the government, and that more revenue may often be obtained by lower rates. There was an old saying that a railroad freight rate should be "what the traffic will bear"; that is, the highest rate at which the largest quantity of freight would move. The same rule applies to all private businesses. If a price is fixed too high, sales drop off and with them profits; if a price is fixed too low, sales may increase, but again profits decline. The most outstanding recent example of this principle is the sales policy of the Ford Motor Car Company. Does any one question that Mr. Ford has made more money by reducing the price of his car and increasing his sales than he would have made by maintaining a high price and a great profit per car, but selling less cars? The government is just a business and can and should be run on business principles.

Experience has shown that the present high rates of surtax are bringing in each year progressively less revenue to the government. This means that the price is too high to the large taxpayer and he is avoiding a taxable income by the many ways which are available to him. What rates will bring in the largest revenue to the government experience has not yet developed, but it is estimated that by cutting the surtaxes in half, the government, when the full effect of the reduction is felt, will receive more revenue from the owners of large incomes at the lower rates of tax than it would have received at the higher rates. This is simply an application of the same business principle referred to above, just as Mr. Ford makes more money out of pricing his cars at $380 than at $3,000.

Looking at the subject, therefore, solely from the standpoint of government revenues, lower surtax rates are essential. If we consider, however, the far more important subject of the effect of the present high surtax rates on the development and prosperity of our country, then the necessity for a change is more apparent. The most noteworthy characteristic of the American people is their initiative. It is this spirit which has developed America, and it was the same spirit in our soldiers which made our armies successful abroad. If the spirit of business adventure is killed, this country will cease to hold the foremost position in the world. And yet it is this very spirit which excessive surtaxes are now destroying. Anyone at all in touch with affairs knows of his own knowledge of buildings which have not been built, of businesses which have not been started, and of new projects which have been abandoned, all for the one reason — high surtaxes. If failure attends, the loss is borne exclusively by the adventurer, but if success ensues, the government takes more than half of the profits. People argue the risk is not worth the return.

With the open invitation to all men who have wealth to be relieved from taxation by the simple expedient of investing in the more than $12 billion of tax-exempt securities now available, and which would be unaffected by any constitutional amendment, the rich need not pay taxes. We violate Adam Smith's first maxim. Where these high surtaxes do bear is not on the man who has acquired and holds available wealth but on the man who, through his own initiative, is making wealth. The idle man is relieved; the producer is penalized. We violate the fourth maxim. We do not reach the people in proportion to their ability to pay and we destroy the initiative which produces the wealth in which the whole country should share and which is the source of revenue to the government.

In considering any reduction the government must always be assured that taxes will not be so far reduced as to deprive the Treasury of sufficient revenue with which properly to run its business with the manifold activities now a part of the federal government and to take care of the public debt. Tax reduction must come out of surplus revenue. In determining the amount of surplus available these factors control: the revenue remaining the same, an increase in expenditures reduces the surplus, and expenditures remaining the same, anything which reduces the revenue reduces the surplus.

The reaction, therefore, of the authorization of extraordinary or unsound expenditures is twofold — it serves, first, to raise the expenditures and so narrow the margin of available surplus; and, second, to decrease further or obliterate entirely this margin by a reduction of the Treasury's revenues through the disturbance of general business, which is promptly reflected in the country's income. On the other hand, a decrease of taxes causes an inspiration to trade and commerce which increases the prosperity of the country so that the revenues of the government, even on a lower basis of tax, are increased. Taxation can be reduced to a point apparently in excess of the estimated surplus, because by the cumulative effect of such reduction, expenses remaining the same, a greater revenue is obtained.

High taxation, even if levied upon an economic basis, affects the prosperity of the country, because in its ultimate analysis the burden of all taxes rests only in part upon the individual or property taxed. It is largely borne by the ultimate consumer. High taxation means a high price level and high cost of living. A reduction in taxes, therefore, results not only in an immediate saving to the individual or property directly affected but an ultimate saving to all people in the country.

It can safely be said that a reduction in the income tax reduces expenses not only of the income taxpayers but of the entire 110 million people in the United States. It is for this basic reason that the present question of tax reform is not how much each individual taxpayer reduces his direct contribution, although this, of course, is a powerful influence upon the individual affected; the real problem to determine is what plan results in the least burden to the people and the most revenue to the government.

87.

Drinking Songs of Prohibition

The Eighteenth Amendment to the Constitution, prohibiting the manufacture, sale, or transportation of alcoholic liquors, was adopted and submitted to the states by Congress on December 18, 1917. Declared ratified on January 29, 1919, the Amendment, along with the Volstead Act enforcing it, went into effect on January 29, 1920. Herbert Hoover in 1928 called Prohibition "a great social and economic experiment, noble in motive, far-reaching in purpose," but the American people on the whole felt differently. The result was that the 1920s — the Amendment was repealed in 1933 — were marked by more flagrant and more widespread disobedience to federal law than probably any decade in our history. The four songs reprinted here give some hint of the attitude that most Americans had toward Prohibition.

❦ AWAY WITH RUM

We're coming, we're coming, our brave little band;
On the right side of temp'rance we now take our stand.
We don't use tobacco because we all think,
That the people who do so are likely to drink!

> *Chorus:*
> Away, away with rum, by gum,
> With rum by gum; with rum by gum.
> Away, away with rum by gum;
> The song of the Salvation Army.

We never eat cookies because they have yeast;
And one little bite makes a man like a beast.
Oh, can you imagine a sadder disgrace
Than a man in the gutter with crumbs on his face?

We never eat fruitcake because it has rum,
And one little slice puts a man on the bum.
Oh can you imagine a sorrier sight
Than a man eating fruitcake until he gets tight?

The man who eats fruitcake leads a horrible life,
He's mean to his children and he beats up his wife.
The man who eats fruitcake dies a terrible death
With the odor of raisins and rum on his breath.

From: *This Singing Land*, compiled and edited by Irwin Silber, © 1965 Amsco Music Publishing Co. Used by Permission.

LITTLE BROWN JUG

My wife and I lived all alone,
In a little log hut we called our own.
She loved gin, and I loved rum,
I tell you what, we'd lots of fun.

Chorus:
Ha! ha! ha! you and me,
Little Brown Jug, don't I love thee!
Ha! ha! ha! you and me,
Little Brown Jug, don't I love thee!

'Tis you who makes my friends and foes,
'Tis you who makes me wear old clothes.
Here you are so near my nose,
So tip her up and down she goes.

When I go toiling to my farm
I take little brown jug under my arm —
Place him under a shady tree,
Little Brown Jug, 'tis you and me.

If all the folks in Adam's race
Were gathered together in one place,
Then I'd prepare to shed a tear
Before I'd part with you, my dear.

If I'd a cow that gave such milk,
I'd clothe her in the finest silk,
I'd feed her on the choicest hay,
And milk her forty times a day.

The rose is red, my nose is, too,
The violet's blue and so are you;
And yet I guess, before I stop
I'd better take another drop.

NO MORE BOOZE

There was a little man, and he had a little can,
And he used to rush the growler;
He went to the saloon on a Sunday afternoon,
And you ought to hear the bartender holler:

Chorus:
"No more booze, no more booze,
No more booze on Sunday;
No more booze, no more booze,
Got to get your can filled Monday.
She's the only girl I love,
With a face like a horse and buggy.
Leaning up against the lake,
O fireman! save my child!"

The chambermaid came to my door,
"Get up, you lazy sinner,
We need those sheets for tablecloths,
And it's almost time for dinner."

HOW DRY I AM

How dry I am,
How dry I am —
Nobody knows
How dry I am.

I'd sell my shoes
For a bottle of booze;
I'd sell my soul
For some alcohol.

One bottle for one,
Two bottles for two,

Three bottles for three,
And a barrel for me.

One barrel for one,
Two barrels for two,
Three barrels for three,
And a hogshead for me.

How dry I am,
How dry I am —
Nobody knows
How dry I am.

Boys playing baseball on the Emerson Wright Playground in Springfield, Mass., 1916; Hine photo

CHANGE AND CONTINUITY

It is well to bear in mind the distinction between a period's view of itself — or, more accurately, its several views of its several selves — and the accustomed view taken in retrospect. Thus, the period from 1914 to the end of Wilson's presidency and even on to the Crash of 1929 is remembered for its upheavals, its excesses and shortcomings, and the inability of leadership to cope with a new world. But to whom was it a new world? The great events little disturbed the really average man who hardly exists for standard history; participating in a mass inertia born partly of exhaustion, partly of cynicism, and partly of a preoccupied apathy, he was content generally to be titillated by the headlines of the Harding scandals and go on about his business. It is probably more than simple coincidence that the creation of the mass audience begun by the press and carried on by radio and the movies was accompanied by a loss of initiative, the gradual abandonment of active involvement in politics. Yet even this hardly touches great numbers customarily estranged from events: the tenant farmers of the South, the surviving homesteaders of the Plains, the immigrants of the urban centers, speaking no English, Negroes almost anywhere, all those who had little interest or involvement to lose. Ordinary daily life continued in spite of "history."

The economic boom of wartime and post-war prosperity did wonders for Southern California. Los Angeles, the central city of the area, had been growing at an incredible pace — its production output increased 100 percent between 1900 and 1910 — and by 1925 ranked as the major manufacturing city in California and one of the largest in the country. The whole Southern California region was prospering on the oil, agriculture, and tourist industries.

(Top) Pantages Theatre on the corner of Seventh and Hill Streets in Los Angeles during the 1920s; (right) Elks Temple in Los Angeles; (bottom) Signal Hill Oil Field near Long Beach, Calif.

(Above) View of Denver, Colo., and the mountains; (left) the great Lucas Oil Gusher in Texas; (below) the Roosevelt Dam in Yuma, Ariz., one of a series in an irrigation project for the Southwest, 1916

Townspeople assembling in the city square of Bonham, Tex., 1920; photo by E. E. Smith

(Above) Itinerant farmers on a rented farm in Texas; (below) Jeffers School near Loveland, Colo.

(Above) Cowboy cutting a steer out from the rest of the herd on the Matador Ranch, Texas, photo by E. E. Smith

(Left) Off-duty cowboys photographed by E. E. Smith somewhere in the Southwest; (below) barbeque at Hougoton, Kansas

New industry in the South: (Top and center) Operations at the Roane Iron Company, Alabama; coke ovens preparing coke for furnaces and "running" molten pig iron; (bottom) dam near Hamlet, N.C.

Scenes in the Appalachian coal regions, representative of the hundreds of isolated mining communities found scattered through the mountains from Pennsylvania and West Virginia to Alabama: (Top) Worker's village at the Consolidation Coal Company mine near Jenners, Pa.; (right) miners at work extending the shaft in a mine in West Virginia; (bottom) line of company-owned cottages in Holden, West Virginia

(Above) Valdosta, Ga., about 1915; (below) Fireman's Cemetery in New Orleans, La.

(Left) Group of persons working in the mill at Salisbury, N.C., photo by Lewis Hine; (center and bottom) three photographs by Doris Ullman of backcountry people in the Appalachian South in the 1920s

Prosperity seemed more attracted to some areas and some people than others. The locale of wealth, the city, was the first to reflect growth, the first to display wealth. By the "filter-down" theory of wealth, the prosperity of the few should eventually reach down through the entire social structure and raise the standard of living for the whole nation. While it no doubt reached the middle class, the lower strata seemed less and less affected.

(Top) Chicago's lakefront skyline as seen from the Field Museum, 1925; (left) postal telegraph messengers in Indianapolis, Ind.; photo by Hine; (bottom) furnace of the National Tube Co., Pittsburgh. **OPPOSITE PAGE:** (Top) Ohio farmer using an elaborate tractor; (center) prize heifers at a 4-H Club fair; (bottom) sorghum mill on a farm near Marion, Ill., 1912

New York City scenes: Looking from Lower Manhattan to the East River and the bridges to Brooklyn; (left) bootblack looking for customers in Union Square; (below) pushcart vendors trying to realize the American dream on Lower East Side

Scenes from the industrial towns of New England. In many areas the textile mills and small factories that had brought prosperity to these towns for a century were closing down. (Top) Noon break outside the Green City Mill in Burlington, Vermont, 1914; (right) a lasting machine operator shaping shoes at a Massachusetts shoe factory, 1920; (bottom) crowded and run-down housing provided by the company for migratory farm workers during the cranberry harvest near Wareham, Massachusetts

Irl G. Whitchurch

(Above) "Apprentice" and (below) "Fog on Mt. Abram"; photographs taken in Maine by Chansonetta
Stanley Emmons, sister of the inventor of the Stanley Steamer, capture images of a passing era

Irl G. Whitchurch

88.

Robert L. Duffus: The Age of Play

Americans learned how to relax during the Twenties as they never had before. They took up golf and tennis; they went to football games, prizefights, and six-day bicycle races; they played Mah-Jongg and bridge and listened to the radio. Robert L. Duffus reported some of the statistical evidence of America's new habits in an article published in the Independent *at the end of 1924. Duffus wondered whether the Puritan ethic of hard work and sober recreation had given way permanently to a less strenuous kind of life.*

Source: *Independent*, December 20, 1924.

AGES OF THE WORLD have been named after materials, such as stone, wood, bronze, gold, and steel; after conspicuous persons, such as Augustus, Elizabeth, Napoleon, and Victoria; after attributed intellectual or moral qualities, such as classicism, romanticism, doubt, and faith; after spiritual stirrings, such as the Reformation and the Renaissance; after political incidents, such as the Crusades; and after movements of population, such as the drift of population into fourth-century Italy or eighteenth- and nineteenth-century America. Our own age may take its place in the historical pageant as the age of the Great War (unless the prophets of despair are right and there are to be greater wars), as the age of cities, or as the age of man's victory over nature — at least of that portion of nature not included in the subdivision called human. But, undoubtedly, the best title for this particular segment of eternity is one that may not readily occur to everyone. This is the Age of Play.

Men and puppies and dolphins and baby lions, it is true, obedient to a kind of play principle in the universe, have disported themselves since the beginning of time. Carvings on Egyptian tombs and frescoes excavated from the ruins of Knossos in Crete tell the story of bullfighting, dancing, and organized sports. The Romans, the Greeks, the Circassians, the ancient Siamese, the Irish of olden times, the Kirgiz, and many of the North American Indians celebrated funeral games in a manner which must have been agreeable for all but the corpse. But play as a ruling impulse is wholly modern and characteristically American.

It is difficult to assign an exact date for the beginning of the Age of Play. If we seek the influences which brought it about, we may go back half a century or more with profit; if we are looking for its external symptoms, a quarter of a century is nearly enough. Obviously, the first prerequisite for play is leisure, although animal spirits and some economic leeway are desirable. Play on anything like the American scale would have been impossible except for the short working day, the Saturday holiday or half holiday, and the annual vacation. These are gifts of a century which also presented us with the World War and the newer pessimism.

With a decrease in the amount of human energy actually required for earning a living has gone a prodigious increase in wealth, thus upsetting what was once held to be an ethical as well as a mathematical law. In 1850 the national income per capita was $95, in 1918, $586 — a rate of progress which far outruns any inflation of the currency. In 1900, according to Mr. Julius Barnes, the average American family spent 60 percent of its income for the basic necessities of life but in 1920 had to devote only 50 percent to the same purpose. Thus there was not only leisure to devote to play but money to spend on it. There was also, no doubt, an increasing restlessness, growing out of the uninteresting nature of the mechanical tasks to which larger and larger armies of workers were being assigned. So the stage was amply set for the Age of Play.

The first unmistakable sign of the coming era was the development of interest in games, a phenomenon faintly manifested in the United States for a decade or two prior to the Civil War and slowly gathering strength thereafter. Baseball first appeared in something like its modern form about 1845 but did not produce its first professionals and thus start on its career as a great national spectacle until 1871. Lawn tennis, first played in America in 1875, and golf, introduced early in the last decade of the century, remained games for the few until very recently. Now there are said to be 2 million golfers and from a quarter to one-half as many tennis players. These are conspicuous instances of a general tendency. The playing of outdoor games was formerly either a juvenile or an aristocratic diversion; it has now become practically universal. There are golf links upon which horny-handed men in overalls play creditable games. And the number of onlookers at professional sports is legion. In a single year there are said to have been 17 million admissions to college football games and 27 million to big league baseball games.

A second phase of the development of play in America is the community recreation movement, which arose from the discovery by social workers that training and organization for leisure were becoming as necessary as training and organization for work. In 1895 the city of Boston took the radical step of providing three sandpiles for the entertainment of young children, model playgrounds came about ten years later, and the first recreation centers were not established until the middle of the first decade of the budding century. As late as 1903 only 18 cities had public playgrounds of any description. Then the growth of such facilities began with a rush. Last year there were 6,601 playgrounds in 680 cities, with an average daily attendance of about a million and a half.

In eighty-nine cities there were municipal golf courses on which any man or woman who could afford clubs, balls, and a small green fee could play. Besides golf courses and tennis courts, upon which many a commoner became proficient in what had been "gentlemen's" games, there were municipal swimming pools, ball grounds, theaters, and, in forty-five instances, summer camps under municipal auspices. Municipal expenditures for public recreation have nearly trebled since 1913, though they are as yet only about one-third of the national chewing-gum bill.

But no spontaneous play and no disinterestedly organized recreation program can for a moment be compared in magnitude with what are commonly known as the commercialized amusements — "the greatest industry in America," as James Edward Rogers of the Playground and Recreation Association has called them. The motion picture, the phonograph, and the cheap automobile came into existence, like the cheap newspaper, because a public had been created which (consciously or not) wanted them and could pay for them. Each had been the object of experimentation during the last quarter of the nineteenth century, but each attained social significance only after the opening of the twentieth, when multitudes, for the first time in history, had money and leisure they did not know how to use.

In 1922 the motion-picture statisticians boasted a daily attendance of 20 million. The federal tax reports showed that in 1921 the American people paid more than $800 million for motion pictures, theaters, concerts, and so forth. And most of this vast sum was spent by persons whose parents had had little or nothing to spend on amusements of a kindred nature as existed prior to 1900. To a slight extent the film drama took the place of cheap vaudeville, the dime museum, and the traveling stock company, yet in its magnitude, its standardization, and its habit-forming properties, it is like nothing on earth or in history but itself.

The great motion-picture audience has other dissipations in common. In 1921 it chewed $44 million worth of gum, ate $408 million worth of candy, drank $448 million worth of soft drinks, bought $231 million worth of musical instruments, and consumed more than $1.7 billion worth of tobacco, or about half enough to pay the entire expenses of the federal government. Its consumption of billiard tables, bowling alleys, and accessories rose from $919,000 worth in 1899 to $9,632,000 worth in 1919; its consumption of peanuts, which are typically a holiday food, from $937,000 worth in 1899 to $4,880,000 worth in 1919. In 1899 it paid $3,953,000 for perfumery and cosmetics; in 1919, $33,466,000. In three years it is said to have spent $175 million upon 3 million radio sets. It also resorts in vast numbers to such characteristically modern places of amusements as Coney Island, which has entertained as many as 600,000 visitors in a single day.

But there is one plaything which dwarfs all the rest. In 1906 there was 1 motorcar for each 1,788 inhabitants; last year there was 1 for each 8. Last year there were 13 million passenger cars in operation, and there is no question that practically every one of them, on Sundays, holidays, after working hours, and during vacations, was used for pleasure. This is not mere humdrum progress; it is more than that — it is revolution. Earl Chapin May, in a recent number of the *Saturday Evening Post,* predicted that "during this current year more than 5 million motorcars will convey 15 million Americans to some campground." In Colorado alone, he says, more than 1,173,000 tourists visited the two national parks and seventeen national forests in 1922, and all but 277,000 of them traveled by automobile. Public camps for motorists have sprung up everywhere during the past four or five years.

But not all motorists keep to the public camps; indeed, most of them, sooner or later, probably try camping out "on their own." The play spirit has never given us so democratic and invigorating a flower. And automobile camping is just beginning. I believe that in time this modern *Wanderjahr,* these swift migrations which broaden the lives of hundreds of thousands who a generation ago would have been sitting stodgily at home, will be just as significant in our social and economic history as the journeyings of the historic Conestoga wagon.

The most significant aspect of the Age of Play, however, is not in its inventions, good and bad, but in an alteration of an ancient attitude — a veritable change in one of the most fundamental of folkways. For uncounted generations man has survived and made progress in the temperate zones only by unceasing industry; in tropical and subtropical areas, where climatic conditions did not encourage industry, he survived without progress. At first the Industrial Revolution did not seem to break down this antique scheme of nature; but in this country, at least, and within this generation, it has become evident that unremitting toil is not necessarily a law of human destiny, and that a thimbleful of brains is worth at any time an ocean of sweat. The mechanical multiplication of labor power by ten, twenty, forty, or a hundred, the replacement of a man by 2 cents' worth of coal, has struck a fatal blow at the ancestral faith in mere hard work.

Less than a hundred years ago the merchants and shipowners of Boston were able to answer the demand of their employees for a ten-hour day with the argument that "the habits likely to be generated by this indulgence in idleness . . . will be very detrimental to the journeymen individually and very costly to us as a community." Fifty years ago a United States commissioner of patents, Mortimer D. Leggett, declared amid the applause of well-meaning persons that "idleness . . . stimulates vice in all its forms and throttles every attempt at intellectual, moral, and religious culture."

The first break in this armor of conservatism occurred when it was discovered that play added to the worker's efficiency and was, therefore, of economic value. Through this chink, heresy has crept in, and it is now apparent that play is coming to be looked upon, whether athletic in character or not, whether "commercialized" or not, as an end justifiable in itself. Blindly, blunderingly, yet with more intense conviction than appears on the surface, the masses of the people are uttering a new moral law. The chains of necessity have been loosened; they are nearer a frank and full enjoyment of life than any people that ever lived.

I do not maintain that all their amusements are wholesome, nor that the excessive standardization and mechanization of work and play alike are without their dangers. I do maintain that such evils as exist are minor in comparison with the great gain for civilization that took place when millions learned to play where only thousands played before. These evils are not to be cured by curbing the spirit of play. Reformers and educators must accept this spirit as more sacred than anything they have to give; they can help by guiding, not by restraining.

The right to play is the final clause in the charter of democracy. The people are king — *et le roi s'amuse.*

———————◆———————

The Era of Wonderful Nonsense.
WESTBROOK PEGLER, of the era which ended in the Crash of 1929

1925

89.

WILL ROGERS: The Normal Majority

Will Rogers won his first theatrical fame as a rope twirler with the Ziegfeld Follies, starting in 1915, but he soon realized that those who talked in the show made a lot more money than those who did not. He is supposed to have asked his wife what he should talk about, to which she is said to have replied: "Talk about what you read in the papers." At any rate, his new routine, which began with the words "Well, all I know is what I read in the papers," soon elevated him to national prominence. He was known and loved by millions of Americans, who saw him on the stage, heard him on the radio, and read his syndicated column. Rogers cheerfully stood up for, but at the same time cheerfully rebuked, the "big normal majority," to which he claimed that he himself belonged. The following selection was originally published as a newspaper column on Washington's Birthday in 1925.

Source: *Autobiography,* Donald Day, ed., Boston, 1949, pp. 107-111.

THE LAST FEW DAYS I have read various addresses made on Lincoln's Birthday. Every Politician always talks about him, but none of them ever imitate him. They always make that a day of delivering a Lecture on "Americanism." When an Office Holder, or one that has been found out, can't think of anything to deliver a speech on, he always falls back on the good old subject, AMERICANISM. Now that is the one thing that I have never delivered an Essay on, either written or spoken. They have all had a crack at it every Fourth of July and Lincoln's Birthday. So now I am going to take up the subject and see what I can wrestle up out of it. Let's get our rope ready and turn it out, and we will catch it and see really what brands it has on it. Here it comes out of the Corral. We got it caught; now it's throwed and Hog Tied; and we will pick the Brands and see what they are.

The first thing I find out is there ain't any such animal. This American Animal that I thought I had here is nothing but the big Honest Majority, that you might find in any Country. He is not a Politician, He is not a 100 percent American. He is not any organization, either uplift or downfall. In fact I find he don't belong to anything. He is no decided Political faith or religion. I can't even find out what religious brand is on him. From his earmarks he has never made a speech, and announced that he was An American. He hasn't denounced anything. It looks to me like he is just an Animal that has been going along, believing in right, doing right, tending to his own business, letting the other fellows alone.

He don't seem to be simple enough minded to believe that EVERYTHING is right and he don't appear to be Cuckoo enough to think that EVERYTHING is wrong. He don't seem to be a Prodigy, and he don't seem to be a Simp. In fact, all I can find out about him is that he is just NORMAL. After I let him up and get on my Horse and ride away I look around and I see hundreds and hundreds of exactly the same marks and Brands. In fact they so far outnumber the freakly branded ones that the only conclusion I can come to is that this Normal breed is so far in majority that there is no use to worry about the others. They are a lot of Mavericks, and Strays.

A bunch of Bobbed Haired men gathered in Madison Square Garden last Sunday at a meeting of these Reds, or Bolsheviki, or whatever they call themselves. It was one of their denouncement meetings. They denounced the heavy snow, Declaration of Independence, 5 cent Street Car Fare, Floods in Georgia, Mayor Hylan's Bathing Suit, Twin Beds, and the Eclipse. A Kid 14 years old delivered such a tribute to Lenine that he made it look like George Washington or Abe Lincoln couldn't have caddied for Lenine. Oh, this Boy had got disgusted with America young in life. Incidentally, while he was making this tirade, NORMALISM of his age, at least a million of them were out skating.

Now some say that a thing like that should not be allowed. Why sure it should be allowed! England can teach any Country in the World how to handle discontent. (Maybe it's because they have more of it.)

United Press International

Will Rogers

They give 'em a Park, Hyde Park, they even furnish the Soap Boxes (as the former contents of the Box is generally as foreign to the Speakers as his Nationality is to the Country he is speaking in). Give 'em a Hall or a Box to stand on and say "Sic 'em; knock everything in sight" and when they have denounced everything from Bunions to Capitalistic Bath Tubs, then they will go home, write all week on another speech for the following Sunday and you never have any trouble with them.

It's just like an exhaust on an Automobile. No matter how high priced the Car, you have to have an exit for its bad Air, and Gasses. They have got to come out. It don't do any particular harm, unless you just stand around behind smelling of it all the time, but who would want to follow a Car to smell of its exhaust when you could just as well be in the Car riding?

Now sometimes there is a loud explosion, and everybody on the Streets will turn around and see what it is. The minute they see, they will go right on their business. They know there has been no damage done. So that's how it is with this so called Radical Element. Let them have a Park or a Hall as an exhaust Pipe. Then when they have some particular Noted Denouncer, why, you will hear a loud report. You will listen, or read what he said and go on about your business the same as the listeners to a back fire. You know its necessary.

Now I am not much on History but I don't think any of these people were drafted over here, nor that there are any Immigration Laws in Europe against this Country. I have often thought what would happen if the Government sent somebody to one of those meetings and he got up and announced that he was instructed to send every one of them back to the Country where they come from, and had been raving about. Say, there would be such a stampede they would tear down the building to keep from going. You couldn't Shanghai them out of here.

No, sir! This country is too big now. To stop this Country now would be like spitting on a Railroad track to stop a Train. These Reds are on their backs snoring and they ain't keeping anybody awake but each other. No Element, no Party, not even Congress or the Senate can hurt this Country now; it's too big. There are too many men just like those Dog Team drivers and too many Women like that Nurse up in Nome for anything to ever stampede this old Continent of ours. That's why I can never take a Politician seriously. They are always shouting that "such and such a thing will ruin us, and that this is the eventful year in our Country's life."

Say, all the years are the same. Each one has its little temporary setbacks, but they don't mean a thing in the general result. Nobody is making History. Everybody is just drifting along with the tide. If any office holder feels he is carrying a burden of responsibility, some Fly will light on his back and scratch it off for him some day. Congress can pass a bad law and as soon as the old Normal Majority find it out they have it scratched off the books.

We lost Roosevelt TR, a tough blow. But here we are still kicking. So, if we can spare men like Roosevelt and Wilson there is no use in any other Politician ever taking himself serious.

Henry Ford has been a big factor in the Industrial development of the Country. Yet if he was gone there would still be enough of those things left to clutter up the Highways for Years. John D. Rockefeller who has done a lot for humanity with his Gifts; yet when he is gone and Gasoline raises 2 Cents, and all expenses and the Estate is settled we will kick along. *Even when our next War comes we will through our shortsightedness not be prepared, but that won't be anything fatal. The real energy and minds of the Normal Majority will step in and handle it and fight it through to a successful conclusion.* A war didn't change it before. It's just the same as it was, and always will be, because it is founded on right and even if everybody in Public Life tried to ruin it they couldn't. This Country is not where it is today on account of any man. It is here on account of the real common Sense of the big Normal Majority. A Politician is just like a Necktie Salesman in a big Department Store. If he decides to give all the Ties away, or decided to pocket all the receipts, it don't affect the Store. It don't close. He closes, as soon as he is found out.

So I can find nothing for alarm in our immediate future. The next time a Politician gets spouting off about what this Country needs, either hit him with a tubercular Tomato or lay right back in your seat and go to sleep. Because THIS COUNTRY HAS GOT TOO BIG TO NEED A DAMN THING.

90.

Frederic C. Howe: Wartime Hysteria

For longtime reformers like Frederic C. Howe, America's participation in the war that was to make the world safe for democracy entailed by-products of hysteria and oppression that threatened the very existence of democracy at home. From 1914 to 1919 Howe was commissioner of immigration at Ellis Island, New York, where he saw the result of the government's indiscriminate and reckless enforcement of the 1917 Espionage Act. In the following selection from his autobiography, Howe describes the effect of the government's anti-alien policy on his work at Ellis Island.

Source: *The Confessions of a Reformer*, New York, 1925, pp. 266-277.

THE ADMINISTRATION OF ELLIS ISLAND was confused by by-products of the war. The three islands, isolated in New York Harbor and capable of accommodating several thousand people, were demanded by the War Department and Navy Department for emergency purposes. They were admirably situated as a place of detention for war suspects. The Department of Justice and hastily organized espionage agencies made them a dumping ground of aliens under suspicion, while the Bureau of Immigration launched a crusade against one type of immigrant after another and brought them to Ellis Island for deportation. No one was concerned over our facilities for caring for the warring groups deposited upon us. The buildings were unsuited for permanent residence; the floors were of cement, the corridors were chill, the islands were storm swept, and soon the ordinary functions of the island became submerged in war activities.

Eighteen hundred Germans were dumped on us at three o'clock one morning, following the sequestration of the German ships lying in New York Harbor. The sailors had been promised certain privileges, including their beer, which was forbidden by law on the island. Several hundred nurses were detained for their training prior to embarka-

tion; each day brought a contingent of German, Hungarian, and Austrian suspects, while incoming trains from the West added quotas of immoral men, and women, prostitutes, procurers, and alleged white slavers, arrested under the hue and cry started early in the war with the passage of the Mann White Slave Act and the hysterical propaganda that was carried on by moralistic agencies all over the country.

I was the custodian of all these groups. Each group had to be isolated. I became a jailer instead of a commissioner of immigration; a jailer not of convicted offenders but of suspected persons who had been arrested and railroaded to Ellis Island as the most available dumping ground under the successive waves of hysteria which swept the country.

In the conflict with concessionaires, I was sustained by the conviction that I was right. I was fortified with evidence and could face the department, committees of Congress, or the public in my fight to clean up the island. In the case of the thousands of suspects, I was merely a custodian; those aliens that had been tried at all had been tried by drumhead court-martials, and such evidence as there might be was not on the island. The justice or injustice of their conviction was no affair of mine; I had no authority to examine the evidence, to concern myself with their stories, to do other than carry out orders, which were to deport aliens when directed to do so, quite irrespective of their guilt.

But the testimony on which men and women were held was so flimsy, so emotional, so illegal in procedure that my judicial sense revolted against the orders which I received. I quarrelled with the commissioner-general of immigration, who was working hand in glove with the Department of Justice; I harassed the secretary of labor with protests against the injustice that was being done. I refused to believe that we were a hysterical people; that civil liberties should be thrown to the winds. But in this struggle there was no one to lean on; there was no support from Washington, no interest on the part of the press. The whole country was swept by emotional excesses that followed one another with confusing swiftness from 1916 to 1920.

The first of the outbreaks had to do with immoral aliens. The Rockefeller Foundation had made exhaustive studies of prostitution. Congress enacted the White Slave Act. The press played up every arrest that suggested organized vice, and soon the country was convinced that it harbored an army of white slavers, mostly recruited from south and central Europe. Prosecutors, chambers of commerce, red-blooded editors were carried away by this emotional righteousness. Prostitution, it was assumed, was an alien vice. It was an immigrant traffic. This crusade, like subsequent ones, needed only a spark to set aflame racial hatred that is today manifesting itself in the Ku Klux Klan.

The white-slave traffic was assumed to be highly organized and financially powerful. It was said to have representatives in foreign countries and to be linked into an international system, like chain stores, with procurers in villages, towns, and cities. Women were said to be held as virtual slaves by procurers; they were sold as so much merchandise; they were shipped from place to place and used in the most inhuman ways by men who trafficked in their virtue. For over a year America seemed convinced that our social and political life was honeycombed with a vice traffic that was threatening the foundations of the nation.

I do not know whether there was any more organized vice in the country in 1916 than there is today. Intelligent agents of the government said that there was no such system. Certainly I could find no evidence of the things portrayed in the press. Of the thousands of arrests made, the number of men and women who might be classed as white slavers or procurers was very small. Many of them were held on slight evidence of guilt. Certainly there was little official evidence to substantiate the assumption that our morality was being undermined by commercialized vice organized into an international system by the most depraved of alien promoters. . . .

Hysteria over the immoral alien was followed by a two-year panic over the "Hun." Again, inspectors, particularly civilian secret-service agents, were given carte blanche to make arrests on suspicion. Again Ellis Island was turned into a prison, and I had to protect men and women from a hue and cry that was but little concerned over guilt or innocence. During these years thousands of Germans, Austrians, and Hungarians were taken without trial from their homes and brought to Ellis Island. Nearly 2,000 officers and seamen from sequestered German ships were placed in my care. Many of them had married American wives. They conducted themselves decently and well. They were obedient to discipline. They accepted the situation, and they gave practically no trouble. They were typical of the alien enemies the country over that were arrested under the hysteria that was organized and developed into a hate that lingers on to this day.

Again I had either to drift with the tide or assume the burden of seeing that as little injustice as possible was done. I realized that under war conditions convincing evidence could not be demanded. I accepted that fact but not the assumption that "the Hun should be put against the wall and shot." From our entrance into the war until after the Armistice my life was a nightmare. My telephone rang constantly with inquiries from persons seeking news of husbands and fathers who had been arrested. On my return home in the evening, I would often find awaiting me women in a state of nervous collapse whose husbands had mysteriously disappeared, and who feared that they had been done away with. I furnished them with such information as was possible. On the island I had to stand between the official insistence that the German should be treated as a criminal and the admitted fact that the great majority of them had been arrested by persons with little concern about their innocence or guilt and with but little if any evidence to support the detention.

Within a short time I was branded as pro-German. I had to war with the local staff to secure decent treatment for the aliens, and with the army of secret-service agents to prevent the island from being filled with persons against whom someone or other had filed a suspicious inquiry.

It is a marvelous tribute to the millions of Germans, Austrians, and Hungarians in this country that, despite the injustices to which they were subjected and the espionage under which they lived, scarcely an americanized alien of these races was found guilty of any act of disloyalty of which the entire German-American population was suspected or accused.

The final outbreak of hysteria was directed against the "Reds" the winter of 1918-1919. It started in the state of Washington in the lumber camps and was directed against members of the I.W.W. organization, which had superseded the more conservative craft unions affiliated with the American Federation of Labor. There was a concerted determination on the part of employers to bring wages back to prewar conditions and to break the power of organized labor. This movement against alien labor leaders had the support of the Department of Justice. Private detective agencies and strikebreakers acted with assurance that in any outrages they would be supported by the government itself. The press joined in the cry of "Red revolution" and frightened the country with scare headlines of an army of organized terrorists who were determined to usher in revolution by force. The government borrowed the agent provocateur from old Russia; it turned loose innumerable private spies. For two years we were in a panic of fear over the Red revolutionists, anarchists, and enemies of the republic who were said to be ready to overthrow the government.

For a third time I had to stand against the current. Men and women were herded into Ellis Island. They were brought under guards and in special trains with instructions to get them away from the country with as little delay as possible. Most of the aliens had been picked up in raids on labor headquarters; they had been given a drumhead trial by an inspector with no chance for defense; they were held incommunicado and often were not permitted to see either friends or attorneys before being shipped to Ellis Island. In these proceedings, the inspector who made the arrest was prosecutor, witness, judge, jailer, and executioner. He was clerk and interpreter as well. This was all the trial the alien could demand under the law. In many instances the inspector hoped that he would be put in charge of his victim for a trip to New York and possibly to Europe at the expense of the government. Backed by the press of his city and by the hue and cry of the pack, he had every inducement to find the alien guilty and arrange for his speedy deportation.

I was advised by the commissioner-general to mind my own business and carry out orders, no matter what they might be. Yet such obvious injustice was being done that I could not sit quiet. Moreover, I was an appointee of the President and felt that I owed responsibility to him whose words at least I was exemplifying in my actions. My word carried no weight with my superior officials, who were intoxicated with the prominence they enjoyed and the publicity which they received from the press.

The bureaucratic organization at the island was happy in the punishing power which all jailers enjoy and resented any interference on behalf of its victims. Members of Congress were swept from their moorings by an organized business propaganda and demanded that I be dismissed because I refused to railroad aliens to boats made ready for their deportation. I took the position from which I would not be driven, that the alien should not be held incommunicado and should enjoy the right of a writ of habeas corpus in the United States courts, which was the only semblance of legal proceedings open to him under the law.

In maintaining this position, I had to quarrel with my superiors and the official force at the island. I faced a continuous barrage from members of Congress, from the press, from business organizations, and prosecuting attorneys. Yet, day by day, aliens, many of whom had been held in prison for months, came before the court; and the judge, after examining the testimony, unwillingly informed the immigration authorities that there was not a scintilla of evidence to support the arrest. For in deportation cases it is not necessary to provide a preponderance of testimony or to convince the court of the justice of the charge; all that the government needs to support its case is a scintilla of evidence, which may be any kind of evidence at all. If there is a bit of evidence, no matter how negligible it may be, the order of deportation must be affirmed.

Again the pack was unleashed. No one took the trouble to ascertain the facts. The press carried stories to the effect that I had released hundreds of persons ordered deported. I had released aliens, but in each case I had been ordered to do so by the courts or the bureau. I had observed the law when organized hysteria demanded that it be swept aside. I had seen to it that men and women enjoyed their legal rights, but evidently this was the worst offense I could have committed. A congressional committee came to Ellis Island and held protracted hearings. It listened to disaffected officials; it created scare headlines for the press; it did everything in its power to convince the country that we were on the verge of a nationwide revolution, of which the most hard-boiled inspectors sent out by the bureau had reported they could not find a trace. When I went to the hearings and demanded the right to be present, to cross-examine witnesses and see the records, when I demanded that I be put on the witness stand myself, the committee ordered the sergeant at arms to eject me from the rooms.

As I look back over these years, my outstanding memories are not of the immigrant. They are rather of my own people. Things that were done forced one almost to despair of the mind, to distrust the political state. Shreds were left of our courage, our reverence. The Department of Justice, the Department of Labor, and Congress not only failed to protest against hysteria — they encouraged these excesses; the state not only abandoned the liberty which it should have protected — it lent itself to the stamping out of individualism and freedom. It used the agent provocateur, permitted private agencies to usurp government powers, turned over the administration of justice to detective agencies, card-indexed liberals and progressives. It became frankly an agency of employing and business interests at a time when humanity — the masses, the poor — were making the supreme sacrifice of their lives.

I had fondly imagined that we prized individual liberty; I had believed that to Anglo-Saxons human rights were sacred and would be protected at any cost.

Latin peoples might be temperamental, given to hysteria; but we were hardheaded, standing for individuality. But I found that we were lawless, emotional, given to mob action. We cared little for freedom of conscience, for the rights of men to their opinions. Government was a convenience of business. Discussion of war profiteers was not to be permitted. The Department of Justice lent itself to the suppression of those who felt that war should involve equal sacrifice. Civil liberties were under the ban. Their subversion was not, however, an isolated thing; it was an incident in the ascendancy of business privileges and profits acquired during the war — an ascendancy that could not bear scrutiny or brook the free discussion which is the only safe basis of orderly popular government.

91.

E. T. Sanford and O. W. Holmes, Jr.: *Gitlow v. New York*

The important case of Gitlow v. New York *originated at the height of the "Red scare" of 1919-1920. Benjamin Gitlow was convicted under New York's Criminal Anarchy statute and appealed to the Supreme Court. His conviction was upheld; but both Justice Sanford's opinion for the majority and Justice Holmes's dissent had far-reaching effects. The two justices agreed that the Fourteenth Amendment forbade a state from impairing rights guaranteed under the First Amendment to the Constitution, but Sanford felt that Gitlow's provocative publication had been more inflammatory than the law allowed. In dissent, Justice Holmes invoked the "clear and present danger" doctrine established in 1919 in* Schenck v. United States *as the standard to be used in determining the constitutionality of any abridgment of freedom of speech. This interpretation has since come to prevail. Parts of the two opinions of June 8, 1925, are reprinted here.*

Source: 268 U.S. 652.

Mr. Justice Sanford. Benjamin Gitlow was indicted in the Supreme Court of New York, with three others, for the statutory crime of criminal anarchy. . . . He was separately tried, convicted, and sentenced to imprisonment. The judgment was affirmed by the Appellate Division and by the Court of Appeals. . . . The case is here on writ of error to the Supreme Court, to which the record was remitted. . . .

The contention here is that the statute, by its terms and as applied in this case, is repugnant to the due process clause of the Fourteenth Amendment. Its material provisions are:

> Section 160. *Criminal anarchy defined.* Criminal anarchy is the doctrine that organized government should be overthrown by force or violence, or by assassination of the executive head or of any

of the executive officials of government, or by any unlawful means. The advocacy of such doctrine either by word of mouth or writing is a felony.

Section 161. *Advocacy of criminal anarchy.* Any person who:

1. By word of mouth or writing advocates, advises, or teaches the duty, necessity, or propriety of overthrowing or overturning organized government by force or violence, or by assassination of the executive head or of any of the executive officials of government, or by any unlawful means; or,

2. Prints, publishes, edits, issues, or knowingly circulates, sells, distributes, or publicly displays any book, paper, document, or written or printed matter in any form containing or advocating, advising, or teaching the doctrine that organized government should be overthrown by force, violence, or any unlawful means . . . is guilty of a felony and punishable by imprisonment or fine, or both.

The indictment was in two counts. The first charged that the defendant had advocated, advised, and taught the duty, necessity, and propriety of overthrowing and overturning organized government by force, violence, and unlawful means, by certain writings therein set forth entitled "The Left Wing Manifesto"; the second, that he had printed, published, and knowingly circulated and distributed a certain paper called *The Revolutionary Age*, containing the writings set forth in the first count advocating, advising, and teaching the doctrine that organized government should be overthrown by force, violence, and unlawful means.

The following facts were established on the trial by undisputed evidence and admissions: The defendant is a member of the Left Wing Section of the Socialist Party, a dissenting branch or faction of that party formed in opposition to its dominant policy of "modern Socialism." Membership in both is open to aliens as well as citizens. The Left Wing Section was organized nationally at a conference in New York City in June 1919, attended by ninety delegates from twenty different states. The conference elected a National Council, of which the defendant was a member, and left to it the adoption of a "Manifesto." This was published in *The Revolutionary Age*, the official organ of the Left Wing.

The defendant was on the Board of Managers of the paper and was its business manager. He arranged for the printing of the paper and took to the printer the manuscript of the first issue which contained the Left Wing Manifesto, and also a Communist Program and a Program of the Left Wing that had been adopted by the conference. Sixteen thousand copies were printed, which were delivered at the premises in New York City used as the office of the *Revolutionary Age* and the headquarters of the Left Wing, and occupied by the defendant and other officials. These copies were paid for by the defendant as business manager of the paper. Employees at this office wrapped and mailed out copies of the paper under the defendant's direction; and copies were sold from this office.

It was admitted that the defendant signed a card subscribing to the Manifesto and Program of the Left Wing, which all applicants were required to sign before being admitted to membership; that he went to different parts of the state to speak to branches of the Socialist Party about the principles of the Left Wing and advocated their adoption; and that he was responsible for the Manifesto as it appeared, that "he knew of the publication, in a general way and he knew of its publication afterwards, and is responsible for its circulation."

There was no evidence of any effect resulting from the publication and circulation of the Manifesto. No witnesses were offered in behalf of the defendant. . . .

Coupled with a review of the rise of Socialism, [the Manifesto] condemned the dominant "moderate Socialism" for its recognition of the necessity of the democratic parliamentary state; repudiated its policy of introducing Socialism by legislative measures; and advocated, in plain and unequivocal language, the necessity of accomplishing the "Communist Revolution" by a militant and "revolutionary Socialism" based on "the class struggle" and mobilizing the "power of the proletariat in action" through mass industrial revolts developing into mass political strikes and "revolutionary mass action" for the purpose of conquering and destroying the parliamentary state and establishing in its place, through a "revolutionary dictatorship of the proletariat," the system of Communist Socialism. The then recent strikes in Seattle and Winnipeg were cited as instances of a development already verging on revolutionary action and suggestive of proletarian dictatorship in which the strike workers were "trying to usurp the functions of municipal government"; and revolutionary Socialism, it was urged, must use these mass industrial revolts to broaden the strike, make it general and militant, and develop it into mass political strikes and revolutionary mass action for the annihilation of the parliamentary state.

At the outset of the trial the defendant's counsel objected to the introduction of any evidence under the indictment on the grounds that, as a matter of law, the Manifesto "is not in contravention of the statute," and that "the statute is in contravention of" the due process clause of the Fourteenth Amendment. This objection was denied. They also moved, at the close of the evidence, to dismiss the indictment and direct an acquittal "on the grounds stated in the first objection to evidence," and again on the grounds that "the indictment does not charge an offense" and the evidence "does not show an offense." These motions were also denied.

The court, among other things, charged the jury, in substance, that they must determine what was the intent, purpose, and fair meaning of the Manifesto; that its words must be taken in their ordinary meaning, as

they would be understood by people whom it might reach; that a mere statement or analysis of social and economic facts and historical incidents, in the nature of an essay, accompanied by prophecy as to the future course of events, but with no teaching, advice, or advocacy of action, would not constitute the advocacy, advice, or teaching of a doctrine for the overthrow of government within the meaning of the statute; that a mere statement that unlawful acts might accomplish such a purpose would be insufficient unless there was a teaching, advising, and advocacy of employing such unlawful acts for the purpose of overthrowing government; and that if the jury had a reasonable doubt that the Manifesto did teach, advocate, or advise the duty, necessity, or propriety of using unlawful means for the overthrowing of organized government, the defendant was entitled to an acquittal.

The defendant's counsel submitted two requests to charge which embodied in substance the statement that to constitute criminal anarchy within the meaning of the statute it was necessary that the language used or published should advocate, teach, or advise the duty, necessity, or propriety of doing "some definite or immediate act or acts" of force, violence, or unlawfulness directed toward the overthrowing of organized government. These were denied further than had been charged. Two other requests to charge embodied in substance the statement that to constitute guilt the language used or published must be "reasonably and ordinarily calculated to incite certain persons" to acts of force, violence, or unlawfulness, with the object of overthrowing organized government. These were also denied. . . . Both the Appellate Division and the Court of Appeals held the statute constitutional. . . .

The correctness of the verdict is not questioned, as the case was submitted to the jury. The sole contention here is, essentially, that as there was no evidence of any concrete result flowing from the publication of the Manifesto or of circumstances showing the likelihood of such result, the statute as construed and applied by the trial court penalizes the mere utterance, as such, of "doctrine" having no quality of incitement, without regard either to the circumstances of its utterance or to the likelihood of unlawful sequences; and that, as the exercise of the right of free expression with relation to government is only punishable "in circumstances involving likelihood of substantive evil," the statute contravenes the due process clause of the Fourteenth Amendment.

The argument in support of this contention rests primarily upon the following propositions: (1) that the "liberty" protected by the Fourteenth Amendment includes the liberty of speech and of the press; and (2) that while liberty of expression "is not absolute," it may be restrained "only in circumstances where its exercise bears a causal relation with some substantive evil, consummated, attempted, or likely," and as the statute "takes no account of circumstances," it unduly restrains this liberty and is therefore unconstitutional.

The precise question presented, and the only question which we can consider under this writ of error, then, is whether the statute, as construed and applied in this case by the state courts, deprived the defendant of his liberty of expression in violation of the due process clause of the Fourteenth Amendment.

The statute does not penalize the utterance or publication of abstract "doctrine" or academic discussion having no quality of incitement to any concrete action. It is not aimed against mere historical or philosophical essays. It does not restrain the advocacy of changes in the form of government by constitutional and lawful means. What it prohibits is language advocating, advising, or teaching the overthrow of organized government by unlawful means. These words imply urging to action. . . .

The Manifesto, plainly, is neither the statement of abstract doctrine nor, as suggested by counsel, mere prediction that industrial disturbances and revolutionary mass strikes will result spontaneously in an inevitable process of evolution in the economic system. It advocates and urges in fervent language mass action which shall progressively foment industrial disturbances and through political mass strikes and revolutionary mass action overthrow and destroy organized parliamentary government. . . .

For present purposes we may and do assume that freedom of speech and of the press — which are protected by the First Amendment from abridgment by Congress — are among the fundamental personal rights and "liberties" protected by the due process clause of the Fourteenth Amendment from the impairment by the states. . . .

It is a fundamental principle, long established, that the freedom of speech and of the press which is secured by the Constitution does not confer an absolute right to speak or publish, without responsibility, whatever one may choose, or an unrestricted and unbridled license that gives immunity for every possible use of language and prevents the punishment of those who abuse this freedom. . . . That a state in the exercise of its police power may punish those who abuse this freedom by utterances inimical to the public welfare, tending to corrupt public morals, incite to crime, or disturb the public peace, is not open to question. . . .

By enacting the present statute the state has determined, through its legislative body, that utterances advocating the overthrow of organized government by force, violence, and unlawful means are so inimical to the general welfare and involve such danger of substantive evil that they may be penalized in the exercise of its police power. . . . We cannot hold that the present statute is an arbitrary or unreasonable exercise of the police power of the state unwarrantably infringing the freedom of speech or press; and we must and do sustain its constitutionality. . . .

It is only necessary to say that, applying the general rules already stated, we find that none of them involved any invasion of the constitutional rights of the defendant. It was not necessary, within the meaning of the statute, that the defendant should have advocated "some definite or immediate act or acts" of force, violence, or unlawfulness. It was sufficient if such acts were advocated in general terms; and it was not essential that their immediate execution should have been advocated. Nor was it necessary that the language should have been "reasonably and ordinarily calculated to incite certain persons" to acts of force, violence, or unlawfulness. The advocacy need not be addressed to specific persons. Thus, the publication and circulation of a newspaper article may be an encouragement or endeavor to persuade to murder, although not addressed to any person in particular. . . .

And finding, for the reasons stated, that the statute is not in itself unconstitutional, and that it has not been applied in the present case in derogation of any constitutional right, the judgment of the Court of Appeals is *affirmed*.

Mr. Justice Holmes. Mr. Justice Brandeis and I are of opinion that this judgment should be reversed. The general principle of free speech, it seems to me, must be taken to be included in the Fourteenth Amendment, in view of the scope that has been given to the word "liberty" as there used, although perhaps it may be accepted with a somewhat larger latitude of interpretation than is allowed to Congress by the sweeping language that governs or ought to govern the laws of the United States. If I am right, then I think that the criterion sanctioned by the full Court in *Schenck* v. *United States*, 249 U.S. 47, 52, applies. "The question in every case is whether the words used are used in such circumstances and are of such a nature as to create a clear and present danger that they will bring about the substantive evils that [the state] has a right to prevent."

It is true that in my opinion this criterion was departed from in *Abrams* v. *United States*, 250 U.S. 616, but the convictions that I expressed in that case are too deep for it to be possible for me as yet to believe that it and *Schaefer* v. *United States*, 251 U.S. 466, have settled the law. If what I think the correct test is applied, it is manifest that there was no present danger of an attempt to overthrow the government by force on the part of the admittedly small minority who shared the defendant's views.

It is said that this Manifesto was more than a theory, that it was an incitement. Every idea is an incitement. It offers itself for belief, and, if believed, it is acted on unless some other belief outweighs it or some failure of energy stifles the movement at its birth. The only difference between the expression of an opinion and an incitement in the narrower sense is the speaker's enthusiasm for the result. Eloquence may set fire to reason. But whatever may be thought of the redundant discourse before us, it had no chance of starting a present conflagration. If in the long run the beliefs expressed in proletarian dictatorship are destined to be accepted by the dominant forces of the community, the only meaning of free speech is that they should be given their chance and have their way.

If the publication of this document had been laid as an attempt to induce an uprising against government at once and not at some indefinite time in the future, it would have presented a different question. The object would have been one with which the law might deal, subject to the doubt whether there was any danger that the publication could produce any result, or in other words, whether it was not futile and too remote from possible consequences. But the indictment alleges the publication and nothing more.

92.

Robinson Jeffers: Two Poems

Robinson Jeffers is probably the most dour and pessimistic of the generation of American poets who rose to prominence during the Twenties. Sharing the general disillusionment that troubled intellectuals after World War I, he was also deeply influenced by the theories of Freud and by the nihilistic trend of thought of some of the leading physicists of the time. Jeffers' preoccupation with universal decay and with the introspective and masochistic tendencies of modern man is reflected in the two poems reprinted here. They appeared in 1925 in a collection that contained some of Jeffers' best-known work.

Source: *Roan Stallion, Tamar, and Other Poems,* New York, 1925.

❧ SCIENCE

Man, introverted man, having crossed
In passage and but a little with the nature of things this
      latter century
Has begot giants; but being taken up
Like a maniac with self-love and inward conflicts cannot
      manage his hybrids.
Being used to deal with edgeless dreams,
Now he's bred knives on nature turns them also inward:
      they have thirsty points though.
His mind forebodes his own destruction;
Actaeon who saw the goddess naked among leaves and his
      hounds tore him.
A little knowledge, a pebble from the shingle,
A drop from the oceans: who would have dreamed this
      infinitely little too much?

❧ SHINE, PERISHING REPUBLIC

While this America settles in the mould of its vulgarity,
      heavily thickening to empire,
And protest, only a bubble in the molten mass, pops and
      sighs out, and the mass hardens,

I sadly smiling remember that the flower fades to make
      fruit, the fruit rots to make earth.
Out of the mother; and through the spring exultances,
      ripeness and decadence; and home to the mother.

You making haste haste on decay: not blameworthy; life is
　　good, be it stubbornly long or suddenly
A mortal splendor. meteors are not needed less than mountains;
　　shine, perishing republic.

But for my children, I would have them keep their distance
　　from the thickening center; corruption
Never has been compulsory, when the cities lie at the
　　monster's feet there are left the mountains.

And boys, be in nothing so moderate as in love of man,
　　a clever servant, insufferable master.
There is the trap that catches noblest spirits, that caught —
　　they say — God, when he walked on earth.

93.

WILLIAM MITCHELL: Military Aviation and National Defense

From the time of his appointment as assistant chief of the air service in 1919, Colonel William ("Billy") Mitchell urged an independent air force and unified control of air power. As he saw little hope of his goals being realized, he became an outspoken critic of the American military establishment. The loss of the Navy dirigible Shenandoah *on September 3, 1925, prompted Mitchell to issue his most severe indictment of the War and Navy departments, for which he expected to be, and was, court-martialed later the same year. Suspended from active duty and stripped of his rank, he left the service early in 1926. The following selection consists of the statements Mitchell made in September 1925. Most of Mitchell's arguments were borne out during World War II, and many of his suggestions were eventually adopted.*

Source: *Aviation*, September 14, 1925.

I HAVE BEEN ASKED from all parts of the country to give my opinion about the reasons for the frightful aeronautical accidents and loss of life, equipment, and treasure that have occurred during the last few days. This statement, therefore, is given out publicly by me after mature deliberation and after a sufficient time has elapsed since the terrible accidents to our naval aircraft, to find out something about what happened.

About what happened, my opinion is as follows: These accidents are the direct result of the incompetency, criminal negligence, and almost treasonable administration of the national defense by the Navy and War departments. In their attempts to keep down the development of aviation into an independent department, separate from the Army and Navy and handled by aeronautical experts, and to maintain the existing systems, they have gone to the utmost lengths to carry their point. All aviation policies, schemes, and systems are dictated by the nonflying officers of the Army or Navy, who know practically nothing about it. The lives of the airmen are being used merely as pawns in their hands.

The great Congress of the United States, that makes laws for the organization and use of our air, land, and water forces, is treated by these two departments as if it were an organization created for their benefit, to which evidence of any kind, whether true or not, can be given without restraint. Officers and agents sent by the War and Navy departments to Congress have almost always given incomplete, miserable, or false information about aeronautics, which either they knew to be false when given or was the result of such gross ignorance of the question that they should not be allowed to appear before a legislative body.

The airmen themselves are bluffed and bulldozed so that they dare not tell the truth in the majority of cases, knowing full well that if they do they will be deprived of their future career, sent to the most out-of-the-way places to prevent their telling the truth, and deprived of any chance for advancement unless they subscribe to the dictates of their nonflying, bureaucratic superiors. These either distort facts or openly tell falsehoods about aviation to the people and to the Congress.

Both the War and Navy departments maintain public propaganda agencies which are supposed to publish truthful facts about our national defense to the American people. These departments, remember, are supported by the taxes of the people and were created for the purpose of protecting us from invasion from abroad and from domestic disturbances from within. What has actually happened in these departments is that they have formed a sort of union to perpetuate their own existence, largely irrespective of the public welfare, and acting, as

we might say about a commercial organization that has entire control of a public necessity, "as an illegal combination in restraint of trade."

The conduct of affairs by these two departments, as far as aviation is concerned, has been so disgusting in the last few years as to make any self-respecting person ashamed of the clothes he wears. Were it not for the patriotism of our air officers and their absolute confidence in the institutions of the United States, knowing that sooner or later existing conditions would be changed, I doubt if one of them would remain with the colors — certainly not if he were a real man.

The story is a long one, beginning practically with the inception of aviation in this country, so I shall mention only a few things in connection with the disgraceful performances which have occurred this summer.

Seeing no progress in our efforts, which had been continued for years, to convince or even seriously interest the governing bodies of the War and Navy departments to better our aeronautical condition, we were stirred to further action by the killing of Lieutenant Pierson and Captain Skeel in the dilapidated racing airplanes during last October's air meet. This was caused by an arrangement between the Navy and Army that the Navy should take the races one year and the Army should take them the next year, thereby equalizing propaganda, not service. Instead of building new airplanes, our men were given the old crates to fly at those terrific speeds. Of course, they came to pieces, as they were designed for only one race two years before. This was done, in spite of the fact that we had sufficient money to build new ships according to entirely advanced patterns and new safety factors.

We in the air fraternity then and there decided to put the issue squarely up to Congress and the people. We received an immediate response from the people and Congress, because they saw the right of our proposition, which was to make a single department of national defense, with subsecretaries for the land, the air, and the water, each to have an equal voice in our national defense system. The general scheme, by the way, has been adopted by practically every civilized country in the world. Had this measure reached the floor of the House of Representatives last winter, it probably would have passed by a large majority.

Congress also provided that not less than $50,000 out of moneys already appropriated should be spent for the aerial bombardment of battleships and shipping board vessels while under their own steam and moving, so as to set at rest any doubt of aircrafts' ability to destroy and sink any seacraft which floats on the water.

It was evident then that the American people were awakening to the necessity for a change and that if this change were to be prevented by the War and Navy departments, that they must act at once. What was the result? Steam was gotten up by the Navy on the one hand to disprove and deprecate the value of air power and show the value of the surface vessels and battleships, and on the part of the Army to fool the public as to the value of antiaircraft, cannon, and machine guns. Any operations by the air service to sink the ships, as provided for by the law of the land, were stopped.

Now, what have the Army and Navy done to show that the existing obsolete systems should be maintained? First, the great Pacific naval maneuvers — the main features of these were the assembling of a fleet of some 148 surface vessels in the Pacific, the parade of our Pacific Coast and entrance into San Francisco Harbor, and then the trip to Honolulu. Press representatives and congressional committees galore were handled, fed, and entertained according to the good old Navy's propaganda system. It

was heralded that the Navy had taken the Hawaiian Islands.

Now, let us see what actually would have happened had there been war. Suppose that we had been at war with a Pacific power and this fleet of surface vessels had been in San Francisco Harbor. Instantly, the Pacific power's submarines would have planted all entrances to the harbor with mines, would have covered all the approaches with these death-dealing engines. If the surface vessels ever got through these, the whole Pacific Ocean would be districted off into squares, and to each of these districts submarines would be assigned for the purpose of tracking the surface ships and attacking them.

These ships would be under constant attack of gunfire from submarines that can carry any size cannon and use projectiles containing gas, high explosives, or armor-piercing shells. They use underwater torpedoes which not only hit the side of the ships but will hit their bottom and can produce gas clouds which will completely envelop any fleet. If any vessels of the fleet survived the submarine attacks, crossed the sea, and came within hundreds of miles of the hostile coast, they would be sent to the bottom forthwith by aircraft.

If the Pacific maneuver showed anything conclusively, it was that aircraft acting from land bases can destroy any surface fleet coming within their radius of operations. This almost had been amply proved by our bombardment tests in 1921.

As far as Honolulu is concerned, it is not a position of decisive influence in the control of the Pacific. Its value consists in being an excellent submarine base to act against hostile surface seacraft and submarines. The control position of the Pacific is our own territory of Alaska and the peninsula of Kamchatka, opposite. It is reported that from $50 million to $80 million has been spent just for this Pacific parade by our Navy — more properly, the vessels belonging to the United States, because, in fact, it is no navy in the modern conception of the term. What would this amount applied to development and improvement of airplanes and submarines have meant?

Next, to get publicity and make a noise about what it was doing with aircraft, this so-called Hawaiian flight was arranged for. Even if it had been successfully made to Honolulu, it would have meant little, either commercially or strategically, compared to what a flight to Europe or Asia would. Three airplanes were built to participate in it. These showed nothing novel in design and were untried for this kind of work. One never got away from the Pacific Coast, another flew a few miles out and was forced to land in the water, and one was lost on account of being out of gas somewhere on the high seas.

Patrol vessels were stationed every 200 miles, a distance entirely too far apart for an experimental flight of this kind, with such primitive flying machines as the PN9's are. Double or triple this number of vessels should have been there. In fact, the whole Pacific Fleet should have been placed there, instead of joyriding around the Antipodes.

As it was, when this slow-moving airplane, going about 75 m.p.h., was first sighted from the destroyers, the destroyers should have steamed out full speed in the direction in which the airplane was going. This would not only indicate the proper course to the plane but would place the destroyer closer to it in case of accident. As the airplane was moving at only about 75 m.p.h., the destroyer could have been speeded up to within 30 miles of that speed.

Why, if they expected to run short of fuel, as indeed they might, did they not make arrangements for refueling the airplane while it was in the air by another airplane, as we have repeatedly done? Why did they carry a crew of five when the weight of two men in fuel might have carried the ship through?

Brown Brothers

Gen. "Billy" Mitchell on the stand at his court martial

What happened to this really good-for-nothing, big, lumbering flying boat when its brave navigators began to run short of gas over a heavy sea? The probability is that they held her up as long as they could. As they neared the water, caught by a sudden gust, she might have been thrown into a stall and gone down straight under the water. Hope was that some passing fisherman may have picked them up as our Lieutenant Wade was picked up in the North Sea. Our Navy did not find him either. All they did was to smash his plane when it was turned over to them by the fishermen. After all, the Hawaiian Islands are not a vital area with our present methods of national defense.

Then the disaster to the *Shenandoah* — killing Captain Lansdowne, the last of our really experienced airship captains — a splendid man, with his companions, following in the wake of Captain Mabry and Captain Maxfield, our airship commanders who have gone before.

I do not know exactly what happened to

the poor *Shenandoah*. She was an experimental ship, built in this country. I believe she was about 50 percent overweight in her structure. She had broken away from her mooring mast — an inefficient way of handling airships, anyway — last spring, and her whole structure was badly strained. I believe that the number of valves in the gas bags containing the helium had been diminished so as to save helium gas, which is expensive in money but which made the ship more dangerous to the crew.

The *Shenandoah* was going west on a propaganda mission for the Navy department to offset the adverse publicity caused by the failures in the Pacific and Arctic. Note: Propaganda and not service is the keynote in these undertakings. What business has the Navy over the mountains, anyway? Their mission is out in the water — not only out in water but under the water, out of sight, away from the land. That is why we have the Navy.

No accurate meteorologist arrangements are available for aircraft in this country. The Weather Bureau is under the Department of Agriculture and primarily organized to turn out weather reports affecting onions, cabbages, and other crops. While this is very necessary, it is a complete failure as far as we are concerned. I say this after having flown across mountains and bucked their storms hundreds of times.

The *Shenandoah*, 50 percent overweight in her structure, had members strained last spring, possibly some of them disintegrated from the action of the nonfreezing compound in the radiators of her engines, wherever this liquid dropped on them, and with the valves in her helium gas bags reduced, strikes a storm. She is caught in an up current of air. Due to her excessive weight, her reserve buoyancy is low. She is carried high up by this current, and her gas bags begin to expand due to the altitude. The crew valves her in an attempt to allow the gas to escape, but the automatic valves, reduced in number, do not allow the escape fast

enough; the pressure of the expanding gas on the structure tears the ship to pieces. Some of her crew go to eternity. Those who do not escape by miraculously good fortune.

No notice of the storm was received in time to avoid it. Her survivors are muzzled by the Navy Department pending a whitewash board. Are these things so, or are they not? I am down here in Texas and have not all the data at hand, but I am sure the facts are practically as stated.

What results? The Navy Department announces that this shows that America cannot be reached by hostile aircraft. What has that to do with it? The way that America will be reached from Asia is by the way of Alaska. The water that has to be crossed is scarcely wider than the English Channel. The route from Europe is by the same course that the round-the-world fliers took to Iceland, Greenland, and North America, whenever a country gets powerful enough to undertake the operation. What has the loss of a seaplane near Honolulu and an airship over the mountain to do with it?

The impression is given to the public at large that the *Shenandoah* was a modern ship, properly constructed, properly operated, and completely equipped. This was not the case. It shakes the faith of the people in airship transportation because they are not given the exact facts on the subject. This is not an argument necessarily for the maintenance of many airships by the government, but it is a demand for the facts in the case, so that we will not be hindered in the commercial development of this splendid aircraft on account of the accident to an airship due to incompetence in the Navy Department and the criminal negligence in the ordering of this trip. If we took the safety valve of a locomotive off to save water in the desert and it blew up, killing the engineer and passengers, would we say that railways were no good in deserts and go back to camels?

An interesting sidelight might be thrown

on the development of airships in this country. When I came back from the war in 1919, I attempted to get warships for the purpose of making them into airplane carriers. That is, having airplanes take off from them and land on them, so that they could get out in the middle of the ocean if necessary and attack hostile vessels in case of war. I obtained permission immediately from the then chief of staff, General March, and the then secretary of war, Secretary Baker. I sent Major Hensley to Europe with money to get the ships. We had even gone so far as to order the gasoline to Germany for the voyage of the ships to this country.

Mysteriously, the order was rescinded — all work was stopped — it was said at the time that it was against the provision of the treaty, which I do not believe was the case. Work had already been begun on the frames by the Germans. This was the ZR-2, rechristened the *Los Angeles*, which the Navy obtained recently, six years after I ordered it. What has it been used for? Nothing but parading around the country. It is evident that whenever a warship is developed as an airplane carrier, the necessity for any naval surface airplane carrier may be done away with. Is this the reason the Navy has the *Los Angeles*?

The Germans are the only people who have had real experience with airships. They had many a disaster before they learned how to handle them. I have seen German Zeppelins years ago in terrific storms. A storm has little effect on an airship properly constructed and ably handled.

What other things has the Navy done this summer? After borrowing some airplanes from the Army that were entirely inadequate to the work in hand, they went on the Macmillan trip to the Arctic. More propaganda! As far as can be learned from a distance, they had a cat-and-dog-fight all the way up and back between Macmillan, the pilots, and the Navy Department and, of course, got nowhere and did nothing. Is there an airman who does not know that

with the little jitneys they took up there the Pole could not be reached? Another example, says the Navy Department, of the incapacity of aircraft.

At last the great antiaircraft tests took place. A battleship goes out into the sea. She takes the airship *Shenandoah* and has her tow a target at thirty-three miles an hour, at a known altitude, in broad daylight and on a certain course. Some officers have told me that the dirigible was heading into the wind of an intensity of many miles an hour and that therefore the target really was almost standing still in the air. The Navy shoots at it all day long in this position and hits it a few times and publishes to the people of the United States the wonderful results obtained to impress them with the fact that battleships can be protected by antiaircraft guns, which is absolutely and entirely false.

What is our Navy for? Presumably it is to control lines of sea communication on the high seas. What is it actually? It is entirely and completely outpointed by Great Britain in the Atlantic. What can it do across the Pacific as at present organized? Nothing — against an insular Asiatic power whom you all know.

The Navy has about $1.5 billion invested in navy yards. The upkeep and depreciation of these amount to about $150 million a year. How many of these are useless and how many of them are of any profit? Probably not many. Suppose we took $50 million of this and applied it to the development of aircraft and submarines under competent airmen and submarine men? What could we do with it?

Every time a battleship is built, the ship itself, when it is completed, may cost from $50 million to $75 million. It has to be protected by submarines, destroyers, cruisers, and aircraft, the total cost of which is around or over $100 million, so that every time a battleship is built, the expenditure of $100 million is necessary. I believe a battleship today is a useless element in the national defensive armament of the United States. Suppose we had even one-half of the cost of a battleship to use in the development of our aircraft and submarines. These are only a few of the things which must be brought up before the people and the coming Congress.

The Navy, to maintain its position, keeps asking for more aircraft, which it cannot use legally because the legal defense of the land is entrusted to armies. In spite of the legal restrictions, however, but to keep control of aviation and not let it get away, the Navy Department continually gets more money from Congress by its Washington lobby so as to keep the political support of the aircraft manufacturers, and possibly some others interested in them.

This year the Navy's estimate for the aircraft amounts to $37,360,248. They only have one aircraft carrier, the *Langley*, which can go about half as fast as a battleship and which is an obsolete collier. It can hold thirty-six small airplanes. They are building two aircraft carriers which can hold sixty to seventy planes. These are practically obsolete before they are completed. Where is the $37 million for aircraft going? It is going into the land aircraft which have nothing to do with the Navy's operations on the seas and which will be used as a political lever for the maintenance of their existing system.

The War Department that now is entrusted by law with the aerial defense over the land areas of the United States and its possessions, including the protection of navy yards, asks for $24,582,000. Consider how foolish this is. The Navy, an organization charged with going to sea and which must operate from surface vessels, which, as a matter of fact, are practically obsolete now and which will afford no real protection to the country in case of an air attack, asking for two-thirds more than the Army does, which acts from land bases and is specifical-

ly charged with the defense of the land areas. The amount allotted to the Navy for new aircraft is three times as much as the Army.

Now, let us turn to the War Department. The War Department has done nothing this summer to develop air power and has undertaken to prove by tests that antiaircraft guns can protect cities, which is known everywhere to be false. They have fixed up a scheme to give constructive hits when the guns firing do not hit the targets at all. The firing has been at targets towed at a constant altitude, over courses which have now been flown hundreds of times, at greatly reduced speeds and never in excess of 75 miles an hour. Even this was only because the wind was helping the plane along and under weather conditions that have been ideal. In spite of all this preparation, the results have been laughable.

As an example of one of these performances, the War Department has taken the lid off for publicity in the II Corps area — that means around New York — with the result that the Coast Artillery tells the papers the story in greatly exaggerated terms, whereas the chief of air service has been completely muzzled. An interesting example of some of the antiaircraft target practice was the testing of the listening device for aircraft at Camp Dix, July 27.

The umpire had told Captain Hall, commanding the airplane bombers at Mitchell Field, that in the next antiaircraft test he was at liberty to fly under conditions which would be used in war. Captain Hall informed the umpire ahead of time that he would glide into the target. Before this, the Coast Artillery had all their practice with planes that had flown over at a fairly constant altitude and with their motors open. The night of the test, planes got their proper altitude, played around a little just out of range of the searchlights and just within range of the listening devices on the ground. The artillery thought that this was easy because they picked up the planes far off and plotted their course absolutely; but all of a sudden sounds from the airplanes stopped. Five or ten minutes later, the bombers dropped their bombs directly on the target. All around not a sound had been heard before this.

The fury of the ground officers, artillery officers, and others was tremendous. The air service had not acted fair and had fooled them, all of which a kind enemy, of course, in war would never do. Discussion even went so far that it had to be pointed out that it was provided in our bombardment manual to attack a place in this fashion. This is only one instance of the ridiculous performance.

So far, practically the only bombardment airplanes we have in this country have been used up towing these targets for ground shooting, which other airplanes could just as well have done. The actual cost out of air service funds appropriated will be approximately $200,000 by the time they are completed this fall.

Why are things done this way? The Coast Artillery now has about ninety-two stations. For the ten years prior to 1920, about $2 billion were spent on coast defense — not $2 million, but $2 billion. What good are these coast defenses? None — except those in the immediate vicinity of large cities, where a submarine might emerge at close range and plant a few shells in the city.

What could the saving do on these useless expenditures if used by the troops of the mobile army stationed in Texas and other frontier points, living in shacks, unequipped with modern conveniences, cut down on every activity and rendered almost incapable, in case the Constitution is menaced, of putting down insurrections or executing the laws when all other means fail and patrolling our frontiers and holding our insular possessions — what would only a small part of this tremendous expenditure mean in the development of aircraft?

Not one heavy bomb has been dropped by the air service line units in target practice for two years. Only about four or five modern sights are on hand with the bombing groups; and today I, who know our personnel better than any living man, can only put my hand on two perfectly capable bombardment crews to handle our aircraft in case we are attacked.

The other thing that the War Department has done this summer is to study how the fliers' pay could be reduced or taken away from them. Think of it, the whole effort of the War Department during the summer was to fool the people into thinking that aircraft cannon are a protection and to keep the rightful flying pay away from the pilots.

To make a long story short, we are utterly disgusted with the conduct of our military affairs applying to aviation. Our pilots know they are going to be killed if they stay in the service, on account of the methods employed in the old floating coffins that we are still flying. Those pilots that still remain have held on so long that if they got out they would starve. They don't dare open their mouths and tell the truth because they and their families might be booted out to some obscure place. No finer body ever existed in the makeup of our country than these men.

There are many able men in the Army — these should be developing the ground Army in accordance with the needs of the nation. There are many able men in the Navy, but the bureaucracies that both of these national services maintain in Washington have passed all bounds of national decency. They are deluding the public, sacrificing our national defense, and not only wasting the money of our citizens but the lives of its ablest men — our flying officers.

This condition must be remedied. It is not in the field of partisan politics — it concerns us all. The American people must know the facts, and with their unfailing common sense and ability, they will surely remedy it.

As far as I am personally concerned, I am looking for no advancement in any service. I have had the finest career that any man could have in the armed service of our United States. I have had the great pleasure of serving in all our campaigns from the Spanish War to the present and of commanding the greatest air forces ever brought together on the planet. I owe the government everything — the government owes me nothing. As a patriotic American citizen, I can stand by no longer and see these disgusting performances by the Navy and War departments at the expense of the lives of our people and the delusion of the American public.

The bodies of my former companions in the air molder under the soil in America, and Asia, Europe, and Africa — many, yes, a great many, sent there directly by official stupidity. We all make mistakes, but the criminal mistakes made by armies and navies whenever they have been allowed to handle aeronautics show their incompetence. We would not be keeping our trust with our departed comrades were we longer to conceal these facts.

This, then, is what I have to say on this subject, and I hope that every American will hear it.

We must apply a remedy to the conditions existing in our whole national defense system, and in our aeronautics in particular. Preliminary steps should be taken at once and in December decisive action by Congress to put these measures into law.

We would consolidate our whole national defense under one head and hold one man responsible for the whole thing. Under him should be three subsecretaries, one for the Army or the land, one for the Navy or the water, and one for our aeronautics.

Policies pertaining to our national defense should be recommended by the secretary of national defense to the President upon the advice of the three subsecretaries. Having three subsecretaries would ensure there being no deadlock, as often occurs at the present time between the Army and Navy. All supplies common to the three services should be gotten by a central agency so as to avoid competition between the different branches of the government.

In time of war or threatened emergency, capital should be conscripted as well as labor. All raw materials for the construction of national defense equipment should be obtained and distributed under one head.

According to this system, the Army organization would remain much the same as it is at present, except that it would be modernized. The Navy organization would also have little change. Any air service that these two departments needed would be permanently assigned to them.

The secretary of the air, however, should be entrusted with the whole aeronautical department of the government, which is even more important in time of peace than it is in time of war, because we can employ aviation in useful pursuits during peace, such as carrying the mail, patrolling the forests, surveying the country, aiding agriculture, animal industry, and exploration.

The Department of Aeronautics should be divided into three principal subdivisions, one charged with the development of civil aviation. This should provide for the airways throughout the country; the aids to air navigation; and provide an efficient weather service and storm warnings; a legal department to make recommendations about all air navigation laws, inspection of pilots and aircraft, so as to be sure the public is safeguarded when traveling or using aircraft. There should also be formed an aeronautical corporation similar to our Inland Waterways Corporation, which should operate between the great centers of population so as to show what things could be carried safely and at a profit through the air. All figures on this should be made public, so that as soon as possible any civilian company desiring to take it over should be allowed to do so. At the present stage of the development of aeronautics, the government must assist, as all aeronautics is a national asset.

The second division should be a section of fabrication or construction. In this department, special studies should be made of the kind of aircraft that are necessary, of their airworthiness and safety. They should be made in accordance with the desires and wishes of the flying men, by experts, and thoroughly tried out before being issued. No aircraft should be built by the government. All should be built by civilian organizations so as to keep up competition, invention, and initiative by the people.

The third division should be the Air Force, that part specifically charged with the air defense of the whole country. Provision should be made for a suitable number of well-trained flying men and good airplanes to defend this country in case of trouble. Only a small part of the total need be kept constantly under arms; the rest should be working in civil life and the mechanics keeping up their work in the factories and in the industries which go to make up aircraft, being called out for a suitable period of training when necessary.

Practically every civilized country has now adopted this sane, economical, and logical system. With a plan of this kind working, the question of who is to command any undertaking is absolutely fixed — if the predominant is to be a sea force, the Navy ought to have command of the undertaking and the Army and Air Force report to it. If it is going to be a land cam-paign, the Army should have charge of it and all the elements of the Navy and Air Force report to it. If it is to be an air campaign, the Air Force should have charge and the Army and Navy report to it. The secretary of national defense could determine this.

With adequate Air Force in this country, it is difficult to see how any hostile host can touch our soil, coming from Europe or from Asia.

Due to the increased understanding of modern implements of defense, it is probable that in the near future civilized nations of the world will agree to eliminate from their national defense arrangements all useless and expensive elements that now enter into it and will confine themselves to a defensive armament consisting of aircraft, submarines, and sufficient land forces for their needs. This is what the influence of air power is bringing about.

For many years we have had to cater to the old Army and Navy system — it now should be stopped and a new one instituted. To sidestep this change, propositions certainly will be made to create a special service of aviation within the Army for work over land; a special service of aviation in the Navy for work over the water; and a special service of aviation within the Department of Commerce to handle civil aeronautics. Although this sounds alluring, it will be even a worse condition than obtains at present, because the old system will still control the aviation in the Army, Navy, and Department of Commerce, and will even entrench it more strongly.

This has been tried in other countries — in England, for instance, before a modern organization was made. The Germans used it to attack London. The Army Air Force would chase them as far as the coast. There would then be no naval air force because they were fooling around in flying boats somewhere and under an entirely separate command. The Germans, therefore, did very much as they pleased.

Civil aviation was assigned to the Board of Trade, which in England is something like our Department of Commerce. It was put under nonfliers who knew absolutely nothing about aviation, and one of the first rules they prescribed was, "When two airplanes meet in a fog, they should blow their fog horns." The utter absurdity of the whole thing was quickly understood by the British people and the whole proposition consolidated under one head. The Germans had done this before them in 1916, and other nations either have done it entirely or are doing it at present.

In addition to the Department of National Defense under one secretary, there should be a Council of National Defense to consist of the secretary of state, the secretary of the treasury, and the secretary of national defense. In case the President desired advice on the conditions relative to a present or to prospective emergencies, he would instruct the secretary of state to convene this council and report to him the result of their deliberations.

The secretary of state, having called together the secretary of national defense and the secretary of the treasury, might say: "Gentlemen, it is probable that a certain country, combined with others, may force us to defend ourselves within five years. Mr. Secretary of National Defense, what do you need in the armed forces of this nation to maintain our independence and institutions?"

The secretary of national defense might answer: "I need an air force of 2,000 airplanes, a naval force of 400 vessels, and an army of half a million men, the cost of which will amount to so much money, with an amount of so much cash immediately available."

The secretary of state would then ask the secretary of the treasury: "How much money have you that can be applied to this proposition, and how much need we raise by taxation at once?"

After the necessary data from the secretary of the treasury, the whole report could be quickly made up and given to the President and an absolutely accurate estimate of the whole situation made.

Under our present system, tremendous complications would result in case of an emergency, as has been the case in the past. The terrible conditions in our national aeronautics today is not so much the result of the absolute ignorance of individuals, because often these are selected on the principle of saying, "tag, you're it; go play with aviation," when they know nothing about it and are really more to be pitied than blamed. The trouble is with the system, and we flying people insist that our views be known and weighed by the American public.

I don't make jokes; I just watch the government and report the facts.
WILL ROGERS

94.

Frederick Jackson Turner: Sectionalism and National Unity

The historian Frederick Jackson Turner is best known for his writings on the frontier, but he also studied other American developments and proposed other theories about the country's history. His theory of sectionalism, first propounded in the lecture from which the following selection is taken and expanded in a book that won the Pulitzer Prize in 1932, was probably as influential as his theory of the significance of the frontier, though not nearly so controversial. His essays and lectures completely revised the old view of uncomplicated rivalries between the North, South, and West in U.S. history. Instead, he revealed intricate economic, social, and geographical forces that divided the country into a number of distinct regions or sections, and at the same time emphasized that a federation of sections was the main source of American unity. The lecture reprinted here was delivered to the State Historical Society of Wisconsin in 1925.

Source: *Wisconsin Magazine of History*, June 1925: "The Significance of the Section in American History."

A GENERATION AGO I published in the *Proceedings* of this society a paper which I had read at the summer meeting of the American Historical Association on "The Significance of the Frontier in American History." The superintendent of the census had just announced that a frontier line could no longer be traced, and had declared: "In the discussion of its extent, its westward movement, etc., it cannot therefore any longer have a place in the census reports."

The significance in American history of the advance of the frontier and of its disappearance is now generally recognized. This evening I wish to consider with you another fundamental factor in American history, namely, the "section." Arising from the facts of physical geography and the regional settlement of different peoples and types of society on the Atlantic Coast, there was a sectionalism from the beginning. But soon this became involved and modified by the fact that these societies were expanding into the interior, following the frontier, and that their sectionalism took special forms in the presence of the growing West. Today we are substantially a settled nation without the overwhelming influence that accompanied the westward spread of population. Urban concentration chiefly in the East has reversed the movement to a considerable extent. We are more like Europe, and our sections are becoming more and more the American version of the European nation.

First, let us consider the influence of the frontier and the West upon American sections. Until our own day, as I urged in that paper, the United States was always beginning over on its outer edge as it advanced into the wilderness. Therefore the United States was both a developed and a primitive society. The West was a migrating region, a stage of society rather than a place. Each region reached in the process of expansion from the coast had its frontier experience, was for a time "the West," and when the frontier passed on to new regions, it left behind, in the older areas, memories, traditions, an inherited attitude toward life that persisted long after the frontier had passed by. But while the influence of the frontier permeated East as well as West, by survival of the pioneer psychology and by the reaction of the Western ideals and life upon the East, it was in the newer regions, in the area called "the West," at any given time, that frontier traits and conceptions were most in evidence. This "West" was more than "the frontier" of popular speech. It included also the more populous transitional zone adjacent, which was still influenced by pioneer traditions and where economic society had more in common with the newer than with the older regions.

This "West" wherever found, at different years, thought of itself and of the nation in different ways from those of the East. It needed capital — it was a debtor region — while the East had the capital and was a creditor section. The West was rural, agricultural; while the East was becoming more and more urban and industrial. Living under conditions where the family was the self-sufficing economic unit, where the complications of more densely settled society did not exist, without accumulated inherited wealth, the frontier regions stressed the rights of man, while the statesmen who voiced the interests of the East stressed the rights of property.

The West believed in the rule of the majority, in what John Randolph, the representative of the Virginia Tidewater aristocracy, called "King Numbers." The East feared an unchecked democracy which might overturn minority rights, destroy established institutions, and attack vested interests. The buoyant, optimistic, and sometimes reckless and extravagant spirit of innovation was the very life of the West. In the East, innovation was a term of reproach. . . .

The West demanded cheap or free lands on which to base a democratic farming population. The ruling interests in the East feared that such a policy would decrease land values at home and diminish the value of lands which its capitalists had purchased for speculation in the interior. It feared that cheap lands in the West would draw Eastern farmers into the wilderness; would break down the bonds of regular society; would prevent effective control of the discontented; would drain the labor supply away from the growing industrial towns, and thus raise wages.

The West opened a refuge from the rule of established classes, from the subordination of youth to age, from the sway of established and revered institutions. . . .

No doubt all this makes too sharply contrasted a picture. But, from the beginning, East and West have shown a sectional attitude. The interior of the colonies on the Atlantic was disrespectful of the coast, and the coast looked down upon the upland folk. The "Men of the Western World," when they crossed the Alleghenies, became self-conscious and even rebellious against the rule of the East. In the thirties the Tidewater aristocracy was conquered by the Jacksonian Democracy of the interior. . . .

To the average American, to most American historians, and to most of the writers of our school textbooks (if one can trust the indexes to their books) the word "section" applies only to the struggle of South against North on the questions of slavery, state sovereignty, and, eventually, disunion.

But the Civil War was only the most drastic and most tragic of sectional manifestations, and in no small degree the form which it took depended upon the fact that rival societies, free and slave, were marching side by side into the unoccupied lands of the West, each attempting to dominate the back country, the hinterland, working out agreements from time to time, something like the diplomatic treaties of European nations, defining spheres of influence, and awarding mandates, such as in the Missouri Compromise, the Compromise of 1850, and the Kansas-Nebraska Act. Each Atlantic section was, in truth, engaged in a struggle for power; and power was to be gained by drawing upon the growing West. . . .

If time permitted, it would be possible to illustrate by such utterances all through our history to very recent times how the Eastern sections regarded the West, with its advancing frontier, as the raw material for power. To New England, until her own children began to occupy the prairies ("reserved by God," as her pioneers declared, "for a pious and industrious people"), this aspect of the West threatened to enable the South perpetually to rule the nation. The first great migration, the most extensive in the area covered, flowed into the interior from the Southern upland. Some of the extreme leaders of the New England Federalists did not so much desire to break away from the South as to deprive that section of the three-fifths representation for its slaves, and either to permit the Western states to leave the Union or to see them won by England. Then the Old Thirteen could be united under conditions which would check the expansion of the South and would leave New England in control. . . .

It was not only the slavery struggle that revealed the Eastern conception of the West as merely the field of contest for power between the rival Atlantic sections, and the West's counterassertion of its own substantive rights. The same thing was shown in many different fields. For example, rival Eastern cities and states, the centers of power in their respective sections, engaged in contests for the commercial control of the Mississippi Valley by transportation lines. . . .

A Southern writer in *DeBow's Review* in 1847 declared:

A contest has been going on between the North and South not limited to slavery or no slavery — to abolition or no abolition, nor to the politics of either Whigs or Democrats as such, but a contest for the wealth and commerce of the great valley of the Mississippi — a con-test tendered by our Northern brethren, whether the growing commerce of the great West shall be thrown upon New Orleans or given to the Atlantic cities. . . .

The middle of the century saw an extension of this sectional contest for economic power derived from the growing West; but it was the railroad trunk lines rather than the canals that occupied the foreground. The goal became the ports of the Pacific. The Memphis convention of 1845 and the Chicago convention of 1847 illustrate how interior cities were now repeating the rivalry for Western trade which had earlier been seen on the Atlantic Coast. The contests between New Orleans, Memphis, St. Louis, and Chicago influenced the Kansas-Nebraska Act and the later strategy of the struggle for position between the Pacific railroads.

Throughout our history, then, there has been this sectionalism of West and East, and this Eastern conception of the West as recruiting ground merely for the rival Atlantic Coast sections. Nationwide parties have had their Eastern and Western wings, often differing radically, and yet able by party loyalty and by adjustments and sacrifices to hold together. Such a struggle as the slavery contest can only be understood by bearing in mind that it was not merely a contest of North against South but that its form and its causes were fundamentally shaped by the dynamic factor of expanding sections, of a West to be won.

This migratory sectionalism has not always been obvious, but it was nonetheless real and important. Year after year new Wests had been formed. Wildernesses equal in area to the greater European nations had been turned into farms in single decades.

But now the era of the frontier advance has ended. The vast public domain, so far as it is suited to agriculture, is taken up. The competent experts of the Department of Agriculture now tell us that "the nation reached and passed the apogee of agricultural land supply in proportion to population about 1890, and that we have entered a period which will necessarily be marked by a continually increasing scarcity of land." The price of lands has risen as the supply of free lands declined. Iowa farmlands mounted from an average of $30 per acre in 1890 to over $200 in 1920.

Shortly after 1890, men began to speak less confidently of the inexhaustible forest supply. The Reclamation Act early in the twentieth century began a new era in governmental conservation and governmental economic activity. The Conservation Congress met in 1908, three centuries after the Jamestown settlers sank their axes into the edge of the American forest. The purpose of the congress was to consider the menace of forest exhaustion, the waste of soil fertility and of mineral resources, the reclamation of the deserts, the drainage of the swamps. Now we are told by high authority that we shall feel the pinch of timber shortage in less than fifteen years. The free lands are no longer free; the boundless resources are no longer boundless. Already the urban population exceeds the rural population of the United States.

But this does not mean that the Eastern industrial type of urban life will necessarily spread across the whole nation, for food must come from somewhere; and the same expert authorities that predict that within about fifty years the United States itself will be unable to feed its population by its home supply also conclude that the deficient food supply will not be available from outside the nation, because the same phenomenon of the encroachment of population upon food is in evidence throughout the world. Already Europe as a whole depends upon importation for its food supply. Its large population in proportion to its area and resources cannot be made the basis for estimates of what is possible in the United States, for Europe's large population was made possible by these imports from the United States as well as from other nations.

If the prediction be true, or if anything like it be true, then there must remain in the United States large rural farming interests and sections. The natural advantages of certain regions for farming, or for forestry, or for pasturage will arrest the tendency of the Eastern industrial type of society to flow across the continent and thus to produce a consolidated, homogeneous nation free from sections. At the same time that the nation settles down to the conditions of an occupied land, there will be emphasized the sectional differences arising from unlike geographic regions.

To President Coolidge, as a speech of his in November last shows, the prospect is of a nation importing its supplies of food and resources, facing "the problem of maintaining a prosperous, self-reliant, confident agriculture in a country preponderantly commercial and industrial." Whether our destiny is to become a nation in which agriculture is subordinate, or one in which it is an equal partner with urban industrial interests, it seems clear that there will be sectional expression of the differences between these interests; for, in certain geographic provinces, agriculture will be entirely subordinate to manufacture, as, in others, such industry will be insignificant as compared with farming.

Unlike such countries as France and Germany, the United States has the problem of the clash of economic interests closely associated with regional geography on a huge scale. Over areas equal to all France or to all Germany, either the agricultural or the manufacturing types are here in decided ascendancy. Economic interests are sectionalized. The sections occupied by a rural population are of course far inferior in numbers of voters to the sections of urban industrial life. The map is deceptive in this respect, for Greater New York City, which would be a point on the map, has almost as many people as live in all the vast spaces of the Mountain and Pacific states. The population of the New England states and the

Middle states of the North Atlantic division is over 30 million, while the population of Wisconsin, Minnesota, North and South Dakota, Montana, Wyoming, Idaho, Washington, and Oregon is less than 10 million. On the map these states take an imposing space, but owing to physical geography a large portion will always remain sparsely settled. Nevertheless, New England and the Middle states together have only eighteen senators, while the states of the section which I have just named have also eighteen senators. New York state alone has a larger population than this Northwestern zone of states; but this wealthy and populous state has only two senators as against the eighteen senators of the other region.

On a map constructed so as to give each state a space proportioned to its population, or to its income tax, instead of to its dimensions in square miles, the Western lands would shrink in their map space in a startling fashion. But in the Senate is exhibited the outcome of the tendencies which statesmen like Gouverneur Morris saw so clearly, namely, the great power of the newer states by their equal representation in the Senate and their ability to take property by taxation from the wealthier section and to distribute it according to numbers, or even according to deficiencies, throughout the Union as a unit. Obviously there is here the certainty of a sectional clash of interests, not unlike those which led to Calhoun's South Carolina Exposition.

Sectionalism will hereafter be shaped by such new forces. We have become a nation comparable to all Europe in area, with settled geographic provinces which equal great European nations. We are in this sense an empire, a federation of sections, a union of potential nations. . . .

That sectionalism which is based on geographical regions has been in evidence from the early colonial period, but it has been obscured and modified by the influence of the unoccupied West. The states have been declining and are likely to continue to diminish in importance in our politics; but the groups of states called sections are likely to become more significant as the state declines. A study of votes in the federal House and Senate from the beginning of our national history reveals the fact that party voting has more often broken down than maintained itself on fundamental issues; that when these votes are mapped or tabulated by the congressional districts or states from which those who cast them came, instead of by alphabetical arrangement, a persistent sectional pattern emerges.

There has been in the earlier periods the sharp clash between New England and the South, with the Middle states divided and unstable, constituting a buffer zone and often holding the balance of power. Then, as population spread westward, the greater parties were composed of sectional wings — normally in the Republican Party there came to be a fairly solid conservative New England, a mixed and uncertain Middle Region, and a more radical North Central wing, ready in the shaping of legislation to join the Democrats in a kind of sectional bloc (even before the days of the bloc) to oppose the conservative and dominant Eastern wing. As time went on, the East North Central states came into closer connection with the Eastern wing, and in the West North Central lay the areas of radical dissent and of third party movements. Legislation was determined less by party than by sectional voting. Bills were shaped for final passage by compromises between wings or by alliances between sections. The maps of presidential elections showing majorities by counties look like maps of North against South; but there was always a concealed East and West which temporarily laid aside their differences.

I think it not too much to say that in party conventions as well as Congress the outcome of deliberations bears a striking resemblance to treaties between sections, suggestive of treaties between European nations in diplomatic congresses. But over an area equal to all Europe we found it possible to legislate, and we tempered asperities and avoided wars by a process of sectional give-and-take. Whether we shall continue to preserve our national, our intersectional, party organization in the sharper sectional conflicts of interest that are likely to accompany the settling down of population, the completer revelation of the influence of physical geography, remains to be seen.

As an illustration of the newer forms of sectionalism, take the movement for the Great Lakes-St. Lawrence deep waterway. Middle Western leaders are arguing that there is "in the heart of the continent a large area beyond the radius of logical rail haul for the movement of bulk commodities to either seacoast." "Nature," runs the argument, "which has indicated the extent of the area which sends its surplus to the Atlantic seaboard and to the Gulf and to the Pacific ports, has provided the American continent with one potential seacoast not yet utilized. Upon the map of economic divides indicated by geography — the Atlantic seaboard, the Gulf territory, and the Pacific slope — there is, as it were, an economic desert 1,000 miles east and west, 500 miles north and south beyond the radius of logical rail haul to either coast." The desire to give an outlet to what is called this "landlocked commerce to the coast" leads to the demand for "a fourth economic divide based upon the Great Lakes as linked with the ocean, giving to the coast of the Great Lakes access to marine commerce" and permitting the erection of each rail system upon the sea base. . . .

But while Duluth writers press the importance of what they call this "frustrated seaway," New York writers protest that the outlet should be through an enlarged Erie Canal, if there is to be such a water route at all, and it is argued that the projected St. Lawrence route would be "Our Dardanelles," liable to be closed against the West by Canadian or British government whenever disagreements invited this mode of co-

ercion. In New England, meantime, there are fears that Boston would be injured as a port, besides the loss of her advantages by seaborne commerce to the Pacific Coast. A few years ago Mayor Curley of Boston indignantly declared that such a waterway "would obliterate New England absolutely." . . .

There is a sense in which sectionalism is inevitable and desirable. There is and always has been a sectional geography in America based fundamentally upon geographic regions. There is a geography of political habit — a geography of opinion, of material interests, of racial stocks, of physical fitness, of social traits, of literature, of the distribution of men of ability, even of religious denominations. Professor Josiah Royce defined a "province" or section, in the sense in which I am using the word, as "any one part of a national domain which is geographically and socially sufficiently unified to have a true consciousness of its own ideals and customs and to possess a sense of its distinction from other parts of the country." It was the opinion of this eminent philosopher that the world needs now more than ever before the vigorous development of a highly organized provincial life to serve as a check upon mob psychology on a national scale, and to furnish that variety which is essential to vital growth and originality.

With this I agree. But I wish also to urge here, as I have elsewhere, that there is always the danger that the province or section shall think of itself naïvely as the nation, that New England shall think that America is merely New England writ large, or the Middle West shall think that America is really the Middle West writ large, and then proceed to denounce the sections that do not perceive the accuracy of this view as wicked or ignorant and un-American. This kind of nationalism is a sectional mirage, but it is common, and has been common to all the sections in their unconscious attitude if not in clear expression. It involves the assumption of a superiority of culture, of *Kultur*, to which good morals require that the nation as a whole must yield.

We must frankly face the fact that in this vast and heterogeneous nation, this sister of all Europe, regional geography is a fundamental fact; that the American peace has been achieved by restraining sectional selfishness and assertiveness and by coming to agreements rather than to reciprocal denunciation or to blows. . . .

Next I wish to emphasize the fact that these regional subdivisions are persistent. Often they remain politically the same for several generations. Probably the mass of voters inherit their party and their political ideas. Habit rather than reasoning is the fundamental factor in determining political affiliation of the mass of voters, and there is a geography, a habitat, of political habit.

There is the same geography of culture, though I am not able in the time that remains to develop this. For example, in a recent map of short story areas (of what the author calls local color areas) almost exactly the same regions are shown as appear on the maps which I have mentioned.

There is, then, a sectionalism of the regions within the larger divisions, a sectionalism of minority areas, sometimes protesting against the policies of the larger section in which they lie and finding more in common with similar regions outside of this section. Herein lies a limitation upon the larger section in case it attempts a drastic and subversive policy toward other sections. As Professor Holcombe has pointed out, in this kind of nation, in this vast congeries of sections, voters cannot hope to have a choice between parties any one of which will stand for all the measures which they oppose. The most they can reasonably hope for, he thinks,

is the formation of a party, resting upon a combination of sectional interests which are capable of cooperation in national politics without too much jealousy and friction, and including that particular

interest with which they are themselves most closely associated. No sectional interest is strong enough, alone and unaided, to control the federal government, and no major party can be formed with a fair prospect of domination in national politics which does not contain more or less incongruous elements.

With this I agree, and indeed have long been on record to this effect. It emphasizes the need for tolerance, for cooperation, for mutual sacrifices by the leaders of the various sections. Statesmanship in this nation consists not only in representing the special interests of the leader's own section but in finding a formula that will bring the different regions together in a common policy. . . .

The significance of the section in American history is that it is the faint image of a European nation and that we need to reexamine our history in the light of this fact. Our politics and our society have been shaped by sectional complexity and interplay not unlike what goes on between European nations. The greater sections are the result of the joint influence of the geologists' physiographic provinces and the colonizing stocks that entered them. The result is found in popular speech in which New England, the Middle States, the South, the Middle West, etc., are as common names as Massachusetts or Wisconsin. The census divisions are more definite and official designations. Of course, the boundary lines are not definite and fixed. Neither are those of European nations. These larger sections have taken their characteristic and peculiar attitudes in American civilization in general.

We have furnished to Europe the example of a continental federation of sections over an area equal to Europe itself, and, by substituting discussion and concession and compromised legislation for force, we have shown the possibility of international political parties, international legislative bodies, and international peace. Our party system and our variety in regional geography have helped to preserve the American peace. By having our combination of sections represented in a national legislative body, by possessing what may be called a League of Sections, comparable to a League of Nations, if it included political parties and a legislative body, we have enabled these minority sections to defend their interests and yet avoid the use of force.

The thing to be avoided, if the lessons of history are followed, is the insistence upon the particular interests and ideals of the section in which we live, without sympathetic comprehension of the ideals, the interests, and the rights of other sections. We must shape our national action to the fact of a vast and varied union of unlike sections.

95.

EDWIN ARLINGTON ROBINSON: "New England"

E. A. Robinson's famous sonnet "New England" was first published in the (London) Outlook *on November 3, 1923. Some American readers declared that Robinson had betrayed his New England heritage, but the poet protested that he was not attacking New England but instead New England's critics. The sonnet, revised, appeared in the volume* Dionysus in Doubt *in 1925. It is the revised version that is reprinted here. Robinson was probably the country's most admired poet during the Twenties; between 1921 and 1928 he was awarded the Pulitzer Prize three times.*

Source: *Collected Poems,* New York, 1929.

NEW ENGLAND

Here where the wind is always north-north-east
And children learn to walk on frozen toes,
Wonder begets an envy of all those
Who boil elsewhere with such a lyric yeast
Of love that you will hear them at a feast
Where demons would appeal for some repose,
Still clamoring where the chalice overflows
And crying wildest who have drunk the least.

Passion is here a soilure of the wits,
We're told, and Love a cross for them to bear;
Joy shivers in the corner where she knits
And Conscience always has the rocking-chair,
Cheerful as when she tortured into fits
The first cat that was ever killed by Care.

1926

96.

Hawthorne Daniel: Living and Dying on the Installment Plan

Personal incomes rose sharply during the 1920s, and with this rise went an equally sharp increase in the demand for consumer goods. Advertising had an important effect on the shaping of consumer preferences, and there was an unprecedented rise in consumer credit purchases. The monthly installment became a familiar feature of family budgets, as many people bought the newly available home appliances (especially refrigerators), radios, and automobiles "on time." The following article by Hawthorne Daniel that was published in January 1926 discussed these new financial habits of Americans.

Source: *World's Work,* January 1926: "Living and Dying on Installments."

So POPULAR has installment buying become, with purchasers as well as with manufacturers and merchants, that it is possible today to buy almost everything from candy to private yachts on the deferred payment plan. Within the last twenty years, and particularly within the last six, installment buying has grown like a mushroom, and now there are few things besides carfare, meals at restaurants, and theater tickets that cannot be paid for at so much down and so much periodically.

Installment buying is useful, is often advisable, and is very convenient. No doubt, it is carried too far in some cases. But customers can often get what they want only by this method of buying; and, since the country really has more money than it needs, the additional cost to the purchaser has not yet caused any vital difficulties.

Installment plan selling originated with the retailer. Conceivably it was first suggested by some customer who, knowing that he was in need of some implement, perhaps in order to increase his income, and realizing that he could buy it for cash only after a long period of saving during which he would have to exist on the reduced income that the lack of the implement enforced, proposed that he be permitted to buy it by paying a part of the total price, with the agreement that he would pay certain set sums regularly at certain set intervals. Such an arrangement, for such an object, is sound enough. It amounts to an advance of credit for the purpose of increasing production; and, while the theorizing economist might see in it some weaknesses, it is sufficiently practical to appeal to businessmen generally.

For many years this scheme of installment buying was in vogue, but with the hearty approval of few. The man who bought on the installment plan was generally considered a ne'er-do-well, and such arrangements were not highly popular. As time went on, however, it came to be recognized that the purchase of goods on installments sometimes encouraged thrift, and the opposition to it grew less violent. . . .

Between 1900 and 1910, however, the installment business began to grow more rapidly. Already there were firms in the field which had for the better part of a hundred years lived almost exclusively on installment business, and workable methods had long since been adopted.

From the point of view of the retailer, the trouble with the installment business had been that he, generally, could not afford to advance long-term credits to many of his customers. His capital was too small. Banks would not accept the agreements he had made with his installment customers as security for loans; and, because the manufacturer or the jobber demanded cash for the goods when the retailer purchased them, their sale on deferred payments was naturally limited. Some houses, of course, were able to finance themselves in this business, but they were few.

This situation brought about the development of a comparatively new feature in American business. That feature is the "finance company." Today, there are about 1,500 of them in the country, although twenty-five years ago they did not exist. And now, when a dealer sells an automobile, or a radio set, or a library table for part cash and the rest on installments, he takes the first payment and has the customer sign a paper agreeing to make his payments regularly, under penalty of forfeiting the goods. This paper, sometimes with other endorsements on it, often including his own, he takes to the finance company with which he is doing business. The finance company accepts the paper as security, and advances the amount represented by the paper, less an agreed upon discount. The retailer may then continue to collect the payments, paying them over to the finance company, or the finance company itself may attend to that; but, whatever happens, the retailer has got his price in cash for the goods he has sold. Generally he has got his full retail price, for, knowing that he has to pay the finance company a discount, he adds enough to the cash price of the goods to cover the difference.

The finance companies have made possible the rapid and tremendous expansion of installment business. But where did they originate? And who, in the last analysis, pays the money that operates their offices and makes possible the profits that now are calling more and more companies into the same field?

Some of these companies, as in the case of the General Motors Acceptance Company, are owned and operated by the companies whose products they help to sell. Others are independent firms, with their own financial arrangements. The Commercial Credit Company, which is the largest company of its kind in America, is of this type. Others are merely individuals, who, in a smaller way, have entered this field.

As to the profits they make — it is obvious that, as always, the consumer pays. Furthermore, and this is one of the uneconomic features of the business, he generally pays handsomely. As a matter of fact, the installment purchaser very often throws away one dollar in every ten by being an installment purchaser. Sometimes, it is true, it costs less than that, but sometimes, again, it costs more.

Suppose a housewife wants a sewing machine, which she may buy, with an electric motor attached, from the local electric light and power company. Let us say that she chooses a machine that retails at $50, and decides to pay $5 down and $5 a month. She will find, probably, that when she signs the paper she is agreeing to pay more than the cash price, which, of course, is proper. But how much more is she paying? A proper interest charge for well-secured loans is 6 percent. It would be proper in this case to charge a somewhat higher rate. But she finds that the machine is going to cost her $55. Each month she will reduce the amount she owes, and in ten months she will have completed her payments. She has owned, then, an average of $25 for ten months. Yet, on this loan, which is really what it is, she has paid $5 interest in advance. That is at the rate of 24 percent a year.

There has been a good deal of criticism of installment business of late. Credit men and others begin to see what they think is a great menace in it. It may be there, and no doubt is, if we consider only the more extreme cases and the "easiest" terms. Critics of the method cite examples — and they are numerous — of installment purchasers who have signed up to pay more in installments than their incomes amounted to. But the system cannot properly be blamed for the weaknesses of such purchasers. It *is* quite possible for the average person to "purchase" more on the installment plan than he can pay for. But it is equally possible with charge accounts. Yet we do not blame the system in this latter case. Invariably we blame the individual.

The greatest trouble with installment selling is that it is new. The entire history of finance companies is covered by twenty-five years, and yet, even in that short time in which to work out sound methods of doing business, there are a number of concerns that are solidly founded and conservative. The danger lies, not with the best but with the poorest of these companies. If a period of "hard times" should come, there will be many that will go to the wall, or will have difficulty in holding on. That will teach them a lesson, and they will not be so likely, thereafter, to overextend themselves. But it is not inconceivable that, before such a crisis comes, many of them will have strengthened their positions by following the sounder methods already being used by the best companies.

It is because they are in a new field in which the principles are not as yet absolutely clear that many companies are weak. Some, of course, as in all businesses, are questionable, but most of them are honest, even though they may be doing business along unsound lines. Given time in which to learn — given sound and successful companies to lead — given the desire on the part of the less sound companies to become sound (and that desire is generally there), and they may surmount their difficulties without any calamitous "period of readjustment."

The installment business has been built up largely by manufacturers desirous of increasing their output. So far it has worked, but there is an interesting possibility that seems to have been overlooked by many whose sales have been increased by this method.

Let us imagine a person who purchases everything on the installment plan. Let us suppose that, in doing so, he pays on the average 10 percent more for the goods than he buys. It is obvious, then, that 10 percent of his expenditures goes to pay the operating costs and profits of finance companies or whatever takes their place. Thus the customer can buy only nine-tenths as much as he could if he paid cash, and consequently the manufacturers who serve him, reduce by 10 percent the goods they can produce for him. Carried to extremes, then, the installment plan may end by forcing a reduction in output, which is the exact opposite of what it is supposed to do. Before the widespread use of the system this was not possible, but today, with more and more merchants utilizing it, there is a real possibility that it will end by killing the goose that lays the golden egg.

Recently, the National Association of Credit Men, an organization representing 30,000 merchants and manufacturers, adopted, at its national convention at Atlantic City, a carefully prepared statement concerning installment credits. It is a clear exposition of the conservative credit man's viewpoint and reads as follows:

Many business executives in their zeal for distribution have failed to understand the explosiveness of credit when it is improperly used. The events of recent years clearly show that the stimulation of business by the unwise use of credits is merely a temporary measure and has a reaction in the serious disturbance of business and prices.

Selling goods at the expense of safe credit tends to cheapen it, to make serious losses, and to disturb business morals. Selling goods on the installment plan when these goods are used for further production or to fill economic needs is perfectly proper, provided the contract has reasonable conditions. Selling goods on the installment plan for individual consumption or for mere pleasure is highly dangerous unless the distribution is reasonable and the credit used in such transactions causes no disturbance of the credit supply.

Making it easy for people to buy beyond their needs or to buy before they have saved enough to gratify their wishes tends to encourage a condition that hurts the human morale and supports a form of transaction for which credit is not primarily intended.

There has been built up in our country a large peak of installment credits, and it is wise for our business people to exercise caution, for undoubtedly in a credit pinch this condition would prove a very disturbing factor.

Some distributors have taken exception to this attitude of caution upon the part of the National Association of Credit Men, but it must be recognized that the preservation of credit is our chief obligation. We must be fearless in pointing out the dangers in the present situation, even though we should, in doing so, go against the ambitions of some for an extended distribution on long and installment credit terms.

If this viewpoint could be accepted by everyone engaged in installment plan selling, many of the dangers that are now evident would be eliminated. The system has been productive of very great benefits. It has made it possible for many people of moderate or even limited means to purchase articles that have been useful and desirable — articles that could or would not have been bought, except for the installment plan.

Many people are capable of wisely using this method of buying. Others are not. The danger to this latter class lies in the fact that they may get permanently ahead of their incomes, buying everything possible on time, and ultimately failing to make good on the payments when sickness or economic changes interrupt the smooth flow of their incomes. Undoubtedly the greater proportion of installment buyers are wage earners, who feel, whether justifiably or not, that their incomes are bound to continue to be regular. Of course, there is no means of telling in advance how regular one's income is going to be. But the person who changes from a pay-as-he-goes to a dollar-down-and-a-dollar-a-week buyer automatically reduces his buying power, and consequently will be able to have fewer of those things which he considers as desirable than if he had been content to save and pay cash.

Now, what are the advantages and disadvantages of this method of selling goods? The advantages are as follows:

First, it increases sales.

Second, it makes possible the purchase of goods that can, by their operation, pay for their own use.

Third, it makes possible the purchase of goods out of income instead of out of capital.

Fourth, it makes possible the purchase of goods by those who cannot pay cash.

On the other hand, installment buying has these disadvantages:

First, the cost to the consumer is always higher.

Second, through excessive use of the method, credit is being improperly used.

Third, irresponsible buyers buy many

things they cannot afford, and in extreme cases buy more than they can pay for.

Fourth, because consumers pay more for their goods, they can buy fewer goods, and consequently the factories will ultimately be forced to produce less for them.

There is much that can be said for the installment method of doing business. But because of its rapid growth there are noticeable weaknesses in it. At present it requires, primarily, more experience and a somewhat more rigid control. The control of the situation lies in the hands of the bankers. If they tighten their purse strings to the borrower who is using the installment system improperly and to excess, the business will come back to normal without any undue difficulties. It is here to stay, for already it has proved its usefulness to manufacturers, merchants, and consumers.

97.

E. E. Cummings: "next to of course god"

E. E. Cummings was one of the many poets and intellectuals who turned bitterly during the Twenties against the "glory" of war and, in their profound disillusionment, launched an assault on patriotism in every form. The attack was not entirely unwarranted, for not only had the nation undergone an orgy of sentimental patriotism during World War I, but the rhetoric of statesmen on both sides had made almost every expression of love of country seem a cliché. The insincerity of such proclamations is satirized in this famous poem of Cummings, published in the volume is 5 in 1926.

Source: *Collected Poems,* New York, 1963.

next to of course god

"next to of course god america i
love you land of the pilgrims' and so forth oh
say can you see by the dawn's early my
country 'tis of centuries come and go
and are no more what of it we should worry
in every language even deafanddumb
thy sons acclaim your glorious name by gorry
by jingo by gee by gosh by gum
why talk of beauty what could be more beautiful than these heroic happy dead
who rushed like lions to the roaring slaughter
they did not stop to think they died instead
then shall the voice of liberty be mute?"

He spoke. And drank rapidly a glass of water

98.

Hiram W. Evans: The Klan's Fight for Americanism

The Ku Klux Klan had been revived in 1915, but it was not until after the war that it exhibited the startling increase in membership that made it a force to be reckoned with during the 1920s. Much of its success was owing to the vigorous leadership of Hiram Wesley Evans, a Dallas dentist who became the Klan's Imperial Wizard in November 1922. Membership exceeded 4,000,000 in the mid-Twenties, and the political influence of the Klan in areas of the South and Middle West was strong enough to control state legislatures and governorships. By the end of the decade the organization had been widely discredited and its membership fell off. The following selection is taken from an article by Evans that outlined the goals of the Klan.

Source: *North American Review*, March-April-May 1926, pp. 33-63.

THE GREATEST ACHIEVEMENT so far has been to formulate, focus, and gain recognition for an idea — the idea of preserving and developing America first and chiefly for the benefit of the children of the pioneers who made America, and only and definitely along the lines of the purpose and spirit of those pioneers. The Klan cannot claim to have created this idea — it has long been a vague stirring in the souls of the plain people. But the Klan can fairly claim to have given it purpose, method, direction, and a vehicle.

When the Klan first appeared, the nation was in the confusion of sudden awakening from the lovely dream of the melting pot, disorganized and helpless before the invasion of aliens and alien ideas. After ten years of the Klan it is in arms for defense. This is our great achievement. The second is more selfish; we have won the leadership in the movement for Americanism. Except for a few lonesome voices, almost drowned by the clamor of the alien and the alien-minded "Liberal," the Klan alone faces the invader.

This is not to say that the Klan has gathered into its membership all who are ready to fight for America. The Klan is the champion, but it is not merely an organization. It is an idea, a faith, a purpose, an organized crusade. No recruit to the cause has ever been really lost. Though men and women drop from the ranks, they remain with us in purpose and can be depended on fully in any crisis. Also, there are many millions who have never joined but who think and feel and — when called on — fight with us. This is our real strength, and no one who ignores it can hope to understand America today.

Other achievements of these ten years have been the education of the millions of our own membership in citizenship, the suppression of much lawlessness and increase of good government wherever we have become strong, the restriction of immigration, and the defeat of the Catholic attempt to seize the Democratic Party. All these we have helped, and all are important.

The outstanding proof of both our influence and our service, however, has been in creating, outside our ranks as well as in them, not merely the growing national concentration on the problems of Americanism but also a growing sentiment against radicalism, cosmopolitanism, and alienism of all kinds. We have produced instead a sane and progressive conservatism along national lines. We have enlisted our racial instincts for the work of preserving and developing our American traditions and customs. This was most strikingly shown in the elections last fall when the conservative reaction amazed all politicians — especially the La Follette rout in the Northwest. This reaction added enormously to the plurality of the President, the size of which was the great surprise of the election. . . .

The Klan, therefore, has now come to speak for the great mass of Americans of the old pioneer stock. We believe that it does fairly and faithfully represent them, and our proof lies in their support. To understand the Klan, then, it is necessary to understand the character and present mind of the mass of old-stock Americans. The mass, it must be remembered, as distinguished from the intellectually mongrelized "Liberals."

These are, in the first place, a blend of various peoples of the so-called Nordic race, the race which, with all its faults, has given the world almost the whole of modern civilization. The Klan does not try to represent any people but these.

There is no need to recount the virtues of the American pioneers; but it is too often forgotten that in the pioneer period a selective process of intense rigor went on. From the first, only hardy, adventurous, and strong men and women dared the pioneer dangers; from among these, all but the best died swiftly, so that the new Nordic blend which became the American race was bred up to a point probably the highest in history. This remarkable race character, along with the new-won continent and the new-created nation, made the inheritance of the old-stock Americans the richest ever given to a generation of men.

In spite of it, however, these Nordic Americans for the last generation have found themselves increasingly uncomfortable, and finally deeply distressed. There appeared first confusion in thought and opinion, a groping and hesitancy about national affairs and private life alike, in sharp contrast to the clear, straightforward purposes of our earlier years. There was futility in religion, too, which was in many ways even more distressing. Presently we began to find that we were dealing with strange ideas; policies that always sounded well but somehow always made us still more uncomfortable.

Finally came the moral breakdown that has been going on for two decades. One by one all our traditional moral standards went by the boards or were so disregarded that they ceased to be binding. The sacredness of our Sabbath, of our homes, of chastity, and finally even of our right to teach our own children in our own schools fundamental facts and truths were torn away from us. Those who maintained the old standards did so only in the face of constant ridicule.

Along with this went economic distress. The assurance for the future of our children dwindled. We found our great cities and the control of much of our industry and commerce taken over by strangers, who stacked the cards of success and prosperity against us. Shortly they came to dominate our government. The bloc system by which this was done is now familiar to all. Every kind of inhabitant except the Americans gathered in groups which operated as units in politics, under orders of corrupt, self-seeking, and un-American leaders who both by purchase and threat enforced their demands on politicians. Thus it came about that the interests of Americans were always the last to be considered by either national or city governments, and that the native Americans were constantly discriminated against, in business, in legislation, and in administrative government.

So the Nordic American today is a stranger in large parts of the land his fathers gave him. Moreover, he is a most unwelcome stranger, one much spit upon, and one to whom even the right to have his own opinions and to work for his own interests is now denied with jeers and revilings. "We must Americanize the Americans," a distinguished immigrant said recently. Can anything more clearly show the state to which the real American has fallen in this country which was once his own?

Our falling birth rate, the result of all this, is proof of our distress. We no longer feel that we can be fair to children we bring into the world unless we can make sure from the start that they shall have capital or education or both, so that they need never compete with those who now fill the lower rungs of the ladder of success. We dare no longer risk letting our youth "make its own way" in the conditions under which we live. So even our unborn children are being crowded out of their birthright!

All this has been true for years, but it was the World War that gave us our first hint of the real cause of our troubles and began to crystallize our ideas. The war revealed that millions whom we had allowed to share our heritage and prosperity, and whom we had assumed had become part of us, were in fact not wholly so. They had other loyalties: each was willing — anxious! — to sacrifice the interests of the country that had given him shelter to the interests of the one he was supposed to have cast off; each in fact did use the freedom and political power we had given him against ourselves whenever he could see any profit for his older loyalty.

This, of course, was chiefly in international affairs, and the excitement caused by the discovery of disloyalty subsided rapidly after the war ended. But it was not forgotten by the Nordic Americans. They had been awakened and alarmed; they began to suspect that the hyphenism which had been shown was only a part of what existed; their quiet was not that of renewed sleep but of strong men waiting very watchfully. And presently they began to form decisions about all those aliens who were Americans for profit only.

They decided that even the crossing of saltwater did not dim a single spot on a leopard; that an alien usually remains an alien no matter what is done to him, what veneer of education he gets, what oaths he takes, nor what public attitudes he adopts. They decided that the melting pot was a ghastly failure and remembered that the very name was coined by a member of one of the races — the Jews — which most determinedly refuses to melt.

They decided that in every way, as well as in politics, the alien in the vast majority of cases is unalterably fixed in his instincts, character, thought, and interests by centuries of racial selection and development, that he thinks first for his own people, works only with and for them, cares entirely for their interests, considers himself always one of them, and never an American. They decided that in character, instincts, thought, and purposes — in his whole soul — an alien remains fixedly alien to America and all it means.

They saw, too, that the alien was tearing down the American standard of living, especially in the lower walks. It became clear that while the American can outwork the alien, the alien can so far underlive the American as to force him out of all competitive labor. So they came to realize that the Nordic can easily survive and rule and increase if he holds for himself the advantages won by strength and daring of his ancestors in times of stress and peril, but that if he surrenders those advantages to the peoples who could not share the stress, he will soon be driven below the level at which he can exist by their low standards, low living, and fast breeding. And they saw that the low-standard aliens of eastern and southern Europe were doing just that thing to us.

They learned, though more slowly, that alien ideas are just as dangerous to us as the aliens themselves, no matter how plausible such ideas may sound. With most of the plain people this conclusion is based simply on the fact that the alien ideas do not work well for them. Others went deeper and came to understand that the differences in racial background, in breeding, instinct, character, and emotional point of view are more important than logic. So ideas which may be perfectly healthy for an alien may also be poisonous for Americans.

Finally, they learned the great secret of the propagandists — that success in corrupting public opinion depends on putting out the subversive ideas without revealing their source. They came to suspect that "prejudice" against foreign ideas is really a protective device of nature against mental food that may be indigestible. They saw, finally, that the alien leaders in America act on this theory and that there is a steady flood of alien ideas being spread over the country, always carefully disguised as American.

As they learned all this, the Nordic Americans have been gradually arousing themselves to defend their homes and their own kind of civilization. They have not known just how to go about it; the idealist philanthropy and good-natured generosity which led to the philosophy of the melting pot have died hard. Resistance to the peaceful invasion of the immigrant is no such simple matter as snatching up weapons and defending frontiers, nor has it much spectacular emotionalism to draw men to the colors.

The old-stock Americans are learning, however. They have begun to arm themselves for this new type of warfare. Most important, they have broken away from the fetters of the false ideals and philanthropy which put aliens ahead of their own children and their own race. . . .

One more point about the present attitude of the old-stock American: he has revived and increased his long-standing distrust of the Roman Catholic Church. It is for this that the native Americans, and the Klan as their leader, are most often denounced as intolerant and prejudiced. This is not because we oppose the Catholic more than we do the alien, but because our enemies recognize that patriotism and race loyalty cannot safely be denounced, while our own tradition of religious freedom gives them an opening here, if they can sufficiently confuse the issue.

The fact is, of course, that our quarrel with the Catholics is not religious but political. The Nordic race is, as is well known, almost entirely Protestant, and there remains in its mental heritage an anti-Catholic attitude based on lack of sympathy with the Catholic psychology, on the historic opposition of the Roman Catholic Church to the Nordics' struggle for freedom and achievement, and on the memories of persecutions. . . .

This is the general state of mind of the Nordic Americans of the pioneer stock today. Many of them do not understand the reasons for their beliefs so fully as I have stated them, but the state of mind is there beyond doubt, and the reasons are true at all vital points. It is inevitable that these people are now in revolt. This is the movement to which the Klan, more through Providence than its own wisdom, has begun to give leadership.

The Ku Klux Klan, in short, is an organization which gives expression, direction and purpose to the most vital instincts, hopes, and resentments of the old-stock Americans, provides them with leadership, and is enlisting and preparing them for militant, constructive action toward fulfilling their racial and national destiny. Madison Grant summed up in a single sentence the grievances, purpose, and type of membership of the Klan: "Our farmers and artisans . . . of American blood, to recognize and meet this danger." The Klan literally is once more the embattled American farmer and artisan, coordinated into a disciplined and growing army, and launched upon a definite crusade for Americanism!

This providential history of the Klan and the providential place it has come to hold give it certain definite characteristics. The disadvantages that go with them, as well as the advantages, may as well be admitted at once.

We are a movement of the plain people, very weak in the matter of culture, intellectual support, and trained leadership. We are demanding, and we expect to win, a return of power into the hands of the everyday, not highly cultured, not overly intellectualized, but entirely unspoiled and not de-Americanized, average citizen of the old stock. Our members and leaders are all of this class — the opposition of the intellectuals and liberals who held the leadership, betrayed Americanism, and from whom we expect to wrest control, is almost automatic.

This is undoubtedly a weakness. It lays us open to the charge of being "hicks" and "rubes" and "drivers of secondhand Fords." We admit it. Far worse, it makes it hard for us to state our case and advocate our crusade in the most effective way, for most of us lack skill in language. Worst of all, the need of trained leaders constantly hampers our progress and leads to serious blunders and internal troubles. If the Klan ever should fail, it would be from this cause. All this we on the inside know far better than our critics, and regret more. Our leadership is improving, but for many years the Klan will be seeking better leaders, and the leaders praying for greater wisdom.

Serious as this is, and strange though our attitude may seem to the intellectuals, it does not worry us greatly. Every popular movement has suffered from just this handicap, yet the popular movements have been the mainsprings of progress and have usually had to win against the "best people" of their time. Moreover, we can depend on getting this intellectual backing shortly. It is notable that when the plain people begin to win with one of their movements, such as the Klan, the very intellectuals who have scoffed and fought most bitterly presently begin to dig up sound — at least well-sounding! — logic in support of the success. The movement, so far as can be judged, is neither hurt nor helped by this process. . . .

The Klan does not believe that the fact that it is emotional and instinctive rather than coldly intellectual is a weakness. All action comes from emotion rather than from ratiocination. Our emotions and the instincts on which they are based have been bred into us for thousands of years; far longer than reason has had a place in the human brain. They are the many times distilled product of experience; they still operate much more surely and promptly than reason can. For centuries those who obeyed them have lived and carried on the race; those in whom they were weak, or who failed to obey, have died. They are the foundations of our American civilization, even more than our great historic documents; they can be trusted where the fine-haired reasoning of the denatured intellectuals cannot.

Thus the Klan goes back to the American racial instincts, and to the common sense which is their first product, as the basis of its beliefs and methods. The fundamentals of our thought are convictions, not mere opinions. We are pleased that modern research is finding scientific backing for these convictions. We do not need them ourselves; we know that we are right in the same sense that a good Christian knows that he has been saved and that Christ lives — a thing which the intellectual can never understand. These convictions are no more to be argued about than is our love for our children; we are merely willing to state them for the enlightenment and conversion of others.

There are three of these great racial instincts, vital elements in both the historic and the present attempts to build an Ameri-ca which shall fulfill the aspirations and justify the heroism of the men who made the nation. These are the instincts of loyalty to the white race, to the traditions of America, and to the spirit of Protestantism, which has been an essential part of Americanism ever since the days of Roanoke and Plymouth Rock. They are condensed into the Klan slogan: "Native, white, Protestant supremacy."

99.

HENRY PRATT FAIRCHILD: American Nationality and the Melting Pot

According to the "melting pot" theory (the phrase had first been used at the turn of the century by the English dramatist Israel Zangwill) the cultural and racial characteristics of the immigrant populations that had flowed into the country up until 1920 had been melted down — assimilated — into the mainstream of American life, with a consequent enrichment of that mainstream. Henry Pratt Fairchild, a sociologist and demographer at New York University, attacked the theory in his book The Melting-Pot Mistake, *a portion of which is reprinted here. Fairchild, not satisfied with the anti-immigrant legislation of the early 1920s that for the first time in American history had reversed the traditional open-door policy on immigration, advocated even more stringent measures that would curb and shape the population by means of birth control and eugenics.*

Source: *The Melting-Pot Mistake*, Boston, 1926: "The Duty of America."

IT IS SO OBVIOUS as to be almost a platitude that the residents of the United States enjoy special privileges. They are certainly more favorably situated than the people of any other great nation on earth with reference to their material well-being, and probably also with respect to their political independence and various other social relationships. The basic stimulus to immigration lies in the desire of persons less fortunately situated to share in these advantages. A policy of restriction makes it impossible for them to do so. It reserves the enjoyment of these unique blessings to those who happen to be established in the country at any particular time and to their descendants.

Is not such a policy, then, on the very face of it, narrow and illiberal? As these words are being written, the morning paper brings an announcement of a proposal made by a person who is described as the "organizer of the Liberal Immigration League" to the effect that in the future there shall be no limit to the number of immigrants, though a rigid selection and control is to be exercised.

If the United States is to be thought of as a gigantic pork barrel or plum pudding, and if only the present and the immediate future are to be considered, an excellent case can be made out for this doctrine. Here is an accumulation of good things which fate has placed in the possession of 110 million people. The remaining 1.6 billion of the earth's population would like their share. Very well! Let them come and take it; and the smaller the portions into which it is divided, the more exactly will the cause of liberalism be served.

It is to reveal the fallacy of just such an interpretation that so much space has been devoted to the exposition of the United States as a nation. The great question of liberalism is: What would be left of the American nation, and what effect would its fate have on the future destiny of mankind, if the natural desire of foreign individuals to share in American advantages were left unrestrained? It has already been suggested that the idea that all immigrants benefit by casting in their lot with the United States is not nearly so well founded on fact as we should like to believe. But for purposes of argument, let it be granted that all immigrants do improve their situation by coming to this country. Does their gain mean a general rise in the average well-being of mankind, not only in the present but in the generations to come?

The answer to this question depends upon what happens to the United States as a result of their coming and to the countries of Europe as a result of their leaving.

As far as the United States is concerned, the first and most direct effect of unrestricted immigration is a retardation, if not a definite lowering, of the standard of living of the common people. It is the search for a higher standard of living which, more than anything else, brings the immigrant here. The standard of the American is higher than his. He can raise his by coming. If in the process he lowers the standard of the American, that is no concern of his. Nor

would this lowering of the American standard, however repugnant to the sentiment of American patriotism, be inconsistent with the principle of liberalism if the final result were an improvement in the general average of comfort of all concerned, native and foreigner alike. If the total gain won by the foreigners more than offset the total loss suffered by the natives, the result would be a more even distribution of benefits wholly consistent with liberalism.

Such, however, is not the case. The nature of the competition between standards of living is such that the lower pulls down the upper much more than it elevates itself. Each successively lower standard that is allowed to enter the competition reduces the level just so much more. The truth has long been recognized by students of the problem, and forcibly expressed by General Francis A. Walker, that the ultimate outcome of unrestricted immigration is a progressive deterioration of the standard until no "difference of *economic level* exists between our population and that of the most degraded communities abroad." Certainly the ideal of liberalism is not to be found in such a denouement as this.

But what may be expected in the countries of source while this is taking place in the country of destination? Does not the departure of their surplus population so relieve the pressure at home as to produce a compensating improvement in their social and economic situation? The complete answer to this question involves a technical analysis too long and complicated to be introduced here. Suffice it to say that the almost unanimous conclusion of scientific students of the problem is that the kind of exodus represented by ordinary emigration produces no relief whatever in the pressure of population and may even make it worse. To put it in concrete terms, we could draw off a million Chinamen a year from China for fifty years, or any other length of time, and at the end of the period there would be just as many Chinamen in China as if not one had emigrated. The same principle holds good for any overcrowded country. No such country can hope to find any permanent relief from its problems of overpopulation — whether they be unemployment, pauperism, disease, or anything else — by shipping its excess nationals to a less crowded region.

There can be only one conclusion. The eventual effect of an unrestricted immigration movement, governed only by the economic self-interest of the migrating individuals, must under modern conditions be a progressive depression of the standard of living of mankind as a whole. It is, therefore, contrary to the liberal spirit, and the label so vigorously exploited and so confidently flaunted in the face of the American public is found to have been falsely applied.

But there is more to the question than this. Other interests than the economic call for consideration.

It has been repeatedly stated that the consequence of nonassimilation is the destruction of nationality. This is the central truth of the whole problem of immigration, and it cannot be overemphasized. An immigration movement that did not involve nonassimilation might be tolerated, though it might have other evil consequences which would condemn it. But an immigration movement that does involve nonassimilation — like the movement to the United States during the last fifty years at least — is a blow at the very heart of nationality and cannot be endured if nationality is conceived to have any value whatsoever. The American nationality has already been compared with a plant. There is, indeed, a striking parallelism between a nation and a noble tree — for instance, one of our own incomparable redwoods — which may be followed a little further, not with any expectation or desire of popularizing a new symbol but merely for the clarification that it affords.

A nation, like a tree, is a living, vital thing. Growth is one of its conditions of life; and when it ceases to grow, there is good reason to fear that it is about to decay and die. Every nation, like every tree, belongs to a certain general type, but it is also uniquely individual within that type. Its peculiar form is determined by various forces, some of which are internal and some external. No nation need fear the changes which come as the result of the operation of natural, wholesome internal forces, that is to say, the ideas and activities of its own true members. These forces may, in the course of time, produce a form and character wholly different from the original, just as the mature plant may have an entirely different aspect from the seedling.

This is nothing to be dreaded or opposed. No change that represents the natural evolution of internal forces need be dreaded. But there are other forces which originate without which threaten not only the form and character but also the vigor and perhaps the very life of the nation. Some of these are the forcible attacks of other nations, like the crowding of trees upon each other, or the unwholesome influence of alien ideas which may be compared with harsh and uncongenial winds which blow upon trees, dwarfing and distorting them.

Most dangerous of all, however, are those foreign forces which, among trees, are represented by minute, hostile organisms that make their way into the very tissue of the tree itself and feed upon its life substances, and among nations by alien individuals who are accepted as immigrants and by a process of "boring from within" (in something much more than a mere trade-union sense) sap the very vitality of their host. In so doing the immigrants may be merely following out their natural and defensible impulses without any hostility toward the receiving nation, any more than the parasites upon a tree may be considered to have any hostility to the tree. Nor can the immigrants, any more than the parasites, be expected to foresee that their activities will eventually destroy the very organism upon which they depend for their existence. The simple fact is that they are alien particles, not assimilated, and, therefore, wholly different from the foreign particles which the tree takes in the form of food and transforms into cells of its own body.

Herein is found the full justification for a special application of the principles of freedom of speech to aliens differing widely from the interpretation in the case of citizens. This is particularly true with reference to attempts at free speech which take the character of criticisms of the form of government or the processes of the governing agencies. The citizen is presumed to be familiar with the genius and spirit of his own government and to be sincerely devoted to it. No check should be put upon his criticisms as long as they are honest and candid. The criticisms of its own citizens are the wholesome internal forces of change in any government, out of which new and more highly developed forms will emerge.

But the criticisms and the attacks of the alien may be malicious and are certain to be ignorant and ill-informed. The alien, just because he is an alien, is not in a position to comprehend the meaning of the various political and social phenomena which he observes about him, he is incapable of interpreting them in the light of their true significance and bearing on the entire scheme of government, and because he has a potential audience of millions equally alien, he may do incalculable harm. False doctrines may be infinitely dangerous even though held by those who cannot express them in votes.

It actually seems as if each nation developed an immunity to certain ideas, just as the trees in a given locality develop a practical immunity to the pests of their own vicinity. Our own Department of Agriculture is constantly on the alert to prevent the introduction of foreign parasites against· which our native plants have no effective protec-

tion. Numerous cases are on record — one of the most spectacular being the chestnut trees of New England — where a type of plant which from time immemorial had been able to hold its own in its native balance of nature has been devastated if not exterminated by the sudden introduction of a parasite against which it had not developed a means of protection. So in a nation, ideas are constantly circulating which are inherently destructive but against which the natives have developed an adequate protection so that they produce no serious harm. But the sudden entrance of new ideas or of foreign varieties of old ideas may find the country unprepared to counteract them. The safest way to guard against such a calamity is to reduce to a small figure the number of those newcomers by which such alien ideas may be introduced.

These considerations do not in any measure justify treating the alien as if he had no rights and were not entitled to express himself on any subject, as has sometimes been done by overzealous patriots under the stress of acute national hysteria. But they do justify the exercise of a wholly different type of control over the public utterances of aliens from that imposed upon citizens, and even more the exclusion of those who in the nature of the case are likely to indulge in un-American utterances because they are imbued with un-American ideas.

There are, it should be noted, a few foreigners whose attitude toward the United States is more positively destructive than that of those who simply cannot understand America because they are not Americans. Among this number are those, very few altogether, who make it their business to launch direct attacks upon the fundamental form and institutions of the American government. To them the deportation acts may most appropriately be applied. But much more dangerous are those who insolently regard the United States as a mere economic catch basin, to which they have come to get out of it what they can, confessing no obligation to it, recognizing no claim on its part to the preservation of its own identity, displaying no intention to contribute to its development or to remain permanently as a part of it.

One type of this group looks forward to a return to the native land as soon as America has been bled of all it has to offer. Another type looks upon America as a sort of no man's land, or every man's land, upon which they can develop a separate group existence along any lines that they see fit. For instance, we are told upon the best of authority that there has already developed in the United States a distinct Polish-American society, which is neither truly Polish nor truly American, but which has a vigorous and distinct character and existence of its own.

More dangerous, however, than any foreign elements are certain individuals of native birth who in an excess of zeal for the foreigner, emanating, it may be presumed, from a misguided and sentimental though well-meaning reaction from the attitude of ethnocentric superiority so characteristic of many Americans, go to the extreme of denying any merit in American institutions and ignoring any claim on the part of America to the perpetuation of its peculiar existence. They are ready to throw any and all distinctly American characteristics into the discard if only we can absorb the "dear foreigners" into our midst. They applaud any expression of national pride on the part of a foreigner as an evidence of sturdy and commendable patriotism but condemn a similar expression on the part of an American as narrow bigotry.

A representative of this type, apparently of native extraction, was talking at an americanization meeting called by a prominent commercial organization in one of our great cities. Working herself up to a fine pitch of emotionalism, she finally exclaimed, "The noblest and finest persons I ever knew in my life were newly arrived immigrants, and the meanest, the lowest, the most contemptible were descendants of the old New England stock!" This was the keynote of the meeting and called forth a tumult of applause.

The central factor in the world organization of the present is nationalism. Strong, self-conscious nationalities are indispensable to the efficient ordering and peaceful promotion of international relations. Every well-developed nationality is a priceless product of social evolution. Each has its peculiar contribution to make to future progress. The destruction of any one would be an irreparable loss to mankind.

Among the nations of the world, America stands out unique, and in many ways preeminent. Favored by nature above all other nations in her physical endowment, favored by history in the character of her people and the type of her institutions, she has a role to play in the development of human affairs which no other nation can play. Foremost in this role is the development of true democracy. In America the stage is set more favorably than anywhere else for the great drama of the common man. Here if anywhere the conditions are auspicious for the upward movement of the masses. If democracy fails in America, where shall we look for it to succeed?

Any program or policy which interferes in the slightest degree with the prosecution of this great enterprise must be condemned as treason to our high destiny. Any yielding to a specious and superficial humanitarianism which threatens the material, political, and social standards of the average American must be branded as a violation of our trust. The highest service of America to mankind is to point the way, to demonstrate the possibilities, to lead onward to the goal of human happiness. Any force that tends to impair our capacity for leadership is a menace to mankind and a flagrant violation of the spirit of liberalism.

Unrestricted immigration was such a force. It was slowly, insidiously, irresistibly eating away the very heart of the United States. What was being melted in the great Melting Pot, losing all form and symmetry, all beauty and character, all nobility and usefulness, was the American nationality itself. Let the justification for checking this force for all time be voiced in the words of two distinguished foreigners. First, Rabbi Joel Blau: "The chief duty that a people owes both itself and the world is reverence for its own soul, the mystic center of its being." Then, Gustave LeBon: "A preponderating influence of foreigners is a sure solvent of the existence of states. It takes away from a people its most precious possession — its soul."

100.

H. L. MENCKEN: Ring Lardner

H. L. Mencken's services to American literature would have been memorable if he had discovered no one except Ring Lardner. Lardner, a sportswriter turned short story writer, depicted in a number of biting satires the effects of the cult of success on ambitious, vulgar, small-town, and lower-class characters. Lardner had already attained substantial popular success, but Mencken, in the following favorable critique of a collection of short stories, brought him to the attention of the intellectuals. The review appeared in 1926.

Source: *Prejudices: Fifth Series*, New York, 1926, pp. 49-56.

A FEW YEARS AGO a young college professor, eager to make a name for himself, brought out a laborious "critical" edition of *Sam Slick*, by Judge Thomas C. Haliburton, eighty-seven years after its first publication. It turned out to be quite unreadable — a dreadful series of archaic jocosities about varieties of *Homo americanus* long perished and forgotten, in a dialect now intelligible only to paleophilologists. Sometimes I have a fear that the same fate awaits Ring Lardner.

The professors of his own day, of course, are quite unaware of him, save perhaps as a low zany to be enjoyed behind the door. They would no more venture to whoop him up publicly and officially than their predecessors of 1880 would have ventured to whoop up Mark Twain, or their remoter predecessors of 1837 would have dared to say anything for Haliburton. In such matters the academic mind, being chiefly animated by a fear of sneers, works very slowly. So slowly, indeed, does it work that it usually works too late. By the time Mark Twain got into the textbooks for sophomores, two-thirds of his compositions, as the Young Intellectuals say, had already begun to date; by the time Haliburton was served up as a sandwich between introduction and notes, he was already dead.

As I say, I suspect sadly that Lardner is doomed to go the same route. His stories, it seems to me, are superbly adroit and amusing; no other contemporary American, sober or gay, writes better. But I doubt that they last: our grandchildren will wonder what they are about. It is not only, or even mainly, that the dialect that fills them will pass, though that fact is obviously a serious handicap in itself. It is principally that the people they depict will pass, that Lardner's Low Down Americans — his incomparable baseball players, pugs, songwriters, Elks, small-town Rotarians, and golf caddies — are flitting figures of a transient civilization, and doomed to be as puzzling and soporific, in the year 2000, as Haliburton's Yankee clock peddler is today.

The fact — if I may assume it to be a fact — is certain not to be set against Lardner's account; on the contrary, it is, in its way, highly complimentary to him. For he has deliberately applied himself, not to the anatomizing of the general human soul, but to the meticulous histological study of a few salient individuals of his time and nation, and he has done it with such subtle and penetrating skill that one must belong to his time and nation to follow him. I doubt that anyone who is not familiar with professional ball players, intimately and at first hand, will ever comprehend the full merit of the amazing sketches in *You Know Me, Al*; I doubt that anyone who has not given close and deliberate attention to the American vulgate will ever realize how magnificently Lardner handles it.

He has had more imitators, I suppose, than any other living American writer, but has he any actual rivals? If so, I have yet to hear of them. They all try to write the speech of the streets as adeptly and as amusingly as he writes it, and they all fall short of him; the next best is miles and miles behind him. And they are all inferior in observation, in sense of character, in shrewdness and insight. His studies, to be sure, are never very profound; he makes no attempt to get at the primary springs of human motive; all his people share the same amiable stupidity, the same transparent vanity, the same shallow swinishness; they are all human Fords in bad repair, and alike at bottom. But if he thus confines himself to the surface, it yet remains a fact that his investigations on that surface are extraordinarily alert, ingenious, and brilliant — that the character he finally sets before us, however roughly articulated as to bones, is so astoundingly realistic as to epidermis that the effect is indistinguishable from that of life itself. The old man in "The Golden Honeymoon" is not merely well done; he is perfect. And so is the girl in "Some Like Them Cold." And so, even, is the idiotic Frank X. Farrell in "Alibi Ike" — an extravagant grotesque and yet quite real from glabella to calcaneus.

Lardner knows more about the management of the short story than all of its professors. His stories are built very carefully, and yet they seem to be wholly spontaneous, and even formless. He has grasped the primary fact that no conceivable ingenuity can save a story that fails to show a recognizable and interesting character; he knows that a good character sketch is always a good story, no matter what its structure. Perhaps he gets less attention than he ought to get, even among the anti-academic critics, because his people are all lowly boors. For your reviewer of books, like every other sort of American, is always vastly impressed by fashionable pretensions. He belongs to the white collar class of labor, and shares its prejudices. He praises F. Scott Fitzgerald's stories of country-club flappers eloquently, and overlooks Fitzgerald's other stories, most of which are much better. He can't rid himself of the feeling that Edith Wharton, whose people have butlers, is a better novelist than Willa Cather, whose people, in the main, dine in their kitchens.

He lingers under the spell of Henry James, whose most humble character, at any rate of the later years, was at least an Englishman, and hence superior.

Lardner, so to speak, hits such critics under the belt. He not only fills his stories with people who read the tabloids, say "Shake hands with my friend," and buy diamond rings on the installment plan; he also shows them having a good time in the world, and quite devoid of inferiority complexes. They amuse him sardonically, but he does not pity them. A fatal error! The moron, perhaps, has a place in fiction, as in life, but he is not to be treated too easily and casually. It must be shown that he suffers tragically because he cannot abandon the plow to write poetry, or the sample case to study for opera. Lardner is more realistic. If his typical hero has a secret sorrow it is that he is too old to take up osteopathy and too much in dread of his wife to venture into bootlegging.

Of late a sharply acrid flavor has got into Lardner's buffoonery. His baseball players and fifth-rate pugilists, beginning in his first stories as harmless jackasses, gradually convert themselves into loathsome scoundrels. The same change shows itself in Sinclair Lewis; it is difficult, even for an American, to contemplate the American without yielding to something hard to distinguish from moral indignation. Turn, for example, to the sketches in the volume called *The Love Nest*. The first tells the story of a cinema queen married to a magnate of the films. On the surface she seems to be nothing but a noodle, but underneath there is a sewer; the woman is such a pig that she makes one shudder. Again, he investigates another familiar type: the village practical joker. The fellow in one form or other, has been laughed at since the days of Aristophanes. But here is a mercilessly realistic examination of his dung-hill humor, and of its effects upon decent people.

A third figure is a successful theatrical manager: he turns out to have the professional competence of a chiropractor and the honor of a Prohibition agent. A fourth is a writer of popular songs: stealing other men's ideas has become so fixed a habit with him that he comes to believe that he has an actual right to them. A fifth is a trained nurse — but I spare you this dreadful nurse. The rest are bores of the homicidal type. One gets the effect, communing with the whole gang, of visiting a museum of anatomy. They are as shocking as what one encounters there — but in every detail they are as unmistakably real.

Lardner conceals his new savagery, of course, beneath his old humor. It does not flag. No man writing among us has greater skill at the more extravagant varieties of jocosity. He sees startling and revelatory likeness between immensely disparate things, and he is full of pawky observations and bizarre comments. Two baseball players are palavering, and one of them, Young Jake, is boasting of his conquests during Spring practice below the Potomac. "Down South ain't here!" replies the other. "Those dames in some of those swamps, they lose their head when they see a man with shoes on!" The two proceed to the discussion of a third imbecile, guilty of some obscure tort. "Why," inquires Young Jake, "didn't you break his nose or bust him in the chin?" "His nose was already broke," replied the other, "and he didn't have no chin."

Such wisecracks seem easy to devise. Broadway diverts itself by manufacturing them. They constitute the substance of half the town shows. But in those made by Lardner there is something far more than mere facile humor: they are all rigidly in character, and they illuminate that character. Few American novelists, great or small, have character more firmly in hand. Lardner does not see situations; he sees people. And what people! They are all as revolting as so many Methodist evangelists, and they are all as thoroughly American.

1927

101.

Calvin Coolidge: Intervention in Nicaragua

Between 1909 and 1927 the United States several times intervened with military force to shore up unpopular regimes in Nicaragua. In 1926 the conservative, pro-American president of that country, Adolfo Díaz, appealed to the United States for aid in suppressing a liberal rival for the presidency, Dr. Juan Sacasa, who was actively supported by the Mexican government. Early in 1927 President Coolidge complied with Díaz' request by sending 2,000 Marines. Coolidge justified the action in his message to Congress of January 10, 1927, which is reprinted here in part. Despite the American presence, the fighting continued; and in April Henry L. Stimson was dispatched to Nicaragua to effect a compromise settlement. Both factions were disarmed and American forces stayed on to supervise the elections of 1928, 1930, and 1932, all of which were won by the traditionally anti-American liberals.

Source: *Record*, 69 Cong., 2 Sess., pp. 1324-1326.

WHILE CONDITIONS IN NICARAGUA and the action of this government pertaining thereto have in general been made public, I think the time has arrived for me officially to inform the Congress more in detail of the events leading up to the present disturbances and conditions which seriously threaten American lives and property, endanger the stability of all Central America, and put in jeopardy the rights granted by Nicaragua to the United States for the construction of a canal.

It is well known that in 1912 the United States intervened in Nicaragua with a large force and put down a revolution, and that from that time to 1925 a legation guard of American Marines was, with the consent of the Nicaragua government, kept in Managua to protect American lives and property. In 1923 representatives of the five Central American countries, namely, Costa Rica, Guatemala, Honduras, Nicaragua, and Salvador, at the invitation of the United States, met in Washington and entered into a series of treaties.

These treaties dealt with limitation of armament, a Central American tribunal for arbitration, and the general subject of peace and amity. The treaty last referred to specifically provides in Article II that the governments of the contracting parties will not recognize any other government which may come into power in any of the five republics through a coup d'état, or revolution, and disqualifies the leaders of such coup d'état, or revolution, from assuming the presidency or vice-presidency. . . .

The United States was not a party to this treaty, but it was made in Washington under the auspices of the secretary of state, and this government has felt a moral obligation to apply its principles in order to encourage the Central American states in their efforts to prevent revolution and disorder. The treaty, it may be noted in passing, was signed on behalf of Nicaragua by Emiliano Chamorro himself, who afterwards assumed the presidency in violation thereof and thereby contributed to the creation of the present difficulty.

In October 1924 an election was held in Nicaragua for president, vice-president, and members of the Congress. This resulted in the election of a coalition ticket embracing Conservatives and Liberals. Carlos Solorzano, a Conservative Republican, was elected president, and Juan B. Sacasa, a Liberal, was elected vice-president. This government was recognized by the other Central American countries and by the United States. It had been the intention of the United States to withdraw the Marines immediately after this election, and notice was given of the intention to withdraw them in January 1925. At the request of the president of Nicaragua, this time was extended to Sept. 1, 1925. Pursuant to this determination and notice, the Marines were withdrawn in August 1925. . . .

Notwithstanding the refusal of this government and of the other Central American governments to recognize him, General Chamorro continued to exercise the functions of president until Oct. 30, 1926. In the meantime a revolution broke out in

May on the east coast in the neighborhood of Bluefields and was speedily suppressed by the troops of General Chamorro. However, it again broke out with considerable more violence. The second attempt was attended with some success, and practically all of the east coast of Nicaragua fell into the hands of the revolutionists. Throughout these events, Sacasa was at no time in the country, having remained in Mexico and Guatemala during this period.

Repeated requests were made of the United States for protection, especially on the east coast, and on Aug. 24, 1926, the secretary of state addressed to the secretary of the navy the following communication:

> I have the honor to suggest that war vessels of the Special Service Squadron proceed as soon as possible to the Nicaraguan ports of Corinto and Bluefields for the protection of American and foreign lives and property in case that threatened emergencies materialize. The American chargé d'affaires at Managua has informed the department that he considers the presence of war vessels at these ports desirable, and the American consul at Bluefields has reported that a warship is urgently needed to protect life and property at that port. An attack on The Bluff and Bluefields is expected momentarily.

Accordingly, the Navy Department ordered Admiral Latimer, in command of the Special Service Squadron, to proceed to Bluefields. Upon arriving there he found it necessary for the adequate protection of American lives and property to declare Bluefields a neutral zone. This was done with the consent of both factions, afterwards, on Oct. 26, 1926, reduced to a written agreement, which is still in force. In October 1926 the good offices of the United States were sought by both parties for the purpose of effecting a settlement of the conflict. Admiral Latimer, commanding the Special Service Squadron, brought about an armistice to permit of a conference being held between the delegates of the two factions. The armistice was originally for fifteen days and was later extended for fifteen days more.

At the request of both parties, Marines were landed at Corinto to establish a neutral zone in which the conference could be held. Doctor Sacasa was invited to attend this conference but refrained from doing so and remained in Guatemala City. The United States government did not participate in the conference except to provide a neutral chairman; it simply offered its good offices to make the conference possible and arranged a neutral zone at Corinto at the request of both parties during the time the conference was held. I understand that at this conference General Chamorro offered to resign and permit the Congress to elect a new designate to assume the presidency. The conference led to no result, since, just at the time when it seemed as though some compromise agreement would be reached, the representatives of Doctor Sacasa suddenly broke off negotiations. . . .

The Nicaraguan constitution provides in Article 106 that in the absence of the president and vice-president the Congress shall designate one of its members to complete the unexpired term of president. As President Solorzano had resigned and was then residing in California, and as the vice-president, Doctor Sacasa, was in Guatemala, having been out of the country since November 1925, the action of Congress in designating Señor Díaz was perfectly legal and in accordance with the constitution. Therefore, the United States government on Nov. 17 extended recognition to Señor Díaz. . . .

Immediately following the inauguration of President Díaz, and frequently since that date, he has appealed to the United States for support, has informed this government of the aid which Mexico is giving to the revolutionists, and has stated that he is unable solely because of the aid given by Mexico to the revolutionists to protect the lives and property of American citizens and other foreigners.

When negotiations leading up to the Corinto conference began, I immediately placed an embargo on the shipment of arms and ammunition to Nicaragua. The Department of State notified the other Central American states, to wit, Costa Rica, Honduras, Salvador, and Guatemala, and they assured the department that they would cooperate in this measure. So far as known, they have done so. The State Department also notified the Mexican government of this embargo and informally suggested to that government like action. The Mexican government did not adopt the suggestion to put on an embargo but informed the American ambassador at Mexico City that in the absence of manufacturing plants in Mexico for the making of arms and ammunition the matter had little practical importance.

As a matter of fact, I have the most conclusive evidence that arms and munitions in large quantities have been, on several occasions since August 1926, shipped to the revolutionists in Nicaragua. Boats carrying these munitions have been fitted out in Mexican ports, and some of the munitions bear evidence of having belonged to the Mexican government. It also appears that the ships were fitted out with the full knowledge of and, in some cases, with the encouragement of Mexican officials and were in one instance, at least, commanded by a Mexican naval reserve officer.

At the end of November, after spending some time in Mexico City, Doctor Sacasa went back to Nicaragua, landing at Puerto Cabezas, near Bragmans Bluff. He immediately placed himself at the head of the insurrection and declared himself president of Nicaragua. He has never been recognized by any of the Central American republics nor by any other government, with the exception of Mexico, which recognized him immediately. As arms and munitions in large quantities were reaching the revolutionists, I deemed it unfair to prevent the recognized government from purchasing arms abroad, and, accordingly, the secretary of state notified the Díaz government that licenses would be issued for the export of arms and munitions purchased in this country. It would be thoroughly inconsistent for this country not to support the government recognized by it while the revolutionists were receiving arms and munitions from abroad.

During the last two months the government of the United States has received repeated requests from various American citizens, both directly and through our consuls and legation, for the protection of their lives and property. The government of the United States has also received requests from the British chargé at Managua and from the Italian ambassador at Washington for the protection of their respective nationals. Pursuant to such requests, Admiral Latimer, in charge of the Special Service Squadron, has not only maintained the neutral zone at Bluefields under the agreement of both parties but has landed forces at Puerto Cabezas and Rio Grande and established neutral zones at these points where considerable numbers of Americans live and are engaged in carrying on various industries. He has also been authorized to establish such other neutral zones as are necessary for the purposes above mentioned.

For many years numerous Americans have been living in Nicaragua, developing its industries and carrying on business. At the present time there are large investments in lumbering, mining, coffee growing, banana culture, shipping, and also in general mercantile and other collateral business. All these people and these industries have been encouraged by the Nicaraguan government. That government has at all times owed them protection, but the United States has occasionally been obliged to send naval forces for their proper protection. In the present crisis such forces are requested by the Nicaraguan government, which protests to the United States its inability to protect these interests and states that any measures which the United States deems appropriate for their protection will be satisfactory to the Nicaraguan government.

In addition to these industries now in existence, the government of Nicaragua, by a treaty entered into on the 5th of August 1914, granted in perpetuity to the United States the exclusive proprietary rights necessary and convenient for the construction, operation, and maintenance of an oceanic canal. . . .

There is no question that if the revolution continues, American investments and business interests in Nicaragua will be very seriously affected, if not destroyed. The currency, which is now at par, will be inflated. American as well as foreign bondholders will undoubtedly look to the United States for the protection of their interests. It is true that the United States did not establish the financial plan by any treaty, but it nevertheless did aid through diplomatic channels and advise in the negotiation and establishment of this plan for the financial rehabilitation of Nicaragua.

Manifestly, the relation of this government to the Nicaraguan situation and its policy in the existing emergency are determined by the facts which I have described. The proprietary rights of the United States in the Nicaraguan canal route, with the necessary implications growing out of it affecting the Panama Canal, together with the obligations flowing from the investments of all classes of our citizens in Nicaragua, place us in a position of peculiar responsibility. I am sure it is not the desire of the United States to intervene in the internal affairs of Nicaragua or of any other Central American republic. Nevertheless, it must be said that we have a very definite and special interest in the maintenance of order and good government in Nicaragua at the present time, and that the stability, prosperity, and independence of all Central American countries can never be a matter of indifference to us.

The United States cannot, therefore, fail to view with deep concern any serious threat to stability and constitutional government in Nicaragua tending toward anarchy and jeopardizing American interests, especially if such state of affairs is contributed to or brought about by outside influences or by any foreign power. It has always been and remains the policy of the United States in such circumstances to take the steps that may be necessary for the preservation and protection of the lives, the property, and the interests of its citizens and of this government itself. In this respect I propose to follow the path of my predecessors.

Consequently, I have deemed it my duty to use the powers committed to me to ensure the adequate protection of all American interests in Nicaragua, whether they be endangered by internal strife or by outside interference in the affairs of that republic.

102.

ROY A. HAYNES: The Success of Prohibition

The federal government tried hard to enforce the Eighteenth Amendment, which went into effect in January 1920. Funds amounting to more than $10 million annually were appropriated, and between 1920 and 1930 more than 300,000 convictions for violations of the law were obtained in the courts. But the task was hopeless, especially in the face of open or covert defiance by several state governments. The mythology of Prohibition includes some amusing institutions — speakeasies, the hip flask, cocktail parties, and bathtub gin — but there was nothing really funny about bootlegging, and there was something more than merely ominous about the takeover of the liquor business by organized crime. The question posed by the federal Prohibition commissioner, Roy A. Haynes, in the speech below — "Is the nation able to enforce its own laws?" — seemed to demand a negative answer, and this was the most serious matter of all. Haynes's speech, part of which is reprinted here, was delivered before a national meeting of the Woman's Christian Temperance Union on January 26, 1927.

Source: *Record*, 69 Cong., 2 Sess., pp. 2505-2507.

ANY REMARKS made at such a gathering on a date near the seventh anniversary of the Eighteenth Amendment, it seems to me, should be both retrospective and prospective. Seven years' experience has taught many lessons; produced many problems; seen many problems solved; disclosed substantial progress; made apparent many needs; and, withal, seven years is but a day in the evolution of a great movement.

In my judgment, the amazing thing about the progress of this first seven years of the operation of the Eighteenth Amendment is not that it is difficult to enforce, and has not been perfectly enforced — as it or no other law ever will be — but that it has been as successfully enforced and as generally observed as it has been. Even a generation is not too long to wait for final judgment concerning a great forward crusade for humanity. . . .

We must remember that prohibition is the greatest effort for human advancement and betterment ever attempted in history, and that while the nearest approach, perhaps, was the destruction of human slavery, let us not forget that that revolutionary policy affected only one section of the nation — whereas the national prohibition policy called for changing the habits and customs of the people in all sections of the nation. Therefore, the most gratifying and enheartening feature of the situation is that so large a majority of our people respect the Constitution and observe this law, and this in spite of the fact that there is a very considerable number of citizens of influence and position who, by nonobservance, are embarrassing the government in the promotion of its great task.

But what has the experience of these seven years taught us? . . . We have learned: (1) size of the task; (2) power of propaganda; (3) inadequacy of our legislation; (4) not enough emphasis on observance; (5) who are the friends and who are the foes, and the real plans of the latter; (6) in spite of all, real progress is being achieved; (7) how to measure progress.

That is, in brief, my summary of the outstanding lessons learned in these seven years. That is the retrospect. What of the prospect for the future?

Our campaign for the immediate future must be based upon the acknowledgment of but one statement of the whole issue, namely — Is the nation able to enforce its own laws — its own charter — in the face of an unsympathetic and actively hostile minority? It is always difficult to think hard and think straight. We are largely governed by our emotions, sympathies, and prejudices. It is but natural that in a nation of 115 million or 120 million people there should not be one mind with reference to policies; but when it comes to obedience to the Constitution, we pass from a matter of policy to a great fundamental principle upon which the perpetuity of the nation depends, and there is no room for division of opinion on that issue.

We must remember that the drink question itself looks different to various groups of persons; to the alien who has been accustomed to beverage liquor in the land of his birth, or to the habitual drinker who likes his drink and who has grown more or less opposed to restraint of any kind hampering his indulgence, the drink question, per se, seems quite different than it does to the Woman's Christian Temperance Union member, the Salvation Army officer, the missionary worker, the army of church people, the charity organizations, and all who have to deal with the effect of drink in its last stages. Yes; we must be broad enough to recognize that this problem must have appeared differently to these groups, but, on the other hand, they must be broad enough to recognize that the time for debate on the use of intoxicating liquor for beverage purposes as a policy has ended under the Constitution, and its observance alone remains as the principle at stake.

Accepting that concept, then, as basic — that general attitude for all citizens, as most to be desired — let us briefly classify the problems and needs immediately ahead of us as I see them:

1. Need of additional legislation, national and state. Unfavorable court decisions, inadequate penalties, twilight zone, indefinite administrative powers, etc., have taught us the imperative need for legislation that is clear-cut in its purpose, broad and powerful in its scope, and unqualified in its intent to do the thing which the framers of the act and the amendment and the people evidently desire. Many state legislatures have yet to pass legislation which is adequate to discharge their full responsibilities under the concurrent power section of the amendment.

From the national standpoint, the department has laid before the Congress and people of America several bills, chief among which are the reorganization bill, the medicinal spirits bill, and the Goff bill, which are imperatively necessary of passage if the department is to properly discharge the duties and responsibilities imposed upon it. No efforts should be spared by the proponents of this law and the friends of the Constitution to bring to speedy enactment these measures.

2. The second need, which comes in my judgment in that order, is the need of a widespread educational program: (a) among the present voters, showing the real progress that is being made and the real benefits achieved, disproving the wet propaganda; (b) and another type of education among the young people of the country, who will soon become first voters and who have not seen the evils of the old saloon days.

The Woman's Christian Temperance Union groups, with its wonderful history in this particular character of work, which was basic to all of the achievements of the past half century, culminating in the Eighteenth Amendment, is the natural leader in such a second crusade as I am now referring to — preachment by word of mouth, by literature in the homes, the public schools, and Sunday schools, on the platform, and in the pulpit.

The teaching in the public schools of scientific temperance once more must be aggressively taken up to meet the future attacks of the enemy, which is more determined and aggressive than ever, and which is looking toward the day when the new voters, untrained and unfamiliar with the facts which brought about the destruction of the beverage liquor business, may be appealed to through their highly prejudicial propaganda for a return to the old order of things. Every agency available to the Christian citizenship of America should be put into action to this end.

Then all will admit the need of a concentration of effort to reach the secular press, asking only for fair treatment and fair presentation of the problem.

In dealing with these educational needs, it must be distinctly realized that special attention must be given to the following classes which are unmistakably asking for a return to preprohibition conditions:

(a) Those who used liquor before the constitutional amendment went into effect, who miss it, and who will go to almost any extreme to have it.

(b) Those few but powerful interests whose finances have been adversely affected by prohibition.

(c) The alien group which has not yet been properly Americanized in this as well as many other American fundamentals.

(d) The reputable, influential business- and society man and woman at the very apex of society who have not yet come to learn the real danger of their nonobservance of this law.

(e) The young people who have never seen the dreadful evils of the drink habit, and from a lack of experience and observation do not realize its dangers.

In this relation this last group, in my judgment, is the most important group in the nation; because from it must come all future support and leadership in the halls of legislatures and Congress, and in high executive and judicial offices. The other groups will comparatively soon pass from the scene of action, but this new generation, not having had to encounter the open saloon with its drink evils, its blatant excitement, and attendant vices, must be educated to the dangers and habits of liquor drinking, must be taught to observe law, revere the Constitution and America's creed, for many are not learning these things by example and precept in the homes of today.

That was the method you followed over the period of the last fifty years and more since the crusade days when agitation for prohibition began and continued successfully on its way; and when the organized liquor traffic believed that a prohibition amendment could never be placed in the Constitution.

3. The next need which I would catalog is that of a more vigorous enforcement policy all down the line — by this I mean not only by the federal agencies but by the state, county, and municipal agencies, with such pressure brought from the electoral constituency that officials sworn to do their duty will in all good conscience courageously discharge their responsibilities and that those officials shall be earnest and on fire with zeal and conviction, not alone as to the letter of the law but as to its righteousness.

Therefore I would briefly summarize the immediately apparent needs: (1) Additional legislation; (2) Education; (3) More vigorous enforcement policies.

In closing, let me suggest in military parlance that, as I see it, we are now in the midst of a counterattack. Great objectives have been won. The Eighteenth Amendment is here. Control of legislatures and Congress has gone from liquor interests. The Supreme Court has spoken as to the constitutionality of the act and the amendment. Great progress in enforcement has already been made. The government is trying to do a decent and constructive thing for the present and future welfare and safety of its people. Having attained these objectives, military experience teaches that a counterattack may always be expected after an advance. The counterattack has in it the element of surprise and possible panic. The counterattack is met by "digging in" and "holding steady." That is the great need of the constitutional army at this moment — to "dig in" and "hold steady."

There is no occasion for panic. We are firmly holding our objectives. That much of the great fight has been won, and there is coming up to the support of the original forces that won these great objectives and that are now "digging in" and "holding steady" great reserves of other and new forces not known in the early days, such as life insurance companies, banks, railroads, fraternal organizations, commercial interests, political economists, scientific investigators, civic commissions, medical specialists, athletic trainers, industrial managers, public health officials, and a host of others.

Verily, prohibition is here, and here to stay. The power of the liquor oligarchy is broken. Three great forces — science, moral sentiment, and business — have so decided and taken their place. We are in the midst of a great historical movement. The spectacle of the people of a great nation, after a century of deliberation and reflection, by self-discipline and self-imposed denial, freeing themselves from the tyranny of centuries of the degradation and demoralization of drink is a sight the like of which has never been witnessed in the history of civilization. Truly the fight has been worthwhile, and the objectives won surpass even our fondest expectations. Let us continue to dig in, hold steady, be not panic-stricken, and go forward to new victories with the host of reserves which are rapidly coming to our support. That is the task ahead.

Q. If you find so much that is unworthy of reverence in the United States, then why do you live here?

A. Why do men go to zoos?

H. L. Mencken, *Prejudices: Fifth Series*, 1926

103.

Bartolomeo Vanzetti: Last Statement in Court

On April 15, 1920, at the height of the patriotic fervor and antiforeign feeling that followed World War I, a paymaster and a guard at a shoe factory in South Braintree, Massachusetts, were murdered in the course of an armed robbery. Two naturalized Italian immigrants, Nicola Sacco, a shoemaker, and Bartolomeo Vanzetti, a fish peddler, were charged with the crime, tried, convicted, and sentenced to death. They were atheists, draft dodgers, and anarchists, and as such, Felix Frankfurter remarked, threatened what the judge and the jury held most dear: "God, country, and property." The trial evoked a storm of protest. After six years of appeals that attracted worldwide liberal support, the two men were still in prison, awaiting execution. The following selection is Vanzetti's last statement, made on April 9, 1927, to the court that examined the evidence and conduct of the trial and, on July 27, sustained the verdict. Sacco and Vanzetti were executed on August 23, but doubt about their guilt continues to this day.

Source: *The Sacco-Vanzetti Case,* New York, 1929, Vol. V, pp. 4896-4904.

WHAT I SAY IS THAT I AM INNOCENT . . . of the Braintree crime . . . That I am not only innocent . . . but in all my life I have never stole and I have never killed and I have never spilled blood. That is what I want to say. And it is not all. Not only am I innocent . . . not only in all my life I have never stole, never killed, never spilled blood, but I have struggled all my life, since I began to reason, to eliminate crime from the earth.

Everybody that knows these two arms knows very well that I did not need to go in between the street and kill a man to take the money. I can live with my two arms and live well. But besides that, I can live even without work with my arm for other people. I have had plenty of chance to live independently and to live what the world conceives to be a higher life than not to gain our bread with the sweat of our brow. . . .

Well, I want to reach a little point far-ther, and it is this — that not only have I not been . . . in Braintree to steal and kill and have never steal or kill or spilt blood in all my life, not only have I struggled hard against crimes, but I have refused myself the commodity or glory of life, the pride of life of a good position, because in my consideration it is not right to exploit man. I have refused to go in business because I understand that business is a speculation on profit upon certain people that must depend upon the businessman, and I do not consider that that is right and therefore I refuse to do that.

Now, I should say that I am not only innocent of all these things, not only have I never committed a real crime in my life — though some sins but not crimes — not only have I struggled all my life to eliminate crimes, the crimes that the official law and the official moral condemns, but also the crime that the official moral and the official law sanctions and sanctifies — the exploitation and the oppression of the man by the man, and if there is a reason why I am here as a guilty man, it there is a reason why you in a few minutes can doom me, it is this reason and none else.

I beg your pardon. [Referring to paper.] There is the more good man I ever cast my eyes upon since I lived, a man that will last and will grow always more near and more dear to the people, as far as into the heart of the people, so long as admiration for goodness and for sacrifice will last. I mean Eugene Debs. I will say that even a dog that killed the chickens would not have found an American jury to convict it with the proof that the Commonwealth produced against us. That man was not with me in Plymouth or with Sacco where he was on the day of the crime. You can say that it is arbitrary, what we are saying, that he is good and he applied to the other his own goodness, that he is incapable of crime, and he believed that everybody is incapable of crime.

Well, it may be like that but it is not, it could be like that but it is not, and that man has a real experience of court, of prison, and of jury. Just because he want the world a little better he was persecuted and slandered from his boyhood to his old age, and indeed he was murdered by the prison. He know, and not only he but every man of understanding in the world, not only in this country but also in the other countries, men that we have provided a certain amount of a record of the times, they all still stick with us, the flower of mankind of Europe, the better writers, the greatest thinkers of Europe, have pleaded in our favor. The scientists, the greatest scientists, the greatest statesmen of Europe, have pleaded in our favor. The people of foreign nations have pleaded in our favor.

Is it possible that only a few on the jury, only two or three men, who would condemn their mother for worldly honor and for earthly fortune; is it possible that they are right against what the world, the whole world has say it is wrong and that I know that it is wrong? If there is one that I should know it, if it is right or if it is wrong, it is I and this man. You see it is seven years that we are in jail. What we have suffered during these seven years no human tongue can say, and yet you see me before you, not trembling, you see me looking you in your eyes straight, not blushing, not changing color, not ashamed or in fear.

Eugene Debs say that not even a dog — something like that — not even a dog that kill the chickens would have been found guilty by American jury with the evidence that the Commonwealth have produced against us. I say that not even a leprous dog would have his appeal refused two times by the Supreme Court of Massachusetts — not even a leprous dog.

They have given a new trial to Madeiros for the reason that the judge had either forgot or omitted to tell the jury that they should consider the man innocent until found guilty in the court, or something of that sort. That man has confessed. The man was tried and has confessed, and the court give him another trial. We have proved that there could not have been another judge on the face of the earth more prejudiced and more cruel than you have been against us. We have proven that. Still they refuse the new trial. We know, and you know in your heart, that you have been against us from the very beginning, before you see us. Before you see us you already know that we were radicals, that we were underdogs, that we were the enemy of the institution that you can believe in good faith in their goodness — I don't want to condemn that — and that it was easy on the time of the first trial to get a verdict of guiltiness.

We know that you have spoke yourself and have spoke your hostility against us, and your despisement against us with friends of yours on the train, at the University Club of Boston, on the Golf Club of Worcester, Massachusetts. I am sure that if the people who know all what you say against us would have the civil courage to take the stand, maybe, Your Honor — I am sorry to say this because you are an old man, and I have an old father — but maybe you would be beside us in good justice at this time.

When you sentenced me at the Plymouth trial you say, to the best of my memory, of my good faith, that crimes were in accordance with my principle — something of that sort — and you take off one charge, if I remember it exactly, from the jury. The jury was so violent against me that they found me guilty of both charges, because there were only two. But they would have found me guilty of a dozen of charges against Your Honor's instructions. Of course I remember that you told them that there was no reason to believe that if I were the bandit I have intention to kill somebody, so that they will take off the indictment of attempt to murder. Well, they found me guilty of what? And if I am right, you take out that and sentence me only for attempt to rob with arms — something like that. But, Judge Thayer, you give more to me for that attempt of robbery than all the 448 men that were in Charlestown, all of those that attempted to rob, all those that have robbed, they have not such a sentence as you gave me for an attempt at robbery. . . .

We were tried during a time that has now passed into history. I mean by that, a time when there was a hysteria of resentment and hate against the people of our principles, against the foreigner, against slackers, and it seems to me — rather, I am positive of it, that both you and Mr. Katzmann has done all what it were in your power in order to work out, in order to agitate still more the passion of the juror, the prejudice of the juror, against us. . . .

What I want to say is this: Everybody ought to understand that the first of the defense has been terrible. My first lawyer did not stick to defend us. He has made no work to collect witnesses and evidence in our favor. The record in the Plymouth Court is a pity. I am told that they are almost one-half lost. So the defense had a tremendous work to do in order to collect some evidence, to collect some testimony to offset and to learn what the testimony of the state has done. And in this consideration it must be said that even if the defense take double time of the state without delay, double time that they delay the case it would have been reasonable, whereas it took less than the state.

Well, I have already say that I not only am not guilty . . . but I never commit a crime in my life — I have never steal and I have never kill and I have never spilt blood, and I have fought against the crime, and I have fought and I have sacrificed myself even to eliminate the crimes that the law and the church legitimate and sanctify.

This is what I say: I would not wish to a dog or to a snake, to the most low and misfortunate creature of the earth — I would not wish to any of them what I have had to suffer for things that I am not guilty of. But my conviction is that I have suffered for things that I am guilty of. I am suffering because I am a radical and indeed I am a radical; I have suffered because I was an Italian, and indeed I am an Italian; I have suffered more for my family and for my beloved than for myself; but I am so convinced to be right that if you could execute me two times, and if I could be reborn two other times, I would live again to do what I have done already.

I have finished. Thank you.

◆

It is awfully easy to be hard-boiled about everything in the daytime, but at night it is another thing.

Ernest Hemingway, *The Sun Also Rises*, 1926

104.

HEYWOOD BROUN: Plea for Sacco and Vanzetti

*"The Sacco-Vanzetti case," Heywood Broun wrote later, "moved me to write the
first violent newspaper pieces I had ever done. And pretty soon I was out of a
job. Never since that time has it been possible to get back entirely into the mood
of the kindly commentator on the less important phases of the passing show."
Broun's feelings about the case were shared by many Americans, who felt that
the anarchists were innocent of the crime for which they had been tried, and that
they had been convicted instead for their radical views. As the day of execution
approached, appeals were made to President Coolidge, Chief Justice Taft, and
others to have the sentence commuted to life imprisonment. Two of Broun's
"violent" pieces of the time are reprinted here. They appeared in his column,
"It Seems to Me," in the* New York World *on August 5 and 6, 1927. Sacco and
Vanzetti were electrocuted on August 23.*

Source: *New York World,* August 5, 6, 1927.

WHEN AT LAST JUDGE THAYER in a tiny voice passed sentence upon Sacco and Vanzetti, a woman in the courtroom said with terror: "It is death condemning life!"

The men in Charlestown Prison are shining spirits, and Vanzetti has spoken with an eloquence not known elsewhere within our time. They are too bright, we shield our eyes and kill them. We are the dead, and in us there is not feeling nor imagination nor the terrible torment of lust for justice. And in the city where we sleep, smug gardeners walk to keep the grass above our little houses sleek and cut whatever blade thrusts up a head above its fellows.

"The decision is unbelievably brutal," said the Chairman of the Defense Committee, and he was wrong. The thing is worthy to be believed. It has happened. It will happen again, and the shame is wider than that which must rest upon Massachusetts. I have never believed that the trial of Sacco and

Vanzetti was one set apart from many by reason of the passion and prejudice which encrusted all the benches. Scratch through the varnish of any judgment seat and what will you strike but hate thick-clotted from centuries of angry verdicts? Did any man ever find power within his hand except to use it as a whip?

Gov. Alvan T. Fuller never had any intention in all his investigation but to put a new and higher polish upon the proceedings. The justice of the business was not his concern. He hoped to make it respectable. He called old men from high places to stand behind his chair so that he might seem to speak with all the authority of a high priest or a Pilate.

What more can these immigrants from Italy expect? It is not every prisoner who has a President of Harvard University throw on the switch for him. And Robert Grant is not only a former Judge but one of the most popular dinner guests in Boston. If this is a lynching, at least the fish peddler and his friend the factory hand may take unction to their souls that they will die at the hands of men in dinner coats or academic gowns, according to the conventionalities required by the hour of execution.

Already too much has been made of the personality of Webster Thayer. To sympathizers of Sacco and Vanzetti he has seemed a man with a cloven hoof. But in no usual sense of the term is this man a villain. Although probably not a great jurist, he is without doubt as capable and conscientious as the average Massachusetts Judge, and if that's enough to warm him in wet weather by all means let him stick the compliment against his ribs.

Webster Thayer has a thousand friends. He has courage, sincerity, and conviction. Judge Thayer is a good man, and when he says that he made every effort to give a fair trial to the Anarchists brought before him, undoubtedly he thinks it and he means it. Quite often I've heard the remark: "I wonder how that man sleeps at night?" On this point I have no firsthand information, but I venture to guess that he is no more beset with uneasy dreams than most of us. He saw his duty and he thinks he did it.

And Gov. Fuller, also, is not in any accepted sense of the word a miscreant. Before becoming Governor he manufactured bicycles. Nobody was cheated by his company. He loves his family and pays his debts. Very much he desires to be Governor again, and there is an excellent chance that this ambition will be gratified. Other governors of Massachusetts have gone far, and it is not fantastic to assume that some day he might be President. His is not a mastermind, but he is a solid and substantial American, chiming in heartily with all our national ideals and aspirations.

To me the tragedy of the conviction of Sacco and Vanzetti lies in the fact that this was not a deed done by crooks and knaves.

In that case we could have a campaign with the slogan "Turn the rascals out," and set up for a year or two a reform Administration. Nor have I had much patience with any who would like to punish Thayer by impeachment or any other process. Unfrock him and his judicial robes would fall upon a pair of shoulders not different by the thickness of a fingernail. Men like Holmes and Brandeis do not grow on bushes. Popular government, as far as the eye can see, is always going to be administered by the Thayers and Fullers.

It has been said that the question at issue was not the guilt or innocence of Sacco and Vanzetti, but whether or not they received a fair trial. I will admit that this commands my interest to some extent, but still I think it is a minor phase in the whole matter. From a Utopian point of view the trial was far from fair, but it was not more biased than a thousand which take place in this country every year. It has been pointed out that the Public Prosecutor neglected to call certain witnesses because their testimony would not have been favorable to his case. Are there five District Attorneys, is there one, in the whole country who would do otherwise?

Again Prof. Frankfurter has most clearly shown that the prosecution asked a trick question in regard to the pistol, and made the expert seem to testify far more concretely than he was willing to commit himself. That was very wrong, but not unique. Our judicial processes are so arranged that it is to the interest of District Attorneys to secure convictions rather than to ascertain justice, and if it would profit his case, there is not one who would not stoop to confuse the issue in the minds of the jurymen.

Eleven of the twelve who convicted Sacco and Vanzetti are still alive, and Gov. Fuller talked to them. He reports somewhat naïvely that they all told him that they considered the trial fair. Did he expect them to report, "Why, no, Governor, we brought in a verdict of guilty just out of general depravity"?

By now there has been a long and careful sifting of the evidence in the case. It is ridiculous to say that Sacco and Vanzetti are being railroaded to the chair. The situation is much worse than that. This is a thing done cold-bloodedly and with deliberation. But care and deliberation do not guarantee justice. Even if every venerable college president in the country tottered forward to say "Guilty," they could not alter facts. The tragedy of it all lies in the fact that though a Southern mountain man may move more quickly to a dirty deed of violence, his feet are set no more firmly in the path of prejudice than a Lowell ambling sedately to a hanging.

I said of Calvin Coolidge that I admired his use of "I do not choose," but he was dealing with a problem wholly personal and had every right to withhold his reasons. For Gov. Fuller I can't say the same. These are the lives of others with which he is dealing. In his fairly long statement he answers not a single point which has been made against the justice of the conviction. The deliberations of himself and his associates were secret, and seemingly it is his intention that they shall remain secret. A gentleman does not investigate and tell.

I've said these men have slept, but from now on it is our business to make them toss and turn a little, for a cry should go up from many million voices before the day set for Sacco and Vanzetti to die. We have a right to beat against tight minds with our fists and shout a word into the ears of the old men. We want to know, we will know — "Why?"

SEVERAL POINTS IN THE OFFICIAL DECISION of Gov. Fuller betray a state of mind unfortunate under the circumstances. It seems to me that the whole tone of Gov. Fuller's statement was apologetic, but this perhaps

is debatable. There can be no question, however, that he fell into irrelevances.

"The South Braintree crime was particularly brutal," he wrote, and went on to describe the manner in which the robbers pumped bullets into a guard who was already wounded and helpless. Surely this is beside the point. Had this been one of the most considerate murders ever committed in the State of Massachusetts, Sacco and Vanzetti would still have been deserving of punishment if guilty. The contention of the defense has always been that the accused men had no part in the affair. The savagery of the killing certainly is wholly extraneous to the issue.

But these references of the Governor are worse than mere wasted motion. Unconsciously he has made an appeal to that type of thinker who says: "Why all the sympathy for those two anarchists and none for the unfortunate widow of the paymaster's guard?" But those of us who are convinced that Sacco and Vanzetti are innocent certainly pay no disrespect to the woes of the widow.

Again Gov. Fuller writes: "It is popularly supposed that he (Madeiros) confessed to committing the crime." Surely this gives the impression that no such statement ever came from the condemned criminal. The Governor may be within his rights in deciding that Madeiros lied, and for some self-seeking reason, but it is not only popularly supposed but also true that he did make a confession.

"In his testimony to me," the Governor explains, "he could not recall the details or describe the neighborhood."

This, I must say, seems to me a rather frowzy sort of psychology. Assuming that Madeiros took part in the crime, fired some shots and sped quickly away in an automobile, how could he be expected to remember the happenings in any precise detail? I have known men who ran seventy yards across the goal line in some football game and after this was over they knew little or nothing of what happened while excitement gripped them. I would be much more inclined to believe Madeiros a liar if he had been able to give a detailed and graphic account of everything which happened during the flurry.

And again, the Massachusetts Executive is far too cavalier in dealing with Sacco's alibi.

"He then claimed," says the Governor, "to have been at the Italian Consulate in Boston on that date, but the only confirmation of this claim is the memory of a former employee of the Consulate who made a deposition in Italy that Sacco among forty others was in the office that day. This employee had no memorandum to assist his memory."

In this brief paragraph I think I detect much bias. By speaking of the witness as "a former employee," Gov. Fuller seems to endeavor to discredit him. And yet the man who testified may be wholly worthy to be believed, even though he eventually took another job. Nor does the fact that his deposition was made in Italy militate against it. Truth may travel even across an ocean.

Assuming that Sacco did go to the Consulate as he has said, why should it be expected that his arrival would create such a stir that everyone there from the Consul down would have marked his coming indelibly? And this witness for the defense, according to Fuller, "had no memorandum to assist his memory." Why in heaven's name should it be assumed that he would? There were other witnesses to whom the Governor gave credence who did not come with blueprints or flashlight photographs of happenings. Memory was all that served them, and yet Fuller believed because he chose to.

One important point the Governor neglected to mention in dealing with the testimony of the Consulate clerk. The employee happened to fix Sacco in his mind by reason of a striking circumstance. The laborer, ignorant of passport requirements, brought with him to the Consulate not the conventional miniature but a large-sized crayon enlargement. And to my mind this should have been a clinching factor in the validity of the alibi.

Gov. Fuller has vindicated Judge Thayer of prejudice wholly upon the testimony of the record. Apparently he has overlooked entirely the large amount of testimony from reliable witnesses that the Judge spoke bitterly of the prisoners while the trial was on. The record is not enough. Anybody who has ever been to the theater knows it is impossible to evaluate the effect of a line until you hear it read. It is just as important to consider Thayer's mood during the proceedings as to look over the words which he uttered.

Since the denial of the last appeal, Thayer has been most reticent, and has declared that it is his practice never to make public statements concerning any judicial matters which come before him. Possibly he never did make public statements, but certainly there is a mass of testimony from unimpeachable persons that he was not so careful in locker rooms and trains and club lounges.

Nor am I much moved at the outcries of admiration from the editorial writers who have expressed delight at the courage of the Governor of Massachusetts. Readily I will admit that in his decision he has exposed himself to the danger of physical violence. This is courage, but it is one of the more usual varieties. To decide in favor of Sacco and Vanzetti would have required a very different sort of courage. Such action upon Fuller's part might very possibly have blasted his political future.

I am afraid there is no question that a vast majority of the voters in the Bay State want to see the condemned men die. I don't know why. Clearly it depends upon no careful examination of the evidence. Mostly the feeling rests upon the fact that Sacco and Vanzetti are radicals and that they are foreigners. Also, the backbone of Massachusetts, such as it is, happens to be up because of criticism beyond the borders of the State. "This is only our business," say the citizens of the Commonwealth, and they are very wrong.

Five times as many telegrams of praise as those of censure have come to the Governor, according to the official statement of his secretary. In such circumstances it seems to me that his courage in the business is of no great importance.

From now on, I want to know, will the institution of learning in Cambridge which once we called Harvard be known as Hangman's House?

105.

Oliver Wendell Holmes, Jr.: *Nixon v. Herndon*

After the Civil War, Southern states sought by various means to evade the requirements of the Fifteenth Amendment to the Constitution, which guaranteed Negroes the suffrage. One common device was to exclude Negroes from the Democratic Party primary elections on the grounds that the primary was a party and hence a private affair. In the one-party South, this was tantamount to exclusion from the election itself. In Nixon v. Herndon, *which had come to the Supreme Court on a writ of error, Justice Holmes ruled that the exclusion of Negroes from party primaries violated not only the Fifteenth but also the Fourteenth Amendment, which forbade states to deprive citizens of their rights without "due process of law." Holmes's opinion, handed down on March 7, 1927, is reprinted here in part.*

Source: 273 U.S. 536.

This is an action against the judges of elections for refusing to permit the plaintiff to vote at a primary election in Texas. It lays the damages at $5,000. The petition alleges that the plaintiff is a Negro, a citizen of the United States and of Texas and a resident of El Paso, and in every way qualified to vote, as set forth in detail, except that the statute to be mentioned interferes with his right; that on July 26, 1924, a primary election was held at El Paso for the nomination of candidates for a senator and representatives in Congress and state and other offices, upon the Democratic ticket; that the plaintiff, being a member of the Democratic Party, sought to vote but was denied the right by defendants; that the denial was based upon a statute of Texas enacted in May 1923, and designated Article 3039a, by the words of which "in no event shall a Negro be eligible to participate in a Democratic Party primary election held in the state of Texas," etc., and that this statute is contrary to the Fourteenth and Fifteenth amendments to the Constitution of the United States.

The defendants moved to dismiss upon the ground that the subject matter of the suit was political and not within the jurisdiction of the court and that no violation of the amendments was shown. The suit was dismissed, and a writ of error was taken directly to this court. Here no argument was made on behalf of the defendants, but a brief was allowed to be filed by the attorney general of the state.

The objection that the subject matter of the suit is political is little more than a play upon words. Of course, the petition concerns political action, but it alleges and seeks to recover for private damage. That private damage may be caused by such political action and may be recovered for in a suit at law hardly has been doubted for over 200 years. . . .

If the defendants' conduct was a wrong to the plaintiff, the same reasons that allow a recovery for denying the plaintiff a vote at a final election allow it for denying a vote at the primary election that may determine the final result.

The important question is whether the statute can be sustained. But although we state it as a question, the answer does not seem to us open to a doubt. We find it unnecessary to consider the Fifteenth Amendment because it seems to us hard to imagine a more direct and obvious infringement of the Fourteenth. That amendment, while it applies to all, was passed, as we know, with a special intent to protect the blacks from discrimination against them. (*Slaughter House Cases*. . . .) That amendment

not only gave citizenship and the privileges of citizenship to persons of color, but it denied to any state the power to withhold from them the equal protection of the laws. . . . What is this but declaring that the law in the states shall be the same for the black as for the white; that all persons, whether colored or white, shall stand equal before the laws of the states, and, in regard to the colored race, for whose protection the amendment was primarily designed, that no discrimination shall be made against them by law because of their color? . . .

The statute of Texas in the teeth of the prohibitions referred to assumes to forbid Negroes to take part in a primary election, the importance of which we have indicated, discriminating against them by the distinction of color alone. States may do a good deal of classifying that it is difficult to believe rational, but there are limits, and it is too clear for extended argument that color cannot be made the basis of a statutory classification affecting the right set up in this case.

Judgment reversed.

GABRIEL: *How about cleanin' up de whole mess of 'em and sta'tin' all over ag'in wid some new kind of animal?*
GOD: *An' admit I'm licked?*

MARC CONNELLY, *The Green Pastures*

106.

Alfred E. Smith: Defense of Catholics in Public Office

Alfred E. Smith, serving his fourth term as governor of New York, became in 1928 the first Catholic to be nominated for the presidency by a major political party. His candidacy for the Democratic nomination, which had been openly proclaimed a year before, had provoked much discussion and made Smith the target of violent anti-Catholic feeling, especially in the South and Southwest. Some of the objections to having a Catholic President were set forth in an open letter to Smith from New York lawyer Charles C. Marshall that was published in the Atlantic Monthly *in April 1927. Smith's prompt rejoinder to Marshall, which is reprinted here in part, appeared in the May issue of the magazine.*

Source: *Progressive Democracy*, New York, 1928, pp. 255-269.

In your open letter to me in the April *Atlantic Monthly*, you "impute" to American Catholics views which, if held by them, would leave open to question the loyalty and devotion to this country and its Constitution of more than 20 million American Catholic citizens. I am grateful to you for defining this issue in the open and for your courteous expression of the satisfaction it will bring to my fellow citizens for me to give "a disclaimer of the convictions" thus imputed. Without mental reservation I can and do make that disclaimer. These convictions are held neither by me nor by any other American Catholic, as far as I know.

Before answering the argument of your letter, however, I must dispose of one of its implications. You put your questions to me in connection with my candidacy for the office of President of the United States. My attitude with respect to that candidacy was fully stated in my last inaugural address as governor when, on Jan. 1, 1927, I said:

I have no idea what the future has in store for me. Everyone else in the United States has some notion about it except myself. No man could stand before this intelligent gathering and say that he was not receptive to the greatest position the world has to give anyone. But I can say this, that I will do nothing to achieve it except to give to the people of the state the kind and character of service that will make me deserve it.

I should be a poor American and a poor Catholic alike if I injected religious discussion into a political campaign. Therefore, I would ask you to accept this answer from me, not as a candidate for any public office but as an American citizen, honored with high elective office, meeting a challenge to his patriotism and his intellectual integrity. Moreover, I call your attention to the fact that I am only a layman. The *Atlantic Monthly* describes you as "an experienced attorney" who "has made himself an authority upon canon law." I am neither a lawyer nor a theologian. What knowledge of law I have was gained in the course of my long experience in the legislature and as chief executive of New York state. I had no such opportunity to study theology.

My first thought was to answer you with just the faith that is in me. But I knew instinctively that your conclusions could be logically proved false. It seemed right, therefore, to take counsel with someone schooled in the church law, from whom I learned whatever is hereafter set forth in definite answer to the theological questions you raise. I selected one whose patriotism neither you nor any other man will question. He wears upon his breast the Distinguished Service Cross of our country, its Distinguished Service Medal, the Ribbon of the Legion of Honor, and the Croix de Guerre with Palm of the French Republic. He was the Catholic chaplain of the almost wholly Catholic 165th Regiment in the World War — Father Francis P. Duffy, now in the military service of my own state.

Taking your letter as a whole and reducing it to commonplace English, you imply that there is conflict between religious loyalty to the Catholic faith and patriotic loyalty to the United States. Everything that has actually happened to me during my long public career leads me to know that no such thing as that is true. I have taken an oath of office in this state nineteen times. Each time I swore to defend and maintain the Constitution of the United States. All of this represents a period of public service in elective office almost continuous since 1903. I have never known any conflict between my official duties and my religious belief. No such conflict could exist. Certainly the people of this state recognize no such conflict. They have testified to my devotion to public duty by electing me to the highest office within their gift four times.

You yourself do me the honor, in addressing me, to refer to "your fidelity to the morality you have advocated in public and private life and to the religion you have revered; your great record of public trusts successfully and honestly discharged." During the years I have discharged these trusts I have been a communicant of the Roman Catholic Church. If there were conflict, I, of all men, could not have escaped it, because I have not been a silent man, but a battler for social and political reform. These battles would in their very nature disclose this conflict if there were any.

I regard public education as one of the foremost functions of government, and I have supported to the last degree the state Department of Education in every effort to promote our public-school system. The largest single item of increased appropriations under my administration appears in the educational group for the support of common schools. Since 1919, when I first became governor, this item has grown from $9 million to $82,500,000. My aim — and I may say I have succeeded in achieving it — has been legislation for child welfare, the protection of workingmen, women, and children, the modernization of the state's institutions for the care of helpless or unfortunate wards, the preservation of freedom of speech and opinion against the attack of wartime hysteria, and the complete reorganization of the structure of the government of the state.

I did not struggle for these things for any single element, but in the interest of all of the 11 million people who make up the state. In all of this work I had the support of churches of all denominations. I probably know as many ecclesiastics of my church as any other layman. During my long and active public career I never received from any of them anything except cooperation and encouragement in the full and complete discharge of my duty to the state. Moreover, I

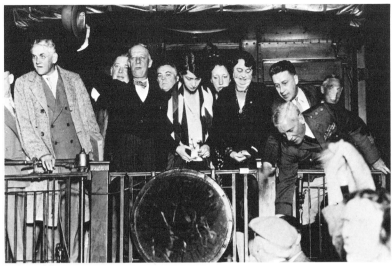

Alfred E. Smith pulling out of Chicago during a whistle-stop campaign for the presidency in 1928

am unable to understand how anything that I was taught to believe as a Catholic could possibly be in conflict with what is good citizenship. The essence of my faith is built upon the Commandments of God. The law of the land is built upon the Commandments of God. There can be no conflict between them.

Instead of quarreling among ourselves over dogmatic principles, it would be infinitely better if we joined together in inculcating obedience to these Commandments in the hearts and minds of the youth of the country as the surest and best road to happiness on this earth and to peace in the world to come. This is the common ideal of all religions. What we need is more religion for our young people, not less; and the way to get more religion is to stop the bickering among our sects, which can have for its effect only the creation of doubt in the minds of our youth as to whether or not it is necessary to pay attention to religion at all.

Then I know your imputations are false when I recall the long list of other public servants of my faith who have loyally served the state. You as a lawyer will prob-

ably agree that the office of chief justice of the United States is second not even to that of the President in its influence on the national development and policy. That court by its interpretation of the federal Constitution is a check not only upon the President himself but upon Congress as well. During one-fourth of its history it has been presided over by two Catholics, Roger Brooke Taney and Edward Douglass White. No one has suggested that the official conduct of either of these men was affected by any unwarranted religious influence or that religion played with them any part other than it should play in the life of every God-fearing man.

And I know your imputations are false when I recall the tens of thousands of young Catholics who have risked and sacrificed their lives in defense of our country. These fundamentals of life could not be true unless your imputations were false.

But, wishing to meet you on your own ground, I address myself to your definite questions, against which I have thus far made only general statements. I must first call attention to the fact that you often divorce sentences from their context in such a way as to give them something other than their real meaning. I will specify. You refer to the apostolic letter of Pope Leo XIII as "declaring to the world that the orders of the Church of England were void, her priests not priests," and so forth. You say that this was the "strange fruit" of the toleration of England to the Catholics. You imply that the pope gratuitously issued an affront to the Anglican Church. In fact, this apostolic letter was an answer to a request made at the instance of priests of the Anglican Church for recognition by the Roman Catholic Church of the validity of their priestly orders. The request was based on the ground that they had been ordained in succession from the Roman Catholic priests who became the first priests of the Anglican Church. The apostolic letter was a mere adverse answer to this request, ruling that Anglican priests were not Roman Catholic priests, and was in no sense the gratuitous insult which you suggest it to be. It was not directed against England or citizens of that Empire.

Again, you quote from the *Catholic Encyclopedia* that my church "regards dogmatic intolerance, not alone as her incontestable right but as her sacred duty." And you say that these words show that Catholics are taught to be politically, socially, and intellectually intolerant of all other people. If you had read the whole of that article in the *Catholic Encyclopedia*, you would know that the real meaning of these words is that for Catholics alone the church recognizes no deviation from complete acceptance of its dogma. These words are used in a chapter dealing with that subject only.

The very same article in another chapter dealing with toleration toward non-Catholics contains these words: "The intolerant man is avoided as much as possible by every high-minded person. . . . The man who is tolerant in every emergency is alone lovable." The phrase "dogmatic intoler-ance" does not mean that Catholics are to be dogmatically intolerant of other people, but merely that inside the Catholic Church they are to be intolerant of any variance from the dogma of the church.

Similar criticism can be made of many of your quotations. But, beyond this, by what right do you ask me to assume responsibility for every statement that may be made in any encyclical letter? As you will find in the *Catholic Encyclopedia* (Vol. V, p. 414), these encyclicals are not articles of our faith. The syllabus of Pope Pius IX, which you quote on the possible conflict between church and state, is declared by Cardinal Newman to have "no dogmatic force." You seem to think that Catholics must be all alike in mind and in heart, as though they had been poured into and taken out of the same mold. You have no more right to ask me to defend as part of my faith every statement coming from a prelate than I should have to ask you to accept as an article of your religious faith every statement of an Episcopal bishop, or of your political faith every statement of a President of the United States. So little are these matters of the essence of my faith that I, a devout Catholic since childhood, never heard of them until I read your letter. Nor can you quote from the canons of our faith a syllable that would make us less good citizens than non-Catholics. In fact and in truth, I have been taught the spirit of tolerance, and when you, Mr. Marshall, as a Protestant Episcopalian, join with me in saying the Lord's Prayer, we both pray not to "My Father" but to "Our Father."

But I go further to demonstrate that the true construction of your quotations by the leaders of Catholic thought is diametrically the opposite of what you suggest it to be.

YOUR FIRST PROPOSITION is that Catholics believe that other religions should, in the United States, be tolerated only as a matter of favor and that there should be an established church. You may find some dream of an ideal of a Catholic state, having no relation whatever to actuality, somewhere described. But, voicing the best Catholic thought on this subject, Dr. John A. Ryan, Professor of Moral Theology at the Catholic University of America, writes in *The State and the Church* of the encyclical of Pope Leo XIII, quoted by you:

> In practice, however, the foregoing propositions have full application only to the completely Catholic state. . . . The propositions of Pope Pius IX condemning the toleration of non-Catholic sects do not now, says Father Pohle, "apply even to Spain or the South American republics, to say nothing of countries possessing a greatly mixed population." He lays down the following general rule: "When several religions have firmly established themselves and taken root in the same territory, nothing else remains for the state than to exercise tolerance toward them all, or, as conditions exist today, to make complete religious liberty for individual and religious bodies a principle of government."

That is good Americanism and good Catholicism. And Father Pohle, one of the great writers of the Catholic Church, says further:

> If religious freedom has been accepted and sworn to as a fundamental law in a constitution, the obligation to show this tolerance is binding in conscience.

The American prelates of our church stoutly defend our constitutional declaration of equality of all religions before the law. Cardinal O'Connell has said:

> Thus, to every American citizen has come the blessed inheritance of civil, political, and religious liberty, safeguarded by the American Constitution . . . the right to worship God according to the dictates of his conscience.

Archbishop Ireland has said:

> The Constitution of the United States reads: "Congress shall make no laws respecting an establishment of religion or prohibiting the free exercise thereof." It was a great leap forward on the part of the new nation toward personal liberty and the consecration of the rights of conscience.

Archbishop Dowling, referring to any conceivable union of church and state, says:

> So many conditions for its accomplishment are lacking in every government of the world that the thesis may well be relegated to the limbo of defunct controversies.

I think you have taken your thesis from this limbo of defunct controversies.

Archbishop Ireland again said:

> Religious freedom is the basic life of America, the cement running through all its walls and battlements, the safeguard of its peace and prosperity. Violate religious freedom against Catholics, our swords are at once unsheathed. Violate it in favor of Catholics, against non-Catholics, no less readily do they leap from the scabbard.

Cardinal Gibbons has said:

> American Catholics rejoice in our separation of church and state, and I can conceive no combination of circumstances likely to arise which would make a union desirable to either church or state. . . . For ourselves we thank God that we live in America, "in this happy country of ours," to quote Mr. Roosevelt, where "religion and liberty are natural allies."

And referring particularly to your quotation from Pope Pius IX, Dr. Ryan, in *The State and the Church*, says:

> Pope Pius IX did not intend to declare that separation is always unadvisable, for he had more than once expressed his satisfaction with the arrangement obtaining in the United States.

With these great Catholics I stand squarely in support of the provisions of the Constitution which guarantee religious freedom and equality.

I come now to the speculation with

which theorists have played for generations as to the respective functions of church and state. You claim that the Roman Catholic Church holds that, if conflict arises, the church must prevail over the state. You write as though there were some Catholic authority or tribunal to decide with respect to such conflict. Of course, there is no such thing. As Dr. Ryan writes:

The Catholic doctrine concedes, nay, maintains, that the state is coordinate with the church and equally independent and supreme in its own distinct sphere.

What is the Protestant position? The Articles of Religion of your Protestant Episcopal Church (XXXVII) declare:

The power of the civil magistrate extendeth to all men, as well clergy as laity, in all things temporal; but hath no authority in things purely spiritual.

Your church, just as mine, is voicing the injunction of our common Savior to render unto Caesar the things that are Caesar's, and unto God the things that are God's.

What is this conflict about which you talk? It may exist in some lands which do not guarantee religious freedom. But in the wildest dreams of your imagination you cannot conjure up a possible conflict between religious principle and political duty in the United States, except on the unthinkable hypothesis that some law were to be passed which violated the common morality of all God-fearing men. And if you can conjure up such a conflict, how would a Protestant resolve it? Obviously by the dictates of his conscience. That is exactly what a Catholic would do. There is no ecclesiastical tribunal which would have the slightest claim upon the obedience of Catholic communicants in the resolution of such a conflict. As Cardinal Gibbons said of the supposition that "the pope were to issue commands in purely civil matters":

He would be offending not only against civil society but against God, and

violating an authority as truly from God as his own. Any Catholic who clearly recognized this would not be bound to obey the pope; or rather his conscience would bind him absolutely to disobey, because with Catholics, conscience is the supreme law which under no circumstances can we ever lawfully disobey.

Archbishop Ireland said:

To priest, to bishop, or to pope (I am willing to consider the hypothesis) who should attempt to rule in matters civil and political to influence the citizen beyond the range of their own orbit of jurisdiction that are the things of God, the answer is quickly made: "Back to your own sphere of rights and duties, back to the things of God."

Bishop England, referring to our Constitution, said:

Let the pope and the cardinals and all the powers of the Catholic world united make the least encroachment on that Constitution, we will protect it with our lives. Summon a general council — let that council interfere in the mode of our electing but an assistant to a turnkey of a prison — we deny the right, we reject the usurpation.

Our Supreme Court has marked out the spheres of influence of church and state in a case from which you quote copiously, *Watson v. Jones*, 13 Wall. 729; but you refrain from quoting this statement:

The right to organize voluntary religious associations, to assist in the expression and dissemination of any religious doctrine, and to create tribunals for the decision of controverted questions of faith within the association, and for the ecclesiastical government of all of the individual members, the congregation and officers within the general association, is unquestioned. . . . It is of the essence of these religious unions and of their right to establish tribunals for the decision of questions arising among themselves that those decisions could be binding in all cases of ecclesiastical cognizance, subject only to such appeal as the organism itself provides for.

That is the state's attitude toward the church. Archbishop Ireland thus puts the church's attitude toward the state: "To the Catholic obedience to law is a religious obligation, binding in God's name the conscience of the citizen. . . . Both Americanism and Catholicism bow to the sway of personal conscience."

Under our system of government the electorate entrusts to its officers of every faith the solemn duty of action according to the dictates of conscience. I may fairly refer once more to my own record to support these truths. No man, cleric or lay, has ever directly or indirectly attempted to exercise church influence on my administration of any office I have ever held, nor asked me to show special favor to Catholics or exercise discrimination against non-Catholics.

It is a well-known fact that I have made all of my appointments to public office on the basis of merit and have never asked any man about his religious belief. In the first month of this year there gathered in the Capitol at Albany the first governor's cabinet that ever sat in this state. It was composed, under my appointment, of two Catholics, thirteen Protestants, and one Jew. The man closest to me in the administration of the government of the state of New York is he who bears the title of assistant to the governor. He had been connected with the governor's office for thirty years, in subordinate capacities, until I promoted him to the position which makes him the sharer with me of my every thought and hope and ambition in the administration of the state. He is a Protestant, a Republican, and a Thirty-Second Degree Mason. In my public life I have exemplified that complete separation of church from state which is the faith of American Catholics today. . . .

I summarize my creed as an American Catholic. I believe in the worship of God according to the faith and practice of the Roman Catholic Church. I recognize no power in the institutions of my church to interfere with the operations of the Constitution of the United States or the enforcement of the law of the land. I believe in absolute freedom of conscience for all men and in equality of all churches, all sects, and all beliefs before the law as a matter of right and not as a matter of favor. I believe in the absolute separation of church and state and in the strict enforcement of the provisions of the Constitution, that Congress shall make no law respecting an establishment of religion or prohibiting the free exercise thereof. I believe that no tribunal of any church has any power to make any decree of any force in the law of the land, other than to establish the status of its own communicants within its own church.

I believe in the support of the public school as one of the cornerstones of American liberty. I believe in the right of every parent to choose whether his child shall be educated in the public school or in a religious school supported by those of his own faith. I believe in the principle of noninterference by this country in the internal affairs of other nations and that we should stand steadfastly against any such interference by whomsoever it may be urged. And I believe in the common brotherhood of man under the common fatherhood of God.

In this spirit I join with fellow Americans of all creeds in a fervent prayer that never again in this land will any public servant be challenged because of the faith in which he has tried to walk humbly with his God.

———————◆———————

Let's look at the record.

ALFRED E. SMITH, repeated phrase in political speeches, "He could make statistics sit up, beg, roll over and bark." — Robert Moses

General Pershing heading a victory parade in Washington, D.C., 1919

HEROES AND HOKUM

Warren G. Harding sounded the official retreat of America in his "normalcy" speech in 1920. Harding spoke for the vast majority in calling for a return to the already mythologized values of the past: middle-class morality, respectability, freedom for business, isolation. None of these was possible; the attempt to restore them and live by them in spite of the radically changed conditions of the world led directly to disaster. The bankruptcy of the public morality, a combination of small town, middle-class, and business virtues, was manifest in the inability of either Harding or Coolidge to make the distant, paternal, and inactive use of the presidency that each preferred an effective guarantee of good, honest government. The approach to business was reactive, based on the obsolete free-competition model and its belief that a fragmented concentration on a multitude of local, private goals would somehow result in a public good. "The business of America is business," said Coolidge, summing up the philosophy that encouraged growth beyond capital limitations and beyond all responsibility, that produced the apparent affirmation of the greatest boom in American history, and that ended in the inevitable Great Depression. The past finally ended.

Scenes in Chicago following announcement of the war's end: (Above) Aftermath of a celebration on Monroe Street; (below) marchers in the Armistice Parade, Nov. 11, 1918

(Above) A modern dance class influenced by Isadora Duncan performing on the grounds at Carnegie Tech, Pittsburgh; (below left) women arrested for indecent bathing attire on a Chicago beach, 1920; (below right) woman having her hair cut in the 1920s, a major event

(Above) Crowd at a Billy Sunday revival meeting in his huge temporary tabernacle in New York

(Right) Clarence Darrow and William Jennings Bryan were opposing lawyers at the celebrated "Monkey Trial" in Dayton, Tenn., 1925. John Scopes, a high school biology teacher, was tried for teaching the theory of evolution in violation of Tennessee law. Darrow used the trial to attack the legal sanctification of Fundamentalist beliefs; (below) John D. Rockefeller, a legend in his own time, with a group of Boy Scouts

(Above) George M. Cohan, popular vaudeville and Broadway performer, remembered for his musical "Yankee Doodle Dandy"; (top) Harry Houdini, the king of escape artists; (right) humorist Will Rogers; (below) Rogers with Billy Mitchell, a pioneer advocate of military air power

There was no lack of outlets for America's apparent need to idolize and richly reward popular heroes. Sports achieved new popularity and every sport, from good old baseball to the newly acceptable game of golf, had heroes to offer. Even more exciting and more accessible to the general populace was the new world of Hollywood movies, custom-made for the hordes of hero-makers. The cultural role of the movie was beginning to be felt, if not understood, as it helped promote the fads and fancies of the Twenties, from fast cars and hip flasks to flagpole sitters and flappers.

(Top) Charlie Chaplin as the little tramp in "Sunnyside," a 1919 film; (left) marquee of a theater in St. Louis; (bottom) motion picture theater in Bisbee, Arizona

(Above) William S. Hart, early Western hero, in "The Aryan," 1916; (below) Clara Bow, the "IT" Girl in "Dancing Mothers," 1926

(Above) Mary Pickford, "America's Sweetheart" of early movies; (below) Gloria Swanson, 1924

(Above) Douglas Fairbanks, dominant figure in Hollywood both as box office attraction and producer, shown in a common dangerous situation in "The Black Pirate," 1926

(Right) Rudolph Valentino, the ultimate matinee idol of the 1920s, with Vilma Banky in a scene from "The Shiek"; (below) part of the enormous crowds that turned out to pay last respects to Valentino following his death at 31 in 1926

(Above) Jack Dempsey after his victory over
Charles Carpentier, 1921; (below) the referee trying to get Dempsey to a neutral corner in the famous "long count" battle with Gene Tunney,
1927. Tunney arose and eventually won the fight;
(right) Tunney during training for the fight

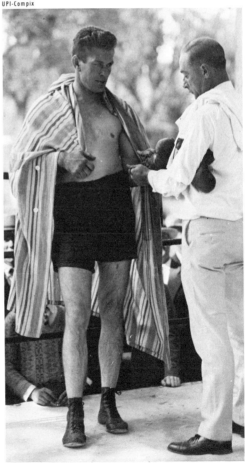

(Above) Babe Ruth hitting his 60th home run in 1927

(Above left) Frank Chance, with cigar and spats, epitomizes the ball player of the day; (above) Walter Johnson, Washington pitcher; (below) crowds watching the World Series in Philadelphia

(Above) Red Grange taking the opening kickoff back 95 yards for a touchdown, an act that, repeated often, made him football's first super-hero; (below left) Bill Tilden, amateur tennis champion of the 1920s; (right) New York reception of golf hero Bobby Jones

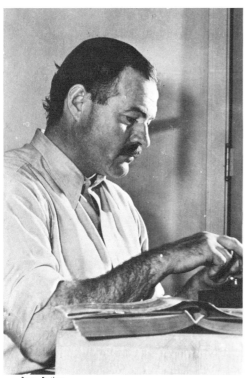

(Top left) Ernest Hemingway; (top right) Gertrude Stein and (bottom left) F. Scott Fitzgerald with his family. All were American writers living in Paris in the 1920s. (Bottom right) Alfred Stieglitz; portrait by Man Ray

(Left) Poet Carl Sandburg photographed by Steichen, 1919; (above) H. L. Mencken and George Jean Nathan in 1928

The literary field in the 1920s has since become best known for the generation of expatriate writers and artists, a group whose migration to Europe was a part of the postwar disillusionment. Reacting against materialism, commercialism, the whole middle-class culture of America, they sought purer airs in Europe. The "lost generation" remained American in its concerns, using native subjects and themes and constantly worrying the twin threads of alienation and anti-intellectualism in American culture.

(Right) Nobel Prize winner Sinclair Lewis; (below) Sherwood Anderson; (bottom right) Lincoln Steffens and Clarence Darrow

Charles Lindbergh and "The Spirit of St. Louis" arriving in Paris, 1927

When the age that made a hero of any-one who captured headlines came upon a real hero, its response was unbounded. On May 21, 1927, an unknown airmail pilot named Charles A. Lindbergh completed the first nonstop transatlantic flight and became the ultimate hero. His return was greeted with a huge tickertape parade and the medal of honor. The celebrations surrounding his feat and the adulation bestowed on him epitomized, more than any other event of the era, the national habit of excess.

(Right) Lindbergh photographed with his plane shortly before leaving New York for Paris; (below) parade for Lindbergh in New York after his return from France, June 1927

107.

CHARLES A. LINDBERGH: Alone Over the Atlantic

Charles A. Lindbergh was twenty-five years old when, on May 20, 1927, he took off from Long Island to fly the Atlantic alone in his monoplane, Spirit of St. Louis. *A good pilot — he had been a barnstormer and had flown a mail run — his ostensible purpose in making the flight was to win a $25,000 prize that had gone unawarded since 1919. Maybe that was all he had in mind, but in fact his exploit turned out to be the single most famous feat in aviation history, and Lindbergh found himself the hero of the Twenties. No one has ever been able to say exactly why, but F. Scott Fitzgerald may have come close to the truth when he wrote: "In the spring of '27, something bright and alien flashed across the sky. A young Minnesotan who seemed to have had nothing to do with his generation did a heroic thing, and for a moment people set down their glasses in country clubs and speakeasies and thought of their old best dreams." President Coolidge, in a gesture that seemed extravagant to no one, sent a cruiser to fetch Lindbergh back from France, and Mayor "Jimmy" Walker remarked after the ticker tape parade up Broadway: "Charles Lindbergh, New York is yours. I don't give it to you. You won it. And one other thing. Before you go, you will have to provide us with a new street-cleaning department to clean up the mess." The following selection is a newspaper interview given by Lindbergh upon his arrival in Paris.*

Source: *New York Times,* May 23, 1927.

WELL, HERE I AM in the hands of American Ambassador Herrick. From what I have seen of it, I am sure I am going to like Paris.

It isn't part of my plans to fly my plane back to the United States, although that doesn't mean I have finished my flying career. If I thought that was going to be the result of my flight across the Atlantic, you may be sure I would never have undertaken it. Indeed, I hope that I will be able to do some flying over here in Europe — that is, if the souvenir hunters left enough of my plane last night.

Incidentally, that reception I got was the most dangerous part of the whole flight. If wind and storm had handled me as vigorously as that Reception Committee of Fifty Thousand, I would never have reached Paris and I wouldn't be eating a 3-o'clock-in-the-afternoon breakfast here in Uncle Sam's Embassy.

There's one thing I wish to get straight about this flight. They call me "Lucky," but luck isn't enough. As a matter of fact, I had what I regarded and still regard as the best existing plane to make the flight from New York to Paris. I had what I regard as the best engine, and I was equipped with what were in the circumstances the best possible instruments for making such efforts. I hope I made good use of what I had.

That I landed with considerable gasoline left means that I had recalled the fact that so many flights had failed because of lack of fuel, and that was one mistake I tried to avoid.

All in all, I couldn't complain of the

weather. It wasn't what was predicted. It was worse in some places and better in others. In fact, it was so bad once that for a moment there came over me the temptation to turn back. But then I figured it was probably just as bad behind me as in front of me, so I kept on toward Paris.

As you know, we (that's my ship and I) took off rather suddenly. We had a report somewhere around 4 o'clock in the afternoon before that the weather would be fine, so we thought we would try it.

We had been told we might expect good weather mostly during the whole of the way. But we struck fog and rain over the coast not far from the start. Actually, it was comparatively easy to get to Newfoundland, but real bad weather began just after dark, after leaving Newfoundland, and continued until about four hours before daybreak. We hadn't expected that at all, and it sort of took us by surprise, morally and physically. That was when I began to think about turning back.

Then sleet began, and, as all aviators know, in a sleetstorm one may be forced down in a very few minutes. It got worse and worse. There, above and below me, and on both sides, was that driving storm. I made several detours trying to get out of it, but in vain. I flew as low as 10 feet above the water and then mounted up to 10,000 feet. Along toward morning the storm eased off, and I came down to a comparatively low level.

I had seen one ship just before losing sight of Newfoundland, and I saw the glow of several others afterward through the mist and storm. During the day I saw no ships until near Ireland.

I had, as I said, no trouble before I hit the storm I referred to. We had taken off at 7:55 in the morning. The field was slightly damp and soft, so the takeoff was longer than it would have been otherwise. I had no trouble getting over the houses and trees. I kept out of the way of every obstacle and was careful not to take any unnecessary chances. As soon as I cleared everything, the motor was throttled down to three-fourths and kept there during the whole flight, except when I tried to climb over the storm.

Soon after starting I was out of sight of land for 300 miles, from Cape Cod over the sea to Nova Scotia. The motor was acting perfectly and was carrying well the huge load of 451 gallons of gasoline and 20 gallons of oil, which gave my ship the greatest cruising radius of any plane of its type.

I passed over St. John's, N.F., purposely going out of my way a few miles to check up. I went right through the narrow pass, going down so low that it could be definitely established where I was at that hour. That was the last place I saw before taking to the open sea.

I had made preparations before I started for a forced landing if it became necessary, but after I started I never thought much about the possibility of such a landing. I was ready for it, but I saw no use thinking about it, inasmuch as one place would have been about as good or as bad as another.

Despite the talk about my periscope, I had no trouble in regard to visibility. The view I had on both sides was quite good enough for navigating the ocean, and the purpose of the periscope was only to enable me to see any obstacle directly in front of me. The periscope was useful in starting from New York and landing in Paris. Other than that I used it very little. I kept a map in front of me and an instrument showing practically where I was all of the time.

Shortly after leaving Newfoundland I began to see icebergs. There was a low fog and even through it I could make out bergs clearly. It began to get very cold, but I was well prepared for cold. I had on ordinary flying clothing, but I was down in the cockpit, which protected me, and I never suffered from the weather.

Within an hour after leaving the coast it

became dark. Then I struck clouds and decided to try to get over them. For a while I succeeded, at a height of 10,000 feet. I flew at this height until early morning. The engine was working beautifully and I was not sleepy at all. I felt just as if I was driving a motorcar over a smooth road, only it was easier.

Then it began to get light and the clouds got higher. I went under some and over others. There was sleet in all of those clouds and the sleet began to cling to the plane. That worried me a great deal and I debated whether I should keep on or go back. I decided I must not think any more about going back. I realized that it was henceforth only a question of getting there. It was too far to turn back.

The engine was working perfectly and that cheered me. I was going along a hundred miles an hour and I knew that if the motor kept on turning I would get there. After that I thought only about navigating, and then I thought that I wasn't so badly off after all.

It was true that the flight was thirty-four hours long, and that at almost any moment in it a forced landing might be what you might call "rather interesting," but I remembered that the flying boys I knew back home spent some hours almost every week in bad flying when a forced landing would have been just as bad for them as a forced landing would have been for me. Those boys don't get credit for it, that's all, and without doubt in a few years many people will be taking just as many chances as I took.

The only real danger I had was at night. In the daytime I knew where I was going, but in the evening and at night it was largely a matter of guesswork. However, my instruments were so good that I never could get more than 200 miles off my course, and that was easy to correct, and I had enough extra gasoline to take care of a number of such deviations. All in all, the trip over the

Atlantic, especially the latter half, was much better than I expected.

Laymen have made a great deal of the fact that I sailed without a navigator and without the ordinary stock of navigation instruments, but my real director was my earth inductor compass. I also had a magnetic compass, but it was the inductor compass which guided me so faithfully that I hit the Irish coast only three miles from the theoretic point that I might have hit it if I had had a navigator. I replaced a navigator's weight by the inductor compass. The compass behaved so admirably that I am ashamed to hear anyone talk about my luck. Maybe I am lucky, but all the same I knew at every moment where I was going.

The inductor compass is based on the principle of the relation between the earth's magnetic field and the magnetic field generated in the airplane. When the course has been set so that the needle registered zero on this compass, any deviation, from any cause, would cause the needle to swing away from zero in the direction of the error. By flying the plane with the needle at an equal distance on the other side of zero and for about the same time the error had been committed, the plane would be back on her course again. This inductor compass was so accurate that I really needed no other guide.

Fairly early in the afternoon I saw a fleet of fishing boats. On some of them I could see no one, but on one of them I saw some men and flew down, almost touching the craft and yelled at them, asking if I was on the right road to Ireland.

They just stared. Maybe they didn't hear me. Maybe I didn't hear them. Or maybe they thought I was just a crazy fool.

An hour later I saw land. I have forgotten just what time it was. It must have been shortly before 4 o'clock. It was rocky land and all my study told me it was Ireland. And it was Ireland!

I slowed down and flew low enough to

study the land and be sure of where I was; and, believe me, it was a beautiful sight. It was the most wonderful looking piece of natural scenery I have ever beheld.

After I had made up my mind that it was Ireland, the right place for me to strike rather than Spain or some other country, the rest was child's play. I had my course all marked out carefully from approximately the place where I hit the coast, and you know it is quite easy to fly over strange territory if you have good maps and your course prepared.

I flew quite low over Ireland to be seen, but apparently no great attention was paid to me. I also flew low over England, mounted a little over the Channel, and then came down close to land when I passed a little west of Cherbourg. From Cherbourg I headed for the Seine and followed it upstream.

I noticed it gets dark much later over here than in New York and I was thankful for that. What especially pleased me was the ease with which I followed my course after hitting the coast of Ireland.

When I was about half an hour away from Paris, I began to see rockets and Very lights sent up from the airfield, and I knew I was all right.

I saw an immense vertical electric sign, which I made out to be the Eiffel Tower. I circled Paris once and immediately saw Le Bourget [the aviation field], although I didn't know at first what it was. I saw a lot of lights, but in the dark I couldn't make out any hangars. I sent Morse signals as I flew over the field, but no one appears to have seen them. The only mistake in all my calculations was that I thought Le Bourget was northeast rather than east of Paris.

Fearing for a moment that the field I had seen — remember I couldn't see the crowd — was some other airfield than Le Bourget, I flew back over Paris to the northwest, looking for Le Bourget. I was slightly confused by the fact that, whereas in America

when a ship is to land, beacons are put out when floodlights are turned on, at Le Bourget both beacons and floodlights were going at the same time.

I was anxious to land where I was being awaited. So when I didn't find another airfield, I flew back toward the first lights I had seen, and flying low I saw the lights of numberless automobiles. I decided that was the right place, and I landed.

I appreciated the reception which had been prepared for me, and had intended taxiing up to the front of the hangars, but no sooner had my plane touched the ground than a human sea swept toward it. I saw there was danger of killing people with my propeller, and I quickly came to a stop.

That reception was the most dangerous part of the trip. Never in my life have I seen anything like that human sea. It isn't clear to me yet just what happened. Before I knew it I had been hoisted out of the cockpit, and one moment was on the shoulders of some men and the next moment on the ground.

It seemed to be even more dangerous for my plane than for me. I saw one man tear away the switch and another took something out of the cockpit. Then, when they started cutting pieces of cloth from the wings, I struggled to get back to the plane, but it was impossible.

A brave man with good intentions tried to clear a way for me with a club. Swinging the club back, he caught me on the back of the head.

It isn't true that I was exhausted. I was tired, but I wasn't exhausted.

Several French officers asked me to come away with them and I went, casting anxious glances at my ship. I haven't seen it since, but I am afraid it suffered. I would regret that very much because I want to use it again.

But I must remember that crowd did welcome me. Good Lord! There must have been a million of them. Other men will fly the Atlantic as I did, but I think it safe to guess that none of them will get any warmer reception than I got.

Finally, I got to Ambassador Herrick's house, and I have certainly been all right since then. . . .

I look forward to the day when transatlantic flying will be a regular thing. It is a question largely of money. If people can be found willing to spend enough to make proper preparations, there is no reason why it can't be made very practical. Of course,

there are many things to be studied, one of the important points being whether the single-motor or multimotor ship is best. . . .

I didn't bring any extra clothes with me. I am wearing a borrowed suit now. It was a case of clothes or gasoline, and I took the gasoline. I have a check on a Paris bank and am going to cash it tomorrow morning, buy shirts, socks, and other things. I expect to have a good time in Paris.

But I do want to do a little flying over here.

108.

ANDREW FURUSETH: Work Is Worship

Organized labor went into a period of decline in the 1920s that was not arrested until the New Deal period. Membership in trade unions and in the American Federation of Labor fell sharply. But the rumbles of discontent were being felt in some areas, even if the unions seemed satisfied with their lot. Mine workers, textile workers, and longshoremen, among others, did not acquiesce in the pattern of cooperation between business and the unions. Andrew Furuseth, president of the International Seamen's Union, was one who declined to accept the idea that all was well between capital and labor even in this era of general prosperity. Yet he was far to the right of the radical Industrial Workers of the World, which advocated overthrowing the capitalist system. In a Labor Day address to students at the University of California in 1927, which is reprinted here in part, Furuseth presented the case for the industrial workingman in terms of traditional American ideals of work and liberty.

Source: *Andrew Furuseth: A Symposium*, New Bedford, Mass., 1927, pp. 175–180.

IN GENESIS WE ARE TOLD that "God created man in His image, in the image of God created He him; male and female created He them." We are further told that man was to take dominion over the earth and that its products were to be to him for meat. Thus we are told that man is the child of God, that men were created equal, with equal right to life, liberty, and the pursuit of happiness. And God rested and saw that all was well. Creation was, so some teachers have told us, finished.

When God made man in His own image — like Himself — it must mean that He gave creative powers to man and that henceforth man was to continue creation, and in freely working — creating — he is obeying the fundamental law of his being.

Whatever we may think of the narrative in the Bible, we cannot doubt that man has creative powers and that creation has continued.

Such historical and archaeological information as we have been able to gather proves, first, that from the earliest times man has been occupied in creating tools, weapons, foods, shelters, customs, laws, religions, and states; second, that while opportunities were equal and man was free to use his creative powers, there were improvements in physical and mental qualities, and that where the free use of the creative powers had been hindered by bondage or prevented by slavery, there has been decay and death. Whether such bondage or slavery was imposed on a group or on the individual, the results have been the same, as we find from the history of India and the history of the nations that have passed away.

Bondage has been the nemesis of nations and of necessity it could not be otherwise, because bondage results in direct negation of the purpose of man's being and is the violation of the fundamental law of life. The bondman can feel no responsibility; he can have no sense of morality, of self-respect, or of honor; he can have no individual will, and for these reasons he cannot exercise his creative power. He — the slave — is alone. Association for mutual aid is unthinkable. Deprived of human estate he is degraded below the animal or vegetable kingdoms. In having thoughts that he cannot utter to men, he is like an animal; in having impulses that he cannot follow, he is less.

In his lack of mobility he is like a tree; in his inability to obey the laws of his being, he is less. His imagination is corrupted, his thoughts darkened. He is dominated by fear — the mother of hate and treachery. He hates his work because it is compelled from without, not an impulse from within. The feeling of his bondage expresses itself in hatred of his master and in a selfishness that knows naught of moderation or restraint, except as it arises from fear. Fear removed, his passions become like a rush of mighty waters with barriers destroyed. Any man compelled to labor against his will, be it by an individual or by society, is a bondman. Let the American people beware of bondage being imposed upon any class. Toleration of it by workers in any field of endeavor is as we shall see treason to American ideals. To resist it is the highest duty, though the result may be prison or death. . . .

The organizations of monster corporations — supermen — capable of action at once over an indeterminate area, of being present in many cities and states at the same time, and endowed with practical immortality, are grinding the faces of the workers. They control wages and this means the control of the clothing that wife and children shall wear, of the food they shall eat, of the shelter they shall enjoy, and of the education the children shall be able to obtain. They control the hours of labor, which means that they determine when the father shall be permitted to be with his family. The worker feels himself controlled at his work and often fears to straighten his back.

Kingly power touched man in spots and at times. The industrial master controls him at his work, blanketing his creative powers; he watches over him at his home, he follows him to his church and to his benevolent society, and finally forbids him to join with his fellows in any trade union to consult about his grievances with the view of having them redressed. As the king punished or rewarded, so does the industrial master; as the king cajoled or bribed, so the industrial master; as the king sent unyielding men to prison or drove them into exile, so the industrial master, by the use of the blacklist, drives men from their homes and compels them to become wanderers, often under assumed names. And yet those laborers will organize and, like Parliament, submit petitions for redress of grievances; and when that fails, they, like the people's representatives in Parliament, will endeavor to compel favorable consideration by withholding the supply of labor which the industrial master needs to continue his business.

The road to freedom and equality on the industrial field is the same as was the road on the political field. The resistance on the part of the Third Estate will, however, be fierce and long. The Third Estate has come into power, it has overcome the opposition of the old governing class, and it feels itself to be "the heir of the castle and the guild." Their power is immense. Some of them control the lives of more men, women, and children than did many a monarch in earlier times. They have seized upon and are using the state. They either control or endeavor to control the churches through the pew; the press through advertising patronage or ownership; the colleges and universities through endowments; the legal profession through employments; the schools through the school boards, and they use the great publishing houses to suppress or rewrite the poets of the past.

They are seeking through the use of the equity power and direct or indirect legislation to deprive the workers of the freedom to quit work and the right to practise mutual aid. They are seeking to compel political obedience through the use of their industrial power, and, finally, they appeal to the young to join in suppressing strikes by a temporary use of even the students at colleges and universities. That these could be used seemed to me to be impossible. Universities are cultural centers. Here the inheritance of past ages [is] studied, classified, and digested; here we are to find through study of the past some guide for the future; here are stored the traditions of the people; here the evolution of man and institutions

as found in history and in religion should be understood; here the real status of labor should be appreciated; here the *laborare est orare* [to work is to pray] of the old monks should be realized as true; here the Declaration of Independence should find its defenders; here is the temple for the keeping of the Covenant, and yet from these places come young men who think it their duty to assist the employers — the just or the unjust — to beat their workers into submission when they have gone on strike to obtain some redress of grievance. The thing seemed monstrous.

I was born in Europe, where the fight was between the old governing class and the Third Estate, and I had never heard of students participating in such struggles except on the side of the workers and the thing hurt. Some thinking, of course, made me understand that there was no such fight here, that while in Europe, as now here, the vast majority of students were from families connected with the Third Estate, and that while in Europe they felt themselves part of a struggle to obtain power, the same class of young men here felt themselves on the defensive to preserve the power which was being attacked. Then I read the report of a distinguished professor describing the strikebreaker as a hero and I began to understand better, but not to excuse the student strikebreaker.

The best that we can do for the strikebreaker is to pity his ignorance or his lack of character; but with this pity will, if he comes from a college or a university, be a mixture of contempt. It is for the man who scabs because of necessity that there may be unmixed pity. The man who knows, as students at a college or university must know, and who out of sport or class-consciousness goes as a strikebreaker, is a traitor to himself and, of course, to fundamental Americanism. When in our hour of trial and communing with "the laws of nature and of nature's God" we agreed that all men are created equal; that they are endowed by their Creator with certain inalienable rights; that among these are life, liberty, and the pursuit of happiness, we enter into a covenant with "nature and nature's God" by which, as a people, we are to live and be judged, and we should realize that if there be a sin against the Holy Ghost, then the failure to keep this Covenant sacred is such sin, and the last place out of which desecration might be expected to come ought to be a college or a university — the cultural centers of our people.

Work is worship — to labor is to pray — because that is to exercise the highest, the divine faculties implanted in us as the sons of God. It matters not if the labor be the writing of a thesis or the digging of a ditch, it is the use of the same divine faculty to labor — to create — and upon its proper and free use depends the life of individuals, nations, and races. Those that have been untrue have shared the fate of the tree without fruit. They have passed away because they encumbered the earth. Those that have been true have lived, and according to history and to religious belief they are to live. Let us try to profit by this lesson and so live that labor shall be free, that it shall come into its own.

109.

WILL ROGERS: America Only

In November 1927 William Hale ("Big Bill") Thompson was reelected to a third term as mayor of Chicago. He had campaigned on the slogan "America First" and emphasized his disapproval of American participation in the World Court and of alleged British machinations to influence American affairs. Immediately after his election, Thompson organized the America First Foundation and invited all other mayors to join it. The membership fee was $10. He thereafter traveled throughout the states advertising his foundation (and himself in the process). Will Rogers satirized the foundation and its founder in his syndicated weekly column on November 13, 1927.

Source: *Autobiography*, Donald Day, ed., Boston, 1949, pp. 160-164.

NOW OF COURSE YOU ALL HAVE READ about Mayor Bill Thompson's Society, "America First," that he is forming. He had asked all the Mayors of the country to join it, and as soon as he gets them in, he will go after some prominent people, and it looks like it might develop into quite a thing. Well, of course, getting my idea from him, I go ahead and form me one "America only."

There has been a terrible lot of various Societys formed to try and instill Americanism into our lagging Patriots. If you have never formed a Society in your life and don't know what to form one about, Why don't let that worry you in the least. Just start to sponsor "Better Citizenship," or "100 percent Americanism," "America for the Americans," or any of those original ideas. There has been quite an epidemic of these, especially since the war.

It seems that before the war come along, we were really kinder lax in our duty toward declaring just what we were. The war come along and about all we could do was to muster up five or six million men of every breed and color that ever been invented. Now these poor fellows dident know whether they were "100 percent Americans" or "Better Citizens," or what they were, and we started them drilling so fast that they dident have time to go through a clinic and find out.

You see up to then they dident know what all this meant. They thought that as long as they paid their taxes, tended to their own business, went to their own churches, kept kinder within the law, that that was all they was supposed to do. And it was like that in the old days. But you see we was a backwards nation and dident know it. What we had to learn was to be better Americans. Why here was old men that had raised a big family and had never paid a cent of dues to prove to the rest of the World that they were for "America First."

Can you imagine such ignorance? How they had ever been able to do this without declaring where they stood was just another one of our lucky blunders. So when the war come along and we found out that all everybody would do was to die, or suffer, or get rich (or whatever the circumstances called for) for their country, why we saw right away that something was needed to instill patriotism. So hence the forming of all these various societies. They come just in the nick of time. For after the war, a lot of young men who had never known much about other men from different parts of the Country, and different Nationalities, during the days in camps and in France had become to know and like and understand each other, and find out each other's viewpoint.

In other words it was just the start of what might a been a bad friendship and un-

derstanding. But it's like everything else, when the necessity arises somebody always arises with the remedy, so on investigation it was found that a lot of these same boys were not 100 percent Americans at all. We had been kinder lax in who we had let into our war, everything had come up so hurriedly. Why a lot of them couldent even speak English. A lot of them dident go to churches, and worse than all, a lot of them went to the wrong churches. In fact, there was a million things we found out that we should have found out before we associated with 'em. Of course it was all too late now and was all over, and we would just have to charge it off to bad management. But let's get organized and don't let it happen again. We all went in 50-50 in war time, but this is peace now and we got time to see who is who, and why.

So these Societys commenced to be formed and they grabbed our little civilization just when it was on the brink and hauled it back to normalcy. You see in America there was originally just one Society (Well it was really two combined): It was the Declaration of Independence, and the Constitution of the United States. If you was here and belonged to that why you was all members of the same Club. You dident know whether you was 100 percent, or 2 and ¾ percent, or what ratio you was. You dident know whether you was a good citizen, or bad one. All you knew was that you belonged to this club called America, and all you had to do was work for it, fight for it and act like a gentleman, that was all the by-laws there was. As long as you did that, you could worship what you wanted to, talk any language you wanted to, in fact it looked like a pretty liberal layout. But after 150 or more years, it was immediately seen that this plan was no good, that the old boys that layed out the Constitution dident know much, that the country should be divided up in various Societys and cliques. So that brings us down to this generation, who really are showing us just what to do to prove that we are not against the old Fatherland.

We used to think that we were for it as long as we dident do anything against it, but now we find we got to join something and announce daily that we are for it. We have got to weed out these ones that are not 100 percent. We got to get around these Luncheons more, and sing some get-together songs. This old thing of eating at home with the folks is never going to get you anywhere. There is no real Americanism in that. Let's get down to the club and do some shouting and get some spirit into the old land.

"Going to be an election coming along pretty soon and we want to stick by the members of the club against all the outsiders." "There is a lot of these people just sitting around and not doing anything for American spirit and they are undermining the very principals of our Government." So you see its stuff like that that will save us. If those kind of clubs and societys hadent been formed just when they was, this would have been a fine looking country now. So get into a club as soon as you can. I don't care what it is just so its banded together to make somebody else's life miserable and yours great.

Now I have looked over all the clubs and none of them seem to have enough scope, or broad minded ideal. So that is why as I told you a few weeks ago that I wanted to get this Society going. "America First" is all right, but it allows somebody else to be second. Now sometimes a thing second can be almost as good as something that's first. So that's the thing my Society avoids. Its with the whole idea of there being no one else. In other words, I am just taking the spirit and foundation of other clubs and societys and making them broader.

They are against something (They got to be against something or they wouldent be formed). Well, mine improves on any of theirs; its against everything. I can take my "America Only" idea and eliminate wars. The minute we extinguish all other nations there will be no more wars, unless its a civil war among ourselves, and that of course we can take care of right here at home without a shipping board. I am getting a lot of applications already, real redblooded go-gettum Americans, that have seen this country trampled under foreign feet enough, and they are right out in the open. Why I figure the patriotism in my organization when I get it formed will run around 165 or 170 percent American. It will make a sucker out of these little 100 percent organizations. Its not too late to send your $20 yet. Remember when you belong to "America Only" you are the last word in organizations.

———◆———

All I know is what I read in the papers.

I never met a man I didn't like.

WILL ROGERS

110.

STEPHEN VINCENT BENÉT: "American Names"

Stephen Vincent Benét was living in Paris in 1927 when he wrote "American Names."
Unlike many expatriates, Benét was neither disillusioned with democracy nor
contemptuous of American life, and the poem — along with John Brown's Body,
another fruit of his stay in France — expressed his deep love for his native land.
The verses, in celebrating the variety of American place-names, not only reflect the
diversity of the nation's cultural origins but also proclaim the plain beauty to be
found everywhere, if one only takes the trouble to look for it.

Source: *Selected Poetry and Prose,* Basil Davenport, ed., New York, 1960.

AMERICAN NAMES

I have fallen in love with American names,
The sharp names that never get fat,
The snakeskin-titles of mining-claims,
The plumed war-bonnet of Medicine Hat,
Tucson and Deadwood and Lost Mule Flat.

Seine and Piave are silver spoons,
But the spoonbowl-metal is thin and worn,
There are English counties like
hunting-tunes
Played on the keys of a postboy's horn,
But I will remember where I was born.

I will remember Carquinez Straits,
Little French Lick and Lundy's Lane,
The Yankee ships and the Yankee dates
And the bullet-towns of Calamity Jane.
I will remember Skunktown Plain.

I will fall in love with a Salem tree
And a rawhide quirt from Santa Cruz,
I will get me a bottle of Boston sea

And a blue-gum nigger to sing me blues.
I am tired of loving a foreign muse.

Rue des Martyrs and Bleeding-Heart-Yard,
Senlis, Pisa, and Blindman's Oast,
It is a magic ghost you guard
But I am sick for a newer ghost,
Harrisburg, Spartanburg, Painted Post.

Henry and John were never so right?
And Henry and John were always
Granted, but when it was time to go
And the tea and the laurels had stood
all night,
Did they never watch for Nantucket Light?

I shall not rest quiet in Montparnasse.
I shall not lie easy at Winchelsea.
You may bury my body in Sussex grass,
You may bury my tongue at Champmédy.
I shall not be there. I shall rise and pass.
Bury my heart at Wounded Knee.

1928

111.

CALVIN COOLIDGE: Veto of the McNary-Haugen Bill

All did not prosper in the prosperous Twenties; farmers, in particular, suffered extremely when the falling off of the foreign market after the war brought about a severe depression in agricultural prices. Various attempts were made to remedy the situation. Notable was the McNary-Haugen Bill, sponsored by the Farm Bloc in Congress and conceived by Hugh S. Johnson and George Peek, farm implement manufacturers from Moline, Illinois. Their plan called for the federal government to purchase farm produce at a price compounded of the world market price, plus the U.S. tariff rate on the item. The government would then sell the surplus at the world price to foreign buyers, and make up the loss by an "equalization fee" assessed against the farmers. With domestic prices thereby raised to a level higher than that obtained on the world market, farmers would receive a better return, since the domestic market was larger than the world market. President Coolidge vetoed the bill in 1927 and again in May 1928, considering it unwarranted legislation in behalf of a special interest. Part of the 1928 veto message is reprinted here.

Source: 70 Congress, 1 Session, Senate Document No. 141.

SENATE BILL 3555, called the Surplus Control Act, is in some respects an improvement over Senate Bill 4808 of the last Congress. It includes several provisions which, if unencumbered by objectionable features, would form a basis for a measure that should do much to develop stronger business organizations in agriculture. But the present bill contains not only the so-called equalization fee and other features of the old measure prejudicial, in my opinion, to sound public policy and to agriculture, but also new and highly objectionable provisions. In its entirety it is little less undesirable than the earlier measure. The bill still is unconstitutional. This position is supported by the opinion of the attorney general. . . .

In its essentials the objectionable plan proposed here is the stimulation of the price of agricultural commodities and products thereof by artificially controlling the surpluses so that there will be an apparent scarcity on the market. This is to be done by means of a board having supposedly adequate powers and adequate funds to accomplish such purpose through various agencies, governmental and private. The surpluses of the different selected commodities so accumulated by the board are then to be sold by export and otherwise directly or through such agencies at whatever loss is necessary in making the disposition. The fund to pay the losses and other costs, while at first furnished by the government, is ultimately to be replaced and thereafter replenished from time to time by means of a tax or fee charged against the product. The theory is that the enhanced price of the commodity would enable the producer to pay the equalization fee and still reap a profit.

The recurring problem of surpluses in farm products has long been a subject of deep concern to the entire nation, and any economically sound, workable solution of it would command not only the approval but the profound gratitude of our people. The present measure, however, falls far short of that most desirable objective; indeed, although it purports to provide farm relief by lessening the cares of our greatest industry, it not only fails to accomplish that purpose but actually heaps even higher its burdens of political control, of distribution costs, and of foreign competition.

It embodies a formidable array of perils for agriculture which are all the more menacing because of their being obscured in a maze of ponderously futile bureaucratic paraphernalia. In fact, in spite of the inclusion in this measure of some constructive steps proposed by the administration, it renews most of the more vicious devices which appeared in the bill that was vetoed last year. This document is much altered from its previous form; but its substance, particularly as to its evident ultimate effect of tending to delude the farmer with a fantastic promise of unworkable governmental price regulation, is still as repugnant as ever to the spirit of our institutions, both political and commercial.

A detailed analysis of all of the objections to the measure would involve a document of truly formidable proportions. However, its major weaknesses and perils may be summarized under six headings:

1. Its attempted price-fixing fallacy.
2. The tax characteristics of the equalization fee.
3. The widespread bureaucracy which it would set up.
4. Its encouragement to profiteering and wasteful distribution by middlemen.
5. Its stimulation of overproduction.
6. Its aid to our foreign agricultural competitors. These topics by no means exhaust the list of fallacious and indeed dangerous aspects of the bill, but they afford ample ground for its emphatic rejection.

1. *Price fixing.* This measure is as cruelly deceptive in its disguise as governmental price-fixing legislation and involves quite as unmistakably the impossible scheme of attempted governmental control of buying and selling of agricultural products through political agencies as any of the other so-called surplus control bills. In fact, in certain respects, it is much broader and more flagrant in its scope.

The heights to which price lifting might be *promised* are freed from the limitations fixed in previous measures. The bill carefully avoids any direct allusion to such price-fixing functions, but there can be no doubt about its intentions and authorizations to the federal Farm Board in this respect. There is apparently no change in the import of the bill in the resolution to impose upon the farmer and upon the consumers of farm produce a regime of futile, delusive experiments with price fixing, with indirect governmental buying and selling, and with a nationwide system of regulatory policing, intolerable espionage, and tax collection on a vast scale.

These provisions would disappoint the farmer by naïvely implying that the law of supply and demand can thus be legislatively distorted in his favor. Economic history is filled with the evidences of the ghastly futility of such attempts. Fiat prices match the folly of fiat money. . . .

2. *The equalization fee,* which is the kernel of this legislation, is a sales tax upon the entire community. It is in no sense a mere contribution to be made by the producers themselves, as has been represented by supporters of the measure. It can be assessed upon the commodities in transit to the consumer and its burdens can often unmistakably be passed on to him.

Furthermore, such a procedure would certainly involve an extraordinary relinquishment of the taxing power on the part of Congress, because the tax would not only be levied without recourse to legislative authority but its proceeds would be expended entirely without the usual safeguards of congressional control of appropriations. This would be a most dangerous nullification of one of the essential checks and balances which lie at the very foundation of our government.

Incidentally, this taxation or fee would not be for purposes of revenue in the accepted sense but would simply yield a subsidy for the special benefit of particular groups of processors and exporters. It would be a consumption or sales tax on the vital necessities of life, regulated not by the ability of the people to pay but only by the requirements and export losses of various trading intermediaries. It would be difficult indeed to conceive of a more flagrant case of the employment of all of the coercive powers of the government for the profit of a small number of specially privileged groups. . . .

3. *Widespread bureaucracy.* A bureaucratic tyranny of unprecedented proportions would be let down upon the backs of the farm industry and its distributors throughout the nation in connection with the enforcement of this measure. Thousands of contracts involving scores of different grades, quantities, and varieties of products would have to be signed by the board with

the 4,400 millers, the 1,200 meat-packing plants, the 3,000 or more cotton and woolen mills, and the 2,700 canners. If this bill had been in operation in 1925, it would have involved collections upon an aggregate of over 16 billion units of wheat, corn, and cotton.

The Bill undertakes to provide insurance against loss, but presumably only against reasonable and unavoidable loss. Just what this might be would involve judgment on the part of government employees upon tens of thousands of transactions running into billions of dollars. This is bureaucracy gone mad. Cooperative associations, flour mills, packing plants, and grain elevators will cease to be private and become public agencies. If there is any conclusion that we can announce as final with regard to governmental business operations, particularly after the bitter and excessively costly wartime experiences with such enterprises, it is that we cannot maintain a bureaucracy of such vast proportions engaged in buying and selling without constant danger of corruption, mismanagement, and prodigious tax burdens. No private agency of so gigantic and complex a character attempting to juggle with profound economic principles in such fashion could survive under such circumstances, and the chances for a governmental trading organization would be even less. . . .

4. *Encouragement to profiteering and wasteful distribution by middlemen.* As was pointed out in the veto last year, it seems almost incredible that the farmers of this country are being offered this scheme of legislative relief in which the only persons who are guaranteed to benefit are the exporters, packers, millers, canners, spinners, and other processors. Their profits are definitely assured. They have, in other words, no particular incentive toward careful operation, since each of them holding a contract, no matter how unscrupulous, wasteful, or inefficient his operations may have been,

would be fully reimbursed for all of his losses.

This would be bound to encourage wholesale profiteering at the expense of the farmer and of the consumer. Every one of these processors could charge what he chose to his domestic trade and recoup the loss incurred on any one of his products thus made unsalable at home through excessive prices by dumping it at reduced rates in foreign markets. With such a complete guarantee of profit, these concerns would be entirely without restraint or limitation as to profiteering and as to slovenly and wasteful processing and selling operations.

Surely there could be no more direct means of destroying the very germ of American commercial genius which is so frankly envied by our foreign rivals — the tireless search for better and more efficient business methods, the competitive zeal for superior service and for adequate returns through large sales of better merchandise at lower prices.

The packers could be commanded by the board to buy hogs enough to create a near shortage at home and then raise the prices to a fixed level. The unsalable surplus would then be dumped abroad at a loss, which would thereupon be made good out of the pockets of all taxpayers, including the farmers. The operations would involve an impenetrable maze of contracts between the board and hundreds of packers and provisioners. The result would be a bewildering snarl of entangled accounting problems because packinghouses buy one kind of product and sell a wide range of highly differentiated specialties. To "equalize" the losses on these would indeed be a task of overwhelming difficulty. . . .

5. *Stimulation of overproduction.* The bill runs counter to an economic law as well settled as the law of gravitation. Increased prices decrease consumption; they also increase production. These two conditions are the very ones that spell disaster to the whole program. The vaguely drawn clause in the measure to meet this obvious danger merely amounts to moral suasion and as a last resort the withdrawal of the equalization fee. Thus, if 90 percent of the growers of a given commodity heed the admonitions of the board and refrain from production, they will, nevertheless, be punished because of the evasions of the remaining 10 percent who have ignored the board's requests. In other words, no farmer will be safe in directing his planning upon his individual judgment; for should the result be a stimulation of an increased yield, the board will be likely to withdraw the support which encouraged the surpluses and allow the prices to collapse under the weight of that artificially created excess. The annals of the industrial and agricultural world are replete with the catastrophes that have come in the wake of such attempted distortions of one of the most fundamental principles of commercial relations.

6. *Aid to our foreign agricultural competitors.* This measure continues, as did its predecessor, to give substantial aid to the foreign competitors of American agriculture and industry. It continues the amazing proposal to supply foreign workers with cheaper food than those of the United States, and this at the expense of the American farm industry, thereby encouraging both the foreign peasant, whose produce is not burdened with the costs of any equalization fees, and also affording through reduced food prices the means of cutting the wage rates paid by foreign manufacturers. The latter step would promptly impair the prosperity of our manufacturing population, which is by far the leading and most profitable market for our farm produce.

It is nonsense to say that our farmers are not interested in such a development, which can only result in unemployment and in consequent decreases in food consumption in the great industrial districts. It is surely poor business to transfer the farmer's market from an employed American workman to the latter's competitor in the low-wage-scale countries across the seas, whose potential buying power and standards of living even at best are far below those of this country.

This is indeed an extraordinary process of economic reasoning, if such it could be called. Certainly it is a flagrant case of direct, insidious attack upon our whole agricultural and industrial strength.

By the inevitable stimulation of production the bill can only mean an increase of exportable surplus to be dumped in the world market. This in turn will bring about a constantly decreasing world price, which will soon reach so low a figure that a wholesale curtailment of production in this country with its attendant demoralization and heavy losses would be certain. Where is the advantage of dragging our farmers into such folly?

Furthermore, as the board undertakes to dump the steadily mounting surplus into foreign countries at the low-cost figures, it will come into direct conflict with the dumping and similar trade laws of many foreign lands which are interested in the maintenance of their own agricultural industries. We might, therefore, expect immediately a series of drastic, retaliatory discriminations on the part of these consumer countries. This will drive our surplus into narrower market channels and force even further price reductions, with consequent increases in the burdens of the equalization tax.

Lastly, and the most important, in connection with this aspect of the bill as an aid to our foreign competitors, the measure will inevitably devastate many of our important farm areas. For instance, the board is expected to obtain higher prices for the American farmer for corn by removing the surplus from the home market and dumping it over our borders at a lower level of prices. In other words, the hog grower in Ontario, Canada, may buy American corn at a very much lower level than the hog grower in the state of Ohio. Both being situated equally as to the European market for their pork products, we shall see immediately the migration of the Ohio hog industries across the border into Canada, with consequent losses to our pork industry by this Canadian competition. . . .

An effort has been made to create the impression that the present bill is an important concession to my recommendations for the control of agricultural surplus. It has been emphasized that the loan provision is what this administration has recommended and that loans to cooperative associations for the control of crop surplus constitute one of two alternatives, with the equalization fee the other alternative. It is said that the first alternative will be tried first and that the equalization fee will be resorted to only if the loan provision should prove inadequate. It becomes apparent, however, upon careful study of the present bill and of the supporting committee reports, that these alleged alternatives can afford no real test of any plan of the kind I have recommended. . . .

The objectives of the type of legislation I have suggested and of this bill are radically different. The two proposals are therefore incompatible as practical alternatives. The object of my proposal is to aid in adjusting production to demand, to afford farmers a greater bargaining power, to handle surplus due to seasonal and other causes beyond the control of producers when unaided by strong business organizations, to minimize price fluctuations, and to reduce the margin between the price paid by the consumer and the price received by the producer.

The real objective of the plan in this bill is to raise domestic prices to artificially high levels by governmental price fixing and to dump the surplus abroad. . . .

I am still hopeful that legislation along the lines suggested in my last annual message, with which many of the provisions of this bill are in harmony, may be enacted, but this bill embodies substantially all of the objectionable features which I said, in that message to the Congress, I could not endorse. I am therefore obliged to return Senate Bill 3555, entitled "An act to establish a federal farm board to aid in the orderly marketing and in the control and disposition of the surplus of agricultural commodities in interstate and foreign commerce," without my approval.

112.

Protest Songs of the Farmers

Farmers never fully recovered from the depression of 1920-1921 and did not share in the celebrated prosperity of the Twenties. The small one-crop farmer has been traditionally victimized by two forces beyond his control, the weather and the market for his goods. In the South, the small farmer had an additional problem; he was often a tenant of the business interests that had bought up plantation land after the Civil War. Whatever the weather and the market, the tenant farmer had to pay his rent. The plight of the poor farmer is portrayed in the two songs reprinted below. "Eleven-Cent Cotton" was written by Bob Miller and Emma Dermer in 1928. "Down on Penny's Farm" was recorded in 1929 but had probably been written earlier. The identity of its original author is not established.

Source: *Songs of Work and Freedom,* Edith Fowke and Joe Glazer, eds., New York, 1960.

☙ ELEVEN-CENT COTTON

'Leven-cent cotton, forty-cent meat,
How in the world can a poor man eat?
Pray for the sunshine, 'cause it will rain,
Things gettin' worse, drivin' us insane;
Built a nice house, painted it brown;
Lightnin' came along and burnt it down.
No use talkin', any man's beat
With 'leven-cent cotton and forty-cent meat.

'Leven-cent cotton, forty-cent meat,
Keep gettin' thinner 'cause we don't eat;
Tried to raise peas, tried to raise beans;
All we can raise is turnip greens.
No corn in the crib, no chicks in the yard,
No meat in the smokehouse, no tubs full of lard;
No use talkin', any man's beat
With 'leven-cent cotton and forty-cent meat.

'Leven-cent cotton, forty-cent meat,
How in the world can a poor man eat?
Our clothes worn out, shoes run down,
Old slouch hat with a hole in the crown.
Poor gettin' poorer all around here,
Kids comin' regular ev'ry year;
No use talkin', any man's beat
With 'leven-cent cotton and forty-cent meat.

'Leven-cent cotton, forty-cent meat,
How in the world can a poor man eat?
Mule's in the barn, no crop's laid by,
Corncrib empty and the cow's gone dry.
Well water's low, nearly out of sight,
Can't take a bath on a Saturday night.
No use talkin', any man's beat
With 'leven-cent cotton and forty-cent meat.

BOB MILLER AND EMMA DERMER

DOWN ON PENNY'S FARM

Come you ladies and you gentlemen and listen to my song;
I'll sing it to you right but you might think it's wrong;
May make you mad, but I mean no harm:
It's all about the renters on Penny's farm.

Chorus:
It's hard times in the country,
Down on Penny's farm.

Now you move out on Penny's farm,
Plant a little crop of 'bacco and a little crop of corn.
He'll come around to plan and plot
Till he gets himself a mortgage on everything you got.

You go to the fields and you work all day,
Till way after dark, but you get no pay.
Promise you meat or a little lard,
It's hard to be a renter on Penny's farm.

Now here's George Penny come into town
With a wagon-load of peaches, not one of them sound.
He's got to have his money or somebody's check;
You pay him for a bushel and you don't get a peck.

Then George Penny's renters they come into town,
With their hands in their pockets and their heads hanging down.
Go in the store and the merchant will say:
"Your mortgage is due and I'm looking for my pay."

Goes down in his pocket with a trembling hand —
"Can't pay you all but I'll pay you what I can."
Then to the telephone the merchant makes a call:
"They'll put you on the chain gang if you don't pay it all."

113.

BENTON MACKAYE: Indigenous America

Benton MacKaye, in his book The New Exploration, a Philosophy of Regional
Planning, *portrayed the conflict in values between the urban industrial society and
rural communal life. He urged that the latter, an indigenous realm of stable values,
be reserved both for its own sake and as a refuge for the urbanized man seeking
escape from the confusion and superficiality of the city. Preservation, MacKaye
felt, could not be achieved by chance, haphazardly and without plan. The natural
realm had to be systematically and synthetically sealed off from urban encroachment.
A selection from MacKaye's book, published in 1928, appears below. In the 1920s
the problem of maintaining separate rural regions engaged the Regional Planning
Association of America, to which MacKaye belonged.*

Source: *The New Exploration,* New York, 1928: "The Indigenous and the Metropolitan."

THIS NEW WORLD is the metropolitan world. It is "a world without a country." Its reactions are born, not of nature's soil but of artificiality; they are reverse to the reactions of the natural normal sphere. Instead of means being adapted to achieve ends, the ends are distorted to fit established means; in lieu of industry being made to achieve culture, culture is made to echo the intonations of industry; oil paints are manufactured not to promote art, art is manufactured to advertise oil paints. Yet this unnatural tendency of the metropolitan process has come about in a seemingly natural way.

The machine spells freedom from primitive industry and rawboned nature, and if one machine makes one unit of freedom, then, we argue, ten machines must make ten units. But, of course, they do no such thing. We wake up to find ourselves no longer serfs to nature's soil but to find ourselves instead the slaves to man's machine. We have within our exogenous world swapped the old boss for a new one. The mastership belongs no longer to nature in the raw but to "nature dressed up in modern clothes."

The great struggle of the immediate future will be between man himself and man's machine. One form of this struggle promises to be a contest between two realms. One of these is that potential realm of permanent human innate desire, whose power awaits its development to actuality even as the potential sphere of waterpower within the mountain stream. This human realm (or sphere) has in America a twofold residence: first, in the gradually awakening common mind of a large portion of the country's people; and, second, in the actual territory and landscape of a large portion of the country itself. This potential, awakening, common mind, groping unconsciously for a complete environment, would base itself on psychologic resource as well as physical, and, to secure man's innate natural ends, would harness *the machine* as the machine has harnessed natural means and power. This we may call the innate or indigenous portion of civilization. The other realm consists of the exogenous or metropolitan portion. Here is the real war of civilization.

This struggle will be taking place, not alone in America but on every other continent. It will be a contest between the aggressive mechanized portion of Western European society (so-called Western civilization) and the indigenous portion of every society invaded, including the indigenous portion of American society. The contest in this country will be between Metropolitan America and Indigenous America. These now stand vis-à-vis, not only psychologically but physically and geographically.

The metropolitan world we have compared to a mechanized framework; also we have compared it to an invading army and to an invading flood of water. It is all of these: it is a mechanized molten framework of industry which flows . . . in accordance with the law of gravitation. First, it occupies the lower valley, such as the locality of the Boston Basin, obliterating the original urban environment of "Boston Town." Next, in fingerlike projections, it flows, glacierwise, toward the outskirts, obliterating such rural village and environment as comes within its wake. Then, its projections narrowing, it flows along the railways and motor roads back through the hinterland, starting little centers of provincial metropolitanism in the Main Street towns and around the numerous gasoline stations. Finally, here and there, it crawls up some mountain summit and obliterates a strategic particle of the primeval environment. It is mightiest in the valleys and weakest on the mountain ridges.

The strategy of the indigenous world is just the other way. It is still mighty within the primeval environment, as along the ridgeways of the Appalachian barrier, including such ranges as the Green Mountains in New England. It is strong also in such regions as upcountry, where, although the farms and villages are depleted, the resources, both physical and psychologic, are still there and are yet open to restoration and renewed development. But down in the lower valleys and around the big centers, the metropolitan world . . . is in virtual possession, and any improvement in environment awaits the complex process of reformation from within.

The metropolitan world, then, may be considered as an exotic intrusion or "flow" into certain portions of the innate or indigenous world. Considered thus, and not merely as a static framework, it becomes the dominant part of the flow of population and of the industrial migration. . . . The control and guidance of this flow and migration we have stated to be the fundamental problem of regional engineering toward the goal set up by Governor Smith of New York, which was "the making of the mold in which future generations shall live." The particular aspect of this problem treated of in this Philosophy of Regional Planning is the strategy of the indigenous world with respect to its contact with this metropolitan flow.

This strategy consists, roughly speaking, in developing the indigenous environments (primeval, rural, and communal) and in confining the encroachments of the metropolitan environment. As applied to this country, therefore, it consists in developing the Indigenous America and in confining the Metropolitan America.

114.

STEPHEN EWING: The Mockery of American Divorce

The increased divorce rate (9 percent to 16½ percent from 1910 to 1928) and the growing social acceptability of divorce were symptomatic of the moral upheaval that took place in the 1920s. Although far from advocating promiscuity, Judge Ben B. Lindsey's proposals that "companionate" marriages (dissolvable by the mutual consent of husband and wife where there were no children) and birth control be legalized caused extensive debate. Lindsey was judge of a special Denver court dealing with juvenile and domestic problems. His proposals were made in 1927 and an article by Stephen Ewing, published in July 1928 and reprinted here in part, was one of the many that appeared in response to them.

Source: *Harper's Monthly*, July 1928.

FOR THE PAST twelvemonth a rather unpleasant nightmare has been disturbing the slumbers of the guardians of our people. That nightmare, evoked so rudely by Judge Ben B. Lindsey, is the vision of a society in which childless couples would be as free to divorce as they have been to marry. Now, the reaction to any nightmare must be — the Freudians to the contrary — as symptomatic as the nightmare itself. It is of interest, therefore, that society should have taken this one seriously, instead of rubbing its eyes and laughing at the incongruity of the picture. Indeed, it is hardly the kind of nightmare which can be dispelled by the strong light of reality; for any person of common sense can see that, although we may not have divorce by mutual consent, technically speaking, we have something very akin to it in actual practice. Why is it, then, that the pillars of our society — and by them we mean not only the pillars of the churches but the greater part of those citizens who concern themselves in one way or another with the public weal — should have delivered themselves of the unalterable opinion that *the enactment of such a law would cause a cataclysmic change in our social mores, if not morals?*

It is true that divorce by mutual consent presupposes an entirely different conception of marriage than our Anglo-Saxon laws have ever countenanced. Indeed, it is a harking back to that Roman system of "free marriage," which was wiped out by the establishment of Christianity and the church's gradual assumption of control over every aspect of man's temporal life. For many centuries, as Mrs. Bromley has already pointed out, the dogma prevailed in western Europe that marriage was an indissoluble state, St. Jerome himself having pronounced: "So long as the husband lives, whether he be an adulterer, or a sodomist, or be steeped in all manner of crime and the wife has left him on account of those crimes, he is still to be regarded as her husband and she is not to be allowed to marry again." As the church lost its temporal power, however, this theory of marriage gave way in western Europe — and later in our own country — to civil laws which permitted divorce when *one party had seriously injured the other.* That is to say, an overt act, an offense on the part of husband or wife, was the only thing which could break the bond.

This theory has never been superseded by any other, either in this country or in England. It follows, therefore, that when two people deliver themselves up to the church or to the civil authorities to be united in wedlock, they forfeit forever their fundamental freedom of action so far as their relationship with each other is concerned. The law becomes the final arbiter of their marital destiny, determining, if called upon to do so, whether an alleged offense on the part of one spouse is sufficient to entitle the other to an absolute divorce and the corresponding privilege to remarry, or whether the so-called innocent party should be allowed only the relief of a separate existence. If there is no alleged offense and the two have simply discovered that their union is a grievous mistake, devoid of positive values — then the law, paradoxically enough, denies them a divorce. The law married them upon their mutual desire, treating them as adults who knew their own minds; but it

will not divorce them upon their mutual desire, for it now presumes that they no longer know what is good for them.

Obviously the law — or society — has maintained this stranglehold upon marriage for the same reason that the church maintained it for centuries — to ensure its own preservation. Society claims, however, that its responsibility in the matter is somewhat more ideal: it must create an ordered existence for its members and it must protect the fate of helpless children — for humanitarian as well as for biological reasons. These ends are justifiable, and yet we beg leave to inquire whether society has chosen the best means to attain them. . . .

To begin with, it may as well be admitted that in a great majority of instances the decree is acceptable to both parties — if not actually desired by them. There were, for example, in this country in 1925 as many as 146,069 uncontested cases, or 84 percent of all divorces granted. Even if one were to subtract those cases in which the defendant was not actually notified, or was such a derelict as to have no defense, it would still leave a large percentage of suits in which the defendant did not care to contest the issue. In this connection Judge C. W. Hoffman of the Domestic Relations Court of Cincinnati found, from an investigation in his court, that at least 75 percent of the defendants had valid grounds for a defense but did not choose to stand upon them. The inference to be drawn is that the majority of divorces are the result of either a tacit or an open understanding between husband and wife. Furthermore, many judges tell us, when suits are contested it is for the sake of the property and the children, and nothing else, in nine cases out of ten.

It would seem rather fortunate that a husband and wife can at least agree to disagree. Yet if they agree to divorce, they must create between them the necessary evidence, and that in itself constitutes the crime of collusion. They may go about committing this crime in a number of ways. The husband may allow himself to be caught in an act of adultery, or one spouse may "desert" the other, or the wife may accuse the husband of failing to support her — it being understood in any event that the offending party will not deny the allegation.

Collusion of an especially flagrant variety is rampant in New York state, where a divorce can be procured only on evidence of adultery. The law, it is true, will permit a husband to confess to an act in the past and to supply his wife with the necessary witnesses. But such witnesses do not grow on rosebushes, for when a man departs from the straight and narrow path he will in all probability seek the greatest possible degree of privacy. It is generally necessary, therefore, for the husband and wife to come to at least a tacit understanding. He may, for instance, conspicuously leave in his smoking jacket an addressed letter to a lady-love making a rendezvous with her on such and such a night, at such and such a hotel. The wife finds it, notes the facts, and sends detectives to apprehend the pair. Later, she turns over the evidence to a lawyer, and, if he is not too scrupulous a member of the bar, he starts suit without inquiring very closely into the methods whereby she obtained the information.

In due time the case is heard as one of many on a crowded calendar; the plaintiff makes her formal complaint by answering a series of routine questions put to her by her lawyer, and *by swearing that she has not connived with her husband to obtain the divorce;* the detectives recite their evidence; the husband puts in no appearance; the plaintiff's attorney makes a request for alimony and counsel fees (already agreed upon by the husband's and wife's attorneys), and the judge must perforce grant the decree since

the lawyer has presented a case that is technically perfect. The procedure appears to be a very simple one, and yet it should be noted that it called for collusion between husband and wife, as well as downright perjury by the latter.

Or if the husband has no lady-love, or does not care to compromise the one he has, he may procure through a firm of detectives a paid corespondent to appear with him in a shocking situation. Or he may fall into the hands of a firm of shyster lawyers who will cut corners by hiring several professional perjurers to swear to the necessary facts.

This, then, is the divorce law on which the Empire State prides itself, the law which has kept the divorce rate down to .41 per thousand, as compared with the national rate of 1.52. . . .

Of the various grounds specified by the laws of the other states, desertion is the least offensive and accordingly one of the most popular — 32 percent of all divorces in 1925 having been obtained on this ground. The percentage would probably run still higher if there were more than twenty-one states which granted divorce for one year's desertion, or more than nine which granted it for two years' desertion.

Yet even when a suit is based on this simple ground, a couple automatically break the law if they agree beforehand that the husband is to desert and the wife to sue him later for that act. Furthermore, when the case comes up, the wife will have to swear falsely on the witness stand or by affidavit that the desertion has been "willful" or "malicious" and that it has been prolonged for the specified time. . . .

Chicago, as everyone knows, is famous, not only for its machine-gun politics but for its swiftly whirring divorce mill, inasmuch as the Illinois law now waives the one-year residence requirement when a suit is based on two successive acts of cruelty which have been committed within a short period of time — from three days to three weeks. In these cases very slight evidence is required, the witnesses as a rule being members of the plaintiff's family. Furthermore, the evidence presented is often of a very tenuous nature. One witness, for instance, testified that she had seen a man strike his wife, when she had only been told that such a thing had happened.

Despite the widespread perjury in Chicago divorce courts, it is the rarest occurrence in the world for a judge to detect perjury or collusion, we are told by several reputable attorneys of that city. . . .

The Nevada laws, when all is said and done, necessitate a minimum of fraud. In the first place, only three months' continuous residence is demanded, but that requirement is now strictly enforced. In the second place, the judges demand very slight evidence to prove mental cruelty. A woman may obtain her freedom on the ground that her husband has been intolerably cool to her, or told her to go to hell once too often. On the other hand, a husband may complain, as one did recently, that his wife has worn him out by making him get up five or six times every night to look after her cat — or that she nags him in public. Such stories of petty irritation may be literally true, so that the plaintiff need commit no perjury in swearing to them. In short, the Nevada legislators appear to have reasoned that since people are bound to get divorced in one way or another, they might as well expedite matters for them — and incidentally line the pockets of the business and lawyer folk of the state. . . .

It is true that there are certain jurisdictions, especially in the East, where the divorce laws are more strictly administered. But the fact remains that a couple determined to be divorced can secure relief in one state or another — if they have the necessary means. Furthermore, by basing their suit on any ground but desertion, they can obtain their freedom practically immediately in a number of states which grant final decrees without imposing an interlocutory period.

To sum up, the divorce laws of our states would seem to work a hardship on two classes of people only — those who are too poor to migrate into another jurisdiction and those who would prefer not to sacrifice their sense of honesty and decency.

If we are going to have laws that work a hardship upon the self-respecting minority who have reason to believe that they are capable of directing their own lives, we must at least make sure that these laws are beneficial to the great run of people. Indeed, that is the big argument advanced — justifiably or otherwise — in favor of the Eighteenth Amendment. Can it be advanced in favor of our divorce laws?

A number of eminent jurists in the East answer emphatically in the affirmative. Even while admitting the necessity of divorce in many instances, they insist that marriage would go to wrack and ruin if people were allowed to part by mutual consent. Nor are they particularly scandalized by the wholesale corruption which goes on in our divorce courts, nor by the fact that the law forces self-respecting citizens to perjure themselves. Indeed, one jurist went so far as to say that if he himself felt entitled to a divorce he would not hesitate to take the necessary steps to get it. All such evading of the law is considered a minor evil. For the jurists think we must have laws that will at least fool the people into thinking that marriage is more difficult to get out of than it really is.

Yet there are numbers of judges, especially in our Middle Western and Western states, who hold quite opposite views. From long experience they have learned that the law serves neither society nor the family by forcing two people to remain together when all concord has gone out of their lives. Furthermore, they have seen with their own eyes the wholesale perjury, the frantic dashing from one state to another — in short, the inflexible determination of individuals to free themselves of irksome bonds. They have seen, too, the tragic results of hundreds upon hundreds of hasty matings, and they know that marriage could not be approached much more lightly than it is today. And so they have arrived at the conclusion that divorce is often a necessary remedy and that, furthermore, no manner of divorce laws can hold marriage together.

For one thing, the realists among the judges have come to believe that incompatibility justifies divorce beyond the shadow of a doubt. "Indeed," says Judge Grier M. Orr, of St. Paul, "I know of no better reason for the granting of a divorce than deep and constant discord. For I consider that there is no physical cruelty to the human body greater than that of mechanically carrying on the marriage relationship after all feeling is cold." He goes on to say quite frankly that when a couple come before him whose chief plea is incompatibility, mental or physical, he satisfies himself that the facts are as presented, and grants them a divorce on the technical grounds of mental or physical cruelty. . . .

More and more judges are coming to look upon divorce as an individual problem, each case to be decided as seems wisest, regardless of the dictates of the law. For this reason, conscientious judges make very earnest attempts at reconciliation. Judge Sabath, who is a leading exponent of the method, firmly believes that no complaint should be filed until the pair have discussed their differences with the judge in his chambers. For he has observed that it is often the charges made in a moment of anger by the husband or wife on the bill of complaint that alienate the other and destroy all possibility of reconciliation. . . .

Judge Hoffman's Domestic Relations Court in Cincinnati has also done remark-able work along this line, for it is equipped with an Adjustment Department that has a psychological clinic and a trained staff of experts attached. Miss Mary Edna McChristrie, who is the referee in charge, reports in a recent article in the *Survey* that out of 400 men and women who came into court threatening to sue for divorce, only 36 actually went ahead with their suits. . . .

Other judges, however, are a little more pessimistic about the possibilities of reconciliation. Judge Orr of St. Paul has found that in the majority of instances the cause of infelicity has become so chronic that it cannot be forgotten. However, when the grievance is based on adultery, he has occasionally been able to convince the husband or wife that the offense was only a passing one and that it has not fundamentally harmed their relationship. In Chicago, Judge Lewis, despite a few very gratifying successes, has found most couples unreconcilable — especially those who have been married five years or more. . . .

With a vast deal of evidence at hand, the realists among the judges have concluded that tragic marriages are the result, not solely of selfishness and materialism, as the moralists are fond of asserting, but to a large extent of *early and hasty matings.* They also blame the appalling ignorance of young people regarding the functions and responsibilities of marriage; but this presents a problem in education that is outside the domain of the law.

The judges complain that our marriage laws are shamefully lax. The marriageable age without the consent of parents is eighteen for a woman and twenty-one for a man in most of our states. But this is easily circumvented, since no birth certificates are required to prove the candidate's age. It would seem, too, that the girl should be twenty-one, as she must be in the Scandinavian countries. . . .

But quite apart from a revision of the marriage laws, we obviously need a more civilized divorce procedure — one that will put a premium on decency rather than on perjury. Whether we should follow the Scandinavian system and impose a "cooling-off period" of one year or so; whether the granting of divorces should be left entirely to the discretion of the judge; or whether each divorce court should be equipped with a highly organized Adjustment Department such as Judge Hoffman's in Cincinnati are questions calling for profound study.

Judge Harry A. Lewis of Chicago, however, has the following concrete suggestion to make:

"I believe all charges for divorce should be eliminated, allowing the complainant to file her bill setting up her reasons for wanting a separation, and to appear before the chancellor to whom it is assigned; and if he thinks there is sufficient reason for the two to be separated, he should sign a decree. This would do away with all fraud entirely, and as a court has power to marry two people upon their mutual request, it should have the power to separate them. Such a system would mean less legal tangle, less expense, less difficulty and sordidness."

This would be an excellent system if we could be sure that all judges would be both wise and human. Whether the law should go a step farther and automatically grant the privilege of divorce to two people after they have submitted themselves to a reconciliation session and have lived apart for a given period of time is a matter for debate, perhaps. It seems to the writer, however, that such a system would not greatly increase the number of divorces being granted today, except among the poor, who cannot now afford the expense involved. In fact, it is quite possible that the great run of divorce-seekers would have to be educated to wait a year and get their decrees by mutual consent rather than sue their spouses in open court; for it is a sad commentary that

even in those states which allow for divorce on grounds of one year's desertion, there are still a great many suits based on charges of cruelty. Perhaps divorce by mutual consent would eventually set a more civilized standard.

For the good of society, men and women must not be forced — or allowed — to recite before the public all the intimate facts of their married life and personal distress. It is nothing short of barbarous to cut open people's hearts and expose them to the public gaze. And it is nothing short of race-suicidal to fill our newspapers with columns and columns of unhealthy divorce scandals. Private hearings under the present laws would hardly solve this particular problem, for they would only open the door to even greater corruption and perpetration of fraud by one party on the other, as happened in Bradford County, Pennsylvania.

Certainly no system of divorce should be countenanced which allows a husband or wife to obtain a decree without the knowledge of the other — as occasionally happens today when the plaintiff goes into another state and the defendant is served by publication. If only one spouse wants a divorce, the law should at least make sure that the other has been personally notified of the impending change in his or her marital status; and perhaps it should also, as in the Scandinavian countries, impose a still longer waiting period than it does when the two are agreed.

Divorce by mutual consent does not necessarily mean that both parties are equally anxious for the decree, but it does mean that they have not parted angrily or furtively. Yet the latter is the technic prescribed by law. It would almost seem as though our lawmakers delighted in putting a premium upon indecency and cruelty. Which action, for instance, is the more decent: for a man to "light out" without warning to his wife, leaving her perhaps without sufficient funds, and exposed to the pity of all the neighbors, or for him to discuss his plans with her and break up the home in a dignified fashion?

The current legal theory seems to be that divorce is not to be allowed until one party — the presumably innocent one — shall have been deeply wounded. The underlying Puritanic principle would seem to be that no human being shall find his salvation in freedom until he has walked through the valley of the shadow of death. But is it not pitifully apparent that every man and woman — with the exception of the very shallow — who feels his marriage going to pieces, walks through the valley of the shadow of death? Why must the law, like a heartless surgeon, drive the knife still deeper?

115.

Felix von Luckner: Prohibition in America

The Wickersham Commission, created by President Hoover in 1929 to investigate the enforcement of Prohibition, disclosed that law enforcement favored the wealthy. "It is easier to shut up the open drinking places and stop the sale of beer, which was drunk chiefly by workingmen," it reported, "than to prevent the wealthy from having and using liquor in their homes and in their clubs. . . . It is much easier to padlock a speakeasy than to close up a large hotel where important and influential financial interests are involved." When Felix von Luckner, the famed commander of a German commerce raider in World War I, visited America in 1927, the easy evasion of Prohibition became apparent to him. Some of his experiences and observations, which are reprinted here from a translation of his book Seeteufel erobert Amerika, *anticipated the findings of the Wickersham Commission.*

Source: TWA, pp. 495-498.

I suppose I should set forth my investigations into the subject of Prohibition. Here is a new experience, at a club's celebration. Each man appears with an impressive portfolio. Each receives his glass of pure water; above the table the law reigns supreme. The brief cases rest under the chairs. Soon they are drawn out, the merry noise of popping corks is heard, and the guzzling begins.

Or, I come to a banquet in a hotel dining room. On the table are the finest wines. I ask, "How come?" Answer: "Well, two of our members lived in the hotel for eight days and every day brought in cargoes of this costly stuff in their suitcases." My informant was madly overjoyed at this cunning.

My first experience with the ways of Prohibition came while we were being entertained by friends in New York. It was bitterly cold. My wife and I rode in the rumble seat of the car, while the American and his wife, bundled in furs, sat in front. Having wrapped my companion in pillows and blankets so thoroughly that only her nose showed, I came across another cushion that seemed to hang uselessly on the side. "Well," I thought, "this is a fine pillow; since everyone else is so warm and cozy, I might as well do something for my own comfort. This certainly does no one any good hanging on the wall." Sitting on it, I gradually noticed a dampness in the neighborhood, that soon mounted to a veritable flood. The odor of fine brandy told me I had burst my host's peculiar liquor flask.

In time, I learned that not everything in America was what it seemed to be. I discovered, for instance, that a spare tire could be filled with substances other than air, that one must not look too deeply into certain binoculars, and that the Teddy Bears that suddenly acquired tremendous popularity among the ladies very often had hollow metal stomachs.

"But," it might be asked, "where do all these people get the liquor?" Very simple. Prohibition has created a new, a universally respected, a well-beloved, and a very profitable occupation, that of the bootlegger who takes care of the importation of the forbidden liquor. Everyone knows this, even the powers of government. But this profession is beloved because it is essential, and it is respected because its pursuit is clothed with an element of danger and with a sporting risk. Now and then one is caught, that must happen *pro forma*, and then he must do time or, if he is wealthy enough, get someone to do time for him.

Yet it is undeniable that Prohibition has in some respects been signally successful.

The filthy saloons, the gin mills which formerly flourished on every corner and in which the laborer once drank off half his wages, have disappeared. Now, he can instead buy his own car and ride off for a weekend or a few days with his wife and children in the country or at the sea. But, on the other hand, a great deal of poison and methyl alcohol has taken the place of the good old pure whiskey.

The number of crimes and misdemeanors that originated in drunkenness has declined. But, by contrast, a large part of the population has become accustomed to disregard and to violate the law without thinking. The worst is, that precisely as a consequence of the law, the taste for alcohol has spread ever more widely among the youth. The sporting attraction of the forbidden and the dangerous leads to violations. My observations have convinced me that many fewer would drink were it not illegal.

And how, it will be asked, did this law get onto the statute books? Through the war. In America there was long a well-developed temperance movement and many individual states already had Prohibition laws. During the war it was not difficult to extend the force of those laws to the whole of the United States. Prohibition was at first introduced only for the period of the war. For the mass of the people it was very surprising when Congress in 1920 adopted the Eighteenth Amendment to the Constitution, which made it a crime to manufacture, transport, or sell intoxicating liquor. The dry states had imposed their will on the whole Union.

A Chicken in Every Pot, a Car in Every Garage.
Republican National Committee advertisement, 1928

116.

JOHN R. TUNIS: The Great God Football

College football, which began as a gentleman's sport in 1873, became big business in the 1920s. To accommodate the increasingly large crowds that flocked to the games, many colleges and universities constructed huge stadiums, with paid admissions often running into millions of dollars. Championship contests between college "conferences" were instituted and postseason games, often played on New Year's Day, multiplied. Inevitably, players were recruited and paid to attend the various schools — by the end of the decade about one-seventh of the college athletes received some form of pay — and special "snap" courses were devised for those athletes who were of doubtful academic promise. Administrators justified their dedication to football on the debatable grounds that it enlarged the institutions' funds. In an article published in November 1928 and reprinted here in part, John R. Tunis tried to account for the college football craze.

Source: *Harper's Monthly,* November 1928.

"RETURNING LETTERMEN are Nagurski, Kabela, Hovde, Lekeseles, Brookmeier, Westphal, Pulbrabek, and Teeter. Emlein and Ukkelberg will supplant Apman and Angevik; and Norgaard and Burquist will provide promising material to guard the flanks."

No, this is not, as you might imagine, a list of future citizens of these United States who have passed or are about to pass the rigid requirements of the Quota; but simply a sample of up-to-date football publicity sent out last summer by one of our large Middle Western state universities. For, at present, every college worthy of the name of an educational institution maintains a press bureau whose function is to keep the name of the university before the public gaze. . . .

Moreover, no longer do these press bureaus wait until the opening of the doors of learning to begin grinding out material for publication. Heavens, no! The advance notices from college press agents start pouring in upon the helpless sporting editors of the nation's newspapers as early as mid-August. By Labor Day the campaign is on in earnest, and the sports pages are full of "Intensive Training to Start Today," and "Preliminary Practice Begins at Notre Dame," or "University of Pennsylvania Squad Takes to Seashore for Early Conditioning." . . .

The volume and stridency of the propaganda steadily increases as the practice sessions become more stern and important in late September, as the early-season games begin in October, and as the end of the year and the "crucial contest" — for nowadays every big football game is a "crucial contest" — approach in the first weeks of November. By this time the sporting pages of the American newspapers have been filled for months with columns of football news and comment, relevant and irrelevant. By this time the chaff has been fairly well separated from the wheat, and the winning teams — as true sports lovers of the most sports-loving nation in the world, we obviously have no use for the losers — have been classified, ticketed, and documented.

There are the Eastern teams, as a rule of small account in the final reckoning, the teams of the Western Conference, the Pacific Coast Conference, the Missouri Valley Conference, the Southwestern Conference, the Minnesota Conference, the Oklahoma Conference, the Rocky Mountain Conference, and a dozen other conferences large and small, important and unimportant from a sporting viewpoint.

There are also several roving teams that make a business, a regular profession, of football. These roving teams are delightfully and refreshingly frank about the game, making no pretenses at all that their halfbacks are members of Phi Beta Kappa; nor do they seek to deny that their coach, with the help of an agile newspaper writer 600 miles away, syndicates his views in the sports pages daily throughout the land to his own profit. There is no pretense made that he is hired to be the moral guardian of the football squad, no twaddle about the manner in which through his precept and example he influences "his boys" for Christian good. No, these teams are a rough-and-ready lot. They do not intend to allow the abnormal functions of a university such as lectures and study to interfere with football.

On a Saturday, one of these elevens will play in Portland, Oregon; the players will dress hastily and catch the evening express from the Coast an hour after the game, in time to run out upon the Yankee Stadium, New York, the following Saturday afternoon. They practise by throwing footballs at one another as they tramp from diners to sleepers, or vice versa. Their studies, if any, are broadcasted to them by radio; yet their degrees are rendered to them at the proper moment — which is to say when their football usefulness to the university is at an end. Much of this, perhaps more, you may learn if you wish, in fact whether you wish or not, by opening the sporting pages of any American newspaper between September and Christmas in any given year.

It is obvious that the sporting public wants all this sort of thing or the newspapers would never publish it. Yes, the sporting public does want it, adores all this football news, eats it, swallows it, almost — I was going to say — wallows in it. And no wonder, too, for the truth is that football is today the Great American Game, at least from the spectators' point of view. . . .

A baseball World's Series crowd of 80,000 is mentioned in the newspaper headlines; on the other hand, a football crowd of 80,000 is a commonplace. At the approximate moment when the Yale Bowl is filled with a gathering of this size, larger numbers are watching Michigan play Illinois at Urbana, Pennsylvania tackle Chicago at Franklin Field, and California play Stanford at Berkeley. For a series of five or six successive Saturdays in October and November each year, football proves its right to be called the King of American Sports.

But, as a matter of fact, football is more to the sports follower of this country than merely a game. It is at present a religion — sometimes it seems to be almost our national religion. With fervor and reverence the college man and the non-college man, the athlete and observer approach its shrines; dutifully and faithfully they make their annual pilgrimage to the football Mecca, be it Atlanta or Urbana, Cambridge or Los Angeles, Princeton or Ann Arbor. From far and near they come, the low and the high, the humble in their sports coupes from the neighboring city, the elect in their special cars from all parts of this football-mad nation. . . .

So devoutly does the American sporting Babbitt worship at the shrine that even the ministers of other and older faiths are duly impressed. Thus, for example, Dean Willard Sperry of the Harvard Theological School:

The only true religious spirit to be discerned among large bodies of undergraduates today is in the football stadium. One of the deepest spiritual experiences I ever had was one Saturday afternoon a few years ago in the Harvard Stadium. It is just that spirit which transforms football from a form of athletics to a religion, which our universities must diffuse through wider channels.

This new religion has its dogma: the doctrine that only through so-called college spirit can a man be saved. According to this doctrine in its purest form, anything done for the purpose of bringing victory to the team is justifiable; any news — learned no matter how — about another eleven, any bit of information garnered publicly or privately must be put to use; any amount of time spent in following and cheering and "supporting" the team counts toward the salvation of the faithful. No less than the undergraduate, the graduate is a traitor to his creed does he fail to turn up in the stadium on the day of days, the Homecoming Day, the Big Game Day, the Day when the college demands his all. So the undergraduate tears away on Thursday afternoon in his rickety flivver to drive the 500 miles to the town where the big game is to be held, and the graduate comes down by express or special train for the same purpose; and if each has a flask upon his hip — well, anything is excused when one realizes the holy motives pervading their acts on behalf of the dear old college.

The religion of football has its high priests and acolytes, its saints and sanctuaries, as do other religions. The saints are those mighty ones of the game who have gone on, whose names are mentioned with hushed breath by sportswriters and football fans alike. The high priests are the saints of the present day; sometime in the future they, too, will have passed away; sometime they, too, will have Memorial Gates and Drives and Locker Buildings constructed in their names and their memory. Today,

Saint Hugo Bezdek and Saint William Roper, Saint Knute Rockne and Saint Chick Meehan fill the places of the great departed. Places which have become more lucrative, let it be added; for today the nest of the high priest is well feathered, and the newspaper ghost writer and the syndicate manager offer him a means of profit not always open in such measure to the men of the days of Percy Haughton.

The acolytes of the religion are of course the players themselves. They serve and wait upon the Great God Football in his sanctuaries — the gridirons of school and college. These humble flagellants are, need it be said, seldom admitted to the inner holy of holies. The hierarchies that rule the game are composed of the Athletic Directors, Graduate Managers, Graduate Treasurers, Chairmen of Football Committees, and the rest who, with the Head Coaches, are merely names for the lowly graduate and undergraduate to bow down before and worship. The hierarchies and the Head Coaches look with benign approval upon the solemn hocus-pocus of the new religion, for after all, high priests, like everyone else, must eat three times daily.

The president of a large college, when he was discussing football informally one day, pointed out a curious thing about this new religion of ours. He mentioned man's natural hunger for ritual in one form or another, and remarked that so fundamental is this emotional craving that when our churches do away with ritual — as the Protestants have largely done away with it in the United States — it springs up in other and most unlikely places. . . .

This ritual has pervaded the game little by little, a bit here and a bit there, without anyone being fully aware of what was going on; it has become a part of college life without anyone permanently attached to the colleges realizing what has happened, until today it is fixed and standardized from Maine to California. Everyone who has attended an American university, large or small, is familiar with its manifestations. By way of preparation for the annual football festival, there are mass meetings at which the high priests and acolytes of the religion speak briefly but passionately and fervently, preaching devotion to the Divine Being. They usually manage to work their audience up to such a pitch that a snake dance follows; headed by the student band playing football songs (which after all are the hymns of the cult), a thousand bareheaded undergraduates swarm across the campus in the dark, swing up Main Street, blocking traffic and pulling the trolleys off the wires, hooting and jeering at the house of Professor Jackson of the Greek Department, who once dared question the sacredness of the gods they worship; and then crowd on to the field back of the gymnasium, where a huge bonfire is lighted and more cheers and songs are heard, until everyone is too hoarse and too tired to continue.

And then on Game Day itself, the day of the great festival, there are the bands parading to the field in uniform, the varsity band leading the procession with its stalwart drum major, the freshman band — in costumes somewhat less elaborate — bringing up the rear. There are the frenzied shouts of greeting as the players race upon the field, the cheers for the captain of the team, for the opponents of the day, for the university; these are the opening prayers, as it were, of the ceremony. Then there are the annual demonstrations of ingeniously organized pageantry, always so important a part of this football ritual; the cheering section that on a blast from a directing whistle suddenly spells out CALIFORNIA in vivid colors or that forms a big blue Y or a big red H made up of colored cards or handkerchiefs. There is the marching and countermarching of the bands between the halves; each year their performance becomes more elaborate, each year they add to the traditional rites some new marvel of disciplined display.

And if, perhaps, by some lucky chance,

the afternoon of the game happens to fall on Armistice Day, so much the better. From the top of the stadium, silhouetted against the dying sun, a bugler in khaki stands with his bugle against his lips. A hush falls upon 90,000 bareheaded spectators and the piercing notes of taps are scattered over the vast arena, penetrating with an exquisite melancholy the hearts of the worshipers. At long last the game is over; there they stand, uncovered in their temple, chanting their Doxology, their closing words of prayer:

In praise of Old Nassau, my boys. . . .
In praise . . . of Old . . . Nassau. . . .

Football today is a complicated affair. Before the time when the merchants of a college town and the Chamber of Commerce subscribed money to the Athletic Association, realizing that 100,000 persons in twenty-four hours can leave a good deal of surplus cash about, before the time when big games were called by name to attract given bodies of citizens — Rotary Day, Kiwanis Day, Dad's Day, and so forth — football was a simple business. . . . Today, the officials — their number has increased until at present there are almost as many officials as players upon the field — are hand-picked for each game by a High Commissioner who receives a salary of $10,000 for the job; a job which does not appear to be working out overwell, either. Last season more than $3,000 was spent for spies to watch the officials and report upon their fairness and the quality of their officiating. The reports, it seems, were not constructive enough, and this fall there is talk of spies being set to watch the spies at an additional cost of $3,000, and so on. Truly, a complicated business, this modern football.

But football was not always quite so involved. In fact it is fair to say that football stole up and caught the colleges unaware; almost before they knew it the vast machine which is modern intercollegiate football had been erected and firmly installed in collegiate life. Thirty years ago it was a game. Today the colleges are waking up to realize that what they have on their hands is a first-class octopus which is strangling many of the legitimate pursuits of the educational institution. . . .

Every year toward the end of the football season, when reports about the vast sums taken in by our colleges flood the press, a rush of printed matter fills the sports pages of the newspapers with arguments to prove how wisely and how well these millions are used. Attempt to question the sacredness of football and any athletic director will immediately overwhelm you with a flood of unanswerable statistics. He will show that football is the godfather of games within and without the walls of the university, that with its gate receipts are built swimming pools and squash courts, that from its profits spring crews fully armed and golf and tennis teams fully clothed. A new baseball cage was built out of football earnings. The lacrosse team made a southern trip upon them. They helped finance the rifle and chess teams, the polo and the debating teams. They maintained and paid for all intramural sports: sports between classes, between the clubs and societies, sports between the dormitories. In fact, they did almost everything but pay the salary of the President. The word intramural to an athletic director takes on a holy significance when he is talking; the intramural sports idea, "athletics for all," is hammered home for all it is worth to show how beneficial modern football really is. . . .

Today, strong and powerful as is the Great God Football, signs are not wanting to show that American college undergraduates are beginning to doubt its divinity. For one thing, the enormous size of our larger universities tends to weaken the overwhelming interest in athletics, and in football especially. Any college graduate of thirty years ago will tell you of class rushes, class suppers, class proms, and the like, such

as have no counterpart today. He will talk of football games and of baseball games and track meets held between college classes, all of which seem strange and impossible to the modern undergraduate. Intense class feeling began to die out years ago; the classes today are far too large in the great universities to permit of much class feeling or class loyalty being shown. So also, the feeling so wrongly called "college spirit" is losing ground in many of the large educational institutions throughout the country. . . .

This does not mean that football will die out and waste away, that football coaches had better cast about for other jobs, that our stadia will crumble and decay, that Athletic Directors will have to return again to the role of humble citizens each fall instead of potentates of sport. It does not even mean that the college president who proposed any major reforms in the game would not still be playing with dynamite. It means simply that a saner attitude is gaining ground among the American undergraduates, and that some day football may cease to be a religion to them and become merely a sport. For football as a game, unless all signs to the contrary fail, will never die out.

And after all, why should it? With all its faults and the faults that creep in with it, football today is a superb spectacle. Considering it simply as a game to watch, what other game can compare with it? . . .

A game and nothing more. A game which ought not to interfere in any way with the educational program of the undergraduate, which ought not to be considered the be-all and end-all of college life, in which it matters not at all who wins or loses; but a magnificent game nonetheless.

No, not *a* game, *the* game of the twentieth century; the game that besides being a sport to play is also one of the most regal spectacles of the present day.

In short, why not take football for what it is: The Great American Game? And let it go at that.

117.

Henry Ford: Youth, Industry, and Progress

Henry Ford, who envisioned an economy of abundance in which high output, low prices, and high wages would be combined to enhance mass purchasing power, revolutionized the life and business philosophy of his time and of the next generation. Ford embodied the American dream of "from rags to riches," and by making good without recourse to underhanded means he reconciled business with religion. Although he was personally eccentric — he hated Jews, Catholics, fat men, prisons, doctors, bankers, and tobacco, carried a gun and believed in reincarnation — his opinions were widely respected. The selection below was first published in 1928 and reprinted in the volume My Philosophy of Industry *(1929).*

Source: *Forum,* October 1928: "Success."

STUDENTS OF WORLD PROGRESS recognize that there is a time for everything. Like the opening of a flower or the budding of a tree, certain events cannot be forced ahead of their time; nor, conversely, can they be disregarded after the time for their appearance has come. Therefore it behooves the man — especially the young man — who wishes to have his part in the progress of this world to watch the signs of the times and be ready at the proper moment to take his place in the procession of human events.

Not only in industry but in all lines of work is this so. In the scheme of progress each unit has its logical place, which no other can fill. As a case in point, the automobile and the airplane could not be successfully developed until the internal-combustion engine had been invented. Earlier engines, such as steam engines, were too heavy; they weighed too much per horsepower to be practical for use in these two new vehicles of transportation. But with the coming of the internal-combustion engine, it was possible to concentrate in a small place and a small weight an enormous amount of power. Thus it enabled us to develop the automobile and, later on, the airplane. One invention makes way for another; one discovery lights up the path ahead so that he who runs may read — and lead.

Similarly, the development of industry was long delayed because one link in the chain of progress was missing. When that had been forged, industry shot ahead to its present high rate of production. I refer to the matter of long-distance-power transmission. Back in the days when machinery had to be run by steam or waterpower, cables and belts were the only means of power transmission. This meant that factories had to be located in the immediate neighborhood of the plant or on the bank of the stream from which power was derived. The natural tendency was for industry to group itself around large sources of power.

Thus centralization was brought about, and on its heels followed quantity production. The mere idea of quantity production was a great step forward, but its consummation was hampered by the very condition that had given rise to it. So long as centralization was necessary, so long as manufacturing could be carried on only by the limited number of factories that could crowd around the various sources of power, quantity production on the present scale was impossible.

Then within our knowledge — within our century — electricity was discovered. Electricity possessed this great advantage over all other kinds of power previously produced — it could be instantaneously transmitted over great distances by wire. Power could be generated in one spot and sent out to any number of factories all over the country. The necessity for centralization had been eliminated, and manufacturing went ahead on a larger scale than ever.

Light, heat, and power — think what has been accomplished by this one idea put into action! And the power age has barely begun. In our own shops we are constantly improving our method of manufacture with an eye to efficiency, economy, and the safety and comfort of our employees. Belt transmission has been entirely supplanted by electrically driven machines, which frees us from the danger and annoyance of wheels and belts whirling overhead. Our furnaces, most of which are electrically heated, are so constructed and insulated that the men work in front of them without discomfort. There is no smoke or gas except in a few processes, and, in these, electric ventilators carry off all disagreeable odors and unhealthful fumes.

The increase in the scale of production does not mean that craftsmanship has gone. From the earliest times machines of some sort have been in use. It took craftsmen to make and use machines then, and it takes craftsmen now. The hand and the brain and the eye have functioned together ever since man came upon the earth. The handmade age is still with us, but it has been refined and advanced until it stands on a higher

plane than when men used wooden plows and primitive potter's wheels. We value the things of the past because of their association; they were steps toward those of the present. But as needs have grown, means of production have been increased and improved.

It has been asserted that machine production kills the creative ability of the craftsman. This is not true. The machine demands that man be its master; it compels mastery more than the old methods did. The number of skilled craftsmen in proportion to the working population has greatly increased under the conditions brought about by the machine. They get better wages and more leisure in which to exercise their creative faculties.

There are two ways of making money — one at the expense of others, the other by service to others. The first method does not "make" money, does not create anything; it only "gets" money — and does not always succeed in that. In the last analysis, the so-called gainer loses. The second way pays twice — to maker and user, to seller and buyer. It receives by creating, and receives only a just share, because no one is entitled to all. Nature and humanity supply too many necessary partners for that. True riches make wealthier the country as a whole.

Most people will spend more time and energy in going around problems than in trying to solve them. A problem is a challenge to your intelligence. Problems are only problems until they are solved, and the solution confers a reward upon the solver. Instead of avoiding problems, we should welcome them and through right thinking make them pay us profits. The discerning youth will spend his time learning *direct methods,* learning how to make his brain and hand work in harmony with each other so that the problem in hand may be solved in the simplest, most direct way that he knows.

— it can live in the future. The world of tomorrow belongs to the young man of today; he can begin shaping the world now. No age has ever presented the tremendous opportunities of the present but along with these opportunities are proportionate responsibilities. With the changing wheel of ambition, boys no longer regard the talkative professions as more important than the manual. They realize that there are gigantic tasks to be done and that these will be accomplished by doers rather than talkers. The man who does things is vastly more important to the world than the clerk who merely makes the record of others' achievements.

Youths have a tremendous advantage over their elders in possessing the power of vision without the drawback of retrospect. They bring fresh eyes and fresh minds to old tasks. They are not tied down by the traditions of the past; they are not slaves to the failures of others. Their concern is not so much with what could have been done in the past as with what can be done in the future. What they make of it will depend on what they make of themselves and the opportunities or tasks which are now before them.

Of course, education has its limits. Education and ability to do things are not interchangeable terms. You cannot educate brains into a man's head, but you can help him to make the most of the brains he has. A man who cannot think is not an educated man, no matter how many college degrees he may have acquired. One who can think things out usually can do them. An education which consists of signposts indicating the failures and fallacies of the past is doubtless useful.

Many men are at work today on theories fundamentally wrong, ignorant that other men have followed that road and have had to come back. So schools are useful if they show the blind alleys of human endeavor. Then they must help to put men in posses-

sion of their own powers. But they cannot do this without the earnest desire of their students to be so helped. Inventors, by the way, are not made by education; but if they have enough education to spare them the mistakes of the past, it saves their time.

Most of us are doing two things — that by which the body is kept alive and that by which the higher part of our nature lives. We go to the job to pay expenses and then we indulge ourselves in what we like to do and maybe were meant to do. The whole secret of a successful life is to find out what it is one's destiny to do, and then do it. Some day there may come to one the duty to do a disagreeable task, to take up a cause which will yield no reward — a cause which will at first surround one with misunderstanding and abuse, and which will make one look like a fool before men. One naturally shrinks from it. But when a man is sure of what he has to do, he should go ahead full speed.

To be right means mainly to be in tune with destiny and willing to obey. It does not necessarily mean to be agreeable, nor to be agreed with, nor to be popular; it does mean to be useful in the purpose which destiny is trying to achieve in us and through us. If a man is right, he need not fear to stand alone; he is not alone. Every right idea that is put forth has many silent adherents.

There is a great deal of nonsense spoken about the "lonely heights" — they may seem to be lonely, but they are only silent. The loneliness comes when a man settles within himself whether he is to be a mere form following a conventional routine or whether he is to listen and obey the voice of a changeable life. It is lonely while he is deciding. If he decides to do what duty bids him, then he is no longer lonely. He comes at once into the fellowship of other people who are thinking as he is but who have been waiting for a leader to declare them and their principles.

118.

HERBERT HOOVER: Rugged Individualism

Near the end of his presidential campaign against "Al" Smith, Herbert Hoover delivered a speech to a New York audience on October 22, 1928. A self-made millionaire who had been born on a small Iowa farm, Hoover's life had, to date, justified his faith in the philosophy first proclaimed in his book American Individualism *(1922), and reiterated on what proved to be the eve of his election. The speech also expressed the Republican philosophy of Harding and Coolidge, under whom Hoover had been an influential secretary of commerce. Even Lincoln Steffens, who since his muckraking days had become an advocate of both Russian communism and Italian fascism, was impressed. "Big business in America is producing what the Socialists held up as their goal; food, shelter and clothing for all," he wrote. "You will see it during the Hoover administration." Hoover's speech, which is reprinted here in part, acquired fame retrospectively as a concise expression of public opinion on the eve of the stock market crash.*

Source: *The New Day: Campaign Speeches of Herbert Hoover,* Palo Alto (Stanford University), 1928, pp. 149-176.

THIS CAMPAIGN now draws near a close. The platforms of the two parties defining principles and offering solutions of various national problems have been presented and are being earnestly considered by our people.

After four months' debate it is not the Republican Party which finds reason for abandonment of any of the principles it has laid down or of the views it has expressed for solution of the problems before the country. The principles to which it adheres are rooted deeply in the foundations of our national life. The solutions which it proposes are based on experience with government and on a consciousness that it may have the responsibility for placing those solutions in action. . . .

When the war closed, the most vital of all issues both in our own country and throughout the world was whether governments should continue their wartime ownership and operation of many instrumentalities of production and distribution. We were challenged with a peacetime choice between the American system of rugged individualism and a European philosophy of diametrically opposed doctrines — doctrines of paternalism and state socialism. The acceptance of these ideas would have meant the destruction of self-government through centralization of government. It would have meant the undermining of the individual initiative and enterprise through which our people have grown to unparalleled greatness.

The Republican Party from the beginning resolutely turned its face away from these ideas and these war practices. A Republican Congress cooperated with the Democratic administration to demobilize many of our war activities. At that time the two parties were in accord upon that point. When the Republican Party came into full power, it went at once resolutely back to our fundamental conception of the state and the rights and responsibilities of the individual. Thereby it restored confidence and hope in the American people, it freed and stimulated enterprise, it restored the government to its position as an umpire instead of a player in the economic game. For these reasons the American people have gone forward in progress while the rest of the world has halted, and some countries have even gone backward. If anyone will study the causes of retarded recuperation in Europe, he will find much of it due to stifling of private initiative, on one hand, and overloading of the government with business, on the other.

There has been revived in this campaign, however, a series of proposals which, if adopted, would be a long step toward the abandonment of our American system and a surrender to the destructive operation of governmental conduct of commercial business. Because the country is faced with difficulty and doubt over certain national problems — that is, Prohibition, farm relief, and electrical power — our opponents propose that we must thrust government a long way into the businesses which give rise to these problems. In effect, they abandon the tenets of their own party and turn to state socialism as a solution for the difficulties presented by all three. It is proposed that we shall change from Prohibition to the state purchase and sale of liquor. If their agricultural relief program means anything, it means that the government shall directly or indirectly buy and sell and fix prices of agricultural products. And we are to go into the hydroelectric power business. In other words, we are confronted with a huge program of government in business.

There is, therefore, submitted to the American people a question of fundamental principle. That is: Shall we depart from the principles of our American political and economic system, upon which we have advanced beyond all the rest of the world, in order to adopt methods based on principles destructive of its very foundations? And I wish to emphasize the seriousness of these proposals. I wish to make my position clear; for this goes to the very roots of American life and progress.

I should like to state to you the effect that this projection of government in business would have upon our system of self-government and our economic system. That effect would reach to the daily life of every man and woman. It would impair the very basis of liberty and freedom, not only for those left outside the fold of expanded bureaucracy but for those embraced within it.

Let us first see the effect upon self-government. When the federal government undertakes to go into commercial business it must at once set up the organization and administration of that business, and it immediately finds itself in a labyrinth, every alley of which leads to the destruction of self-government. Commercial business requires a concentration of responsibility. Self-government requires decentralization and many checks and balances to safeguard liberty. Our government to succeed in business would need become in effect a despotism. There at once begins the destruction of self-government.

The first problem of the government about to adventure in commercial business is to determine a method of administration. It must secure leadership and direction. Shall this leadership be chosen by political agencies or shall we make it elective? The hard, practical fact is that leadership in business must come through the sheer rise in ability and character. That rise can only take place in the free atmosphere of competition. Competition is closed by bureaucracy. Political agencies are feeble channels through which to select able leaders to conduct commercial business.

Government, in order to avoid the possible incompetence, corruption, and tyranny of too great authority in individuals entrusted with commercial business, inevitably turns to boards and commissions. To make sure that there are checks and balances, each

Wide World

Calvin Coolidge and President-elect Herbert Hoover en route to Hoover's inauguration, March 1929

member of such boards and commissions must have equal authority. Each has his separate responsibility to the public, and at once we have the conflict of ideas and the lack of decision which would ruin any commercial business. It has contributed greatly to the demoralization of our shipping business. Moreover, these commissions must be representative of different sections and different political parties, so that at once we have an entire blight upon coordinated action within their ranks which destroys any possibility of effective administration.

Moreover, our legislative bodies cannot in fact delegate their full authority to commissions or to individuals for the conduct of matters vital to the American people; for if we would preserve government by the people we must preserve the authority of our legislators in the activities of our government.

Thus, every time the federal government goes into a commercial business, 531 senators and congressmen become the actual board of directors of that business. Every time a state government goes into business, 100 or 200 state senators and legislators be-

come the actual directors of that business. Even if they were supermen and if there were no politics in the United States, no body of such members could competently direct commercial activities; for that requires initiative, instant decision, and action. It took Congress six years of constant discussion to even decide what the method of administration of Muscle Shoals should be.

When the federal government undertakes to go into business, the state governments are at once deprived of control and taxation of that business; when a state government undertakes to go into business, it at once deprives the municipalities of taxation and control of that business. Municipalities, being local and close to the people, can, at times, succeed in business where federal and state governments must fail. We have trouble enough with logrolling in legislative bodies today. It originates naturally from desires of citizens to advance their particular section or to secure some necessary service. It would be multiplied a thousandfold were the federal and state governments in these businesses.

The effect upon our economic progress

would be even worse. Business progressiveness is dependent on competition. New methods and new ideas are the outgrowth of the spirit of adventure, of individual initiative, and of individual enterprise. Without adventure there is no progress. No government administration can rightly take chances with taxpayers' money.

There is no better example of the practical incompetence of government to conduct business than the history of our railways. During the war the government found it necessary to operate the railways. That operation continued until after the war. In the year before being freed from government operation, they were not able to meet the demands for transportation. Eight years later we find them under private enterprise transporting 15 percent more goods and meeting every demand for service. Rates have been reduced by 15 percent and net earnings increased from less than 1 percent on their valuation to about 5 percent. Wages of employees have improved by 13 percent. The wages of railway employees are today 121 percent above prewar, while the wages of government employees are today only 65 percent above prewar. That should be a sufficient commentary upon the efficiency of government operation. . . .

Bureaucracy is ever desirous of spreading its influence and its power. You cannot extend the mastery of the government over the daily working life of a people without at the same time making it the master of the people's souls and thoughts. Every expansion of government in business means that government in order to protect itself from the political consequences of its errors and wrongs is driven irresistibly without peace to greater and greater control of the nation's press and platform. Free speech does not live many hours after free industry and free commerce die.

It is a false liberalism that interprets itself into the government operation of commercial business. Every step of bureaucratizing of the business of our country poisons the very roots of liberalism — that is, political equality, free speech, free assembly, free press, and equality of opportunity. It is the road not to more liberty, but to less liberty. Liberalism should be found not striving to spread bureaucracy but striving to set bounds to it. True liberalism seeks all legitimate freedom first in the confident belief that without such freedom the pursuit of all other blessings and benefits is vain. That belief is the foundation of all American progress, political as well as economic.

Liberalism is a force truly of the spirit, a force proceeding from the deep realization that economic freedom cannot be sacrificed if political freedom is to be preserved. Even if governmental conduct of business could give us more efficiency instead of less efficiency, the fundamental objection to it would remain unaltered and unabated. It would destroy political equality. It would increase rather than decrease abuse and corruption. It would stifle initiative and invention. It would undermine the development of leadership. It would cramp and cripple the mental and spiritual energies of our people. It would extinguish equality and opportunity. It would dry up the spirit of liberty and progress. For these reasons primarily it must be resisted. For 150 years liberalism has found its true spirit in the American system, not in the European systems.

I do not wish to be misunderstood in this statement. I am defining a general policy. It does not mean that our government is to part with one iota of its national resources without complete protection to the public interest. I have already stated that where the government is engaged in public works for purposes of flood control, of navigation, of irrigation, of scientific research or national defense, or in pioneering a new art, it will at times necessarily produce power or commodities as a by-product. But they must be a by-product of the major purpose, not the major purpose itself.

Nor do I wish to be misinterpreted as believing that the United States is a free-for-all and devil-take-the-hindmost. The very essence of equality of opportunity and of American individualism is that there shall be no domination by any group or combination in this republic, whether it be business or political. On the contrary, it demands economic justice as well as political and social justice. It is no system of laissez faire.

I feel deeply on this subject because during the war I had some practical experience with governmental operation and control. I have witnessed not only at home but abroad the many failures of government in business. I have seen its tyrannies, its injustices, its destructions of self-government, its undermining of the very instincts which carry our people forward to progress. I have witnessed the lack of advance, the lowered standards of living, the depressed spirits of people working under such a system. My objection is based not upon theory or upon a failure to recognize wrong or abuse, but I know the adoption of such methods would strike at the very roots of American life and would destroy the very basis of American progress.

Our people have the right to know whether we can continue to solve our great problems without abandonment of our American system. I know we can. We have demonstrated that our system is responsive enough to meet any new and intricate development in our economic and business life. We have demonstrated that we can meet any economic problem and still maintain our democracy as master in its own house, and that we can at the same time preserve equality of opportunity and individual freedom.

In the last fifty years we have discovered that mass production will produce articles for us at half the cost they required previously. We have seen the resultant growth of large units of production and distribution. This is big business. Many businesses must be bigger, for our tools are bigger, our country is bigger. We now build a single dynamo of 100,000 horsepower. Even fifteen years ago that would have been a big business all by itself. Yet today advance in production requires that we set ten of these units together in a row.

The American people from bitter experience have a rightful fear that great business units might be used to dominate our industrial life and by illegal and unethical practices destroy equality of opportunity.

Years ago the Republican administration established the principle that such evils could be corrected by regulation. It developed methods by which abuses could be prevented while the full value of industrial progress could be retained for the public. It insisted upon the principle that when great public utilities were clothed with the security of partial monopoly, whether it be railways, power plants, telephones, or what not, then there must be the fullest and most complete control of rates, services, and finances by government or local agencies. It declared that these businesses must be conducted with glass pockets.

As to our great manufacturing and distributing industries, the Republican Party insisted upon the enactment of laws that not only would maintain competition but would destroy conspiracies to destroy the smaller units or dominate and limit the equality of opportunity among our people.

One of the great problems of government is to determine to what extent the government shall regulate and control commerce and industry and how much it shall leave it alone. No system is perfect. We have had many abuses in the private conduct of business. That every good citizen resents. It is just as important that business keep out of government as that government keep out of business.

Nor am I setting up the contention that our institutions are perfect. No human ideal is ever perfectly attained, since humanity itself is not perfect.

The wisdom of our forefathers in their

conception that progress can only be attained as the sum of the accomplishment of free individuals has been reinforced by all of the great leaders of the country since that day. Jackson, Lincoln, Cleveland, McKinley, Roosevelt, Wilson, and Coolidge have stood unalterably for these principles.

And what have been the results of our American system? Our country has become the land of opportunity to those born without inheritance, not merely because of the wealth of its resources and industry but because of this freedom of initiative and enterprise. Russia has natural resources equal to ours. Her people are equally industrious, but she has not had the blessings of 150 years of our form of government and of our social system.

By adherence to the principles of decentralized self-government, ordered liberty, equal opportunity, and freedom to the individual, our American experiment in human welfare has yielded a degree of well-being unparalleled in all the world. It has come nearer to the abolition of poverty, to the abolition of fear of want than humanity has ever reached before. Progress of the past seven years is the proof of it. This alone furnishes the answer to our opponents, who ask us to introduce destructive elements into the system by which this has been accomplished.

119.

James R. Randolph: Rockets and World Politics

The first liquid-propelled rocket test was made by Dr. Robert H. Goddard on March 16, 1926, at Auburn, Massachusetts. "It looked almost magical as it rose," Goddard wrote in his diary the following day, "without any appreciably greater noise or flame, as if it said 'I've been here long enough; I think I'll be going somewhere else, if you don't mind.'" The rocket, which burned gasoline and liquid oxygen, remained airborne two and one-half seconds after take-off and landed eighty-four feet from the launch site. Goddard is considered to have founded the modern science of liquid-fuel rocketry. Liquid-fuel rockets attracted little attention in the United States, but they were successfully developed by the Germans who, by attaching an explosive warhead, used them as weapons in World War II. In 1928 James R. Randolph speculated on the effects of Goddard's work on rockets in an article titled "Can We Go to Mars?" part of which is reprinted here.

Source: *Scientific American*, August 1928.

Today man looks through his telescope at the other members of the solar system and wonders what is there. Will he ever be able to go there and see?

Several of these heavenly bodies might repay at least a passing visit, should such a thing prove possible. The moon is too airless for anything more, but would be interesting to look at more closely than is now possible. Also, its invisible back portion would be worth seeing. Venus and the large outer planets hide themselves behind dense veils of cloud, but there is a possibility that Venus might prove habitable for man.

But of them all, Mars presents the most interesting possibilities, and would probably be the first visited. Its skies are generally clear, permitting an easy view of the surface, and this surface appears to resemble our own in some respects, although in others it is very different. There is a possibility that men might be able to live there, although scientists are far from agreement on this question.

And over all this surface is a network of fine dark lines, the "canals" of Mars, which many people believe are the work of beings having intelligence comparable to our own. None of the other theories advanced to explain them have proved satisfactory, at least in the case of certain of these canals. Even a flying visit might settle this question beyond a reasonable doubt and would show whether or not there really are "people" there.

The space between the two planets is devoid of air or any other kind of matter. Hence, there is only one way in which such a trip could be made. A projectile of some sort would have to be thrown off from the earth with sufficient velocity to clear the earth's attraction and would then have to be directed into an orbit that would touch the orbit of Mars at the time Mars got to that particular part of it. Then, its velocity would have to be reduced so that it could be captured by the planet and become a satellite. Such it would remain for about a year, at the end of which time its speed would have to be increased, returning it to its own orbit, and thence back to the earth.

Thus the projectile would have to be able to change its velocity in a vacuum, and at the start it would have to attain a velocity of seven miles per second, as that is the velocity needed to escape the earth's attraction.

There is only one device known to science at the present time with which these requirements could be met. That is the high-altitude rocket invented by Professor Robert H. Goddard of Clark University. The shells from the largest naval guns have a muzzle velocity of little more than half a mile per second.

The Goddard rocket is now in a stage of development corresponding to the small airplanes built by Langley. Small rockets have been built to test the principle that would be employed in constructing one to reach very high altitudes. The theory has been proved sound, and it has been shown that the problems to be encountered in going from these to large rockets capable of infinite range are no more serious than those involved in the design of huge transatlantic liners. Engineering difficulties may be looked for because of the enormous size of the machine, and the cost will be very great, but the plan is by no means impossible. . . .

The Goddard rocket differs from the ordinary rocket much as a modern turbine differs from a hurdy-gurdy, or flutter wheel. It works on the same principle, but it has been designed for the highest possible efficiency and power output. Some of the latest rockets use liquid fuel, whose nature is being kept secret, but the earlier ones used smokeless powder. . . .

Because of its high cost and the lack of a financial motive for the trip, it is likely to be a long time before such large rockets are built.

The Goddard rocket in its present size could be used for exploring the upper atmosphere, beyond the range of sounding balloons. The next development that is planned is the study of the Heaviside layer, which is supposed to exist at an altitude of about sixty miles above the earth's surface, and to play an important part in the transmission of radio signals.

It is also planned to take astronomical photographs from outside the earth's atmosphere.

A further development of the Goddard type of rocket is likely to be that for war.

Experiments along this line were begun during the World War, but were dropped when the Armistice was signed. At that time they had resulted in a multiple-charge rocket that fired several charges in succession, and traveled straight. It was shown that these rockets could be made at least as accurate as a long-range gun, with vastly greater possibilities as to size and range.

Rockets are possible that could shoot halfway around the earth, carrying loads of hundreds of tons — and this offers interesting possibilities for the next war. They could be steered to a limited extent, the pilot staying in the rocket until the last possible moment, and then going off in a landing plane.

Decided changes in world politics would follow the introduction of such a weapon. The armored horseman brought in the feudal system. The gun restored democracy. The modern battleship suppressed piracy and abolished the rights of small nations. The airplane made the League of Nations a necessity by bringing possible enemies entirely too close for comfort. The rocket would bring America and Russia as close together, in a military sense, as France and Germany now are.

In the right hands the rocket would bring universal peace. In the wrong hands it would lead to conquest more absolute than anything the world has ever known. The largest empires of past and present could not exist without great numbers of loyal soldiers to hold them together. An empire using rockets would need only governors and spies. The mechanics who made the rockets could be slaves, and a mere handful of men could direct them.

120.

ALLEN TATE: "Ode to the Confederate Dead"

During the 1920s one of the most distinguished literary movements in the country was centered at Vanderbilt University in Nashville, Tennessee. This Southern regional group included such figures as John Crowe Ransom — in many respects its guiding spirit — Robert Penn Warren, Donald Davidson, and Allen Tate. They had in common a profound affection for a romanticized view of the Old South that they attempted to express in novel and experimental literary forms. The following example of Tate's work, "Ode to the Confederate Dead," was published in Mr. Pope and Other Poems *(1928) but underwent many subsequent revisions.*

Source: *Poems 1922-1947*, New York, 1948.

ODE TO THE CONFEDERATE DEAD

Row after row with strict impunity
The headstones yield their names to the element,
The wind whirrs without recollection;
In the riven troughs the splayed leaves
Pile up, of nature the casual sacrament
To the seasonal eternity of death;

Then driven by the fierce scrutiny
Of heaven to their election in the vast breath,
They sough the rumor of mortality.

Autumn is desolation in the plot
Of a thousand acres where these memories grow
From the inexhaustible bodies that are not
Dead, but feed the grass row after rich row.
Think of the autumns that have come and gone! —
Ambitious November with the humors of the year,
With a particular zeal for every slab,
Staining the uncomfortable angels that rot
On the slabs, a wing chipped here, an arm there:
The brute curiosity of an angel's stare
Turns you, like them, to stone,
Transforms the heaving air
Till plunged to a heavier world below
You shift your sea-space blindly
Heaving, turning like the blind crab.

   Dazed by the wind, only the wind
   The leaves flying, plunge

You know who have waited by the wall
The twilight certainty of an animal,
Those midnight restitutions of the blood
You know — the immitigable pines, the smoky frieze
Of the sky, the sudden call: you know the rage,
The cold pool left by the mounting flood,
Of muted Zeno and Parmenides.
You who have waited for the angry resolution
Of those desires that should be yours tomorrow,
You know the unimportant shrift of death
And praise the vision
And praise the arrogant circumstance
Of those who fall
Rank upon rank, hurried beyond decision —
Here by the sagging gate, stopped by the wall.

   Seeing, seeing only the leaves
   Flying, plunge and expire

Turn your eyes to the immoderate past,
Turn to the inscrutable infantry rising
Demons out of the earth — they will not last.
Stonewall, Stonewall, and the sunken fields of hemp,
Shiloh, Antietam, Malvern Hill, Bull Run.
Lost in that orient of the thick and fast

You will curse the setting sun.

   Cursing only the leaves crying
   Like an old man in a storm

You hear the shout, the crazy hemlocks point
With troubled figures to the silence which
Smothers you, a mummy, in time.

                         The hound bitch
Toothless and dying, in a musty cellar
Hears the wind only.
                Now that the salt of their blood
Stiffens the saltier oblivion of the sea,
Seals the malignant purity of the flood,
What shall we who count our days and bow
Our heads with a commemorial woe
In the ribboned coats of grim felicity,
What shall we say of the bones, unclean,
Whose verdurous anonymity will grow?

The ragged arms, the ragged heads and eyes
Lost in these acres of the insane green?
The gray lean spiders come, they come and go;
In a tangle of willows without light
The singular screech-owl's tight
Invisible lyric seeds the mind
With the furious murmur of their chivalry.

   We shall say only the leaves
   Flying, plunge and expire

We shall say only the leaves whispering
In the improbable mist of nightfall
That flies on multiple wing:
Night is the beginning and the end
And in between the ends of distraction
Waits mute speculation, the patient curse
That stones the eyes, or like the jaguar leaps
For his own image in a jungle pool, his victim.

What shall we say who have knowledge
Carried to the heart? Shall we take the act
To the grave? Shall we, more hopeful, set up the grave
In the house? The ravenous grave?
                   Leave now
The shut gate and the decomposing wall:
The gentle serpent, green in the mulberry bush,
Riots with his tongue through the hush —
Sentinel of the grave who counts us all!

121.

James Weldon Johnson: Race Prejudice and the Negro Artist

In the atmosphere of nativism and xenophobia that followed the war, it was perhaps not surprising that the American Negro continued to be victimized by the social, political, and economic exclusion that had increasingly been his lot since the end of Reconstruction. The Negro was savagely persecuted in the 1920s and the prosperity of the period passed him by. Nonetheless, Negroes began to make their presence felt in the cultural life of the nation: in literature, drama, and the concert stage. James Weldon Johnson, poet, professor, and secretary from 1916 to 1930 of the National Association for the Advancement of Colored People, argued, in an article that is reprinted here in part, that this renaissance had softened the prejudice that many Americans felt toward Negroes.

Source: *Harper's*, November 1928.

WHAT AMERICANS call the Negro problem is almost as old as America itself. For three centuries the Negro in this country has been tagged with an interrogation point; the question propounded, however, has not always been the same. Indeed, the question has run all the way from whether or not the Negro was a human being, down — or up — to whether or not the Negro shall be accorded full and unlimited American citizenship. Therefore, the Negro problem is not a problem in the sense of being a fixed proposition involving certain invariable factors and waiting to be worked out according to certain defined rules.

It is not a static condition; rather, it is and always has been a series of shifting interracial situations, never precisely the same in any two generations. As these situations have shifted, the methods and manners of dealing with them have constantly changed. And never has there been such a swift and vital shift as the one which is taking place at the present moment; and never was there

a more revolutionary change in attitudes than the one which is now going on.

The question of the races — white and black — has occupied much of America's time and thought. Many methods for a solution of the problem have been tried — most of them tried *on* the Negro, for one of the mistakes commonly made in dealing with this matter has been the failure of white America to take into account the Negro himself and the forces he was generating and sending out. The question repeated generation after generation has been: what shall we do with the Negro? — ignoring completely the power of the Negro to do something for himself, and even something to America.

It is a new thought that the Negro has helped to shape and mold and make America. It is, perhaps, a startling thought that America would not be precisely the America it is today except for the powerful, if silent, influence the Negro has exerted upon it — both positively and negatively. It is a certainty that the nation would be shocked by a contemplation of the effects which have been wrought upon its inherent character by the negative power which the Negro has involuntarily and unwittingly wielded.

A number of approaches to the heart of the race problem have been tried: religious, educational, political, industrial, ethical, economic, sociological. Along several of these approaches considerable progress has been made. Today a newer approach is being tried, an approach which discards most of the older methods. It requires a minimum of pleas, or propaganda, or philanthropy. It depends more upon what the Negro himself does than upon what someone does for him. It is the approach along the line of intellectual and artistic achievement by Negroes and may be called the art approach to the Negro problem. This method of approaching a solution of the race question has the advantage of affording great and rapid progress with least friction and of providing a common platform upon which most people are willing to stand. The results of this method seem to carry a high degree of finality, to be the thing itself that was to be demonstrated.

I have said that this is a newer approach to the race problem; that is only in a sense true. The Negro has been using this method for a very long time; for a longer time than he has used any other method, and, perhaps, with farther-reaching effectiveness. For more than a century his great folk-art contributions have been exerting an ameliorating effect, slight and perhaps, in any one period, imperceptible, nevertheless, cumulative. In countless and diverse situations song and dance have been both a sword and a shield for the Negro. Take the spirituals: for sixty years, beginning with their introduction to the world by the Fisk Jubilee Singers, these songs have touched and stirred the hearts of people and brought about a smoothing down of the rougher edges of prejudice against the Negro. Indeed, nobody can hear Negroes sing this wonderful music in its primitive beauty without a softening of feeling toward them.

What is there, then, that is new? What is new consists largely in the changing attitude of the American people. There is a coming to light and notice of efforts that have been going on for a long while, and a public appreciation of their results. Note, for example, the change in the reaction to the spirituals. Fifty years ago white people who heard the spirituals were touched and moved with sympathy and pity for the "poor Negro." Today, the effect is not one of pity for the Negro's condition but admiration for the creative genius of the race.

All of the Negro's folk-art creations have undergone a new evaluation. His sacred music — the spirituals; his secular music — ragtime, blues, jazz, and the work songs; his folklore — the Uncle Remus plantation tales; and his dances have received a new and higher appreciation. Indeed, I dare to say that it is now more or less generally acknowledged that the only things artistic that have sprung from American soil and out of American life, and been universally recognized as distinctively American products, are the folk creations of the Negro. The one thing that may be termed artistic, by which the United States is known the world over, is its Negro-derived popular music. The folk creations of the Negro have not only received a new appreciation; they have — the spirituals excepted — been taken over and assimilated. They are no longer racial, they are national; they have become a part of our common cultural fund.

Negro secular music has been developed into American popular music; Negro dances have been made into our national art of dancing; even the plantation tales have been transformed and have come out as popular bedtime stories. The spirituals are still distinct Negro folk songs, but sooner or later our serious composers will take them as material to go into the making of the "great American music" that has so long been looked for.

But the story does not halt at this point. The Negro has done a great deal through his folk-art creations to change the national attitudes toward him; and now the efforts of the race have been reinforced and magnified by the individual Negro artist, the conscious artist. It is fortunate that the individual Negro artist has emerged; for it is more than probable that with the ending of the creative period of blues, which seems to be at hand, the whole folk creative effort of the Negro in the United States will come to a close. All the psychological and environmental forces are working to that end. At any rate, it is the individual Negro artist that is now doing most to effect a crumbling of the inner walls of race prejudice; there are outer and inner walls. The emergence of the individual artist is the result of the same phenomenon that brought about the new evaluation and appreciation of the folk-art creations. But it should be borne in mind that the conscious Aframerican artist is not an entirely new thing. What is new about him is chiefly the evaluation and public recognition of his work.

When and how did this happen? The entire change, which is marked by the shedding of a new light on the artistic and intellectual achievements of the Negro, the whole period which has become ineptly known as "the Negro renaissance," is the matter of a decade, it has all taken place within the last ten years. More forces than anyone can name have been at work to create the existing state; however, several of them may be pointed out.

What took place had no appearance of a development; it seemed more like a sudden awakening, an almost instantaneous change. There was nothing that immediately preceded it which foreshadowed what was to follow. Those who were in the midst of the movement were as much astonished as any-

one else to see the transformation. Overnight, as it were, America became aware that there were Negro artists and that they had something worthwhile to offer. This awareness first manifested itself in black America, for, strange as it may seem, Negroes themselves, as a mass, had had little or no consciousness of their own individual artists.

Black America awoke first to the fact that it possessed poets. This awakening followed the entry of the United States into the Great War. Before this country had been in the war very long there was bitter disillusionment on the part of American Negroes — on the part both of those working at home and those fighting in France to make the world safe for democracy. The disappointment and bitterness were taken up and voiced by a group of seven or eight Negro poets. They expressed what the race felt, what the race wanted to hear. They made the group at large articulate. Some of this poetry was the poetry of despair, but most of it was the poetry of protest and rebellion. Fenton Johnson wrote of civilization:

I am tired of work; I am tired of building
    up somebody else's civilization.
Let us take a rest, M'lissy Jane.

You will let the old shanty go to rot, the
    white people's clothes turn to dust,
    and the Calvary Baptist Church sink
    to the bottomless pit.

Throw the children into the river; civilization has given us too many. It is better to die than it is to grow up and find out that you are colored.
Pluck the stars out of the heavens. The stars mark our destiny. The stars marked my destiny.
I am tired of civilization.

Joseph Cotter, a youth of twenty, inquired plaintively from the invalid's bed to which he was confined:

Brother, come!
And let us go unto our God.
And when we stand before Him
I shall say,
"Lord, I do not hate
I am hated.
I scourge no one,
I am scourged.
I covet no lands,
My lands are coveted.
I mock no peoples,
My people are mocked."
And, brother, what shall you say?

But among this whole group the voice that was most powerful was that of Claude McKay. Here was a true poet of great skill and wide range, who turned from creating the mood of poetic beauty in the absolute, as he had so fully done in such poems as "Spring in New Hampshire," "The Harlem Dancer," and "Flame Heart," for example, and began pouring out cynicism, bitterness, and invective. For this purpose, incongruous as it may seem, he took the sonnet form as his medium. There is nothing in American literature that strikes a more portentous note than these sonnet-tragedies of McKay. Here is the sestet of his sonnet, "The Lynching":

Day dawned, and soon the mixed
crowds came to view
The ghastly body swaying in the sun:
The women thronged to look, but never
a one
Showed sorrow in her eyes of steely
blue;
And little lads, lynchers that were to be,
Danced round the dreadful thing in
fiendish glee.

The summer of 1919 was a terrifying period for the American Negro. There were race riots in Chicago and in Washington and in Omaha and in Phillips County, Arkansas; and in Longview, Texas; and in Knoxville, Tennessee; and in Norfolk, Virginia; and in other communities. Colored men and women, by dozens and by scores, were chased and beaten and killed in the streets. And from Claude McKay came this cry of defiant despair, sounded from the last ditch:

If we must die — let it not be like hogs
Hunted and penned in an inglorious spot,

Oh, Kinsmen! We must meet the
common foe;
Though far outnumbered, let us still be
brave,
And for their thousand blows deal
one deathblow!
What though before us lies the open
grave?
Like men we'll face the murderous,
cowardly pack,
Pressed to the wall, dying, but —
fighting back!

But not all the terror of the time could smother the poet of beauty and universality in McKay. In "America," which opens with these lines:

Although she feeds me bread of bitterness,
And sinks into my throat her tiger's
tooth,
Stealing my breath of life, I will confess
I love this cultured hell that tests my
youth

he fused these elements of fear and bitterness and hate into verse which by every test is true poetry and a fine sonnet.

The poems of the Negro poets of the immediate post-war period were widely printed in Negro periodicals; they were committed to memory; they were recited at school exercises and public meetings; and were discussed at private gatherings. Now, Negro poets were not new; their line goes back a long way in Aframerican history. Between Phillis Wheatley, who as a girl of eight or nine was landed in Boston from an African slave ship, in 1761, and who published a volume of poems in 1773, and Paul Laurence Dunbar, who died in 1906, there were more than thirty Negroes who published volumes of verse — some of it good, most of it mediocre, and much of it bad.

The new thing was the effect produced by these poets who sprang up out of the war period. Negro poets had sounded similar notes before, but now for the first time they succeeded in setting up a reverberating response, even in their own group. But the effect was not limited to black America; several of these later poets in some subtle way affected white America. In any event, at just this time, white America began to become aware and to awaken. In the correlation of forces that brought about this result it might be pointed out that the culminating effect of the folk-art creations had gone far toward inducing a favorable state of mind. Doubtless it is also true that the new knowledge and opinions about the Negro in Africa — that he was not just a howling savage, that he had a culture, that he had produced a vital art — had directly affected opinion about the Negro in America. However it may have been, the Negro poets growing out of the war period were the forerunners of the individuals whose work is now being assayed and is receiving recognition in accordance with its worth.

And yet, contemporaneously with the work of these poets, a significant effort was made in another field of art — an effort which might have gone much farther at the time had it not been cut off by our entry into the War, but which, nevertheless, had its effect. Early in 1917, in fact on the very day we entered the War, Mrs. Emily Hapgood produced at the Madison Square Garden Theater three plays of Negro life by Ridgley Torrence, staged by Robert Edmond Jones, and played by an all-Negro

cast. This was the first time that Negro actors in drama commanded the serious attention of the critics and the general public.

Two of the players, Opal Cooper and Inez Clough, were listed by George Jean Nathan among the ten actors giving the most distinguished performances of the year. No one who heard Opal Cooper chant the dream in the *Rider of Dreams* can ever forget the thrill of it. A sensational feature of the production was the singing orchestra of Negro performers under the direction of J. Rosamond Johnson — singing orchestras in theaters have since become common. The plays moved from the Garden Theater to the Garrick, but the stress of war crushed them out.

In 1920, Charles Gilpin was enthusiastically and universally acclaimed for his acting in *The Emperor Jones*. The American stage has seldom seen such an outburst of acclamation. Mr. Gilpin was one of the ten persons voted by the Drama League as having done most for the American theater during the year. Most of the readers of these pages will remember the almost national crisis caused by his invitation to the Drama League Dinner.

And along came *Shuffle Along*; and all of New York flocked to an out-of-the-way theater in West Sixty-third Street to hear the most joyous singing and see the most exhilarating dancing to be found on any stage in the city. The dancing steps originally used by the "policeman" in *Shuffle Along* furnished new material for hundreds of dancing men. *Shuffle Along* was actually an epoch-making musical comedy. Out of *Shuffle Along* came Florence Mills, who, unfortunately, died so young but lived long enough to be acknowledged here and in Europe as one of the finest singing comediennes the stage had ever seen and an artist of positive genius.

In 1923 Roland Hayes stepped out on the American stage in a blaze of glory, making his first appearances as soloist with the Boston Symphony Orchestra, and later with the Philharmonic. Few single artists have packed such crowds into Carnegie Hall and the finest concert halls throughout the country as has Roland Hayes; and, notwithstanding the éclat with which America first received him, his reputation has continued to increase and, besides, he is rated as one of the best box-office attractions in the whole concert field. Miss Marian Anderson appeared as soloist with the Philadelphia Symphony Orchestra and in concert at the Lewisohn Stadium at New York City College. Paul Robeson and J. Rosamond Johnson and Taylor Gordon sang spirituals to large and appreciative audiences in New York and over the country, giving to those songs a fresh interpretation and a new vogue.

Paul Robeson — that most versatile of men, who has made a national reputation as athlete, singer, and actor — played in Eugene O'Neill's *All God's Chillun* and added to his reputation on the stage, and, moreover, put to the test an ancient taboo; he played the principal role opposite a white woman. This feature of the play gave rise to a more acute crisis than did Gilpin's invitation to the Drama League Dinner. Some sensational newspapers predicted race riots and other dire disasters, but nothing of the sort happened; the play went over without a boo. Robeson played the title role in a revival of *The Emperor Jones* and almost duplicated the sensation produced by Gilpin in the original presentation.

There followed on the stage Julius Bledsoe, Rose McClendon, Frank Wilson, and Abbie Mitchell, all of whom gained recognition. At the time of this writing each of these four is playing in a Broadway production. Paradoxical it may seem, but no Negro comedian gained recognition in this decade. Negro comedians have long been a recognized American institution and there are several now before the public who are well known, but their reputations were made before this period. The only new reputations made on the comedy stage were made by women, Florence Mills and Ethel Waters. In addition there are the two famous Smiths, Bessie and Clara, singers of blues and favorites of vaudeville, phonograph, and radio audiences. . . .

During the present decade the individual Negro artist has definitely emerged in three fields, in literature, in the theater, and on the concert stage; in other fields he has not won marked distinction. To point to any achievement of distinction in painting, the Negro must go back of this decade, back to H. O. Tanner, who has lived in Europe for the past thirty-five years; or farther back to E. M. Bannister, who gained considerable recognition a half century ago. Nevertheless, there is the work of W. E. Scott, a mural painter, who lives in Chicago and has done a number of public buildings in the Middle West; and of Archibald J. Motley, who recently held a one-man exhibit in New York which attracted very favorable attention. The drawings of Aaron Douglas have won for him a place among American illustrators. To point to any work of acknowledged excellence in sculpture the Negro must go back of this decade to the work of two women, Edmonia Lewis and Meta Warrick Fuller, both of whom received chiefly in Europe such recognition as they gained. There are several young painters and sculptors who are winning recognition.

But the strangest lack is that with all the great native musical endowment he is conceded to possess, the Negro has not in this most propitious time produced a single outstanding composer. There are competent musicians and talented composers of songs and detached bits of music, but no original composer who, in amount and standard of work and in recognition achieved, is at all comparable with S. Coleridge-Taylor, the English Negro composer. Nor can the Negro in the United States point back of this decade to even one such artist. It is a curious fact that the American Negro through his whole history has done more highly sustained and more fully recognized work in the composition of letters than in the composition of music. It is the more curious when we consider that music is so innately a characteristic method of expression for the Negro.

What, now, is the significance of this artistic activity on the part of the Negro and of its reactions on the American people? I think it is twofold. In the first place, the Negro is making some distinctive contributions to our common cultural store. I do not claim it is possible for these individual artists to produce anything comparable to the folk-art in distinctive values, but I do believe they are bringing something fresh and vital into American art, something from the store of their own racial genius — warmth, color, movement, rhythm, and abandon; depth and swiftness of emotion and the beauty of sensuousness. I believe American art will be richer because of these elements in fuller quantity.

But what is of deeper significance to the Negro himself is the effect that this artistic activity is producing upon his condition and status as a man and citizen. I do not believe it an overstatement to say that the "race problem" is fast reaching the stage of being more a question of national mental attitudes toward the Negro than a question of his actual condition. That is to say, it is not at all the problem of a moribund people sinking into a slough of ignorance, poverty, and decay in the very midst of our civilization and despite all our efforts to save them; that would indeed be a problem. Rather is the problem coming to consist in the hesitation and refusal to open new doors of opportunity at which these people are constantly knocking. In other words, the problem for the Negro is reaching the plane where it is becoming less a matter of dealing with what he is and more a matter of dealing with what America thinks he is.

Now, the truth is that the great majority of Americans have not thought about the Negro at all, except in a vague sort of way and in the form of traditional and erroneous stereotypes. Some of these stereotyped forms of thought are quite absurd, yet they have had serious effects. Millions of Americans have had their opinions and attitudes regarding their fellow colored citizens determined by such a phrase as, "A nigger will steal," or "Niggers are lazy," or "Niggers are dirty."

But there is a common, widespread, and persistent stereotyped idea regarding the Negro, and it is that he is here only to receive; to be shaped into something new and unquestionably better. The common idea is that the Negro reached America intellectually, culturally, and morally empty, and that he is here to be filled — filled with education, filled with religion, filled with morality, filled with culture. In a word, the stereotype is that the Negro is nothing more than a beggar at the gate of the nation, waiting to be thrown the crumbs of civilization.

Through his artistic efforts the Negro is smashing this immemorial stereotype faster than he has ever done through any other method he has been able to use. He is making it realized that he is the possessor of a wealth of natural endowments and that he has long been a generous giver to America. He is impressing upon the national mind the conviction that he is an active and important force in American life; that he is a creator as well as a creature; that he has given as well as received; that he is the potential giver of larger and richer contributions.

In this way the Negro is bringing about an entirely new national conception of himself; he has placed himself in an entirely new light before the American people. I do not think it too much to say that through artistic achievement the Negro has found a means of getting at the very core of the prejudice against him by challenging the Nordic superiority complex. A great deal has been accomplished in this decade of "renaissance." Enough has been accomplished to make it seem almost amazing when we realize that there are less than twenty-five Negro artists who have more or less of national recognition; and that it is they who have chiefly done the work.

A great part of what they have accomplished has been done through the sort of publicity they have secured for the race. A generation ago the Negro was receiving lots of publicity, but nearly all of it was bad. There were front page stories with such headings as, "Negro Criminal," "Negro Brute." Today, one may see undesirable stories, but one may also read stories about Negro singers, Negro actors, Negro authors, Negro poets. The connotations of the very word "Negro" have been changed. A generation ago many Negroes were half or wholly ashamed of the term. Today, they have every reason to be proud of it.

For many years and by many methods the Negro has been overcoming the coarser prejudices against him; and when we consider how many of the subtler prejudices have crumbled, and crumbled rapidly under the process of art creation by the Negro, we are justified in taking a hopeful outlook toward the effect that the increase of recognized individual artists fivefold, tenfold, twentyfold, will have on this most perplexing and vital question before the American people.

122.

STEPHEN VINCENT BENÉT: To the American Muse

Stephen Vincent Benét was born into a military family with literary inclinations, a fact that proved important not only for him but for his brother and sister, for all became writers. Benét spent a year in France in 1926-1927 on a Guggenheim Fellowship and there wrote John Brown's Body, *his best-known work. Of epic length, if not of epic grandeur, the poem portrays the impact of the Civil War on America, on groups of Americans, and on individuals who are intermittently brought to the fore.* John Brown's Body *was immensely popular. With it Benét won the Pulitzer Prize in 1929; Henry Steele Commager judged it "not only the best poem about the Civil War, and the best narrative" but also "the best history"; and for a time its author was probably more read than any American poet. The passages from the Invocation that are reprinted here reflect Benét's feeling for the physical vastness and historical richness of his country.*

Source: *John Brown's Body*, New York, 1928.

American muse, whose strong and diverse heart
So many men have tried to understand
But only made it smaller with their art,
Because you are as various as your land,

As mountainous-deep, as flowered with blue rivers,
Thirsty with deserts, buried under snows,
As native as the shape of Navajo quivers,
And native, too, as the sea-voyaged rose.

Swift runner, never captured or subdued,
Seven-branched elk beside the mountain stream,
That half a hundred hunters have pursued
But never matched their bullets with the dream,

Where the great huntsmen failed, I set my sorry
And mortal snare for your immortal quarry.

You are the buffalo-ghost, the broncho-ghost
With dollar-silver in your saddle-horn,
The cowboys riding in from Painted Post,
The Indian arrow in the Indian corn,

And you are the clipped velvet of the lawns
Where Shropshire grows from Massachusetts sods,
The grey Maine rocks — and the war-painted dawns
That break above the Garden of the Gods.

The prairie-schooners crawling toward the ore
And the cheap car, parked by the station-door.

Where the skyscrapers lift their foggy plumes
Of stranded smoke out of a stony mouth
You are that high stone and its arrogant fumes,
And you are ruined gardens in the South

And bleak New England farms, so winter-white
Even their roofs look lonely, and the deep
The middle grainland where the wind of night
Is like all blind earth sighing in her sleep.

A friend, an enemy, a sacred hag
With two tied oceans in her medicine-bag.

They tried to fit you with an English song
And clip your speech into the English tale.
But, even from the first, the words went wrong,
The catbird pecked away the nightingale.

The homesick men begot high-cheekboned things
Whose wit was whittled with a different sound
And Thames and all the rivers of the kings
Ran into Mississippi and were drowned.

They planted England with a stubborn trust.
But the cleft dust was never English dust.

Stepchild of every exile from content
And all the disavouched, hard-bitten pack
Shipped overseas to steal a continent
With neither shirts nor honor to their back.

Pimping grandee and rump-faced regicide,
Apple-cheeked younkers from a windmill-square,
Puritans stubborn as the nails of Pride,
Rakes from Versailles and thieves from County Clare,

The black-robed priests who broke their hearts in vain
To make you God and France or God and Spain.

These were your lovers in your buckskin-youth.
And each one married with a dream so proud
He never knew it could not be the truth
And that he coupled with a girl of cloud.

And now to see you is more difficult yet
Except as an immensity of wheel
Made up of wheels, oiled with inhuman sweat
And glittering with the heat of ladled steel.

All these you are, and each is partly you,
And none is false, and none is wholly true.

So how to see you as you really are,
So how to suck the pure, distillate, stored
Essence of essence from the hidden star
And make it pierce like a riposting sword.

For, as we hunt you down, you must escape
And we pursue a shadow of our own
That can be caught in a magician's cape
But has the flatness of a painted stone.

Never the running stag, the gull at wing,
The pure elixir, the American thing.

Index of Authors

*The numbers in brackets
indicate selection numbers
in this volume*

BEARD, CHARLES A. (Nov. 27, 1874-Sept. 1, 1948), historian and educator. Professor of politics (1907-17) at Columbia University; a founder of the New School for Social Research, N.Y.C.; wrote *American Government and Politics* (1910), *An Economic Interpretation of the Constitution* (1913), *The Rise of American Civilization* (1927), *A Basic History of the United States* (1944). [27] See also Author Index, Vols. 13, 15.

BENCHLEY, ROBERT (Sept. 15, 1889-Nov. 21, 1945), journalist and humorist. Managing editor (1919-20) of *Vanity Fair,* columnist for the *New York World,* drama editor of *Life* magazine, and drama critic (1929-40) for the *New Yorker;* radio and motion picture personality; wrote *Of All Things* (1921), *My Ten Years in a Quandary* (1936), *Benchley Beside Himself* (1943). [48]

BENÉT, STEPHEN VINCENT (July 22, 1898-March 13, 1943), author. Wrote novels, short stories, and poetry (*Heavens and Earth,* 1920; *John Brown's Body,* 1928; *Ballads and Poems, 1915-30,* 1931; *Western Star,* 1943). [110, 122] See also Author Index, Vol. 16.

BOAS, FRANZ (July 9, 1858-Dec. 21, 1942),

anthropologist. Born Germany; first professor of anthropology (from 1899) at Columbia University; curator of anthropology (1901-05) at the American Museum of Natural History, N.Y.C.; wrote *Anthropology and Modern Life* (1929), *Race, Language and Culture* (1940). [17, 55]

BORAH, WILLIAM E. (June 29, 1865-Jan. 19, 1940), lawyer and public official. U.S. senator from Idaho (from 1907); chairman (1924-33) of the Senate Foreign Relations Committee; sponsored constitutional amendments for a national income tax and direct election of senators. [76] See also Author Index, Vol. 15.

BOURNE, RANDOLPH (May 30, 1886-Dec. 22, 1918), pacifist and essayist. Contributed to the periodicals *The Masses* and *Seven Arts;* wrote *Youth and Life* (1913), *Education and Living* (1917), *The History of a Literary Radical* (1920). [28] See also Author Index, Vol. 13.

BROUN, HEYWOOD (Dec. 7, 1888-Dec. 18, 1939), journalist. Writer (1908-09, 1910-12) for the *New York Morning Telegraph;* baseball writer and drama critic (1912-21) for the *New York Tribune;* wrote a column, "It Seems to Me," for the *New*

York World (1921-28); a founder and first president (from 1933) of the American Newspaper Guild. [104]

BRYCE, JAMES (May 10, 1838-Jan. 22, 1922), British historian, jurist, and diplomat. Professor of civil law (1870-93) at Oxford; undersecretary for foreign affairs (1886) in Gladstone's cabinet; ambassador to U.S. (1907-13); wrote *The American Commonwealth* (1888), a classic study of American government, and *Modern Democracies* (1921). [57] See also Author Index, Vol. 11.

CARTY, J. J. (April 14, 1861-Dec. 27, 1932), electrical engineer. Chief engineer (1907-19) and vice-president (1919-30) of American Telephone and Telegraph Co.; pioneer in switchboard construction and a principal developer of the telephone. [3]

COFFIN, HOWARD E. (Sept. 6, 1873-Nov. 21, 1937), industrialist and automotive engineer. Co-founder (1909) of the Hudson Motor Car Co.; chairman (1915-16) of the Committee on Industrial Preparedness of the Naval Consulting Board; a founder and president (1923) of the Air Transport, Inc. (later United Air Lines). [4]

COHAN, GEORGE M. (July 3, 1878-Nov. 5, 1942), actor, playwright, and producer. Wrote and acted in plays (*Little Johnny Jones,* 1904; *The Song and Dance Man,* 1923), and composed popular songs ("I'm a Yankee Doodle Dandy," "You're a Grand Old Flag," "Give My Regards to Broadway," "Over There"). [22] See also Author Index, Vols. 12, 13.

COLBY, FRANK MOORE (Feb. 10, 1865-March 3, 1925), editor. Professor of history (1890-91) at Amherst College, and professor of economics (1895-1900) at New York University; editor (from 1898) of the *International Year Book* and (1900-03, 1913-15) of the *New International Encyclopaedia;* wrote *Outlines of General History* (1899). [67]

COOLIDGE, CALVIN (July 4, 1872-Jan. 5, 1933), lawyer and statesman. Thirtieth President of the United States (1923-29); mayor of Northampton, Mass. (1910-11); Massachusetts state senator (1912-15), lieutenant governor (1916-18) and gover-

nor (1919-20); Vice-President of the United States (1921-23) under Harding; succeeded to the presidency upon Harding's death (Aug. 2, 1923). [77, 101, 111]

COUNTS, GEORGE SYLVESTER (Dec. 9, 1889-   ), educator. Professor of education (1924-26) at Yale, (1926-27) at the University of Chicago, and (from 1927) at Columbia Teachers College; wrote *The American Road to Culture* (1930), *The Social Foundations of Education* (1934), *Education and the Promise of America* (1945). [60]

CUMMINGS, E. E. (Oct. 14, 1894-Sept. 3, 1962), poet and artist. Wrote prose works (*The Enormous Room,* 1922, and *Eimi,* 1933), plays, and poetry characterized by typographical nonconformity and stylistic originality (*XLI Poems,* 1925; *Is 5,* 1926; *&,* 1926; *Collected Poems,* 1938; *One Times One,* 1944; *95 Poems,* 1958). [74, 97] See also Author Index, Vols. 15, 16.

DANIEL, HAWTHORNE (Jan. 20, 1890-   ), author. Editor (1927-35) of *Natural History Magazine;* curator of printing and publishing (1927-35) for the American Museum of Natural History; editor (1936-39) of *The Commentator;* wrote books on travel and the sea, biographies, and works on foreign affairs. [96]

DAY, WILLIAM R. (April 17, 1849-July 9, 1923), jurist. Secretary of state (1898) under McKinley; chairman (1898-99) of U.S. commission to negotiate peace with Spain; associate justice (1903-22) of the U.S. Supreme Court. [51]

DENSMORE, JOHN B. (Nov. 25, 1877-July 29, 1937), lawyer and public official. Attorney (1913-18) and director general of employment (*c.* 1918), U.S. Department of Labor. [35]

DERMER, EMMA (fl. 1928), songwriter. [112]

DUFFUS, ROBERT L. (fl. 1924), journalist. [88]

ELIOT, CHARLES W. (March 20, 1834-Aug. 22, 1926), educator. Assistant professor of chemistry and mathematics (1854-63) at Harvard; professor of analytical chemistry (1865-69) at Massachusetts Institute of

Technology; president (1869-1909) of Harvard. [14] See also Author Index, Vols. 10, 11.

EVANS, HIRAM WESLEY (fl. 1926), social agitator. Imperial Wizard and Emperor (from 1925) of the Ku Klux Klan. [98]

EWING, STEPHEN (fl. 1928), journalist. [114]

FAIRCHILD, HENRY PRATT (Aug. 18, 1880-Oct. 2, 1956), social scientist. Professor of economics (1910-12) and of the science of society (1912-18) at Yale University; professor of social economy (1919-24) and of sociology (1924-45) at New York University; wrote *Immigration* (1913), *Elements of Social Science* (1924), *Economics for the Millions* (1940). [99]

FORD, HENRY (July 30, 1863-April 7, 1947), automobile manufacturer. Organizer, president (1903-18, 1943-45), and sole owner after its first few years, of Ford Motor Co., during his tenure the world's largest auto manufacturer; sailed for Europe aboard the Ford "Peace Ship" (1915-16) in a futile attempt to end World War I. [117] See also Author Index, Vol. 15.

FOSDICK, HARRY EMERSON (May 24, 1878-), Baptist clergyman. Professor of practical theology (from 1915) at Union Theological Seminary, N.Y.C.; pastor (1926-46) of Riverside Church, N.Y.C.; wrote *The Second Mile* (1908), *The Meaning of Prayer* (1915), *On Being a Real Person* (1943), *The Man From Nazareth* (1949). [63]

FROST, ROBERT (March 26, 1874-Jan. 29, 1963), poet. Professor of English (1916-20, 1924, 1926-38, 1949-63) at Amherst; professor of poetry (1939-43) at Harvard and (1943-49) at Dartmouth; among his books of poetry are *A Boy's Will* (1913), *North of Boston* (1914), *Mountain Interval* (1916), *New Hampshire* (1923), *West-running Brook* (1928), *A Further Range* (1936), *A Witness Tree* (1942), and *In the Clearing* (1962). [79] See also Author Index, Vols. 13, 15, 16.

FURUSETH, ANDREW (March 12, 1854-Jan. 22, 1938), labor leader and authority on the American Merchant Marine. President (from 1908) of the International Seamen's Union of America. [108]

GEORGE, WALTER LIONEL (March 20, 1882-Jan. 30, 1926), English journalist and author. Wrote novels, short stories, literary and social criticisms, including several books in support of the women's rights movement. [54]

GRIFFITH, D. W. (Jan. 22, 1875-July 23, 1948), motion-picture actor, director, and producer. A founder (1919) of United Artists studio; credited with such innovations in camera technique as the fade-out and the flashback; produced and directed *The Birth of a Nation, Intolerance, Orphans of the Storm,* and *America.* [7]

HARDING, WARREN G. (Nov. 2, 1865-Aug. 2, 1923), lawyer, editor, and political leader. Twenty-ninth President of the United States (1921-23); owner and editor (from 1884) of the *Marion* (Ohio) *Star;* lieutenant governor of Ohio (1904-06); U.S. senator (1915-21). [58]

HAUSER, HENRI (July 19, 1866-1946), French historian and economist. Wrote *The Sources of French History* (1906-16), *The Beginning of Capitalism* (1927). [84]

HAYNES, ROY A. (Aug. 31, 1881-Oct. 20, 1940), editor and public official. Editor (from 1908) of *Hillsboro* (Ohio) *Dispatch;* federal prohibition commissioner (1921-27). [102]

HOLMES, OLIVER WENDELL, JR. (March 8, 1841-March 6, 1935), jurist. Son of physician and author Oliver Wendell Holmes; professor of law (1882) at Harvard Law School; associate justice (1883-99) and chief justice (1899-1902) of the Massachusetts Supreme Court; associate justice (1902-32) of the U.S. Supreme Court. [47, 73, 91, 105] See also Author Index, Vols. 12, 13.

HOOVER, HERBERT CLARK (Aug. 10, 1874-Oct. 20, 1964), mining engineer, relief administrator, and statesman. Thirty-first President of the United States (1929-33); chairman of American relief commissions (1914-15) in London and (1915-19) in Belgium; U.S. food administrator (1917-19); director (1921) of relief in Eastern Europe; secretary of commerce (1921-28) under Harding and Coolidge; organized U.S. relief operations in Europe after World War II; chairman (1947, 1953) of federal Commissions on Organization of the Executive Branch. [82, 118] See also Author Index, Vols. 15, 17.

HOWE, FREDERIC C. (Nov. 21, 1867-Aug. 3, 1940), lawyer and political scientist. Director (1911-14) of the People's Institute, N.Y.C.; commissioner of immigration at the Port of New York (1914-19); special adviser to the secretary of agriculture (from 1935). [90]

JEFFERS, ROBINSON (Jan. 10, 1887-Jan. 20, 1962), poet. Wrote *Tamar and Other Poems* (1924), *Cawdor* (1928), *Thurso's Landing* (1932), *Be Angry at the Sun* (1941); adapted Euripides' *Medea* for American production (1946). [92] See also Author Index, Vol. 15.

JOHNSON, JAMES WELDON (June 17, 1871-June 26, 1938), lawyer and poet. First Negro lawyer admitted to Florida bar (1897); U.S. consul (1906) in Venezuela and (1909-12) in Nicaragua; a founder and secretary (1916-30) of the National Association for the Advancement of Colored People; professor of creative literature (from 1930) at Fisk University; wrote *Fifty Years and Other Poems* (1917), *God's Trombones* (1927); edited *The Book of American Negro Poetry* (1922). [121]

KNIGHT, FRANK H. (Nov. 7, 1885-   ), economist and educator. Instructor in economics (1916-17) at Cornell and (1917-19) at the University of Chicago; professor of economics (1919-28) at Iowa and (from 1928) at the University of Chicago; wrote *Risk, Uncertainty and Profit* (1921), *The Economic Order and Religion* (1945), *The Economic Organization* (1951), *Intelligence and Democratic Action* (1960). [72]

LA FOLLETTE, ROBERT M. (June 14, 1855-June 18, 1925), lawyer and political leader. U.S. representative from Wisconsin (1885-91); governor (1901-06); U.S. senator (from 1906); organized (1911) National Progressive League; Progressive Party candidate (1924) for President of the United States. [19]

LAWRENCE, D. H. (Sept. 11, 1885-March 2, 1930), English author. Wrote novels (*Sons and Lovers*, 1913; *The Rainbow*, 1915; *Lady Chatterley's Lover*, 1928), short stories, plays, critical essays, travel

books, and poems (*Birds, Beasts and Flowers*, 1923; *The Ship of Death*, 1933); translated works from Russian and Italian, including Giovanni Verga's *Cavalleria Rusticana* (1928). [64]

LENIN, V. I. (April 22, 1870-Jan. 21, 1924), Russian revolutionist and statesman, and chief ideologist of Bolshevism in its original form. Founded (1900) the revolutionary journal *The Spark;* principal organizer of the Marxian Socialist Congress (1903) and subsequently of the Bolshevik Party; a founder (1919) of the Communist Third International; leader of the 1917 Revolution; head of the Soviet People's Commissars (1917) and premier (1918-24) of the U.S.S.R.; wrote *The Development of Capitalism in Russia* (1899), *The State and Revolution* (1917). [33]

LEWIS, SINCLAIR (Feb. 7, 1885-Jan. 10, 1951), novelist and playwright. Worked (1908-16) as a journalist and editor; wrote *Main Street* (1920), *Babbitt* (1922), *Arrowsmith* (1925), *Elmer Gantry* (1927), *Dodsworth* (1929), *Cass Timberlane* (1945); first American to receive the Nobel Prize for Literature (1930). [78] See also Author Index, Vol. 15.

LINDBERGH, CHARLES A. (Feb. 4, 1902-   ), aviator. Made first solo nonstop transatlantic flight, from Roosevelt Field, New York, to Le Bourget Air Field, Paris (May 20-21, 1927); toured U.S. for Guggenheim Foundation to promote aeronautics; worked on physiological experiments that resulted in development of the "artificial heart" (1936); consultant to U.S. Army Air Force during World War II. [107] See also Author Index, Vol. 16.

LINDSAY, VACHEL (Nov. 10, 1879-Dec. 5, 1931), poet. Wrote *General William Booth Enters into Heaven and Other Poems* (1913), *The Congo and Other Poems* (1914), *The Chinese Nightingale* (1917), *The Golden Whales of California* (1920), *Going-to-the-Sun* (1923). [46] See also Author Index, Vol. 13.

LIPPMANN, WALTER (Sept. 23, 1889-   ), editor and author. Assisted in preparation of the Fourteen Points and the League of Nations plan for the Paris Peace Conference (1918-19); a co-founder (1914) and editor of the *New Republic;* syndicated political columnist (1931-67) for the *New York Herald Tribune;* wrote *Public Opinion* (1927), *A Preface to Morals* (1929), *The Good Society* (1937), *U.S. Foreign Policy: Shield of the Republic* (1943), *Essays in the Public Philosophy* (1955). [8] See also Author Index, Vols. 13, 15, 16, 17, 18.

LODGE, HENRY CABOT (May 12, 1850-Nov. 9, 1924), public official and author. U.S. representative from Massachusetts (1887-93); U.S. senator (from 1893); wrote *The Story of the American Revolution* (2 vols., 1898), *The Senate and the League of Nations* (1925), and several biographies. [41] See also Author Index, Vols. 12, 13.

LOWELL, A. LAWRENCE (Dec. 13, 1856-Jan. 6, 1943), political scientist and educator. Professor of science of government (1897-1909) at Harvard and president (1909-33) of the university; wrote *Essays on Government* (1899), *Conflicts of Principle* (1932). [49]

LOWELL, AMY (Feb. 9, 1874-May 12, 1925), poetess and critic. Edited *Some Imagist Poets* in three yearly anthologies (1915, 1916, 1917); wrote critical essays, biographies, and poetry (*A Dome of Many-Coloured Glass,* 1912). [8]

LUCKNER, FELIX VON (June 9, 1881-April 13, 1966), German naval officer. As commander of the commerce raider *Seeadler* during World War I, destroyed much Allied shipping and earned the nickname "Sea Devil"; toured U.S. (1927). [115]

MacKAYE, BENTON (March 6; 1879-   ), forester and authority on regional planning. Proposed (1921) construction of the Appalachian Trail from Maine to Georgia; planned (1931-32) a Connecticut highway system; regional planner (1934-36) for the Tennessee Valley Authority and (1942-43) for the Rural Electrification Administration. [113]

McKENNA, JOSEPH (Aug. 10, 1843-Nov. 21, 1926), jurist, U.S. representative from California (1885-92); judge (1892-97) of U.S. Circuit Court; U.S. attorney general (1897-98) under McKinley; associate justice (1898-1925) of the U.S. Supreme Court. [51]

MAHONEY, JOHN J. (fl. 1920), public official. Massachusetts state supervisor of Americanization. [50]

MARSHALL, LOUIS (Dec. 14, 1856-Sept. 11, 1929), lawyer and civic leader. Mediator in the New York cloakmakers' strike (1910) and the clothingmakers' strike (1919); a founder of the Jewish Welfare Board; chairman of the American Jewish Relief Committee. [81]

MELLON, ANDREW W. (March 24, 1855-Aug. 26, 1937), financier and public official. Held large interests in coal, coke, and iron enterprises and aluminum manufacture; president of the Mellon National Bank, Pittsburgh; secretary of the treasury (1921-32) under Harding, Coolidge, and Hoover; ambassador to Great Britain (1932-33); principal benefactor of the National Gallery of Art, Washington, D.C. [44, 86]

MENCKEN, H. L. (Sept. 12, 1880-Jan. 29, 1956), editor and satirist. Editor and writer (from 1899) for four Baltimore newspapers; literary critic (1908-23) and co-editor with G. J. Nathan (1914-23) of *Smart Set;* co-founder with Nathan and editor (1924-33) of the *American Mercury;* wrote *Prejudices* (in series, 1919-27), *In Defense of Women* (1917), *The American Language* (1919 ff.), and an autobiography (3 vols. 1940-43). [23, 68, 100] See also Author Index, Vol. 15.

MILLER, BOB (fl. 1928), songwriter. [112]

MITCHELL, SIDNEY D. (fl. 1918), lyricist. [29]

MITCHELL, WILLIAM (Dec. 29, 1879-Feb. 19, 1936), army officer and early advocate of a separate air force. Served with U.S. Army in Spanish-American War, Philippine Insurrection, on Mexican border, and in France in World War I; commander of air forces (1917-18) for the Allies; court-martialed (1925) and convicted of insubordination for criticizing War and Navy Department mismanagement of aviation service; conviction condemned by congressional resolution in 1946. [93]

MUMFORD, LEWIS (Oct. 19, 1895-   ), writer and social critic. Lecturer (1925) at the New School for Social Research, (1931-35) at Dartmouth College (1942-44) at Stanford, (1948-52) at North Carolina State College, (1951-59) at the University of Pennsylvania, and (1957-60) at M.I.T.; wrote *Sticks and Stones* (1924), *American Taste* (1929), *The Culture of Cities* (1938), *The Condition of Man* (1944), *The City in History* (1961). **[85]**

NATHAN, GEORGE JEAN (Feb. 14, 1882-April 8, 1958), editor, author, and drama critic. Drama critic (1908-23) and co-editor with H. L. Mencken (1914-23) of *Smart Set;* drama critic (1922-35) for *Judge,* (1924-30 and 1940-51) for the *American Mercury,* (1930-35) for *Vanity Fair,* and (from 1943) for King Features News Syndicate; co-founder (1924) and co-editor (1924-30) with Mencken of the *American Mercury* and co-founder (1932) of the *American Spectator;* author of numerous books on the theater. **[65]**

NORRIS, GEORGE W. (July 11, 1861-Sept. 2, 1944), lawyer and legislator. U.S. representative from Nebraska (1903-13); U.S. senator (1913-43); secured passage of an act creating the Tennessee Valley Authority (1933) and an act that became the 20th Amendment to the Constitution (1933). **[19]**

O'HARA, GEOFFREY (Feb. 2, 1882-January 31, 1967), composer and songwriter. Born Canada; a founder (1914) of the American Society of Composers, Authors and Publishers; wrote operettas, hymns, and popular songs. **[29]**

PAGE, KIRBY (Aug. 7, 1890-Dec. 16, 1957), social evangelist and author. YMCA worker (1916-17) in France and Great Britain; editor (1926-34) of *The World Tomorrow;* contributing editor of *The Christian Century;* wrote 20 books on peace and religious life. **[61]**

PETTIGREW, R. F. (July 23, 1848-Oct. 5, 1926), lawyer and public official. U.S. representative from South Dakota (1881-83); U.S. senator (1889-1901); wrote *The Course of Empire* (1920), *Triumphant Plutocracy* (1922). **[5]**

POUND, EZRA (Oct. 30, 1885-   ), poet and critic. Foreign editor of *Poetry* maga-

zine; arranged for publication of Wyndham Lewis' *Tarr* and James Joyce's *Portrait of the Artist as a Young Man* and *Ulysses;* edited T. S. Eliot's *Waste Land;* translated Oriental classics; confined to a hospital (1946-58); major poems include *Homage to Sextus Propertius* (1917), *Hugh Selwyn Mauberley* (1920), *The Cantos* (from 1925). **[24]**

PURINTON, EDWARD E. (April 24, 1878-1945), author. Lecturer on health, psychology, and efficiency; efficiency analyst; wrote *Efficient Living* (1915), *Practical Course in Personal Efficiency* (1917), *Personal Efficiency in Business* (1919). **[59]**

RANDOLPH, JAMES R. (fl. 1928), journalist. **[119]**

ROBINSON, EDWIN ARLINGTON (Dec. 22, 1869-April 6, 1935), poet. Wrote *The Children of the Night* (1897), *The Man Against the Sky* (1916), *Merlin* (1917), *Lancelot* (1920), *Collected Poems* (1921), *Tristram* (1927). **[95]**

ROCKEFELLER, JOHN D., JR. (Jan. 29, 1874-May 11, 1960), financier and philanthropist. Son of John D. Rockefeller; associated with his father's business and philanthropic interests in the Standard Oil Co. and the Rockefeller Foundation; planned and built Rockefeller Center, N.Y.C., and donated land for the United Nations Building. **[6]**

ROGERS, WILLIAM PENN ADAIR (Nov. 4, 1879-Aug. 15, 1935), humorist, writer, and actor. Starred in vaudeville, the Ziegfeld Follies, and motion pictures; wrote a syndicated column of satire and homely philosophy for the *New York Times* (from 1926); author of *The Cowboy Philosopher on Prohibition* (1919), *Illiterate Digest* (1924), *Will Rogers's Political Follies* (1929). **[89, 109]**

ROOSEVELT, THEODORE (Oct. 27, 1858-Jan. 6, 1919), soldier, historian, and statesman. Twenty-sixth President of the United States (1901-09); assistant secretary of the navy (1897-98) under McKinley; served in Cuba (1898) as colonel of "Roosevelt's Rough Riders" volunteer cavalry regiment; governor of New York (1899-1900); Vice-President of the United States (1901) under McKinley;

succeeded to the presidency upon McKinley's death (Sept. 14, 1901); received Nobel Peace Prize (1906); wrote *The Naval War of 1812* (1882), *The Winning of the West* (4 vols., 1889-96). [26] See also Author Index, Vols. 11, 12, 13.

ROOT, ELIHU (Feb. 15, 1845-Feb. 7, 1937), lawyer and statesman. Secretary of war (1899-1903) under McKinley and Theodore Roosevelt, and secretary of state (1905-09) under Roosevelt; U.S. senator from New York (1909-15); member (1910-17) of The Hague Tribunal; president (1910-25) of the Carnegie Endowment for International Peace; received Nobel Peace Prize (1912); headed special diplomatic mission to Russia (1917). [16] See also Author Index, Vol. 13.

SANDBURG, CARL (Jan. 6, 1878-July 22, 1967), poet and author. Poetry collections include *Cornhuskers* (1918), *Smoke and Steel* (1920), *The People, Yes* (1936), and *Complete Poems* (1950); edited collections of folk songs (*The American Songbag*, 1927); wrote histories (*Abraham Lincoln — The Prairie Years*, 1926; *Abraham Lincoln — The War Years*, 1939). [9, 36] See also Author Index, Vols. 13, 15.

SANFORD, EDWARD T. (July 23, 1865-March 8, 1930), jurist. Judge (c. 1908-23) of U.S. District Court in Tennessee; associate justice (from 1923) of the U.S. Supreme Court. [91]

SANTAYANA, GEORGE (Dec. 16, 1863-Sept. 26, 1952), philosopher, poet, novelist, and literary critic. Born Spain; teacher of philosophy (1889-1912) at Harvard; wrote *The Sense of Beauty* (1896), *The Life of Reason* (5 vols., 1905-06), *Scepticism and Animal Faith* (1923), *The Realms of Being* (4 vols., 1927-40), *The Last Puritan* (1935), and an autobiography, *Persons and Places* (3 vols., 1944-45, 1953). [53] See also Author Index, Vol. 13.

SMITH, ALFRED E. (Dec. 30, 1873-Oct. 4, 1944), political leader. New York state legislator (1904-15), Democratic leader of the Assembly (1911) and speaker (1913); sheriff of New York County (1915-17); president (1917) of the New York Board of Aldermen; governor (1919-20, 1923-28); Democratic Party candidate (1928) for President of the United States. [106]

STEVENS, DORIS (Oct. 26, 1892-March 22, 1963), author and women's rights advocate. Organizer (1915) of first National Convention of Women Voters; managed campaign of women for Congress (1924); chairman (1928-39) of Inter-American Commission of Women; member (1924-48) of national council of National Woman's Party and (1931-36) of Women's Consultative Committee on Nationality; wrote *Jailed for Freedom* (1920). [25]

STODDARD, LOTHROP (June 29, 1883-May 1, 1950), writer on social and political problems. Wrote *Present Day Europe — Its National States of Mind* (1917), *The Rising Tide of Color Against White World-Supremacy* (1920), *Racial Realities in Europe* (1924), *Scientific Humanism* (1926). [52]

STRUNSKY, SIMEON (July 23, 1879-Feb. 5, 1948), editor and essayist. Born Russia; staff member (1900-06) of the *New International Encyclopedia*, (1906-24) of the *New York Evening Post*, and (from 1924) of the *New York Times*; wrote *The Patient Observer* (1911), *The Rediscovery of Jones* (1931). [13]

SULLIVAN, LOUIS (Sept. 3, 1856-April 14, 1924), architect. Father of modernism in architecture and employer of the concept that "form follows function"; designer of the Auditorium, Gage, and Stock Exchange buildings in Chicago, the Union Trust Building in St. Louis, and the Bayard Building in New York; wrote *The Autobiography of an Idea* (1924). [75] See also Author Index, Vols. 11, 12.

SUTHERLAND, GEORGE (March 25, 1862-July 18, 1942), jurist and public official. U.S. representative from Utah (1901-03); U.S. senator (1905-17); U.S. counsel (1921) at The Hague; associate justice (1922-38) of the U.S. Supreme Court. [73] See also Author Index, Vol. 15.

TAFT, WILLIAM HOWARD (Sept. 15, 1857-March 8, 1930), jurist and statesman. Twenty-seventh President of the United States (1909-13); U.S. solicitor general

29, 1944), journalist and author. Known as "the Sage of Emporia" for his work as owner and editor (from 1895) of the *Emporia* (Kan.) *Gazette;* wrote *The Real Issue and Other Stories* (1896), *A Puritan in Babylon* (1938), *The Changing West* (1939), *Autobiography* (1946). [56] See also Author Index, Vols. 12, 13, 15.

WILLIAMS, WILLIAM CARLOS (Sept. 17, 1883-March 4, 1963), physician and writer. Wrote poetry (*Complete Collected Poems 1906-1938*, 1939), novels, short stories, and an autobiography (1951). [70]

WILSON, WARREN H. (May 1, 1867-March 2, 1937), Presbyterian clergyman and sociologist. Taught rural sociology (1914-23) at Teachers College, Columbia University; lecturer (from 1927) on rural religion at Union Theological Seminary; wrote *Quaker Hill* (1908), *The Church of the Open Country* (1911), *The Evolution of the Country Community* (1912), *Rural Religion and the Country Church* (1927). [2]

WILSON, WOODROW (Dec. 28, 1856-Feb. 3, 1924), lawyer, historian, educator, and statesman. Twenty-eighth President of the United States (1913-21); instructor in history (1885-88) at Bryn Mawr College and (1888-90) at Wesleyan University; professor of jurisprudence and political economy (1890-1902) at Princeton University; president (1902-10) of Princeton; governor of New Jersey (1911-13); received Nobel Peace Prize (1919); wrote *A History of the American People* (5 vols., 1902). [15, 18, 34, 38, 40] See also Author Index, Vols. 11, 13.

WORK, JOHN M. (fl. 1916), Socialist politician. Affiliated with the national office of the Socialist Party and author of pamphlets on the Socialist cause. [11]